ANTI-AMERICANISM

Paul Hollander

ANTI-AMERICANISM

IRRATIONAL & RATIONAL

With a new introduction by the author
Including Reassessment, Comment on Reviews, and Update

Transaction Publishers
New Brunswick (U.S.A.) and London (U.K.)

New material this edition copyright © 1995 by Transaction Publishers, New Brunswick, New Jersey 08903. Originally published in 1992 by Oxford University Press, Inc.

This book is printed on acid-free paper that meets the American National Standard for Permanence of Paper for Printed Library Materials.

Library of Congress Catalog Number: 94-26253
ISBN: 1-56000-774-5
Printed in the United States of America

Library of Congress Cataloging-in-Publication Data

Hollander, Paul, 1932-
   Anti-Americanism : irrational and rational / Paul Hollander, with a new introduction by the author.
      p. cm.
   Originally published : Oxford University Press, 1992.
   "Includes reassessment, comment on reviews, and update"—CIP galley.
   Includes bibliographical references and index.
   ISBN 1-56000-774-5
   1. Anti-Americanism.   2. United States—History—1969-   3. United States—History—1961-1969.   4. Radicalism—United States—History—20th century.   5. Political alienation—United States—History—20th century.   I. Title.
E839.H65   1994
305.892'4073—dc20   94-26253
                                                                               CIP

This book is dedicated to my daughter
Sarah L. Hollander

What did the personal troubles of Americans amount to? Did they really suffer? The world looked into American faces and said, "Don't tell me these cheerful well-to-do people are suffering!" Still, democratic abundance had its own peculiar difficulties. America was God's experiment. Many of the old pains of mankind were removed, which made the new pains all the more peculiar and mysterious.

Saul Bellow
Humboldt's Gift

Contents

Introduction to the Transaction Edition: Anti-Americanism Reconsidered

It is an undeniable source of satisfaction to comment on a new edition of a book one has written, especially when the author's relationship to the publisher is long-standing. Transaction Publishers has published three of my other books, prior to the current reprinting of *Anti-Americanism*,[1] but this is not the only reason for my appreciation of this publishing enterprise, without which American intellectual life and the social sciences in particular would be greatly impoverished.

The new edition of one's book provides a welcome opportunity, indeed necessity to reexamine from a new vantage point the ideas and findings which were conveyed in the original work, a chance to rethink and reflect on what one would have done differently in light of new ideas, more information, and the responses of reviewers and readers. It is especially fruitful and stimulating to reassess one's work in the light of unfriendly critical reaction.

On three previous occasions I commented on reviews of books I wrote when they were reprinted in paperback edition.[2] Such authorial reflections and responses should be of special interest to the readers curious about the relationship between critics and writers.

Besides such reflections a new introduction also seeks, in a small way, to be a substitute for bringing up to date and otherwise improve the original work. Taking another look at the work (such an introduction affords) is an opportunity for the author to rethink some of his own ideas (independent of what the critics thought), his major premises, propositions, and conclusions in the light of new events, developments, and information since the book was originally written. This is all the more in order when he changes the title of the book for the new edition (as is the present case), which in itself suggests that he had done a certain amount of rethinking.

Additionally, the most obvious question to raise here is whether any changes have taken place in the last few years in the condition of anti-Americanism, at home or abroad; have there been new eruptions in different parts of the world and what impact does the fall of communism continue to have on the attitudes the work refers to?

The New Title

Several considerations prompted me to change the title. Although I still believe that the original one correctly informed readers of what the book was about, it failed to convey one of its major messages, namely, that anti-Americanism cannot only be divided into domestic and foreign varieties but also into irrational and rational ones, that is to say, unjustified and justified. Some of the discontents and criticisms stimulated by American cultural influences abroad, or by traits of American culture at home, are well founded.[3] In particular to the extent that anti-American sentiments have been a response to modernization (as I argue in the book) they reflect legitimate apprehensions. Modernity and modernization (the latter often justifiably called "Americanization") have been mixed blessings and the United States has been in the forefront of spreading these disruptive processes, hence it is understandably identified with them. On the other hand blaming capitalism (also justifiably identified with the United States) for all the ills of the world, from sexism to pollution, is a much more dubious practice.

Critical sentiments toward American society and culture are far from groundless when the United States, capitalism, and modernity are conflated and the United States becomes linked to the endemic problems of modernity, such as the decline of community and social solidarity, the growth of impersonality, bureaucratization, social isolation, the loss of meaning and sense of purpose, the assault on nature (or the physical environment) and an excessive rationalism. Each of these phenomena appear to impinge on deeply felt personal needs and thus creates a critical disposition toward the broader social setting in which they originate and which they permeate. Possibly, these aspects of modernity may also help to explain why the sense of victimization and the claims of victimhood (themselves a form of social criticism) have become so widespread in American society during the past quarter century—a development that was perhaps not given adequate attention in *Anti-Americanism* but will be further commented on in this introduction.

While a substantial portion of the book itself conveyed that a separation of the unwarranted and well grounded varieties of anti-Americanism is feasible, the title failed to do so, yet arguably this is one of the more important and less predictable propositions of the book.

The title change was also prompted by the realization that the many versions and varieties of the adversarial sensibility and radical social criticism discussed in the book were not always successfully or illuminatingly encompassed by the term "anti-Americanism."

Finally it also became evident that the concept "anti-Americanism," while readily associated with the phenomenon abroad, did not, for some readers, satisfactorily designate the domestic varieties. Apparently the notion of a domestic anti-Americanism in some instances evoked memories and associations that produced misinterpretation and even hostility toward the whole idea that such a complex of attitudes exists and is worthy of critical analysis. The term, it seemed, conjured up the era and ethos of the subcommittee on un-Americanism (of the U.S. House of Representatives), even McCarthyism and its demagoguery.

It is difficult to make a respectable argument with a concept some readers may regard as tainted, or discredited. This I am afraid was sometimes the case with anti-Americanism, notwithstanding the discernible realities it denoted and my efforts to explain what I did and did not mean by it. The new title, I trust, has somewhat rectified this state of affairs conveying as it does a more differentiated view of the phenomenon and making it clear that not all of its shadings and varieties merit unqualified rejection and scorn, or deserve to be ranked with racism, sexism or anti-Semitism.

At the same time I still believe that anti-Americanism, more often than not, *is* irrational and misdirected; it consists of attitudes and sentiments that reveal more about those displaying them than about the target of the hostile critiques. Domestic anti-Americanism in particular may be distinguished from the foreign varieties by its more personalized quality, by giving voice to "a culture of complaint."[4] These complaints, as will be further discussed below, seem to rest on the determination to hold the social order and institutions responsible for highly personal discontents and unhappiness, a trend that continued through the early 1990s.[5] This is not to suggest that all radical domestic critiques derive from personal grievances or neuroses; rather, I am suggesting that the domestic ones have a more personal quality and more often involve an effort to link the personal realm to the social and political, in the spirit of the venerable feminist claim that "the personal is political." Anti-Americanism abroad rarely makes such claims.

To reiterate briefly what is discussed at far greater length in the book: anti-Americanism is a metaphor that stands for alienation, estrangement, radical social criticism, or an adversarial view of American society and culture; it usually entails the misperception and exaggeration of the flaws and failings of American institutions and values; it also leads or amounts to an unrealistic and inflated view of the responsibility that the (American) social system has for the problems and difficulties of particular groups and individuals. A recent definition, though applied to the phenomenon abroad, helpfully joins together the essentials of both types: "What is essential in determining anti-Americanism is the nature and range of grievances and the intensity of feeling."[6]

Other understandings of the phenomenon supplied by Marcus Cunliffe (discovered since the book was completed) are also useful to cite here, as for instance a conception of anti-Americanism as "a force of unthinking, uncharitable hostility aimed at the United States." He also pointed out that "European anti-Americanism comes to look much less puzzling or pernicious" when seen as simply a reaction to the power of the United States and that "U.S. 'anti-Americanism' may be the most eloquent and passionate variety." But he ends up by suggesting that quite possibly the only genuine and "inveterately biased" form of anti-Americanism is the "emanation from the propaganda machines within the Soviet bloc, in which anything American tends to be caricatured as evil, plutocratic, genocidal." Unhappily such sentiments and their frequent ventilation have not been limited to communist propaganda as is repeatedly shown in this book. Indeed some of the examples Cunliffe himself gives suggest that highly irrational critiques of the United States have been expressed by distinguished Western intellectuals. E. P. Thompson may well have been the forerunner of a type of anti-Americanism that found many imitators in subsequent decades:

> The "American Dream" really is...childish and...debased and its poison can be found in every field of American life. Those who have never been to the United States and who fool themselves... that Hollywood, the Hearst Press and the comics, represent only a lunatic fringe of the American bourgeoisie, sometimes suggest that Babbit is an out-of-date joke on the twenties: unfortunately it only foreshadows the horror of today.[7]

More recently the term *political correctness* (pc) has acquired wide currency and has become comparable in its implications to the attitudes and sentiments characteristic of the adversary culture and thus domestic anti-Americanism. The difference is that more often than not pc refers to the institutionalization of these attitudes (mostly on college campuses) expressed in various regulations, most notoriously the speech codes that embody the values and beliefs of the adversary culture and are eagerly supported by radical social critics.

It may be useful at this point to direct the attention of the reader to the Preface, and parts of chapters 1, 8, and 10, where anti-Americanism is defined.

The Critiques of the Book

Anti-Americanism attracted less review attention than my previous major work, *Political Pilgrims*. This in itself was surprising given the title and topic; I thought that a book claiming to deal with anti-Americanism would arouse considerable interest among Americans, (and more so than one that dealt with the political misjudgments of Western intellectuals) given their long-standing concern with how they are seen by the rest of the world. In fact this was not the case; *Political Pilgrims* got far more review and media attention, occasioned more correspondence and public discussion, and sold more copies in a comparable period.

Among the important publications that chose not to review *Anti-Americanism* were the *New York Review of Books* (which, with admirable consistency has refused to review anything I have written, regardless of its topic), *The Atlantic,* and *Harper's* (neither of which ever reviewed any of my books). More surprisingly the *Washington Post, LA Times, New Republic, American Spectator,* and *National Review* (all of which reviewed books of mine in the past) also declined to review it. The two major scholarly publications most closely associated with my own discipline and work (sociology and political science), *Contemporary Sociology* and the *American Political Science Review,* also passed by the opportunity to inform their readers about the existence of the book (I take this to be simply a matter of not wasting space on a politically incorrect volume). On the other hand, the book was reviewed (and favorably) by the *New Yorker,* which never before took notice of my publications.

I am still not sure how to interpret the relatively limited review attention the book received: Was it a reflection of the perceived decline of anti-Americanism abroad in the early 1990s? If so, was it connected, in some obscure fashion, to the fall of communism in the Soviet Union and Eastern Europe? And, as regards the domestic variety, was that of little interest because of a widespread perception of the 1980s, the Reagan-Bush decade, as one redolent with the triumph of conservative beliefs and the corresponding virtual extinction of the adversary culture?[8] If so, I was perhaps presumed

to be "flogging a dead horse" as a reviewer had said about an earlier effort of mine to document and examine the existence and nature of the adversary culture.[9] Or, as noted above, was the whole
notion of "anti-Americanism" distasteful for some reviewers, reminiscent of McCarthyism and related phenomena disposing them to
ignore a book dealing with it?

The most striking pattern of the reviews, whether they were
favorable or not, was their extraordinarily limited scope, addressing, as they did, only a small portion of what the book dealt with,
while leaving untouched much of what the book was about—major topics and arguments were not engaged. Perhaps one explanation of this was the sheer size of the book and the demand it imposed
on the reader and reviewer. One of them, Herbert Mitgang of the
New York Times, appeared to base his entire sweeping critique on
one (!) chapter, which dealt with the American mass media, and
which he called, "a major section of the book"; this "major section"
was one of ten chapters and encompassed exactly 40 pages out of a
total of 514.

Some reviews chose to discuss only the domestic aspects, others only the anti-Americanism of intellectuals, or only the most
bizarre and irrational aspects of the phenomenon. Hardly any
made reference to a major explanation of domestic anti-Americanism discussed, namely, the high expectations built into American culture. Few if any reviewers bothered to say anything about
anti-Americanism abroad, the structure or organization of the
book, about my findings of the relationship between the domestic
and foreign varieties, about the issue of domestic anti-Americanism and decadence, or about the strength or weakness of my data.
None noted or commented on the quote by Saul Bellow (from his
Humboldt's Gift) at the very beginning of the book, which obviously was intended to convey some of its flavor or key message.
In order to reduce the chances of it being overlooked again, this is
what I quoted from Bellow:

> What did the personal troubles of Americans amount to? Did they
> really suffer? The world looked into American faces and said, "Don't
> tell me these cheerful well-to-do people are suffering!" Still, demo-
> cratic abundance had its own peculiar difficulties. America was
> God's experiment. Many of the old pains of mankind were removed,
> which made the new pains all the more peculiar and mysterious.

These "more peculiar and mysterious" pains are central to the
understanding of the heartfelt rejections of American culture and

society within the United States. In these few sentences Bellow managed, inimitably, to suggest a vital connection between "personal troubles" and their social roots. It was the attempt to turn personal troubles into social criticism that often emerged as a domestic variety of anti-Americanism. In turn the pains of Americans that Bellow alludes to are inseparable from the high expectations American culture has always generated and from the ambivalence that affluence more recently has created.

Aside from the sparse coverage of both the major propositions and the specifics of the book, the other major pattern in the reviews—even more astonishing—was the recurring assertion that I made no distinction between unjustified and justified critiques of the United States and American society, that I considered all critiques anti-American.

Herbert Mitgangs's review, largely consisting of the repetition of this idea, exemplified the type of hostility that can blind a reviewer not merely to the major arguments of a book, but its contents as well. He wrote that I defined anti-Americanism as the failure "to run up the flag for...undisguised neoconservative cheerleading" and that I confused "200 years of devoted and often idealistic American self-criticism...with anti-Americanism."[10] Mr. Mitgang also regarded as self-evidently absurd the idea that Hollywood movies made for entertainment could possibly have social-political themes of a highly critical, left-of-center character.

Mitgang's sentiments were echoed by a reviewer in the *New Statesman* (London) who called me "a sort of neo-McCarthyite...he treats opposition to US foreign and domestic policy...as tantamount to betrayal of the nation's core values."[11] (Other British reviews were far more favorable, notably those in the *Times Literary Supplement, Sunday Telegraph, The Spectator,* and *Times Educational Supplement*).

Donald Lyons in the *Wall Street Journal* claimed that "there is no thorough effort to define any basic terms.... This is a book that puts *Nine to Five*'s Dolly Parton in the dock with Oliver Stone.... And it is thus throughout the book: Criticize, say, American education and you may find yourself on the same page with Noam Chomsky."[12] Readers of this review had no way of knowing that the reference to the movie *Nine to Five* was made in the context of films I described as "dwell[ing] on the corruption of American life and domestic institutions: corporations, law enforcement etc." What I actually said about *Nine to Five* was that it dealt with "sexism in the office," which it certainly had; no reference was made to Dolly Parton [p. 237]. As to Chomsky and critics of American education (which includes me), many are attacking it from the same vantage point as Chomsky and if such writers found themselves on the same page with him it was for that obvious reason.

The reviewer in the *San Diego News* faulted me for "fail[ing] to appreciate the value of metaphor";[13] the case in point was my quoting Mary Daly, the radical feminist, who compared Nazi medical experiments to American gynecology. There was nothing discernibly metaphorical in Ms. Daly's determination to show connections between American medical research and Nazi experiments in "perpetrating and legitimating atrocities" [p. 72]. Metaphorical or not, her book was permeated by comparisons between the United States and Nazi Germany (and not just in medical research), which struck me as a fine specimen of hostile and irrational social criticism.

These and similar objections were all the more remarkable since, in anticipating such critiques, I went to considerable length to make clear what I did and did not mean by anti-Americanism; in fact I began the book, in the Preface, with a discussion of what I understood by the concept. Among other things I wrote: "I should make clear at the outset that I did not equate all criticism of this country with hostility toward the United States, nor did I intend to discredit or dismiss all critiques of the United States with the term 'anti-Americanism'" [p. viii]. This was followed by extensive discussion of what I did mean by the term. Such definitions and clarifications continued throughout the Preface and in the first chapter and were also to be found in other parts of the book.

A French reviewer (in the *Journal of American History*) was critical of my lack of definition of the "adversary culture"[14] (which I tended to use as a synonym for domestic anti-Americanism), while he thought that I defined anti-Americanism abroad "clearly."

It is apparent in retrospect that had the book been confined to anti-Americanism abroad—which in fact is the more customary usage—its reception would have been more favorable. That critics abroad entertain a certain amount of groundless hostility toward the United States is evidently more acceptable than assertions that such hostility exists among the "pampered intellectuals" at home (as Bellow once called them).

Richard Pipes in a fair review made an interesting and unusual criticism I would like to comment on here. He wrote:

> It is unconvincing to argue that the intellectuals who fill the pages of this book with their inanities are inspired by the quest for "a more stable and traditional way of life." If this were the case why would so many of them sympathize with revolutionary movements...? Surely the problem facing contemporary intellectuals is not that they are trying to make life "meaningful" since, judging by the litera-

ture, literary criticism or, philosophy they turn out, they are doing their best to rob it of meaning. I believe Hollander takes too idealistic a view of his protagonists. They are in fact motivated not only by the difficulties of coping with modern life...but also by frustrated ambition.[15]

It was not my intention to argue that it is a longing for a "more stable and traditional way of life" as such that was the mainspring of anti-Americanism among intellectuals; rather, I sought to convey that modernity (which the United States embodies)—depriving them of accessible moral certainties and a sense of community—creates the resentments that find expression in anti-Americanism (or the adversarial outlook).

Regarding the attitude of American intellectuals I emphasized a factor peculiar to the American setting: the high expectations American culture has always generated, a process that intensified during the 1960s. Intellectuals were in the forefront of experiencing, articulating, and internalizing such expectations. These high and unrealistic expectations (of what a society can do for groups and individuals) have not been realized, nor could they be. Confronted with such a state of affairs these intellectuals turned on the society that seemingly let them down, unleashing their social critical impulses with a new intensity and diminished rationality. This in a nutshell is a theory of domestic anti-Americanism.

It is true that I have not given major emphasis to "frustrated ambition," lust for power, and sense of entitlement, the frustration of which is surely another factor contributing to the anti-Americanism of many American intellectuals. However plausible a conjecture it is, I found it hard to prove, even to illustrate these connections. At the same time it appeared to me that the attitudes in question were also in evidence among numerous intellectuals who have gone a long way to satisfy their cravings for high status, recognition, and influence, if not actual power.

Such then were the major themes and patterns in the critiques of the book. Quite possibly it could have been criticized on other grounds too, but the reviewers' attention was single-mindedly riveted on the few points of contention noted above.

There is at last another view of the ideas the book sought to convey that was expressed in a letter to the *Times* occasioned by the op-ed piece I wrote a few months after the book was published. It deserves to be quoted here because it conveys a point of view that none of the critics expressed and yet provides another refreshing critical perspective. Padma Desai, a professor of economics at Columbia University argued that while I correctly identified the United

States as "the major form and carrier of modernity" I was wrong in considering the associated anti-Americanism "well founded." She also wrote: "The change…that traditional societies fear derives essentially from our [American] egalitarianism and our respect for individual rights…. These American ideas…have a universal and powerful appeal. Spreading everywhere, they threaten to upset the restrictive and exploitative social order in more traditional societies. They naturally prompt anti-Americanism."[16] What she suggests is that the ideas associated with modernity represented by the United States have a wide appeal, while they disturb the guardians of tradition; in other words, anti-Americanism of this type need not embarrass Americans! Admittedly, inclined as I was to accept the critiques of modernity I did fail to consider its liberating aspects, focusing instead on the subversive ones. In turn Professor Desai did not seem to acknowledge that the liberating and demoralizing aspects of modernity cannot for long be insulated from one another. Likewise the problematic long-term effects of modernity are inseparable from the egalitarianism, the individualism, and the greater range of choice it brings about. It is of course the unintended results of modernization, such as family instability and incipient normlessness that create difficulties.[17]

Of the positive critical responses I will only make reference to one, both because of its source (by no means associated with conservative thinking) and because it is in such sharp contrast to what the critics typically charged. Naomi Bliven wrote in the *New Yorker*:

> Hollander avoids cheap shots…his sober tone, deliberate space and methodical compilation will infuriate not only the anti-Americans among his readers but also many patriots, who would like him to brandish the red-white-and-blue instead of doggedly trying to explain why other people don't. One of his appealing traits is an intellectual honesty that allows him to admit to uncertainty.[18]

Anti-Americanism at Home

In November 1993 an article by Charles Krauthammer appeared in the *New Republic* entitled "Defining Deviancy Up"; a year earlier an article by Senator Moynihan was published in the *American Scholar* entitled "Defining Deviancy Down." In February 1994 Richard Rorty, the liberal philosopher, published an article on the op-ed page of the *New York Times* entitled "The Unpatriotic Academy" in which he criticized left-wing academic intellectuals who in the name of "the politics of difference" refuse to identify with their country and to take pride in any of its accomplishments. He observed that "it is important to insist that a sense of shared national identity is not an evil."[19] Taken together these articles provide important recent indicators of (and responses to) the persistence of the radical critiques and rejections of American society. Krauthammer's in particular provides a summary of major shifts in American cultural norms in the adversarial or radical-critical direction.

The main thrust of Moynihan's article was that "we are getting used to a lot of behavior that is not good for us" as he took note of "the great wave of moral deregulation that began in the mid 1960s" when "the poor and the insane were freed from the fetters of middle class mores." Moynihan was especially concerned with the growing moral acceptance of one-parent families despite the abundant indications of the link between such families and a wide range of social pathologies, including crime, low educational achievement, and even medical-health problems.[20] Krauthammer in turn observed "a vast social project of moral levelling...the moral deconstruction of middle class normalcy...it is not enough for the deviant to be normalized. The normal must be found deviant."

These redefinitions of deviancy parallel, in their radical implications, the far-reaching rejections of traditional Western values and ideas upon which the edifice of multiculturalism rests (discussed below). The redefinitions of deviance reflect (as does multiculturalism) a contradictory mix of moral relativism and absolutism. The old values are attacked and "deconstructed" in the name of a skeptical relativism; the new ones are pursued uncompromisingly on behalf of fierce, new value commitments. The new values inspire the discovery of new types of deviance: "entirely new areas of deviancy—such as date rape and politically incorrect speech— have been discovered."

It is in three areas of life that these redefinitions are most prominent: family, heterosexuality, and "thought crimes" (or politically incorrect expression). Krauthammer wrote:

> Under the new dispensation it turns out that the ordinary middle-class family is not a warm, welcoming font of "family values," not a bedrock of social and psychic stability.... It is instead a cauldron of pathology, a teeming source of the depressions, alienations and assorted dysfunctions of adulthood.... deep in the family lies the worm, the 1990s version of original sin: child abuse.[21]

The "new ideology of child abuse" (not unlike the new versions of racism) greatly expands the meaning of "abuse" and encourages over-reporting. At the present time, Krauthammer writes, about two-thirds of child abuse cases reported are dismissed for lack of evidence. It is not only "the helping professions committed to a belief in endemic abuse [who] have encouraged a massive search to find causes and where they cannot be found invent them"; of equal significance here is the social-cultural receptivity to this new, ever-broadening version of victimization.

From the radical-social critical standpoint it is hard to think of a better indictment of a social system than endemic child abuse. From the standpoint of individuals on the lookout for a new source, or legitimation of a sought after victimhood, and new relief from personal responsibility, the discovery of such abuse is equally welcome.

The other area of redefinitions has occurred in heterosexual relationships:

> A second vast area of human behavior that until recently was considered rather normal has had its threshold for normality redefined up so as to render much of it deviant. Again we start with a real offense: rape. It used to be understood as involving the use of, or threat of force. No longer. It has now been expanded by the concept of date rape to encompass an enormous continent of behavior that had long been viewed as either normal or ill-mannered, but certainly not criminal.[22]

Here again the radical social-critical implications are vast; what is one to think of a society where, according to Catherine McKinnon and her supporters, "Some 47% of women are victims of rape, or attempted rape...and 25%...are victims of completed rape." To be sure none of these figures correspond to those compiled by the FBI under the United Crime Reporting Program (undoubtedly dismissed by the believers in the higher figures as part of a male conspiracy to hide the truth). In a well-known study by Mary Koss, "73% of the women she labeled as rape victims did not consider themselves to have been raped. Fully 42% had further sexual relations with the so-called rapist."

Rape figures become inflated because of "the extraordinarily loose definition of sexual coercion and rape." Such looseness, presumably originates in the desire to magnify the numbers of those victimized in order to further dramatize, and prove conclusively, the evils of the male-dominated social order. But the radical-critical feminist agenda is even more ambitious: "[B]ehind these numbers is an underlying ideology about the inherent aberrancy of all heterosexual relations.... The date rape epidemic is just empirical dressing for a larger theory which holds that because relations between men and women are inherently unequal, sex can never be fully consensual. It is always coercive." According to McKinnon, rape victims' reports of rape and women's reports of normal sex "look a lot alike." And, as Krauthammer points out, "if there is no such thing as real consent, then the radical feminist ideal is realized: all intercourse is rape."

These allegations cumulatively yield an image of society in which the brutalization of half of its members is endemic—a truly radical and devastating social criticism that ranks with the claims of similarly endemic child abuse. Such critiques arise out of an extraordinary degree of hostility that might be a product of the experience of the abuses alleged, or of other, largely undiagnosed, unidentified discontents.

At last the third area in the "moral deconstruction project" is free speech. Here the notion of "sensitivity" has been summoned to justify repressions of free expression. Thus, for instance,

> A University of Michigan student...offers the opinion *in class* that homosexuality is an illness, and finds himself hauled before a formal university hearing on charges of harassing students on the basis of sexual orientation....It used to be that homosexualitty was considered deviant. But now that it has been declared a simple lifestyle choice, those who are not current with the new definitions, and have the misfortune to say so in public, find themselves suspected of deviancy.... Under the new dispensation it is not insanity but insensitivity that is the true sign of deviant thinking, requiring thought control and re-education.[23]

There is little doubt that the thought control referred to is informed by the values and beliefs of the radical social critics.

Since the repression of politically incorrect ideas cannot be justified in the manner such things used to be, or are, in political dictatorships (where the state itself exercises these controls), "sensitivity," the desire not to offend (a seemingly apolitical motive), provides legitimation for the definition and pursuit of thought crimes. However, the speech codes protect only certain types of sensitivities; they seek to ban and banish the expression of views that directly or indirectly question or undermine the post-1960s code of correct beliefs, the beliefs of those on the Left and its further reaches. Another new device for enforcing politically correct "diversity" has been the threat of withholding accreditation from colleges which fail to live up to the required proportional distribution of victim groups.[24]

These redefinitions represent momentous trends. In any society or culture when "the deviant is declared normal [and] the normal is unmasked as deviant" vast changes are underway. Krauthammer offers one explanation for what has been an intensification of adversarial sentiments entailed in these redefinitions and reversals of moral sentiment:

> Defining deviancy up, like defining deviancy down is an adventure in moral equivalence. As such, it is the son of an old project that met its demise with the end of the Soviet empire. There once was the idea of moral equivalence between the East and the West...we were really as bad as they were. We could match them crime for crime...this species of moral equivalence is now dead.... But ideology abhors a vacuum. So we have a new version of moral equivalence: the moral convergence within Western society of the normal and the deviant. It is a bold new way to strip the life of the bourgeois West of its moral sheen. Because once it becomes, to use McKinnons' words, "difficult to sustain the customary distinctions between pathology and normalcy," the moral superiority to which bourgeois normalcy pretends vanishes.... Defining deviancy up is a new way of satisfying an old ideological agenda.[25]

Much of the book that follows this introduction describes and examines that old ideological agenda.

It is most likely that if we asked a radical critic what was most seriously wrong with American society today he would begin the litany of defects and injustices with racism. Since the second half of the 1980s (when most of this book was conceived and written) adversarial or radical social criticism in the United States crystallized around the continued assertion of the *inherently* racist character of American society. These critiques have become increasingly routinized, a form of conventional wisdom that rarely goes challenged especially when made by black critics. An appearance of Sister Souljah, the rap singer, at Amherst College in 1992 typified such charges and their enthusiastic acceptance by "a standing room-only crowd" that greeted her "by cheers of support." The audience was informed that "'[t]he purpose of your education is to maintain a state of racism....' [and] Education is geared to making you become corporate slaves,'" that children starved in Africa "as a result of exploitation by white people"; furthermore, that "American society, higher education, corporate America, the media, and the music industry...are rife with racism."[26] Denial or criticism of such charges becomes further irrefutable evidence of racism.

During the late 1980s and early 1990s multiculturalism emerged both as a new remedy against racism (and some of its alleged consequences) and as a new and more ambitious source of the radical critique of American culture and society. While this book includes a short discussion of multiculturalism (or "cultural diversity") as a new component of the curriculum [pp. 181–88], since I wrote it multiculturalism has emerged as the most influential vehicle of radical social criticism, indeed, rejection of American culture and society and as such deserves further comment.[27]

In higher as well as lower education multiculturalism is promoted as a remedy for the effects of racial discrimination by acquainting those victimized with the accomplishments of their people and culture and thereby raising their self-esteem; in this endeavor multiculturalism has embraced and transferred to the intellectual-educational realm a major device of combating racism, namely, affirmative action or quotas. Thus, multicultural (or cultural diversity) studies seek to ensure that authors of a particular race or ethnicity and women (sometimes also those of a nonheterosexual orientation) will be *represented* in the curriculum, making such representation the new and major criterion in curriculum design. Thus, "representation" or "representativeness" are moved from the political to the educational realm—a logical extension of affirmative action to the realm of ideas.

"Multicultural" studies, despite their evident nonacademic and nonintellectual thrust met little opposition from the educational establishment or from intellectual elite groups. The ready acceptance of these programs has, in all probability, resulted from the claim that they would remedy discrimination, cultural deprivation, and insufficient self-esteem among the protected minorities and especially black Americans. It is important to emphasize that these programs have been driven largely by (and modeled after) the Afrocentric variety.

While multiculturalism usually presents itself as an effort to broaden the curriculum by including deserving authors hitherto neglected (for reasons of racism or sexism), and as a benevolent tool of raising self-esteem, it has been a highly politicized source of social criticism, often more fundamental than the other varieties examined in this book. Multiculturalism rejects not merely the ideas and beliefs that are integral parts and bases of American culture and society, but Western culture as a whole. Multicultural studies while ostensibly dedicated to the idea of introducing students to non-Western cultures also advance the startling and truly radical proposition that Western culture or civilization bears a unique responsibility for racism, sexism, elitism, "classism," homophobia, and whatever else is inhumane and objectionable according to the radical social critics.

Arguably, the abundant social-critical strain in multiculturalism has also been enriched by the contribution of erstwhile social critics of a Marxist persuasion. As Robert Hughes observed, "The academic left professes to see in it [multiculturalism] the seeds of radical promise: Marxism...reborn as...multiculturalism." He also pointed out: "[M]ulticulturalism means something less than genuine curiosity about other cultural forms....many 'radicals' seem to assume that, in looking at other cultures under the rubric of 'multiculturalism,' one should gaze mainly at their versions of Marxism, 'liberation struggle' and so forth."[28]

While multiculturalism utilizes intellectual currents that have a strong antirational, relativizing message in order to dispute the importance or superiority of Western culture, at the same time it glorifies non-Western cultures on the assumption that doing so will uplift the minorities no matter how tenuous a connection they have with these cultures. This objective is most evident in the Afro-centric branch of multiculturalism, which is the most widespread and advances the most dubious intellectual claims.[29]

The success of multiculturalism is among the larger, cultural reflections of the institutionalization of the radical critiques of American society and Western culture: "It alleges that European institutions and mental structures are inherently oppressive, and that non-Eurocentric ones are not."[30] The multiculturalist critique of the West and the United States brings together the critiques of several contingents of the adversary culture: black nationalists and separatists, radical feminists, various types of Marxists and Maoists, opponents of heterosexuality, as well as postmodernists and deconstructionists irritated by Western rationality and linear thinking.

The varieties of radical social criticism discussed here and especially the charges of racism (as well as the policies for its hoped-for alleviation) could not have been successfully sustained for three decades without a widespread, rarely questioned acceptance of social determinism, without the belief that uncontrollable social forces are responsible for the fate of various victim groups and especially black Americans. Such a determinism—and the open-ended indictment of the social order it entails—has been an integral part of the adversarial worldview. Orlando Patterson, a black sociologist noted over two decades ago the advantages of embracing the social deterministic view for black Americans (subsequently adopted by other victim groups as well):

[D]eterminism explains not only failure in the sense of failure to achieve...but also failure interpreted to mean an involvement with wrong, shameful and humiliating acts. Thus, the unusually high crime rate among black adults, the high rate of juvenile delinquency, the high rate of marital instability and parental irresponsibility, and the unusually high dependence on welfare...are explained with almost ridiculous ease by social determinism.... For the black American who is...troubled by the apparent failure of his group...the simple answer is the determinist social philosophy and explanatory system.... for all disadvantaged groups seeking equality, the most strategically useful moral system is determinism. We have then a paradox of a group of people seeking for the preconditions of moral autonomy by appealing to the opposing ethic of determinism.[31]

Two events (and the public responses to them) since this book was written demonstrate the continued prevalence of social determinism in the public explanation of the conduct of victim groups and its connection with radical social criticism. One was the Los Angeles riots in April 1992, the other the murders on the Long Island Railroad in December 1993.

The LA riots were treated by the media, academics, and politicians almost exclusively as the product of the racist repression of racial-ethnic minorities sparked by the acquittal of policemen accused of beating Rodney King (a black man); the riots were self-evident expression of the accumulated frustration and despair of these minorities. Rarely was the possibility raised that the rioters, looters, and murderers had any moral responsibility for their behavior—a stereotypical response to such riots since the mid 1960s and a powerful reflection of massive societal guilt.[32]

John Bracey, a professor of Afro-American studies at the University of Massachusetts at Amherst "called the young rioters 'our warriors' and said they deserved protection not condemnation. 'It is standard tactics...to label black people who resist as criminals.... It is absolutely imperative to...not allow the scapegoating of those people who took the chance.'"[33]

U.S. Representative John Conyers said, "Those weren't criminals, those were outraged citizens." Maxine Water, their U.S. representative, insisted (on CBS's "60 minutes," on 27 March 1994) that they were "rebels." President Clinton, presidential candidate at the time, said: "[T]o be sure it was heartbreaking to see some little children going into the stores in Los Angeles and stealing from their neighbors, but they live in a country where the top one percent of Americans have more wealth than the bottom 90 percent." Shortly after the riots, Leonard Fein wrote in the *Los Angeles Times*: "We have, as a nation, decided to bequeath to our children the rotten fruit of racism and bigotry."

In the aftermath of the riots the *Los Angeles Times* also reprinted Andrew Hacker's musings on race relations suggesting that white America may embark on the extermination of its black citizens:

> At times, the conclusion seems all but self evident that white America has no desire for your presence.... Can this nation have an unstated strategy for annihilating your people? How else, you ask yourself, can one explain the incidence of death and debilitation from drugs and disease; the incarceration of a whole generation of your men; the consignment of millions of women and children to half-lives of poverty end dependence?...
>
> ...could it be that if white America begins to conclude that you are becoming too much trouble, it will find itself contemplating more lasting solutions?[34]

Hacker does not merely embrace the well-worn deterministic explanation of social pathologies among the black population, he actually invites his readers to entertain the possibility of the impending genocide ("lasting solution" only a small step removed from "final solution").

The comments cited above help to better understand the symbiotic relationships between white guilt and black rage. Black rage (and the demands for compensatory measures it generates) is legitimated by the reflexive display of white guilt; in turn white guilt is sustained and reinvigorated by the recurring eruptions of black resentment. It is difficult to envisage one without the other.[35]

Extremists within the black community will gladly share their conspiracy fantasies with sympathetic whites. Colin Ferguson, originally from Jamaica, claimed to be a victim of racism and, in December 1993, killed six white passengers on the Long Island Railroad without any provocation. Jim Sleeper wrote:

> In the weeks since the...Long Island Railroad massacre, scores of commentators cited...Colin Ferguson's grievances against Caucasians, Chinese, "Uncle Tom Negroes"...to argue that he is a deranged loner.... But none of the reports took into account the most compelling explanation of his malevolent worldview: the dangerous political subculture in which he was steeped. No one, it seems, is willing to entertain even the possibility that Ferguson's delusions were fed by the politics of Crown Heights, Tawana Brawley, the Central Park jogger, the Korean boycott...a politics of paranoia

and rage about white and Asian racist conspiracies that has dominated New York City's black media.[36]

It is then no cause for surprise that William Kunstler, who is in the forefront of those voicing the most extreme and irrational critiques of American society, (and is, not coincidentally, Ferguson's lawyer) took the position that Ferguson "was driven insane by racial injustice":

> Minutes after the court session ended...Mr Kunstler and Mr Kuby [the other lawyer] were before a bank of cameras, explaining that "black rage," the anger that many black Americans feel over centuries of their unjust treatment would be a cornerstone of their insanity defense...."If you treat people as second-class citizens, they're going to snap."[37]

The climate of opinion these incidents and their interpretation reflect will assure that the preferential treatment of those officially classified as victim groups will remain entrenched and probably expand, since the new (Clinton) administration explicitly supports "representativeness" or "diversity." Among the recent examples of such policies a critic noted:

> Quotas have run amok in the first year of the Clinton administration. At the Justice Department...Merit and bonus awards must be racially apportioned along with promotions, training programs...and disciplinary actions. Discipline cannot be "initiated against any group of employees at a statistically significant higher rate than any other group." Performance reviews are race-normed...
> ...at the Dept. of Housing & Urban Development...To obtain an "outstanding" rating, managers must be actively engaged in "promoting diversity." This requires managers to be active members of minority, feminist or homosexual organizations, to ensure career advancement of those with diversity status...
> ...Mr Clinton's health plan requires that medical students be allocated to medical specialties according to race in order to achieve a racially balanced medical profession.[38]

It is relevant in this context to recall that serious consideration was given to Johnetta Cole—a formerly fiery radical and Castro loyalist (currently president of Spellman college in Atlanta) who is a black woman—in the first Clinton cabinet.[39] Such policies of the Clinton administration invite reference to the political beliefs and attitudes of an unusually activist presidential wife, Hillary Rodham Clinton:

Her sense of purpose stems from a world view rooted in the activist religion of her youth and watered by the conviction of her generation that it was destined... to teach the world the error of its ways. Together, both faiths form the true politics of her heart, the politics of virtue.... Driven by the increasingly common view that something is terribly awry with modern life, Mrs. Clinton is searching...for The Answer.... The Western world, she said, needed to be made anew. America suffered from a "sleeping sickness of the soul"...[the] nation was in the throes of a "crisis of meaning."[40]

As of this writing (in the Spring of 1994) it is too early to say whether or not the Clinton administration, or certain personalities and influences in it, would significantly contribute to the reinvigoration of the adversary culture in the highest places, or merely represent echoes of a faded youthful idealism of the presidential couple. Certainly the president himself has received much criticism from leftist liberals for his moderation (as in the Lani Guinier case and regarding his policies about the homosexuals in the military).

In the period here discussed, the early 1990s, venerable voices of radical social criticism remained active and vocal and helpful for defining and redefining the most unambiguously irrational varieties of radical social criticism, or domestic anti-Americanism. Noam Chomsky in particular (described an exemplar of "the genuine left") persisted in his satanic visions of American society where

if you are rational and honest, you are pretty much excluded from the educated classes, from the privileged classes [Did *he* consider *himself* irrational and dishonest, *or* excluded from the educated and privileged classes?].... The norm is [in the United States] that if you subordinate yourself to the interests of the powerful, whether it is parent or teacher or anybody else...you will get ahead. Go to any elite university and you are usually speaking to...people who have been selected for obedience.... The Sixties left an enormous legacy.... That's why everyone hates the Sixties. It might lead to real democracy.... The court system [in the United States] has collapsed.... Another four years of this will institute—I am not joking—a fascist-style legal system in which civil rights don't exist...most Americans would be horrified if they knew what they were doing in the world....our leaders...want to control the international oil system...to establish the principle that the world is ruled by force, because that's the only thing that we are good at.[41]

In the same interview Chomsky also averred that "We have been celebrating genocide for 500 years" (since the discovery of America by Columbus) and that the United States was "crucially responsible for" the death of tens of millions of people in the Third World.

Ramsey Clark too has remained "one of the harshest and most unrelenting critics" of American society equal in intensity if not volume to that of Chomsky. He believed that "America's legacy abroad was one of 'violence, poverty, authoritarian governments and turmoil.'" He was described by one of his detractors as giving "automatic support for anyone opposed to the United States for any reason whatsoever." William Kunstler called him "the voice of conscience in the American bar."[42]

Bernardine Dohrn, former Weather Underground leader (after thirteen years underground, and after refusing to cooperate with the grand jury investigating the 1982 Brink's robbery-murders in Nanuet, N.Y.) also preserved her old values and commitments. As revealed in an admiring article in the *New York Times* "Home Section" (complete with photos of her and her former fellow radical activist husband, William Ayer), "She still seeks radical change, but with different methods." The readers were informed that "for a real-life taste of what Mr. Ayers calls 'movement culture,' each summer the couple send the children to a camp where they stay in bunks named after Harriet Tubman and Eugene V. Debs and study subjects like South Africa and the campaign against nuclear power."[43]

Among the prominent radical critics Oliver Stone deserves mention here for his recent contribution to the demonization of American society performed in his movie *JFK*, made since this book was written. Even Tom Wicker, himself a hardy social critic, observed that

> if *JFK* and its wild assertions are to be taken at face value, Americans will have to accept the idea that most of the nation's major institutions, private as well as governmental, along with one of its Presidents, conspired together and carried out Kennedy's murder to pursue the war in Vietnam and the Cold War, then covered up the conspiracy until Mr. Garrison and Mr. Stone unearthed and exposed it.[44]

As George Will summed up the major message of the film:

> Much of America's establishment conspired to kill Kennedy because he loved peace and "they" wanted war.... [Stone] perhaps...is just another propagandist frozen in the 1960s like a fly in amber, combining moral arrogance with historical ignorance. He is a specimen of 1960s arrested development, the result of self-absorption encouraged by all the rubbish written about his generation being so unprecedentedly moral, idealistic, caring, etc.[45]

The significance of the movie was not limited to being a costly expression of one man's alienation from American society (receiving eight Academy Award nominations) but that it was a powerful instrument of denigrating America in the eyes of the audiences, and especially those of younger age, unable to summon the knowledge its critical scrutiny required. As another critic noted, "The children of the video age get their information more from images than from words. They tend to believe what they see. They will swallow *JFK* whole." And to supplement the influence of the film there was a "*JFK* Study Guide" for high school social studies and college history departments, which Warner Brothers helped to distribute.[46]

The adversarial spirit was also alive and well in some of the entertainment Broadway offered. As a review noted of a recent play "'The Kentucky Cycle' portrays a nation full of rampant greed.... The playwright Robert Schenkkan...sees a country born of greed and deceit and single-mindedly devoted to the notion that all men are fleeceable. In 'The Kentucky Cycle'...he tallies the costs of our national duplicity. They are enormous."[47] The socialist-realist-style play undertook to present the evils of America all the way from 1775 to 1975. A similarly critical-revisionist view of American history emerged and spread in various major museums around the country; the Smithsonian in Washington, D.C., exemplified this idea in its exhibition "The West as America: Reinterpreting Images of the Frontier," which dealt with the period 1820–1920. Daniel Boorstin, the historian and former librarian of Congress called it "a perverse, historically inaccurate, destructive exhibit."[48] There was of course a certain logic, from the radical critic's point of view, in the wide-ranging efforts to discredit the American past: trying to show how deep the roots of present days evils were, they sought an indestructible foundation for the rejection of American society and culture.

The same process of critical "deconstruction" and adversarial delegitimation has also continued in the textbooks in social studies and American history (discussed in the chapter on higher education). The historian Bernard Lewis noted of this process: "We live at a time when great efforts are being made to falsify the record of the past and to make history a tool of propaganda; when governments, religious movements, political parties and sectional groups of every kind are busy rewriting history as they would wish it to have been."[49]

In this update of the radical domestic critiques of American culture and society further reference must be made to the proliferation of victims groups over the past few years.

There has been a steady, relentless expansion of these groups since the early 1960s. What began as the recognition of the historic wrongs suffered by the black population gradually led to the definition of approximately 80 percent of Americans belonging to some victim group, a process that promises to end with the entire population perceiving itself as victimized.

These developments unfolded as blacks, 12 percent of the population, were followed by women, who constitute half of the population (within the general victim group of women there is the steadily expanding category of rape victims as the theme of victimization becomes increasingly popular among feminists);[50] Hispanics are approximately another 10 percent; Asian Americans and Native Americans add a few more percentage points; then come the handicapped, 10–20 percent of the population depending on the criteria used for their definition. (To be sure some of these groups overlap: Hispanic women may also be handicapped, etc.) At last, though not officially incorporated into the protected categories assisted by affirmative actions programs, there are the lesbians and homosexuals, 3–10 percent of the population, depending on whose figures we accept. There are also the homeless and AIDS victims and those overweight. At the present time the only nonvictim group left is that of white, healthy, heterosexual males. They cannot be more than 15 percent of the population.

Generally speaking, the trend has been for each and every victim group to claim expanding numbers, assisted in this endeavor by what came to be known as advocacy research.[51] As Robert Hughes put it,

> The range of victims available ten years ago…has now expanded to include every permutation of the halt, the blind, the lame and the short…. Never before in human history were so many acronyms pursuing identity…
> …to be vulnerable is to be invincible. Complaint gives you power…the power of emotional bribery, of creating previously unnoticed levels of social guilt.[52]

Paradoxically the claims of victimhood are sometimes accompanied by the semantic denial that the group in question is in any way debilitated, hence the proliferation of euphemisms seeking to disguise the condition that was the original basis of the claim of victimhood (as in "differently abled," "vertically challenged" or even in the adoption of "gay" by homosexuals; nor are we supposed to call the old just that, they are "senior citizens," etc).

It is notable how little resistance has met the growing claims of victimhood, how readily these claims have been granted by the powers that be. Rarely has it been asked if indeed every woman is a victim regardless of social class, education, and occupation, if dark pigmentation alone confers victim status regardless, again, of income, education, social position, and political power.

Of late even those who have so far remained outside the officially recognized boundaries of victimhood have been finding new ways to be included, and those already inside are reaching for additional forms of victimhood that need not exclude whites, males, heterosexuals, or those healthy (or apparently so). It is now within reach to have a society where every citizen, in the best egalitarian tradition, has one (or several) claims to victimhood.

The latest avenue to victim status is the most widely available: it is provided by our parents who "abused" us during childhood. A recent check at a bookstore in New York revealed eighty-four current titles on child abuse, sometimes referred to as "soul murder" by the experts. According to John Bradshaw, one of the experts, such "soul murders" takes place in 96 percent of American families.[53] In the vast literature on the subject the "first cause of all our ills [is] the American family...a stricken institution that churns out nothing but emotionally crippled individuals...everywhere...celebrities and plain folk alike are absorbed in surviving, repenting and pointing an accusing finger at parents, relatives, spouses or lovers."

Perhaps the most significant aspect of these developments has been the "melodramatic...refus[al] to distinguish among levels of suffering and victimization."[54]

The incest variety of child abuse has been another strong contender among the expanding categories of victimhood. Social psychologist Carol Tavris wrote:

> The sexual-abuse-victim story...draws like a magnet those who wish to invoke a measure of sympathy in these unsympathetic times. It is no wonder that publishers and talk shows have a thriving business exploiting stories of abuse.... The childhood abuse explanation of all one's current problems...with or without the incest variation, is now *de rigeur* for any aspiring celebrity autobiographer...
> ...the survivor books rely on definitions that are as expandable as a hot-air balloon. In these books the rule is: If you feel abused, you were abused...anything your parents did that you didn't like is a violation.[55]

David Rieff observed:

> Imagine a country in which millions of apparently successful people...have come to believe fervently that they are really lost

souls—a country where countless adults allude matter-of-factly to their "inner children," who, they say, lie wounded and in desperate need of relief within the wreckage of their grown-up selves. Imagine the celebrities and opinion-makers among these people talking nightly on TV and weekly in the magazines not about their triumphs but about their victimization, not about their power and fame but about their...childhood persecutions.[56]

The child-abuse species of victimhood, like all the others, takes it for granted that "no blame for these addictions or dependencies [results of the abuse suffered] can be assigned to those who exhibit them. Terms such as 'character', 'weakness' and 'individual responsibility' are no longer deemed appropriate."[57] Even a professional criminal specializing in attacks on old people and injured in the course of committing a serious crime is entitled to sympathy and lavish financial compensation and becomes enlisted among the ranks of deserving victims as was the case of "a young man who was crippled after being shot by the police while attempting to rob a 76-year-old victim in the subway"; he was awarded $4.3 million.[58] At last it should also be noted that the mass media has played a major role in popularizing victimhood and victims, making them part of the world of entertainment, as self-declared victims populate talk shows, among other programs.[59]

From a broader social-historical perspective these developments raise the questions of why and how does culture encourage victimhood and what does it mean when it is encouraged with such zeal, determination, and lack of discrimination? Or, as Aaron Wildavsky asked, how does one account for "the almost compulsive urge to cry suppression in the midst of the most licentious period in the last several hundred years"?[60] For the present discussion I will focus on the social-critical implications of spreading victimhood (rather than on its association with decline or decadence to be taken up later).

It is self-evident that when a society is teeming with victims whose claims to victimhood are not merely unchallenged but warmly supported by the political system and by the elite groups of society (legislators, educators, therapists, churchmen, media people, etc.) there is an implicit challenge or questioning of the legitimacy of the entire social order. Each and every victim in these groups owes its suffering, in the final analysis, to social factors beyond the control of specific human beings; each and everyone of them is a victim of some malevolent social force: racism, sexism, "heterosexism," homophobia, "ableism," elitism, "classism" capitalism, a consumer society, or uncaring parents, themselves the products of this hideously deformed social system. The implied claim that society or culture turns virtually everybody into some type of a victim constitutes the most radical critique of a society anyone can think of.

Several factors may account for these developments. The most obvious is that the successful claim to victimhood brings tangible rewards in the form of the various compensatory and entitlement programs supported both by the government and private institutions and business. But the moral rewards may be even more important. The accredited victim is accorded respect, an elevated moral status and sense of entitlement. The sense of grievance also justifies the endless preoccupation with the self, a predisposition that, as such, is independent of the penchant for victimhood but is congenial with it. Gradually the focus on grievance and victimization becomes a source of identity for both individuals and groups.[61] These preoccupations also "lend an inflated self-importance" to people preoccupied with "relationships, creative difficulties and self fulfillment."[62] Thus have the notions of the "personal" and "political" become intertwined, expanding both the conceptions of what constitutes victimhood *and* the volume and intensity of social criticism.

Anti-Americanism Abroad

It calls for some comment why this book has more to say about the domestic than the global varieties of anti-Americanism. Of the ten chapters six are devoted to the former and only three to the latter. Under ideal circumstances a book on anti-Americanism should provide a better balance between these two prototypes; it should also have more to say about the numerous regional varieties in order to present a truly global picture bolstered by every available attitude and opinion survey.

An examination of anti-Americanism abroad would also have benefited from a fuller discussion of the hostile stereotyping of Americans as people whereas my emphasis was placed on the critiques and caricatures of American institutions, values, and policies. If I were to undertake such a study again I would make greater use of literary and journalistic sources to capture these stereotypes, perhaps following the example set by Art Buchwald. In 1957 he placed the following advertisement in the *London Times*: "Would like to hear from people who dislike Americans and their reasons why."[63] While the hundred plus responses were obviously not representative of either the readers of the *London Times* or of English people in general they do suggest the range and flavor of such stereotypes.

The explanation of this imbalance (between my treatment of anti-Americanism at home and abroad) may be found, in part, in the fact that I began the book with the domestic aspects and by the time I finished it I used up much of the space that was available for the volume. But probably a better explanation of the imbalance may be found in the feeling that the domestic variety was the more puzzling and challenging phenomenon that required more documentation, explanation, and critical analysis, whereas the corresponding attitudes and sentiments abroad have been more readily acknowledged and their explanation seemed less problematic. I also believed that given the connections between the two prototypes (domestic and foreign) and the cross-fertilization between them, a more thorough exploration of the domestic one would also shed light on the foreign version. I felt that my understanding of the essentials of the phenomenon, as for instance expressed in the following quote, illuminated both of the prototypes:

> What holds together the varieties of anti-Americanism is a sense of grievance and the compelling need to find some clear-cut and morally satisfying explanation for a wide range of unwelcome circumstances associated with either actual states, or feelings of backwardness, inferiority, weakness, diminished competitiveness, or a loss of coherence and stability in the life of a nation, group or individual. [p. 343]

While some of the above is perhaps more readily applicable to the foreign than to the domestic type, the sense of grievance, the loss of coherence, the need for a morally satisfying explanation (of various discontents, frustrations, deprivations) are all essential for the states of mind that the concept captures, at home as well as abroad. In other words, the scapegoating impulse is central to anti-Americanism and its many varieties; what is to be explained, and what I tried to explore in this book, is why the United States has become the focus of these impulses at a particular point in time in history.

Of the three major types of anti-Americanism abroad I outlined in the book (nationalistic, anticapitalistic, and antimodernist), probably the anticapitalist type has lost the most ground in the last few years as the fall of the Soviet Union (and other communist systems) made it more difficult to uphold the anticapitalist alternative. Despite much protestation to the contrary among some Western intellectuals, these developments damaged the prestige and credibility of Marxism as well as its anticapitalist messages, which were among the most solid foundations of anti-Americanism.

Not only did the former communist systems in Eastern Europe proclaim the pursuit of private enterprise, even the remaining communist states, foremost among them China, have increasingly adopted a market economy and capitalist methods of production. More specifically the fall of the pro-communist regime in Nicaragua, the weakening of Cuba and the absorption of Marxist guerrillas in El Salvador into a basically pro-American system also helped to discredit Marxist, anti-capitalist sentiments in Latin America. But the observation of Jorge Castenada about the Latin American left applies to leftist radical critics within the United States as well:

> the self-destruction of the basic model signified the disappearance of the left's framework for conceiving of an alternative.... The effects of the passing of the paradigm extended beyond those sectors of the left directly identified with the socialist experience. They helped discredit the central concept that was equally dear to every segment of the Latin American left: the role of the state in economic and social policy.[64]

At the same time cultural anti-Americanism that seeks to protect indigenous cultural traditions and national identity remains vigorous; often it is part of a broader anti-Western, antimodern (or "counter-modernising" in Peter Berger's words) movement most virulent in Islamic countries and most zealously pursued by Islamic fundamentalist movements.

Arab anti-Americanism (one of the most colorful varieties) probably gained strength from the Gulf War—a development that occurred while this book was in press. Thus, an Egyptian writer believed that the invasion of Kuwait by Iraq "was a trap set by Washington" to be used as a pretext for destroying Iraq's military assets. A Lebanese journalist blamed the United States for turning Lebanon into one of the "poverty-stricken, hungry and destroyed countries." A professor of sociology in Tunis suggested that the United States "wanted to force upon the world a 'universal totalitarian character'" and another Lebanese writer castigated the United States for its "aggressive culture" and "colossal contempt shown to their [the Arab peoples'] religious and cultural identity—Islam." The subtitle of a collection of writings by a famous Arab intellectual was "From Cultural Invasion to the Gulf War." As the author of an unusual critique of Arab intellectuals pointed out, "Victimhood has turned into something like a new Arab art form."[65] If so, Arabs and Americans had, after all, something in common.

The demise of the Soviet Union as a superpower left the United States as the only superpower—a position that may help to refocus and stimulate nationalistic grievances and resentments against the United States. On the other hand, the demise of the Soviet Union has also meant that a major force supporting these sentiments is no longer present. This can be seen in the United Nations where expressions of anti-Americanism (discussed on pp. 343–55), in the absence of a Soviet Bloc actively supporting them, have greatly diminished in the last few years.

There is nonetheless no reason to expect nationalistic anti-Americanism to diminish substantially worldwide except under circumstances when national identity and interest are more obviously threatened from other sources. This may be the case in Western Europe, which at the present time is preoccupied with the growing problems of illegal immigration from Islamic and other Third World countries, in addition to the difficulties created by the presence of those already within their borders.

The decline of anti-Americanism in Western Europe is perhaps best exemplified by the case of France [pp. 384–87]. Since I wrote those pages a new study sheds further light on the ups and downs of French anti-Americanism and provides a better understanding in general of anti-Americanism abroad and its connection with modernization and matters cultural. French anti-Americanism, Richard Kuisel argues, was above all a response to perceived threats to national identity, to the specter of cultural homogenization and colonization, which, in the case of France, goes back to the 1930s. Such fears were combined with the strong left-wing sentiments that used to prevail among French intellectuals at least until the late 1970s.[66]

For reasons discussed both in my book and in the new study, the French left and the reputation of Marxism in France went into a sharp decline over the past ten to fifteen years, which put a major dent into the political and anticapitalist version of anti-Americanism. However, the apprehension over the influx of American mass culture survived and led to the pursuit of measures seeking to stem its tide.[67] These apprehensions are not without foundation, neither in France nor globally: "Statistically, America's impact is overwhelming. Of the world's 100 most attended films last year 88 were American.... As the millennium approaches... American popular culture has never been more dominant internationally, nor more controversial."[68]

American cultural products stimulate anti-Americanism in two ways: first, by their impact on indigenous culture (even indigenous mass culture) that arouses the protective instinct of the elite groups and intellectuals in particular; and second, by presenting images of

American life which are far from reassuring, including violence, anomie, addictions, instability, corruption, and the unbridled pursuit of money and power.

Thus, while there has been a growing recognition that France too has become an eager consumer society, the United States did not cease to be a "cultural menace" as was shown by the protests over the opening of the Walt Disney amusement park near Paris in 1992. The theme park was branded as "a cultural Chernobyl" as well as

> a horror made of cardboard, plastic and appalling colors, a construction of hardened chewing gum and idiotic folklore taken...out of comic books written for obese Americans...
>
> ...[a] kingdom of profit [that] will create a world that will have all the appearance of civilisation and all the savage reality of barbarism.[69]

French intellectuals also voiced fears about the crushing of the imagination of children and turning them into consumers and spectators.

Kuisel's book confirms the connections between the domestic and foreign critiques of the United States I emphasized, pointing to the influence (in France) of American social critics such as C. Wright Mills, William H. Whyte, John Kenneth Galbraith, Sidney Lens, Vance Packard, Michael Harrington, Herbert Marcuse, and Jack Kerouac. In the late 1960s in particular the confluence between American radical social critics and the critiques by the French left became pronounced ("What America's young rebels disliked about their society...were those features of America that the French left has habitually scorned").[70] Similar links between domestic and foreign critiques were also noted by Marcus Cunliffe.[71]

Studies of German anti-Americanism, which came to my attention after the book was finished, also emphasized the cultural dimensions and their historical roots going back to Heine, Jacob Burchhardt, and Nietzsche.[72] As Andrei Markovits observed, "For these intellectuals, America was the soulless juggernaut, threatening 'Kultur' and true nobleness which only a long history could create."[73] Not surprisingly, given both such traditions and the massive American political and cultural (and until recently military) presence, "In today's generation, the political condemnation of the United States inherited from the 1968 generation is joined by a cultural antipathy, a knee jerk tendency to equate all things American with the McDonalds invasion" In Germany, given the pronounced ecological concerns, there was a strong anti-industrial strain in the anti-American protests, the United States being seen as a "major embodiment of alienating...technology and culture."[74] (The aversion to technology was much less of an issue in France and elsewhere in Western Europe.)

There was at last another component of anti-Americanism more prominent in Germany than other parts of Europe: the preoccupation with a more fragile national identity in post World War II Germany associated with the rapid Americanization of West Germany.[75]

Since this volume was written a new and unexpected source of cultural anti-Americanism may be emerging in post-communist Eastern Europe. With the removal of political controls over cultural life and mass communications, Western and primarily American cultural products began invading Eastern Europe. As in other parts of the world, while generally popular, the new influx has been troubling for the native intellectuals and has begun to have an adverse effect on local film industries and book publishing. Commenting on American movies, a Hungarian journalist wrote: "An unprecedented wave of filth has been sweeping our movie threatres this summer. The cultural pollution has assumed such proportions that this writer is wondering about the possibilities of controls for pollution of this type as well."[76]

It is quite possible that such sentiments will intensify and perhaps spread beyond the intelligentsia (in Eastern Europe) as part of a broader disillusionment with the West and especially the United States for failing to provide economic assistance proportionate to expectations. The difficulties of adjusting from a state controlled to a privatized economy and capitalist methods of production are also likely to contribute to anti-American, anti-Western feelings. There is at last also the resurgence of nationalism in some of these countries (Hungary, Slovakia, Russia in particular), which, as in the rest of the world, remains a dependable source of anti-American sentiment.[77]

The persistence and variety of anti-Americanism in diverse parts of the world may be further illustrated by a virtually random selection of recent newspaper reports. Farley Mowat, "Canada's most widely read author" and "a life long socialist" said that he is "'terrified' of the United States and intends to keep his distance." He added: "I'm a bit like somebody who lived in one of the Greek city states watching Rome grow bigger and bigger and more and more ominous, more and more imperial, more and more careless of the other people in the world."[78] In expressing such sentiments he was well within the Canadian strain of anti-Americanism discussed on these pages [see chapter 9].

Another striking example of continuity was provided by recent reports from Guatemala which echoed an unusually lurid and irrational expression of anti-Americanism earlier reported from Mexico [p. 363]:

> Fed by rumors that Americans were coming to kidnap children, cut out their vital organs and ship them to the United States for transplantation, an extraordinary panic has swept Guatemala over the last month.... The situation has become so serious that the United States Embassy is recalling some 200 Peace Corps volunteers from the countryside to the capital...and the State Department has warned Americans not to travel to the country.[79]

In Japan, too, anti-Americanism has gone hand in hand with a partial Americanization and has been strengthened by the information the Japanese public receives from and about the United States, both fictional (American mass entertainment) and journalistic; it is further stimulated by the clash of economic interest in trade relations. Of late the cases of Japanese visitors to the United States victimized by criminals (in Los Angeles) or by a trigger-happy citizen (in Mississippi) provide all too plausible confirmation of America as a hopelessly violent society. An American reporter from Tokyo wrote:

> You can kill your parents while they are eating ice cream in front of the TV. You can ravage your wife. You can maim your husband. You can pull out a gun...and blow the life out of an innocent 16 year old foreign exchange student who rings your doorbell on Halloween. You can do any of these things and then find an American jury that will let you get away with it.
>
> For the most part this is a grotesque parody of the United States, probably inspired in large part by resentment and jealousy.... But that dangerous, decadent America...is the America the foreign media love to portray.[80]

Even in Israel, old ally and protégé of the United States, anti-Americanism can flare up, as was the case recently in the wake of the Hebron massacre committed by an American immigrant. "It's a common perception that if you come from America you have to be crazy" an Israeli journalist said. Concurrently, "The newspaper *Maariv* complained about American parents who 'send their lunatic children to Israel.'" The recent report suggested that many American immigrants were seen in Israel as idealistic and unrealistic extremists,[81] thus displaying an unexpected affinity with radical American social critics who stay at home.

If the burden of the foregoing remarks has been that anti-Americanism abroad (though somewhat reduced and transformed) is not likely to disappear in the foreseeable future, reference must be made to an unusual opposing argument put forward by John Gray. In his view anti-Americanism is already in sharp decline, though for reasons neither he nor this writer would consider desirable.

Gray suggests two reasons for this development. The first and less problematic one, that with the collapse of the Soviet Union the global presence of the United States is being reduced and hence it stimulates less suspicion, hostility, or apprehension. In addition, the United States has also become a weaker nation less able and willing to exercise global leadership or take initiatives:

> [T]his perceived eclipse of American global hegemony—America's inability to confront its own domestic problems, and its increasing unwillingness to project its still massive military power...has been associated with a waning of anti-Americanism.... As America suffers a creeping Brazilianization of its institutions, economy and public life, its status as a unique exemplar of modernity is ever more compromised and anti-Americanism loses much of its rationale.... The prospect is that America will no longer be perceived as a threatening embodiment of modernity.

The other source of the changed perception of the United States, Gray argues, is the growing influence—within American culture and society—of what used to be called the adversary culture, and what he calls "universalist liberalism" (a somewhat problematic concept since present-day liberalism cheerfully endorses multiculturalism and feminism, hardly universalistic beliefs).

According to Gray, former left-wing critics of the United States in Western Europe at any rate "praise American radical feminism, gay rights and multiculturalism as models to be copied by European countries"; hence "America [is] being adopted as the last best hope of universalist liberalism, the one remaining utopian experiment."[82] In other words, if his analysis is correct, the United States will neither be a suitable target on account of being a great interventionist power, nor will its domestic social arrangements stimulate hostility as its politics and culture are increasingly taken over by the liberal left and its national identity eroded by multiculturalism. While certain policies and personalities of the Clinton administration lend some plausibility to this thesis, numerous aspects of American society and culture are likely to retain characteristics which have always stimulated anti-American sentiments abroad.

Anti-Americanism and the Fall of Communism

There used to be a close relationship between the idealization of and sympathy for communist systems, and the deeply felt rejection of American society. It is for that reason that the fall of these systems is relevant to this updating of anti-Americanism.

During the period discussed in the book (1965–1990), communist systems, though their reputations in some instances were already tarnished, by their very existence represented an alternative to the much despised capitalist social order the United States exemplified. Even the Soviet Union, while often criticized even by those on the left, had the potential to be reformed as long as it existed, to become a socialist system with a human face. This alternative is no longer available.

An even more direct connection used to exist between communist systems and anti-Americanism. These systems sought, to the best of their abilities, to keep the flames of anti-Americanism alive globally. Insofar as anti-Americanism abroad and at home (in the United States) helped to sustain one another, the communist efforts were not altogether inconsequential, though by no means decisive for the persistence of the phenomenon.

For all these reasons the collapse of communist states mattered most to two groups of people. Not surprisingly, one consisted of those who had lived under them; the other consisted of Western intellectuals, deeply invested in the critiques of their own societies and looking for alternatives to them, many among them harboring affection toward the various incarnations and especially theories of communism.

For the purposes of this discussion it may be useful to think of intellectuals as those among the educated and leisured strata in the West who are the most driven to and capable of articulating their discontent with the experience of living in modern (secular, rich, pluralistic, and technologically advanced) societies. They constitute a group most adept at and frequently engaged in public moralizing in this century.

Numerous well-known and influential intellectuals responded to the fall of communist systems. Their responses range from unmitigated delight to thinly disguised regret and in-between encompass a variety of efforts to reconcile these events with strongly held ideas and beliefs and especially with their estrangement from Western societies. (Those who were delighted by the collapse are rarely found among the anti-American social critics and can safely be excluded from this discussion.)

Among the intellectuals responding to the collapse, those located at various points on the left-of-center spectrum deserve the most attention not only because they often tend to be radical social critics but also because they are people who followed with particular interest, sympathy, or ambivalence the rise, evolution, and decay of communist societies (which always called themselves socialist, an appellation that was rarely challenged by outsiders, although sometimes was modified by "state," "existing," "actually existing," or "bureaucratic").

My observation of such attitudes made at the beginning of the turmoil in the communist countries remains for the most part valid:

> The decay of communism failed to set into motion any major reassessment of the political attitudes and sympathies of Western social critics, and occasioned little soul searching on account of their profound misjudgments of existing socialist systems. This reluctance to confront the implications of the moral and material bankruptcy of communist systems (and of the ideas which inspired them) is more pronounced in the United States than Western Europe.[83]

Most of the group here discussed has been made up of people who wished to preserve their core (left-of-center) beliefs through a variety of intellectual and psychological efforts and mechanisms.

Left-of-center intellectuals, generally speaking, rarely questioned the legitimacy of communist states even when they were critical of them on other grounds. Their reluctance to seriously question their legitimacy was nurtured by a venerable source of the misapprehensions of these systems, namely, the fear of "ethnocentrism" that goes back to the 1930s. Being critical of communist states was supposed to be ethnocentric because it implied attributing to their citizens the same needs and values members of Western pluralistic societies cherished. The critics of ethnocentrism disbelieved in generalized human needs which would conflict with social and political institutions seeking to shape or overcome these needs. This anti-ethnocentric view was more often than not associated with a highly critical disposition toward American and Western social arrangements, institutions, and values, which were evaluated in a far from relativistic manner.

The notion of moral equivalence (between West and East, or the United States and the Soviet Union) used to be an important device with which to neutralize criticism of communist systems and the Soviet Union in particular. While, if taken at face value, this appears to be a neutral concept, the idea has in fact been closely associated with the rejections of American society. Dominant since the late 1960s it led to equating the Moscow Purges with the Hollywood Purges, the U.S. invasion of Grenada with the Soviet occupation of Afghanistan, the powers of the CIA with the powers of the KGB, the treatment of American mental patients with that of political prisoners in Soviet psychiatric hospitals, and so forth. Central to these equations was the insistence that nothing in American (or Western) social and political practices and institutions was morally superior to their communist equivalent. This point of view denied or seriously obscured moral as well as institutional differences between the United States and the Soviet Union and consequently made it difficult to discern the substantial qualitative differences between the stability, legitimacy, and durability of these two systems.

Those who viewed communist systems with indulgence and regarded them as relatively successful modernizing societies perceived their stability as resting on their capacity to satisfy the (modest) material needs of the population. Since Gorbachev's rise to power the stability of these systems was further predicated (in these circles) on the policies of reform.

The current discussion focuses on the short term. We do not know what impact in the long run the disintegration of communist systems and ideas will have on new generations of American radical social critics and their attitude toward their own society. It remains to be seen, for instance, what will be the fate of the attitude of anti-anti-communism, prevalent among left-of-center intellectuals. As may be recalled, anti-anti-communism was a product of the reaction against the obsessive and often irrational anti-communism associated with the late Senator McCarthy. Diana Trilling observed: "It was Joseph McCarthy who took anti-communism out of the realm of respectable discourse and created for people of liberal impulse an automatic association between any voiced opposition to communism and reaction."[84] Anti-anti-communism has also been closely linked, throughout its entire existence, to a highly, indeed often radically critical disposition toward American society.[85]

I will first deal with those who have clearly learned something from these historic events. Richard Rorty, the philosopher who would not object to being described as a man of the left, was clearly among them. He wrote in 1992: "It is going to take a long period of readjustment for us Western leftist intellectuals to comprehend that the word 'socialism' has been drained of force—as have been all the other words that drew their force from the idea that an alternative to capitalism was available."[86]

What survives of the idea of socialism is at the heart of the debates sparked by the collapse of communism. The latter accelerated a trend that has been discernible well before the disintegration of the communist systems, namely, the dilution of the concept of socialism.

For a growing number of left-liberal American intellectuals socialism has come to mean an increasingly undifferentiated set of attitudes, a form of private morality of limited political content that includes a basic decency, caring, generosity, sensitivity to the needs of fellow human beings, capacity for some self-sacrifice, and so forth. The position of being a socialist (or a man of the left) has gradually become transformed from a specific political agenda into a diffuse source of self-esteem for many American intellectuals. This is especially the case when such a self-identification is colored by associations of youthful vitality and idealism, and of a time when the concept was less tarnished by the policies and deeds committed on its behalf in the course of its attempted realization.

The late Irving Howe arrestingly summarized (well before the fall of communism) the attitudes that used to draw idealistic intellectuals to socialism in the United States and elsewhere: "They became socialists because they were moved to fervor by the call of brotherhood and sisterhood; because the world seemed aglow with the vision of a time in which humanity might live in justice and peace."[87]

Paul Berman of similarly impeccable credentials as solid left-liberal is also among the minority of leftist intellectuals willing to admit that "what has just now collapsed is…more than Communism in its traditional Soviet model." He continued: "The idea of a detotalitarianised, reform Communism is just as dead, or even deader. So is the third world impulse for a watered-down semi-Soviet, semi-indigenous system to be called, depending on the region, 'African socialism', 'Arab socialism' or 'Sandinismo.'"[88]

Eugene Genovese, a historian with well established Marxist and left-wing credentials, has gone further in challenging left-of-center conventional wisdom than most others of a similar background. His observations go a long way explaining the persistence of domestic anti-Americanism: "unable to offer a coherent alternative to capitalism as a social system, and with no socialist countries left to identify with, many left-wingers now wallow in a mindless hostility to Western Civilization and to their own identity as Americans."

Genovese also spotted another interesting trend that suggests how tenaciously the political attitudes and values of the 1960s survive in present day political reflexes: "Those who indulge in the fantasy of a socialism risen phoenix-like from the ashes no longer equate socialism with working class power and the abolition of private property. Rather, they embrace a caricature of classic liberalism that would free individuals from virtually all social restraint."[89] In support of these observations it should be noted that ever since the 1960s there has emerged in American society a peculiar combination of attitudes among those on the left (or the New Left). The latter, while suspicious of the centralized, bureaucratic, communist states (and especially the Soviet Union), embraced a no-enemies-on-the-left mentality together with the anti-anti-communism that the late Senator McCarthy inspired. To this amalgam was added the volatile component of radical individualism (Genovese referred to) strangely contradicted and undercut by an abject willingness to retreat from a defense of individualism, and especially the notion of individual achievement and merit, when the flag of preferential treatment of selected victim groups was raised.

Genovese does not shrink from the conclusion that the "collapse of socialism, understood as a social system based on state ownership of the means of production, has tellingly exposed the disease—the futility of the communist ideal of a radically egalitarian society of free and autonomous individuals." The decay of communist systems occasioned another profound stock taking by Roger Gottlieb, an English Marxist (or former Marxist) who is distinguished by his willingness to confront the "basic flaws" of the theory (and not merely of the praxis it had inspired). In his 1992 study he concluded that "[t]here are certain limitations which Marxism—no matter how transformed, modernized or joined with other perspectives (Marxist-feminism, black Marxism etc.)—cannot overcome."[90]

Gottlieb is among the handful of authors coming out of a Marxist tradition willing to raise the crucial question of the relationship between the nature of the theory and the practices it had inspired, or stimulated: why has it been so difficult to realize the theory, or what is in it that lends itself to distortion or misapplication: "[Do]...the roots of Stalinist terror lie in Marxism's fundamental lack of respect for the individual person and for universal human rights? Will Marxism just *have* to sacrifice innocent lives to some mythical higher purpose? Does the absence of principles held without regard to final consequences mean that Marxist morality will always justify means by utopian ends?"[91]

Elsewhere he draws attention to one of the deepest flaws of the Marxist theoretical edifice, the shallow optimism about human nature:

> [B]ecause the Marxist tradition presupposes...that human fulfillment results from the proper arrangement of human relations and consumption, its model ignores a basic dimension of human experience. The problem arises from some unstated—and unexamined—premises: If we are given enough bread and justice, we will be

satisfied and not want more. We will no longer be driven by greed, insecurity, envy, boredom or the fear of death.... We will accept ourselves and others. Having achieved equality we will not seek superiority.... Having so much we will not want more. In short, once external injustice is ended, internal mysery will dwindle.[92]

These observations are helpful for understanding the radical rejections of American society (especially by American social critics) fueled as they have been by high expectations stimulated in part by American cultural traditions (see pp. 15–17 in the book) and, in many cases, by Marxism.

Gottlieb's comments on Marxism and righteous anger in social activism are also helpful for appreciating the bitterness that enters into the radical rejections of America:

> The uses of suffering and anger in Marxism and feminism are repeated in the *new social movements*: racial struggles, gay and lesbian liberation, ethnic liberation movements of all kinds.... a certain kind of aggressive, unreflective, self-righteous anger simply becomes an entrenched habit of mind, a basic, pervasive and potentially limiting viewpoint.... this politicized anger has a real tendency towards self-righteousness.... Part of my identification with my rage is also a permanent sense of being treated unfairly...[thus becoming]... righteously angry victims.[93]

Some of the responses to the fall of communism on the left may also be examined with the help of the concepts Leon Festinger developed over three decades ago. While the situations and groups he investigated and the handling of the collapse of communism by those on the left are by no means identical there are similarities. In our case in point it was widely believed that the Soviet Union, and the ancillary systems it spawned and controlled, would survive in the foreseeable future, perhaps with some modifications, (reforms), and that these systems represented valid paths to modernity. Contrary to such expectations the Soviet Union and the systems it supported abruptly collapsed under conditions totally unforeseen and this constituted what Festinger calls "dissonance" given the belief in their durability. Such dissonance was presumably more strongly felt by those who not only believed these systems to be durable but also preferred them to capitalist ones. By contrast, the same intellectuals often anticipated and dwelt on the crisis and impending collapse of Western capitalism, which, however, failed to materialize. The ensuing situation is similar to what Festinger dealt with in his study (*When Prophecy Fails*), when "the convinced person has some investment in his belief" and a "variety of ingenious defenses [spring up] with which people protect their convictions...to keep them unscathed." Festinger also noted that "[d]issonance produces discomfort and...there will arise pressures to reduce or eliminate dissonance."

Virtually all the mechanisms or forms of dissonance reduction that Festinger specified came into play in the wake of the collapse. Of these, two have been particularly prominent. One was a redefinition of the situation, that is, denial that the Soviet Union was socialist or Marxist, in which case the collapse did not matter and did not challenge belief in the durability of such systems, or reflect on the capacity of Marxism to inspire just societies, or undermine the belief that capitalist systems were more corrupt and doomed to earlier unraveling than socialist ones. The second popular strategy in the words of Festinger is "to forget or reduce the importance of those cognitions that are in a dissonant relationship." This meant ignoring the collapse, forgetting about communist systems and how their durability and legitimacy compared to those in the West, that is, ceasing to dwell on matters that contradict established beliefs and preferences. This was a path chosen by many academic intellectuals who, rather than to reflect on the collapse, instead immersed themselves with renewed vigor in other matters such as multiculturalism, postmodernism, critical legal theory, revisions of American history, the many branches of feminism, and so forth.

Another reaction to the fall of communism that is in line with Festinger's observations has been to predict improved opportunities for socialist movements in the West. (Festinger noted that true believers often respond to the failure of the prophecy by redoubling their activism.)[94] Christopher Chase-Dunn, a sociologist at Johns Hopkins University, reassuringly concluded that "The revolutions in the Soviet Union and the People's Republic of China have increased our collective knowledge about how to build socialism despite their only partial successes."[95] Geoff Eley, a historian at the University of Michigan saw "a rich source of possibilities" in the socialist tradition for new organizational efforts on the left.[96] Even in the United States, according to Chase-Dunn, "there should be new openings for building socialism."[97] Maurice Isserman, a historian, was hopeful that "[t]he collapse of international communism and the end of the cold war may well prove to be the prelude to another, more enduring, rise of the American left."[98]

Such responses to the collapse gained strength from the ample social support that was available for them in various subcultural settings of American society (especially the campuses) where such beliefs and attitudes have flourished, indeed, have become institutionalized since the 1960s. This too was a condition Festinger specified among those helpful "to withstand disconfirming evidence."

Erstwhile political pilgrims and tourists constitute another group of radical social critics of the United States likely to resist sweeping reevaluation of the wreckage of the social systems they were irresistibly drawn to. There have been tens if not hundreds of thousands of such people in this century, most recently admirers of Sandinista Nicaragua.

Of these countries, Cuba under Castro remains the only one that can still count on a measure of sympathy of those on the left for its defiance of the United States, its refusal to compromise with capitalism and unwillingness to follow the former Soviet Union and its former allies along the path of political-economic reform. Even as recently as the summer of 1993 "seeing the bright side of Castro" was a fair description of an American TV documentary of Cuba; Cuba was also praised on the correspondence page of the *Times* for "pioneering energy conservation" (as if it had a choice) and friends of Castro campaigned across the nation to lift the economic blockade motivated doubtless as much by the impulse to diminish human suffering as the desire to save the system.[99] At Hampshire College in Amherst, Massachusetts, on April 14, 1994 sympathetic faculty members joined in a public presentation entitled "Cuba: Socialism Under Duress." As of 1993 Gunter Grass, the famous German writer (and a leading anti-American, see also pp. 381–82 in the book), still believed that Cubans "were less likely to notice the absence of liberal rights" having been given "self respect" by the revolution, and that Cuba still "has something to offer besides shortages and a nice climate."[100]

Another example of durable affection for Cuba was provided by Carol Brightman, author-editor of the volume *Venceremos Brigade: Young Americans Sharing the Life and Work of Revolutionary Cuba* (New York, 1971)—perhaps the most fulsome and morbidly fascinating rapture about Castro's Cuba that has ever been published. (It was discussed at some length in my *Political Pilgrims*). In 1994, following yet another visit, Brightman was still impressed by "Castro's efforts to devise 'a different kind of socialism.' She also boasted [in *The Nation*] about getting Castro to autograph a baseball cap for her 14-year-old son."[101] At last it should also be noted here that the venerable social critic Benjamin Spock, as of September 1994, still found much to admire and nothing to criticize in Castro's Cuba.[102]

Those still desirous of going on a conducted political tour of Cuba could take advantage of a ten-day "Cuba Study Tour" offered by the "Florida Coalition for Peace and Justice," complete with visits to day-care centers, schools, cooperative farms, mental hospitals, and representatives of the Cuban Peace Movement, among other things.[103]

It has been conventional wisdom, repeated on the evening news, that the U.S. economic blockade, and not the policies Castro pursued for decades, was responsible for the difficulties of the Cuban economy. Thus, Cuba under Castro remains the only communist state that still elicits warmth among some Western intellectuals in part because the current economic hardships have reinvigorated its aura of victimhood and because it is the last uncompromising communist system.

Bizarre examples of the idealization of other communist systems may also be encountered occasionally, illustrating the uncommon persistence of belief in face of overwhelming evidence. Mary Lou Greenberg, a former editor of *New China* magazine and a 1971 pilgrim to China wrote in a recent *New York Times*:

> In 1971 during the Cultural Revolution workers spoke to me with pride of their efforts to build a new...China. They were making prodigious economic gains.... But even more important, new social relations were being forged...the Chinese I saw were characterised by dignity and optimism....
>
> It is no wonder that, in this centennial year of the birth of Mao Zedong, many in China as well as around the world, are looking at the experience of the Maoist years not only with nostalgia, but also for lessons for the future.[104]

Former President Jimmy Carter's assessments of North Korea and its supreme leader, Kim Il Sung, (following his visit in June 1994) are also worth mentioning here, dealing as we are with the survival of breathtaking misperceptions of the remaining communist systems and the affinity such misperceptions have with a highly critical view of American society. President Carter may also be remembered as the incarnation of anti-anti-communism at the highest level. During his presidency he warned against the "inordinate fear of communism" and was stunned that Brezhnev, after their public huggings and joint commitment to the cause of peace, proceeded to invade Afghanistan.

Mr. Carter was evidently most favorably impressed by Kim Il Sung, whose police state ranks among the most ruthless and repressive in our times and who created around himself the most grotesque cult of personality. According to a press report, "Mr. Carter heaped praise on Kim Il Sung...'I found him to be vigorous, intelligent...well informed...and in charge of the decisions about his country."[105] It was also possible for him to observe, in the course of his brief and doubtless carefully chaperoned visit, "the reverence with which they [the North Korean people] look upon their leader.'"[106] And as if determined to compete with the political tourists of the past (in projecting unhesitatingly the familiar on the unfamiliar) he reportedly said that "Pyongyang [the capital] is full of pep—its shops remind him of the 'Wal-Mart in Americus, Georgia', and at night the neon lights remind him of Times Square."[107]

The survival of the skewed comparative moral perspectives of some Western intellectuals is reflected in a recent book on political imprisonment by the prominent feminist social critic, Kate Millett. As in so many other instances, what at first sight appears as an exercise in moral equivalence (between the West and communist powers), on closer inspection "reveals some odd disproportions."[108] Thus, in this study of "political cruelty":

> Out of a total of eleven chapters, the Gulag and the Holocaust get one chapter each, while the evils of Western colonialism get six...Mao's China gets a third of a chapter, Iran half a chapter—and British Ireland a whole chapter.... Cuba is not mentioned once in Millett's chapters on Latin America. From her account you would not know that Cuba successfully concealed its own torture of political prisoners and so in the early '70s it seemed like a wonderful success story.... [moreover] she never mentions that the cold war was fought by two sides.[109]

At last, like other radical critics of the United States Millett suggests that American policies and the outrages they have given rise to "are worse than anything preceding them in our century."[110]

Unhappily for many Western intellectuals positioned on the further reaches of the left, not only has the supply of appealing communist systems been exhausted, there is also a critical shortage of guerrilla movements with suitable credentials. The Shining Path guerrillas in Peru were described by Jorge Castaneda as "the last movement to openly proclaim its allegiance to 'Marxism-Leninism-Maoism,' to unabashedly put forward the goal of Communist revolution and to unhesitatingly reject any notion of electoral contention or dialogue with existing authorities or institutions."[111] As such it has come closest to having the proper credentials and appeals for radical leftist intellectuals (such as William Kunstler and John Gerassi who were among the supporters of a Berkeley, California, based Pro-Shining Path group).[112] Such sympathizers must be capable of accepting large quantities of bloodshed in a good revolutionary cause. The supporters in Berkeley were not alone. As was reported in the *Times*, "From Berkeley to London to Stockholm, solidarity groups have formed to support a group [Shining Path] that one human rights advocate, Juan E. Mendez of Americas Watch recently called 'the most brutal guerilla group that ever has appeared in the Western Hemisphere.'"[113]

It is hardly surprising that past assessments of the communist systems conditioned the reaction to their collapse. Many Western intellectuals used to regard them (even in more recent times) with bemused tolerance and understanding while regretfully noting their occasional (or frequent, as the case may be) departure from the early ideals or the guiding theory. For I. F. Stone the Soviet Union represented (in 1983) a "distortion of socialism," nonetheless it was "still socialism."[114] For him as for many other intellectuals on the left what mattered were the good intentions; even a deformed socialist system was preferable to an unreconstructed capitalist one; someday, actually existing socialist states might become more authentic incarnations of the ideal. In the meantime the Soviet Bloc and the Soviet Union in particular were given credit for restraining American imperialism, aiding Third World liberation movements and propping up the supposedly more authentic socialist states such as Vietnam, Cuba, and Nicaragua. Moreover, according to the authors of a Marxist textbook in sociology, "The Soviets were trying something for the first time in history and it is hardly surprising that they made mistakes."[115]

Robert Heilbronner wrote wistfully that "the collapse of the Soviet system, hailed as a victory for human freedom, was also a defeat for human aspirations."[116] The same viewpoint was eloquently conveyed by the main character (an Italian communist) contemplating the wreckage of both theory and practice in a recent novel of George Steiner:

> Marxism did man supreme honor. The Moses and Jesus and Marx vision of the just earth, of a neighbour's love, of human universality, the abolition of barriers between lands, classes, races...of tribal hatreds: *that* vision was...an over-estimate of man. A possibly fatal, possibly deranged but none the less magnificent, jubilant over-estimate of man. The highest compliment ever paid him.[117]

For some radical social critics in the United States the fall of communist systems provided yet another opportunity to level new charges at American society. This development was discussed in the last chapter [esp. pp. 460–67]. Most characteristically the commentaries of leftist social critics (of the West) have been pervaded by the concern that the collapse might legitimate capitalism and actually existing Western democracies. Their reaction to the unraveling was also colored by the impression that only under capitalism did serious social problems—such as crime, substance abuse, prostitution, family instability, ethnic discrimination, dissatisfaction with work, environmental destruction and others—flourish. Many tacitly assumed that communist systems, whatever else might be wrong with them, were largely free of anomie, self-centeredness, and the many types of spiritual malaise afflicting capitalist societies.

Thus, a continued suspicion and hostility toward capitalism have remained major determinants of the responses to the collapse. Some even succeeded in blaming capitalism for the difficulties of the socialist states. A professor of anthropology at the University of Massachusetts (Amherst) averred:

> the communist countries should have stayed on a road of purely socialist development instead of giving in to their citizens' demand for a more consumer-oriented economy. But because the West had the consumer goods, it was able in the 1980s to hoodwink the communist world into becoming trading partners which tied its economic well-being to the West's.... "The decline in the 1980s of world capitalism nailed Eastern Europe" Cole says, explaining the collapse of the East bloc.[118]

According to Christopher Chase-Dunn

> The communist states have been important experiments in the construction of socialist institutions, but they were perverted...by the necessities of survival...in the context of the capitalist world market.... The communist states failed to institutionalise a self-reproducing socialist mode of production because of the strong threats and inducements emanating from the larger capitalist world-system....
>
> The existence of a dynamic and competitive world market encouraged corruption, consumerism, and political opportunism by the "new class" of technocrats and bureaucrats [in the communist states].[119]

In short, in the words of a Cuban émigré scholar, Dario Fernandez-Morera, "Socialism would have turned out much better had capitalism not continued to be around to corrupt it."[120]

These attitudes help to understand why, for example, a resolution proposed in 1990 at the annual meeting of the Organization of American Historians was defeated with only one vote in its support. The defeated motion wished to express

> wholehearted support of the new initiative from the leaders of the Soviet Union seeking to place history on a footing of respect for truth and avoiding deliberate falsehood.... [the resolution also proposed to express]...profound regret that during the period when history in the Soviet Union and the commmunist states in Eastern Europe was controlled by powers hostile to the pursuit of truth, the Organization never protested the forced betrayal of the historians' responsibility to truth imposed upon Soviet and East European historians by their political leaders.[121]

By contrast, American professional associations in the social sciences and humanities routinely passed political resolutions supportive of various left-of-center political systems, causes, or movements.

Another recurring theme on the left has been that the collapse did not vindicate American foreign policies. A columnist in the *Chronicle of Higher Education* spoke for many of his fellow academics on this matter:

> We set out to break the back of Soviet Communism but simply broke our own bank instead. The cost of the cold war to the United States was perhaps even more spiritual than economic.... The United States emerged from the cold war burdened by debt and poverty and carrying numerous scars from wounds to our cherished institutions—self-inflicted for the sake of superpower competition. In turning our nation into a hard-line cold-war combatant we undermined our "best traditions"...Considering what might have been, the United States was the loser in the cold war.[122]

A volume devoted to the reassessment of the Cold War argued that it served largely domestic political and psychological purposes for the United States, gratifying in particular the need to find enemies and "to affirm American identity and Americans' basic goodness." Gorbachev "deprived" Americans of their major enemy, suggesting again that there was no enemy, only a fantasy. As the revisionist historians saw it, "The Cold War had resulted largely from the efforts of the United States to export capitalism across the globe.... The Soviet Union, far from being the aggressor, found itself on the defensive...the burden of responsibility for the Cold War rested on the United States."

In this perspective, anti-communism, as a domestic issue, was the root of the Cold War, providing Americans with "psychological security" according to Mr. Brands, author of this study. Moreover, "the most important reason for detente's demise was that Americans loved the Cold War too much to let it go."

As these suggestions so well illustrate, anti-anti-communism rested on the premise that there was no substance to the fears of or aversion to communism (represented by the Soviet Union), neither domestically nor globally. The author concludes that the collapse raised the question "whether it had been necessary for Americans to get so worked up over an enemy that proved to be a shell." He too believed that "the call to arms against communism" subverted the principles on behalf of which the Cold War was fought; Americans had little reason to rejoice in their victory in the Cold War, so the volume concludes.[123] Similar views were expressed in the popular history of the 1950s written by David Halberstram who focused on the delusions driving U.S. foreign policy during those years.[124] E. L. Doctorow, the novelist-social critic described American Cold War policies "as an act of national self mutilation"[125]

As the communist ideals ceased to have even the most rudimentary embodiment or discernible approximation in actually existing political systems (with the possible and partial exception of Cuba), and as most of the systems that used to legitimate themselves by Marxism have ignominiously collapsed, it has become all the more important to rescue and reaffirm the ideals (for those who believed in them), and to separate them from the disagreeable realities they were linked to. Such efforts were also prompted by the disturbing, indeed wholly undreamed of possibility that the Marxian developmental scheme could be reversed and socialist systems be replaced by capitalist ones.

Shlomo Avineri among many others maintained that "the Soviet system was not and could not have been a socialist system.... Marxism saw socialism as a stage that would follow capitalism and take its place.... This [Soviet] society and socialism have nothing in common."[126] Authors of the textbook already mentioned (*Crisis & Change*) wrote: "We do not believe that the failure is a failure of Marxism. Still less is it the final 'triumph of capitalism'.... Capitalism is still in crisis.... The main reason that communism has not been realized is that sufficient numbers of people do not *understand* why it is required and what it requires."[127] At a conference entitled "Rethinking Marxism" at the University of Massachusetts at Amherst (attended by 1500) one participant said: "The old model of statist, authoritarian socialism...had been dealt a blow. That sweeps the slate clean." He advised American Marxists to keep the faith proposing the slogan: "[S]ocialism is dead. Long live socialism." On the same occasion Bertell Ollman suggested that "the collapse of the Soviet Union provided a new opportunity for purer Marxist theories to thrive."[128]

Stuart Hall wrote in *Marxism Today* that "we should not be alarmed by the collapse of 'actually existing socialism' since, as socialists, we have been waiting for it to happen for three decades."[129] If such commentators had been anxiously awaiting the collapse of existing socialist systems for decades they succeeded in keeping such attitudes to themselves. In fact many leftist intellectuals in the West pointedly abstained from the criticism of existing socialist states, trying to find virtue in their anticapitalist policies.

It appears at the present time that those among the academic intellectuals who have remained most faithful to their Marxist beliefs and are the most radical critics of American culture and society, can most often be found in departments of English, or "Cultural Studies." As John Searle observed, "Having been refuted as theories of society, these views have retreated into departments of literature, where they still...flourish as tools of interpretation."[130] Presumably this group is furthest removed from social and political realities (and feel the least disciplinary pressure to close the gap). John Diggins rightly observed of them that they "[clung] to a theory that bore no relations to the simple desires of people living under oppressive regimes."[131] Any program of the annual meetings of the Modern Language Association of the last two decades provides support for these observations.

For the radical social critics attracted to any variety of Marxism, the fall and attendant final discreditation of communist systems made it especially urgent to prove that the ideas of Marxism and the now defunct political systems had *nothing* in common. It is one thing to say that communist states disgraced the Marxian ideals, that Marx would have disapproved of their practices, that theory and practice diverged; it is something quite different to propose that Marxism and communist systems had nothing whatsoever to do with one another. While it is not the purpose of this introduction to examine the relationship between Marxist theory and the practices of communist states, a few obvious convergences may be mentioned to refute the claims noted above. They include the conviction that private property and the profit motive are the sole source of most social and human evil; the intense hostility toward religion and peasants; and, especially consequential, the dismissal of the importance of the individual in the historical process—these aspects of theory were certainly upheld by existing communist states. Frank E. Manuel observed: "[F]ollowers of a religious cult or a secular messianic movement have been known to reflect the temper of their founder....the regimes that spoke in his [Marx's] name derived their justification from the idea that the individual was of no moment in the period before the dawn of true human history.... prophets and messiahs must share blame for the excesses of their followers."[132]

While left-liberal intellectuals in the United States could accept the idea that the Soviet empire collapsed because of its economic crisis and institutional malfunctioning, because "the system did not work," the notion that its unraveling was a form of "moral collapse" was rarely entertained by this group. Irving Kristol's comment helps to explain this phenomenon: "[S]ocialism is dead but versions of the collectivist impulse live.... Today the old-fashioned animus against the market economy is being sublimated into an aggressive animus against the bourgeois society that is organically associated with our market economy. If you delegitimate this bourgeois society, the market economy...is also delegitimized."[133]

This animus is in turn stimulated by the belief in the unique moral failures of capitalist, that is, Western or American society, quite different from, and supposedly more profound, than the failures of communist systems.

The Moral Collapse of Communism was the title and theme of John Clark and Aaron Wildavsky's book in which they proposed that "every evil attributed to capitalism turns up under socialism" and that the most decisive failure of these systems was moral rather than economic. As these systems approached their final disintegration Clark and Wildavsky wrote: "The final irony is that a political economy that was to alter human relations from selfish isolation to altruistic communitarianism actually created a caricature of capitalism in which everyone was forced to fend for themselves."[134]

Martin Malia's response to the collapse is probably the most radically opposed to those prevalent among intellectuals positioned on the left. For him the crucial explanation of the decay and the fall was to be found not in the system's deviation from the Marxist-socialist blueprint but in the attempt to realize it:

> [T]he relevant basic concept [for understanding the Soviet phenomenon] is not modernization, or even totalitarianism; it is socialism. "Building socialism" is what the Soviet Union was all about.... We should take this claim seriously.... Still less should we dismiss Soviet ideology as no more than hortatory rhetoric....in this perspec-

tive the term socialism designates first of all a moral idea.... Only
if this moral basis is recognized is it possible to account for the extraordinary emotional charge that has always surrounded the socialist project. The essence of the moral idea of socialism is that
human equality is the supreme value.[135]

This being the case, the supreme goal of politics under socialism was the removal or alleviation of inequality: "The practical, instrumental program of socialism therefore consists in the
equalization of wealth by political means; in...the subordination of
economics to politics."[136]

As noted earlier, many radical social critics of America preferred
to avert their eyes from events in the former Soviet Bloc. Given their
preoccupation with the impending, ongoing, or approaching crisis
of capitalism (or late capitalism) it is hardly surprising that they
missed the actual crisis of communism.

The multiplication of the causes, which today mobilize and
motivate various adversarial groups in the United States, is probably linked, indirectly at least, to these escapist attitudes and the
decline of the universalistic vision of Marxism to which communist
systems at least paid lip service. It would be difficult at the present
time to find expressions of belief in the eventual emergence of "the
new socialist man" (or woman), in the prospects of greatly improving human nature, let alone the human condition, (as distinct from
alleviating the lot of selected victim groups), or in the worldwide
unity of the working classes and so forth.

Multiculturalism is perhaps the best example of how universalistic ideals and aspirations have been replaced by strongly felt and
divisive assertions of ethnic pride and superiority. Much of the
adversarial energy that at earlier times led to the idealization of
putative embodiments of socialism in various locations (most recently in Nicaragua) found new outlets in the pursuit and advocacy of multiculturalism.

Postmodernism, structuralism, deconstructionism, critical-legal
theory, and varieties of radical feminism may be added to the types
of radical social criticism that provided preoccupations and diver-
sions for many intellectuals who might otherwise have been under
greater pressure to ponder the lessons of the decay and collapse of
existing socialism and its legitimating ideas.

Anti-Americanism and Decadence

Decadence is another topic that is touched upon at the end of this
book. Have any of its alleged symptoms intensified since this book

was completed? Is a declining super power more or less likely to inspire anti-Americanism? Is the United States in decline?

Decadence and anti-Americanism may be linked in two ways (see also pp. 456–59). In the first place domestic anti-Americanism itself may be seen as a symptom of decadence especially when it takes the form of an irrational self-flagellation conducted by members of elite groups, foremost among them academic intellectuals, but also politicians. There is reason to question the vitality of a social system when some of its key groups appear to have lost faith in its dominant values and institutions, when they readily assent to its most radical critiques (or themselves put such forward), when an exaggerated belief in the discrepancy between theory and practice seems to prevail, when radical social criticism becomes a thriving industry, and when even mass entertainment echoes the themes of radical social criticism (see pp. 228–42).

There is much truth in the observation of Richard Bernstein a cultural correspondent of the *New York Times*:

> The Vietnam War…ended with the most powerful episode of self doubt, of questioning America's role in the world that the country had ever experienced.
> That self doubt, the ambivalence about America's nature, remains a part of the collective heritage even now…many who came of age during the 1960s have never regained the confidence in the essential goodness of America and the American Government that prevailed in earlier periods.[137]

In turn anti-Americanism abroad may be linked to decadence when American culture and society are rejected because they are perceived as decadent.

Many meanings may be attached to decadence. A society may be considered decadent when it is incapable or unwilling to defend itself against external threat while commanding the necessary resources to do so; a society of declining productivity and economic know-how, of falling educational standards and declining interest in maintaining them; a society pervaded by growing fear of risk taking, one of administrative chaos, ungovernability, intensified competition among interests groups contributing to governmental paralysis; a social system whose institutions are incapable of exercising necessary social control; a society of diminishing work ethic, immersed in rising tides of self-indulgence, hedonism, and escapism, and increasingly incapable of socializing the young and maintaining family cohesion—all such symptoms are usually associated with decadence.

The rising rates of illegitimacy are a particularly serious threat to family cohesion and the upbringing of children, indeed to the integrity of the social order as a whole. Whereas in 1960 the illegitimacy rate was only 5%, by the early 1990s about one-third of all American children were born out of wedlock; two-thirds of black children. However, illegitimacy rates among the white population have been rising faster than among other groups. An anthropologist observed: "For an anthropologist the widespread failure to marry is a sign of impending disaster. Cultures differ in many ways, but all societies that survive are built on marriage...the history of human society shows that when people stop marrying, their continuity as a culture is in jeopardy."[138]

Most often discussions of decline and decadence focus on matters economic: declining productivity, competitiveness, entrepreneurial spirit, and growing trade deficit.[139] Seymour Itzkoff linked such difficulties to "educational and cultural decline" in turn based on an even more basic problem: "falling intelligence levels" and "a demographic shift...toward lower levels of intellectual and thus cultural, educational and inevitably, economic achievement."[140]

The cultural shift to an expansive social determinism that relieves the individual (or some groups) of responsibility for their actions might also be included in this inventory of decline. Some observers would add the decline of meaningful religious participation and belief.

Some statistical indicators of decline have been assembled by William J. Bennett:

> Since 1960, the population has increased 41%; the Gross Domestic Product nearly tripled; and total social spending by all levels of government (measured in constant 1990 dollars) has risen from $143 billion to $787 billion—more than a five-fold increase. Inflation-adjusted spending on welfare has increased 630%...on education...225%....
>
> But during the same 30-year period there has been a 560% increase in violent crime; more than a 400% increase in illegitimate births; a quadrupling in divorce rates; a tripling of the percentage of children living in single-parent homes; more than a 200% increase in teenage suicide rate; and a drop of almost 80 points in the SAT scores. Modern day social pathologies...seem impervious to government spending on their alleviation.[141]

Probably the most telling symptoms of decadence are to be found in the realm of values, difficult as it is to provide clear-cut, quantifiable evidence of them. The spread of moral relativism is certainly a part of the picture.

Mass entertainment, among other things, fully reflects these trends. It is in itself noteworthy, and far from unrelated to decadence, that entertainment has expanded into areas of life earlier thought to be quite distinct and far removed from it. The provision of information by the mass media, formal education, and some religious activities increasingly partake of entertainment presumably in order to attract, or keep large audiences. Even personal misery and pathology have become the staple of mass entertainment as in the many television talk shows where

> indecent exposure is celebrated as virtue....there was once a time when personal failures, subliminal desires, and perverse taste were accompanied by guilt or embarrassment, at least by silence. Today these are a ticket to appear as a guest on the Sally Jessy Raphael show, or one of the dozens or so shows like it....a list of some of the daytime talk-show topics...include: cross dressing couples; a three-way love affair; a man whose chief aim in life is to sleep with women and fool them into thinking that he is using a condom...women who can't say no to cheating; prostitutes who love their jobs; a former drug dealer...a young girl caught in the middle of a bitter custody battle.[142]

There are of course also endless televised confessions by sufferers of diverse victimhoods and abuses.

Why does all this constitute further evidence of decadence? Because suffering or personal pathology is converted into entertainment; because of the growing inability of entertainers and their audiences to distinguish between the private and the public, entertainment and therapy, voyeurism and empathy, exhibitionism and intimacy, between friends and strangers.

The embrace of social-cultural determinism helps to explain the phenomenon: when people displaying what used to be considered pathologies are encouraged to disclaim *any* responsibility for these conditions they feel more at liberty to talk about them to huge audiences. The craving for publicity, the longing to emerge, however briefly, from anonymity (by being on a television program watched by millions) is another powerful incentive.

The popularity of joining victim groups (discussed earlier in another context) may also be associated with decadence. First, by doing so the victim reduces or completely abandons responsibility for his behavior as he combines a sense of implicit moral superiority with a sense of entitlement and passivity. Second, as David Rieff wrote, only in a rich and self-indulgent society can such self-absorption become widespread: "It is a measure of the continued economic success of the United States that so many of its citizens could be so buffered from the real harshness of the world that they can spend their time anatomizing the state of their own feelings and speculating, often deep into middle age, about whether or not their parents have always behaved as well as they should have."[143]

The idea Rieff is conveying is similar to the notion of "excess security" discussed early in the book [pp. 43–48]. Other examples of the phenomena here discussed come from Berkeley, California, the city with probably the most radical municipal government in the United States, one that barely regards itself as part of the country, and nearby Marin country, nearly as politically correct. A recent arrival "dumbfounded by the ease with which life is conducted here" noted: "issues on the local political agenda...[included] banning gas-powered leaf blowers...[and] segregating perfume-wearers in public places."[144]

The so-called postmodernists, the most extreme and articulate representatives of moral (and intellectual) relativism in the United States at the present time, have made a signal contribution to the ethos of decadent self-indulgence: "They belong to what is today the most secure stratum of the most secure society in the world. Their generation...has never had to face catastrophe."[145]

When the generous attribution of victimhood becomes institutionalized in legislation it may also have tangible economic consequences. While the economic costs of the preferential treatment of racial-ethnic minorities is unknown, the cost of recent legislation regarding the disabled is projected to be high. Gary Becker, an economist, wrote:

> The [disability] act covers not only people with hearing, sight or mobility impairments but also those with emotional illness, dyslexia, AIDS, and past drug or alcohol addiction. This is why some of the act's supporters claim that it will help 40 million Americans.... The new law defines disability so ambiguously that whether or not a person has been excluded from a job unfairly will often be impossible to determine with any confidence. Are people handicapped— and hence entitled to special consideration—simply because they cannot work under stressful conditions or because they object to any criticism of their work that may mean a return to alcohol or drug dependency?.... Most of the costs will be passed on to workers, consumers, and, eventually, the disabled themselves.[146]

Connections may also be established between decadence, the preoccupation with victimhood, and self-esteem. In effect the pursuit of self-esteem seeks to provide a shortcut to a variety of improvements and accomplishments, to personal and social uplift. Whereas at earlier times (and in other cultures) it was believed that self-esteem is a product of tangible achievements and accomplishments, and the disciplined effort they require, at the present time therapeutic exhortations promise easy access to a flattering view of the self that is unrelated to any notion of underlying merit, and is offered as the egalitarian remedy against any notion of failure or guilt.

Just as the attainment of victimhood has become easy and within the reach of all, so—the other side of the coin—attaining self-esteem is said to be easy and unproblematic as "the distinction between therapy and the rest of American life has eroded."[147]

The apparently easy access to *both* victimhood and self-esteem may also be seen as part of the intensifying egalitarianism that has swept the country over the past three decades. Each of these three phenomena involves a decline in making important distinctions: between real and questionable victimhood, between genuine and spurious grounds of self-esteem, and between groups and individuals in society at large. The latter is what Aaron Wildavsky called "radical egalitarianism," by which he meant

> not only an approach to the distribution of economic resources, but...the idea of a culture or way of life devoted to diminishing differences among people [or] the belief in the moral virtue of diminishing differences among people of varying incomes, genders, races, sexual preferences and...power.... Distinctions are seen as the beginnings of inequality, an hierarchical ordering of the world. Consequently egalitarians guard against such differentiation and seek to erode it wherever possible.[148]

The most obvious and consequential results of these beliefs are to be found in education and cultural life in general. Grade inflation for instance has been associated with the distaste of teachers for making sharp distinction between the performance of students and regarding such formal evaluation as somehow inauthentic and invidious. Concern with the performance of the beneficiaries of affirmative may also increase reluctance to pursue high standards and make distinctions, which would "penalize" these minorities, possibly expressing discrimination or racism. Abhorrence of "elitism" is then the inescapable counterpart of radical egalitarianism that strives for equal outcomes rather than equal opportunities. Thus, education for the gifted becomes a luxury.[149]

Educational standards are also severely compromised when teachers are under pressure not to discipline disruptive students who may turn out to be overrepresented among certain minorities.[150] Albert Shanker noted for example that a discipline code in the Cincinnati School System was challenged in courts because it had "a disparate impact" on African-American students; disparity in disciplinary referral was treated as a form of racial discrimination. Evidently it was resolved that teachers must discipline students in proportion to their presence in the student population. The same principle has been at work in legislation proposed by members of the Black Caucus in Congress seeking to regulate the proportion of those sentenced to capital punishment to reflect their distribution in the general population.[151]

The growing fear of elitism and the attendant reluctance to differentiate has also had its impact in the arts. Symphony orchestras, for instance, are becoming uneasy about playing the classics and—according to a report of the American Symphony Orchestra League—of "creating the image of an 'exclusive, arrogant, possibly racist institution.'" The orchestras have been advised "to become more 'representative' of their communities." These concerns have their origins in the scarcity of Hispanics and blacks among both musicians and audiences of symphony orchestras. The report was an example of "diversity" or "representativeness" becoming code words for lowering standards.[152] A peculiar confusion of art, religion, and social causes was revealed in an exhibition hosted by the Harvard Divinity School (as well as the Episcopal Divinity School earlier) called "Sacred Condoms" that featured, among other things, "dolls dressed up in condom rainwear" and "condoms...filled with honey [and]...alphabet soup."[153]

The hostility to science should also be noted among the symptoms suggestive of decadence. Few outside the academic world (and not many within) are aware that by the early 1990s the critiques of science have become a major form of social and culture criticism in the United States. While earlier critiques focused on particular social institutions or practices, the most recent, anti-scientific variety seeks a fundamental conceptual transformation, the revision of ways of looking at the world.

The question, of course, is whether or not such hostility would actually interfere with scientific work, slow down scientific discoveries, or their application, and discourage people from entering the scientific vocation. While it is hard to know what part the anti-scientific trends have played in the process, graduate students in the sciences are increasingly recruited from other countries; minorities show little interest in the hard sciences and the proportion of white males entering such fields has been declining.

Perhaps the most serious threat the anti-scientific attitudes represent is the undermining of cognitive clarity, the ascendance of the belief that one opinion is as good as any other, that it is impossible to find agreement on what is a fact and what is an opinion, that there is no reality outside subjective consciousness, that every perception is hopelessly tainted by personal (or group) interest and partiality. Paul R. Gross and Norman Leavitt wrote:

> [P]ostmodern scepticism rejects the possibility of enduring universal knowledge in any area. It holds that all knowledge is...rigidly circumscribed by interests and prejudices....The traditional Marxist view that what we think of as science is really 'bourgeois' science...recurs with predictable regularity in its own right, or refurbished as the doctrine of 'cultural constructivism'. The radical feminist view [is] that science like every other intellectual structure in modern society is poisoned and corrupted by ineradicable gender bias...multiculturalists...view "Western" science as inherently inaccurate and incomplete by virtue of its failure to incorporate the full range of cultural perspectives...radical environmentalism condemns science as embodying instrumentalism and alienation from direct experience of nature.... What enables [these views] to coexist congenially...is a shared sense of injury, resentment, and indignation against modern science.

The hostility to science postmodernists share with radical feminists and assorted "multiculturalists" (Afrocentrists in particular) amounts to the rejection of logic, rationality, and often common sense as well, and, in the final analysis, allows "no ground for distinguishing reliable knowledge from superstitution."

At last these attitudes also conjure up decadence insofar as "the health of a culture is measured in part by the vigor with which its immune system responds to nonsense." American culture, for far too long, has been very accommodating to nonsense of every description, and of late, this tendency has been given vocal support by the militant relativism of postmodernist intellectuals.[154]

Decadence is further reflected not merely in the rising rates of crime, and especially violent ones, but in the declining ability or willingness of juries to differentiate guilt from innocence. This development appears to have two explanations. One is the spread of the social-deterministic mentality: conditions under which individuals can be held accountable for their behavior have greatly diminished as new forms and definitions of "abuse" and "temporary insanity" find acceptance in the courtroom. Even such an unexpected body as the Iowa Board of Corrections declared (in connection with domestic violence) that "[v]iolence does not result from a personal or moral defect; it stems from the ideology of patriarchy which permeates all levels of society."[155]

The much publicized case of the Menendez brothers in California was far from unique in the successful use of the claim of "abuse" by a defense lawyer. In a lesser known case in Rochester New York: "A former Niagara Falls Honor Student who bludgeoned his mother to death...will not spend a day in prison or have a criminal record.... Instead the court granted him youthful offender status and ordered him sent to a youth correctional institution for 16 months to four years. His juvenile record will be sealed." Alleged maternal abuse was the mitigating circumstance.[156]

In conclusion it may be reaffirmed that there is a connection between the rejections of American culture and society and the phenomena of decline and decadence. Domestic anti-Americanism is a symptom of decadence as it paradoxically combines a nihilistic cultural relativism with the lashes of a bitter moralistic criticism that feeds on the discontents of modernity, arising out of a perception of life that is *both* meaningless and unjust.

Northampton, Mass.   P.H.
April–August 1994

NOTES

1. Paul Hollander, *The Many Faces of Socialism*, New Brunswick, NJ: Transaction Publishers, 1983; Paul Hollander, *The Survival of the Adversary Culture*, New Brunswick, NJ: Transaction Publishers, 1988; Paul Hollander, *Decline and Discontent*, New Brunswick, NJ: Transaction Publishers, 1992.

2. "Introduction to the Phoenix Edition: A Reassessment" in *Soviet and American Society: A Comparison*, Chicago: University of Chicago Press, 1978; "Preface to the Paperback Edition: Political Pilgrims and Estrangement Today," New York: Harper & Row, 1983; and "An End to the Political Pilgrimage? Introduction to the University Press of America edition of *Political Pilgrims*," Lanham, Md.: University Press of America, 1990.

3. This point was reaffirmed in the only piece I wrote on the topic since the book was published, an op-ed article in the *New York Times* (July 3, 1992) entitled "Why Don't They Like Us?" In it I wrote, among other things, that "ambivalence tempered with respect is the most appropriate attitude with which to contemplate the United States."

4. That is the title of the book by Robert Hughes, New York: Oxford University Press, 1993.

5. It is an attitude Edmund Wilson spotted in an encounter with a representative of the 1960s generation: "He was a disturbing example of... the idiotic desire of young people to blame everything wrong on somebody else, and to manufacture grievances" *The Sixties,* New York: Farrar Straus and Giroux, 1993, p. 753.

6. Richard F. Kuisel, *Seducing the French: The Dilemma of Americanization,* Berkeley: University Press of California, 1993, p. 8.

7. Quoted in Marcus Cunliffe, "European Anti-Americanism" in *In Search of America,* New York: Greenwood Press, 1991, pp. 394, 399, 400, 401.

8. For a study showing that, contrary to popular belief, the Reagan era did not usher in sweeping conservative social-cultural transformations, see Larry M. Schwab, *The Illusion of a Conservative Reagan Revolution,* New Brunswick, NJ: Transaction Publishers, 1991.

9. Dennis Wrong in his review of my *Survival of the Adversary Culture* in *Contemporary Sociology,* September 1990.

10. Reviewed by Herbert Mitgang, *New York Times,* Jan. 2, 1992.

11. Reviewed by Boyd Tonkin, *New Statesman,* April 17, 1992.

12. Reviewed by Donald Lyons, *Wall Street Journal,* May 11, 1992.

13. Reviewed by Maura Reynolds, *San Diego Union,* Jan. 5, 1992.

14. *Journal of American History,* September, 1992. If indeed I did not provide precise definitions this might have been because I dealt with the concept (adversary culture) in my book of almost the same title (see above). I defined and discussed the concept and its origin in the introduction of that volume, especially on pp. 10–14.

15. *Partisan Review,* no.1., 1994, pp. 168–69.

16. Correspondence, *New York Times,* Nov. 23, 1992.

17. Durkheim was well aware of these problems of modernity and of the psychological difficulties people experience outside familiar structures and upon being inundated with many choices. More recently Robert Nisbet addressed this issue in his classic *Quest for Community* (1957). At a broader philosophical level this has also been an issue preoccupying Isaiah Berlin in his *Four Essays on Freedom.*

18. *New Yorker,* June 7, 1992.

19. Charles Krauthammer, "Defining Deviancy Up—the New Assault on Bourgeois Life," *New Republic,* Nov. 22, 1993; Daniel Patrick Moynihan, "Defining Deviancy Down," *American Scholar,* Winter 1993; Richard Rorty, "The Unpatriotic Academy," *New York Times,* op-ed, Feb. 13, 1994.

20. Moynihan, *cited,* pp. 30, 21.

21. The other "original sin" prominent in the radical critiques of America is "racism," a stain that, in the eyes of the critics, is virtually irremovable and is present even when no actual manifestation of it can be observed.

22. Krauthammer, *cited,* pp. 20, 22, 23, 24, 25.

23. Ibid.

24. See, for example, "The Diversity Standard," *Wall Street Journal* (editorial), Dec. 29, 1993.

25. Krauthammer, *cited,* p. 25.

26. "Rap Artist Decries Racists Society," *Daily Hampshire Gazette,* Feb. 27, 1992.

27. An exceptionally illuminating, article-length examination of multiculturalism is to be found in John R. Searle, "Is There a Crisis in American Higher Education?" *Partisan Review,* no. 4, 1993; see also Hollander, *Decline and Discontent, cited,* pp. 14–19, 26–28.

28. Robert Hughes, *Culture of Complaint*, New York: Oxford University Press, 1993, pp. 75, 99, 101.

29. See, for example, "Teaching Reverse Racism," *Time Magazine*, April 4, 1994. A widely used text that advances unsupported claims of African scientific and moral superiority was produced by a former technician (at Argonne National Laboratories in Illinois) lacking any discernible educational or intellectual credentials or qualifications. "Yet despite the essay's bizarre claims, it has been accepted not only by Afrocentric extremists but also by...school boards." Perhaps the potential critics feared that had they voiced their apprehensions they would have been branded racist.

30. Hughes, *cited*, p. 102.

31. Orlando Patterson, "The Moral Crisis of the Black American," *Public Interest*, Summer 1973, pp. 44, 47, 48. See also Lawrence Mead, "Job Programs and Other Bromides," op-ed, *New York Times*, May 19, 1992.

32. Of late even the term *underclass* came under attack because of its "connotations of undeservingness and blameworthiness." Mickey Kaus pointed out that "[Herbert] Gans [a critic of the concept]...is enforcing, through semantic guilt-tripping, a liberal orthodoxy in which distinguishing good behavior from bad among the poor is somehow forbidden" (Mickey Kaus, "'Underclass' sums it up well," *Daily Hampshire Gazette*, Sept. 22, 1990).

33. "Don't Label Blacks as Criminals," *Campus Chronicle* (Amherst), May 15, 1993, p. 4.

34. Quoted in Dennis Prager, "Blacks, Liberals and the Los Angeles Riots," *Ultimate Issues*, (Culver City, Calif.) April-June 1992, pp. 4,5,7,6.

35. There is also a white-liberal, or left-liberal anger nurtured by sources independent of the condition of black Americans. Dennis Prager wrote: "The rage at America that liberalism cultivates in blacks...emanates from a rage within many liberals themselves. Angry people want other people to be angry at the same things they are" (Prager, *cited*, p. 13).

36. Jim Sleeper, "The Origins of Colin Ferguson's Hate—Psycho-Killer?" *New Republic*, Jan. 10 and 17, 1994 p. 17. The most popular black talk show in New York City, "The Gary Bird Show," was also described as purveying conspiratorial fantasies: "The underlying emotion dictates the facts; no fact can be too strange if it vindicates the emotion." Regarding the conditions of blacks in America, "Nothing changed: domination simply assumed a new shape" (James Traub, "A Counter-Reality Grows in Harlem," *Harper's*, August 1991); see also William McGowan, "The Media's Race Taboo," *Wall Street Journal*, April 14, 1994.

37. "Racial Injustice Seen in Murder Defense," *New York Times*, March 16, 1994; for a critique of the "black rage" defense see Alan Dershowitz, "When the Plea is Black Rage," *Washington Times*, April 3, 1994.

38. Paul Craig Roberts, "Awash in an Unremitting Tide of Quotas," *Washington Times*, Feb. 23, 1994.

39. See among the many media responses "Notebook," *New Republic*, Jan. 4 and 11, 1993; Carl T. Rowan, "Smearing Johnetta Cole," *Washington Post*, Dec. 17, 1992; A. M. Rosenthal, "The Special Interests," *New York Times*, Dec. 15, 1992. For references to Cole in this book see pp. 140, 152, and 214.

40. Michael Kelly, "Saint Hillary," *New York Times Magazine*, May 23, 1993.

41. Quoted in Charles M. Young, "Noam Chomsky: Anarchy in the USA," *Rolling Stone*, May 1992, pp. 46, 47, 71, 73. Bernard Sanders, another veteran social critic and voice of the 1960s, currently U.S. representative from Vermont, doubtless would have seconded the views of Chomsky. In a *Los Angeles Times*

editorial Sanders proposed that "The United States of America is, increasingly, an oligarchy...the U.S. is becoming a Third World Economy...[and] is fast becoming a non-democratic country" (*Los Angeles Times*, Jan. 16, 1994).

42. David Margolick, "The Long and Lonely Journey of Ramsey Clark," *New York Times*, June 14, 1991.

43. Susan Chira, "Same Passion, New Tactics," *New York Times*, Nov. 18, 1993.

44. Tom Wicker, "Does 'JFK' Conspire Against Reason?" *New York Times* (Arts and Leisure), Dec. 15, 199.

45. George Will, "'JFK' Libels America," *Daily Hampshire Gazette*, Dec. 27, 1991.

46. Brent Staples, "Hollywood: History by Default," *New York Times*, Dec. 25, 1991; David W. Belin, "Earl Warren's Assassins," *New York Times* (op-ed), March 7, 1992.

47. David Richards, "Smashing America's Favorite Myths," *New York Times* (Arts and Leisure), Nov. 21, 1993.

48. Eric Gibson, "Smithsonian Politics on Exhibit," *Insight*, June 24, 1991.

49. Quoted in *History Textbooks—a Standard Guide* (1994–95 edition), New York: American Textbook Council, 1994, pp. 30–32.

50. This trend was spotted among others by Jean Bethke Elstain over a decade ago. See "The Victim Syndrome: A Troubling Turn in Feminism," *Progressive*, June 1982. For a recent examination of the exaggeration of victimization by rape see Katie Roiphe, *The Morning After: Sex, Fear and Feminism on Campus*, Boston: Little, Brown, 1993; for an inside report of radical-social critical trends at a feminist conference see Christina Hoff Somers, "Sister Soldiers," *New Republic*, Oct. 5, 1992, and her book.

51. For a recent scrutiny of advocacy research see Neil Gilbert, "Miscounting Social Ills," *Society*, March-April 1994. The incentive for such (upward only) miscounting is obvious: the bigger the numbers and the problem they signify, the more funds may become available for its alleviation; no less important is the moral satisfaction to be had by demonstrating, by the sheer magnitude of the problem, the defective character of the social system that produces it. See also Hans Toch, "Politically Correct Approaches to Violence and Aggression," *Criminal Justice Research Bulletin* 7, no. 5, 1992. This type of research, Toch shows, tends to encourage women and children to report experiences of victimization and allows "respondents themselves to define what they now consider sexual abuse" (p. 4).

52. Hughes, *cited*, pp. 9, 17.

53. Dana Mack, "Are Parents Bad for Children?" *Commentary*, March 1994, pp. 30, 33.

54. Michael Vincent Miller, "How We Suffer Now," *New York Times Book Review*, May 17, 1992, pp. 43, 44.

55. Carol Tavris, "Beware the Incest-Survivor Machine," *New York Times Book Review*, January 3, 1993 pp. 16, 17. Notes and allegations of sexual victimization have become so widespread that even fourth graders would use such charges to make trouble for a teacher. In a Chicago school a nine-year old offered to pay $1 each to ten of her classmates "if they falsely claimed that Thompson [the teacher] fondled them.... One of the children finally admitted they concocted the story to get the substitute teacher in trouble" ("Children Plot-Sex-Abuse Claims" [AP], *Daily Hampshire Gazette*, May 18, 1994).

56. David Rieff, "Victims All?—Recovery, Co-dependency, and the Art of Blaming Somebody Else," *Harpers*, Oct. 1991, p. 49; see also , Charles J. Sykes: *A Nation of Victims*, New York: St. Martin's Press, 1992.

57. Rieff, cited.

58. "Court Upholds Award to Crippled Robber," *New York Times*, Feb. 21, 1992; see also "The Mugger and His Millions," *Washington Times* (editorial), Dec. 5, 1993. See also Margot Slode, "In a Growing Number of Cases Defendants are Portraying Themselves as Victims," *New York Times*, May 20, 1994.

59. See, for example, Walter Goodman, "When Even Victimizers Say They are Victims," *New York Times*, March 28, 1994.

60. Aaron Wildavsky, *The Rise of Radical Egalitarianism*, Washington, D.C.: American University Press, 1991, p. xxv.

61. See Shelby Steele, "The New Sovereignty: Grievance Groups have become Nation unto Themselves," *Harper's*, July 1992.

62. Michiko Kakutani, "Beyond Iron John? How About Iron Jane?" *New York Times*, Aug. 27, 1993.

63. Cunliffe, *cited*, pp. 391–92.

64. Jorge G. Castaneda, *Utopias Unarmed: The Latin American Left After the Cold War*, New York: Knopf 1993, p. 245.

65. Kanan Makiya, *Cruelty and Silence*, New York: Norton, 1993, pp. 255, 279, 259.

66. Kuisel, *cited*.

67. Mario Vargas Llosa, "Fields of Dreams," *National Interest*, Winter 1993–94.

68. John Rockwell, "The New Colossus: American Culture as Power Export," *New York Times*, Jan. 30, 1994.

69. Alan Riding, "Only the French Elite Scorn Mickey's Debut," *New York Times*, April 13, 1992; see also Kuisel, *cited*, pp. 227–30.

70. Kuisel, *cited*, pp. 110, 114, 187, 199, 210.

71. He mentions the influence of C. Wright Mills, David Riesman, Sloan Wilson, William H. Whyte, Vance Packard, Henry Miller, as well as the nineteenth-century critics. He notes that all these "would be cast into insignificance by some of the stories and commentaries on their native land produced by Americans during the past quarter century. The tally is longer and angrier than comparable literature from elsewhere"; Cunliffe, *cited*, p. 395.

72. Andrei S. Markovits, "On Anti-Americanism in West Germany," *New German Critique*, Winter 1985, p. 11.

73. Andrei S. Markovits, "Anti-Americanism and the Struggle for a West German Identity," in Peter H. Merkl, ed., *The Federal Republic of Germany at Forty*, New York: New York University Press, 1989, pp. 11, 39.

74. Markovits 1985, *cited*, pp. 17, 18, 25.

75. Markovits 1989, *cited*, p. 37; see also pp. 379–80 in this book.

76. Kolozsvari Papp Laszlo, "Itatnak," *Elet es Irodalom* (Budapest), Aug. 14, 1992.

77. Vladimir Zhirinovsky, the newly popular Russian politician recently observed that "the Americans" were trying to subvert Russia with "chewing gum, stockings and McDonalds" and were generally intent on destroying his country ("The Zhirinovsky Phenomenon," *New York Times*, April 5, 1994). For further information on the new Russian anti-Americanism, see also Michael Specter, "The Great Russia Will Live Again," *New York Times Magazine*, June 19, 1994.

78. Clyde H. Farnsworth, "Writer Turns Tables: It's U.S. That's Non Grata," *New York Times*, March 28, 1994.

79. "Foreigners Attacked in Guatemala," *New York Times*, April 5, 1994.

80. T. R. Reid, "Overseas Image of the U.S.: Do Anything, Get Away With It," *Daily Hampshire Gazette* (Times-Post News Service), Feb. 24, 1994.

81. Clyde Haberman, "Massacre at Hebron Exposes Anti-American Mood in Israel," *New York Times*, March 20, 1994.

82. John Gray, "The Left's Last Utopia," *National Review,* July 19, 1993, pp. 34, 35.

83. Paul Hollander, *Decline and Discontent, cited,* pp. 241–42. In the context of the reluctance to reexamine past critiques of the United States it may be noted here that whereas social critics (such as Tom Wicker and Seymour Hersh) were, in 1984, convinced of U.S. (CIA, Pentagon, etc.) responsibility for the loss of the Korean airliner near Sakhalin, they felt no obligation, after subsequent revelations from the former Soviet Union, to publicly reassess their conspiratorial scenarios. (For the conclusive evidence coming out of the former Soviet Union, see Murray Sayle, "Closing the File on Flight 007," *New Yorker,* Dec. 13, 1993.) The same may be said about the radical social critics' routine denials and ridiculing of the possibility that the Soviet Union funded the American Communist Party—a fact once more affirmed by Soviet and post-Soviet sources in recent years.

84. Diana Trilling, "How McCarthy Gave Anti-Communism a Bad Name," *Newsweek,* Jan. 11, 1993.

85. For a recent example, see Joel Kovel, *Red Hunting in the Promised Land: Anticommunism and the Making of America,* New York: Basic Books, 1994.

86. Richard Rorty, "For a More Banal Politics," *Harper's,* May 1992, p. 16.

87. Irving Howe, *Socialism and America,* New York: Harcourt, 1985, p. 215.

88. Paul Berman, "Still Sailing the Lemonade Sea," *New York Times Magazine,* Oct. 27, 1991, p. 32.

89. Eugene D. Genovese, "The Collapse of Socialism: A View from the Left," Washington, D.C.: American Enterprise Institute, Bradley Lecture Series, 1992, pp. 2, 3.

90. Roger Gottlieb, *Marxism 1844–1990: Origin, Betrayal, and Rebirth,* New York: Routledge, pp. 199.

91. Ibid., 208.

92. Ibid., 210.

93. Ibid., 211.

94. Leon Festinger, *When Prophecy Fails,* Minneapolis: University of Minnesota Press, 1956, pp. 3, 26.

95. Quoted in Louis Kriesberg and David R. Segal, eds., *The Transformation of European Communist Societies, Research in Social Movements, Conflict and Change,* Greenwich, Conn.: JAI Pres, 1992, p. 182.

96. Quoted in C. Lemke and G. Marks, eds., *The Crisis of Socialism in Europe,* Durham: Duke University Press, 1992, p. 26.

97. Chase-Dunn in Kriesberg, *cited,* p. 182.

98. Maurice Isserman, "Left Out," *New York Times Book Review,* March 8, 1992, p. 9.

99. Walter Goodman, "Seeing the Bright Side of Castro's Cuba," *New York Times,* Aug. 26, 1993; "Cuba Pioneering Energy Conservation" (letter), *New York Times,* Dec. 13, 1990; "Cuban Rally Draws Thousands: Speakers Call for an End of U.S. Economic Blockade," *Massachusetts Daily Collegian* (Amherst), Jan. 29, 1992; "An Inhumane Embargo," *Valley Advocate* (Hatfield, Mass.), Sept. 16, 1993; "The Time Has Come to End the Embargo Against Cuba" (full page advertisement), *New York Times,* May 2, 1994.

100. Gunther Grass, "Pity on Cuba," *Dissent,* Fall 1993, pp. 415, 416.

101. Quoted in Paul Mulshine, "The Unbearable Lightness of Being in Cuba," *Heterodoxy,* May-June 1994, p. 15.

102. Correspondence, *New York Times,* Sept. 4, 1994.

103. Flyer.

104. "Is China Taking a Great Leap Backward?" *New York Times* (letter), Jan. 2, 1994.

105. David E. Sanger, "Two Koreas Agree to Summit Meeting on Nuclear Issue," *New York Times*, June 19, 1994, p. 12.

106. Ibid.

107. George Will, "Carter Misreads North Korea's Kim," *Daily Hampshire Gazette*, June 24, 1994.

108. Michael Scammell, "Of Human Bondage," review of Kate Millett's "The Politics of Cruelty—an Essay on the Literature of Political Imprisonment," *New Republic*, May 16, 1994, p. 35.

109. Ibid., p. 36.

110. Ibid., p. 35.

111. Castaneda, *cited*, p. 128.

112. See "Who Speaks for the Victims," *Hemisphere*, Fall 1991, p. 18.

113. James Brooke, "Shining Path Supporters Abroad Anger Peru," *New York Times*, Dec. 18, 1991; see also Simon Strong, "Where Shining Path Leads," *New York Times Magazine*, May 24, 1992.

114. John Judis, "A Majority of One," *New York Times Book Review Section*, Dec. 20, 1992, p. 9.

115. Peter Knapp and Alan J. Spector, *Crisis & Change: Basic Questions of Marxist Sociology*, Chicago: Nelson-Hall, 1991, p. 245.

116. Quoted from Robert Eisner, "Why Long Faces?" *New York Times Book Review Section*, Sept. 19, 1993.

117. George Steiner, *Proofs and Three Parables*, London: Granta 1992, pp. 41–42.

118. Quoted in R. Grossman, "The Marxist Brothers," *Chicago Tribune*, March 18, 1991.

119. Chase-Dunn in Kriesberg, *cited*, p. 168–69.

120. Dario Fernandez-Morera, "Materialist Discourse in Academia During the Age of Late Marxism," *Academic Questions*, Spring 1991, p. 18.

121. Wilcomb E. Washburn, "The Treason of Intellectuals" (pamphlet), Herndon, Va.: Young America's Foundation, 1989, p. 2.

122. Wade Huntley, "The United States was the Loser in the Cold War," *Chronicle of Higher Education*, March 31, 1993.

123. H. W. Brands, *The Devil We Knew*, New York: Oxford University Press, 1993, pp. 194, vi, vii, 163, 165, 221, 224.

124. David Halberstam, *The Fifties*, New York: Villard, 1993.

125. Quoted in Arnold Beichman, "Cold War Blame Frame," *Washington Times*, November 7, 1993.

126. *Dissent*, Winter 1992, pp. 7, 8.

127. Knapp and Spector, *cited*, pp. xi–xii, 251.

128. Quoted in John Patrick Diggins, *The Rise and Fall of the American Left*, New York: Norton, 1992, pp. 361–62; see also Anthony Flint, "Marxists Adjust to Capitalist World—Seek Silver Lining in Fall of Kremlin," *Boston Globe*, Nov. 14, 1992.

129. Quoted in Lemke and Marks, *cited*, p. 25.

130. John Searle, *cited*, p. 701.

131. John Diggins, "Power, Freedom and the Failure of Theory," *Harper's*, January 1992, p. 16.

132. *Daedalus*, Spring 1992, pp. 9, 18, 19.

133. Irving Kristol, "Vision of the Capitalist Future," *Washington Times*, January 3, 1992, p. 4.

134. John Clark and Aaron Wildavsky, *The Moral Collapse of Communism*, San Francisco: Institute for Contemporary Studies, 1990, pp. 16–17, 311, 336.

135. *National Interest*, Spring 1993, pp. 85, 86, 87.

136. Ibid., p. 88.

137. Richard Bernstein, "Long Conflict Deeply Marked Self Image of Americans," *New York Times*, Feb. 2, 1992.

138. David W. Murray, "Poor Suffering Bastards: An Anthropologist Looks at Illegitimacy," *Policy Review*, Spring 1994, p. 9.

139. For one such discussion see Stanley Rothman, "American Entrepreneurship," *World and I*, November 1991, with responses from Robert Heilbroner and Christopher Lasch, among others. See also Edward Luttwak, *The Endangered American Dream*, New York: Simon and Schuster, 1993. For a critique of the idea of American decadence see Alfred Balk, *The Myth of Ameican Eclipse*, New Brunswick, NJ: Transaction Publishers, 1990.

140. Seymour Itzkoff, "America's Unspoken Economic Dilemma: Falling Intelligence Levels," *Journal of Social, Political and Economic Studies*, no. 3, Fall 1993, pp. 319, 322.

141. *The Index of Leading Cultural Indicators*, Washington, D.C.: Heritage Foundation, 1993, p. i.

142. William J. Bennett, "Getting Used to Decadence," Washington, D.C.: Heritage Foundation Lecture, 1993, p. 4.

143. Rieff, *cited*, p. 56.

144. Ann Cooper, "Lenin to Go," *New Republic*, Feb. 3, 1992, p. 16.

145. Michael Howard, "Facing Monsters," *New York Times Book Review*, March 6, 1994; see also Gertrude Himmelfarb, *On Looking Into the Abyss*, New York: Knopf, 1994.

146. Gary S. Becker, "How the Disabilities Act Will Cripple Business," *Business Week*, Sept. 14, 1992, p. 12.

147. "Hey, I'm Terrific! the latest national elixir—self esteem—is supposed to cure everything from poor grades to bad management," *Newsweek*, Feb. 17, 1992.

148. Wildavsky 1991, *cited*, pp. 235, xviii, 71.

149. Jon Nordheimer, "Education for the Gifted, Seen as a Luxury, Faces Cutbacks," *New York Times*, Nov. 29, 1992. See also p. 455 in this book.

150. Albert Shanker, "Discipline by Numbers," *New York Times*, Jan. 16, 1994.

151. Stanley Rothman, "Execution by Quota," *Public Interest*, Summer 1994.

152. Edward Rothstein, "Be Smart as a Leming, Orchestras are Told," *New York Times* (Arts and Leisure), July 11, 1993.

153. Martin Peretz, "Sacred Condoms," *New Republic*, May 18, 1992, p. 50.

154. Paul R. Gross and Norman Levitt, *Higher Superstition: The Academic Left and Its Quarrels with Science*, Baltimore: Johns Hopkins University Press, 1994, pp. 5, 45, 217.

155. William Petroski, "Prison Program Guidelines Opposed," *Des Moine Register*, Oct. 17, 1992.

156. "Court Lowers Sentence for Slaying Mother," *New York Times*, Nov. 18, 1990.

Preface

The preface provides the last opportunity for an author to address his readers, to update his work, to make reassessments and last-minute qualifications, to modulate sweeping generalizations, or to confide his true intentions. Such impulses are particularly pressing in the case of a lengthy volume written over a long period of time that also happened to be a fairly tumultuous period in history.

I started work on this book in the early 1980s, but my interest in the topic goes back further, finding its first published expression in an article written in 1978.[1] The same interest also found expression in *Political Pilgrims,* a book I began in the early 70s, which sought, among other goals, to understand the rejection of American society by many of its privileged members, although in it there was nothing concerning the hostility the United States inspired abroad.

Much has happened and changed in the world in those years and it is entirely legitimate to ask whether or not these changes have made the concerns and findings of this study in any way obsolete, irrelevant, or otherwise unworthy of interest?

Even if the events of the past decade would have diminished the topicality of this study—which I do not believe to be the case—it could still make a claim on the interest of present-day readers as social or intellectual history, or a chapter in the history of twentieth-century ideas between 1965 and 1990. I do believe, however, that the major findings and information gathered in this volume reach into the present and that the phenomena examined will be with us in the foreseeable future. The phenomena in question, as the title makes clear, are the hostile critiques of the United States (or American society) both at home and abroad, neither of which attracted much social scientific or other scholarly interest.[2] As regards the relationship between critiques "at home" and "abroad," it has been a subject totally unexplored, except for a few impressionistic remarks here and there. Yet it seems highly plausible that hostility toward the United States abroad and hostility at home are interdependent and nurture one another. This is not to say that critiques abroad are predicated on domestic confirmation or vice versa, but only that each group of critics finds welcome supporting evidence in the reproaches of the other group.

It may also be pointed out—as will be discussed at some length later on—that no foreign critic has ever discovered ills of American society that had not been noted before by the natives. As C. Vann Woodward has observed: ". . . few could equal native American critics in the harshness and severity with which they have written of the stupidities and crudities of their own civilization."[3] One may add, that this was sometimes the case even when the targets of criticism were neither stupidities nor crudities, but aspects of American society of which more charitable judgments could also be made.

Even at this early stage readers may wish to know how I managed to separate the just critiques from the unfair ones and how I avoided designating all critiques of American society as anti-American? Although this matter too will be discussed at some length in the book, I should make clear at the outset that I did not equate all criticisms of this country with hostility toward the United States, nor did I intend to discredit or dismiss all critiques of the United States with the term "anti-Americanism." Rather, that term has been employed to denote a particular mindset, an attitude of distaste, aversion, or intense hostility the roots of which may be found in matters unrelated to the actual qualities or attributes of American society or the foreign policies of the United States. In short, as here used, anti-Americanism refers to a negative predisposition, a type of bias which is to varying degrees unfounded. I regard it as an attitude similar to its far more thoroughly explored counterparts, hostile predispositions such as racism, sexism, or antisemitism.

A preliminary example of these attitudes should make clear what type of utterances I am ready to label as "anti-American" (or "intensely alienated" as far as the domestic variant of these attitudes is concerned). An American reader of the radical-left publication the *Guardian* wrote in the aftermath of the war with Iraq:

> It is depressing that segments of the "left" in this country have been using the flag in antiwar endeavours to demonstrate that they too are patriotic. Steven Miller's letter exemplifies this approach. . . . Which aspect of our "national identity" is it that Miller likes so much? Is it the genocide of native peoples and the theft of their land? Or is it slavery and the slaughter of millions of Africans and the continued mutilation and attempted destruction of Black people? . . . perhaps it is the "the war on drugs" that so enthralls those who like the flag. Or how we stole part of Mexico; our bombing of Hiroshima and Nagasaki . . . Or perhaps it was . . . U.S. support for South Africa and Israel, and the continuing colonization of Puerto

Rico . . . the refusal to launch a meaningful campaign against AIDS . . . the denial of reproductive rights for women and the destruction of the world's environment.

The flag is not mine. The "national identity" of this country is one of continued and unparalleled destruction, the likes of which have never been seen anywhere in history. Just imagine that one day the left is victorious. Is it the U.S. flag that we will then hoist? Let's hope not. The U.S. flag is the symbol of the evil empire. Progressive people should reject it.[4]

For a preliminary example of the anti-American mindset abroad, I will refer to a report of attitudes of French intellectuals who used to believe that "Eldridge Cleaver's *Soul on Ice* was boycotted by white Americans but became a bestseller anyway because so many Negroes bought it . . . If you ask a New York policeman for directions, he will threaten you with his nightstick . . . The leading New York restaurants try to exclude Jews . . . American capitalists fought the California grape strike by importing grapes from Israel."[5]

Two sets of recent historical events and trends may cast doubt on the continued usefulness, or timeliness, of concern with anti-Americanism, domestic or foreign. The first is the decomposition or crisis of communist systems that not only stimulated anti-Americanism by their official propaganda, but some of which were seen by social critics in the West as possible or partial counter-models or alternatives to capitalist systems such as the United States. Specifically, Eastern Europe ceased to be part of the Soviet empire and several of its countries are being transformed into political democracies; Germany has become united; there is both turmoil and democratization in the Soviet Union; in Nicaragua the Marxist-Leninist government was voted out of office; the Chinese authorities while resisting democratization have been seeking to improve productivity by reducing state control over the economy; worldwide, "existing socialism" has been discredited.

The other major set of historical events with implications for anti-Americanism has been the war with Iraq. In early 1991 the United States with United Nations backing expelled Iraq from Kuwait and destroyed much of Iraq's military might, while suffering minimal casualties in a war many critics thought would exact huge American losses or be another Vietnam—and in any event another immense stimulant of anti-Americanism in the Third World and especially in the Middle East. None of the dire predictions have materialized as of this writing.

The dramatic disintegration of communist systems by itself reduced the volume of anti-Americanism as these states used to target the United States with their huge propaganda machinery. At the present time neither the governments nor the people of these countries nurture such attitudes—not that the people ever shared the officially fostered animosity.

But this book is not concerned with the type of anti-Americanism that amounted to little more than official state propaganda. My major interest has been anti-Americanism as a more or less spontaneous sentiment, or one easy to arouse, a sense of grievance and apprehension when originating abroad, and a profound sense of alienation and readiness to moral indignation as experienced by the native critics. The latter believe (as exemplified above) that America's is a uniquely unjust, dangerous, and corrupt social system.

Those who believe that the bankruptcy of communist systems has provided vindication for the virtues and advantages of the American system of government and free enterprise underestimated the durability of the feelings that fuel anti-Americanism. As will be shown in the last chapter, the decline of communism has had little impact on the hostility toward the United States, especially among the critics in the United States. Many social critics at home now contrast improvements in the Soviet Union with what they consider the stubborn resistance to desirable change in the United States.[6]

The war with Iraq concluded shortly before these lines were written, was seen by many as signaling the end of the Vietnam syndrome: isolationism, hostility toward the military establishment, and collective self-doubt. While clearly the quick and successful war with Irag did lead to an upsurge of national pride and sympathy toward the military forces, a new peace movement also promptly emerged and once more became a voice of intense social criticism, reflecting the negative predisposition which is the central topic of this book. For many peace activists the Gulf war appeared to provide new and welcome vindication of a set of feelings that had been much in evidence during the Vietnam war and during the years when the U.S. supported the anticommunist guerillas in Nicaragua. As with its predecessors, the latest peace movement attracted a large corps of individuals fully convinced of the systemic defects of the United States and deeply disturbed by any assertion of its military power. The successful prosecution and conclusion of the war in particular disheartened these activists. Speaking for many of her fellow protestors, Margaret Hummel, a community organizer from Underhill, Vermont, said, "This is one victory I am not celebrating." Earlier, commenting on the relative weakness of the peace movement, she remarked: "'. . . this will all change when we start bringing them [the soldiers] home in human pouch containers.'" A similar sentiment was expressed by another activist: "'Horrible as this sounds,'" said Jim Cloviel at a Los Angeles rally, "'what we really need to get people out here is boys coming home in body bags.'"[7] Michael Klare a professor at Hampshire College in Amherst, Massachusetts, entertained the prospect of a prolonged and costly war with grim relish:

To pay for these overseas adventures, American citizens can expect diminished medical care, reduced food assistance and a deteriorating housing supply.

Many Americans will resist these new demands and deprivations. Protests will abound,—and thus the other major consequence of Pax Americana II: increased repression, jingoism, intolerance at home . . . draft evaders and tax resisters will be hunted down . . . We will become a garrison society, like the one George Orwell had envisioned in *1984*.[8]

It may also be noted here that little expression of outrage was heard from these quarters over the fate of the Kurds in the wake of their uprising which followed the coalition victory over Iraq. Although it could be argued that the refusal of the United States to intervene on the Kurds' behalf, and on those of other minorities which rose up against Sadam Hussein, deeply tarnished the whole enterprise in the Gulf, the fate of the Kurds prompted little audible moral indignation among these critics of the United States.

Though diminished in numbers and influence, those belonging to the adversary culture retained the old beliefs and patterns of selective moral indignation and compassion; for them time stood still.

It may be of some interest to the reader that the momentous and unexpected political changes in the world noted above have been paralleled by some similarly unexpected if less momentous changes in the attitude of the author as this study progressed. While this book began as, and has in most respects remained, a critique of anti-Americanism (as defined above), I have also come to a broader realization that hostility toward the United States, and especially certain aspects of American culture, is not always or entirely irrational, and even some of its irrational manifestations may originate in conditions that warrant concern. It has become increasingly clear that to the extent that "Americanization" is a form of modernization, the process can inspire understandable apprehension and anguish among those who seek to preserve a more stable and traditional way of life in various parts of the world. As to those who reject this social system with great passion at home, I have come to the conclusion that they too feel, deep down, victimized by modernity and they confuse American capitalism (a major target of their critiques) with modernity and with what it stands for in the realm of values and human relationships. At the heart of their protest is unhappiness about living in a basically secular, excessively individualistic society which, while providing a wide range of choices and options, offers little help for its members to make their lives more meaningful. Since I share Emile Durkheim's notions as to what human beings require for a modicum of balance and emotional stability, I can understand that the openness, the freedoms, and the moral-ethical free-for-all characteristic of American society and culture can become troubling and burdensome. Durkheim would doubtless agree that the American way of life at the present time is lacking in solid structures and necessary limitations and instead endlessly raises expectations, material as well as spiritual, which cannot be met.

More recently, Leszek Kolakowski has remarked on aspects of modernity increasingly characteristic of American society which give rise to the discontents the alienated critics of society experience and express: ". . . the most dangerous characteristic of modernity . . . [is] the disappearance of taboos . . . Various traditional human bonds which make communal life possible, and without which our existence would be regulated only by greed and fear, are not likely to survive without a taboo system . . . no society, not even an open society, can do without trust of tradition . . . or,—to put it another way—some 'irrational' values that are characteristic of a closed society are indispensable to an open society."[9]

It will thus be one of the conclusions of this study that the cultural relativism and moral uncertainty associated with American culture may contribute more to anti-Americanism than many of the more commonly expressed reproaches aimed at the more obvious defects of the United States. Of course, as will be discussed later, anti-Americanism has many other less reputable sources, including envy, resentment, dogmatic leftism, simple-minded anticapitalism or mindless utopianism, and an expectation that a social order can be constructed which will be free of the conflict among major human values and aspirations. But I am also suggesting that anti-Americanism, and especially the domestic and Western (as distinct from Third World) varieties, can also grow out of a confusion of the personal and social realms. To misidentify, willfully or innocently, the sources of personal problems and discontents as social or sociological in origin seems to have become a chracteristic of our times in the West and especially in the United States.[10]

Part of the contemporary predicament of Americans (or those among them who are not obliged to invest much of their energy in sheer survival) is an old one; it is that we cannot have everything: we cannot live in a society that is materially rich, individualistic, open to all currents of ideas, one that allows and encourages free expression and mobility of every kind, where we can shop around for our favorite religion, experiment with new identities, and sample available options and life styles and at the same time also enjoy the benefits of stable communal ties, sustaining beliefs, taken-for-granted values, and a solid sense of purpose. Domestic anti-Americanism and the associated readiness for chronic moral indignation is in part a response to these perplexities and frustrations which became increasingly widespread in the second half of the twentieth century.

While I do not favor the idealization of the past, certain fundamental differences exist not only between the population densities and technologies of societies today (particularly those in the West) and those of earlier times, but also between some of their basic ideas or conceptions of reality. As Isaiah Berlin has so eloquently shown, a central problem of the contemporary world is the breakdown of consensus regarding either the solubility of human and societal problems or agreement as to what they are. He wrote:

> . . . what none of the contending parties denied [in earlier times, that is— P.H.] was that these fundamental questions were in principle answerable; and that a life formed according to the true answers would constitute the ideal society . . . that the central problems . . . of men are in the end, the same throughout history; that they are in principle soluble; and that the solutions form a harmonious whole . . . Thinkers from Bacon to the present have been inspired by the certainty that there must exist a total solution: that in the fullness of time, whether by the will of God or by human effort, the reign of irrationality, injustice and misery will end; man will be liberated, and will no longer be the plaything of forces beyond his control. . . .
>
> . . . It is this great myth . . . that came under attack towards the end of the eighteenth century. . . .[11]

There is no indication that we are any closer today to an agreement on the nature of these fundamental questions, let alone their solubility.

While anti-Americanism abroad differs from the domestic variety, enriched as it is by grievances peculiar to nationalism, the two varieties also resemble one another (besides both being nurtured by certain problems of modernization) in sharing a determination (as Berlin put it) ". . . not to be impinged upon by what is not one's own, by alien obstacles to self realisation, whether on the part of individuals or civilisations."[12] As regards the nationalistic grievances, this determination (not to be impinged upon) is a reaction to American cultural or economic influences; as far as domestic hostility is concerned, the same determination is associated with the excesses of individualism and especially the preoccupation with self-realization.

The United States is likely to remain a symbolic scapegoat both for trends and developments which *can be* associated with it, and for which it bears responsibility as the major force for modernity in recent history, and *also* for the kind of alienation that emerges from the murkier depth of personal discontents and the refusal to come to terms with the imperfections and conflicts of the world, human nature, and social existence.

It is a pleasure to acknowledge the many forms of assistance I received in the course of writing this book from a number of institutions and individuals.

The first draft of the first chapter was written in August 1984 at Villa Serbelloni, the Study and Conference Center of the Rockefeller Foundation in Bellagio, Italy, where I was scholar in residence at the time. Further research, and some writing, was done at the Hoover Institution in Stanford, in the summers of 1985 and 1986, where I was a visiting scholar. A sabbatical leave in the Spring semester of 1984 from my institution, the University of Massachusetts at Amherst, made it possible to spend time in Mexico and Western Europe collecting information, including interviews with people in different walks of life involved with the subject matter in various ways. On this as on other occasions my research and travel expenses were met through the generosity of the Earhart Foundation, which since 1983 has provided me a research grant that was used throughout the project to support a part-time research assistant and to pay for the costs of collecting and analyzing survey data used in various chapters.

I am especially grateful to the Bradley Foundation, which awarded me a grant at a crucial stage of this study. It enabled me to take a leave of absence for the full year of the 1988–89 academic year and I used it for writing most of the book. It is hard to know how much longer it would have taken to complete this study or whether it would have been possible to carry it out without the various forms of assistance I have cited.

I also had help of a purely intellectual kind from a number of friends and colleagues. Given the length of the manuscript I was reluctant to ask any single individual to read all of it and instead asked different people to read different chapters, depending on their particular interests and expertise. They include my colleagues Jay Demerath and Christopher Hurn in my own depatment of sociology; Steven Balch, editor of *Academic Questions;* Peter Berger of Boston University; Richard E. Bissell, former director of research of the U.S. Information Agency; Alain Gagnon of McGill University; Irving Louis Horowitz of Rutgers University; Seymour Martin Lipset of the Hoover Institution and Stanford University; Lothar Knauth of the National Autonomous University of Mexico (who also organized the Mexican survey research and interviews); David Riesman of Harvard University; Clark Roof, my former colleague, now of the University of California at Santa Barbara; Stanley Rothman of Smith College; Maurice Tugwell of the Mackenzie Institute of Toronto; and Josephina Vazquez of El Colegio de Mexico. Each provided written comments and much good advice. Mr. Marcus Raskin of the Institute of Policy Studies graciously agreed to have a lengthy and wide-ranging discussion with me about the Institute and its place among the critics of American society. My wife, Mina Harrison, made many excellent suggestions to improve my style of writing.

I also benefited from exposing some of the ideas of this book to audiences at the American Enterprise Institute, the Heritage Foundation, the

Ethics and Public Policy Center, the Foreign Policy Research Center in Philadelphia; at the first annual meeting of the National Association of Scholars in New York; to the Boston chapter of the National Association of Scholars; and to a group of the staff of the U.S. Information Agency in Washington, D.C. I also continued to benefit from living in a part of the world where many of the attitudes and ideas examined in this book have been the staple of public discourse and widely held conventional wisdom for decades.

Northampton, Mass.   P.H.
April 1991

NOTES

1. Paul Hollander, "Reflections on anti-Americanism in Our Times," *Worldview*, June 1978. It was reprinted in *The Many Faces of Socialism*, New Brunswick: Transaction, 1983.

2. References to existing literature on the subject will be provided throughout the volume and especially in Chapters 1, 7, and 8. It should be noted, however, that most of the existing literature deals with anti-Americanism abroad. Here I would like to draw attention to two studies which have much bearing on the domestic variety. They are: Arnold Beichman, *Nine Lies About America*, New York: Library Press, 1972; and Rael Jean Isaac and Erich Isaac, *Coercive Utopians*, Chicago: Regnery, 1983. See also Paul Hollander, *The Survival of the Adversary Culture*, New Brunswick: Transaction, 1983.

3. C. Vann Woodward, *The Aging of Democracies*, 1990, p. 8 (manuscript).

4. Ralph King, Chicago, Ill., "Not My Flag," Letter, *Guardian*, March 6, 1991.

5. Quoted from Tom Wolfe's Foreword to Beichman cited p. xix.

6. For example, William Kunstler, the radical lawyer, said: "The struggle for individual rights and liberties is an endless one, and it seems highly paradoxical that, just as it is reaching a climax in Eastern Europe, it should be slackening here." In his "The Rise and Fall of the Bill of Rights," *The Voice*, Univ. of Massachusetts, Amherst, Nov. 1990, p. 5.

7. B. Drummond Ayres, Jr., "For Foes of Gulf War, Nation's Victory Is Bitter," *New York Times*, March 17, 1991; Peter Applebome, "Antiwar Rallies," *New York Times*, Jan. 27, 1991; David Gonzales, "Talk of Ground War Intensifies Mood at Antiwar Demonstration," *New York Times*, Feb. 18, 1991.

8. Michael Klare, "Pax Americana II," *Nation*, Feb. 11, 1991, p. 149.

9. Leszek Kolakowski, *Modernity on Endless Trial*, Chicago: Univ. of Chicago Press, 1990, pp. 13, 164.

10. For an excellent and much neglected analysis of this development (i.e., the deflection of discontent from the personal to the public sphere) see "The Root of American Alienation" and "Rejection of the Prevailing American Society" in Don E. Fehrenbacher, ed., *History and American Society—Essays of David M. Potter*, New York: Oxford Univ. Press, 1973.

11. Isaiah Berlin, *The Crooked Timber of Humanity*, New York: Knopf, 1991, pp. 211, 212, 213.

12. Berlin, *cited*, p. 225.

PART I

INSTITUTIONAL
SETTINGS

1

Introduction:
The Persistence of
the Radical Critiques

These people are still committed. The impulse didn't end. It just scattered.

Eric Foner, 1988

I'll always miss the 1960s . . . miss the music and the drugs and the demonstrations and the sense of power. I'll miss the clarity of purpose . . .

Elsa Dixler, 1986

Miss America: "Society has lost its bearings."

Associated Press report, 1988

Over the last couple of years, the demands on me to speak have escalated beyond anything imaginable.

Noam Chomsky, 1989

Of his life today, a rueful sociology professor says, "I make myself comfortable within a rotten system."

Vincent Canby, 1990

[We are] the most hated nation on Earth.

Kurt Vonnegut, 1986

I

When even Miss America feels called upon to make pronouncements on the sorry state of American society it is clear how pervasive the radical critiques of American society have become, how widely they permeate public awareness. In turn the belief of Kurt Vonnegut—blending guilt, masochism, and projection—exemplifies the symbiotic relationship between the domestic and the foreign critiques of the United States.

While there is a good deal of consensus about the character of the 1960s—recalled as a decade of turbulence, protest, change, challenge to established authority, etc.—far fewer people would agree to the propo-

sition that the values and beliefs of the 60s have remained a major influence in American life in the decades that followed (for an example of
such denial see Wrong 1989). Indeed there are those in considerable
numbers who not only lament the passing of the 60s but insist that its
good works have been undone, its idealism obliterated by the successive
generation of self-centered yuppies and Reaganites. Many intellectuals
and journalists look upon the 1980s as "the age of Ronald Reagan and
Alan Bloom, of academic anti-theory and political passivity," insisting
that Reagan "had radically transformed the political and moral landscape" [Euben 1989:18]. Dr. Spock "is dismayed by the apolitical nature
of many of the nation's young. 'I'm very disappointed that so few young
people are interested in politics . . . They seem . . . interested only in getting good grades and getting a good job'" [Reed 1983]. Another author
devotes a book to the proposition that not only have the young protestors
of the 60s vanished but the older generation of influential social critics
has also fallen by the wayside due to the "professionalization of cultural
life"; the remaining social critics—cloistered in academia, immersed in
arid abstractions—no longer reach the public, having themselves ceased
to be "public intellectuals," no longer acting as the "moral conscience
of society" [Jacoby 1987; Bernstein 1987]. Christopher Lasch, the well-
known social critic, summed it all up, suggesting that "The dream of a
better world collapsed in the late 60s and nothing has taken its place"
[Lasch 1989]. For Barbara Ehrenreich the 1980s was "a decade of greed"
[Mittgang 1990].

In the course of the last ten to fifteen years it has become widely
accepted that the spirit and values of the 1960s have been replaced by a
new materialism, a new ethic of self-seeking and amoral indifference to
the poor and unconcern for social justice. In fact the very insistence on
the loss of the ethos of the 1960s and its putative idealism and high-
mindedness has been turned into a new form of social criticism, a new
measure of the degeneration of American society. The Republican victories in the last three presidential elections made a major contribution
to these beliefs.

By contrast it is a major theme of this book that over the past quarter-
century a generally critical disposition toward existing social arrangements has established itself and spread among the educated strata and
especially elite groups of American society. (For some evidence of survey
research on "the liberal political attitude of professionals" see Brint
1984.) Moreover this critical disposition has become a cultural belief,
entirely taken for granted and by now part of conventional wisdom (in
these strata), namely, that this is a severely flawed, and possibly doomed
society, though still a menace to its citizens and humanity. Or, as a former
activist of the 60s generation put it: ". . . the left as a cultural force . . .

provided a continuing 'adversarial' thread in our culture that has counter-balanced cultural themes that promote conformity to . . . capitalism and the nation-state" [Flacks 1988:189–90].

The cultural, taken-for-granted aspects of these enduring adversarial beliefs were humorously captured in an article written for a local newspaper in one of the notable enclaves of the adversary culture, the Pioneer Valley of Massachusetts.

> Politically correct people know each other's opinion without having to talk about it much . . . Politically correct conversation is really more like a laundry list to make sure everyone at the table has her or his politics in line. The important thing to know when to nod affirmatively or tsk in disgust. This is how it goes:
> "Nelson Mandela."
> "Yes. Animal Rights."
> "Good point and don't forget Nicaragua."
> "What a shame about Ortega."
> "Pass the sun-dried tomatoes and blackened tofu please. The hierarchical patriarchy of the capitalist West." . . .
> Everyone agrees on everything and then go out for 16% butterfat ice cream made by people who only use their first names (far less patriarchal, you know) and who donate money to politically correct causes [Gibson 1990:17].

In similar circles ". . . you were likely to be assaulted at a cocktail party if you didn't support the nuclear freeze and believe . . . that otherwise the world was faced with the . . . absolute certainty of nuclear war. Now it is backing *contra* aid that makes you a pariah and an embarrassment to your kids at school" [Peretz 1986].

It is no mystery why there is disagreement about the persistence of the sixties ethos. For those who identified with and thrived on the spirit of the 60s any diminuition of that ethos is experienced as a painful loss; they feel that too little of it survives. By contrast for those who opposed the same values and movements whatever survived of them is too much—an all-too-human reaction that explains the divergence between the impressionistic judgments about the impact of the period and controversial social phenomena in general.

This book seeks to show in some detail that the radical rejection of American society which emerged and prevailed through the 1960s and early 1970s is far from extinct despite the political changes which seemed to mark the end of that period. In fact the political changes themselves have been overstated. As Lipset pointed out, "the conclusion that America has been in a conservative mood . . . is challenged by the results of the races for Congress and state offices and by the findings of opinion polls" [Lipset 1985]. In 1988 the U.S. House of Representatives was found to have "the most liberal record" since such ratings began in 1947 ["House in '88 Rated Most Liberal in 40 Years" 1989]. The election of Bush for president combined with Democratic congressional victories continued this trend. In 1981, the Reagan presidency notwithstanding—and at a time of defense build-up—entitlement programs still amounted to 47.9 percent of the federal budget, while defense was 26.2 percent [Pear 1981].

This study examines the character and substance of the critiques of American society which survived the 1960s and some of the social movements and groups which embody them and the institutions which sustain them. As such it also represents an effort to understand better why so many educated, articulate, and often idealistic people have adopted these critiques in full or in part. I would especially like to shed further light on the attitudes of a substantial number of American intellectuals[1] and members of other elite groups which formulated or embraced the radical critiques of American society.

These interests of the author are longstanding and found partial expression in a book entitled *Political Pilgrims* first published in 1981. In it I analyzed not so much the social criticism directed at the United States (and other Western countries) but a particular (and paradoxical) product of the highly critical mentality: the embrace of other, idealized social-political systems and the process of projecting upon them the desirable qualities the critics felt to be in short supply in their own society. While that book was mainly an inquiry into the idealization of communist political systems (or that of the pursuit of utopia) it took note of the underlying estrangement that produced in most instances these pursuits and visions. Still, relatively little space and attention were devoted to mapping out the dimensions of rejection and estrangement that preceded the wishful look for alternatives.

A subsequent collection of essays, entitled *The Survival of the Adversary Culture* [Hollander 1988], reflects a similar preoccupation in a more fragmentary fashion.

Anti-Americanism intends to provide a detailed account of the contents and characteristics of the contemporary critiques of American society and to examine their apparent sources. In doing so it will extend the scope of my earlier work in several respects. The present inquiry will not be limited to "certified," full-time intellectuals and social critics (usually associated with the academic or literary world) but will also include members of the clergy, journalists, and others. Chronologically it also goes beyond *Political Pilgrims* (which ended with the late 1970s), as it spans approximately a quarter-century, from the mid-1960s to the end of the 1980s.

This study departs from my earlier work in yet another important respect: It will also examine some of the more common critiques of the United States abroad, often subsumed under the term "anti-Americanism." (I had written one essay in 1978 anticipating these interests; see Hollander 1983: 299–311.)

The concept of anti-Americanism implies more than a critical disposition: it refers to critiques which are less than fully rational and not necessarily well founded. It usually alludes to a predisposition, a free-floating hostility or aversion, that feeds on many sources besides the discernible shortcomings of the United States. In the words of two commentators on the phenomenon, anti-Americanism "involves perceptual distortion such that a caricature of some aspect of behavior or attitude is raised to the level of general belief" [Doran and Sewell in Thornton ed. 1988:106]. Among the major sources of such anti-Americanism we find nationalism (political or cultural), the rejection of (or ambivalence toward) modernization and anti-capitalism—each to be discussed below.

Although the foreign critiques of the United States have been with us for a long time and in great abundance surprisingly little has been written about them and especially about their relationship to domestic social criticism. This study will compare the domestic and foreign critiques of American society and seek to understand how these two strands of thought and feeling influence, cross-fertilize, and legitimize one another.

Not being a historian I have been more interested in the persistence and recurrence of the critiques of the United States in recent times and in the renewed receptivity of the general public to many of these indictments in the United States, than in the more distant origins of these attitudes. I have been impressed by the observation that—even in a period of relative calm, such as the last twenty years, when the pendulum swung away from militant protest and political unrest—a reflexive disparagement of American society (at home) has maintained itself and became absorbed in some measure into the whole culture and many of its institutions.

It is then one of the major propositions of this book that the contrasts between the 1960s (seen as the period of the most vocal rejection of American society in recent times) and the decades that followed (the 70s was sometimes called the apolitical "me-decade") have been greatly overdrawn. This author sees far more continuity where others discerned a spectacular swing of the pendulum and a virtual reversal of the attitudes and trends of the 1960s. In these by now stereotyped views ". . . the sixties are represented as a morally generous, energetic time of political, personal and communal action . . . the seventies in contrast are an apolitical, devitalized decade of intense, morally debilitating preoccupation with the self" [Clecak 1983:4].

Perhaps one reason for this tendency—to exaggerate the differences between these two periods—may be found in the more general inclination to believe that in America nothing endures, that social-political events and cultural trends follow rapidly one another in endless and ephemeral succession and that attitudes and values are not markedly different from articles of consumption and styles of fashion.

A brief chronological clarification may be helpful here. What most people mean by the 60s—i.e. the period of protest, conflict, and militance—actually began in 1964 and ended in the early 1970s. By the same token the 1970s, seen as a decade of greater tranquility and a time of return to more conventional attitudes and values, began sometime around 1973–75 and continued into the early 1980s, capped by the election and re-election of Ronald Reagan as president.

The reader will notice that more space is given in this volume to the domestic than the foreign critiques of American society. There is a reason for this besides the vast space a comprehensive global examination of the foreign critiques would require. It is my belief that anti-Americanism abroad is a far more comprehensible phenomenon than the rejection of American society by its domestic detractors. Nor is there much dispute about the existence of the phenomenon abroad whereas the domestic variant is both more puzzling and more controversial in regard to both its character and impact. This being the case I devote more space to exploring, documenting, and seeking to understand the domestic critiques.

II

The radical critiques of American society here examined have their source in the type of alienation (or estangement, used interchangeably throughout) that is an attribute of highly "judgmental" intellectuals and quasi-intellectuals[2] and not of the (supposedly) downtrodden, and exploited masses, incapable of comprehending their true condition and its causes. Such "false consciousness" is at any rate the explanation social critics offer to account for the quiescence of "ordinary" people and in justification of their own readiness to become their spokesmen.

Although estrangement, as here understood, has in contemporary America become quite routinized, debates about the proper meaning of the term have not ceased. It still remains to be settled whether it applies to the insightful or the benighted, those who can or who cannot grasp the nature of the social realities that confront them, those who conform because of their ignorance or those who stand apart because of their understanding.

Some of these problems arise from the earlier association of the concept of alienation with false consciousness. If alienation leads to false consciousness, as in the most obvious case of religion—as Marx and Engels argued—then alienated intellectuals could not claim to be trustworthy analysts of society. But intellectuals confidently offer radical critiques of existing social arrangements precisely because they claim to be free of false consciousness, including the "religious reflexes" of the world. The social critics whom I call alienated intellectuals see as their central task the demolition of false consciousness in others, the raising of the level of consciousness of those who cannot grasp the nature of social-political realities which oppress, imprison, and dehumanize them. The estrangement of critical intellectuals is supposed to originate in and hinge upon their correct understanding of an unjust social world and to lead to their prescriptions for transforming it. (On the other hand it is an intriguing possibility that in the case of intellectuals, as in that of less exalted strata of society, alienation has led to another type of false consciousness: the embrace of secular religions and political utopia-seeking.)

In this book the concept of alienation will not be applied to people who are judged by others (such as Marx, Marcuse, or Fromm and their numerous followers) to be alienated but who are themselves totally unaware of being in such a state and appear to be free of discontent or critical sentiment toward their society. Nor will the concept be used in reference to the personal injuries and sense of loss ascribed by Urie Bronfenbrenner to neglected children growing up without "caring and supportive adults" [Hechinger 1986], although such personal difficulties may sometimes sensitize individuals to the injustices of the social order. Instead alienation as here used has most in common with the concept of "middle-class radicalism" developed by the English author Frank Parkin, who also stressed the rejection of dominant values as its key component [Parkin 1968:14].

The alienation of the social critics here discussed leads not to the resigned acceptance of the status quo but to determined efforts to change it. This view of the relationship between alienation and social criticism is quite different, for example, from that of Michael Walzer, who wrote that ". . . the class of alienated intellectuals doesn't coincide with the class of social critics . . . Alienation is most often expressed in political withdrawal, disinterest or radical escape; and then there is no engagement at all with the critical enterprise" [Walzer 1988:6]. It will not be the first time that alienation has been is used in different ways by different authors.

The kind of alienation here examined merges into an intense hostility toward the existing social order; it usually takes the form of a highly developed capacity for moral indignation, sometimes rage, provoked by the perceived inequities of (American) society. Peter Clecak described the same phenomenon when he wrote ". . . radical sensibility . . . is a compound of moral anger, self-righteousness, and personal resentment that goes beyond ideology . . . [it] releases itself in moral outrage at existing arrangements (and, sooner or later at people) allegedly responsible for deforming human potentiality" [Clecak 1983:56]. Todd Gitlin described alienation during the 60s as taking the form of a wide-ranging rejection of American society and culture:

> Little by little, alienation from American life—contempt even for the conventions of flag, home, religion, suburbs, shopping, plain homely Norman Rockwell order—had become a rock-bottom prerequisite for membership in the movement core.

He recalled how after an uplifting visit to Cuba he had to change seats at Mexico City airport because he could not bear looking at a billboard advertising Cutty Sark whiskey: "capitalist propaganda disgusted me" [Gitlin 1987: 271, 279].

Such attitudes need no longer define alienation or represent its only expression; to be alienated today is compatible with many things one did not associate with this state of mind and social role at earlier times. Estrangement has become compatible with holding fashionable and popular opinions, being the recipient of social honors and material recognition, belonging to cohesive subcultures or communities, being active in public affairs and securely entrenched in various hierarchies. It may provide access to a new source of self-esteem and sense of self-assurance that derives from the role of the righteous critic of society and its evils [see also Hollander 1983: 323–343].

The joys of consumption too may be compatible with being a militantly estranged social critic. Paul Cowan, working for the *Village Voice,* was astonished to discover that

> literary people lived as luxuriously in 1965 as the rest of America's middle class. They seemed eager to spend the money . . . as quickly as possible, purchasing new pleasures with the words and pictures they created; even the radicals who loudly proclaimed their willingness to make any sacrifice that would end the slaughter in Vietnam . . . The committed life that Camus had described . . . seemed . . . monkish, even priggish, from the vantage point of the Big Fiesta. [Cowan 1970:71]

A more recent example of the life-style of the radical social critic (by no means atypical except for the lack of permanent academic employment) is provided by

[Marge] Piercy [who] lives mostly in Wellfleet on Cape Cod where, with her housemates, she grows many vegetables and some fruit. Too much of the time she travels giving poetry readings and workshops. She has been politically active since later adolescence, a state she sometimes feels she has prolonged into her forties . . . She was involved in civil rights and worked in Students for Democratic Society from 1965 to 1969. Since the late 60s she has been active primarily in the women's movement, but works on other issues when she feels impelled to do so. [Piercy 1979:413]

Many critics of society can boast of similar settled circumstances and security that do not set them apart from millions of other comfortable Americans. Such conditions help to explain why today estrangement is widespread yet often overlooked: experiencing it is less unpleasant than used to be the case when social critics were more isolated, beleaguered, and marginal.

Much of the alienation in the United States today takes the form of a widespread skepticism and pervasive suspicion (besides the outrage noted above) directed at existing American institutions and social arrangements. As such it has become an established part of our intellectual discourse and a form of conventional wisdom, so much taken for granted that it is barely noted any more. What was once daring and unconventional criticism and a form of non-conformity, and as such noteworthy, is today self-evident truth in many subgroups, settings, and enclaves of our society. Albert Camus was ahead of his time time when he observed in 1957 that "today conformity is on the Left" [Camus 1974:170–71].

Thus, at the present time, the feeling that the society one is a part of is totally worthless and, hopefully, doomed is compatible with a reasonably cheerful personal disposition and the untroubled enjoyment of the available pleasures of life—material, aesthetic, and social. The gloom, withdrawal, pessimism, and marginality associated in the past with alienation and sustained radical social criticism have receded, certainly in the United States. To read the remarks of an otherwise hardnosed critic of American society dating from 1958 is not merely quaint, it illustrates the enormity of change in such matters. Norman Birnbaum wrote: "The nearer he [the intellectual] comes to the everyday world, the more remote he is likely to feel from it. Material rewards are irrelevant: his needs are spiritual" [Birnbaum 1958:46].

The changes in the substance and context of estrangement here noted had numerous consequences. While the critiques of American society have become increasingly standardized, repetitive, and unoriginal, the groups and institutions devoted to the articulation and dissemination of these critiques multiplied. There are now not only proliferating college courses imbued with the spirit of the radical critiques of American society but entire institutions and centers of study dedicated to the adversarial analysis of existing American institutions and values, as for example the Institute for Policy Studies in Washington.

The Institute has been notable for its longevity (it was founded in 1963) and for its capacity to accommodate many varieties of leftism and to nurture virtually every adversarial current in American society during the past quarter-century. It has exemplified the durability of the radical-critical sensibility and exerted considerable influence on what used to be the liberal center of the political spectrum. Perhaps the most steadfast and predictable producer of a great variety of radical social criticism and policy proposals, it has also been influential in Congress, the mass media, and various protest movements. A unique quality of the IPS has been its ability to conceal or play down its radicalism and attain a certain respectability among policy-makers in Washington and elsewhere. Its influence was illustrated, among other things, by producing an "alternative budget" (in 1977 and again in 1981) at the request of 54 Democratic members of Congress. Associates of the Institute had easy access to major publishing houses, newspapers, magazines, national television, elite college campuses, and the liberal churches. The celebration of its twentieth anniversary was attended by a wide range of public figures, prominent social critics, and celebrities. They included politicians James Abourezk, Les Aspin, Marion Barry, Birch Bayh, George Brown, Frank Church, George Crocket, Ron Dellums, Christopher Dodd, Don Edwards, William Fulbight, Gary Hart, Tom Harkin, George McGovern, Pat Schroeder, and Ted Weiss; also Helen Caldicott (the peace activist), Noam Chomsky, John Kenneth Galbraith, Averell Harriman, Seymour Hersh, Grace Paley, and I.F. Stone, among hundreds of others. Senior Institute figures served as advisers to Jesse Jackson in his presidential campaigns.

The 1983 Report of the Institute summed up its objectives as follows:

> The Institute for Policy Studies is engaged in a longer and deeper struggle, a struggle over the underlying principles and future direction of the political bankruptcy of the ideas and assumptions now governing America . . . [IPS Report 1983:6]

There are many critics whose rejection of society remains shrill and self-conscious and who do not seek to dilute these attitudes in the broader strata of the adversary culture. They include writers "who pride themselves on their alienation from society" as an observer of the 1986 PEN Congress put it, which provided an opportunity for the self-consciously alienated to assemble [Pollit 1986].

Whether or not the radical-critical disposition here outlined is more conducive to deeper insight into the nature of the social-political world than is a less adversarial perception is an important but unsettled question. If, as Thomas Sowell proposes, "alienation is a misconception of reality" borne out of deep frustrations [Sowell 1985:34] and if such alienation and the radical critique are intertwined—then by definition it will not lead to superior insights.

Both hostile and favorable predispositions toward the existing social order mold, and sometimes distort judgment. Intellectuals as other mortals, and perhaps more so, seek to find support and confirmation for their basic values in the social-political world; they too have their limitations in rising to unbiased detachment or impartiality.

Not surprisingly, the estranged intellectuals are persuaded that the hostile-critical vision yields a deeper understanding and is an essential requirement of the intellectual role itself. Time and again intellectuals have taken pride in thinking of themselves as "troublemakers" or "disturbers of peace" alerting a smug or corrupt society to its vices and hypocrisy. "The modern social critic is a specialist in complaint," Walzer wrote [Walzer 1988:4]. It is widely held that intellectuals are tradition- and duty-bound to be critical, questioning, iconoclastic, non-conformist, and, to some degree, adversarial toward the social order of their country. As an English author transplanted to these shores put it, "Who really expects happy, grateful, well-adjusted scribes to emerge and flourish these times?" [Hitchens 1983:1020]. Susan Sontag observed at the 1986 PEN Conference that "the task of the writer is to promote dissidence" [Pollitt 1986]. But some felt that American writers fell short of that ideal, arguing that "While the Russians turn their writers into courageous dissidents, we turn ours into trivial apologists" [Pemberton 1986].

What precisely qualifies intellectuals to become not merely social critics, but purveyors of secular morality? Many, including Walzer, come close to equating the social critic and the prophet. Paraphrased by Richard Neuhaus: "They are those with a special gift . . . The social critic is a 'sage' . . ." with a moral mandate. It is the duty of these prophetic-critics to castigate their society for not living up to its moral pretensions [Neuhaus 1987:49, 51]. According to Norman Birnbaum (one of the authors whose critiques span the entire period here discussed), the intellectual "bear[s] the responsibility for deciding anew how the world really is, or how it ought to be" [Birnbaum 1958:46]. Thirty years later Birnbaum still held a similarly exalted notion of the role of intellectuals: "Installed, with all due modesty, in the vanguard of an aroused citizenry, we may set forth once again to redeem a not quite fallen world . . . We secular thinkers will find outselves in the midst of those who take their

social conscience and . . . their self-definition from ecclesiastical tradition" [Birnbaum 1988:174]. He does not tell us who "installed" them
and bestowed this mandate upon them or why their judgments are to be
trusted.

More modestly, Richard Flacks proposed that "Leftist activists and
intellectuals who are true to their identity . . . do not want to lead others
or convert them. Instead their goal is to empower and enlighten." And
what is this "true identity"? His reflections (following a reunion in 1977
of one hundred former SDS activists) provide an answer:

> . . . what they had in common . . . was that they were each intellectuals
> hoping to connect their work to historical transformations . . . they per-
> ceived themselves to be struggling to ensure that their work—and indeed
> their total way of life—had a meaning in history . . . the intellectual who
> . . . challeng[es] the legitimacy of established authority . . . guided by
> visions of a newer world . . . is a kind of activist. [Flacks 1988:235, 280,
> 199]

By contrast Paul Johnson expresses grave misgivings about "the moral
and judgmental credentials" of many leading intellectuals who "tell mankind how to conduct its affairs . . . [and] proclaim a special devotion to
the interests of humanity." Finding a huge chasm between the conduct
of their private lives and their public pronouncements and theories he
finds little ground for heeding their advice or regarding them as the moral
conscience of society [Johnson 1988:ix, 1]. In fact he finds intellectuals
singularly unsuited for such a role due to their immoderation, impracti-
cality, extreme self-centeredness, and detachment from ordinary people.

It would appear then that becoming a radical social critic-moralizer
is a matter of self-selection often associated with some sort of academic
certification or accreditation. While Leszek Kolakowski thinks that a
"tendency common to intellectuals is their constant and desperate search
for their own legitimacy" [Kolakowski in "The Responsibility of Intellectuals" 1986:165], they generally appear quite successful in suppressing
such doubts and find the basis of their legitimacy in a combination of
good intentions, a higher level of education, and an articulateness.

The negative essence of alienation was expressed with unusual clarity
in a very different political and cultural setting by a Hungarian intellectual describing his own and his fellow intellectuals' disposition toward
his society:

> . . . here in Eastern Europe the foundation of our entire intellectual (as
> well as non-intellectual) life has been the rejection of the system under
> which we live . . . I don't know what would we do with ourselves if the

system suddenly and dramatically improved. We are lucky that there is little likelihood of this happening. If such as change would come about we would lose not only our livelihood but also our sense of identity and social function . . . we, East European students of society . . . live off the analysis of a diseased society . . . we would not know what to do with ourselves in a wholesome, normal society. We would have to relearn our skills . . . [Hankiss 1989]

While these remarks (dated by the recent changes in Eastern Europe) fully, if unintentionally, capture the attitude of Western intellectuals harshly critical of their society it does not follow that *their* alienation has the same foundations as its counterpart had in Eastern Europe. It is possible that an East European intellectual had or still has better grounds for estrangement than an American or Western European. Who is to decide? What is beyond doubt that the amount or intensity of public social criticism is not necessarily proportional to the evils which prevail in a society; such criticism also depends on the encouragement the social setting provides (or withholds) for expressing it, on the availability of means to disseminate the critiques, on the absence or presence of supportive audiences, or consumers of social criticisms, and on the expectations of the critics—an especially important subjective factor. As Michael Walzer put it, "Disappointment is one of the most common motives for criticism. We have an idea about how institutions ought to function or how people ought to behave. And then something happens . . . and we feel ourselves thrust into the company of social critics" [Walzer 1988:22].

This brings us to the heart of the debate about estrangement: how much of it derives from high and, by implication, unrealistic expectations (and the murkier underworld of personal grievances and injuries) and how much from the dispassionate observation of existing social arrangements and institutions?

While high expectations about both personal fulfillment and social justice appear to be a trait of intellectuals and other trend-setting groups, following the 1960s high expectations trickled down, as it were, to large numbers of college-educated, middle-class youth. One of them, Jane Alpert (former underground activist and companion of Sam Melville, convicted for many bombings) wrote:

We believed that the world could be cleansed of all domination and submission . . . that power playing between nations, sexes, races, ages, between animals and humans, individuals and groups could be brought to an end. Our revolution would create a universe in which all consciousness was cosmic . . . untainted by fear, possessiveness, sickness, hunger, or the need for a drug to bring happiness. [Alpert 1981:175]

In American society it is difficult to arrive at more restrained critiques of society due to a social-cultural tradition of excessive individualism that combines a highly optimistic view of individual potential with a correspondingly sanguine assessment of their institutional realization [see also Kreilkamp 1976]. Such a conception of the individual with virtually unlimited innate possibilities for self-improvement—but needlessly enslaved or handicapped by social institutions and practices—stimulates the kind of impatience and rejection that has been characteristic of radical social criticism in this country since the 1960s. (Though of course these attitudes go back to Rousseau.) Paradoxically this outlook has also been associated with an insistent social-cultural determinism that refuses to allow that this individual bursting with potential must share some responsibility for his circumstances with the forces of the social environment. Hence the radical critiques of American society are nurtured by high expectations about the possibilities of both self-realization and the perfectibility of social institutions. Given these expectations a reactive anger follows when major improvements fail to materialize. Todd Gitlin well described this state of mind: "Only true-blue believers in the promise of America could have felt so anti-American. Ours was the fury of a lover spurned" [Gitlin 1987:263].

The 60s was certainly a period when these expectations intensified and spread: ". . . the open-ended search for salvation itself became an ever more fertile source of dissent during these years: it heightened material and political as well as psychic expectations, thereby widening perceived disparities between aims and achievements" [Clecak 1983:103]. As another author put it, there was, at the time, "frustration and disillusionment with the society's seeming failure to enact its own highest ideals . . ." [Tipton 1982:2].

It was said of Tom Hayden, the prominent 60s radical (who was subsequently elected to the California State Assembly), that

> . . . he held and popularized unrealistic expectations of what any individual could achieve. Echoing the individualism inherent in the popular American belief that anybody could become anything through effort, courage and hard work, Hayden's New Left insisted on pushing the idea of self-transformation beyond achievable limits . . .
>
> . . . Hayden became an angry young man who sought to confirm in the larger world of political action his true identity . . . [Jacobs 1989:108]

Such a mingling of social idealism and personal frustration became a hallmark of the period. Take for instance the recollections of Jane Alpert of her state of mind at a civil rights demonstration

> I had stopped thinking about . . . the citizens of Chester, the evils of racism and poverty. The utopian vision that had tugged at me yesterday was gone.

In its place was something else, a fury that tore out of me with a life of its own . . . I was screaming against everyone and everything that stood in my way—the boys who had rejected me, the man who had fired my father when I was nine, my absent father, my mother, my brother . . .

[On another occasion, she recalled] . . . By yelling the phrases at the top of my lungs, I was saying no not only to the draft, not only to the war, but to all the values of the military and of corporate enterprise—to the religious and patriotic ideas my parents had tried to compel me to respect from the time I was a child. [Alpert 1981:56, 93]

Such connections between the personal and social (and political) are also illustrated by the belief of Sam Melville, who "used to say that his marriage had convinced him that monogamy was simply one of the oppressive structures of capitalism [Melville 1972:18]. The feminist movement in particular made the links between matters personal and social-cultural its major theme, insisting (not unlike Melville) that bad marriages invariably resulted from faulty social arrangements and specifically the oppression of women, and that disputes, marital or other, between men and women can never be free of social determinants. Arguably, the feminist critiques of American society went further than any other in seeking to find sociological explanations for even the most intimate personal problems, especially those of women.

Well into the post-Vietnam period, when most former protestors turned to more prosaic preoccupations (such as making money or getting degrees), high expectations persisted as did the moral indignation *and* social determinism of the social critics. As of 1980 Tom Hayden reproached Americans "for refusing to explore inner frontiers" and for fearing self-knowledge "that could cause us to despise ourselves or make us feel inferior, weak, worthless, shameful" [Hayden 1980:32]. He did not say in which culture did people delight in the kind of self-exploration he recommended. In turn, Michael Lerner, another veteran 60s activist, complained that

"the 1970s and 80s in the U.S. were dominated by this belief that the individual had only him/herself to blame if s/he faced a life that was unfulfilling." In fact . . . the blame should rest not on the individual but on the "system" that is perpetuated by encouraging self blame. [Rothstein 1989:19]

III

The radical critiques of American society persisted not merely because they were nurtured by cultural tradition, including individualism, optimism, and high expectations. There have also been specific developments during the 1970s and 80s that helped to sustain the seemingly paradoxical

trends discussed here, namely, the continued vigorous growth and elaboration of social criticism in the universities and colleges (see Chapter 3)
taking place within a larger social context that had become more quies-
cent.

The most obvious explanation of this phenomenon has been that
many of the student radicals, activists, and protestors stayed in academia,
resuming their studies and joining the faculties in the social sciences and
humanities in substantial numbers (". . . the politics of the 60s are now
to be found mainly in the classroom, among the faculty . . . Yesterday's
radical students are today's restive junior faculty . . . They are the children of the 60s. They were marching then, but now the political action
takes place in the classroom and in scholarly books . . ." [Dickstein
1988:68]). They ceased to be full-time political activists but they became
(almost) full-time social critics; the material well-being and occupational
security attained did not change their worldview while providing new
opportunities for critical reflection.

A more general proposition should also be entered into the argument
at this point. It is that, all things considered, there are few incentives for
most people to revise significantly the fundamentals of their political-ideological outlook.[3] Such revisions, if the beliefs in question were deeply
held, are an unpleasant, wrenching experience which in the end, more
often than not, are met with scorn or skepticism directed at the newly
converted. Moreover in the decades following the 1960s there were hundreds of thousands of people who held similar, if by then partially discredited beliefs, who found sufficient mutual support in their huge numbers to persist in these beliefs if in a more muted way. This helps to
explain why there have been for every Susan Sontag who rejected her
former radical beliefs and ceased to make apologies for left-wing dictatorships [Sontag 1982], hundreds and thousands of unrepentant members of the adversary culture who found her change of heart distasteful
or contemptible and who continue to pour forth their critiques of the
evils of American society on the pages of *The Nation, The Village Voice,
Mother Jones, The Rolling Stone, In These Times, The Monthly Review, The
Progressive, The Guardian, The Socialist Review,* the countless "alternative
publications" (see Chapter 4) as well as the op-ed pages of the *New York
Times* and *Washington Post* (in addition to the courses many of them
teach at elite colleges and universities).

An open break with the values and beliefs of 60s radicalism would
inspire expressions of contempt or outrage such as greeted the desertion
of Peter Collier and David Horowitz on the part of their ertswhile comrades who did not waver. Among them were Michael Klare, formerly of
the Institute for Policy Studies, and Edward S. Herman of the University
of Pennsylvania (who with Noam Chomsky had the distinction of defend-

ing the Pol Pot regime on the pages of *The Nation* [Chomsky and Herman 1977]. Michael Klare, currently a professor at Hampshire College in Massachusetts, wrote:

> ... there are a handful of former 60s radicals who have followed David Horowitz and Peter Collier in repudiating the militant New Leftism of their youth and embracing the crass materialism of the Reagan epoch. But the majority retain allegiance to the egalitarian and antimilitaristic values of their student days ... most of my former associates in the Columbia [University] SDS remain active in citizen movements—as environmentalists, women's and gay-rights advocates, volunteers at AIDS centers or homeless centers or as peace activists. [Klare 1989]

Similar indignation met the efforts of Ronald Radosh, Joyce Milton, and Alan Weinstein, who established (or re-established) through diligent research the guilt of the Rosenbergs and Alger Hiss respectively and thereby provoked the outrage of many old believers to whom such findings were nothing short of sacrilege and to whom the innocence of the aforementioned has remained a vital article of faith and centerpiece of a tightly structured belief system. (See for example Goodman 1983 and "Guilty or Innocent?" 1983.)

Alger Hiss has been honored by an endowed chair (of social studies) named after him at Bard College currently occupied by Joel Kovel, an appropriately embittered critic of American society [Evanier and Klehr 1989]. As of this writing I am unaware of a Rosenberg chair (in peace studies, social criticism, or Soviet-American relations).

The celebration of the Rosenbergs intensified during the 70s and 80s, constituting a part of the effort to rehabilitate the Old Left, including the American communist movement. Besides being commemorated in an idealized literary form (by E.L. Doctorow in *The Book of Daniel*) they have also become subjects of "The Rosenberg Era Art Project ... an exhibit of drawings and paintings ..." and a book entitled *The Rosenbergs: Collected Visions of Artists and Writers* [Brown 1988]. Such a focus on the victims of a social system is among the most effective forms of social criticism; their posthumous popularity is a reminder of the inhumanity of the social order. The Rosenbergs have also been put to good use in the ideology of anti-anticommunism as for example reflected in an article of an alternative newspaper ("Anticommunism and the Rosenbergs: A Lesson from the Past?") which suggested that anticommunism leads to the execution of innocents [Carroll 1988]. Thus the fate of the Rosenbergs has been converted into the message that anticommunism is and has *always* been an irrational and destructive attitude culminating in murderous injustices such as the execution of the Rosenbergs or the mass killings of the Vietnam war.

The acclaim regularly bestowed on the campuses on Angela Davis (who became "a permanent fixture on the American political landscape") supports the proposition that "In America . . . one need only be perceived as a victim of government persecution to be given a platform from which to declaim political banalities . . ." [Lester 1989]. In 1988 she was key-note speaker at Dartmouth College at the celebration of fifteen years of coeducation and "received a standing ovation after her speech." As a critic of the occasion further noted: "It was truly chilling to see Dart-mouth students, some of the most privileged human beings on . . . earth, stand up and applaud a speech that attacked everything America is today" [Dhillon 1988].

Lesser victims of anticommunism and especially McCarthyism have also been the subject of idealization in a new historiography aptly char-acterized by Theodore Draper as reflecting "the peculiarly protective post-New Left attitude toward the American Communist movement." In this new vision "Communist professors were highly trained academics who, despite their radicalism, shared with their colleagues commitment to the standards of their profession, in particular objectivity and fairness" and would not dream of imposing their views on their students) [Kaplan and Schrecker ed. 1983:31]. Of a book-length study these professors "emerge . . . as self-righteous, high-minded political innocents." The author's attitude "appears to be that communism was a venial sin, for which one need have no regrets; but anti-communism is a mortal sin which cannot be forgiven" [Draper 1987:35, 29, 34].

The survival of these attitudes is also apparent in the romanticization of former members of the American communist movement and some of its leading figures in books such as Vivian Gornick's *The Romance of American Communism* (1978). Of the latter a critic wrote: "One some-times has to remind oneself that in her evocation of coziness and warmth she is writing about the CP in the time of Stalin and not about a summer camp" [Howe 1978].

These trends are less than surprising given the fact that many of the activists of the 60s were "red diaper babies" (or were influenced by them), that is, raised by families who had been members or supporters of the American communist movement. Many had "grown up in the CP net-work of summer camps and political clubs" [McConnell 1987:33]. Todd Gitlin wrote:

> They had grown up breathing a left-wing air . . . being different, touched by nobility and consecrated by persecution . . . The majority of the original New Leftists were not the children of Communist or socialist parents, but some in adolescence were . . . influenced . . . by children who were. From

them the rest of us absorbed, by osmosis, the idea and precedent, and romance of a Left. [Gitlin 1987:67]

Another former New Left activist of such parentage put it this way: "Beneath the incredible blindness and political failures of the Communist Party . . . there had been a rather remarkable achievement—the socialization of a large band of people who learned to be effective catalyzers of popular struggle" [Flacks 1988:158].

This background helps us to understand the evolution of attitudes among the 60s activists from anticommunism to anti-anticommunism and sometimes to procommunism. The latter came to be manifested in admiration for Marxist-Leninist regimes such as those in Cuba, North Vietnam, Nicaragua, and others in the Third World. A fictional character in a novel of the radical author Marge Piercy personifies this revolutionary-functionary type, quite unlike the romanticized the 60s idealist-radical:

> Lark was too influenced by the Vietnamese [communists, that is] to charge around waving his prick. He wanted to . . . persevere for the long haul. He thought of himself with pride as an organization man. What went on in Rhodesia and in Angola was as important to him as what happened in his room; distant battles fed and drained him. He read long articles on the latest ideas of Kim Il Sung and Enver Hodza. [Piercy 1979:310–11]

Such fictional characters resembled some real life political activists, as for example David Gilbert, one of the convicted members of the Weather Underground and participant in the Brinks hold-up in 1981, who was described as ". . . a decent, sensitive, fully emotional human being . . . a humanitarian who was outraged at what people could do to one another . . . he sees himself as having a small but necessary part in history." He also used to "argue that communism and 'Third World Revolution' carried out through 'peoples' war' were the only paths to equal justice" [Farber 1982:B4]. Another activist convicted of many bombings, Sam Melville, was characterized by Wiliam Kunstler, the radical lawyer, as "a caring and sensitive and deeply moral person" [Kunstler in Melville 1972:ix].

Todd Gitlin, also a former activist, had a somewhat different view of these figures: "They had permuted class guilt into a theory that permitted them to abase themselves before a stereotyped, united Third World and yet retain for themselves a special mission" [Gitlin 1981:669].

A new apotheosis of anti-anticommunism was reached on the occasion of a conference entitled "Anti-Communism and the United States: History and Consequences," held in November 1988 at Harvard University and attended by the entire radical-social-criticism establishment. Speakers included Philip Agee, Eqbal Ahmad, Ricardo Alarcon (deputy foreign minister of Cuba), Carl Bernstein, Leonard Boudin, Alexander, Andrew, and Patrick Cockburn, Harvey Cox, Angela Davis, Daniel Ellsberg, Richard Falk, Richard Flacks, Stephen Jay Gould, Gus Hall, Edward S. Herman, Saul Landau, Joel Kovel, Ring Lardner, Jr., John Mack, M.D. (of the peace movement), Karl E. Meyer, Ralph Miliband, Jessica Mitford, Carl Oglesby, Jack O'Dell (an adviser of Jesse Jackson), Michael Parenti, Victor Rabinowitz (a former president of the National Lawyers Guild and partner of Leonard Boudin), Margaret Randall, Nora Sayre, Ellen Schrecker, Paul Sweezy, Howard Zinn, and approximately another hundred speakers.

The sponsors of the conference included Bella Abzug, Julian Bond, Noam Chomsky, Dave Dellinger, Barbara Ehrenreich, J. William Fulbright, John Kenneth Galbraith, Gabriel Garcia Marquez, Bishop Thomas Gumbleton, LaDonna Harris, Pete Seeger, Sandra Levinson, Rose and William Styron, Gore Vidal, George Wald, Howard Zinn, and others.

The Institute for Media Analysis in New York City, which sponsored the conference, lists among its board of advisers Noam Chomsky, Ramsey Clark, Alexander Cockburn, Joel Kovel, Michael Parenti, Abby Rockefeller, and Mikis Theodorakis, among others.

According to information provided by the program about half of the speakers were academics; the second major group was lawyers (generally associated with the National Lawyers Guild), followed by journalists and freelance writers and assorted radical activists and organizers (including several functionaries of the Communist Party of the U.S.), three representatives of the American Friends Service Committee, plus a sprinkling of foreign dignitaries from leftist Third World countries or movements (Angola, Cuba, Guyana, Nicaragua, El Salvador, and South Africa, including the former ambassador from Grenada) ["Anticommunism and the U.S." 1988; "Come Home Anti-Communism" 1988; Evanier and Klehr 1989].

Among the reasons for overlooking the survival of the ethos of the 60s is the disappearance of many of the organizations which used to promote the political agenda of that era. But as Harvey Klehr (among others) pointed out this did not mean that the spirit of the New Left has vanished; rather, it found new organizational expressions and causes [Klehr 1988:131). A broad rejection of American society has remained the emotional point of departure of these newer groups and causes, as used to be that of their predecessors.

In 1978 "the children of the 1960s" came together to establish the National Conference on Alternative State and Local Policies ("led and organized by some of the prominent young radical political activists of the 1960s") to serve as a "clearinghouse for activists across the country" [Broder 1978:A4]. It has become an effective political instrument assisting at the grassroots level the establishment of what I called "enclaves of the adversary culture."

Another nationwide organizational expression of the adversarial energy has been ACORN, the Association of Community Organizations for Reform Now "aimed at voicing the grievances of working-class and middle class neighborhoods . . ." among them Tom Hayden's Campaign California [Flacks 1988:219].

In 1987 an attempt was made to organize an American Green Movement: "Ecologists, anti-nuclear organizers, feminists, community leaders, American Indian representatives, Marxists, Socialists, anarchists, libertarians and trade unionists were among more than 500 people from all over the country who came . . . for the first national conference of the American Green Movement." There was an agreement among those assembled "that there was an urgent need for alternatives to existing political, economic and environmental institutions and practices" [Shabecoff 1987]. Another earlier effort similar in spirit was the formation in 1979 of the Citizens Party, established to "address the needs of people rather than cater to the needs of big business." In that year the party nominated as its presidential and vice presidential candidates Barry Commoner, the environmentalist, and LaDonna Harris, a feminist American Indian leader. The ticket won over a quarter-million votes. In 1984 the Citizens Party nominated as its presidential candidate Sonia Johnson, a Virginia feminist who once chained herself to the White House fence in an equal rights protest [Barron 1984].

Another development of some importance that tends to obscure the survival of the radical sensibilities is that many social critics have ceased to be marginal in any sense. (It is precisely for that reason that, contrary to Walzer, it *does* make sense "to call Herbert Marcuse, who worked for the Office of Strategic Services and moved on to the American professoriat, an alienated intellectual" [Walzer 1988:8].)

Many people who, by the criteria here used, are called alienated, work within the system although they do not have a sense of allegiance toward it. There has in fact developed a whole philosophy of justification of such affiliations and occupational ties, in particular the claim that the system will be changed by the critics working within it. In West Germany this was called the "march through the system" and it cannot be dismissed as mere rationalization of occupational security and material advantages such participation yields. In the words of Richard Flacks

... many former sixties activists refocused their activist identities into professional careers in human services, education, communications, planning—seeking in these ways to find institutionalized channels for the
implementation of their values ... thousands, in one way or another,
retained their committment to activism. [Flacks 1988:167]

Even former leaders of the Weather Underground found niches in
the system and easy access to the media. Bill Ayers, one of its leaders,
could expound on National Public Radio in defense of "our little satchel
of dynamite hidden under a coat" regretfully contrasting such supplies
with the superior resources of the armed forces of the United States
["Our Anti-Government Radio" 1982:1]. Another former Underground
leader Bernardine Dohrn joined a prestigious law firm in New York but
her view of the United States remained unchanged as did her justification
of "the necessity of underground work" [TRB, 1985]. Homer L. Meade,
one of the group of armed black students who occupied a building at
Cornell University in 1969, is "continuing the struggle" as a teacher and
administrator at the University of Massachusetts at Amherst [Wise 1984].
"Roger Wareham, one of a group of black revolutionaries known as the
New York Eight, landed a job at the Center for Law and Social Justice
[a branch of the Medgar Evers College in Brooklyn]." Both he and
another member of the "New York Eight" hired by the Center "had been
convicted on various weapons changes during the 1984 trial." The
administrator who hired them said "Everybody here has some kind of
activist background. I've made that a criterion. No matter what kind of
degree you have, you have to have a history of sensitivity and interest in
community work" [French 1988].
    The continuity between the 60s and 80s also found expression in the
sympathy and moral support some well-known social critics extended to
convicted felons of the violent Weather Underground (and other violent
groups). Thus for example following the Brinks hold-up and trial in 1981
"Some of Boudin's supporters issued a statement after she pleaded guilty,
lauding her idealism ... they denounced her sentence ... as unduly
harsh and criticized the legal system for various repressive measures that
violated human rights. Among the signers were Daniel Berrigan, Anne
Braden, Noam Chomsky, Arthur Kinoy and Benjamin Spock." Members
of the May 19th Communist organization and the Black Liberation Army
received support "despite the documented record of their violence and
support for violence" from Ti-Grace Atkinson, Daniel Berrigan, Anne
Braden, Emile Di Antonio (producer of a sympathetic film about the
Weather Underground), Frank Donner, Arthur Kinoy, William Kunstler,
and Morton Sobel [Klehr 1988:113, 115].

Further illustration of yet deeper affinities between the Old Left and the New Left, and its violent offspring, is provided by the family ties of Kathy Boudin, whose father Leonard Boudin has been a member in good standing of the Old Left and whose "home has always been a salon for leftist intellectuals . . . Kathy grew up immersed in their ideas." It was noted of the Weathermen in general that "Many of their parents were leftists or at least liberals." [Franks 1981: 38, 44] The father of another defendant in the Brinks case, Judith Clark, was Moscow correspondent of *The Daily Worker* until 1957 [Farber 1982].

Despite much evidence to the contrary the influence of the 60s has also been called into question—among those who mourn the passing of that decade—in connection with the rise and the alleged power of the neo-conservative intellectuals during the 1970s and 80s. Amitai Etzioni, the sociologist, described them as ". . . benefiting from the past few years' shift to the right in the national mood . . ." [Etzioni 1977]. Given their contacts in the Republican administration in Washington and their association with new or more influential foundations and research institutions (such as Heritage, American Enterprise, and Hoover), there has been a tendency among those regarding them with distaste to overstate their impact on American political and intellectual life and thereby magnify the threat they are supposed to represent to liberal, left-of-center values.

Michael Kinsley, an editor of the *New Republic,* advised that "It is time for the neoconservatives to grow up and admit they've won." He believed that today "a young intellectual on the make with no ideological predispositions but an enormous hunger for ego rewards . . . would choose to become a neoconservative." He disputed the prevalence of "moral equivalence thinking" criticized by neoconservatives but admitted that "Western intellectuals spend far more time criticizing the societies they live in than they do criticizing communism. So what?" [Kinsley 1985:29].

Anthony Lewis, columnist of the *New York Times* and another critic of the neoconservatives, was convinced that "Few intellectual movements in this country have won so much political influence so fast" as did the neoconservatives. Examining neoconservative claims of left-wing influence on campuses he "wondered what country Miss Decter [who made these claims] was in—what century." He agreed entirely with George McGovern, who disputed vigorously neoconservative assertions of leftist influence, observing that "The 'left' is so small in the United States that one has difficulty finding it'" [Lewis 1985]. In the same spirit the *Village Voice* referred to the Committee for the Free World (a neoconservative group that publishes a monthly newsletter and organizes annual conferences) as "powerful," to *Commentary* as "the nation's most influential political journal," and to conservatives like Jeane Kirkpatrick and Eliot Abrams as "run[ing] riot across Washington, D.C., Latin America and half the globe during the last eight years" [Berman 1988]. It is notable that those who belittle the survival of the left-of-center beliefs themselves belong to the part of the political spectrum which in their view lost all power and influence.

Presumably these conflicting claims of which political ideas and movements prevail have something to do with the moral and popular credit and psychological gratification that is associated with the underdog status in American culture, with the glory of the "uphill struggle" and the admiration for those who challenge established powers and vested interests.

The dispute over the degree of influence exercised by neoconservative vs. leftist intellectuals and their respective beliefs also has its roots in the sense of identity and self-conception of intellectuals who prefer to think of themselves as original, iconoclastic, nonconformist or unorthodox— beliefs which are difficult to reconcile with being a best-selling author, lecture circuit celebrity, campus guru, Washington insider, or purveyor of what has become conventional wisdom for cheering audiences.

IV

Nostalgia for the 1960s is among the expressions of the influence that period and its values continue to exert over the imagination and beliefs of important groups in our society.

While outbursts of nostalgia for the past are always among the signs of unease with the present, the nostalgia for the 1960s has a greater political significance and is among the more obvious indications of the impact and lingering influence of that period and the values it encapsulates. Although such nostalgia is also due to the fact that those nostalgic were younger at the time fondly recalled, it cannot be doubted that the 60s nostalgia has an ideological component that spans, by now, a quarter-century.

In articles, book-length memoirs, or at reunions of former activists there is evidence that basic values survived and continue to nourish adversarial attitudes and often activities as well. An author of a study of the student movement concluded that for the committed activist life in the 60s was one of "uncommon intensity and political seriousness . . . [part of] a creditable effort to hasten the end of an unjust and cruel war . . . [and] moments of almost unbearable excitement" [Miller 1987:14]. Tom Hayden wrote in his memoir that we of the sixties accomplished more than most generations in American history . . . Why conclude that life's most powerful moments already are behind us? . . . it is up to the sixties generation to . . . apply our ideals with a new maturity to our nation's future. [Hayden 1988:xix, 596]

At a reunion of University of Wisconsin student activists of the mid-1960s "hard-core intellectual protestors seemed relieved that old friends did not become bankers and Wall Street wheeler-dealers" [Rosenthal 1987]. Appropriately, the mayor of Madison, Wisconsin, a former activist turned into corporate lawyer, subsequently into mayor, declared "The issues have changed. I've changed. But my values haven't changed" [Johnson 1989].

A typical "then and now" summary in the *Alumni Magazine of Northeastern University* (in Boston) tells the reader about Wini Breines, who

> in the 1960s was a student activist . . . chanting anti-war anthems and carrying hand-painted signs. In the 1980s Breines . . . rarely attends demonstrations. Yet she doesn't feel that she or her fellow former activists have "sold out" . . . "We're not all stockbrokers," said Breines, associate professor of sociology . . . Her friends' career choices include teaching, social work, therapy, labor union organizing and counseling . . . They have remained true to certain values . . . [Watts 1985]

Participants of the 20th anniversary of the building occupations at Columbia University "included poets, novelists, doctors, film-makers, housing organizers, legal services lawyers, professors, construction workers . . . In the . . . biographies they submitted they wrote about traveling to Cuba, harvesting coffee in Nicaragua, joining anti-apartheid and anti-nuclear arms protests, working with the poor." One of them, for eleven years "an active Trotskyite" and participant in a sister cities program with Nicaragua, was "Still hoping to see socialism in the USA." Mark Rudd, who dominated the proceedings,

> paid tribute to two former Columbia Weatherman, Ted Gold and David Gilbert. Mr. Gold was killed in 1970 . . . in a Greenwich Village townhouse where he was building bombs . . . Mr. Gilbert is serving a 75-year-to-life sentence . . . for the armed robbery of a Brinks armored truck in which two security guards and a police officer were killed. [Riner 1988:B22]

Mario Savio, 60s student leader at Berkeley, at a commemoration of the "free speech movement" told his audience that "Our government is preparing a blood bath in Central America . . ." ["'Free Speech Orator' Savio Gives Call to Action" 1984] and that "Nicaragua would become this generation's Vietnam." According to a critical observer "'it was an anti-Reagan rally' not a commemoration of free speech" ["Student Movement of '64 Remembered at Berkeley" 1984].

Interviews with participants of the Harvard Strike of 1969 (many of them academics today) inspired the observation that "the radicals have retained many of the ideals of the sixties . . . they may have changed the world more than the world has changed them." A former SDS organizer said "we had to bust ass to get 25,000 for a national demonstration protesting the war. Last year, on a few days' notice, there were 50,000 people protesting against involvement in El Salvador. You didn't have to tell these people about the issue—they'd been through it before. The movement is still there" [Stark 1984:112, 174]. David Dellinger, longtime radical activist, inclined to the same view:

> . . . more people are actively committed to human familyhood today, and to a holistic relationship with the natural universe, than at any other time in my 71 years. More people are arrested every year for nonviolent resistance to the country's military insanities and domestic cruelties than during any year in the '60s . . . [McCarthy 1987]

Dellinger, who has also been an unusually durable apologist for Third World dictatorships (such as communist Vietnam and Cuba), "has been called the ultimate in unrepentant radicals." According to the same *Washington Post* editorial writer (McCarthy) he had nothing whatsoever to repent of.

The death of Abbie Hoffman provided another occasion for a surfacing of 60s nostalgia. The Los Angeles City Council voted unanimously to adjourn in his memory and a correspondent in a Massachusetts newspaper compared him to Jesus Christ [Engel 1989]. According to a *Nation* editorial "he shines with incredible brightness as a *real* national hero," who "articulated the consciousness of the counterculture that realized that the ultimate extension for arresting kids for smoking marijuana in this country was dropping napalm on other kids in Southeast Asia" [Krassner 1989:617, 616]. At the memorial service David Dellinger claimed that "the report of his suicide was a conspiracy and a lie" [King 1989].

There is also less impressionistic evidence of the survival of the political values of the 1960s. A study of 145 committed activists over a period of twenty years found that they "held on to their essentials beliefs" and displayed "a remarkable level of stability regarding a very wide range of issues" connected with their political-ideological positions [Marwell, Aiken, and Demerath 1987:375, 373]. Similar conclusions were reached by Whalen and Flacks based both on the findings of their own research and a review of other studies [Whalen and Flacks 1989; esp. 4, 160–63].

Likewise a study of public interest activism concluded that "the flames of liberal political protest" continued to burn through the 1970s, indicated by, among other things, "over one hundred citizen organizations representing more than six million dues-paying members" and a similar number of legal advocacy firms [McCann 1986:15].

By the 1980s standardized indictments of American society have been voiced not only by full-time critics but by other less prominent or unknown citizens similarly estranged. No longer limited to academic intellectuals concentrated in the social sciences and humanities, clerics, journalists, elected officials, members of the welfare bureaucracies, social workers, and educated housewives active in their communities echoed critiques of American institutions.

The people I have in mind—who belong to this broader adversary culture—can be identified by a number of beliefs. Among them is that American intervention almost anywhere in the world is without moral justification. They also aver that the United States bears the lion's share of responsibility for the sufferings of the poor in the Third World. They include prosperous white middle-class people who voted for Jesse Jackson ("a delayed effect of the sixties" according to Norman Birnbaum [Birnbaum 1989:150]), those who would not register for draft (or who support and encourage nonregistration). They are citizens for whom all American military expenditure is wasteful, who claim to have sleepless nights over the prospect of nuclear war and press for making their towns "nuclear free zones" (and "sister cities" of those in the USSR or Nicaragua), people who in any conceivable conflict between the U.S. and other powers instinctively place the blame on the U.S., those among the college educated who are persuaded that Orwell's *1984* captures most aptly the characteristics of contemporary America. They can also be identified by sporting bumper stickers proclaiming "US out of North America" and "This Country Was Built on the Bones of Indians." They are inclined to believe that the United States is a uniquely hypocritical and destructive society that failed to live up to its promises. They are for the most part people of goodwill and frustrated idealism, persuaded that in no other country are social ideals and practices so far apart as in the United States of America.

Correspondence columns and guest editorials in local and other newspapers are a goldmine of such attitudes.[4] A columnist of a student newspaper in Massachusetts writes ". . . this country is still the Land of Opportunity: there is an infinite opportunity here to lie, cheat, bribe, blackmail, swindle, buyout, coerce and 'bump off' that you will not find elsewhere" [Caldeira 1984:13]. Another one believes that "We are all products of a society that tries its damnedest to tear our humanity from limb to limb and replace our real selves wih an anxiety-ridden, materialistic clone" [Galitsky 1989:5]. Such examples of the intact survival of 60s rhetoric is not limited to a few impressionable students. A retired professor of English at the same university finds five parallels between the support for Reagan and Hitler [Barnard 1984]. A correspondent to a local newspaper warns: "The American people should worry less about terrorists lurking in European airports and more about the ones occupying the seats of power in the nation's capital" [Engel 1986]. Another correspondent intones: "It is time for us to awake from our delirium of power and virtue . . . The only terrorism we can really stop is our own" [Holt 1988]. Another citizen rebukes President Reagan for his insufficient concern with American terrorism and asks, "Who are the terrorists? Who should be punished? Are any of us without guilt?" [Myers 1985]. A "longtime environmental activist" and regular contributor to the *Palo Alto Weekly* offers more extended analysis:

> Our democratic political system seems to be for sale . . . our nation will be owned and run by a relatively few corporations within a few years . . . Militarism has become the supreme value . . . [Whereas in the past] "Getting ahead" didn't seem to be the supreme value . . . A *feeling* value dominated and there was warmth in men's and women's affairs . . . Are you aware of a dangerous disease now with us? I call it [the] . . . hardening of the heart . . . it causes divorce, drug abuse and hatred of neighbors . . . [Crozier-Hogle 1986]

A former military chaplain advised: "We must stop this insanity of worshipping the gods of metal. We must stop this insanity of making the military an honorable profession" [Dipalazzo 1985]. A tax resister wrote, "We owe it to humanity and our creator to resist evil openly, and the task begins at home . . . Let us be rid of all implements of destruction . . . Let us arm ourselves with love, courage and ingenuity" [Buchanan 1982]. Another grassroots activist believes that American goodwill is the key to the solution of the hostage crisis and in the same breath expresses dismay about "the rich giant being stingy with poor countries," that is, cutting back on foreign aid [Matteson 1981]. A field representative of the American Friends Service Committee perceived of crime as a form of "poor decision making" induced solely by poverty which should not be dealt with by imprisonment [Weaber 1985].

A middle-class couple (formerly of New Rochelle, N.Y.) in a small New England town decides not to celebrane Thanksgiving since it commemorates what in reality was the genocidal extermination of the Indians. This insight came to them from Howard Zinn, the radical historian [Loisel 1985]. In a public kindergarten in Brooklyn the school authorities resolve that traditional Thanksgiving celebration (degrading to Native Americans) be replaced by "international" Thanksgiving, insisting that each child identify him or herself by national origin. As an indignant parent wrote, "On one of the country's truly national holidays [the children] are encouraged to think of themselves as anything but American . . ." [Ticker 1990]

An anti-nuclear activist arrested for unlawfully entering a plant that builds submarines explains her motives for joining the peace movement:

> I had a gradual awareness that something essentially was wrong . . . that there was a connection between the arms race and hunger, globally and locally. I'm committed to staying in this movement. I've found a calling here. [Wilson 1984]

Another activist specializing in protest against military bases is "almost like a driven person" who "admits that beneath the surface is a simmering rage at what he sees as injustice . . . He seeks to find the connection between different issues—the C5 [military transport plane] and militarization, the C5 and environmental policies, the C5 and . . . social services . . ." [Pollard 1987]. A young man refusing to register for the draft believes that his act "will promote peace and justice" [Mager 1985]. A graduate of Columbia University characterized by the police as "an intelligent individual" and a "self-described 'revolutionary Communist'" inundates New York City with graffiti which "assail everything from the CIA and FBI to racism and imperialism" and includes the warning "AIDS is Germ Warfare by U.S. Government" [Purdum 1986]. His small-town colleague in an interview with the local "alternative" newspaper reveals that "he's fighting against 'the U.S. screwing over and destroying the people of Central and South America. I'm very angry at this government,' he says. 'I'm doing graffiti in my commitment to educate people in this area.'" The graffiti gives him a "a feeling of power and victory over a system he thinks is oppressive" [Singer 1982:3A].

A member of the so-called Ohio Seven ("who do not deny that they went underground . . . to pursue their program of resistance to American imperialism"), convicted and given long sentences for multiple bombings, told the sympathetic interviewer of the same alternative newspaper that "We represent an alternative way of struggling which the government sees as a threat . . ." [Hundley 1987:3, 6]. A small-town restaurateur and dropout of a graduate program in education ("it was a system of slave labor") fantasizes about disrupting the Pentagon by telephone: "I got this idea to bring the country to a standstill. Everyone around would get on the phone for two days straight and keep calling the Pentagon and tie up their phone lines" [French-Lankarge 1985:8]. A "tireless" American Friends Service Committee activist already as a fifth grader formed an International World Peace Friendship Club, now in her sixties has been arrested 18 times and "faces incarceration without fear." She "has worked on a variety of issues ranging from the atmosphere testing of nuclear weapons to the sale of war toys, she sees them all as one issue . . . her work is all part of a single effort to create a world based on the simple moral values she learned as a child in Missouri" [Ayvazian 1986].

Such are a few sketches from the adversary culture.

V

Indications of the survival (and revival) of the adversarial attitudes of the 60s have not been confined to the correspondence pages of newspapers and the reminiscences of activists. There has been a wide variety of social, political, and cultural phenomena suggesting that the attitudes here discussed developed institutional roots and an organizational reality, that beliefs often translate into action.

For example by the early 1980s antimilitary sentiments were once more in evidence on the campuses even if their intensity remained below the levels reached in the late 60s and early 70s. In the spring of 1985 a student strike was held across the nation to "increase awareness of militarism" complete with the rhetoric that was prevalent in the 60s:

> . . . our passivity and non-resistance to the status quo is what keeps the war machine rolling onwards to the eventual annihilation of the human race . . . By the very existence of military science and research in this institution and by the presence of ROTC . . . on campus, it is clear that the University itself is an active part of the war machine. [G. Brown 1985; "No Business as Usual April 29" 1985]

It was also characteristic of the ethos of academia that measures by the State Department to prevent "leakage of high technology" to Soviet exchange scholars or students met with widespread resistance at universities, "academics contend[ing] that the Pentagon's premise that Soviet scholars would use the machines [advanced computers] for critical military applications is ridiculous" [Sanger 1985]. At the Jet Propulsion Laboratory in Pasadena, California, faculty voted that "The Army's new study center . . . should be thrown out 'at the earliest possible time' . . ." ["Faculty Opposes" 1984]. There was a nationwide movement centered in academic communities to prevent the Air Force from building a chain of radio towers (GWEN) designed to maintain military communications during a nuclear attack [Kelliher 1989]. These protests took place against the background of declining national public support for military expenditures. In 1985 a Gallup survey found that "Americans by a ratio of 4-to-1 believe that too much rather than too little is being spent by the

Government on the military" ["Gallup Finds Support for Military Cut-backs" 1985]. A few years later another poll confirmed that the public favored "sharp cuts" in defense spending and displayed pronounced iso-lationist sentiments [Dionne 1989].

The U.S. Marines were physically prevented from recruiting at the University of Massachusetts at Amherst in 1987 [Elliot 1987]. On the same campus in the same year Amy Carter and Abbie Hoffman were among the highly publicized protestors of CIA recruitment; charged with trespassing (for their occupation of an academic building) they were acquitted by a local jury, a verdict that was seen as "a statement against the CIA" and suggested that the jury accepted the defense argument that the building takeover was to prevent CIA crimes around the world. In yet another replay of the 60s, Leonard Weinglass, one of the defenders of the Chicago Seven, was a member of the defense team [McDermott 1987]. A "necessities defense" led to the acquittal of 26 protestors in Vermont who occupied the office of a state senator "to dramatize their opposition to United States policy in Central America" ["Protestors Unusual Defense Ends in Controversial Victory" 1984].

Anti-CIA demonstrations in the 80s were also popular. At Amherst College it was the faculty rather than students who protested CIA recruit-ment [McKay 1982]. Sometimes the visits of CIA recruiters were can-celled in anticipation of the protests ["CIA Calls Off Visit to Columbia" 1983]. Bella Abzug in a speech "calling for activism" conveyed her "understanding" of the anti-CIA protests [Britton 1986].

Demonstrations were not the only manifestations of the anti-CIA fer-vor, one of the legacies of the 1960s that surfaced in the 80s. The climate of opinion in these years was such that an organization could flourish that specialized in publicizing the names of American intelligence agents abroad. Its founder, Louis Wolf, "boasts of having helped to disclose the identities of more than 2000 American intelligence agents stationed around the world" including one in Jamaica who was gunned down 48 hours after his identity was thus revealed. Mr. Wolf, charitably described by the *New York* Times reporter as a "gadfly," "grew up in a wealthy Philadelphia family ... [and] became a Quaker" [Taubman 1980; Thomas 1980]. In a further illustration of the adversarial sensibility a group of 60 legal scholars voiced strong objections to a proposed bill ("an infringement of First Amendment rights of free speech and free press") that would have made a crime the disclosure of the identity of intelli-gence agents [Mohr 1981].

The adversary culture was almost as hostile toward the FBI as it was toward the CIA as witnessed by the benefit concert for Leonard Peltier, the convicted murderer of two FBI agents, celebrated as a political pris-oner ["Benefit for Indian Activist Draws Support" 1987].

The invasion of Grenada was another occasion for the expression of outrage at the American use of force. It was denounced not only on dozens of campuses but also in the strongholds of the adversary culture such as Berkeley (by its mayor) and cities such as Boston, Detroit, Minneapolis, and New York. In Aurora, New York, at Wells College, Bernardine Dohrn was the speaker at the meeting protesting the invasion ["2500 Rally at UN to Oppose Invasion" 1983]. On the first anniversary of the invasion forty college student-body presidents issued a statement registering retroactively their disapproval and also taking the opportunity to protest U.S. policies in Central America ["Grenada Debate" 1984]. The bombing of Libya evoked similar responses, at any rate on elite campuses, complete with teach-ins, rallies, and letters to the editors.

The Soviet shooting down of the Korean airliner in 1984 provided another occasion for a display of the attitudes here discussed. *The Nation* magazine, Tom Wicker, and Seymour Hersh, among others, were persuaded that the United States was to be blamed for the loss of the plane. Wicker, in particular, basing his charges on a *Nation* article (and, one might suspect, his own intuition) was ready to believe that the various American agencies, fully aware that the plane strayed into Soviet airspace "deliberately chose not to guide the airliner back to safe course . . ." in order to find out how Soviet air defenses will respond and thus gain a "bonanza of intelligence information" [Wicker 1984; see also Helms 1984].

A new domestic social problem that stimulated justified social criticism, while also reflecting a free-floating estrangement in search of justification, was the spread of homelessness. For some observers it was largely a result of well-intentioned deinstitutionalization (the release of the mentally ill from mental institutions); for the social critics it was a direct consequence of the economic policies of Reagan such as reduced federal subsidies for housing, curtailed welfare benefits, and unemployment. For the most radical among the social critics homelessness was the latest vindication of the incurable ills and injustices of American society. Among them Jonathan Kozol was sufficiently inspired "to liken homeless families to concentration camp inmates" on ABC television [Whitman 1988:19]. (Elsewhere Kozol argued that the oppressed of this country were "purposefully maleducated" [Wattenberg 1985].)

The sentiments associated with homelessness were also illustrated by the indignation that greeted the findings of a painstaking empirical study that sought to establish their actual numbers. Its author, Peter Rossi, a distinguished sociologist, was subject to "torrents of criticism" and the "longest stretch of personal abuse" he ever suffered (since his basic military training); he became "persona non grata" and a "non-person" among homeless advocates for finding their numbers smaller than those put forward by the advocacy groups [Rossi 1987:79]. Civil libertarians championed the rights of the homeless to be on the streets. In the celebrated case of a homeless woman in New York removed from the street for involuntary hospitalization,

> [the] judge ordered her released . . . [and] said that society, not she is sick ("the blame and shame must attach to us") and, anyway, the sight of her may improve us. By being "an offense to aesthetic senses" she may spur the community to "action" . . . The judge was unimpressed by the fact that the woman had a history of drug abuse and psychiatric hospitalization, defecated on herself, destroyed paper money . . . ran into traffic, shouted obscenities, was inadequately clothed for winter sleeping outdoors, and was found by city psychiatrists to suffer from paranoid schizophrenia . . . The Civil Liberties Union psychiatrists found her rational . . . and diagnosed her destruction of money as an assertion of autonomy. [Will 1987]

These were not the only signs of the presence of the adversarial spirit in the legal profession. The National Lawyers Guild ("its agenda . . . still unabashedly and unapologetically left-wing") now has 10,000 members in 200 chapters (it had 500 in 1953 and the earlier high was 4000). Ten of its members are judges in New York City, many are high-profile political activists [Margolick 1987]. Much of the Pro Bono work and that of public interest lawyers also reflects an "eager[ness] to challenge the system . . ." Remarkably it is the government that funds much of this litigation often directed against various government agencies [Goode 1986]. The left-of-center trends in the legal profession were also illustrated by the topics and panels at the 18th National Conference on Women and the Law (e.g., "Lesbian Family Recognition," "The Future of the Sanctuary Movement," "Colonized Peoples Within U.S. Borders: Self Determination or Slavery?," "The Global Assembly Line and the Hometown Response," "Feminist Values in the Courtroom," "No Safe Place: Systemic Violence," "Historical Perspectives of Women of Color/Third World Women in the Law," and many others of a similar political thrust).

The attention given to the homeless connects with broader issues. The media and social critics rallied to their cause both on laudable humanitarian grounds and also because they were the latest victims whose deprivation offered new, dramatic, and incontrovertible evidence of the inhumanity and malfunctioning of the system. Their emergence into public awareness continued a process that began in the 1960s, namely the multiplication of groups claiming victim status. This development had dual origins: on the one hand the more victims, the easier to indict the system; on the other hand certified victim status resulted in various benefits and preferential treatment (enshrined in federal legislation), as in the case of racial minorities and women. Robert Nisbet, the sociologist, wrote, "In this special, very modern social sense of victimhood, there can be no end to the process of creating victims. At this moment at least 75% of the American people are victims . . . all women . . . the blacks, Hispanics, Indians, farmers exposed to drought, [the] unemployed, mentally disturbed . . ." [Nisbet 1982]. He might have added the most recent group, those infected with AIDS. A political scientist noted that "America [has] gone from being 'land of liberty' to the home of the oppressed . . . Entire regions seek official designation as 'underprivileged' as if it were a badge of honor . . ." [Wildavsky 1982:56]. The rewards of victimhood are also moral and psychological, imbuing one's life with drama and a sociologically certified moral rectitude [Epstein 1989]. In 1990 the victim status of the handicapped (or disabled, in the currently correct usage), their numbers estimated close to 50 million, was enshrined in new far-reaching legislation seeking to provide them with equal employment and other opportunity.

The process of creating victims, or readily granting victim status, reflected a growing sense of guilt among the elite groups of society, the prolonged impact of the protest movements of the 60s, and the readiness to hold society responsible for the difficulties of various groups and individuals. The growing popularity of the doctrine of social-cultural determinism has been directly related to the growth of victim groups. Even a high school principal arrested for drug use was not to be judged, according to Richard Green, Chancellor of the City Schools of New York:

> ". . . we have a principal who unfortunately made a bad decision about the use of crack . . . And when we see an individual human being out there . . . powerless to do anything about his circumstance, you don't feel good about it." He [the Chancellor] was not going to put the principals further under "assault." [Weiss 1988:44]

The public and institutional response to the case of Tawana Brawley, a black teenager of Wappinger Falls, New York, who claimed to have been raped and brutalized by a group of white men, was another unusually instructive example of the connections between societal guilt, social determinism, and radical social criticism. The allegation generated vast investigations mobilizing numerous law enforcement agencies and their highest officials; it preoccupied the governor of the state, inspired many demonstrations and protests, and provided a new forum for castigating American society for its racism. At last, after lengthy investigation, the case was deemed to be a fraud [see, for example, "Evidence Points to Deceit by Brawley" 1988; see also McFadden 1990]. But according to Stanley Diamond, distinguished professor of anthropology at the New School for Social Research,

> The case cannot be measured by legal canons, official justice or received morality . . . The grand jury has responded to the technical questions of the case, weighing the evidence but necessarily blind to its deeper meanings. In cultural perspective, if not in fact, it doesn't matter whether the crime occurred or not . . . What is most remarkable about this faked crime is that traditional victims have re-created themselves as victims in a dreadfully plausible situation. [Diamond 1988:409, 410]

Professor Diamond apparently sought to convey that the incident justified moral outrage not because of what happened but because what might have happened and because such things had happened at other times. In another incident where allegations of racial harassment at Emory University, Atlanta, turned out to be a hoax by the alleged victim, the president of the Atlanta chapter of NAACP said, "It doesn't matter . . . whether she did it or not . . . because of all the pressure these black students are under at these predominantly white schools. If this [i.e., the phony allegation of racial harassment] will highlight it [i.e., these pressures] . . . I have no problem with that" [Applebome 1990].

Feelings of white guilt toward the black community had a wide variety of expressions ranging from the reflexive granting of black student demands on campuses to apprehension about expressing criticism of blacks' job performance, to supporting Jesse Jackson as a presidential candidate as "the right thing to do" regardless of unease about his qualifications. Such solicitousness is a form of social criticism—reaching out to the victim intended as criticism of the victimizer.

The effort to identify with the underdog sometimes found grotesque expressions as in the case of the middle- (or upper-middle-) class youngster who on the op-ed page of the *New York Times* earnestly explained why what he himself defined as an unprovoked attack on him by young black males (leaving him with a broken nose) was totally understandable because of what he "symbolized" for them [Strozier 1988]. A replay of the story was published two years later by a former inmate of a Nazi camp who "felt a keen sympathy for the robber" (a young black man) and excused him on the grounds that "in this kid's mind he was not committing a crime, according to his peers and the circumstances of his upbringing" [Horn 1990]. Evidently, it did not cross his mind that the same might have been said of his former campguards who did not think that mistreating Jews was a crime, given the attitude of their peers and the circumstances of their upbringing.

Such attitudes may also be part of a more general decline of personal accountability that was also evident in the moral and material support a Catholic order gave to Richard Herrin, self-confessed murderer of his former girl-friend, instructed by a Roman Catholic priest right after the murder to "immediately begin the process of self-forgiveness"—advice he diligently followed [Gaylin 1986].

The survival and entrenchment of the radicalism of the 60s found an especially tangible expression in what I called elsewhere [Hollander 1988:17–19] the political-administrative enclaves of the adversarial worldview. They go back to the 1960s when Tom Hayden proposed to create what he considered "'liberated territories' built from youth ghettos like Berkeley, Cambridge and Ann Arbor. From these places revolution would spread to the rest of America" [Jacobs 1989:107]. Although the revolution did not spread, the enclaves persisted. They are mostly campus towns (such as those mentioned earlier) where many of the 60s activists, their supporters, and descendants settled in the shadow of academic institutions hospitable to these survivors of the 60s. These towns, usually dominated by left-of-center or radical town governments, often declared themselves "nuclear free zones," "sister cities" of Nicaraguan or Soviet cities, passed resolutions at town meetings on U.S. foreign policy, divested of firms doing business with South Africa (or producing nuclear weapons), offered sanctuary to refugees from noncommunist countries such as El Salvador and Guatemala, ostentatiously refused to participate in federal civil defense programs, loudly protested the presence of any military installation or activity in their vicinity, and so on[5] [for a case study of Berkeley, see "A Tale of Socialism in One City" in Collier and Horowitz 1989].

Estrangement is also given institutional recognition in studies and research addressed to the documentation and criticism of the ills and evils of American society generously supported by major foundations, on the well-paid lecture circuit of prominent and popular social critics. Textbooks, too, used in secondary and other schools present an increasingly negative portrait of American society and history as will be shown later. The process here described also manifests itself in the large number of instructors at colleges and universities whose professional identity is stamped by the commitment to persuade their students about the endemic and systemic nature of injustice in the United States.

Bertell Ollman for instance, reviving Marcuse's notion of repressive tolerance, dismissed academic freedom under capitalism as ". . . part of the problem . . . because the ideal of academic freedom helps to disguise and distort an essentially repressive practice . . ." For a genuine change "we shall have to await the coming of a society that no longer needs its universities to reproduce and rationalize existing inequalities, that is a socialist society" [Kaplan and Schrecker, eds. 1983:53, 54].

The growing involvement of the churches in the radical criticism of American society has been another major development in the "routinization of estrangement" since the 1970s. Why and in what manner they added their voices to these critiques will be examined in subsequent chapters. Clerics as other critics of American policies and institutions found it irresistible to connect their disapproval of particular policies to the sweeping and far-reaching indictments of American institutions.

In this preview of the symptoms and factors connected with the survival and renewal of the radical critiques of American society we must also take further note of the Reagan presidencies. While in themselves they may be seen as representing the triumph of social and political forces hostile to the spirit of estrangement which emerged in the 1960s, they actually reinvigorated them. With Reagan in the White House social critics could point with renewed confidence to the ingrained ills of American politics, the ascendance of social forces obstructing beneficial social change.

While the earlier ambivalently wishful predictions of an emerging police state or American-style fascism failed to materialize (Tom Hayden reportedly announced in 1969 that "Fascism is here, and we're all going to be in jail by the end of the [Vietnam] war" [Collier and Horowitz 1985:2]), there was at least a Republican president in the White House: a believer in free enterprise, the strengthening of the American military forces, American self-assertion abroad, traditional religious values, and the general goodness of American society. As a former movie actor, he was also intimately associated with the ethos of Hollywood, its escapist entertainment, glittering materialism, show-business celebrities, and the techniques of public relations—the whole milieu of inauthenticity that antagonized intellectuals and other social critics for generations.

Possibly the social critics' dislike of Reagan was even stronger than that reserved earlier for Nixon. Reagan's personal characteristics were more infuriating—the jovial, genial attributes he could deploy in the service of political objectives. Thus both his personality and policies helped to revive the rejections of American society—they proved that the dreams and aspirations of the 1960s were under serious attack. If a person like Reagan could be president—many critics felt—it proved that their alienation was justified. In a poll of 51 foreign policy experts published by *Parade* magazine Reagan was rated below Castro, Pol Pot, Le Duan (Vietnam), Kim Il Sung (North Korea), Mengitsu (Ethiopia), and Jaruzelski [Sobran 1983]. The Reagan presidency generated new organizational energies, stimulated social protest and a mobilization of political discontent most directly focused on nuclear arms and American policies in Central America.

The persistence of the radical critiques of American society, needless to say, also owed much of its vigor to the memories (and "lessons") of Vietnam and Watergate, the most often cited symbols of discredit to American political institutions in recent times. Guilt feelings connected with Vietnam were assiduously nurtured by social critics. Robert Jay Lifton argued, ". . . since all of us are part of America and we . . . live in the American realm and contribute to national and military efforts, we share a certain culpability . . ." It was tempting to move from Vietnam to the past: ". . . the fact that Indians have been massacred or that blacks have been ill-treated, and I am an American enjoying the fruits of American life, gives me a sense that I have some responsibility toward reparation . . ." Richard Sennett, participant in the discussion, observed that "the middle class is on every side subjected to a demand that it feel guilty about something. There's almost a glorification of guiltiness . . ." [Farber et al. 1972:523, 524, 525]. Such ostentatious confessions of guilt on the part of social critics became widespread since the 60s, presumably contributing to their feelings of moral courage and superiority.

Vietnam had another, less obvious impact, also of long-term significance. The retreat of the United States demonstrated that it was far from invincible, a development that not only gave pleasure to radical critics but also contributed to a generally increased receptivity to all critiques of American society, to the decline of trust in major American institutions (see for example Lipset and Schneider 1983), and to an overall decline in the levels of collective self-esteem, especially among elite groups. For example it has become conventional wisdom, mouthed by U.S. congressmen and high school teachers of social studies alike, that the U.S. is responsible for Third World poverty. Daniel Moynihan observed, discussing guilt feelings among American elite groups, that "We have allowed the problems of Third World poverty to be defined as something we created and for which we are responsible . . . this definition represents a triumph for our foes . . . guilt as a political weapon is poorly understood" [Moynihan 1978:37, 38].

Hamilton Fish III, son and grandson of long-term Republican congressmen and former publisher of *The Nation* magazine, personified these elite attitudes. "He was born during the Korean war and came of age with Vietnam. He was freshman at Harvard in the spring of 1970 when President Nixon ordered the Cambodian incursion. Harvard . . . exploded. He was transformed. 'I was influenced by all the traditional elitist values . . . Vietnam changed everything. I didn't grow up believing what leaders say is true but that they lie to you . . . I lost automatic faith in institutions

. . ." Mr. Fish was also very disturbed by the American bombing raid on Libya [Curtis 1986].

Watergate served similar functions by revealing domestic corruption in the highest places and depriving the president's office of the respect it has enjoyed at other times. Both Vietnam and Watergate have remained powerful reference points for national self-denigration and delegitimation.

It is then not so surprising that even a moderate and reasoned social critic, such as Irving Howe, concluded by the end of the 1980s that American society was as deeply flawed as ever before:

> Everyone with eyes to see is coming to recognize that beneath the surface of affluence and the ideology of "free market," there is taking place in this country a steady, grinding process of social decay. Drugs, violence, poverty, gangs, homelessness, shootouts are but few of the symptoms. Malaise, disintegration, pathology, "underclass": these are some of the key words. The reality is a terrible dehumanization, the worst we have known in fifty years . . . [Howe 1989:423]

VI

The entrenchment of the attitudes discussed so far took place, for the most part, among people who themselves rarely suffered the ills and injustices they described and decried. It is quite likely that never before in history have such large numbers of people, comfortable and privileged to various degrees, come to the conclusion that their society was severely flawed or thoroughly immoral.

The reflexive questioning or rejection of the social order that became characteristic of this subculture developed and maintained itself in combination with an unstated sense of security which itself became a source of embarrassment if not outright guilt. I call this an "excess security"— an overdeveloped, sometimes suffocating sense of security a Marxist would be tempted to call "surplus security" (see also Schlesinger 1980).

These attitudes were perhaps the most common among some of the younger rich, but not limited to them:

> In the 1970s they were a phenomenon in philanthropy: rich young people with avowedly leftist politics using their inheritance to promote "change, not charity."
>
> Around the country they organized community groups opposing the Vietnam war, picketed nuclear plants and demonstrated for desegregated housing. On the local level they gave money for battered women and

abused children, the homeless and disabled, homosexuals, lesbians, minority members . . .
    The political activism of the network members has not changed,
although the causes have. Network members oppose United States involvement in Central America and dealings with South African business. They
organize demonstrations by rent-strikers, support farmers, boycotts and
rally against growth in military spending . . .
    Some young donors said inheriting money evoked feelings of
guilt, embarrassment, fear of envy, or doubts about self-worth. [Teltsch
1990]

   These attitudes were not limited to the socially conscious rich. Similar
feelings were in evidence even among the middle classes and especially
their critically disposed segments who experienced a tug of war between
the untroubled enjoyment of their relatively privileged way of life and a
deeply felt need to renounce it in the name of more authentic values and
as a gesture of solidarity with the truly disadvantaged. These attitudes
were discernible both among the (more or less) full-time social critics and
members of the larger adversary culture who embraced the critics' diag-
nosis of American society. Economic and political security was at once a
source of unease and the foundation for developing "alternative life-
styles."
   Identifying with and championing various "underdogs" or selected
victim groups, more and more broadly defined, was another way of trying
to resolve the tension between middle-class comfort and security on the
one hand and youthful idealism or homage to the values of the 60s and
the other. A lesbian activist-lawyer in Northampton, Massachusetts,
decided to move to San Francisco because she found the locally available
cultural-ethnic "diversity" and the supply of underdog groups inadequate: there were not enough disabled people among them. She said:
" 'There is something else I want: [that is, besides a vibrant lesbian community—P.H.] cultural diversity, ethnic diversity. There are also more
people in the San Francisco area than there are here with physical differences, with what we call disabilities.' The mild climate in the Bay Area
makes life easier for people in wheelchairs, she explains. 'This is another
way in which my life will have people in it who are different from me.' "
She referred to her freedom from disabilities as her "abilism" as if that
too was a questionable attitude like sexism and racism [Brown 1989]. As
such remarks—no longer confined to the campuses—suggest, the pursuit
of "diversity" has emerged as a new goal among the estranged, something
self-evidently desirable. It is usually not made clear why diversity in itself
is or should be automatically admirable, since diversity of belief, value,
ethnicity, or ways of life by themselves are value-neutral. In a middle-
class suburb a neighbor who belongs to an organized crime syndicate rep-

resents diversity; so do drug dealers. People afflicted with a wide range of pathologies are "diverse." (It is another matter that on closer inspection the "diversity" touted on the campuses turns out to favor certain beliefs, groups, or styles of thought as will be shown later.)

The politically committed and economically secure often agonized over money, that is, over having it rather than not having it: "Money was an embarrassment, a political stumbling block," one of them confessed. "The political vow of poverty was as sacred as the religious one . . . we realized . . . that all money was blood money, earned—or rather won—at someone else's expense." This too was probably unique to our times: not the feeling of guilt about being privileged, but the large number of people who entertained these feelings. There was more to it: "While we identified economically with the working class, we had in fact created a new and separate class—one of privileged poverty—we were for the most part young, healthy, flexible, without dependents; we could at any time take better-paying jobs, or write home for help." Finally the activist in question realized that she could not "embrace the purer collectivism of radical economics" [Babize 1978], which was her way of saying that she was ready to earn a good living.

"Excess security" does not prevent those afflicted with it from pre-occupation with distant, apocalyptic threats such as a nuclear holocaust, or some type of ecological disaster at some unspecified time in the future. What this group of people find truly difficult to conceive of are more tangible and serious material, economic, or political deprivations: real and prolonged poverty; loss of some valued item of consumption or service; restrictions on physical mobility, recreational activity, or choice of enter-tainment; subordination to higher authorities; helplessness in the face of political power; any hardship of political origin. Even Angela Davis, despite her often voiced belief in the uniquely repressive qualities of the American political system, could confidently point out—after being detained by the police—that "I knew they could not hold me for any period of time without allowing me to contact a lawyer" [Davis 1974:16].

The attitudes here discussed are also evident when demonstrators seek to interfere with the military authorities by blocking roads or damaging equipment but obviously do not expect serious consequences to follow, such as imprisonment for any length of time and certainly not under inhumane conditions; nor do they expect such transgressions to endanger their job or place in college. They don't in fact anticipate any significant or durable disadvantage to ensue from political protests including "civil disobedience."

Institutional arrangements, constitutional and legal guarantees—

woven into the fabric of political pluralism and democracy—create and maintain such a sense of security. In recent decades the prevailing patterns of upbringing, in both the family and schools and colleges have strengthened the phenomena here discussed. Excess security in adults resembles the attitudes and expectations of well-to-do teenagers who engage in the customary rebellion against parental authority. It is a rebellion conditioned by the underlying belief that parents will accommodate to the hostilities of their offspring and will not respond punitively (an attitude paralleled on the campuses to this day by the routine demand that every politically motivated infraction of regulations be met with amnesty).

Since the 1960s college administrators and authorities came to be perceived in similar ways by their students; they too have shown patience, tolerance, and understanding. They refused to take seriously the sometimes questionable conduct of their charges; whenever possible they reinterpreted disruptive behavior in a more positive light, usually as an understandable response to the frustration of some idealistic impulse. Campus misconduct, as for instance the shouting down of unpopular speakers or "sit-ins," have been treated with lenience and explained away with reference to higher values. Many teachers and college administrators could thus be perceived as extensions of parental authority and as such not particularly threatening. Even when the police and the courts were more stern there were usually helpful and supportive counterauthority figures, so to speak, available in such confrontations: lawyers, college deans, parents. But the courts have not been especially harsh either. Even former fugitives from justice, members of the violent Weather Underground "who resurfaced in the late 1970s received gentle wrist pats from the judiciary, as did Abbie Hoffman . . . caught selling cocaine" [McConnell 1987:37]. Bernardine Dohrn's treatment was similar.

Thus for many who came of age in the 1960s the secure world of childhood stretched into young adulthood infused with an implicitly unshakable sense of security. They had reason to believe that there will always be bail money, a place in college, a way to make ends meet. Often people possessed of such a sense of security are convinced that they lead a charmed existence and take great risks, not all of them political. (Risk-taking may include casual drug smuggling from countries where the legal system is not especially anxious to protect the rights of the accused, like Turkey or Mexico, and prison conditions can turn out to be far worse than these offenders would imagine.) A reporter commented on the attitudes of members of the Weather Underground: "They lacked a good healthy fear of life, having received few of its blows. Sheltered and protected so long, they felt invincible. Even when they went underground . . . they felt they could always go back" [Franks 1981:46].

The attitude of Cathy Boudin in prison most strikingly exemplifies the mentality here described. She was, as may be recalled, a prominent fugitive from justice for two decades, a leading member of the Weather Underground, deeply involved in numerous acts of violence against "the System," which she regarded as exceptionally brutal, inhumane, and unjust. She was also author of *The Bust Book,* a handbook for political prisoners. She was finally apprehended on the scene of the Brinks murder-robbery in 1981 and subsequently given a long sentence for her participation. (She was defended in court by her father, Leonard Boudin, a prominent figure on the American left.) A hardened revolutionary, one would think. Yet after her arrest and imprisonment she appeared astonished and pained to discover that being in prison is quite unlike being free and she complained bitterly of the restrictions placed on her life by virtue of being a prisoner:

> I cannot have friends visit me from outside prison. I have been totally isolated from any community of friends inside the prison walls or outside.
>
> The prison is cutting me off from a necessary part of any and every human being's life. The need for talking to people, building friendships, sharing day-to-day life . . .
>
> For the first four weeks the entire lighting in my cell consisted of one 60-watt bulb over the sink and toilet . . . In order to get enough light to read I had to sit on the open toilet or move my bed next to the open toilet to catch the light . . . Finally the prison put in a glaring 135-watt high-intensity bulb with no shade.
>
> The window has bars on it and looks only into walls. There is . . . no sense of the weather . . . Only when I go to an attorney visit, make a phone call or take my hour recreation do I catch a glimpse of the sky. Only in the afternoon is there a sense of the sun . . . [There is] the dehumanizing solitude. Moreover my lawyers have legal work to do; they cannot spend all their time providing personal contact and support for me. Moreover my relationship to an attorney is no substitute for relationships with other women here to help deal with the difficulty of the prison experience . . . And my legal visits are not a substitute for being able to have a connection to my own friends and the community outside the prison . . .
>
> I must make a written request for every single thing . . . Another policy designed to harass us . . . concerns plastic crochet needles. I requested [them] to help pass time . . . It is punitive to deny us plastic crochet needles . . .
>
> . . . our rooms were extremely overheated . . .
>
> . . . each prisoner gets salad. This was missing from our trays for the first week. I finally insisted on it and did get it . . .
>
> . . . [one day] we couldn't get boiled water to make tea. [Frankfort 1983:44, 45, 47, 52, 53, 54, 70]

The author of the book about Boudin noted, "Even in prison Boudin writes as if she is entitled to all the amenities of civilized living, forgetting

entirely that she is there as an accused murderer" [Ibid.:91]. Her indignation attendant upon the discovery of the limitations of prison life
reflects a deep and serene sense of immunity and entitlement. Not even
the evil, repressive system she was fighting was expected to inflict discomfort and deprivation. Sam Melville, another embittered enemy of the system, convicted of many bombings, was enraged for not receiving in Attica
maximum security prison his favorite radical journal, *The Monthly Review*
[Melville 1972:60].

The underlying sense of security and the resulting confident expectation that defiance of law and physical attacks on authority will not have
an adverse effect or cause lasting discomfort also carried over into foreign
affairs. If it was hard to imagine that domestic political forces could
threaten one's way of life (no matter how hard one tried to bait them and
defy them), it was much harder to believe that distant, outside forces
could exert disagreeable influence. John Updike captured these attitudes
in his reminiscences of the antiwar movement of the 1960s:

> These privileged members of a privileged nation believed that their pleas-
> ant position could be maintained without anything visibly ugly happening
> in the world. They were full of aesthetic disdain for their defenders, the
> business-suited hirelings drearily pondering geopolitics . . . down in Wash-
> ington. The protesters were spitting on the cops who were trying to keep
> their property—the USA and its many amenities—intact. A common
> report in this riotous era was of slum-dwellers throwing rocks . . . at the
> firemen come to put out fires; the peace marchers . . . seemed to me to be
> behaving identically, without the excuse of being slum-dwellers. [Updike
> 1989:24–25]

The entire American historical experience has reinforced the confident expectation that no foreign power can ever tread on American soil
or impinge on the American way of life. Nobody has ever invaded, occupied, or bombarded the continental United States. There have been no
violent seizures of power, military takeovers, abrupt and unanticipated
changes of government leading to the mistreatment of those on the losing
side. Americans had little chance to learn about such forms of political
violence (except for the Civil War) and the dramatic shifts in power
which take little notice of the consent of the governed.

The unstated sense of invulnerability to foreign threats here touched
upon is also connected with an implicit belief in the strength of this
country. As the radical critics see it, the United States is still excessively
strong, a country with an all too powerful military establishment and
bloated will to global power. While the critics disapprove of such
strength, their belief in it helps to brush aside a sense of any foreign

threat. The social critics recognize only the unresolved social problems of American society as a threat to its survival or integrity.

As already noted the prospect of a nuclear holocaust has been a major exception. Although historically and experientially unparalleled, an increasing number of Americans in the 1970s and 80s claimed to be able to conjure up its horrors vividly. This attitude probably derived in part from the aversion to modern technology, seen as the major and most familiar source of evil in the world today especially in the hands of capitalist corporations.

The fear of nuclear war could thus be assimilated into broader social criticism and its familiar targets: capitalism, imperialism, the Western industrial way of life, the aggressiveness of the United States, and so on. There is a greater readiness to entertain any disaster if familiar targets of hostility can be implicated, such as the military-industrial complex or the "corporate power structure."

The sense of security here discussed is also nurtured by the disposition to view the United States in isolation from other parts and trends of the world. During the 1960s the experience and growth of material wealth led to a more general questioning of the reality and necessity of scarcities in human affairs as well. Herbert Marcuse, the major exponent of this point of view, claimed that the global satisfaction of material needs in our times was within reach and delayed only because of the irrational social-economic arrangements prevailing in the modern industrial societies of the West, pre-eminently the United States.

The overdeveloped sense of security while contributing to the isolationism here discussed was not the only factor accounting for it; nor was the defeat in Vietnam, important as it has been, its singular source. Isolationism between the late 60s and the 1980s can also be linked to the radical critiques of American society which postulate, among other things, that the survival of American capitalism depends on its foreign involvements and sources of support; hence, cutting off such involvements will hasten its demise. As Robert W. Tucker put it:

> Far from being an end in itself, the radical rejection of American foreign policy is primarily intended as a means of the transformation of domestic society. If for no other reason than this, the isolationism of the radical left ought not be confused with the isolationism of yesterday . . . which found in America's involvement abroad a threat to the nation's institutions. [Tucker 1971:8–9]

In the same spirit Staughton Lynd proposed that "to oppose Vietnam without opposing capitalism is to acquiesce in future Vietnams . . .," while Susan Sontag suggested that ". . . Vietnam offered a key to a systematic criticism of America" [Lynd quoted in Tucker 1971:17; Sontag 1968:87]. Two former radicals observed that "Vietnam was a universal solvent—the explanation for every evil we saw and the justification for every excess we committed" [Collier and Horowitz 1985:2]. The critiques of American foreign policy were an integral part of a radical critique of American society.

In the final analysis "excess security" may be a useful concept because it connects and helps us to understand a wide range of social phenomena and forms of behavior associated with the rejection of American society, or at any rate the predisposition to such rejection. It helps to explain attitudes ranging all the way from isolationism in foreign policy to an ostentatious preference of college students for wearing patches and tattered clothing; why students in elite colleges leave their rooms and cars unlocked; why others postpone college secure in the knowledge that the opportunity to do so will still be there after the grand tour of Europe or the coast-to-coast exploration of this country. The concept also helps us to understand young people or young urban professionals who move into "funky" slum neighborhoods feeling protected by this sense of invulnerability (besides being lured by cheap real estate). It also helps to account for the growing taste for adventure among the materially comfortable groups of the population (however stereotyped and commercialized such pursuits may become when large numbers of people engage in them) and the varieties of bohemian or countercultural life-styles which entail elements of risk taking [Speier 1952]. It is this sense of security, bordering on invulnerability, that also helps us to grasp why so many people of the materially comfortable and college-educated strata of the population are opposed to both military service and expenditures.

The sense of security here outlined also illuminates short-term orientations of various kinds which presuppose unconcern with or confidence in the future. The enlarged sense of security underlies the apparent contempt for safety, planning, and deferred gratification as well as practical measures of personal or collective self-protection. Loren Baritz, the cultural historian, also observed that middle-class youth of that period ". . . felt safe enough to postpone decisions about their economic futures, or to assume that somehow everything eventually would turn out to be fine" [Baritz 1988:283].

It bears restatement that estrangement in our times, unlike in the past—when the outspoken public rejection of the prevailing social order was associated with marginality, insecurity, and various social, political, or economic disadvantages—emanates from groups and individuals who are generally privileged, well integrated into society at large (or some of its subcultures), and enjoy a substantial sense of security that can be inferred from their behavior. The adversarial disposition here discussed is indeed a form of "middle-class radicalism" [Parkin 1986].

VII

What emerges from this sampling of the rejections of American society? What precisely did the estranged critics object to most, what inspired their suspicion, bitterness, or disenchantment, as the case may be?

We cannot understand and appreciate radical social criticism without an awareness of the standards against which the critics measure this society. For example, Studs Terkel, whose critiques span half a century, "states flatly that his purpose 'is not to seek out facts in the lives of contemporary Americans ...' ... Instead he recalls how he once was inspired by *'a vision of what still could be'"* [Elfin 1988; my emphasis]. Not only is this vision overdetermined by extraordinary expectations; more unusually in the case of Terkel, it remains anchored in the Depression years, and in the refusal to acknowledge that they had passed and the ensuing conditions have been a substantial improvement.

The volume of the critiques of American society produced over the past quarter-century is huge and its boundaries sometimes in dispute: one person's radical social criticism is another's taken-for-granted verity. Nonetheless the principal themes can be charted. They coalesce around the four clusters of charges and attributions.

    1) Inauthenticity;
    2) Capitalism, the associated injustices and inequalities and decline of the quality of life;
    3) Aggressiveness and repressiveness, their cultural sources and byproducts;
    4) The loss of meaning and the deformation of the individual; the critiques of individualism.

Let us examine each of these clusters and how each theme has been developed and interpreted by major social critics.

1) The forms of inauthenticity subjected to criticism range from the use of synthetic materials to personal relationships, from manipulated politics to manipulated consumer tastes. American society as experienced by the critics is permeated by falsehood, hypocrisy, pretense. Nothing is genuine, original, or trustworthy. Critiques of inauthenticity often combine with hostility toward technology which creates obsolescent, poorly made, and unnecessary objects, articles of consumption, nurtured by false needs. Such technology is, in turn, associated with capitalism and its

manipulated consumers who seek things not becuase they are truly needed but because they have been persuaded to buy them, or because they enhance social status.

In public as well as in private lives there is a substantial gap between the way things are supposed to be and the way they really are, a discrepancy between ideals and realities, theories and practices, aspirations and achievements. American society does not live up to its beliefs and promises; the critics—enraged or saddened by this—seem to believe that nowhere are such divergencies as profound as in this society.

E.L. Doctorow, the popular writer (and relentless social critic) warns: "Our psychic deterioration goes beyond intellectual life. In the past ten years there has been a terrible loss of moral energy in art, politics, in social expectation . . . In the name of rugged individualism, we celebrate greed, gluttony and social coercion . . ." [Doctorow 1983:6, 7]. The mendacity and corruption of the entire political-economic system and the people running it also radiate inauthenticity, Norman Birnbaum refers casually to the "arrogance, exploitativeness and venality of our elites" and to their "thieving incompetence" [Birnbaum 1988:174, 190]. Marcus Raskin, the prolific social critic and cofounder of what has been an institute of social criticism (Institute for Policy Studies), offers this version of inauthenticity in the polity: ". . . the American system . . . is jerry-built. It never quite resolves fundamental problems. It merely engulfs them in new ones . . . masking them through the pleasing language of problem-solving, coordination and efficiency" [Raskin 1974:6, 127].

According to the critics, we are kept in the dark, misled, routinely lied to, manipulated, imprisoned in a state of false consciousness. George Wald, the Nobel Prize-winning scientist, believes that ". . . we Americans . . . are the most brainwashed people in the world" [Bernstein 1982]. Kurt Vonnegut complained on a television program: "The lies we have been fed about nuclear energy have been as cunningly crafted as the masterpieces of Benvenuto Cellini. If we let them, they will kill everything on this . . . planet . . . with their vicious, stupid lies." Normal Mailer (who in a similar spirit often described the United States as "carcinogenic" and "plastic") focused his mistrust (on the same program) upon the Watergate case. "Watergate, he says, involved 'five different conspiracies' and we will not know the truth about what really happened for 50 years" [Corry 1985]. Walter Cronkite thought this to be an Orwellian society in its manipulative distortion of reality:

> Could Smith see the seeds of his Oceania in our society, in which the Federal government tries to shroud more and more of its activities with "security" classifications . . . where a Vietnam village can be destroyed so it can be saved; where the President names the latest thing in nuclear

missiles the "Peacekeeper"—in such a world can the Orwellian vision be far away? [Cronkite 1983]

Gore Vidal too addressed the gap between the way things were supposed to be and the way they really are: "The United States is now in serious disrepair . . . Inner cities resemble Calcutta . . . Our success story is turning sour indeed . . . fantasy now governs in that Disneyland by the Potomac where the Great Cue-card Reader preaches simple-minded sermons of hate, and the last best war of all draws nearer and nearer" [Vidal in Friedman ed. 1983:x]. The Reagan presidency gave a great boost to the theme of inauthenticity given his Hollywood background and "great communicator" image.

Inauthenticity, manipulativeness, and repression come together in the dark vision of John Barth (the famous novelist) as he contemplates the American past and present: "Our beautiful wisterias and rhododendrons are fertilized with blood, our hybrid tea roses mulched with crime we do not approve of, but have made uneasy peace with that circumstance." For Barth as for other critics, the CIA has become the matchless symbol for manipulativeness and underhanded repression as it haunts an entire lengthy novel of his, and the private lives of its main characters: "Covert government security operations, like organized crime operations, are cancers in the body democratic . . . They widen the gap between what things represent themselves to be and what they are . . . The famous links between the Mafia and the CIA . . . they're quite natural" [Barth 1987:246, 261].

The loss or breakdown of the moral foundations of society is another form of criticism that may be noted here. The popular writer John Irving "makes it all too plain, and with positive rage, that in his eyes American society has been a moral disaster since the 1960s" [Kazin 1989:1]. For Adrienne Rich, the feminist author, the social order is "morally bankrupt" [Rich 1979:270]. Christopher Lasch surveying the decade of the 80s concluded that "The moral bottom has dropped out of our culture" [Lasch 1989]. For the social critics inauthenticity and loss of moral grounding are inseparable.

In its apolitical forms inauthenticity enters the bloodstream of commerce; it becomes "emotional labor" in the smiles of sales people who pretend (and are painstakingly trained to do so) that they care about the strangers who are their customers. Capitalism "turn[s] feeling into a commodity"; human feelings become commercialized, spontaneity vanishes as the marketplace intrudes upon the ways we define ourselves [Hochschild 1983]. These reflections arise out of a study of airline hostesses, but examples abound outside such specialized callings; the advertising and public relations industries provide further evidence.

The type of inauthenticity here discussed may also be seen as rooted in the original idea of alienation defined as "the structured inability of individuals to control conditions and consequences of their labor; the inability of individuals . . . to achieve community . . ." The result is the "impoverishment of the spirit" [Flacks 1988:38]. Inauthenticity thus leads to and reflects the deformation of the individual—another major theme of the critiques of American society discussed below.

Inauthenticity and impersonality often go together as in the case of salespeople who seek to transform an essentially impersonal situation into one of make-believe warmth and concern in the hope of improving sales, maximizing profits. Inauthenticity of this type can plausibly be ascribed to modern capitalism and its marketing techniques. Yet much of what pass as critiques of capitalism, including especially impersonality, are in fact criticisms of modernity.

Critiques of inauthenticity (and those of capitalism and its technology) also have an aesthetic component as in the concern with the destruction of the natural environment and all that is "natural" in our lives. Marge Piercy complained: "Technology is monstrous . . . because our values are monstrous . . . They are killing us . . . with cancer, drugs, contraceptives, food, asbestos . . . bad schools and television" [Glaenzer 1983:4]. Technology also becomes a tool of inauthenticity when it deforms the political process:

> Technology . . . comes to serve as an effective instrument of social control—in the case of mass media, by short-circuiting the electoral process through opinion surveys . . . and by presenting the choice of leaders and parties as a choice among consumer goods. [Lasch 1984:26]

The critiques of inauthenticity often merge with that of the quality of life, inspired by environmental concerns as in the writings of the late Edward Abbey, a romantic nature lover *par excellence:*

> I am thinking, what incredible shit we put up with most of our lives—the domestic routine (same old wife every night), the stupid and useless and degrading jobs, the insufferable arrogance of elected officials, the crafty cheating and the slimy advertising of the business men, the tedious wars in which we kill our buddies instead of our our real enemies back home in the capital, the foul, diseased and hideous cities and towns we live in, the constant petty tyranny of automatic washers and automobiles and TV machines and telephones . . . what intolerable garbage and what utterly useless crap we bury ourselves in day by day, while patiently enduring at the same time the creeping strangulation of the clean white collar . . . Such are my . . . feelings . . . as we float away on the river . . . [Abbey 1971:177–78]

The critiques of false consciousness—often intertwined with those of inauthenticity—are indispensable to these critiques of American society: they not only represent an attack on inauthenticity but also explain (or purport to explain) how the political and economic systems can maintain themselves. Richard Flacks writes: "What is wrong [with America is] . . . that people lack the historical awareness and the language to articulate a generalized vision of democracy." He is especially distressed by the fact that "Little in our culture or politics enable us to ask how life would be enriched and institutions improved if every morning we all woke up knowing that some of our day would involve us in decisions that affected the social future" [Flacks 1988:286].

Flacks, as other radical critics, considers the reluctance to participate in public affairs on a daily basis a serious deficiency in one's life. Norman Birnbaum too is alarmed by the lack of authentic participation of the citizenry, "the loss of the public space, the decline of public existence, the inauthenticity of substitutes we have for it . . ." He believes that "Our fellow citizens are quite unwilling to venture into a public sphere . . . They see no connection between it and their own lives" [Birnbaum 1988:92, 186–87]. Presumably Birnbaum would also regard as a manifestation of false consciousness that the American public "has much difficulty in entertaining the idea that our social arrangements as a whole constitute a permanent catastrophe" [Birnbaum 1988:176].

Alan Wolfe, a sociologist, uses the concept of "ideological repression" which is "the attempt to manipulate people's consciousness so that they accept the ruling ideology" [Wolfe 1978:8]. But false consciousness may take more unexpected forms, as discovered by another prolific social critic, Michael Parenti: "Self-hate becomes a valuable asset for the powers that be, directing antagonism of racial minorities, women, children and other oppressed groups on themselves." And the same goes for consumerism, since "The socialization of people into consumerism serves to retard class consciousness." (The definition of consumerism is easily accomplished by Parenti: it is the desire "to accumulate more than they need"— a definition most social critics implicitly embrace, assured of their ability to distinguish between real and spurious needs.) [Parenti 1978:99, 101].

Yet another form of false consciousness was spotted by Alan Wolfe and called "atheoreticalism," the inability "to relate isolated events . . . in a way that makes sense . . . The democratic state has a vested interest in preventing the emergence of patterns of thought in which two things can be related to a common third thing that caused them" [Wolfe 1978:118]. False consciousness is also inculcated when ". . . elaborate institutional arrangements . . . conceal[ed] the alliance of state and property . . . [and] the economic activities of the government on behalf of property were rendered almost invisible ..." [Piven and Cloward 1982:81].

The system of education (besides the mass media) plays a major part in the inculcation of false consciousness. According to Gore Vidal, ". . . our educational system has seen to it that 95.6% of the population grow up to be docile workers and consumers, paranoid taxpayers and eager warriors ..." [Vidal 1982:227]. In Parenti's view "The real goal of education is ... to produce ... the person conditioned to working at compulsive and mindless tasks, able to suspend autonomous judgements ... and to assume his or her place in the elite-controlled institutions" [Parenti 1978:118].

Birnbaum views higher education as responding to "labor market transformations" and "to tasks of preparation and social selection assigned to them" [Birnbaum 1988:152]; he too sees the media as a tool of the power-holders although he admits that "the fragmented American public[6] has in the recent past shown a strong capacity to resist total indoctrination" by the media [Birnbaum 1988:185].

The critiques of inauthenticity while greatly intensified during the 1960s resemble earlier critiques of the "soullessness" of modern civilization which have been with us at least since the industrial revolution.

2) The critiques of capitalism. Much of the criticism directed at American society is part of a general critique of capitalism of which the United States is not only the pre-eminent example but also the global defender. While the traditional critiques of capitalism focused on exploitation, social injustice, and the irrationalities of the production process, during the period here examined the critics have been more preoccupied with the spiritual damages it inflicts. They dwelled on the ways in which capitalism undermines wholeness, true individuality, the sense of community, social bonds, self-realization, authentic values. Concern with the meaninglessness of work has been common to both older and more recent critiques.

To be sure capitalism is also held responsible for massive social injustices and inequalities; it is blamed for nurturing greed that not only undermines human relationships but also contributes to the destruction of the physical environment for the sake of short-term profit. Sometimes it is also held responsible for the mistreatment of women and discrimination against ethnic minorities.

Why has capitalism inspired so much aversion among Western intellectuals, and why has this aversion so successfully perpetuated itself over a century and a half despite a substantial transformation of capitalism and the discrediting of alternative socio-economic systems? Probably because capitalism has increasingly become something of a metaphor for modernity and, even more broadly, for all the evils and ills of organized society, for the endemic presence of conflict and scarcity, and for the timeless problems of the relationship between the individual and society.

The critiques of capitalism divide into several partly overlapping categories:

a) Capitalism as creator of injustice and inequality;

b) capitalism as a source of economic irrationality and wastefulness (in the modern version: consumerism, false needs, the imbalance between the private and public as in Galbraith's critique of the "affluent society");

c) capitalism as destroyer of social bonds and community (through competition, mobility, modernization);

d) capitalism as a promoter of global inequality, as in the critiques of "imperialism" (modern version: neo-colonialism, multinationals), and capitalism as exploiter of the poor countries or regions of the world;

e) the aesthetic-romantic and cultural critique: capitalism as a homogenizing force undermining diversity and the traditional ways of life; also, as the destroyer of the natural environment; and

f) the culmination and convergence of all these critiques: the supreme charge that capitalism is the ultimate source of the deformation of the individual, depriving him of his spirituality, human essence, work satisfaction, higher aspirations.

The venerable critique of capitalism was of late rendered by Noam Chomsky as "greed and the desire to maximize personal gain at the expense of others" [Chomsky in Moyers 1989:47]. Much of this is a critique of social injustice, of poverty and the inequities of income distribution. As a radical journalist recently put it: "On the one hand the swag-bellied plutocrats, on the other the needy and the desperate . . . Little has changed . . . the Stinking Rich . . . and . . . the exploited masses" [Cockburn 1985].

Two professors at Stanford University made the case against capitalism on more traditional grounds:

> The persistence of poverty, unemployment, and differential access to schooling is not the result of the inefficiencies in capitalist development but the direct product of that development. In order to have a society in which human needs . . . are put before the accumulation of capital and the production of goods as ends in themselves, it is a necessary condition to dismantle the capitalist system of production [Carnoy and Levin in Raskin ed. 1978:257]

The critiques of capitalism tend to expand; they may start with specific objections to socio-economic arrangements but soon become sweeping indictments, holding it responsible for an ever-broadening range of human problems and discontents. The critics often remove the distinction between discontent and suffering along the lines suggested by an advertisement for the *National Review*:

> CBS reports that though the unemployment rate is down, many people aren't happy with the jobs they're getting. One of the problems of the modern world is that people confuse discontent with suffering. Next we expect CBS to report that though nobody is starving the food tastes lousy. [Advertisement in *NY Review of Books*, April 9, 1987]

Indeed the line between suffering and discontent is hard to draw; discontent may turn into genuine suffering, but some forms of suffering are more substantial than others. It is characteristic of modernity that judgments about the sources of suffering become increasingly subjective and relative; in this climate of opinion the boundary between discontent and suffering becomes elusive.

Therein lie the attractions of the critiques of capitalism: they give a handle to the critic to conflate all suffering and discontent, to locate every source of frustration, deprivation, and human misery in a single system or concept. Gar Alperowitz credits capitalism with ". . . horrendous problems, including exploitation, inequality, ruthless competition, individual alienation, the destruction of community, expansionism, imperialism, war . . ." [Lynd and Alperowitz 1973:55].

Joel Kovel, a radical psychoanalyst, is concerned with the victims of capitalism, who may include in contemporary America "the denied child, the 'useless' female, the 'imperialized' Puerto Rican, the thwarted proletariate" [Leonard 1982].

Capitalism puts profits above people. Tom Hayden wrote: ". . . inherent in the process of doing business under capitalism is a marked tendency to put profits above people, to lure the consumer into the highest price possible while conceding the lowest wage possible to the workers . . ." [Bunzel 1983:55]. Stokeley Carmichael, the black radical prominent in the 60s, "likened capitalists to 'animals' whom he claimed merely consumed, 'eat and die,' assuming no responsibility toward others." As of 1982 he still averred that capitalism will inevitably fail (presumably due to its internal contradictions) and that "socialism is the inevitable economic system sweeping the world" [McKay 1982]. Paul Wachtel, a psychologist discernibly following in the footsteps of Erich Fromm, argued that "our society's preoccupation with goods and material productivity is in large measure irrational and serves needs similar to those which motivate neurotic defense mechanisms in individuals" [Wachtel 1983:1].

Norman Birnbaum entertained an apocalyptic vision of American society at the root of which he would undoubtedly locate the current ways of capitalism: "Menaces to human health and to nature, an attack on values that cannot be homogenized or sold on the cultural market, restrictions on the most fundamental of democratic rights . . . the reduction of the living standard of the American labor force . . . and the possibility of total extirpation in nuclear war . . ." were some of the prospects he contemplated [Birnbaum 1988:174].

E.L. Doctorow, focusing on the ravages of the Reagan era, suggested that

> Something poisonous has been set lose in the last several years as we have enjoyed life under the power and principles of political conservativism . . . And that degradation of discourse, that too, is part of this something that is really rotten in America right now . . . The Pentagon and the Stock Exchange are in the eighties the twin images of our idolatry . . . we have seen a national regression to the robber baronial thinking of the nineteenth century . . . [Doctorow 1989:352, 354]

Sheldon Wolin was concerned not only with "the power of the corporations" but more broadly with inequality and elitism: "every one of this country's primary institutions is antidemocratic in spirit, design and operation . . . Government institutions, educational institutions, communications institutions—they are all hierarchical structures and hierarchy means inequality of power" [Wolin in Moyers 1989:100–101]. Such concerns highlight the utopian streak in the critiques here examined.

The critiques of capitalism over the past quarter-century fluctuated between the traditional emphasis on social injustice, inequality, and poverty on the one hand, and, on the other, the more intensely felt contemporary concern with psychic damage, the deformation of the personality and harm to the spiritual essence of human beings. Competition and competitiveness remained the major villains. In the words of Jonathan Kozol, "Winning is all; the solitary runner, tuned in to a headset that excludes the cries of his less fortunate competitors, becomes a national ideal" [Kozol 1988:138].

As American society has become increasingly affluent during the period here examined it has become more difficult to attack capitalism on the more traditional grounds; not even the harshest critics could deny that people were living better, at least materially speaking, that there was less unemployment, less poverty, less deprivation. For that reason— beginning in the 1960s—the critiques shifted to some degree to the "quality of life" or spiritual impoverishment theme, pioneered, among others, by Marcuse and the Frankfurt School. But even these critiques had venerable historical roots, in the romantic sensibility of 19th-century writers, poets, artists, and social critics, including of course Marx himself.

As Irving Kristol put it, ". . . throughout history artists and writers have been contemptuous of commercial activity . . . regarding it as an activity that tends to coarsen and trivialize the human spirit. And since bourgeois society was above all else a commercial society . . . their exasperation was bound to be all the more acute" [Kristol 1983:32]. Such trivialization of the human spirit, and especially its manifestations among ordinary people, led Marcuse to complain about a social order (the American) that allowed ordinary people "to break the peace wherever there is still peace and silence, to be ugly and to uglify things, to ooze familiarity, to offend against good form . . ." [Walzer 1988:184]. Bertolt Brecht had similar objections: ". . . his hatreds extended from the flimsy architecture to the store-bought bread . . . the air was unbreathable and there was nothing to smell. America . . . was all marketplace, all selling" [Simon 1989:275–76].

In the final analysis the deepest roots of the hostility to capitalism lie not in the economic but in the spiritual, metaphysical, or psychological realms, in its putative responsibility for "alienation" understood as a fall from grace, linked to the Marxist version of original sin, the division of labor. David Horowitz, the former radical, observed that "'Alienation' is the Marxist name for the catastrophe that has befallen human existence . . . that there are not merely particular injustices to be remedied by particular reforms but that there is injustice in general—in the very structure of mankind's being in the world" [Horowitz 1988:5]. Thus the persistence of anticapitalism is a form of a secular messianism, a universal protest against injustice, frustration, meaninglessness—against secularization and modernization, and the attendant loss of transcendence. Although only one variety of modernity, capitalism is especially vulnerable to such charges. Again, as Kristol pointed out: "Bourgeois society is without doubt the most prosaic of all possible societies . . . uninterested in . . . transcendence . . . It is a society organized for the convenience and comfort of common men and women, not for the production of heroic, memorable figures" [Kristol 1983:28–29]. Robert Heilbroner the economist also noted these attributes of capitalism and found them unappealing. He wrote: "Capitalism would be impossible in a sacralized world to which men could relate with awe and veneration, just as such attitudes cannot arise in a society in which exchange value has reduced to a common denominator all use-values" [Heilbroner 1985:135]. Other important social thinkers in our times such as Daniel Bell [1976], Joseph Schumpeter [1950], Erich Fromm [1955], and Leszek Kolakowski [1977] reached similar conclusions about the problems capitalism faces in legitimating itself, lacking a transcendent worldview.

This is not to say that the more obvious failings of capitalism ceased to attract the attention of the critics. Homelessness for instance has become, as noted earlier, the subject of much criticism as it seemingly confirmed the belief that capitalism must harshly and spectacularly victimize some groups of people, proving that its flaws are "systemic" (a favorite word of the critics). It means that these defects cannot be eradicated without a fundamental transformation of the system. For example:

> We ... try to understand and explain the housing crisis not in isolation but as a central and emblematic part of a broader crisis of the U.S. economy and social system ... Just as the current system cannot house its people decently, it cannot feed them adequately, or provide them with decent health care, education, environmental protection, and bodily security ..."
> [Hartman ed. 1983:8]

The same goes for matters of health: "... even the most liberal form of national health insurance is incapable of dealing with the structural inadequacies of the American health system ..." [Lander in Raskin ed. 1978:312].

Just as the changing characteristics of capitalism in the United States necessitated at least a partial shift from concern with unemployment, poverty, and so on to the depersonalization, spiritual loss, lack of self-realization, and so forth, so the changed attitude and condition of the American working classes prompted the critics to find more appealing classes of victims. They succeeded in locating them in what came to be known as the Third World. Capitalism, and its strongest and most avaricious representative, the United States, has now been cast into the role of the victimizer and exploiter not so much of its own working classes (duped into soporific false consciousness and sometimes dismissed as virtual accomplices of their masters) but of the "people of color" around the globe. For example "... the United States, with 6% of the world's population, uses more than 60% of the world's resources for itself ... to keep this society going ..." [Raskin 1969:18]. The multinational corporations in particular became the new focus of criticism representing the tentacles of capitalism in the Third World: "... the multinational corporation, in pursuit of its own interests, constitutes a clear and continuing threat to the interests of millions of people around the world ... Corporate planners have become a public menace ..." [Barnet 1975].

The argument here pursued about the deeper roots of hostility toward capitalism is, paradoxically enough, strengthened by the recent developments in what used to be considered socialist systems and the reaction of the critics of capitalism to these developments (see also Chapter 10). Although most of these state socialist countries have since the mid-1980s sought to reinvigorate their economies by allowing more free enterprise and capitalist forms of production and management, and since 1989 moved to discard rapidly many forms of public ownership—none of these changes has inspired reassessments among the critics of America, many of them also erstwhile admirers of these systems. The critics of capitalism here discussed have not been impressed by the fact that formerly anti-capitalist societies are now increasingly emulating capitalism despite huge investments of resources, energy, and political effort over long periods of time in finding alternatives to it.

3) Repression at home and aggression abroad. It is routinely asserted by social critics that the United States exploits and brutalizes Third World countries . These activities are said to be rooted in capitalism and its hunger for new markets, profits, cheap labor, and so on. Parallels are sometimes drawn between such treatment of the Third World countries and "Third World People," that is, racial-ethnic minorities within the United States.

Domestic repression, as we have learned since Marcuse, has become more subtle, as conveyed by the concept "repressive tolerance." The idea has remained popular among intellectuals, since on the one hand it suggested the insidiousness of the new forms of repression and on the other it implied that its discernment takes unusual powers of observation and analysis possessed only by intellectuals. The anniversary of Orwell's *1984* provided new opportunities for expanding on this theme. Gary Marx, a sociologist at MIT, warned:

> Over the last four decades subtle, seemingly less coercive forms of control (some of which Orwell anticipated) have emerged. Their existence within societies that have not become less democratic, may . . . blind us to their ominous potential . . . We are moving closer to the manufacture and control of culture found in Orwell's society, though private interests are involved to a much greater extent than is the state . . . Mass media persuasion is far more subtle and indirect than the truncheon over the head . . . [and] not necessarily less coercive . . . There is nowhere to run or hide. There is no exit from the prying eyes, ears and data-processing machines of government and business. Citizens' ability to evade surveillance is diminishing. [Marx in Short ed. 1986:137, 139, 153]

Jonathan Kozol found the system of schooling the most deadly instrument of repression (besides being the major device for inculcating false consciousness). He wrote:

> U.S. education is . . . an ice-cold and superb machine. It does the job . . . The first goal and primary function . . . is not to educate good people but good citizens. It is the function which we call—in enemy nations—"state indoctrination" . . . The words are different but the function is the same:

twelve years of mandatory self-dehumanization, self-debilitation, blood loss.

... Public education, for most children, is a twelve-year exercise in ethical emaciation.

Thanks largely to the ministrations of the system of education the United States ... is a rich, benevolent, sophisticated, murderous, well-mannered and exquisite social order. There is time and money and resources to conciliate us all ... psychoanalysis for the indignant, prison cells for those—too few— who will not break and buckle in the requisite positions of capitulation, self-cancellation or surrender ... We cannot continue with our theater evenings, garden clubs and tea if we would like to redirect priorities and salvage dying children. The passive, tranquil and protected lives rich people lead depend on strongly armed police, well-demarcated ghettos. The price of liberation for more than a million children in New York City schools might well be loss of sleep ... for people fifty miles away. The price of plans to cure ten thousand heroin addicts in the Boston slums might well be a lack of private space for wealthy men and women in the most expensive hospitals ... Art shows, string quartets, luncheon clubs and pleasant dining places might well suffer loss of customers ... [Kozol 1975:1, 130, 181, 184]

Repression and false consciousness are most obviously joined together when people think that they are enjoying political and intellectual freedoms when in fact they are oppressed. Or, again as Kozol so colorfully put it, education "enable[s] the imprisoned to feel free and the crippled to interpret their toe-movements as real ambulation." Adding a new twist to the inculcation of false consciousness through education, Kozol writes: "My concern ... is a great deal less with the destructive education of the victim, more with the desensitizing education of the victimizer ..." [Ibid.:4, 12]. As this concern suggests, Kozol has embraced more perfervidly than many other critics a seamless scheme of victim and victimizer which not only elevates the victim to a state of unsullied, virtuous innocence but overflows with an unusually intense vindictiveness toward the (alleged) victimizer.

None of this is intended to suggest that the critics ignore what they regard as the more traditional and cruder forms of political repression and its contribution to the failure of various radical or socialist movements to become influential (see for example Goldstein 1978). Victor Navasky, among others, believed that "the search for scapegoats [for the failed policies and scandals of the Reagan era—P.H.] will take us farther down the road to a police state." He feared that those "responsible for the progressive agenda of the sixties—affirmative action, gay rights, feminism, the antiwar movement," will be blamed and victimized [Schulz and Schulz 1989:xix]. Norman Mailer was not to be outdone in anticipating similar trends. On the occasion of declaring his support for Salman Rushdie he pointed out that ". . . if he were not supported, then 'fundamentalist groups in America . . . will know how to apply the same methods to American writers.'" [Hartley 1989:74].

Racism, sexism, and homophobia feature most prominently among the repressive aspects of American society; they may be deduced either from capitalism or American culture.

The cultural critiques of such repression (especially congenial to feminist authors, as will be shown below) focus on a unique "macho" mentality, insensitivity, brutality, propensity to violence, and aggressive competitiveness peculiar to Americans. Cultural critiques often also suggest that there is a fatal asymmetry or disjunction between the development of American technology on the one hand and values and social practices on the other.

While some critics would argue that domestic repression is more subtle (due to the successful inculcation of false consciousness), others continue to portray the government as harshly repressive at home and even more so abroad.

Racism is often found to be the most obvious form of repression in the United States, although that too is increasingly portrayed as "more subtle"—which usually means that its observable manifestations are harder to find. When this is the case it may be called "insensitivity." For William Kunstler, the radical lawyer, "all white people are cursed with the sin of racism," and "he likened police to an army of occupation in urban ghettos" ["Police Don't Applaud William Kunstler" 1984]. Increasingly since the 1960s, racism (and later sexism) was discussed by the radical critics as original sin used to be: presumed to exist, deep in the hearts of (white) people and in the hidden recesses of social institutions (hence "institutional racism"), whether or not its carriers were aware of it, whether or not it had any tangible expression.

In the 1980s a new wave of concern with racism emerged pre-eminately on the campuses but not limited to them. One of its hallmarks has been an inordinate extension of the concept of racism itself originally referring to groundless discrimination or denigration based on race but of late applied even to critics of reverse discrimination. As Russell Baker observed, the term "'Racist' now has a punishing power similar to the power of 'Communist' in Red-hunting days when a politician calling you 'Communist' expected your boss to fire you immediately" [Baker 1990]. By the late 1980s the word was so broadly used that virtually any criticism of an individual who happened to be black and especially of black officials or office holders would elicit the automatic attribution of racism; by the same token black or Hispanic students placed in lower ability groups (tracks) in schools were victims of racism. Gus Savage, a black congressional representative from Chicago, attributed to racism all criticisms of his performance as an elected official and of his sexual harassment of a black Peace Corps worker [Johnson 1990]. Indictments of Marion Barry, mayor of Washington, D.C., on drug charges were also seen by many black voters as expression of racism. The *Philadelphia Inquirer* was accused of racism for suggesting that the black mayor Wilson Goode was unpopular; the "Philadelphia Association of Black Journalists charged 'insensitivity' and demanded that the *Inquirer* both apologize and make amends by appointing a black city editor." In turn the *Washington Post* was accused of racism for its meager coverage of the Miss America contest at which a young black woman was crowned. Ironically the limited coverage was the result of pressures from feminist groups deploring these contests as demeaning to women [Harwood 1990]. In the same year the black superintendents of schools in both Boston, Massachusetts, and Selma, Alabama, explained the termination of their contracts as unmistakable and self-evident consequences of racism although in both cases specific critiques of their performance had been made. Amiri Baraka, the black writer, upon being refused tenure at Rutgers University explained this not merely by racism but by the influence of Klansmen and Nazis in the English Department [Hanley 1990].

The assumption of the Boston Police Department (based on what turned out to be false information) that a white couple might have been attacked by a young black male in the inner city (the notorious Stuart case) provoked a wave of indignation and was treated as the penultimate proof of racism, although ample data support the plausibility of such crimes being committed by young black males in major urban areas. (If "stereotyping" was responsible for such beliefs, similar stereotyping of white males was at work when Tawana Brawley's story was readily accepted.) Likewise the report in the winter of 1990 that one-quarter of young black males is either in prison or on probation or parole was treated in many quarters as further proof of racism held responsible for the condition of these black males.

Blacks who did not subscribe to the conventional wisdom about the nature of and remedies to racism could not be called racist, but they too could count on generous portions of abuse. Randall Kennedy, a black Harvard Law School professor who was skeptical about "critical race studies" or "new minority scholarship" (that is, "a unique minority perspective on legal issues"), was urged by his colleagues not to publish these views. "'There was a sort of lynch Randy Kennedy mind-set,' said a white professor, speaking on condition of anonymity. Since the article was published . . . some academics have made attempts to exclude Mr. Kennedy from professional forums where he could express his views" [Rothfeld 1990]. Ann Wortham, another black academic who has opposed reverse discrimination, had much difficulty finding a job at a time when black women Ph.D.s were treasured and zealously pursued by elite institutions. In her own assessment it bothered many people that she did not act as if she had been "scarred by racism . . . [or as a person] who was very race conscious, who was suspicious of whites" [Wortham in Moyers 1988:129]. Thomas Sowell, the black political scientist, has been persona non grata in liberal academic circles for decades for his outspoken criticism of reverse discrimination, most recently expressed in a thorough demolition of the numerous unexamined premises and unsatisfactory results of these policies in several countries [Sowell 1990]. Shelby Steele, the black author who had the temerity to suggest that it may not be helpful for blacks to cultivate endlessly the helpless victim image and blame the social environment for all their problems, was also denounced for deviating from the conventional wisdom. Seeking to disgrace him, one of his critics, Martin Kilson, branded him a right-winger and neo-conservative (using these terms a total of twenty-two times in a three-page article) [Kilson 1990].

It is conceivable that the renewed concern with racism among the critics of society intensified during the 1980s in part because other issues and indictments of American society lost some of their plausibility or failed to generate sufficient moral indignation. Glen Loury (another black intellectual who did not subscribe to the prevailing verities of race relations) suggested that there may be a "need for a victim class whose inevitable alienation proves the backruptcy of American ideals . . ." [Loury 1989:6]. The charge of racism has been used more often than any other to indict American society, especially at a time when massive efforts (including preferential treatment) have been under way for decades to rid society of its legacy. Nor can the possibility be excluded that since claims of racism often result in remedial or compensatory action, there are powerful incentives at work to inflate issues and incidents of racism.

As the critics see it repression in the United States is not limited to blacks. Hispanics, Native Americans, women, and those of an unconventional sexual orientation are all victims. Gore Vidal explained why they were oppressed: "Any sexual or intellectual or recreational or political activity that might decrease the amount of coal mined, the number of pyramids built, the quantity of junk food confected will be proscribed . . ." He proposed that discrimination against homosexuals exists "because men who don't have wives or children to worry about are not as easily dominated as those men who do" [Vidal 1982:151]. Adrienne Rich also addressed this issue and offered a somewhat different interpretation: "A concerted attack is now being waged against homosexuality, by the church, . . . the media, by all the forces of this country that need a scapegoat to divert attention from racism, poverty, unemployment, and utter, obscene corruption in public life." She added that this attack was also designed to divert attention "from the psychic and physical destruction of . . . women by institutionalized hetero-sexuality, in marriage and the pursuit of 'normal' sexuality" [Rich 1979:224].

The latest victims whose existence was to prove further the moral bankruptcy of American society were those suffering of AIDS. Victimized for their unconventional sexual orientation (homosexuality), AIDS victims often blamed the social system for their disease. According to an AIDS activist, Larry Kramer,

> . . . the AIDS pandemic is the fault of the white, middle-class, male majority. AIDS is here because the straight world would not grant equal rights to gay people . . .
>
> AIDS is our holocaust and Reagan is our Hitler. New York City is our Auschwitz . . .
>
> I have come reluctantly to believe that genocide is occurring: that we are witnessing . . . the systematic, planned annihilation of some by others with the avowed purpose of eradicating an undesirable portion of the population.[Kramer 1989:178, 173, 263]

Thus was the holocaust once again used to authenticate the sufferings of yet another victim group.

It was also proposed that ". . . AIDS was becoming a useful tool for the far right in its never ending battle to scare people away from unconventional sex . . ." [Leavitt 1989:31].

AIDS sufferers were singled out by the social critics for special compassion and solicitousness which those afflicted with other, comparably severe and life-threatening diseases rarely if ever received. And although clearly infectious there was a fierce battle regarding its definition as such and judicial decisions preventing it to be declared as such (as in the case of the State Supreme Court in New York which "rejected an effort to force the Health Commissioner to declare AIDS and HIV infection to be communicable and sexually transmitted diseases . . . New York state doctors must report AIDS cases, but do not have to identify the patient" [Lewin 1988]). In all probability these attitudes resulted from the combination of a debilitating disease with an unconventional sexual orientation which by itself merited sympathy as a form of defiance of prevailing moral codes.

A more unusual choice of the admirable underdog victim was made by a small but distinguished group of intellectuals who perceived violent criminals as victims of society and authentic witnesses to its inhumanity, who by their lawless behavior challenged its repressiveness. These attitudes surfaced in the case of Jack Henry Abbott, championed for a while by a group of New York intellectuals and Norman Mailer in particular. If his behavior was culpable it was entirely due to social forces beyond his control. Similar attitudes were more widespread in the case of George Jackson, a violent black criminal in California who was also a political activist (see also Chapter 10).

Ronald Dellums, a member of the U.S. House of Representatives, offered this panoramic view of the victims of American society: "America is a nation of niggers . . . If you are black, you're a nigger. If you are an amputee, you're a nigger. Blind people, women, students, the handicapped, radical environmentalists, poor whites, those too far to the left are all niggers . . ." [Tolchin 1983]. Marge Piercy found American society teeming with "oppressed peoples—women laborers, the poor, native Americans, older people—whose lives are controlled by the ruling class" [Glanzer 1983:4]. Michael Parenti believed that "The Freedom of Information Act is the only thing we have left to keep them from rounding us up" [Quoted in Powell 1988:82]. Bertram Gross saw "a new despotism creeping slowly across America" [Gross 1980:2].

Richard Barnet provides the best summary of the cultural approach to institutionalized repression and aggression in both domestic affairs and foreign policy:

> . . . a strategy of peace remains only a pious hope unless it is rooted in institutional change . . . For more than a generation American society has been organized for war rather than peace . . .
>
> What can we conclude from our attempt to trace the roots of war in American society? . . . there is no single revolutionary stroke that will cut the roots of war. They are deeply entwined around every institution, including our schools and family life. The number one nation is dedicated to winning. In kindergarten games and high school football contests, in power plays in offices and board room of great corporations, in the . . . academic rivalries of universities . . . in the struggles of politics, the overriding objective is to win. The myth of competition and the glory and excitement of victory are fundamental to the American way of life. [Barnet in Friedman ed. 1983:138–39]

A criminologist found parallels between criminal violence and the American conduct of war in Vietnam and its domestic underpinnings:

> So it is appropriate to begin a study of the seductions of crime with cases of the use of torture by the American military to interrogate Vietnamese peasants and to close . . . by suggesting that, in the late twentieth century, the great powers of the West [of which only the U.S. is mentioned—P.H.] find themselves in one dubious foreign, militarized situation after another

... achieving victories that bring them only the prize of emotional domestic support ... all because ... not to use violence would signal loss of meaning in national history. Like the bad nigger, who ... draws innocent blood to construct a more self-respecting career ... Western democracies, still seduced by the colonial myth of omnipotence, must again and again strike down thousands so that when the inevitable retreat comes, it will lead over masses of corpses toward "peace with honor." [Katz 1988:324]

I.F. Stone told an audience at Harvard University (protesting the domestic and foreign policies of the Reagan administration) that "this country is suffering from wounded macho" ["Notes on People" 1981].

Loren Baritz, a cultural historian, entitled his book: *Backfire: A History of How American Culture Led Us into Vietnam and Made Us Fight the Way We Did* (1985) and argued that "Something in the culture led the public to support a succession of U.S. presidents ... in Southeast Asia, no matter how murderous their decisions were ..." He "inexorably link[ed] the American way of war with the American way of life," which included "Our idea of moral superiority wedded to our perception of technological invincibility ..." He believes that since the war "there has been no fundamental change in American attitudes. Our faith in technology and our belief in our moral superiority remain unshaken, he contends ..." [Wise 1985:3, 4]. Baritz, as some other critics, seems to suggest that "something" in the American character and culture predisposes the nation to act in foolish and destructive ways.

A classical, if more than usually impassioned formulation (she may no longer care to uphold) was offered by Susan Sontag at the time of the Vietnam war:

A small nation of handsome people ... is being brutally and self-righteously slaughtered ... by the richest and most grotesquely overarmed, most powerful country in the world. America has become a criminal, sinister country—swollen with priggishness, numbed by affluence, bemused by the monstrous conceit that it has the mandate to dispose of the destiny of the world. [Sontag in Menashe and Radosh eds. 1967:346]

A broader vision of a world victimized by the West, including the United States, has been central to the writings of Theodore von Laue, the historian who pointed out that "All-too-few people in the immensely privileged West realize the depths of despair, frustration and fury to which ... Westernization has reduced its victims" [Johnson 1988].

The cultural approach to such matters is also evident in the reminder of Dr. Benjamin Spock (in a discussion of violence against children) that "ours has always been a rough society, slipping easily into brutality, as in our treatment of Native Americans, slaves and each new wave of immigrants" [Fields 1988].

Noam Chomsky towered above all other critics of American imperialism, repression, and overall viciousness. (His loathing for Israel was close second to similar sentiments directed at the United States.) While his critiques encompass each major theme here noted he made a special effort to expose and denounce American activities abroad. His view might best be compared to those of the Ayatollah Khomeni persuaded that America is the Great Satan of the world. This conviction enabled Chomsky (and his followers) to remain profoundly indifferent toward the failings of all other systems, since those were invariably, and by necessity, dwarfed by the crimes of the United States. Chomsky said in a moment of candor to the historian Ronald Radosh: "You notice I never said anything about what I saw in Vietnam when I went there during the war. My responsibility was to address myself only to the U.S. war against Vietnam. That's why I never went to Cuba. I knew Cuba would be horrible—a real Stalinist nightmare—but because there was no war like in Vietnam I wouldn't have the excuse not to say what I thought" [Collier and Horowitz 1989:240].[7]

Chomsky excelled in explaining why no other country or movement (unless allied with or friendly to the United States) should be held accountable for its misconduct, since their political misdeeds or deformities have always been provoked or necessitated by American actions and policies. As two commentators put it, "The heroic dimensions of Chomsky's status derive from his performance of an absolutely critical service to the contemporary Left—developing the devil theory that holds America and the West responsible for all the world's evil" [Collier and Horowitz 1989:228]. The ravages of Pol Pot (at first denied or minimized) were just one of many such examples of Chomsky's attitude. More generally he insisted that Third World revolutions which degenerated into corrupt tyrannies did so because of American pressures; otherwise independent and honorable governments became Soviet puppets because of American intrigues and campaigns of subversion or intervention. Chomsky argued that the United States wants to overthrow these progressive and bountiful systems because of the feared demonstration effect; if they were to be allowed to continue to prosper, the oppressed masses in the West would demand similar enlightened policies and benefits in their own countries. He wrote:

> If peasants starving to death in Honduras can look across the border [that is, to Nicaragua—P.H.] and see health clinics, land reform, literacy programs, improvement in subsistence agriculture . . . the rot may spread; and it may spread still farther, perhaps even to the United States, where the

many people suffering from malnutrition or the homeless in the streets in the richest country of the world may begin to ask some questions. It is necessary to destroy the rotten apple before the rot spreads through the barrel. [Collier and Horowitz 1989:237]

Chomsky's argument had broader appeals and applications. If the United States was ultimately responsible for moral outrages committed everywhere around the world it could also be blamed for the "excesses" and destructiveness of radical groups at home (e.g. the Weathermen) who, in any event, legitimized their activities by the desire to change an (allegedly) unresponsive social system. Increasingly, former radicals of the 60s era and their supporters argued that "whatever excesses they had committed had resulted from America's madness, a social insanity that had temporarily diminished their capacity" [Collier and Horowitz 1989:240]. Here was yet another example of what I called "selective determinism" [Hollander 1983:241–51].

Noam Chomsky reportedly also proposed that "Some societies are so organized that they lead themselves to a 'quite predictable' destruction . . . The U.S. is such an example of 'inevitable, global' suicidal direction." He also referred to the U.S. as "global terrorist" and perpetrator of indiscriminating, worldwide interventions [Dempsey 1987]. Chomsky's all-purpose theory of American foreign policy proposed that it was based on the determination to preserve "the freedom to rob and exploit" other nations, an impulse "rooted in the unchanging institutional structure [of] military-based state capitalism" [Tonelson 1986; see also Chomsky 1988].

This was a congenial theme for other critics as well. "The weapons merchants have a strong hold on U.S. policy," observed Norman Cousins [Cousins 1987], and Michael Klare elaborated:

> . . . the ultimate arm of our national policy—the military—has been used consistently to defend, expand and maintain our informal empire . . . the deployment of U.S. forces abroad has been governed by the principle of business expansionism . . . to guarantee our access to key markets and . . . raw materials . . . to protect American properties from expropriation . . . Expansionism is not a matter of choice for capitalist America: it is a way of life of this society. [Klare 1972:24, 13]

Critics were fond of linking aggression abroad and repression at home, American imperialism and domestic social injustice. For Daniel Berrigan, "The American ghetto and the Hanoi 'operation' were a single enterprise—total war in both cases" [Berrigan 1969:xiv]. Chester Hartman proposed that "The struggle against the poor in this country is similar to the struggle against the poor in the Third World" [Colloquium 1982:14]. According to the Rev. William Sloan Coffin, "We see the effects of the arms race everywhere—rotting, rat-infested housing, inadequate programs of health care and education, rampant unemployment, soaring inflation . . . the poor . . . have become modern-day lepers in this country while we spend billions upon billions on armaments . . ." [Coffin in Rockman ed. 1979:7, 9].

The cultural explanations of American aggression abroad gradually gained wider acceptance. Prominent political figures often expressed sentiments remarkably similar to those of the social critics, fixing blame on both a cultural legacy and national character. Such beliefs have become conventional wisdom among Democratic politicians since the Vietnam war, including presidential contenders George McGovern, Jesse Jackson, Michael Dukakis, Paul Simon, and others. Former Senator Fulbright said, for instance:

"We are such a young county . . . We feel we're the good guys. Every contest with the Russians we've got to win. There is no thought that you can compromise. We have this football mentality. Win, win, win." He also observed "with sadness, even dismay, that United States foreign policy remains perennially stamped by a 'macho,' 'John Wayne approach.'" [Weinraub 1983]

Senator Fulbright's attitudes in such matters were further illuminated on the occasion when it was reported to him ". . . that his book, the *Arrogance of Power,* had been published in the Soviet Union but it had been censored [with both chapters and paragraphs removed] . . . Fulbright looked down at the ground for a while and then up . . . and said, 'You know this story makes me very sad. It will only provide ammunition to the enemies of detente'" [Puddington 1987:1].

The feminist critiques of American society and its repressiveness were in many ways similar to those developed by the radical left except of course for focusing on women as the pre-eminent, uniquely victimized group, whose sufferings exceed and overshadow those of all other groups. Andrea Dworkin wrote:

The nature of women's oppression is unique: women are oppressed as women, regardless of class or race . . . women live with those who oppress them . . .

. . . we were the ultimate house-niggers, ass-licking, bowing, scraping, shuffling fools . . .

. . . extraordinary violence has been done to us . . . our minds are aborted in their development by sexist education . . . our bodies are violated

by oppressive grooming imperatives . . . the police function against us in
cases of rape and assault . . . the media, schools, and churches conspire to
deny us dignity and freedom . . . the nuclear family and ritualized sexual
behavior imprison us in roles . . . which are degrading to us. [Dworkin
1974:23, 21, 20]

Feminists also rejected capitalism. For example Zillah Eisenstein proposed that there was a "mutuality reinforcing dialectical relationship
between capitalist class structure and hierarchical sexual structuring . . ."
As most feminists she too found the nuclear family especially culpable
for the condition of women: "Patriarchy today, the power of the male
through sexual roles in capitalism, is institutionalized in the nuclear family" [Eisenstein 1979:5, 25]. Not only the nuclear family but the middle-
class way of life itself was anathema. Dworkin believed that "the destruction of the middle-class lifestyle is crucial to the development of decent
community forms in which all people can be free and have dignity." The
nation-state was another major source of oppression: "We want to
destroy patriarchal power at its source, the family; in its most hideous
form, the nation-state. We want to destroy the structure of culture as we
know it . . ." [Dworkin 1974:22, 153].

Insistence on the universality of the oppression of women diminished,
at least by implication, the responsibility of capitalism. Yet feminists, like
most other critics of American society, tended to discuss the flaws of
America, sexism included, as if they were peculiar to the United States
and capitalism. While sexism in state socialist societies was occasionally
noted, there was greater reluctance to point to its presence in Third
World countries. It was difficult to admit that many supposedly progressive Third World countries, especially in Africa and parts of Asia, treated
women far worse than capitalist ones, including the United States. For
some feminists it was especially hard to be critical of Cuba even when
they were confronted with what they would undoubtedly have regarded
as repellent sexist practices in the United States, such as an old-fashioned
floor show in a nightclub featuring ample display of female flesh [Radosh
1976:64–65]. Some radical feminists faced a somewhat similar problem
in regard to sexism among American blacks. While they felt duty-bound
to sympathize with blacks—another major victim group whose condition
added weight to the indictment of American society—the sexism widespread among black males was difficult to deny and created "cognitive
dissonance." Diana Russell observed that a "reverse racism" emerged:
"white women put[ting] themselves in situations they would not otherwise enter if the men were white" [Russell 1975:175].

Feminist critics of American society also shared with other social critics the concern with false consciousness the system allegedly implanted

into its many victims. Mary Daly referred to it as a form of "colonization" that has become "internalized, festering inside women's heads, even feminist heads." She also wrote:

> Women's minds have been mutilated and muted . . . Moronized women believe that male-written texts (biblical, literary, medical, legal, scientific) are true. Thus manipulated, women become eager for acceptance as docile tokens mouthing male texts, employing technology for male ends, accepting male fabrications as the true texture of reality. [Daly 1978:1, 5]

In the final analysis it was the insistence on the uniquely degrading and universal nature of the oppression of women that was central to the feminist critiques. Sometimes this claim took an apocalyptic form, as in the writings of Mary Daly. She wrote: "This is an extremist book, written in a situation of extremity . . . on the edge of a culture that is killing itself and all of sentient life. The Tree of Life has been replaced by the neocrophilic symbol of a dead body hanging on dead wood. The Godfather insatiably demands more sacrifices, and the fundamental sacrifices of sadospiritual religion are female" [Daly 1978:17–18]. Feminists such as Daly had little difficulty linking the oppression and suffering of women to a generalized state of violence, injustice, and even the degradation of the physical environment:

> Patriarchy as the Religion of Rapism legitimates all kinds of boundary violation. It blesses the invasion of privacy, for example, by . . . agencies such as the FBI and CIA . . . It extends its blessing also to the violation of life itself by scientifically "created" pollution, by the metastasizing of a carcinogenic environment . . . and by the hideous weapons of modern warfare . . . [Daly 1978:69–70]

Daly, like many other feminist critics, held the medical profession and therapists in an especially virulent contempt and responsible for what she called "the Ice Age of Gynocidal Gynecology." And like many nonfeminist critics of American society, she could not resist the Nazi metaphor, the ultimate denigration of American society by comparing it to, indeed equating it (or aspects of it) with Nazi Germany. (In turn, Dworkin in the book cited consistently spells America as Amerika, the 60s codeword for equating it with Nazi Germany.) Daly wrote: "It is my intention . . . to show some threads of connectedness between manifestations of the medical re-search [sic] mania as it worked itself out in Nazi death camps and as it has manifested itself in gynecology practiced in America. There are striking similarities in style and method of perpetrating and legitimating atrocities." She believed that violence against women, or "patriarchal gynocide," was "the root and paradigm" of all genocide, that "the Nazi medical atrocities and American gynecological practices" had "common roots" and there was a "deep kinship" between their respective practitioners [Ibid.:224, 298, 306, 309].

The uniqueness of the repression of women found its major expression in rape and the generalized male hatred of women, of which rape was only the most vivid manifestation. Adrienne Rich wrote: "Beneath sexism . . . lies gynephobia. It is an ancient and well-documented phenomenon . . . male contempt and loathing for women and women's bodies is embedded in language, art, folklore, and legend . . ." She also wrote: "The beating of women in homes across the country, the rape of daughters by fathers and brothers . . . the casual male violence that can use a car to run two jogging women off a country road, the sadistic exploitation of women's bodies to furnish a[n] . . . empire of pornography, the decision taken by powerful white males that one-quarter of the world's women shall be sterilized . . . are some of the examples of the hatred and resulting mistreatment." Heterosexuality itself harms women, Rich suggests:

> The question finally . . . is whether women's bodies are to be viewed as essentially at the service of men; and to what extent the institution of heterosexuality promotes . . . the belief that they are . . . It is high time the institution [of heterosexuality] receive the same searching scrutiny that class and race have received . . . and that the indoctrination of women toward heterosexuality be challenged . . . [Rich 1979:263, 17]

The preoccupation with rape was understandable on several grounds. It was a form of violence experienced mostly by women (homosexual rape was far less common and mostly limited to prisons) and as such provided a particularly powerful illustration of their victimization; it was also a form of violence and violation that mobilized the deepest revulsion and indignation; moreover, women were raped by men, and many feminists, especially the lesbians among them, did not like men, whether they raped women or not.

The critiques of rape could also be transformed into critiques of American society as a whole. It has become an article of faith among radical feminists that, far from being an isolated, deviant, or psychopathological act, held in contempt by society at large, rape not only has been far more widespread than anyone had ever suspected but has also been systemic, culturally sanctioned, a mere extension of the way men treat women even when not raping them. In particular rape has been seen as "a political act," analogous to the lynching of blacks by whites to keep them in their place. It was also described as "the logical expression of the stereotyped male," rooted in the patterns of culture and socialization. Diana Russell wrote: ". . . being trained since childhood to separate sexual desire from caring . . . or loving . . . many men regard women as sexual objects . . . the virility mystique stresses the importance of having access to, and keeping score on, many women . . . If males and females were to be liberated from their sex roles, the rape situation would change dramatically" [Russell 1975:231, 256, 263, 274]. In her later work Russell also linked the sexist culture of American society, its notions of masculinity and "a critical problem in the collective male psyche" to other forms of violence against women and to the abuse of children [Russell 1984].

Pornography was often viewed as encouraging rape and the general brutalization of women; demands for its suppression were vocal, resting on both this belief and the assertion that it demeans women. In such and other instances radical feminism (earlier a companion of sexual liberation) embraced a peculiar puritanism which also inspired elaborate codes of behavior (at places of work and in colleges) designed to protect women from sexual harassment, which, like racism, came to be defined more and more broadly (as in the famous University of Michigan code which proscribed the observation that women are not as good as men in mathematics or the sciences). Another far from atypical example of these attitudes was revealed in the decision of the (male) principal of a high school in Northampton, Massachusetts, who proposed to remove an issue of *Sports Illustrated* from the school library featuring women wearing the "latest swimwear" which "might be demeaning to women" [Haddad 1990].

Some readers may consider the feminist critiques here sampled atypical, unrepresentative, or extreme and as such unacceptable even for many women who think of themselves as feminists. Even if this were the case—and it is not easy to determine which of the feminist writings are more or less typical or representative—the radical feminist critiques, just as the radical critiques in general, had considerable impact, and not necessarily because they were accepted in their totality. Their major effect was the radicalization of critical discourse: they redefined its boundaries, the meanings of "moderate" and "mainstream." Against the background of the radical rejections of American society, feminist or other, the less extreme critiques have become easier to accept; they could more smoothly enter and be absorbed in the realm of conventional wisdom.

4) The last cluster of criticisms here examined has to do with the loss of meaning in American society, the excesses of individualism, and the deformation of the individual.

Critiques of individualism (or its inauthentic forms) often go off in opposite directions. Sometimes American society is accused of fostering attitudes which are excessively individualistic, that is, uncaring, selfish, hedonistic, lacking in compassion and sense of community. On the other hand it is often also argued that people do not have enough control over their lives, that American society is far too homogenized, it oppresses the individual, prevents personal growth, or authentic self-expression and is indifferent to individual needs (as in the critiques of formal education that imposes a "lockstep march" on the unique needs of students).

It is not difficult to connect the defects of the social and normative order with excessive individualism, that is, the preoccupation with the self as the sole source of meaning in life. When the social order does not provide meaning and sustaining values, when a sense of purpose and community is more and more elusive, the individual is overwhelmed by "intense feelings of emptiness and inauthenticity" [Lasch 1978:39]. The greater the vacuum outside, in the social and institutional realm, the greater the freedom and temptation to focus on the self and exaggerate its importance. This is not a peculiarly American or capitalist phenomenon but one that is central to modernity and secularization which lead to "the growing determination to live for the moment" [Lasch 1978:188]. Norman Birnbaum talks about ". . . an increase in moral and psychological disorientation, a deeply rooted rootlessness. A flight into an entirely private sphere is but part of the result . . . when the larger setting offers so little . . . There is, it appears, no substitute for a sustaining public life" [Birnbaum 1988:189]. Despite the recurring references to it, Birnbaum never makes clear just what šuch a "sustaining public life" may consist of, or where it could be found at the present time or in the past.

As noted above, the problems and critiques associated with individualism can be of a diametrically opposed character. On the one hand American society is criticized for being excessively individualistic, that is, insufficiently communitarian, giving undue weight to private over public concerns. On the other hand it is also rebuked for diminishing "true" individuality by fostering inauthentic concerns, and an inauthentic individualism, or a narcissistic personality type. At last American society has also been criticized for fostering conformity, for smothering the individual by its fads, fashions, institutions, policies, its sheer weight and size, and by becoming increasingly "massified" or undifferentiated.

In the Marxian tradition society is accused of "crushing" the individual primarily through its exploitative work situations, unyielding institutions, restrictive cultural norms, and—as argued more recently—by the very existence and imposition of social roles and daily routines. The individual is powerless and he may be both materially deprived and hindered in self-fulfillment of loftier kinds. Such critiques popular in the 60s began to emerge already in the 1950s as part of the critique of "mass society." It is hard to be authentic in a mass society permeated by mass culture, advertising, public relations, role playing, "other-directedness," "escape from freedom," and the "quest for community." Inauthenticity is also associated with ideas and concepts such as "popularity," "interpersonal skills," "visibility," "celebrity," and "image" [Boorstin 1961].

Above all, the ravages of individualism can be linked to capitalism and its American variety. Competition and competitiveness are the root cause; they spill over into an unabashed "looking out for number one," an exaggerated quest for self-sufficiency and autonomy; this excessive and unsound individualism also undermines personal relationships, cuts the individual off from the group, and virtually wipes out communal life.

Robert Bellah and his associates found discontent and bewilderment in the lives of middle-class Americans devoted to "personal ambition and consumerism"; they were "seeking in one way or another to transcend the limitations of a self-centered life" [Bellah 1985:290]. The study also warns against "restless competition and anxious self-defense," the neglect of "the larger issues of existence," the decline of "public virtue" and meaningful civic participation and especially the danger of the citizen being "swallowed up in 'economic man'"—an "individualism [that] may have grown cancerous" [Ibid.271, viii]. *The Habits of the Heart* amounted to yet another rediscovery of the problems of a secular society which overemphasizes the private at the expense of the public, the individual over the communal, and leaves the individual disoriented, isolated, in an unsuccessful pursuit of meaning.

For Christopher Lasch "it is a way of life that is dying—the culture of competitive individualism, which in its decadence has carried the logic of individualism to the extreme of a war against all, the pursuit of happiness to the dead-end of a narcissistic preoccupation with the self" [Lasch 1978:xv]. This preoccupation with the self, and the irresistible overestimation of its uniqueness and unique needs also represent continuities between the 60s and 70s (the latter designated as the "Me Decade" by Tom Wolfe) and the 80s.

Tom Wolfe described the phenomenon as "The new . . . dream . . .; changing one's personality—remaking, remodelling, elevating and polishing one's very self . . . and observing, studying, and doting on it . . . By the mid-1960s this . . . luxury had become available for one and all, i.e. the middle classes . . ." The popularity of the burgeoning encounter, therapy, support, and consciousness-raising groups was easy to grasp. Again as Wolfe put it: ". . . the appeal was simple enough. It is summed up in the notion: 'Let's talk about Me' . . . the most fascinating subject on earth. Not only that, you also put me onstage before a live audience . . . my life becoming a drama with universal significance . . ." [Wolfe

1977:126, 128, 129]. Such emphasis on the unique attributes and needs of the self also becomes a source of interpersonal conflict. Lasch observed: "our society, far from fostering private life at the expense of public life, has made deep and lasting friendships, love affairs, and marriages increasingly difficult to achieve" [Lasch 1978:30].

Consumerism does contribute to this state of affairs by making it plausible to treat people and personal relationships as items of consumption: to be discarded when no longer needed, when a new product comes on the market, when the putative, vaunted "personal growth" demands new relationships as on other occasions it may demand new products. Lasch points out, "Advertising serves not so much to advertise products as to promote consumption as a way of life. It 'educates' the masses into an unappeasable appetite not only for goods but for new experiences and personal fulfillment" [Ibid.:72]. But personal relations also become difficult when they represent virtually the only source of emotional sustenance, when "men and women make extravagant demands on each other and experience irrational rage and hatred when their demands are not met" [Ibid.:199].

While capitalism is most frequently held accountable for these developments, Lasch is also critical of what he calls "welfare liberalism, which absolves individuals of moral responsibility and treats them as victims of social circumstances" [Ibid.:218]. He is critical of a capitalist ruling elite on the ground that "it has replaced character building with permissiveness, the cure of souls with the cure of the psyche, blind justice with therapeutic justice, philosophy with social science, personal authority with an equally irrational authority of professional experts" [Ibid.:221].

These critiques have less to do with the Marxian preoccupation with exploitation, oppression, profit hunger, and the pursuit of self-interest than with the concern over the loss of meaning, the inability of society to legitimize itself, to socialize the young in a coherent manner. (They also resemble the type of foreign critique of American society I called anti-Americanism as a reaction to the crisis of meaning.)

Other critics describe the condition of the individual in capitalist America in still more dire terms: ". . . the majority of Americans . . . are at the edge of economic, social and psychological panic . . . [their] sensibilities deformed through economic privations and societal dislocations" [Raskin 1978:xi and 1974:19]. Michael Parenti envisioned "the mass of middle Americans" afflicted by "occupational disability, job insecurity, job dissatisfaction, constant financial anxieties, mental stress and depression, alcoholism and conflictual domestic relations . . . Even if not suffering from acute want, few if any exercise much control over the condition of their lives" [Parenti 1978:66–67].

Thus American society not merely exploits and mistreats the individual, it also deforms him in a durable way.

As the decade of the 1980s came to a close Christopher Lasch concluded that "The moral bottom has dropped out of our culture" and "young people in our society are living in a state of almost unbearable, though mostly inarticulate agony" [Lasch 1989].

A summary of the domestic or internal critiques of American society must in conclusion also take note of a characteristic that many of these critiques have in common, namely the reluctance or refusal to make differentiated judgments about various forms and degrees of social evil, moral, or political corruption. For example the critics routinely equate U.S. intervention in Grenada with Soviet intervention in Afghanistan; a Catholic bishop compares American submarines with Nazi extermination camps; Chomsky believes that a major mission of American schools is to teach the young how to brutalize the peoples of the Third World; for James Baldwin, Harvard and life in the ghetto destroy black people in equal measure; a sociologist insists that crime flourishes in the United States because it helps to improve the self-conception and complacence of the middle classes; various scholars (besides Walter Cronkite) propose that the United States bears "deep similarities" to the totalitarianism depicted in *1984* [for the sources of these examples see Hollander 1986].

Not only in the comparisons with the Soviet Union—which gave rise to the school of moral equivalence between "superpowers"—but whenever any iniquity in the world crops up the critics find comparable evils in the United States.

More recently a columnist in the *New York Times* managed to detect a close resemblance between the Ayatollah's death sentence of Salman Rushdie and the indignation of American veterans in Chicago over the purposeful trampling of the American flag presented as an art exhibit (". . . many of our fellow citizens are as willing as the mullahs in Tehran to silence dissident voices that offend their sacred symbols and beliefs" [Lukas 1989]). Mr. Lukas, as other social critics—irritated or embarrassed when anybody finds evil outside the United States without hastening to point out that its equivalents exist here too—overlooked a few differences between these incidents. Nobody called for the death of the art student who proposed to desecrate the flag (and who is not hiding under police protection); if anybody had, few would have approved it or volunteered to implement it. But these are small matters for those for whom the most enduring legacy of the 60s has been the instinctive belief that no society can be inferior to this one and there are no deformities of social institutions and political behavior which do not flourish in the United States.

NOTES

1. I used the word "substantial" because there is no obvious way to quantify these attitudes and the people who display them. Certainly some segments of the intelligentsia are occasionally surveyed or polled on various issues which have relevance to the concerns of this book, but I have yet to hear of a survey addressed to "intellectuals" as such. Hence the quantitative dimensions of the phenomena here discussed cannot be ascertained with much precision.

2. I use the term quasi-intellectual to refer to people with intellectual aspirations and developed critical attitudes who do not however quite measure up to widely used definitions of intellectuals which incorporate a measure of distinction, creativity, influence, and access to a wider public. Quasi-intellectuals are far more numerous than "intellectuals" (and somewhat similar to what others called the New Class), whereas intellectuals have been thought of as more of a vanguard, or elite.

Part of the difficulty of applying the older understanding of intellectual to present-day conditions is that the spread of higher education stimulated—in Western countries at any rate—critical impulses on a large scale without necessarily imparting the attitudes which also used to accompany such a critical disposition, in particular a sustained preoccupation with ideas.

3. George Kennan's reflections on the serenity of Andrei Gromyko, revealed in his memoirs, sheds further light on the reluctance to seriously rethink one's political past and on the associated propensity to repress memories of questionable activities. These remarks of Kennan are especially relevant and illuminating as regards the "unrepentant" radicals of the 60s who also often justified their actions by reference to larger causes and collectivities. Kennan wrote: ". . . repression . . . reconciles the errant, bewildered soul to the painful record of its own mistakes . . . the active awareness of which, if allowed to accompany the subject as a companion through life, would paralyze the will and destroy the enthusiasm for life itself."

"What is not so often understood is that this capacity for repression of memory can be easily transferred from the individual's sense of responsibility for his own conduct to the behavior of a political collectivity into whose hands he has committed his . . . loyalty. When this transference occurs, it is—in the personal psychic sense—enormously health giving . . . for here the moral responsibility is shifted entirely to someone else. . . . For anything undertaken . . . in response to the will of the collectivity . . . no matter how distasteful . . . from the standpoint of individual morality, there could be no guilt, no questioning, no remorse. And if it turned out that what the Party required to be done . . . involved apparent injustice or cruelty—well, one might regret that it was found necessary; one might wish that it could have been otherwise. But it was not one's own responsibility; and one was justified in later years . . . in pushing the memory back into those dim precincts of forgetfullness that already veiled so many other evidences of man's savagery and nastiness . . ." [Kennan 1988:3].

4. I am well aware that the correspondence columns of newspapers published in New England campus towns, such as my own, yield information about political attitudes quite different from what one would find in corresponding publications in a suburb of Dallas or St. Louis or Pittsburgh. On the other hand there is nothing unique about the Amherst-Northampton area, as far as such political beliefs are concerned; the country is sprinkled with similar enclaves of the adversary culture where the 60s survived both demographically and attitudinally speaking. I have in mind places like Berkeley and Santa Cruz, Calif.; Cambridge-Boston, Mass.; Madison, Wisc,; Ann Arbor, Mich.; Boulder, Colo.; Burlington, Vt.; and many others.

5. For example the town of Amherst, Mass., in 1988 supported various local groups suing the federal government and/or the Department of Defense because of the overflight of C5 transport planes on training exercises.

Attitudes of many members of the Town Meeting of Amherst toward the military have also been illustrated by their opposition to an article that was to grant exemptions to former prisoners of wars on their auto excise taxes; the article passed 105 to 75 votes after acrimonious debate [Barrett 1983].

In Berkeley, California—probably setting a new record in such matters—the City Council declared the entire city a sanctuary for undocumented Central American aliens (presumably excluding Nicaraguans who fled a communist state). "The resolution is similar to one adopted in 1971 when the City Council declared Berkeley a refuge for military personnel who refused to be sent to Vietnam" ["Berkeley in Sanctuary Move" 1985]. So much for continuity in a stronghold of the adversary culture.

Berkeley also attempted to apply enlightened principles to the lives of animals. A special park was set aside for dogs in the hope that they would "[co]exist harmoniously once separated from their owners' ethic of possessiveness." One of the activists involved in this endeavor observed: "Some people were sure that the dogs would prove to be egalitarians . . . But they aren't. They come here and immediately join the pack, which is . . . controlled by the top dog . . . they have a great time in the pack, but they aren't really very progressive. It was a hard lesson for some of the radical pet owners . . . to swallow. Not only have we failed to create the New Man in Berkeley. We haven't even created the New Dog" [Collier and Horowitz 1989:216]. Berkeley has also gone to great lengths to find "a politically correct" police dog that does not have aggressive attributes [Bishop 1990].

6. The concern with "fragmentation" (he shares with many social critics) is a recurring theme in Birnbaum's volume. We are rarely told what precisely constitutes "fragmentation" or how much of it is dangerous to the health of society or the polity. Perhaps we are expected to grasp intuitively the nature and evils of fragmentation as we are to grasp the meaning of "totality," "wholeness," and "organic"—other favorites of Marxist authors.

Birnbaum also wrote: "Cultural and social antagonisms, often unavowed, divide what was once the body politic. It now is something between a corpse and a chronic invalid" [Ibid.:190].

In such comments Birnbaum, otherwise a stern critic of the consensual views of society, betrays an unexpected longing for harmony and an unbecoming aversion to social conflict and division he ought to consider inevitable and even wholesome under corporate capitalism.

7. In a conversation with the author (on March 18, 1989) Ronald Radosh reaffirmed the accuracy of the quote.

2

The Churches: New Voices of Social Protest

"The religious left is the only left we got."

Michael Ferber, 1985

I

By the early 1980s large portions of the clergy of various denominations (Protestant fundamentalists excepted) have become the predictable voices of social criticism in American society. There has been since the 1960s something of a "religious revival on the left," as a sympathetic observer of the phenomenon put it. According to his estimates, ". . . of every five people actively working for progressive causes, at last three draw energy and conviction from their religious beliefs." He explained this state of affairs by the confluence of the ideas of sin and alienation: ". . . some churchpeople would define sin as a state not so different from the alienated, one-dimenstional, male-supremacist, imperialist and technocratic world the left has been at pains describing" [Ferber 1985;10, 12].

A Roman Catholic sister who also served as national secretary of Christians for Socialism from 1976 to 1983 made similar observations about what she called "The emergence of the Christian left." She wrote: "Perhaps no change in the U.S. landscape is as notable over a 20-year horizon as what has occurred in the role of the Christian sector in the movements and processes of social change" [Schultz 1984:56].

Notable of the social criticism these clerics and their followers have engaged in is that it cannot to any significant degree be distinguished from its secular counterparts. Moreover, these critiques, as their secular counterparts, have become increasingly cultural or subcultural; that is to say, assimilated into the thinking and attitudes of substantial segments of American society, constituting an unquestioned, natural, taken-for-granted view of the world and the United States. So deeply ingrained have these perspectives become that often they strike those upholding them as self-evident truth, statements of a descriptive rather than critical character. Thus in many instances a zealous attachment to increasingly secular causes has come to supplement residual religious convictions. As observed by a former director of the Cathedral Peace Institute of the Episcopal Church in New York City: "I finally concluded that the mindset of the 1960s clergy, which tended to direct their attention to issues of this world, has not in any fundamental way diminished their need for religious certainty. These clergy merely seek the equivalent of religious certainty in the causes they advocate" [Kennedy 1986; see also Robb and Robb 1986:192–208].

An English observer describes the same phenomenon in Britain as a new "alliance between Christianity and Marxism," an observation also applicable to some segments of the religious community in the United States. He believes that the churches in Britain—at the level of church leadership —have largely been taken over by public figures hostile to both capitalism and liberal democracy and totally unimpressed by the rejection of state socialist systems by the people upon whom such anticapitalist governments had been imposed [Minogue 1990:9].

Although the clergy has been actively involved with various social and political causes since the mid-1960s, through the 1970s and 80s such involvements have deepened and become institutionalized, cutting across an increasingly broad range of denominations. For instance at a celebration to honor peace in Leverett, Massachusetts, "Slow Turtle, chief medicine man of the Wampanoag Nation gave the opening prayer . . . Leaders of the Jewish, Christian and Baha'i faiths offered prayers, and the keynote speakers—an exiled Catholic priest from El Salvador and an American lawyer who recently participated in a protest in Central America—addressed the crowd" [Jones 1988].

While some of the older causes of the 60s have been retained—such as racial justice in the United States and disarmament—new ones have been added: South Africa, Nicaragua, gay liberation, AIDS, and sanctuary for certain groups of Central American fugitives. As far as the Protestant denominations have been concerned,". . . if one looks at the public posture of mainline liberal Protestantism on the great majority of issues . . . there is no doubt where these churches come out: Their social and political views are highly consonant with those of one camp—the one intended by the 'New Class' designation . . ." [Berger in Michaelson and Roof eds. 1986:28]. The renewal of such political activism on the part of the clergy has also been reported in the mass media [e.g., Briggs 1984 Sept.; Teltsch 1985; "36 Religious Leaders" 1985].

This is not to suggest that the political activism has been limited to or dominated by those of liberal and left-liberal denominations. A reactive, right-wing religious activism and social criticism have also emerged during the 1970s and 80s, preoccupied, above all, with abortion and generally opposed to the various causes embraced by clerics at the other end of the spectrum. However, it was not my purpose to sketch the entire spectrum of political activism and social protest the various churches have engaged in but rather to show that the left-of-center, adversarial voices in the secular realm had ample support and resonance among the churches.

By the early 1980s not only the National Council of Churches (the activist, organizational arm of these Protestant denominations) and the American Friends Service Committee (the left-of-center organizational offshoot of the Quakers) but substantial elements of the Catholic hierarchy too have embraced what came close to a reflexively adversarial position toward many aspects and institutions of American society and a corresponding benefit-of-doubt posture toward its foreign critics and adversaries. Presumably the politicization and radicalization of the Catholic Church in Latin America also exerted influence on the trends here discussed; in turn the "Third Worldism" of Latin American churches might have influenced the Pope. At any rate in the 1988 encyclical "The Social Concerns of the Church" he too embraced the moral equivalence of liberal capitalism and Soviet-style socialism, as will be further discussed below.

The developments noted above have been somewhat paradoxical on several grounds. First, while many secular groups and movements which emerged in the 1960s have in the course of the 1970s withdrawn from radical activism and the hostile questioning of American society, the immersion of the churches in radical social criticism and activism did not subside with the passage of time. Rather, it has continued to grow gradually and surged in the early 1980s with causes such as nuclear disarmament and U.S. involvement in Central America.

Second, while during the 1960s and 70s a growing number of those dissatisfied with American society turned to religious or quasi-religious pursuits and communities, by contrast several churches increasingly embraced a series of secular, political issues removed from the central and fundamental concerns of religion itself. To be sure, spokesmen of these churches and denominations would insist that their worldly preoccupations were in fact spiritual and sanctioned by their respective religious commitments and values—that the struggle against poverty, racism, sexism, homophobia, inequality, or material greed were in fact religious causes as well.

Although a cause-and-effect relationship is unclear, the politicization of the churches here discussed more or less coincided with the beginning (in the mid-1960s) of a decline of membership and church attendance in the liberal (or mainline) Protestant denominations. According to Clark Roof, a sociologist of religion, "Since the 1960s the more liberal, mainline Protestant churches have been in a downward spiral, suffering from a loss of confidence and institutional vitality" [Roof 1988; see also Roof 1982:17].

Tom Wolfe's theory is also helpful for understanding these developments:

> Ever since the late 1950s both the Catholic Church and the leading Protestant denominations had been aware that young people . . . were drifting away . . . The key—one and all decided—was to "modernize" and "update" Christianity. So the Catholics gave the nuns outfits that made them look like World War II WACS. The Protestants set up "beatnik coffee houses" . . . Both the priests and preachers carried placards in civil rights marches, gay rights marches, bondage lovers' rights marches or any other marches, so long as they might appear hip to the urban young people.
>
> In fact all these strenuous gestures merely made the churches look like rather awkward and senile groupies of secular movements . . .
>
> Today it is precisely the most rational, intellectual, secularized, modernized, updated, relevant religions . . . that are finished . . . What the Urban Young People want from religion is a little . . . *Hallelujah!* . . . and *talking in tongues* . . . *Praise the God!* . . . "charismatic Christianity" . . .
>
> This curious development has breathed new life into the existing fundamentalists, theosophists, and older salvation seekers of all sorts. [Wolfe 1977:132–34].

In these Protestant churches there has been a growing divergence between the leadership that embraced largely secular and left-of-center causes and the ordinary members of congregations, far less concerned with the favorite issues of the church elite. It should be kept in mind that much of what follows refers to the orientation of these elites within the churches rather than the beliefs and attitudes of the rank-and-file membership.

Similar trends were evident in the Catholic Church. Since 1966 some 11,000 priests and 35,000 sisters resigned; weekly mass attendance too declined significantly [Glynn 1983:11]. Under these circumstances the embrace of activism, of various secular social and political causes offered a path toward reinvigorating religious institutions by associating them with issues many people, especially the young, deeply cared about. As David Martin observed, "The clergyman is peculiarly sensitive to the charge of marginality and irrelevance and feels compelled to divest himself . . . of the specific clerical character . . . [he] is anxious to be where the action is" [Martin 1983:133].

Paul Seabury noted the same phenomenon, in connection with the Episcopal Church: "The excitement lay outside the institutional church . . . What would be the marching orders? Civil rights? Poverty? Whose poverty? Colonialist exploitation? The Vietnam war? All these crusades found eager recruits among newly ordained priests and among older priests and rectors who had come to doubt the significance of the unchanging church in a violently changing society" [Seabury 1978:21].

As far as the Catholic Church was concerned,". . . there has been an enormous redirection of religious energy into the secular realm . . ." Moreover, ". . . after two decades of change and inner turmoil, it is the Church's politically oriented institutions that have emerged the most vital and unscathed" [Glynn 1983:12, 13]. Peter Berger suggested that ". . . the Catholic bishops are following in the well-worn footsteps of a major segment of official mainline Protestantism," and their pastoral letters reminded him of "the left wing of the Democratic party gathered for prayer" [Berger 1985:35].

Another paradox of the emerging orientation of the churches has been that although their concerns have also expanded geographically, encompassing many aspects and areas of global politics, they have remained steadfastly unmoved by issues of religious freedom itself when such freedoms have been under massive attack in numerous countries including those these churches have singled out for their respectful attention, indeed affection.

Several speculative explanations of this state of affairs may be put forward. The most general, as alluded to above, is that the churches in the United States, aware of the long-term trends toward secularization (undiminished by the periodic religious and quasi-religious revivals, as those of the 60s and 70s), have been seeking to preserve their influence by associating themselves with issues attracting the greatest public attention and appearing to have the strongest moral appeal.

Kenneth Minogue, the British political scientist, offered a convincing theory of such developments:

> . . . institutions which lose their faith will soon abandon their identity. In the case of the Churches, awareness of the growing erosion of support in what Max Weber called a "disenchanted" world has led to the search for a new role. "Searching for a new role" is a typically bureaucratic expedient employed by those who manage an institution which is visibly under threat and it often runs into resistance from rank-and-file members who retain the original beliefs. [Minogue 1990:9]

While in the 1960s and early 70s the protest against the war in Vietnam and the struggle for civil rights were the issues to rally around, in the late

1970s and early 1980s the new causes have been discrimination against women, lesbians, and homosexuals; assistance to AIDS victims; apartheid in South Africa; the conflicts in Central America; and the threat of nuclear annihilation. The focus on minorities or underdog groups has been retained. The domestic designations of underdog groups had their foreign counterparts, usually in the vague entity called the Third World, which, as will be seen later, acquired a certain spiritual-religious aura or mystique [Berger 1983]. The idiosyncratic nature of these underdog designations was well exemplified by Cuba, seen by sympathizers, church-related and other, as the underdog pitted against the American colossus. Yet Cuba fielded the biggest army in all of Latin America in both relative and absolute terms with enough manpower to spare for large expeditionary forces in Africa.

The selectivity of these moral concerns and commitments was further illustrated by the relative indifference these activist and globally involved churches have shown toward Afghanistan and the suffering of its people, perhaps because those sufferings did not offer possibilities for holding the United States, the West, capitalism, or the multinational corporations responsible.

The churches' designations of countries, movements, or groups as underdogs deserving of moral and material support and sympathy reflected clearly patterned political values and predispositions. Even the military might of such countries, organizations, or movements could be played down by redefining it as defensive in purpose. Defensiveness and aggressiveness have increasingly been defined in relation to what particular observers regarded as legitimate threats, or the overall context of particular conflicts. It was frequently overlooked that even the most powerful and repressive political systems and their leaders were capable of feeling threatened by vast imaginary conglomerations of enemies, and that the claim of being threatened has become the major legitimation of aggression in our times. Abhorrence of violence, not unlike moral indignation and compassion, has become highly selective in many clerical circles, even among those professionally committed to evenhandedness in matters of morality—as will be further shown below. Such trends, spearheaded by the American Friends Service Committee (see below), have transformed some church-related (and other) pacifist organizations into highly politicized advocacy groups [for a book-length study of these trends see Lewy 1988].

The increasingly conspicuous selectivity in moral passion and compassion will be a recurring theme in our examination of the attitudes of the unrelenting critics (secular or religious) of American society and institutions.

II

Daniel Berrigan, Jesuit priest and prominent Vietnam-era activist, author of 37 books, was an early and, some would argue, atypically extreme representative of the trends outlined above. Examining his views will nonetheless be rewarding given our interest in the continuities between the adversarial beliefs of the 1960s and 1980s. We may begin with his views of violence conveyed in a letter to the Weathermen in 1971:

> I have a great fear of American violence, not only out there in the military and the diplomacy, in economics, in industry and advertising, but also in here, in me, up close among us.
> On the other hand, I must say, I have very little fear, from first-hand experience, of the violence of the Vietcong or Panthers (I hesitate to use the word violence), for their acts come from the proximate threat of extinction, from being invariably put on the line of self-defense . . .[Casey 1971:211]

Thus the violence of the favored groups is justified as defensive and legitimated by the ends pursued. It is, in any event, socially determined. Here is Daniel Berrigan again:

> Well, I look upon the Weathermen as a very different phenomenon because I have seen in them very different resources and purposes. I believe that their violent rhythm was induced by the violence of the society itself. And I can excuse the violence of those people as a temporary thing . . . I feel that the best way to understand the violence and alienation of our young radicals is to look at America's violence. [Berrigan and Coles 1971:76, 84]

Berrigan also found mitigation in Weathermen violence by seeing it as "the American character emerging" [Casey 1971:187]. Such exculpatory, contextual or social determinism has however been selectively used [Hollander 1983:241–51].

While Berrigan was reluctant to designate as violence the activities of the Vietcong or the Black Panthers—although such activities clearly entailed physical violence or destruction of property—he was inclined to ascribe violence to activities which, morally questionable or not, are certainly not violent as the word is generally understood. In doing so Berrigan and other social critics have demonstrated considerable skill in the use of language designed to either defuse or inflame moral passions depending on the purpose at hand. For example he designated as "latent violence" or institutionalized violence the *policies* of the administration at Cornell University in order to excuse and mitigate the actual violence of black students against it [Berrigan and Coles 1972:84]. He also explained to students at Cornell that "old ladies who work as secretaries for draft boards are the equivalent of the Beast of Belsen and deserve no more respectful treatment than she did" [Bloom 1987:326].

Thus ideological-political alignments can be traced by the semantic choices made in labeling activities or processes as violent or nonviolent and by designating groups as victims or victimizers respectively, and the ways in which their claims of being "threatened" and victimized are denied or given credit.

The policy statements of the World Council of Churches (which the American National Council of Churches supports and belongs to) on political violence reflect an outlook strikingly similar to Berrigan's. For example: "Revolutionary violence is permissible as a last resort in over-throwing oppressive elites if it will eliminate '*the vast covert violence which the existing order involves*'" [Quoted in Lefever 1979:25]. Here again actual violence is equated with "vast covert violence" which can mean anything those using this concept wish to refer to and want to discredit.

Redefinitions of political violence have been especially impressive when originating with religious groups which used to claim pacifist credentials, such as the American Friends Service Committee. The AFSC, not unlike most secular political partisans, came to the conclusion that violence that brought about results they favored was acceptable as means to good ends whereas violence used for ends they disapproved of was morally abhorrent. The AFSC also redefined and broadened the concept of violence by introducing ideas such as "the violence of the status quo" or "economic violence" (meaning inequality or social injustice). Or else a distinction was made between the *quality* (as distinct from the purpose) of violence employed by the forces of good as opposed to the forces of evil, suggesting that the forces of good used violence in a restrained manner whereas the forces of evil employed it lavishly and with indulgent brutality. Philip Berryman, a Latin American specialist of the AFSC, argued that "there were clear differences in the way violence was used by the army and by the guerilla groups [in Latin America] . . . the army practiced systematic torture and terrorism . . . and was largely indiscriminate in its violence whereas guerilla violence was targeted . . . [guerillas] made every effort not to endanger innocent bystanders" [Berryman 1984:209–10; for a further discussion of the AFSC and political violence see Lewy 1988].

Whether or not such assertions were empirically correct is another question; often they were not, as exemplified by the guerilla practice of planting mines on highways which blew up buses carrying civilian passengers in El Salvador.

In the light of these attitudes toward violence among representatives of religious faiths it is not surprising that, according to a "young war resister," "Meeting Phil Berrigan [Daniel's brother and fellow-activist] was not like meeting a priest, but like meeting a military man, a general or a guerilla leader." [Casey 1971:front matter, unpaginated]

The reinvigorated entry of the churches into the area of secular moralizing and social criticism may also be related to a latent competition for moral leadership between the clergy and the secular intellectuals. In the words of David Martin, the clergyman ". . . compares himself enviously with the committed intellectuals, whose role appears to consist in researching the contours of the real world and proposing how it may be reformed" [Martin 1983:133]. The latter, especially in their incarnations as college teachers and administrators, journalists and publishers, foundation officials, and so on, have in recent years become aspirants to the role of the conscience of society. Sometimes the clerical and secular roles are no longer sharply differentiated as in the case of clerics attached to colleges who teach, perform religious rituals, may informally dispense therapy, appear on television, and publish. Occasionally the reverse may also be the case when secular intellectuals hold positions of leadership in a particular church. Thus, for example, Richard Barnett (better known as a founder and head of the Washington-based Institute for Policy Studies) was listed among the leaders of the World Peacemakers, which is "a mission of the Eighth Day Faith Community of the Church of the Saviour, an ecumenical church in Washington" [World Peacemakers pamphlet, n.d.]. It would also be difficult to decide where the lines were drawn between the secular-political and religious-spiritual concerns and roles of the Rev. William Sloan Coffin Jr., who has in 1987 assumed leadership of a national peace/disarmament organization, SANE/FREEZE, after advocating a variety of political causes from the pulpit of the Riverside Church in New York City and earlier as chaplain at Yale University.

Thus the two groups continue to contend for moral leadership: secular intellectuals have incorporated vigorous moralizing into their occupational roles (especially as publishing academics in the humanities and social sciences), while clergymen, eager to reclaim and expand their moral authority and influence, have invaded the secular political realm.

Although occupationally distinct, activist clerics and secular intellectuals have become increasingly united in both the style and substance of their social criticism, in their eagerness to champion what they perceive to be the underdog, in their aversion or outright hostility to Western political and economic institutions and capitalism in particular, and in their reflexive rejection of American society. Among the examples of such ideological united fronts we might note the close ties between the Riverside Church in New York and the Institute for Policy Studies in Washington, D.C. The support of secular social critics for their clerical allies was also demonstrated by the eagerness on the part of well-known social critics such as Robert J. Lifton, George Wald, and Richard Falk to testify in support of Daniel Berrigan when he was tried for damaging missiles at a General Electric Plant in 1981 [Robbins 1981].

Thus the estrangement of secular intellectuals and portions of the clergy has converged. We can best capture the quality of this shared estrangement by turning to a sampling of the social criticism of the clergy, less familiar than that of the secular intellectuals.

Once more Daniel Berrigan provides an excellent point of departure. Although he has been characterized as belonging to "the shock troops of the peace movement" [Gray 1970:44] and positioned at what might be called the cutting edge (or the extremity) of social criticism—castigating the ills of American society with greater intensity and passion than other critics among the clergy—his views are far from unrepresentative of much of the social criticism offered in less colorful language by other clerical critics of American society. Indeed, some of his pronouncements redolent of the ethos of the 60s and early 70s have become, somewhat unexpectedly, conventional wisdom by the early 1980s among many churchmen.

It has been correctly noted that Daniel Berrigan is possessed of a "dawning realization that practically nothing of traditional civilized structures is functioning for human welfare [in the United States]. This is true of medicine, education, communication, arts, the Church, and indeed, God help us, the courts" [Quoted in Casey 1971:16]. He also believed that

> American power is locked into its method, its sleep-walking, its nightmare, its rampant and irreversible character. No change in the personnel of power seems to bring about any serious change in the functioning and direction of power, in the misuse and grinding under of human beings. [Ibid.: 19]

A similar statement, capturing the essence of alienation, was made by one of Berrigan's admirers, Gordon C. Zahn:

> One need not deny that this nation may have reached a critical point in its history where revolution, in the sense of a total and rapid restructuring

of the social order, is the only way by which it can free itself for its own and the world's good from the chains of war, militarism, racism and economic imperialism. [Casey 1971:104]

Zahn also illustrates the characteristic incapacity of many social critics to make distinctions, a development that can be traced to the rhetoric and hyperbole of the 1960s:

When an Agnew attacks the news media, how far are we from Goebbels? When a Julius Hoffman displays a level of judicial temperament and decorum that would have won the admiration of Roland Friesler and his *Volksgericht*, is it really enough to send off a new flurry of telegrams to Congressmen and Senators? [Ibid.:100]

Daniel Berrigan, on his part, averred that "there *is* a uniqueness to the threat posed by American power right now" [Berrigan and Coles 1972:100], a sentiment that is crucial for understanding the quality of embittered alienation he embodies. Such a perception of and insistence on this alleged "uniqueness" holds the key to the nature of estrangement we are here concerned with, among both the clerics and their secular colleagues.

How did such beliefs develop? Why have many intelligent, sensitive, and well-meaning people in recent decades become convinced that the United States represents a uniquely evil and dangerous social-political system that deserves nothing but, hostility, and contempt, that nothing short of total and radical destruction of the existing structure could bring improvement?

Another follower of the Berrigans, Edward Duff, S.J., correctly summed it up: "Believing 'that times are inexpressibly evil' Daniel Berrigan believes also that they are irretrievably beyond lawful remedy" [Casey 1971:23].

Here then is the other crucial component of profound alienation: the belief that given the uniqueness of the evils of the social order, its non-violent correction is not an option. Such a belief either becomes the counsel of despair and inaction, or in the case of impassioned activists like the Berrigans, the justification of quasi-revolutionary activity, of "extraordinary measures" (civil disobedience in his case) and also the source of sympathy toward those wishing to change the systems by force. Hence Daniel Berrigan hoped, as Duff put it, "that he could build bridges to the Weathermen and the Black Panthers; certainly as a priest he was pleased by his appeal to the New Left" [Casey 1971:24].

The far-reaching ramifications of evil in American society were further described by another of the Berrigans' admirers, David J. O'Brien:

"All of America, its governments and courts, its businesses and unions, its churches and its schools are implicated in the evils of war and oppression. All of us are implicated . . ."[Casey 1971:75].

The embrace of collective guilt has been a much-sought-after attitude among social critics for reasons not entirely clear. Did Professor O'Brien and other critics truly and literally mean that "all of us," including presumably himself, are implicated in the evils he described?

Such an eager, overzealous embrace of collective guilt raises interesting questions. Empirically speaking, it is clearly untrue that "all of us" are implicated in many of the evils in question. Yet the Berrigans and their followers vigorously advocate the curious belief that not resisting a particular evil equals, morally speaking, the actual commission or perpetration of that evil. It is a position that was also taken by other prominent social critics as J. P. Sartre and Noam Chomsky [Hollander 1981:62, 56].

Belief in collective guilt has two consequences. One is the dilution of clear responsibility for whatever reprehensible action took place: when all are responsible in some abstract sense no one can be held specifically culpable. The second consequence of insistence on collective guilt is an enhanced moral indignation: somewhat illogically, the Berrigans and others can rise to a higher level of moral indignation about the social ills or evils supposedly created by or contributed to by "all of us."

How is it possible to be so outraged about forms of behavior or attitudes allegedly so common, or widespread? How is one to account for the popularity of the collective-guilt school? Why are its advocates generally seen as upholders of a higher degree of moral virtue? The answer may in part be found in the popularity of the "banality of evil" thesis put forward by Hannah Arendt in connection with Nazi war criminals such as Adolf Eichmann.

Perhaps the most obvious explanation of the appeal of collective guilt has been that it helps to dramatize evil: it suggests that not only a clearly identifiable minority of wrongdoers but an entire society is implicated, thus an image of monumental and seemingly intractable evil is conjured up. Correspondingly Hannah Arendt popularized the view that in our times the most unremarkable individuals are capable of perpetrating moral outrages of colossal proportions, as for example Eichmann organizing the Holocaust. In turn, Stanley Milgram's experiments showed how easily ordinary people can be pressured into inflicting pain. His work supported the idea that almost anybody can be enlisted, under appropriate conditions, in the service of morally reprehensible activities or policies [see also Hollander 1983:187–91]. If so, there is not much of a dividing line between the virtuous and the guilty, innocent bystanders and active wrongdoers all of them products of a vicious social order.

It is also likely that the confessional embrace of collective guilt contributes to a favorable self-conception as it projects a sense of heightened responsibility, sincerity, moral seriousness, and adherence to high principles. (At the same time, such a stance may be combined with the comforting underlying knowledge that there are no concrete and specific grounds for the profession of guilt.)

But above all, the avowals of collective guilt are tools of social criticism: as they diminish personal responsibility they magnify that of society and its institutions by proposing that the whole social system is corrupt and not only particular individuals guilty of specific wrongdoing. "We are all guilty" translates into saying that "this is a society rotten to the core" that corrupts everybody. Professions of collective guilt and impassioned social criticism spring from the same source.

The radical rejections of American society here discussed combine sweeping, generalized indictments (noted above) with the critique of specific institutions. Here again is Daniel Berrigan:

> The family [in the U. S.] is a sitting duck before the war machine. Its needs keep magnifying and it supports the system as consumers. The middle class breeds kids to become social engineers, the poor breeds kids to kill. [Casey 1971:187]
>
> [Elsewhere he noted] . . . marriage as we understand it and family life as we understand it in this culture both tend to define people in a far more suffocating and totalizing way than we want to acknowledge . . . [Berrigan and Coles 1972:52]
>
> . . . many of our children are taught to hate, not only taught so in homes, but by sheriffs, mayors, governors and on up . . . the kinds of families that have been "flourishing" in this society . . . especially the white middle classes have become what they have embraced: consumerism; militant self-interest; and wars to subdue "natives" . . . [Ibid.:56]
>
> [Moreover] . . . families too can be virtual armies: the child is segregated, indoctrinated, isolated in order to be injected with a world view . . . And armies succeed, as do many of our homes and schools: lives are controlled, spirits crushed, wars of one kind or another waged and won. [Ibid.:57]

Daniel Berrigan regarded the family as hopelessly compromised by its involvement in consumption and the profit-making machinery of the capitalist system:

> . . . in a consumer society, the family is the means by which most people become tied to a cycle like this: go along with things, so long as you get enough to buy more and more things even though the whole world is

exploited so that a relatively small number of people in this country—
us!—can live well. [Berrigan and Coles 1972:50–51]

Berrigan's followers fully shared these views:

> I saw that shopping center as the real state of the nation, its image repro-
> duced a thousandfold across the American landscape. A thick haze of *artifi-
> cial* light overhead, food deceptively *packaged* and dangerously *processed,*
> people cramming their carts with goods, transacting *faceless business,*
> dressed in *plastics* . . . This was the consumer society. [Casey 1971:193]
> [My emphasis]

Why did "consumerism" inspire such loathing among the social critics of both the churches and the secular world? For the clerics it was an
all-to-obvious distraction from spiritual concerns, or at any rate their sec-
ular-religious values and purposes. As for the Berrigans,

> They are men sworn to poverty by their religious orders, and a conversion
> to poverty is perhaps the only conversion they desire to impose on man-
> kind. With a sometimes maddening simplicity, they view the problems of
> racism, of war, and of most human suffering as created by a system of
> unequally distributed wealth, by human beings' greed for private property.
> [Gray 1970:73]

Immersion in consumption was seen not only as crassly materialistic
but also as self-centered and distracting from higher moral values and
social consciousness. Above all consumption was associated with capitalism and its contemptible pursuit of profit. Moreover—as seen by the critics of this type—the consumer society succeeded in masking its defects
and injustices and reduced poverty sufficiently enough to remove it from
among the major objects of public concern and compassion. American-
style consumption was also linked with "inauthenticity," as witness the
preoccupation with plastic, packaging, processing, mass production, and
faceless business transactions. Perhaps if people could have consumed
the individualized products of autonomous and creative craftsmen or
small-scale farmers made out of "natural" materials, consumption might
have been less alienating and more acceptable aesthetically too. Hence,
there was an element of "elitism" in the critiques of consumer society:
its goods were tawdry, cheap, mass-produced, made of "inauthentic"
materials. They symbolized the more profound inauthenticity of the
entire social order: nothing was real, honest, natural, down to earth, or
straightforward. According to a vocal social critic, Barbara Ehrenreich,
one of the telling symptoms of social polarization in contemporary Amer-

ican society was the emergence of "two cultures . . . natural fiber vs. synthetic blends; hand-crafted wood cabinets vs. mass-produced maple; David's Cookies vs. Mister Donuts"[Ehrenreich 1986:44]. Production and marketing signified the falsehood institutions incorporated and social relationships entailed. The religious and secular critiques converged as social critics such as Marcuse, Berrigan, and their followers agreed that consumption was bad for the soul and society by helping to obscure the true interests of the very people who indulged in it so blindly.

The ambivalent or selective admiration of poverty in turn helps to explain the attraction exercised by Third World countries for the clerics sharing the Berrigans' worldview. If poverty is seen in a positive light, associated with spiritual graces and a purer life, poor countries will be found appealing, especially if they also espouse a socialist ideology of some variety designed to reduce poverty without falling prey to the indulgences of capitalistic consumption. Minogue's observation sheds further light on this matter:

> One set of people—"the poor"—has been entrenched as exclusively the bearer of rights because being the "products" of society, its behaviour cannot be morally judged . . . Because they are construed in terms of victimhood, the poor are the only class of persons who can . . . thus constitute an indispensable resource in the cultivation of righteousness. [Minogue 1989:11, 13]

Bertrand Russell's observation further illuminates the same mindset and places it into a broader historical context:

> One of the persistent delusions of mankind is that some sections of the human race are morally better or worse than others . . . A rather curious form of this admiration for groups to which the admirer does not belong is the belief in the superior virtue of the oppressed: subject nations, the poor, women and children. [Russell 1950:80]

The Berrigans' rejection of American society is of importance because it has been characteristic of the social criticism that has arisen in the late 1960s and has been with us ever since. Many of its themes have become incorporated into the critiques of American society and capitalism adopted by the churches in more recent years. Such critiques have become increasingly comprehensive in character, finding, time and again, linkages between one reprehensible social institution or practice and another. Daniel Berrigan's linking the undesirable aspects of the family to consumption resembles Marcuse's distaste for the family as an (unwanted) unit of social cohesion infected by the values of consumer society. On the other hand, the particular animus displayed by Daniel Berrigan toward the family approaches the intensity of the aversion found only among the radical feminist critics of the same institution. Possibly in Berrigan's case these attitudes are related to his clerical status and the attendant detachment from and incomprehension of the institution. More likely they also have a biographical component. (His father was either absent or uncaring while he grew up, but ready to exact "obedience [and] humiliation from his wife and family." But for his mother "he [the father] would have broken our spirits, in somewhat the way his had been broken. He was a failure in the eyes of others; and inevitably, in his own" [Berrigan 1987:18–19].)

The rejection of the status quo displayed by Berrigan often seems associated not only with a utopian vision of alternatives but also with a somewhat exalted view of the self. Daniel Berrigan wrote:

> . . . we are teachers of the people, who have come on a new vision of things. We struggle to embody that vision day after day . . . instead of thinking of the underground as temporary or exotic or abnormal, perhaps we are being called upon to start thinking of its implications as an entirely self-sufficient, mobile, internal revival community, so that the underground may be the definition of our future.[Casey 1971:210]

Elsewhere he remarked in the same spirit: "I just don't belong to myself" [Berrigan and Coles 1972:50]. He also believed that "the biology of the spirit is really exploding in this country, hence the inner turmoil that is all around us today. Biologically and spiritually we are trying to break through to another stage of human development"[Ibid.:52; see also 47].

As is often the case, the lack of specificity of the vision of the future and of the new ways of life following the "breakthrough" in no way diminished the desire to achieve it. Estrangement is nurtured by negation, rather than by a clear grasp or vision of the alternatives which were to replace it. Thus Daniel Berrigan said:

> I believe from my own experience and from what I have seen happen to others that a new kind of life, a new way for people to live with one another is quite possible—though I can't be as clear about the details of that life as you might wish, except to tell you . . . : I am trying to live now . . . in a way that points to the future and indicates the direction I believe we must all take . . . [Ibid.:93]

The significance of the Berrigans as social critic-activists is also reflected in the manner they were perceived by some of their contem-

poraries. They were sometimes seen as "avenging angels," people committed to "life-affirming social change," "truly prophetic witnesses," or
as a "slender man [Daniel Berrigan] . . . asking Americans to stop consuming one another and the world" [Casey 1971:156, 170, 64, 192].
According to *Commonweal*, they (the brothers) "summon their fellow
Americans to . . . a moral revolution, a regeneration that is based on the
personal conversion of individuals through acts which break them off
from established powers . . . and which link them, through suffering and
the fate of being outcast with the poor and the oppressed" [quoted in
Casey 1971:74].

According to John C. Raines:

> . . . the activity of the Berrigans is best understood as fundamentally
> *priestly activity*. They are attempting to regain an ancient heritage and
> power: to become practitioners of the healing of souls. They have sensed
> the demons at loose in the spiritual depths of modern man and society . . .
> they have undertaken to recapture the original priestly task and calling—
> the struggle of exorcism and liberation. [Ibid.:95]

How "the activity of the Berrigans is best understood" raises further
interesting questions regarding the connections between self-esteem and
participation in social protest. Certainly in recent times participation in
the type of social-political protest in which the Berrigans excelled has not
been a lonely or isolating activity; on the contrary, it has been associated
with a rewarding sense of community and good fellowship. Glimpses of
such an atmosphere are provided by the accounts of sympathetic observers:

> On the way to Catonsville, Daniel was in joyous spirits. "This is like going
> on a picnic," he said . . .
> The [Catonsville] nine cheerfully got in, smiling, bracing and congratu
> lating each other, and extending their fingers in the peace movement's V
> of protest. It was a handsome, photogenic group. [Gray 1970:101, 44]

A Catholic protester referring to the raid on a draft registration office
as a "party" culminating in the public burning of draft documents, reminisced: "Everyone began moving out with his loot . . . We came across
the street shouting and singing and making all kinds of noises . . . It was
liberating and we truly felt a great joy . . . We felt spurred with new life
. . ." Another participant in the same protest recalled:

> . . . I was pretty excited, so I don't remember the specifics . . . About all I
> remember was dancing up and down and singing "Ding Dong, the Witch

is Dead." The group linked arms, sang, read scripture and waited a full
ten minutes before the police finally arrived. As in Baltimore and Catonsville, the media had been notified in advance and were there in force—
television, radio and newspaper reporters. [Meconis 1979:30]

There are remarkable similarities between these sentiments and those
of more recent protesters who demanded to sever all economic ties with
South Africa. A Stanford University student wrote:

> The value of my act of civil disobedience . . . does not hinge upon the
> results which it brings about . . . I was able through my arrest, to make a
> personal statement, relishing my own identity.
>   . . . a picture [in the *Stanford Daily*] . . . captures most effectively my
> sentiments on the civil disobedience experience. In this photograph, I am
> standing upright, strong and defiant . . . my arrest was a liberating experi-
> ence . . . I chose civil disobedience as the best manner in which to express
> myself . . . [Ramming 1985]

These quotes also provide a reminder of the persistence of the spirit
of the 1960s into the 1980s and especially the blending of the preoccupation with the self and matters public-political.

Participation in social protest for white middle-class Americans
(including activist-clerics) was an emotionally rewarding experience
rather than one associated with deprivation, ostracism, or isolation. Defiance of the authorities in the manner pursued by the Berrigans and their
followers rarely led to serious retribution and more often to fame, popularity, supportive publicity, and the admiration of devoted followers.
Therefore, up to a point Daniel Berrigan could plausibly aver that "jail
was the most beautiful experience in the world . . . It's only in prison that
you can place yourself at the edge of mankind's suffering, that your conscience can be absolutely free" [Gray 1970:50].

It may be noted here that the experience of imprisonment may lose
some of its attractions when its circumstances are truly degrading and
when the associated social isolation deprives the protester of supportive
publicity. Under such conditions the protester would find it far more difficult to preserve his sense of dignity and serenity and to rejoice in his
imprisonment as Berrigan did. Neither serious physical deprivations nor
isolation from favorable publicity have been typical conditions of imprisonment for most Americans involved in acts of civil disobedience in
recent decades. Hence participation in the political protests, and the associated (modest) risks, sometimes led to an exalted self-conception bordering on euphoria. Daniel Berrigan actually compared the Catonsville
destruction of draft documents to "Christ's overthrowing the tables of the
moneychangers" [Gray 1970:48]. In those days

He held court for a while, greeting everyone in the casual manner of the
hip college chaplain ... He was dressed in a style reminiscent of the
French worker-priests—a black turtleneck, a beret, an old ski jacket ...
His eyes were kind and knowing; they had the guarded warmth of a mat-
inee idol who knows the power of his seductiveness ... '[Ibid.:46]

Of Philip Berrigan it was observed that ... the greatest joy of this
modest man's life is to flaunt his rigorous conscience in the face of all
institutions" [Gray 1970:74]. In turn a critic of the Berrigans noted that
". . . those who victimize themselves transfigure themselves into new people, into an ethical elite ... The ultimate dividend of such an investment
of religious energies in politics is arrogant self-exaltation ... Self-abase-
ment is indeed a precondition of self-righteousness . . ." [Vree 1975:285–
87].

The attitudes associated with social-political protest sketched here have
endured, as both passionate social criticism and active protest continue
to confer substantial benefits on the participants, including the gift of
heightened self-esteem. The role of social critic has come to play an
important part in the sense of identity of many people, helping them to
occupy the "moral high ground" without, as a rule, substantial injury to
their social position or personal safety. Being a social critic or active protester in the United States has come to offer a combination of idealistic
self-assertion and security, political commitment and group support. The
satisfactions of alerting the seemingly uncaring world to evil and injustice
have not ceased with the 1960s. This is not to deny that some of the
protestors were willing to face risks greater than those which actually
confronted them.

The end of the 70s and the beginning of the 80s found the Berrigans
engaged in the same type of activities they have specialized in during the
protest against the Vietnam war: prostrate on the driveway of the White
House, protesting in New London the launching of nuclear submarines,
smashing nose-cones of missiles in a plant in Pennsylvania. Most recently
Daniel Berrigan was found guilty for contempt of court (for failing to
appear for his arraignment) and for blocking an elevator in a federal
building to protest American military aid to El Salvador ["Chronicle"
1990:30]. Thus there remains an unbroken continuity between the
stands taken—in word and deed—by the Berrigans (and especially Daniel) in the 1960s and 80s.

In a foreword to a volume edited by Jim Wallis, a pastor of the
Sojourners community (a highly politicized, left-of-center Protestant
denomination), ² Daniel Berrigan resumed his apocalyptic discourse sampled before. On this occasion his focus of attention was the law:

. . . We live in an atmosphere in which law and order have become sacred shibboleth, unexamined, self-justifying . . . isolating Americans . . . The government has become a law unto itself . . . The courts have . . . never offered less of justice, equity . . .

The law-abiding and the lawless are one and the same . . .

. . . the law as presently envisoned . . . and administered in America literally and mercilessly descends, crushes all who impede, subverts conscience . . . The law is the omni-Mafia of history . . . [it] crushes the powerless and holds the powerful unaccountable. The law kills—conscience first of all. The law creates and maintains a system of mysery, exclusion and mindless violence . . .

How victimized Americans are, how conned, how lied to . . .

Ahead of us, a vast concrete wasteland; we have no clear sense of future emerging, of relief, intervention or vision . . . Indeed the only future is a more horrid vision of the past: permanent hardened terror. [Berrigan in Wallis, ed. 1987:xiii–xvii]

III

While the activities and attitudes of the Berrigans may have been more extreme and risk-seeking than those of other social critics (clerical or secular), the gulf separating them from the church hierarchy and its policies had significantly narrowed by the beginning of the 1980s. By then the Catholic Church as a whole and its various leaders and orders had gotten increasingly involved in a wide variety of protest activities embracing causes similar to those the Berrigans championed. It has been correctly observed that "The Berrigan tradition, born during the Vietnam War . . . has nourished a new generation of activist-witnesses . . ."[Ferber 1985:10].

The Berrigans' rhetoric also found echo, among others, in the pronouncements of the Archbishop of Seattle, Raymond G. Hunthausen, who called the Trident submarine of the U. S. Navy "the Auschwitz of Puget Sound" [Turner 1982:16; see also "Secretary of Navy Critical" 1982]. Nor were the views (voiced in the more placid 1980s) of George Hunsinger, a theologian at the Bangor Theological Seminary, different from those of the Berrigan brothers in the feverish 60s. Hunsinger reached the conclusion that "today to be an American is to be an executioner or, what is much the same, an accomplice to the executioners" [Hunsinger 1985:18]. Like other impassioned critics preceding him he found little difference between the United States and Nazi Germany and the moral predicament of those failing to protest the evils of each system. Although the idea has been commonplace in the adversary culture ever since the 1960s (often conveyed by the spelling "Amerika"), he claimed,

"That there might be some dark continuity between our society and Nazi Germany is a deeply forbidden thought . . . Unconscionable criminal parallels can exist in a qualitative rather than quantitative sense" [Hunsinger 1985:15]. By proposing that "quality" be the basis of comparing and equating moral outrages Hunsinger breaks new ground for equating altogether different atrocities, making it virtually impossible to make any distinction between them since "quality" is a far more subjective matter than quantity.

As is emphasized throughout this study a hallmark of the critiques of American society developed over the past two decades has been the refusal (or inability) to make distinctions between its shortcomings and those of others, nurtured by the refusal (or inability) to apply the most rudimentary comparative-historical standards. Even when the so-called moral equivalence thesis is ostensibly applied (on the part of these critics) to the United States and its adversaries, in particular the Soviet Union, it soon becomes clear that it is the United States that bears the brunt of the criticism and especially its emotional sting. Hunsinger, as other critics, dismisses this issue quite casually by remarking that ". . . why concentrate on the crimes of others when they are constantly held aloft . . . for all to behold? . . . why protest against crimes one can do almost nothing about instead of against those one might, in concert with others, still do something to rectify?" [Hunsinger 1985:18].

This seemingly pragmatic argument is deeply flawed from both the moral and empirical standpoint. Morally speaking one's attitude toward crimes or injustices should not depend on what one can do to alleviate them, yet Hunsinger is singularly devoid of moral indignation in regard to crimes committed by powers other than the United States (or its perceived allies). Moreover it is simply untrue that little is said in this country about the crimes and flaws of the United States while those of its adversaries "are constantly held aloft." Even more astonishing is the claim for anybody who lived in this country over the past quarter-century that "Atrocities committed by our own side do not meet with our disapproval, and we have developed a remarkable capacity for not hearing about them" [Ibid.:16]. In fact the space and time devoted to the defects of American society—in the mass media, in scholarly writing, in college courses, in sermons and public gatherings of all sorts—has been immense, but apparently no matter how much of it has been produced and disseminated, it remains insufficient in quantity or quality for critics like Hunsinger.

It is also untrue that nothing can be done about the crimes of other systems: pressure can be brought upon them, public protests can be organized, as can boycotts of trade and cultural relations, and so on. Their victims too can be welcome (if and when released). At last there is an interesting contradiction buried in the argument here advanced (i.e., that one should only protest the crimes of the United States because such protests yield results): those fond of this argument are the same critics who on other occasions portray this society as coldly repressive and singularly unresponsive.

Drawing parallels between the American government and Nazi Germany and the moral necessity of taking a stand against both has not been limited to Archbishop Hunthausen and theologian Hunsinger. Evoking Nazism to indict the United States also proved irresistible to many social critics and activists in the 1980s who protested American involvement in Central America and American possession of nuclear weapons. These protestors have been endlessly repeating—as did their predecessors in the 1960s—the cliche' of refusing to be "good Germans," that is, passive, law-abiding, morally uninvolved citizens in the face of massive evil. Antinuclear activists routinely compared the trains carrying nuclear weapons in the American West with the trains carrying the Jews to the gas chambers, and Dachau, a Nazi concentration camp, with American nuclear weapons plants [see for example Douglas and Kellerman in Wallis ed. 1987]. In the 1980s as in the 1960s such rhetorical excesses have served the same two goals: to inflame moral indignation by associating current American policies with those of Nazi Germany and, second, to legitimate civil disobedience, or what amounted to sabotaging the military policies of the country.

Underlying these perceptions we confront not only the unwitting or willful incapacity to differentiate but also the visceral rejection of the American social system and a characteristic exaggeration of American power: the alleged evils and injustices of American society become particularly threatening and morally energizing when associated with vast strength. Jim Wallis believed that "The arms race rushes on as the production of even more dangerous nuclear weapons and increased military spending wipe out remains of already gutted social programs. Military interventionism has become a way of life . . . and the projection of American power . . . has completely superseded any concern for human rights in the conduct of U. S. foreign policy" [Wallis ed. 1987:xxvii]. Another Sojourner, Danny Collum, conjures up similar images of the ominously tilting balance between the forces of good and evil in the United States:

> . . . this is a tough time to be working for social change in these United States . . . all this activity has . . . done little or nothing to slow the juggernauts of war and injustice. We all know the litany of horrors—contra aid, Star Wars, rollback of civil rights for minorities and women, broken obligations to the poor and unemployed . . .

... our corporate elite is trying to recapture ... the ground lost in the 1960s and 1970s to domestic reform and Third World revolution. The battlefields range from Central American villages ... to U.S. day-care centers, union picket lines and the mass media. But they are all part of the same protracted war.

... the people who run America ... are ... sitting astride an empire that requires trade, raw materials, labor and markets across the planet. Protecting that economic reach ... requires a global projection of military power. And the maintenance of a global military capacity ultimately requires that the citizens of the mother country ... be convinced, through a combination of material rewards and cultural conditioning, that the whole imperial enterprise is worth the cost. [Collum in Wallis ed. 1987:3-5]

The reinvigorated social-political activism of the churches found a wide variety of expression. Leroy Matthiesen, a bishop in Texas, urged his parishioners not to work in the local nuclear arms plant and received the support of all twelve bishops of Texas [Marzani 1982:2]. In turn twelve Catholic bishops in the West expressed great displeasure over the production and transportation of nuclear warheads, among them Raymond Hunthausen of Seattle, who did not miss the opportunity to "compare the trains that move nuclear weapons ... to the trains to the Nazi death camps" [Lindsey 1984]. The bishops "urged direct action to impede deploying nuclear weapons ..." [Ibid.]. The bishops also went on record opposing a space-based defense against missiles [Steinfels 1988], and they had earlier expressed grave doubts about the morality of nuclear deterrence in general [e.g., Chira 1983]. A "major religious coalition" went even further in opposing not only nuclear weapons but also nuclear power plants ["Church Coalition Assails Utility Power Ads" 1984]. The anti-nuclear stand taken by the Catholic bishops was heartily endorsed by Marcus Raskin [Raskin 1983].

The Maryknoll order in particular remained in the forefront of political activism, its support of liberation theology a cornerstone of its policies in the Third World and proudly counting among its priests Miguel d'Escoto, foreign minister of Marxist-Leninist Nicaragua. A spokesman for the order averred that "Maryknoll's involvement with poor and oppressed peoples in the third world has indeed politicized us... But we engage for moral reasons, not for partisan interests ..." [Briggs 1984; see also Roelofsma 1986].

The stands taken by the Catholic bishops in their pastoral letter on the American economy further reflected these social-critical trends and especially an aversion to capitalism. As a critic put it, ". . . from the beginning a suggestion has been planted that there is something basically wrong with *our* economic arrangements . . ." [Berger 1985:32]. The bishops took a social-deterministic position toward poverty and inequality in the United States, making reference to "our punitive attitude toward the poor" and the necessity to "struggle with our own selfishness." They also proposed a "global affirmative action," "to restructure the international order along the lines of greater equity" ["Excerpts from Draft of Bishops' Letter" 1984; see also "Excerpts from Final Draft" 1986]. Among the sources consulted for the 1984 Draft has been *Global Reach*, a leading anticapitalist text by Richard Barnett and Ronald Muller.

It should be noted here that the social criticism of the churches, and their anticapitalism in particular, was highly congenial with the secular branches of the adversary culture. In particular the growing preoccupation with and aversion toward the multinational corporations was shared in equal measure by the National Council of Churches (see below) and organizations such as the Institute for Policy Studies and the Interfaith Center on Corporate Responsibility, which claimed to represent 17 Protestant denominations and 170 Catholic orders and dioceses [see for example Nickel 1980].

The gradual movement of the Catholic Church toward social-political activism (of the left-wing variety) may be attributed to the factors mentioned earlier which account for similar trends among other denominations as well. They include above all the desire to find causes which would revitalize organized religion and extend its popular appeal. This approach has been especially tempting to the Catholic Church since its doctrinal base is more forbidding and less apt to attract popular enthusiasm than is the case in the mainline Protestant churches:

> In the end the modern Church is faced with an almost insuperable dilemma. The fact is that its traditional teaching on sexual matters, and indeed on much of private life, retains little popular appeal. Inevitably it is the "social Gospel" that proves most resonant for modern Catholics. . . . it is the message of justice and peace that electrifies . . . For many Catholics today, religious feeling has been redefined in political terms . . . the old preoccupation with scrupulous personal virtue has been replaced by a generalized sense of good intentions and series of impeccably "virtuous" stances on public issues. Otherworldliness has given way to utopianism; as a result, the spiritual has come to be understood by many as something in opposition not so much to the profane world as a whole as to the established political order. [Glynn 1983:14, 13, 11]

Thus, it is not so surprising that, as Patrick Glynn further observed,

... to speak on such matters as birth control and priestly celibacy has been to risk a torrent of abuse. In the attempt to gain the ear of the clergy and laity alike, it has proved infinitely more gratifying and productive to turn to political themes.

... Clergy at all levels have been galvanized by the antinuclear theme ... [Correspondingly] the Church bureaucracy devoted to the promotion of peace and justice has dramatically expanded ... Over the last ten years 90% of the nation's Catholic religious orders and 60 percent of its 173 dioceses and archdioceses have established "peace and justice commissions" of their own ... it has become routine for a Catholic diocese to take public stands and even lobby on a whole range of domestic and foreign policy issues ... The more active diocesan commissions employ full-time activists ... as the Church awakened to its new political role, enormous institutional power fell into the hands of these well-meaning but other-worldly sisters and priests. [Ibid.:12, 13]

Such policies and trends in the Church led at least one observer to suggest that the Catholic Church has globally moved toward becoming "an ally of the Left" and that conventional Marxist wisdom about religion (as buttressing the forces of reaction) needs revision in the light of both such developments and a reinterpretation of Marxism itself. Carl Marzani quoted approvingly the late Palmiro Togliatti (former head of the Italian Communist party), who said: "We must understand that deep desire for a socialist society not only can exist in those of religious faith but may be stimulated by a tormented religious conscience confronting the stark problems of the contemporary world" [Quoted in Marzani 1982:15].

Indeed a tormented, or at least mildly tormented, religious conscience seems to underlie some of the stands taken by the churches in the United States and has much in common with its secular versions found in the adversary culture. A free-floating sense of guilt appears to motivate many of those who lash out against their society, a guilt readily transformed into avowals of collective guilt (discussed earlier) and deployed as a tool of social criticism.

While the Catholic Church moved into the arena of political activism more recently (in the United States at any rate) the "mainline" Protestant churches had a longer and more consistent record of involvement in such matters. William Sloane Coffin, Jr., who was senior minister at the Riverside Church in New York City during much of the 1980s, played in the Protestant context a role somewhat analogous to that of the Berrigans—except for having a lesser appetite for melodramatic acts of civil disobedience than they had. Coffin rose to prominence during the Vietnam era and became a leader of the antiwar movement when he was chaplain at Yale University. Like Daniel Berrigan he too visited North

Vietnam during the war and returned with glowing accounts of the humaneness of that system and its leaders. With the fading appeals of the victorious North Vietnamese regime his political affections were transferred to a more colorful revolutionary country closer to home:—Nicaragua—and to the causes of disarmament and the subjugation of the Third World by multinational corporations. Already in 1978, well before the groundswell of opposition to nuclear arms had arisen in the United States, he was in the forefront of a program called "Reverse the Arms Race" (which was also supported by Cora Weiss, another prominent former antiwar activist, also active in the Riverside Church and presiding over the foundation financing the Institute for Policy Studies).

At a conference organized in late 1978 Coffin said that "The Pentagon has become just like the Rev. Jim Jones," and asked: "Who should refuse the civil-defense drills, who should refuse the giant vat of Pentagon poison, more than the religious community?" [Vecsey 1978].

A few years later at another conference he proposed: "We need to save our people from the self-serving delusions of a superpower," referring to the United States. On that occasion he and other speakers called for "more socially activist preaching" which "should address the ills of society in the uncompromising terms of the Old Testament prophets" [Austin 1982]. He was described by a reporter as "An activist preacher . . . less likely to rail against personal immorality and more apt to denounce economic and social systems that oppress the poor" [Ibid.].

Coffin was also an enthusiastic advocate of the moral equvalence thesis:

> In repentance lies our hope . . . Were we Americans to repent of the self-righteousness . . . we would realize that if we are not yet one with the Soviets in love, at least we are one with them in sin . . . Were we to repent of our self-righteousness, the existence of Soviet missiles would remind us of nothing so much as our own; Soviet threats to rebellious Poles would call to mind American threats to the Sandinistas; Afghanistan would suggest Vietnam. Soviet repression of civil liberties at home would remind us of our own complicity in the repression of these same civil rights abroad . . . Jesus would never be "soft on communism" any more than he would be soft on capitalism. [Coffin 1985:32]

In his latest incarnation as president of SANE/FREEZE, a major disarmament organization, he proclaimed his goal "a warless world" and he linked the underfunding of vital social programs to capitalism. "'I watched deterioriation of everything not connected with profit-making' [between 1977 and 1987 while living in New York] . . . Schools, monuments and services suffered, he said, in an effort to make the rich richer"

[Munoz 1988]. He quoted with approval John Kenneth Galbraith (the well-known secular social critic, professor at Harvard, and former Ambassador to India), who termed this a "heartless society," and the playwright Eugene O'Neill, who considered the United States "the greatest failure" in the world [Coffin 1985:83].

Two other new causes emerged in the 1980s claiming the attention of socially conscious clergy: the sanctuary movement and AIDS victims.

The sanctuary movement sought to provide assistance to illegal aliens from El Salvador and Guatemala viewed as economic refugees by the U. S. government but favored by the organizers of the sanctuary movement as victims of the political systems they regarded as right-wing allies of the United States. It was a movement mixing charitable-humane and political-ideological objectives and utilizing the moral appeals of its charitable goals to legitimate its political agenda. In championing these particular groups of refugees the movement also sought to indict American foreign policy and the governments of El Salvador and Guatemala. A major sanctuary coordinating organization, the Chicago Religious Task Force on Central America, made clear in a 1984 position paper that the sanctuary movement is worthless unless it also becomes an opponent of U.S. foreign policy in Central America ["The Sanctuary Movement: A Time for Reappraisal" 1985]. Coincidentally organizers of the movement have been sympathetic toward and supportive of the Marxist guerillas in El Salvador and the Marxist-Leninist government in Nicaragua. The sanctuary movement showed no interest in or sympathy toward refugees from Marxist systems such as Nicaragua or Cuba: "Oscar Herreras, Director of Father Moriarty Refugee Program in San Francisco, doesn't consider Nicaraguans to be political refugees. 'They are not leaving because they are persecuted. You don't find arbitrary arrests and executions in Nicaragua'" [Brock 1986:20].

Coffin too was a supporter of the sanctuary movement and stressed its political aspects: "The sanctuary movement can no longer separate foreign policy and domestic policy. We must change the former through the latter. A successful revolution in Central America would . . . cast a few hopeful rays in our direction" [Ibid.]. The point is not peculiar to Coffin; a Maryknoll publication on the sanctuary movement expressed the same hope: "What the refugees have brought to North America is a liberation gift—they brought us revolutionary hope" [Golden and McConnell 1986:195].

AIDS was another new concern for some of the churches in the 1980s (as it was for other groups more directly associated with the adversary culture). While it was in large measure a charitable preoccupation, the selection of this particular group of victims was not without social-political significance. The churches (and many other secular groups concerned with AIDS) never campaigned with the same fervor (if at all) against, say, lung cancer or coronary heart disease and other crippling and lethal illnesses unrelated to matters of sexual morality. Nobody made quilts celebrating victims of muscular dystrophy or leukemia, but there have been quilts listing and commemorating AIDS victims [see for example "AIDS Quilt to Visit Amherst" 1990]. The latter were characteristically perceived as "victims" not merely of physiological processes but of human ill will and faulty social arrangements.

At a conference of clerics, "Several of the clergymen [among them Paul Moore, Jr., the politically active Episcopal bishop of New York] compared those who work with AIDS victims to figures in Christian history" [Goldman 1985]. A review of official statements on AIDS by 45 different religious groups concluded that there was "'remarkable consensus' uniting Catholics, Protestants and Jews"; "most of the statements stressed compassion over judgement"; special ministries to serve AIDS victims were also proposed [Steinfels 1989].

As is often the case with other self-appointed advocates of victims, those supporting AIDS patients almost invariably embraced some form of social criticism; the victim irresistibly drew attention to the victimizer. But who could be blamed for AIDS, who could be held responsible? (other than those persisting in particular sexual practices or drug habits—but that would be a judgmental attitude, "blaming the victim," a forbidden notion since the early 1970s when a book of the same title appeared [Ryan 1971]). It was not as easy to locate societal responsibility for AIDS as, say, for racism or sexism. But the impulse to do so was there: society could be implicated for not providing sufficient resources to devise cures for the illness; in turn such (alleged) reluctance could be linked to homophobia since homosexuals were among the prime victims of the disease. To a lesser extent racism could also be invoked since the other major group affected were intravenous drug users, often black. But another reason for the surge of sympathy toward AIDS victims (among liberal and adversarial groups) was that by virtue of their sexual preferences and practices they constituted a deviant, underdog group defying conventional standards of (heterosexual) morality. For this reason they could also count on support from feminists favoring alternative sexual standards and practices. Supporting AIDS victims and fund-raising activities on their behalf became especially popular not only among clerics but also among Hollywood celebrities.

The churches' attitude toward AIDS victims can be better understood when compared with stands taken earlier toward criminals and criminal justice. It is an attitude that reminds one of the concept of "conspicuous compassion" introduced by George Will. He characterized it as one "flaunted by people too exquisitely evenhanded to 'single out' the raped from the rapist. It is the moral ostentation of people so delicately sensitive that they will not discriminate . . . between the wielder of the hammer and the one whose skull was hammered" [King 1990]. In a policy statement in 1979 the National Council of Churches (NCC) proposed that "law itself is unjust and the 'criminal justice system' is poisoned at its source" [Isaac and Isaac 1981:10]. The statement firmly embraced the kind of social determinism widely held by critics of American society and essential for its indictment. But as is often the case such social determinism was selective: opposition to imprisonment of street criminals could be reconciled with demands for stern penalties for corporation executives guilty of white-collar crimes. This double standard was once more linked to a particular notion of victim and victimizer, derived from the extreme and selective social determinism noted above.

Thus the NCC president at the time, the Reverend M. William Howard, derided the notion that we do not have political prisoners and pointed out that ". . . much of our prison population is comprised of people who are victims of the social, economic and political structures of our society" [Ibid.]. This outlook also helped to define those suffering of AIDS as victims of an uncaring society, penalized for their unconventional sexual practices.

By the end of the 1980s many of the policies of the NCC have become more controversial and its leaders recognized that the unmoderated pursuit of its social-political agenda would alienate some member churches and reduce the number of supporters and funding. However, the "restructuring" proposed has not been substantial [Goldman 1988; "NCC Shaken by Crisis" 1989]. Nor has been there any indication, as of early 1990, that the NCC has confronted and learned from the issues raised by the collapse of communist systems around the world and their turning to market economies and political pluralism ["The Churches and the Cold War" 1990].

Even if the power of the NCC declined and if members of congregations have been deserting the mainline churches their influence is not to be underrated. As Clark Roof pointed out,

> Liberal Protestantism's *cultural* influence is greater than its lack of religious vitality suggests . . . Persons within this tradition are disproportionally represented among the nation's civic and corporate elite . . . Politically the power of liberal Protestants continues to be fairly strong despite the gradual erosion of WASP influence throughout this century: all three reli-

gious groups [Episcopal, Presbyterian, and United Church of Christ—
P.H.] have far more members in the U.S. Senate and House of Representatives than would be expected based on their aggregate sizes . . . the old-
line liberal Protestant community accounts for slightly less than 10% of
the American population. [Roof 1987:87; my emphasis]

On the other hand it has also been argued by Jay Demerath that the
churches themselves are "undergoing marginalization . . . [that] the civil
rights movement of the 1960s represented the last concerted effort of
social activism on the part of American religion. Since then we have seen
a steady process of differentiation and fragmentation, which has, on the
one hand led the prophetic few to be more desperately strident, while on
the other hand, reduced their political effectiveness"[Demerath 1990].

These remarks are also given indirect support by a recent report
dwelling on the difficulties liberal churches have encountered seeking to
maintain ministries in the inner city catering to the needs of poor ethnic
groups. For an increasing number of newly graduated seminary students
these positions have become unattractive both for economic reasons and
due to the lack of personal safety in these neighborhoods. Those left are
increasingly "women and gay men. Most have been influenced by Liberation Theology . . ." A black minister in New York also criticized these
programs: "'The mainline denominations see these inner-city churches
as outlets for missions, not places where black or Hispanic people become
empowered . . .These churches get funds from outside. They serve the
function of assuaging the guilt of white Christians in the suburbs who
support them'"All these circumstances led to the conclusion that "for
mainline Protestantism, the inner city grows remote" [Hedges 1990].

IV

Numerous examples have been given above of the social criticism and
social-political activism of the clergy. There is also substantial evidence
to show that the examples provided and the attitudes discussed were not
isolated or atypical during the past quarter-century and had a clear institutional focus and origin. A sympathetic study from the late sixties provides important clues to this phenomenon in its finding that

Many of the high-status and high-quality seminaries in America have long
traditions as centers of liberal theology and progressive political thought.
Thus higher-status churches in seeking out clergy who have the credentials of the higher-status educational institutions are systematically hiring
men who are politically more liberal than the constituency of the congregation. [Hadden 1969:85]

A similar pattern was found in the Presbyterian church whose staff "... who run the boards, offices and agencies ... tend consistently to occupy positions on the political spectrum that are decidedly to the left. Only 20% of church members support the Sanctuary movement for example, while 76% of the clergy employed in the denomination's boards and offices support the movement" [Duggan 1986:11].

The political orientation of the clergy emerging (or crystallizing) in the 60s was thus summed up in the conclusion of Hadden's study: "Clergy have come to see the church as an institution for challenging man to new hopes and new visions of a better world ... the seminaries are producing an increasing proportion of clergy who are committed to a challenge-oriented ministry ..." [Hadden 1969:85, 206–7].

More recent survey data provide abundant indications of the spread and institutionalization of such a "challenge oriented ministry" and the specifics of "new visions of a better world." Conducted by the Roper Center at the University of Connecticut in the early 1980s, the survey explored the moral, religious, and political attitudes and opinions of 2000 randomly selected professors in the major Christian theology schools and seminaries, 57% of whom responded.

Asked to indicate "If an individual could consistently be a good member of your denomination and at the same time adhere to these positions," 36% thought this would apply to Marxism but 53% of those with incomes over $50,000 (the highest category used in the survey) felt that there was no conflict between Marxism and their religious beliefs.

In a question asked to describe general political inclinations, 14% of the respondents chose "very liberal" and 34% "somewhat liberal," but among those with incomes over $50,000 26% professed to be "very liberal" and 40% "somewhat liberal," whereas in the same (highest) income group only 2% were "very conservative" and 7% "somewhat conservative"! In the 1972 presidential elections 56% voted for McGovern but among those with an income over $50,000, 76% did so. On almost every issue those with the highest income were the furthest to the left - yet another indication, if more is needed, that radical social criticism and political belief do not derive from economic insecurity, as was once believed.

Some 74% of the total sample regarded U.S. defense expenditures as excessive and 68% favored reducing such expenditures. Of the respondents, 45% disagreed with the proposition that "economic growth is a better way to improve the lot of the poor than redistributing existing wealth," and 37% agreed that "The U.S. would be better off if it moved toward socialism" (45% of those with incomes over $50,000 agreed).

Over half, or 57% favored reducing the sale of arms and military assistance to countries which are opposed to communism. Some 71% found the nuclear bombing of Hiroshima morally unjustified, and 35% believed that if the Soviet Union launched a full-scale nuclear attack on the U.S. "the moral course would be . . . to do nothing."

Of all respondents, 32% believed that the (American) private business system, the federal system, and the judicial system each was in need of "major amendment"; 45% believed that the American political ideology and distribution of power were in need of "major amendment," and 43% felt the same way about the distribution of income.

In response to the question "Do you think the United States is in general a force for good or ill in the world?" 18% thought it was a force for ill and 25% were "neutral." But of those with incomes over $50,000, 25% felt it was a force for ill and 30% were neutral. A more informal survey conducted by Richard Neuhaus on the same issue produced similar results. He wrote:

> In admittedly unscientific research I have asked scores of mainline Protestant leaders what the response would be if a certain question were put to the middle and upper management at 475 Riverside Drive [headquarters of the National Council of Churches] and at various denominational headquarters. The question is this: On balance, and considering the alternatives, is America a force for good in this world? . . . no more than 10 to 15 per cent of mainline leadership would readily answer that question in the affirmative. The great majority either would add so many equivocations as to make their answer tantamount to negative, or would baldly state that America is a force for evil. [Neuhaus in Griffith ed. 1981:13]

As to the conflict between the U.S. and the Soviet Union, for 80% (in the Roper survey cited above) it was "fundamentally a struggle in power politics" and only for 20% was it a "moral struggle."

Some 70% believed that multinational corporations hurt the poor countries of the Third World and the same number believed that "as a nation we generally treat people of the Third World unfairly." There was a 50-50 split regarding the question: "Which is the greater problem in the world today: repressive regimes aligned with the U.S. or Communist expansion?" but among those with incomes over $50,000 only 37% believed that communist regimes were the greater problem [Theology Faculty Survey 1983:32, 36, 37, 39, 40–44, 46, 48, 49].

These figures gain added significance when compared with the attitudes of the general public. Thus for example while 50% of the theology faculties subscribed to some degree of liberalism only 21% of the general public did so; 74% of the theologians found expenditures on defense excessive but only 29% of the general public did so.

But compared with other (secular) faculties the similarities were more pronounced: for example, of all faculty, 41% identified themselves as liberal versus 49% of those teaching religion and theology; 4% as "left" among the general faculty and 7% among the latter group [Ibid.: 68, 69, 70].

Summarizing the findings of the survey (cited above), Ladd and Ferree, who designed it, wrote:

> Those who teach candidates for the clergy and other religious vocations in the United States are distinguished by a general socio-political "liberalism" in the everyday American usage of that term . . . They are . . . social critics—believing that the central political institutions and values of the society need revision . . . They are notably critical of the United States' role in world affairs and they are troubled by what they believe to be an undue emphasis on the military . . .[Ibid.:80–81]

Michael Novak drew the conclusion from these findings that "the relationship between their religion and their politics seems to flow less from their theology than from their academic surroundings since the profile of their political views closely matches the profile of professors of the humanities and social sciences . . . [Moreover] The survey makes clear that professors in theological schools are an elite in terms of education, income and status . . . a substantial minority [of them] is nonetheless adversarial to the system" [Novak 1982:101].

One more study may be cited here that lends further support to the findings discussed above and also highlights the differences between Catholics and mainline Protestants on the one hand and fundamentalists on the other. It was a survey of the attitudes and beliefs of 178 religious leaders of Christian denominations based on a reputational sample.

Some 59% of the Catholic and 80% of the mainline Protestant leaders considered themselves liberals in politics (as against only 13% of the fundamentalists); 31% of the Catholics and 25% of the mainline Protestants (Protestants below) believed that the United States should move toward socialism (as against only 4% of the fundamentalists). Slightly more Catholics than Protestants, 44% versus 41%, were of the opinion that the social structure of the United States alienates its citizens; 39% of the Catholics and 51% of the Protestants believed that basic institutions of American society need to be overhauled. Some 77% of the Catholics and 68% of the Protestants believed that the poor are poor because of circumstances beyond their control; 81% of the Catholics and 83% of the Protestants favor government intervention to reduce the income gap between poor and rich.

Almost two-thirds of these two groups favored affirmative action in hiring blacks. Close to half of the Catholics and two-thirds of Protestants believed that nuclear plants are unsafe. The authors of the study also concluded that "Many Catholics and Mainliners . . . believe that national security is an unimportant national goal."

Indicative of their interest in political power, "When asked whom they think *should* have the most influence in America, religious leaders, regardless of faith, believe that they should be the top leadership group . . ." [Lerner and Rothman 1988:9, 11, 12, 13, 16, 17, 24, 25].

Why do many clergymen, including teachers of theology and church leaders, share the social-critical disposition widespread among the secular intellectuals of the adversary culture? Part of the answer is suggested by Novak and the findings of the survey cited: the theologians at any rate are influenced by and associated with a broader, campus-based adversary culture. What of the rest of the clergy, parish priests and ministers in particular? Many of them are doubtless influenced by the messages emanating from higher levels of church hierarchy: the NCC, the Catholic bishops; they are also bound to reflect in some measure the teachings they were exposed to at their seminaries in the course of their training.

Generally speaking it is plausible that the adversarial attitudes of the clergy (even more than those of secular intellectuals) originate in a peculiar idealism and in an idiosyncratic, selective designation of and identification with the "underdog." Even the most cynical among us cannot dispute that the clerical role attracts those with an idealistic disposition which in an increasingly secular age comes to be channeled into a social-political direction. Perhaps it is easier to move from concern with religious salvation to worldly salvation (or from religious to secular utopia-seeking) than to embrace such high expectations without a religious background. The affinity of clerics toward secular religious ideologies (socialism, liberation theology) reflects these tendencies and their historical roots.

James V. Schall traced these attitudes to "The Enlightenment effort to domesticate and secularize Christian salvation history [which] was revived by men of our century" [Schall in Griffith ed. 1981:25]. When all is said and done Marxist socialism is the only major contemporary ideology in the West that has such a salvationist or millenarian component. To be sure it remains to be explained how—in view of the monumental and destructive failures of that ideology and of the efforts to implement it—clerics could continue to be drawn toward it. Perhaps, as again Schall put it, it is "the weakness of practical judgement against actual historical experience, the curious tendency of ostensibly pious Christians to allow the real Marxists to take power with religious blessings" [Ibid.:33].

In the final analysis the alienation of clerics has not only similar manifestations but also similar sources to that of other elite groups in American society (i.e., academic and literary intellectuals, media people, public interest lawyers, welfare officials, and so on). To the extent that there is a persuasive general explanation of these broader trends among American elite groups we will also better understand the attitudes and positions discussed in this chapter.

V

The steady critique of American social institutions and domestic policies undertaken by the liberal churches was closely paralleled by a corresponding critique of American policies abroad. These churches developed a foreign policy of their own, generally at odds with that of the administration in Washington but in broad agreement with the secular critics of American society. While it is tempting to characterize this policy as isolationist, on closer inspection it turns out to be a blend of selective isolationism and interventionism.

On the one hand these critics are opposed to American intervention against political systems which call themselves socialist such as Grenada, Cuba, Nicaragua, or Angola and also vehemently object to support for anticommunist guerilla movements seeking to weaken or overthrow such systems. (They also disapproved of the overthrow of Manuel Noriega in Panama not because he headed a putatively socialist government but because it was—in the eyes of the critics—a display of naked American power in a small Central American country.) The same logic compels these groups to lobby against assistance to several countries friendly to the United States and strongly anticommunist in their domestic policies. Thus the liberal churches have been in favor of cutting off all assistance to countries such as El Salvador, Guatemala, South Korea, and the Philippines under Marcos.

In 1981 the National Conference of Catholic Bishops urged the U.S. administration to end all military assistance to El Salvador. Bishop Hurley said, "We do not believe in a military solution" [Briggs 1981; see also Briggs 1982], seemingly unaware that the communist guerillas and their suppliers did not share his point of view. Church leaders including the Rev. William Sloane Coffin, Jr., were also among a group of 75 lobbying Congress to end all military aid to El Salvador, Guatemala, and the anticommunist guerillas in Nicaragua [Herbut 1983]. Not surprisingly the American Friends Service Committee (AFSC) took the same position, its representative Philip Berryman testifying before a House Subcommittee against military assistance to El Salvador [Lewy 1988:157]. According to the *Washington Post* the churches' influence over the legislative process also found expression in the responsivess of the then speaker of the

House, Thomas P. O'Neill, to the views of Maryknoll missionaries ada-
mantly opposed to American military assistance to anticommunist guerillas and sympathetic to the left-wing governments and movement in
Central America [Shapiro 1985; for a further discussion of the political
sympathies and activities of the Maryknoll order or the Catholic Foreign
Mission Society, see Frawley 1983]. *The Nation* credited church activists
with persuading the Congress to vote down Reagan's request for military
aid to the contras [Ferber 1985:10].

While some of the countries the churches wished to disarm have been
undemocratic, their varying degrees of authoritarianism do not explain
the churches' hostility toward them since, as will be shown below, the
same churches have shown great warmth toward and understanding of
authoritarian systems on the left—hence authoritarianism *per se* cannot
be the mainspring of their critiques.

South Africa has been a special case attracting the greatest hostility
on the part of the churches and eliciting the most far-reaching demands
for intervention, if not by force of arms, by economic blockades and boycotts. Church groups have also been supportive of the African National
Congress guerillas seeking to destroy the system by force. In fact "the
National Council of Churches [NCC] has endorsed the 'Harare Declaration' which calls upon churches to support liberation struggles in South
Africa. In Executive Committee debate the objection was raised that the
Harare document was 'a blanket endorsement of any group that purports
to act on behalf of liberation' and it was urged that NCC declare itself in
favor of 'nonviolent' change. That amendment lost . . ." ["The NCC on
South Africa" 1986; on church support of the African National Congress
and other guerilla movements see also Isaac and Isaac 1981]. There was
certainly truth to the observation that these churches were among those
for whom the word "liberation" (and, one might add, "national liberation
movements" was a "Pavlovian stimulus" [Minogue 1990:5].

According to the *Washington Post* American missionaries in the Philippines have also been supportive of the communist guerilas (the
National Democratic Front) in that country and opposed military aid not
only to the Marcos government but also to that of its democratic succes-
sor, Corazon Aquino. Their campaign against such assistance was conveyed in a letter sent to over 1000 churches in this country and other
lobbying efforts based in Washington, D.C. [Branigin 1986].

In 1983 the *60 Minutes* news program aired a segment by Morley
Safer reporting on the support the NCC has given to left-wing causes
around the world, including pro-Cuban and pro-Soviet guerila movements. The Episcopal Church too was subsidizing Third World liberation
movements as well as Puerto Rican nationalists not averse to violence
[Seabury 1978:2]. The Methodist Church was funding the Palestine Lib-

eration Organization through its support groups in this country including the Palestine Solidarity Committee and the Middle East Resource Center reportedly directed by Sheila Ryan, a former member of the Weather Underground [Isaac and Isaac 1981:9]. Likewise the Quakers and the AFSC have a long record of unwavering support for the PLO, hardly a pacifist group. At an AFSC conference on Israel and the Palestinians it was proposed to erase "stereotypes" which suggest that the PLO is tied to terrorism [Maurer 1977:39]. Championing the PLO also afforded new opportunities for applying the moral equivalence approach, as I.F. Stone compared the mistreatment of Arabs by Israel to that of the Jews by Nazi Germany [Maurer 1979:12].

Another pro-Western and increasingly democratic society that inspired the hostility of numerous American churches and in particular the NCC has been South Korea. It has apparently earned this animosity by combining a vigorous capitalist economy with strong anticommunist policies and close military ties with the United States. South Korea is one of the few countries where large numbers of American troops have been stationed for decades (whose presence helps to protect it from North Korean attack). It may have been the presence of these troops and their symbolic identification with American assertion of military power that contributed to the concerns of these churches. As is often the case the dependence of a country on American military assistance made it possible to combine the denunciation of that country with that of American foreign policy. Thus a statement of the NCC proclaimed:

> We are deeply conscious of the roles our nation's government, and military and economic interests, have played in creating, maintaining and deepening divisions of Korea. . . . The churches too have much to confess. Korea has suffered from the uncritical acceptance by many in our churches and nation of the virulent anti-communism which gripped our society hard in the 1950s and has kept it in its grasp to varying degrees ever since. [NCC Policy Statement 1988:5]

In the same spirit the General Assembly of the Presbyterian Church adopted a resolution in 1986 on "Reconciliation and Reunification in Korea." The Assembly also offered "prayers of repentance for the complicity of our nation . . . in helping to create and perpetuate the tragic division and conflict that beset the people of Korea" [Ibid.:6].

The churches' treatment of South and North Korea have been classic examples of the skewed moral equivalence approach (and its combination with double standards) otherwise most prominent in discussions of Soviet-American relations and comparisons but also present whenever communist and anticommunist systems are compared. It carried little weight in these comparisons that North Korea has remained one of the few steadfastly Stalinist systems dominated by a dictator surrounded by a grotesque personality cult and one that virtually obliterated organized religion, whereas South Koreans enjoyed religious freedom, growing political pluralism, and rapidly rising living standards. Particularly noteworthy is that religious freedom in the South earned no moral credits whatsoever while religious repression in the North failed to elicit any discernible moral indignation on the part of these churches. In their eyes the South was irremediably tainted by its anticommunism, capitalism, and association with the United States, while the North was free of such stigma.

More than being just engaged in projections of moral equivalence the NCC combined a barrage of no-holds-barred criticism of South Korea with urging the U.S. government "to refrain from hostile and inflammatory rhetoric about the Democratic People's Republic of Korea," that is, North Korea [Ibid.:5].

Another memorable example of how the moral equivalence premise can be turned into criticism of the United States was provided by the Rev. William Sloane Coffin, Jr., quoted earlier. In a speech on disarmament at Smith College (in Northampton, Massachusetts) the Reverend Coffin said that "Can you trust the Russians?" is not the point . . . The point is, he said, "can you trust the State Department, the CIA, the Defense Department, the scientists?" [Munoz 1988]. A critic of such attitudes aptly observed that "Many of the 'peace' people who tell us we can trust the humane instincts of the Soviets also tell us that our own leaders are dangerous fanatics" [Hitchcock 1983].

The Catholic Church too was susceptible to the moral equivalence approach, as was most clearly indicated by the 1988 Papal Encyclical "The Social Concerns of the Church." In it the Pope spoke of

> . . . the *existence of two opposing blocs*, commonly known as the East and the West . . .
>
> In the West there exists a system which is historically inspired by the principles of *liberal capitalism* . . . In the East there exists a system inspired by *Marxist collectivism* . . .
>
> It was inevitable that by developing antagonistic systems and centers of power, each with its own forms of propaganda and indoctrination, the *ideological opposition* should evolve into growing *military opposition* and give rise to two blocs of armed forces, each suspicious and fearful of the other's domination.
>
> . . . the Church's social doctrine adopts a critical attitude toward both liberal capitalism and Marxist collectivism.

... Each of the two *blocs* harbors in its own way a tendency toward *imperialism* ... or towards forms of neo-colonialism ... [Myers ed. 1988:22–24]

The moral equivalence approach in foreign policy embraced by the liberal churches colors the position taken on the American role in world affairs. It also nurtures unilateralism in disarmament and a benefit-of-doubt attitude toward the Soviet Union. "Moral equivalence" is also relevant to policies in the Third World insofar as it tends to conceal a belief in the moral inferiority and guilt of the United States especially in its alleged role as exploiter of poor countries, bulwark of capitalism, and home of the multinationals.

The one-sided determinism associated with dependency theory (and liberation theology) blames not only poverty but even the political repression and human rights violations in the Third World on "the rich countries." Thus Juan Luis Segundo, a theologian, said that

> in principle he was in agreement with the military of his own country, Uruguay, in their rejection of foreign criticism of their human rights abuses ... Segundo asserted that the root of human rights violations was to be found in the impossible conditions laid on Third World countries by the rich countries ... Hence it was hypocritical for those countries to ... criticize the regimes that carried out the repression. [Berryman 1987:117]

"Dependency theory" represents a revitalized version of Marxism that assigns the role of the proletariat to the poor nations of the world, defined as helpless, victimized, dependent entities whose well-being (or, rather, misery) depends entirely on the capitalist countries and the United States in particular. Liberation theology is similarly infused with strong anticapitalist impulses and concern with the welfare of the poor in the Third World and especially Latin America, where it has been most popular.

According to one of its best-known American interpreters, Phillip Berryman (an AFSC expert on Latin America), "liberation theology is an interpretation of Christian faith out of the experience of the poor ..." or "1. An interpretation of Christian faith out of the suffering, struggle, and hope of the poor. 2. A critique of society and the ideologies sustaining it. 3. A critique of the activity of the church and of Christians from the angle of the poor". [Berryman 1987:4, 6].

But liberation theology is more than a theory; it also seeks to be a guide to action aimed at changing society, the distribution of wealth and power. This makes it especially appealing to intellectuals, in or outside the church. Berryman explains further:

Liberation theologians are intellectuals. They produce a steady output of books and articles and take part in conferences. What makes their enterprise different from most academic theology, and from the usual role of the intellectual, however, is the connection to grass-roots work and popular movements. [Berryman 1987:81]

It is the latter aspect of liberation theology that leads its adherents to the support of movements and systems which are guided by some version of Marxism-Leninism. As I have shown elsewhere [Hollander 1981] a major appeal of Marxist-Leninist political systems and their leaders for Western intellectuals has always been that these systems supposedly united theory and practice, that their leaders were not cut off from the masses but were steadily uplifting them, raising their level of consciousness—another major tenet of liberation theology (concientization).

Dependency theory and liberation theology come together in blaming capitalism and the United States in particular for the poverty of underdeveloped countries. As summarized in the Medellin document of 1968, Episcopal bishops of Latin America averred that ". . . the principal guilt for the economic dependence of our countries rests with . . . foreign powers inspired by uncontrolled desire for gain."

Liberation theology has particular appeals for American clerics predisposed to hold the United States responsible for the ills of the world, since it explicitly designates the United States as the main enemy of progress and liberation [see for example Novak 1984:84, 51]. Liberation theology also re-emphasizes the commitment of the church to the poor and hence makes its upholders susceptible to the appeals of political systems which espouse egalitarian policies and claim to make the uplifting of the poor their major goal. As will be seen below, those who find this theology congenial are, as a rule, sympathetic to political systems such as those prevailing in Nicaragua and Cuba and movements such as those of the Marxist guerillas in El Salvador.

Not only has liberation theology found favor with those critically disposed toward American society and U.S. foreign policy, its attractions are enhanced by providing religious sanction and legitimation for political objectives and agendas. Liberation theology also struck a responsive chord in all those who have been seeking to reconcile Marxism and Christianity or obscure the conflict between them.

Anticapitalism and antimilitarism are closely linked in the churches' outlook on global affairs and their policy recommendations. The spokesmen of the churches here discussed appear to believe unhesitatingly that the causes of war can be traced to capitalism and its ruthless pursuit of profit at the expense of all other values.

The antimilitarist rhetoric of the churches and religious groups has been given durable legitimation by the bitter lessons of the Vietnam war, regularly invoked by the churches in their antimilitarist crusade. In turn antimilitarism finds receptive audiences in a peaceful and consumption-oriented society susceptible to the argument that military expenditures are wasteful except in times when politicians can persuade the public of some imminent and tangible threat. Thus religious groups can at one stroke protest both the "misplaced domestic priorities" (guns before butter) and wrongheaded foreign policies.

Few groups have been more determined in the pursuit of unilateral disarmament through such arguments than the American Friends Service Committee. Characteristically it would argue that

> U.S. citizens daily feel the effects of our government's military support for the war in Central America. Instead of our tax dollars going to improving our schools, revitalizing our communities, creating jobs and providing food and housing for the poor, sixty-one cents of every tax dollar go to the military. [Nuclear Weapons and Intervention in Central America and the Caribbean, n.d.]

The assertion that 61% of the tax dollars constituted military expenditures was highly inaccurate: the actual portion in the 1980s was around 30% [*Statistical Abstract of the U.S.* 1988:314]; in 1982 military expenditures were 26% of the budget, down from 45% or more during much of the 1950s and 60s [Hershey 1982].

The main purpose of the argument was to delegitimate military expenses in general (and especially in Central America) by juxtaposing them to other, far more appealing uses of public funds. Such was the hostility of the Quakers and their supporters toward the American military establishment that not only nuclear weapons but even a large transport plane like the C-5A was perceived, by an AFSC activist, as an evil device since it was capable of projecting American power: "These large planes . . . are part of our policy of 'low intensity warfare' against poor small countries . . . it is our duty to endeavor to discourage United States domination of the 'Third World'" [Crowe 1988].

It is the power and the potential (or actual) assertiveness of the United States that inspires the deepest, visceral aversion among the critics of America rather than nuclear weapons per se. No such aversion is ever discernible in their comments (if any) on the military forces of other countries, especially those they perceive as socialist.

The Quakers did not limit their activities to general critiques of U.S. foreign policy; their political arm, the AFSC, in particular has been an energetic, full-time lobbying organization addressing a wide range of foreign policy issues. Among many projects aimed at curbing the military establishment, it led the movement of "tax resistance" against military expenditures. In 1983 some 10,000 Quakers participated in such a protest, according to a member of the "War Tax Committee" of the denomination ["Quakers Leading Tax Protest" 1983].

The Quakers were not alone in such endeavors; Archbishop Hunthausen noted earlier for his fondness for comparing American submarines with Nazi death camps was among those urging taxpayers to withold half of their taxes, which by his calculations supported the military [Turner 1982; Novak 1982]. Another example of Quaker opposition to the military has been support and counseling for draft resisters, that is to say, advising those eligible for the draft on how to avoid registering, or how to face the legal consequences of the refusal to do so [see for example "Quaker College in Indiana Aiding Draft Resisters" 1982]. There have been no reports of the Quakers attempting to offer assistance, solidarity, or moral support for those resisting the draft (not mere registration) in any other country and in particular those whose military establishments confronted the United States.

VI

The critical disposition of the churches toward American society, U.S. foreign policy, and capitalism has not been replicated in a similarly critical attitude toward political systems outside the United States or the Western sphere of influence. Even the Soviet Union, although ostensibly a moral equal of the United States—and if so equally culpable for the sorry state of global affairs—has largely escaped criticism. Not even its invasion of Afghanistan has been a suitable occasion for criticism for either the NCC or the AFSC. The latter, astonishingly enough, blamed the deterioration of detente for the invasion *and* the American response to it [Wieseltier 1982:39]. In the same spirit the World Council of Churches (WCC) (whose policies mirror those of the NCC especially in foreign affairs) at its 6th Assembly in 1983 refused to condemn the Soviet invasion of Afghanistan while demanding the outside aid to the anti-Soviet guerillas be cut off ["World Church Assembly Proves Bias" 1983].

The WCC also refused to condemn the Soviet Union for denying religious freedom to its citizens. "Church officials . . . defended their actions by contending that open attacks against the Soviet Union would result in additional suffering for Russian believers . . ." [Briggs 1983:A6]. The same clerics have shown no hesitation to make impassioned public attacks on South Africa or Chile under Pinochet presumably on the assumption that those repressive governments will not be enraged by such critiques and impose additional suffering on the oppressed in their countries.

There has also been a longstanding reluctance to criticize the Soviet Union not only for its impressive range of human rights violations but specifically for its repression of religion and harassment of people seeking to practice their religion [see for example "Religious Freedom and the WCC" 1983].

A major explanation of the lack of criticism of Soviet policies and activities may be found in the churches' involvement in the peace movement. If and insofar as lack of conflict between the "superpowers" was the overriding goal and the precondition for global peace, tension or ill feeling between them would seem to hinder the cause of peace. A "breakdown in communications" was to be averted at all costs. Any criticism of the Soviet Union thus came to be regarded as poisoning the atmosphere and interfering with cordiality. According to the *National Catholic Reporter,* "Protesting Soviet policies has had the unfortunate effect of cutting us off from fruitful contact with the Russians . . ." [Hitchcock 1983].

Given their highly critical disposition toward their own country, the churchmen felt, "Who are we to criticize the Soviet Union? Let us remember the Native Americans, black slavery, the Depression, the internment of the Japanese during World War II, Vietnam, the homeless, and so on, and so on." Since the social critics deeply believed in the sins of the United States they considered it morally unacceptable and distasteful to criticize the Soviet Union. Moreover, the Soviet Union, too, criticized the United States (and capitalism), hence there was an affinity between such a system and American social critics, both religious and secular.

The peace movement also championed the reduction of American political-military presence and influence around the world. Closing U.S. bases, the cessation of military assistance to particular countries (e.g., South Korea), cutting military expenditures, establishing nuclear-free zones, and so on were always justified by promoting peace in the world. Coincidentally these proposals would reduce American political-military presence and influence.

The attention of the World Council of Churches even extended to remote regions of the Pacific seeking to make them "independent and nuclear free," which would in effect reduce or remove American military-political presence from the region [Tanham 1988:88–90]. In the same spirit the Pacific Resource coordinator of the United Methodist office for the U.N. protested the Compact of Free Association of Micronesian Islands with the United States, perceiving it as "a colonial type compact between a superpower and two developing microstates" which provided for extensive U.S. military presence [Quass 1985].

The concern with peace was not the only factor silencing criticism of the Soviet Union. While in the 1970s and 80s the Soviet Union no longer inspired the type of admiration that had animated many Western intellectuals and clergymen in the 1930s and 40s there remained a residue of goodwill toward it among these groups. It was inspired by a largely dated conception of the Soviet Union as an underdog nation ravaged by invaders time and again and struggling to overcome backwardness and underdevelopment but hindered from doing so by the arms race of which it was a reluctant participant, compelled by the United States. In any event it was a long-suffering country and people which deserved the benefit of doubt. Most important, its failings, including religious repression, were not to be allowed to distract from the cause of peace. Thus Dr. Bruce Rigdon, a professor at McCormick Theological Seminary in Chicago (and spokesman of a 266-member delegation of the National Council of Churches that visited the Soviet Union in 1984), was "irritated" by a demonstration of Soviet Baptists in a Moscow church during their visit. Even more remarkable was the position taken by Ms. Agnes Marsh, national vice president of United Presbyterian Women, who suggested that those suffering religious persecution in the Soviet Union were imprisoned for other, ordinary crimes just as a "percentage of our prison population are members of Christian churches" [Sysyn 1985:14].

The Rev. Billy Graham on his peace mission in 1982 "stayed clear of any references to religious freedom . . . or other topics potentially offensive to Soviet authorities" [Schmemann 1982:3] and stated that "he had seen no evidence of religious persecution by the Soviet Government" [Briggs 1982]. Methodist Bishop James Armstrong, former president of the National Council of Churches, returned from the Soviet Union impressed by the "vigor" of religion there [Hitchcock 1983].

If the Soviet Union was treated in an uncritical but at least restrained fashion the same cannot be said about various repressive left-wing governments in the Third World which elicited outright admiration and have been treated with warmth and sympathy, as will be shown below. Such warmth increased in proportion with the degree to which such countries were seen as victims, or former victims, of the United States.

Correspondingly the churches' concern with social injustice and political repression did not, as a rule, extend to countries in the Third World which espoused leftist or Marxist-Leninist values and called themselves socialist. It was aptly observed of the NCC that "what it condemns as 'wrongs' and 'injustices' in pro-Western nations become 'mistakes' or 'bad judgement' in socialist countries" [Billingsley 1990:180]. In this regard too, the political stances taken by the churches were similar to those of the secular critics of America. While occasionally brief, unspecific critiques were directed at injustice and repression outside the West, such statements were perfunctory, lacking in moral fervor and conviction. For the most part they were made, once more, in the framework of a questionable moral equivalence between the failings of the United States and its adversaries. Characteristically criticisms of these systems would immediately be coupled with critiques of (allegedly) corresponding flaws of the United States; often the United States would actually be held responsible for Soviet (or Cuban, Nicaraguan, Vietnamese, Cambodian, and so on) violations of human rights. Thus the Episcopal Bishop of New York, Paul E. Moore, said in his Easter sermon a few years ago, "I am not saying the Sandinistas are perfect any more than I am saying that the young United States of America was perfect after the Revolutionary War" [Hart 1984]. Even in a critique of religious fundamentalism around the world Jim Wallis (quoted earlier) managed to equate the Ayatollahs of Iran with American fundamentalist sects:

> The resurgence of religious fundamentalism around the world has often made matters worse by offering religious sanction to war and racism and sexism, the suppression of freedom and the abuse of human rights, and the domination of the rich over the poor. From the holy war crusades of the Iranian Ayatollahs to the nuclear Armageddon theology of the American religious Right, the danger of such fundamentalist nationalism is increasingly clear. [Wallis 1987:xxviii]

The churches' solicitousness toward the Third World and their critiques of American foreign policy were closely linked to a questionable but firmly held premise. It is that the United States is virtually the only powerful actor in international relations, the only one who takes significant initiatives, and that all other countries merely respond to what the United States does—a belief that obviously multiplies American responsibility and maximizes the opportunity to blame the United States. Thus according to a religious activist:

> Even in the current age of rough military parity, the United States' clear economic, political and technological superiority makes it the dominant partner in the superpower relationship. For better or worse, we set the tone of the relationship and the terms of the conflict. If there is to be a turn toward peace, it will have to begin here. And it will have to begin with a change of heart among the American people. [Collum in Wallis ed. 1987:226]

Exactly the same belief was held by secular critics of the United States intent on holding it responsible for the sorry state of world affairs in general and Soviet-American relations in particular.

Not surprisingly attitudes toward political violence abroad were as inconsistent as they were toward its domestic varieties, as was noted earlier. Not only did some of these churches provide material assistance and moral support to guerilla movements in the Third World, there was also an attempt to redefine violence itself and thereby justify double standards. One way to do so was to introduce the idea of "the violence of the status quo," or "structural violence" whereby social injustices were simply equated with violence. Pacifist religious groups were also capable of joyously celebrating the military victories of their favored movements, as in the case of the communist victory in Vietnam [see for example Lewy 1988:48-49, 109].

The double standards used to judge political or military violence were also displayed when the NCC in 1973 condemned the downing of a Libyan airliner by Israel but had no comment on the shooting down of a civilian plane by the guerillas in Zimbabwe in 1978, nor did it protest the Soviet destruction of yet another civilian airliner, the Korean flight 007 in 1983 [Billinglsey 1990:61]. The AFSC, which was free of apprehensions about the state of civil liberties while Grenada was communist-controlled, expressed grave concern with alleged restrictions on civil rights as soon as the communist regime was deposed ["Quaker Group Reports Rights Curbs in Grenada" 1984].

VII

In the 1980s U.S. policy in Central America and toward Nicaragua in particular became the focal point of criticism mounted by church groups and organizations. These critiques of U.S. foreign policy were stimulated largely by the sympathy toward its alleged victim, Nicaragua. Not only did the churches lobby forcefully and successfully against aid to the anticommunist guerillas, they organized their own aid programs to assist the Nicaraguan authorities and supported the so-called "pledge of resistance" which obligated those signing it to engage in civil disobedience ("necessary acts of resistance") in the event the United States "significantly escalates its intervention in Nicaragua, El Salvador, or the Caribbean and Cuba." (The pledge was sponsored and endorsed by the Witness for Peace [an offshoot of the Quakers], the Inter-Religious Task Force on Central America, Southern Christian Leadership Conference, Pax Christi, World Peacemakers, AFSC, United Church of Christ, and other religious and secular organizations [see Pledge of Resistance leaflet, n.d.].)

The churches were also in the forefront of organizing political tours to Nicaragua which not only aimed at acquainting the American visitors with the alleged accomplishments of the government but also entrusted them with disseminating their favorable views at the grass-roots level upon their return—exactly as the minister of interior Tomas Borge had intended.[3]

As was the case during the Vietnam war, once more the Rev. William Sloane Coffin, Jr., typified widely held attitudes, endorsed by both the religious and secular groups associated with the adversary culture. His sentiments regarding Marxist-Leninist Nicaragua reflected the same predisposition which determined the stand he took on Vietnam. There is to begin with the irresistible impulse to feel friendly toward "the enemy of my enemy." That is to say, if the United States is hostile toward a country or political system, the latter must be doing something right and deserve support and sympathy. Thus the American attempts to overthrow or weaken the Sandinista regime almost automatically made it a recipient of the sympathy and solidarity of a full-time social critic of the United States, such as Coffin. As in the case of Vietnam, it was also tempting to cast the conflict in terms of David against Goliath, the courageous little nation, strong on spirit but poor in lethal machinery, against the technological colossus.

Coffin wrote: "A single American plane flying out of southern California, Texas or Florida could obliterate Nicaragua in 20 minutes . . ." [Coffin 1983]—a proposition which invites the rejoinder: "What if it could?" A single Soviet plane flying out of Siberia could obliterate the Aleutian Islands or a good chunk of Alaska in less time but this is just as unlikely as Coffin's fantasy conjured up to ridicule the idea that Nicaragua could be a threat to the United States.

Coffin's vision of the potential nuclear annihilation of Nicaragua also failed to address the question of why American nuclear capabilities did not restrain Nicaraguan attempts to export the revolution. Evidently he failed to observe over the past decades how little political leverage nuclear weapons afford in conventional and especially guerilla wars and particularly in conflicts between a superpower such as the U.S. and smaller countries, whatever the distance between them. The American capacity to obliterate Cuba with nuclear weapons has made no difference whatsoever either to Castro's domestic or foreign policy, although the distance from Florida to Cuba is even shorter than from the southern U.S. to Nicaragua. Coffin also overlooked the possibility that even a small nation can become a military-political base for powers hostile to the United States (such as Cuba and the Soviet Union) and even a small nation such as Nicaragua is capable of maintaining substantial conventional military forces dwarfing those of its neighbors, which has in fact been the case. (That such forces were not set up merely to counter the anticommunist guerillas was suggested by the fact that following the virtual cessation of their activities, as American military assistance came to an end, Nicaragua did not reduce the size of its armed forces.) At last even a small nation can support guerillas seeking to overthrow its neighbors as the Sandinistas have also done.

Coffin like other sympathizers with communist systems before him also disputed that Nicaragua had a Marxist-Leninist government (although it would probably not have unduly disturbed him if he thought that it had one). He asked rhetorically: ". . . how 'Marxist-Leninist' is a country when four well-known Roman Catholic priests and no Communists serve in the Cabinet?" [Ibid.]. But it is quite clear by now that the four priests in question have chosen to put their political-ideological commitments ahead of their religiosity, or else succeeded in convincing themselves (as probably Coffin himself had) that there is no real conflict between Marxism and Christianity—after all, that is what "liberation theology" is all about. In disputing the Marxist-Leninist credentials of the Sandinista regime Coffin steadfastly ignored the statements these leaders themselves made about their ideology, although they would play down—for the benefit of non-Marxist visitors—their Marxist political values and thrust into prominence their residual Christianity, stressing their religious credentials and affiliations.

Coffin was also a member of the board of the Nicaragua Education Project in Washington, D.C., which organized group tours to promote a more favorable image of the regime. Other board members included Julian Bond, the black politician, and Adele Simmons, former president of Hampshire College in Amherst, Massachusetts—an institution that may not unfairly be characterized as a surviving, active enclave of the radical chic of the 1960s and outpost of the counterculture in "higher" education. (In 1988 she was appointed president of the wealthy MacArthur Foundation in Chicago, thereby providing yet another example of the close ties between left-leaning academic institutions and foundations similarly disposed.)

In a further example of the suspension of disbelief Coffin also accepted at face value the stated objectives of the Nicaraguan regime as for instance "to stop the exploitation of the many by the few and to end foreign domination" [Ibid.].

Coffin's beliefs are largely defined by his anti-anticommunism; for him anticommunism is simply an "obsession" ("Obsessed with Communism, the Reagan Administration sees a 'Marxist-Leninist' under every Central American bush" [Ibid.]). His attitude resembles those of the sympathizers' with far-left movements or systems who nonetheless indignantly protest being labeled a communist (or Marxist-Leninist) while being concurrently attracted to these ideas and their institutional or organizational embodiments. On the one hand it is slanderous to be called a communist and it evokes righteous indignation—on the other there is much hidden or open flirtation with the same ideology and the movements it inspires.

The benign view of the allegedly non-Marxist Sandinistas was complemented by the denial that they provided assistance to other Marxist-Leninist movements or guerilla groups—a claim that also used to be made about the North Vietnamese authorities and their relationship to the Vietcong guerillas in the South. (The alleged autonomy of the Vietcong was among the major arguments used against U.S. intervention in what was said to be a civil war.) Coffin in all probability was among those who asserted that the Vietcong got no help from North Vietnam; more recently he made the same claim regarding the guerillas in El Salvador: "As for the charge that the Sandinistas are exporting violence . . . Anyone with commonsense knows that you can't have revolt without revolting conditions . . ." [Ibid.]. "Revolting conditions" have certainly abounded in history but the successful overthrow of governments takes more than the presence of such conditions.

The attempt to deny or play down the Marxist-Leninist attributes of the Nicaraguan regime has also been similar to the earlier denials of the Marxist-Leninist character of Castro's Cuba. As on other occasions in the past (e.g., Vietnam) the nationalism of the Sandinista regime was invoked to make its Marxist-Leninist commitments implausible. Coffin and his followers apparently could not entertain the possibility that political systems can at once be nationalistic and Marxist-Leninist and that getting rid of American influence in Nicaragua (as in Cuba) is not an automatic guarantee of remaining free of the influence of another big power—the Soviet Union. Nicaragua has repeatedly shown the limits of its "independence" in a symbolic way by voting with the Soviet Union on virtually every issue in the United Nation and especially by supporting Soviet policy in Afghanistan. (Grenada acted the same way before the U.S. intervention, providing another example of how small nations do not necessarily assert their autonomy after shaking off American or other Western influences and controls.)

Coffin was by no means unique in sympathizing with the Nicaraguan regime and criticizing American policies in Central America (and around the world). More than 300 religious leaders, including 22 Roman Catholic bishops, denounced these policies in a joint statement in 1982 [Austin 1982]. "Ruth Harris, an executive with the United Methodist Church Board of Global Ministries, said that after a recent visit to Nicaragua and Costa Rica she felt 'humiliated and angry' about American policies in the Caribbean. The Reagan Administration policies in Central America 'dismayed us beyond words,' she said, quoting a letter a delegation of Church officials wrote to farmers in Nicaragua after their visit . . ." [Ibid.]. Likewise the U.S. National Conference of Catholic Bishops went on record opposing American aid to the Nicaraguan resistance movement *and* to the government in El Salvador to fight the communist guerillas. ["American Bishops Visiting Nicaragua" 1985]. And in 1986 "Nearly 200 religious figures formed a human cross on the steps of the Capitol," once more protesting the proposal to send military aid to the Nicarguan resistance. Those participating and signing a formal statement of protest included "21 Roman Catholic, Methodist, Episcopal and Unitarian bishops, officials of the United Church of Christ, the Christian Church, the Mennonite Church, the Unitarian Universalist Association and the National Council of Churches and about a dozen rabbis" [Religious Figures Protest Contra Aid" 1986].

Some church groups and clergymen were also anxious to convey their appreciation and support for the Nicaraguan government on the occasion of President Daniel Ortega's visit to New York in 1986. Invited to address the congregation at the Park Slope Methodist church in Brooklyn, Ortega was informed by the pastor, the Rev. Finley Scheaf, that "his congregation had a 'deep sense of shame' over American support of the contras . . ." ["Sandinista Makes His Case on a Brooklyn Church Visit" 1986]. In the course of the same visit Ortega was also "honored at a Riverside Church luncheon with appreciative comments from the Rev. William Sloane Coffin" (the church people assembled mingled with secular celebrities such as Morley Safer of CBS, Betty Friedan, the feminist author, former senator Eugene McCarthy, Bernadine Dohrn, former Weather underground activist, and Bianca Jagger of Rolling Stone fame [Motavalli 1985]. Those promoting the Sandinistas in the United States also included Blase Bonpane, a former Maryknoll priest, liberation theologian, and professor at the University in California in Los Angeles. He organized "delegations of prominent American celebrities to Nicaragua," with an emphasis on Hollywood stars, at the request of Rosario Murillo, wife of President Ortega [Ingwerson 1984].

An evangelical group, the Sojourners (mentioned earlier) devoted an entire issue of their publication (also called *Sojourners*) to the celebration of Nicaragua. Every major stereotyped misconception of Marxist one-party dictatorships reappeared as the authors retraced, figuratively speaking, the path traversed by their ideological forebears who had visited, in the same spirit, the Soviet Union, China, North Vietnam, and Cuba. The new "sojourners" were similarly impressed by the various accomplishments (real or claimed) of the new regime and were ready to accept all the official arguments and rationalizations regarding the less appealing aspects of life in revolutionary Nicaragua. For instance they had no difficulty accepting the official explanation of the deportation of the Miskito Indians as a "political necessity" and the postponement of elections as understandable and justified, and they unhesitatingly supported the claim that the new regime dealt humanely with former supporters of Somoza. Like Coffin, they too dismissed the importance of Marxism in shaping the outlook of the leaders and found no cause for concern in the official policies toward the freedom of religion ["Nicaragua: A Fragile Future" 1983; see also Hollander 1983 May].

A member of the Witness for Peace (the Quaker group championing Nicaragua) on his return in 1986 found the closing down of the opposition newspaper *La Prensa* justified on the grounds of government suspiciousness "of an opposition newspaper given aid by an American organization" [Pogson 1986]. Another Quaker, an AFSC activist in Massachusetts, was indignant over the criticism a *New York Times* editorial expressed of the authorities in Nicaragua. She wrote: "Tens of thousands of American citizens who have been in Nicaragua, including AFSC Central American staff, do not see Nicaragua as a 'police state' but as a small, poor country under attack . . . Restrictions on personal liberties and civil rights have come not in response to dogmatic ideology but rather in response to conditions of war" [Crowe 1986]. The dependability of the judgments of the same writer may be further pondered in the light of her earlier account of China under Mao:

> With three weeks spent in the People's Republic of China I have such a wonderful picture in mind of a society . . . which is alive and engaged in constructive building. Every one is moving in a positive way, working hard, enjoying their work, bent on top productivity . . . The children seem happy and highly motivated, family life seems relaxed and meaningful. [Crowe 1974]

Her views of China under Mao were shared by those speaking for the National Council of Churches, an official publication of which "compared the Cultural Revolution with the Protestant Reformation 'in its drive to restore the vigor and purity of revolutionary goals and practices'" ["The Churches and the Cold War" 1990:5].

AFSC activists, while among the most vocal supporters of the Nicaraguan authorities, were far from unusual in going to Nicaragua with favorable preconceptions and a determination to find support for their criticism of American foreign policy in Central America. Other church-sponsored tourists displayed a similar outlook. Belonging to a group of "Christian pacifists," Sister Joyce Barrett, R.S.M., of Burlington, Vermont, "expressed her concern about the link between U.S. policy on Central America and the arms race, a concern shared by others on the tour . . . We see the arms buildup that takes food from the poor . . ." She "admitted that the group's whirlwind four-day tour would not offer an opportunity to sample all aspects or opinions of the revolution. 'It's a tight schedule,' she said, 'But I expect it will confirm what I already thought about what the present government had done to gain rights for the people.'" Another participant of the tour group, Father William Brisotti, a diocesan priest and member of the Catholic Peace Fellowship, wanted to use his experiences "to push for change in American policy toward Nicaragua." Going a step further, "a member of the Vermont contingent took her turn at the microphone [during the vigil in front of the U.S. Embassy in Managua] promising that she would try to export Nicaragua's democracy to the American system" [Frawley 1983 July].

The "Christian Pacifists" on this tour also went on record refusing to blame the communist guerillas in El Salvador for their violence, quite comparable with that generated by the contras in Nicaragua. "In the case of El Salvador, it appeared that the guerillas were justified in fighting, according to the vigilers, while the Nicaraguan opposition forces were not. When Ebener [one of the participants in the tour group] refused as a pacifist to support violence on the right or the left, he found few supporters" [Ibid..].

The highlights of the tour—and that of many others organized by church groups—included "A visit with Commandante Tomas Borge, minister of interior . . . Speaking at a lecture and dinner at the former country club (now reception center), Borge received sustained applause from his generally enthusiastic audience as he discussed . . . reports of the state's persecution of the Catholic Church and the Miskito Indians" [Ibid.].

Borge's credibility with church groups (as reported by a defector from his own ministry) was enhanced by the practice of displaying crucifixes and Bibles in the office he used for meeting such delegations and frequently quoting the Bible [Baldizon 1985]. Borge, it may be recalled, was one of the most radical and authoritarian figures in the government (hence his job as head of the Nicaraguan secret police) yet for a Quaker publication he came to exemplify "a gentleness in the Nicaraguan nature" ["Nicaragua Visited" 1984].

There was an enormous outpouring of enthusiastic Nicaraguan travel accounts by participants of church-sponsored tours and members of the clergy in particular. As in other impoverished and mismanaged Marxist-Leninist systems of earlier times, the favorably predisposed visitors always managed to discover "an atmosphere of youth, vitality and hope," as did a Catholic activist in Nicaragua [Scherer 1984]. Others, as for example a director of a Theological Seminary in California, advised "to discard our U.S. ideological lenses . . . and enter into networks of trust . . ." Given such determination it may not be surprising that he concluded that ". . . Nicaragua has achieved more freedom, justice and grass-roots democracy in five years than any of its neighbors (with the exception of Costa Rica) has achieved in five hundred years" [Kinsler 1986:16, 15].

This however was an understatement compared with the conclusion reached by Father Richard Preston of Lansing, Michigan, who wrote that "From my Christian perspective, it seems correct to me to believe that, in some real way, the reign of God has arrived in Nicaragua" [Preston 1983].

The churches' support for Nicaragua has not been limited to lobbying, tour organizing, and media events. Various church organizations (in particular the National Council of the Churches of Christ) have also been providing substantial financial-material assistance for various government or pro-government organizations in Nicaragua [see *Church Support for Pro-Sandinista Network* 1984].

Some church activists, such as the Witness for Peace group, also took it upon themselves to observe and report on guerilla activity in border regions, or to interpose themselves protectively between the U.S. Navy and Nicaragua. Thus in 1984 ". . . with the U.S. State Department threatening to 'eliminate' alleged Soviet fighter planes if they were unloaded, over thirty members of Witness for Peace began a 24 hour vigil in the port of Corinto. On that same day they took a small boat out 12 miles and met U.S. Navy vessels monitoring Nicaraguan waters. Over megaphones they called out to the Navy ships to leave Nicaragua in peace" and, by implication, free to receive its shipment of Soviet fighter planes undetected. ["Letter from Corinto" 1984]. Other church-affiliated activists, including Maryknoll missionaries, showed their support by living and working in Nicaragua, swelling the ranks of secular supporters known as *internacionalistas*.

VIII

Even Cuba, a solidly Marxist-Leninist police state, continued through the 1980s to find supporters and favorably predisposed visitors among clerics and religious journalists. They included members of the Associated Church Press, an organization affiliated with the major Protestant churches, "invited by the Cuban Institute for Friendship with nations" (as was reported in *Granma,* official Cuban newspaper). The tour of this group followed closely the pattern established in the Soviet Union as early as the 1920s and continued through the decades in other Marxist-Leninist regimes [see Hollander 1981:chs. 4 and 8]. Then as now, the objective of such tours, as far as the hosts were concerned, was to maximize the favorable impressions of the visitors and use them to neutralize criticisms of the regime abroad. The visitors were encouraged to influence the public opinion in their own countries by "telling the truth" about countries allegedly misrepresented in the capitalist media.

In all these objectives the Cuban hosts were highly successful, as the article published in *Granma,* indicates. Here is part of the record of the trip and the interpretations offered by *Granma:*

> For 7 days they [the "religious journalists" from the U.S. and Canada] were able to journey to numerous churches . . . headquarters of the Ecumenical Council of Cuba, the Evangelical Theology Seminar in the city of Matanzas . . . the Catherdral Plaza, the Tropicana cabaret, Varadero Beach, the Psychiatric Hospital of Havana . . .
>
> In the meeting . . . with the members of the Ecumenical Council of Cuba they received a detailed explanation of the work and social activities of the Council and were given the correct view of the life and work of the Cuban Church within the Socialist Revolution . . .
>
> One of the places that had the greatest impact, according to their own accounts, was the Psychiatric Hospital of Havana . . . The journalists were impressed by the gardens, the poultry farm and the occupational therapy areas . . . [Oliva 1983]

As this author noted in his earlier work, similar sights and establishments found in the native countries of the political tourists rarely elicited similar elation; but then, how could one compare a socialist poultry farm with a capitalist one, or an occupational therapy room of a capitalist mental hospital with its socialist counterpart? I had written:

> Many Western visitors seemed to forget that they were describing inherently ordinary objects—factories, hydroelectric plants, bridges, school houses or movie theatres . . . which under capitalism would provoke little excitement. All such inherently ordinary or prosaic projects and constructs were transformed, in the eyes of the beholders, by their new purpose and context. [Hollander 1981:137]

Gertrude Himmelfarb's comments of similarly disposed visitors in the USSR half a century ago go to the heart of the matter: "The marvel was not that there should be parks, hospitals, factories; after all, these could be found in England as well. The marvel was that they should all, as the Webbs thought, be inspired by a collective ideal, a single moral purpose" [Himmelfarb 1971:11].

Evidently this was exactly the frame of mind in which the group of religious journalists (and other sympathetic visitors) toured Cuba in 1983, earning the praise of *Granma.* Even a nightclub (the Tropicana), complete with floorshow and chorus girls, was heartily endorsed by these visitors, unlikely to applaud such entertainments under capitalism—but then again it was a socialist nightclub. *Granma* described the visitors' reactions:

> The journalists were astounded by Matanzas and Varadero. After meeting with the Christians in Evangelical Theology Seminary they enjoyed the attractions of the internationally famous Playa Azul. Returning to their countries they commented on Varadero, and the no less famous Tropicana cabaret: "we liked it a lot and enjoyed ourselves very much." [Oliva 1983][3]

In keeping with the spirit of such tours the religious journalists were also "hosted by the 63 farm families that inhabited the Vietnam Victory Commune . . . the farmers and the northerners [the visitors, that is] chatted, took photos and toasted the friendship between the peoples of Cuba, the United States and Canada" [Ibid.]

At the end of the trip this group of visitors obliged their hosts by telling them what they wanted to hear at the press conference organized at the Cuban Institute for Friendship. Here are examples of these proceedings as reported in *Granma:*

> Q: It is said that human rights are violated in Cuba. Have you seen anything that indicated that this is true?
>
> Dennis Earl Shoemaker, Director of *Communique,* responded: We saw no sign of human rights violations. [Ibid]

Armando Valladares, the Cuban poet who had spent 22 years in Cuban prisons, recalled the uses the authorities made of such support by American Christians:

> During those years [i.e., while in jail] with the purpose of forcing us to abandon our religious beliefs and to demoralise us, the Cuban communist indoctrinators repeatedly used the statements of support for Castro's revolution made by some representatives of American Christian churches. Everytime that a pamphlet was published in the United States, everytime a clergyman would write an article in support of Fidel Castro's dictatorship, a translation would reach us and that was worse for the Christian political prisoners than the beatings or the hunger. [Valladares 1983]

Another member of the same group, Marie Louise Suhor (director of *The Witness,* identified as a Protestant publication in St. Louis), who reportedly was on her fifth visit to Cuba, was thus cited by *Granma:*

> Q: Do you believe there is religious freedom in Cuba?
> A: I believe so, as I have seen the churches open and the people in them.[4]

Q: Do you see some of the ideals of Christ carried out in our society?
A: The group in the press conference affirmed much of these. We have seen it in the social work of the Revolutionary government. It is the task of all Christians to do this and here we see that the government does carry it out. We are happy that the Cuban government does do it. [Ibid.]

Not only were these visitors immune to the all-too-painful lessons of history—and in particular of the identical misjudgments of the Soviet regime under Stalin and China under Mao—they succeeded in brushing aside the repeated outflow of people from Cuba who voted with their feet against the regime on both economic and political grounds. Indeed the most startling examples of reverential travel reports of Cuba in more recent years have been produced by clerics, Protestant as well as Catholic.

"A Report from Cuba" signed by seven dignitaries of different churches[5] made these points: "As Christians we are profoundly impressed—and humbled—by a 'secular' government that is carrying out the gospel demand to feed the hungry, clothe the naked and minister to 'the very least' of the brothers and sisters of the human family . . ." [Armstrong and Dilley 1977].

Such perceptions had a venerable ancestry. D.F. Buxton, an English Quaker, and Hewlett Johnson, the late Archbishop of Canterbury, among others, were profoundly impressed with the Soviet system under Stalin on similar grounds. Their assessment matched in both spirit and substance evaluations of Cuba under Castro by American clerics. Buxton wrote:

> The Communists have in fact revived and applied what are, historically, essentially Christian ideas and applied them where they always ought to have been applied, i.e. to society and our social duties . . . in spite of all their irreligious jargon their society is a more Christian one than ours . . . [Buxton 1928:82, 85]

As for Hewlett Johnson, he thought that ". . . this Soviet programme regards men as persons and plans for them as brothers. There is something singularly Christian and civilized in this atittude and intention . . ." [Johnson 1940:5].

The visitors to Cuba quoted above also defended its human rights record:

> We believe that it [the Cuban government] has also preserved individual human rights more fully than many outsiders concede . . . We need to

remember that whereas at home dissent must often be directed *against* policies designed to favor the rich at the expense of the poor, in Cuba the task is to *improve* policies designed to help the poor . . .

. . . there is a significant difference between situations where people are imprisoned for opposing regimes designed to perpetuate inequities (as in Chile and Brazil, for example) and situations where people are imprisoned for opposing regimes designed to remove inequities (as in Cuba). [Armstrong and Dilley 1977, Quoted in *Time for Candor* 1983:80, 81] ·

Thus the moral endorsement of the coercive policies of the Castro regime was predicated on the simple (and questionable) belief that it was "designed to remove inequities." As at other times in recent history approval of the stated ends of a political system was sufficient to silence moral indignation over the questionable means used to attain them. To be sure the equanimity about Cuban human rights violations rested not only on the approval of the putative goals of the regime (which justified the means used) but also on the observers' profound ignorance of the nature of these coercive policies. They could thus assert without hesitation—presumably on the basis of assurances received from Cuban officials—that "In the process of change in Cuba it is freely acknowledged by the Cubans that there have been arrests, trials and sentences, not for verbal dissent but for specific acts directed against the government" [Ibid.:81]. Did these visitors trusting their hosts' assurances ever hear of Armando Valladares and many other Cuban writers imprisoned for their writings and other forms of "verbal dissent"? Did they know that Cuban laws made it possible to punish people for verbal dissent and criticism of the regime? Or would they have agreed with the Cuban government that such criticisms are "specific acts directed against the governemnt"?

Present-day admirers of Cuba could also take the position that the Dean of Canterbury (Hewlett Johnson) was wrong about the USSR under Stalin but *they* are right about Cuba under Castro. They might even have believed that while Stalin made mistakes his errors should not detract from his accomplishments. *Gulag* was the price to be paid for advances in social justice outside the camps.

A delegation of United Methodists in the early 1980s reached even more startling conclusions:

. . . Cuba represents a vision of the future shared by many poor and working people in the U.S. today . . .

We learned how arrogant it appears to others that the United States government, which cannot provide adequately for its own citizens, presumes to advise another people how they should plan their future. We learned about the narrow (and incorrect) perspective we have been taught about democracy . . . We learned that apathy, so prevalent in our country, is virtually non-existent in today's Cuba where powerlessness and hopelessness no longer prevail . . .

We saw . . . a country where the great majority of people believe they are makers and the beneficiaries of a new society . . .

. . . We were inspired. Cubans are characterized by a tremendous spirit of enthusiasm for building a new society . . . and a burning desire for the rest of humanity to gain the freedoms that Cubans have so recently won . . . We returned hoping that our communities can lead America in developing the humility we need to learn from Cuba. [Davenport 1983:83–85]

As recently as 1988 at a time when Cuba was singular in its rigid attachment to a failed and repressive Marxist-Leninist system, a member of an ecumenical delegation, the Rev. Loey Powell, had nothing but praise for Cuba and especially the condition of women and took at face value every bit of information she was given as part of the organized hospitality. Her delegation was "the honored guest" in a Havana neighborhood courtesy of the local Committee of Defense for the Revolution. ("Cuba is a revolutionary country and the process has made remarkable advances for workers, for women, for those who had been left out of society and whose labor had been exploited." And so forth. [Powell 1988])

The National Council of Churches study-guide series on "Peoples and Systems" waxed similarly eloquent about the Cuban educational system: "Permeating Cuban educational practice is the concept that a new type of society will develop a new type of human being . . . cultured, self-confident and self-disciplined, [who] regards work as the creative center of life and is bound to others by solidarity, comradeship and love . . .

"Today, such people are just appearing on the horizon . . . a new consciousness [is] being developed . . . through the tutoring of the island's head teacher, Fidel Castro" [Muravchik 1983:18]. Another pamphlet on Cuba in the Friendship Press series of the National Council of Churches concluded that ". . . at home Cubans have found a new dignity . . . Internationally, the island-nation . . . has been adopted as a symbol of revolutionary hope and courage by the Third World and has the long term support of a country [presumably the Soviet Union!—P.H.] which does not seek economic domination . . ." [*Time for Candor* 1983:90].

Such statements on the part of clergymen and various church officials and their publications were not the only reflections of the sympathy American churches have shown toward Castro's Cuba. There were other forms of institutional support as well, in particular funds provided for an organization designed to disseminate pro-Cuban propaganda, the Cuba Resource Center (CRC). Established in 1971 and supported in part by grants from a variety of churches, the CRC "... was and remains a 'solidarity organization' which supports the communist government in Cuba. In addition to publishing a quarterly magazine, the CRC sponsors exhibitions, concerts and tours of Cuban speakers. Its sympathies are so straightforward that it even offered its supporters a 14" × 25" poster of Fidel Castro as an 'excellent memento or gift'" [Ibid.:17].

At a time when support for Cuba has significantly diminished (though by no means disapppeared) within the (secular) intellectual community, numerous church leaders, clergymen, and groups associated with various churches have persisted giving every benefit of doubt to a regime the moral credentials of which have long been called into the most serious question.

IX

Another example of the dated political sympathies of certain church leaders in recent years may be found in their attitudes toward communist Vietnam. As will be recalled such sympathies were widespread during the years of American involvement in the war, but were sharply reduced after the communist takeover and the outpouring of the boat people which dramatically illuminated both the severe economic and political privations. Numerous native supporters and officials of the communist regime, now disillusioned, joined the refugees providing information about the practices and policies of the system established in South Vietnam. Such sources of information, however, made little impression on those predisposed to look upon communist Vietnam sympathetically.

Jim Wallis (of the Sojourners, quoted earlier) suggested in 1979 that the Indochinese refugees had been "inoculated with a taste for Western lifestyle" and were escaping "to support their consumer habit in other lands" ["Truth in Book Advertising" 1987:6]—in short they were suffering from false consciousness and fleeing for unworthy reasons which reflected their own moral corruption. The alleged corruption and untrustworthiness of refugees from communist countries has been a longstanding claim among those reluctant to allow their testimony to be weighed in the indictment of these systems. Such indictments and the resulting comparisons (with the West) would cast a more favorable light upon the countries which the critics were attacking, hence the experiences of refugees were to be discounted. (Noam Chomsky for instance went to great length to discredit and scorn refugee information about Pol Pot's Cambodia [Chomsky and Herman 1977] while similar efforts were made regarding Cuban refugees by Philip Brenner of the Institute for Policy Studies, Andrew Zimbalist, an economist of Smith College in Mas-

sachusetts, and Johnetta Cole, an anthropologist, now president of Spellman College in Atlanta [Hollander 1981:233, 473].)

Cora Weiss—a close associate of the Rev. Mr. Coffin—also disapproved of the Indochinese refugees on the ground that "Every country is
entitled to its own people . . . [they] are a basic resource that belongs to
that country" [*Time for Candor* 1983:14].

It was difficult for the critics of American society to forgive the refugees for risking their lives to enter a country the critics held in deep
contempt. At the same time information originating with the officials of
the countries the refugees fled, including Vietnam, was deemed reliable
as it coincided with the preconception of the critics.

It was difficult to accept criticism of the new political system that
would have vindicated its enemies. As was the case in the past, when
supporters of the Soviet Union under Stalin were reluctant to discuss its
defects in public, now hardcore supporters of communist Vietnam were
unwilling to do so for similar reasons. Thus AFSC staff in Philadelphia
in 1976 took the position that critique of human rights violations in communist Vietnam "Regardless of the intentions of its sponsors . . . plays
into the hands of the U.S. government . . ." [Lewy 1988:116].

Thus it came to pass that the grotesque spectacle of well-meaning
and gullible Westerners visiting Soviet (or Chinese) model prison camps
and praising them for their humane and enlightened treatment of prisoners was repeated in the "re-education camps" of communist Vietnam.
Given the number of former inmates who made their way to the West as
well as other information available of the characteristic treatment of
political prisoners in communist systems including Vietnam, it is hard to
explain the inordinate gullibility of the group of church officials who testified before a Subcommittee of the U.S. Congress on the subject of Vietnamese re-education camps in the spring of 1983. They were Dr. Paul
F. McCleary, Executive Director of Church World Service, and Midge
Austin Meinertz, Director for Southern Asia, Church World Service,
accompanied by Dr. Harry Haines, board member of the CWS and Executive Director of the United Methodist Committee on Relief. Excerpts
from their testimony follow:

> Arrangements for our delegation's visit to a reeducation camp in Vietnam
> were made through the efforts of Vietmy, the committee for Friendship
> and Solidarity with the American People, located in Hanoi, in cooperation
> with the Vietnam Fatherland Front Committee of Ho Chi Minh City, both
> of which applied to the offices of the Army for permission to see such a
> place. The request was made in connection with our stated concern
> regarding human rights violations reported by the press in relation to reed-
> ucation centers established following the end of the war in 1975. We were

accompanied by two members of the Vietmy Committee, including our translator . . . and two representatives of the Army (one press officer) . . .

. . . At the camp itself, although there was a small open sentry stand at the gate, there were no guard towers, no barbed wire, none of the traditional "prison" appurtenances.

. . . we observed that the men appeared to be sufficiently fed and in general good health . . .

. . . When asked directly about punitive measures for would-be "escapees' the camp commanders indicated that there were none.

Although the camp commanders assured us that no punitive measures were employed to assure that camp regulations would be followed, they did indicate that positive reinforcement for meritorious behavior was common (extra cigarettes, extra soap, towels, whatever) . . .

. . . While the rest period for camp members was still in effect our group walked through staff quarters . . . Following our tour . . . we joined a broader grouping of staff for lunch. The meal was entirely of camp-grown produce and livestock prepared by camp members. It was delicious: chicken, pork, rice, fruit . . .

. . . As we walked into the U-shaped central area, the men were mostly sitting on their sleeping platforms in small groups talking, playing cards, playing guitars, smoking homemade water pipes . . . When we asked as to the limitation on personal effects we were informed that there was none.

As we neared the closed end of the U near the volley ball court, we began to hear singing from one assembly hall. A camp chorus practicing, but certainly not surprised at our visit. When our visit was explained to those assembled, there was the group applause we had grown used to in orphanages, rehabilitation centers, any formal presentation.

The remarkable naïveté of these visitors is also reflected in their surprise and inablility to grasp why the inmates (who were being "reeducated" precisely because of their earlier association with Americans) were unwilling to converse with them or ask them any questions (". . . no hands were raised") or why other inmates were not surprised to see the visiting delegation inspecting them.[6] It may be imagined what unflattering thoughts these inmates might have entertained about their American visitors who were treated with utmost cordiality by their captors.

Thus despite repeated requests there were no questions:

Instead a group spokesman stood up and delivered remarks . . . The substance of both camp members' presentation focused on the new government's policy of leniency, the realization that there had been no bloodbath, the value of reeducation and manual labor; statements recognizing that they were trying to understand mistakes of the past and learn skills to contribute to the new society so that they could be reunited with their loved ones.

> After we left the hall, the camp commander asked whether we wanted personal interviews, which they would be glad to arrange.

They declined, given the earlier fiasco, to converse with English-speaking inmates (they delicately insisted on calling them "camp members"). So the tour of inspection continued:

> As we moved away from the meeting hall, we passed tool workshops, gardens, furniture-making workshops, dining halls, latrines. All neat, sufficient, well-constructed wood and bamboo woven mat with thatched roofing. Small touches, flowers in a vase made of a painted can caught my eye. And the beautiful location itself—tall and ancient trees against the blue sky . . . In some ways the camp looked as though it could have been a small tropical resort area . . .
>   . . . We came away from Vietnam impressed at the government's apparent commitment to providing opportunities for individuals to prepare for a role in the new society . . .
>   . . . the men we saw seemed to have their basic life needs met, and they can work toward the day they are united with their families and full citizens' rights are restored. [*Time for Candor* 1983:63–67]

There were other on-the-spot reports of the good life in newly liberated Vietnam, including one provided by an AFSC delegation in 1977. One of its members noted among his most memorable experiences a visit to a "new economic zone" where the delegation saw "the homes of the pioneer families who have moved out of the city and are dedicating themselves to reclaiming the land [and] to building a new life of productive work. It reminded me of the American pioneers . . ." [Lewy 1988:124]. Apparently unknown to the AFSC delegation was the fact that these "new economic zones" were basically penal settlements where people were forced to settle under extremely harsh and depriving conditions. It may be noted here that in a similar spirit Owen Lattimore visiting similar (or worse) penal colonies in the Soviet Far East in 1944 was reminded (by them) of the Hudson Bay Company and the Tennessee Valley Authority [Hollander 1981:157].

The durable misconceptions of these systems—climaxing in the tragicomic misperceptions of their penal colonies—cannot be fully explained by the belief in the regimes' apparent commitment to social justice and the eradication of poverty, although this belief has played a major role. To these beliefs we must add the mystique of the Third World, which in conjunction with liberation theology was influential among American church groups and clerics. This mystique has several components. To start with the idea of a "Third" World suggests that the countries belonging to it avoid the pitfalls of both the First and the Second World, that is of the West and the East; in particular they are not going to repeat the mistakes and imitate the vices of Western, capitalist-style modernization (nor those of Soviet-style socialism). The Third World is also supposed to be judiciously non-aligned, uninvolved in the sordid squabbles of the superpowers. Most important since much of the Third World consists of former colonies, these new states are morally superior victims of the West—of capitalism, colonialism, or neo-colonialism.

In their capacity as victims of the West (including the United States) these countries have provided excellent opportunities for continued collective self-flagellation on the part of Western and American social critics; the very existence and misery of these countries serve as a reminder of the sins of the West and thus constitute an essential theme in adversarial social criticism. At last, as far as the United States is concerned, its own minority groups—blacks, Hispanics, Native Americans—are sometimes designated as outposts or representatives of the Third World within American society, their alleged exploitation echoing that of the Third World. (The reader may be reminded here that most clerics in the survey cited earlier subscribed to the belief that the United States was responsible for Third World problems.)

The Third World also benefits, morally and psychologically, from the dependency theory which insists that its poverty and underdevelopment are to be blamed on the West. At the same time underdevelopment has certain moral-aesthetic appeals in the eyes of some beholders. The premodern countries of the Third World get credit for being possessed of a measure of innocence or wholesome simplicity; they are free of the corruptions of the advanced urban-industrial nations, expecially those in the West. Their inhabitants are somehow purer in their (authentic) poverty, closer to nature, more communal, less alienated. To be sure these mythical views of the Third World have minimal basis in reality.

The World Council of Churches in particular has virtually institutionalized Western guilt toward the Third World, making it a cornerstone of its pronouncements and policies. These attitudes surfaced perhaps most memorably at its Nairobi Assembly in 1975:

> The mood of the Nairobi Assembly was sounded in a keynote address by Robert McAfee Brown, an American professor of Christian ethics. Brown said he was ashamed of the evil his country had done "and continues to do, to so many countries," adding that many persons in the Third World were starving because "American business exploits them." Brown felt so guilty about America's sins that he delivered his address in Spanish to avoid the language of "imperialism." [Lefever 1979:41]

There was little difference between the WCC and the National Council of Churches in the United States [see also Lefever 1987:81] regarding the spectacular misjudgments of various left-wing dictatorships sampled above. By 1990 it was increasingly clear that the hope and confidence placed in such political systems were grotesquely misplaced, yet the writers and spokesmen associated with the NCC—not unlike other adversarial critics of American society and U.S. foreign policy—made no effort to re-examine these beliefs. A recent study of the NCC concluded that

> The extensive research for this study turned up no evidence that the NCC had ever, in any council document, publicly acknowledged or apologized for factual error, poor judgement or political bias . . . Only such error, poor judgement or political bias . . . can account for the NCC's failure to see that Marxist-Leninist regimes persecute Christians for their faith . . . [and] seek to eradicate all religious belief. NCC officials have visited these states, but they have often failed to reach out to their oppressed brothers and sisters . . . Worse still, the council has on occasion applauded the tormentors for "fulfilling" the Gospel—which is a little like cheering for the lions at the Roman Coliseum. [Billingsley 1990:188–89]

Such refusal to re-examine profoundly mistaken beliefs and assumptions about political systems and movements abroad continues to rest on the unshakable conviction that citizens of a society so riddled with social injustices and moral corruption as the American have no moral standing to criticize others (perceived to be) engaged in rectifying such flaws in their own society. The tendency to support these systems abroad is also based on an irrepressible affinity toward those who share the social critics' negative sentiments toward their own society. As long as the alienated sensibility continues to stamp the beliefs of church officials the temptation to misjudge other societies will be with us.

NOTES

1. These observations are corroborated by the photographs taken of Daniel Berrigan and included in his autobiography; they show him, when under arrest, displaying what can only be described as a triumphant and self-satisfied smile [Berrigan 1987:248].

2. The Sojourners have been described as "a growing and increasingly influential group of evangelicals whose conservative theology has led to radical—some would say leftist—political action." They are an energetic activist group favoring civil disobedience and public protest. Far from isolated they also "maintain close contact with mainline Protestant peace groups" and also Roman Catholics and especially "the more peace minded bishops and the Catholic Workers." Their influential secular contacts and allies include Republican Senator Mark Hatfield of Oregon, who is a contributing editor of *Sojourner* magazine [Monroe 1985:1, 10]. Another important ally of Sojourners is Richard

Barnett of the Institute of Policy Studies, another contributing editor of *Sojourner* ["An Interview with Clark Pinnock" 1985:5].

3. Similar miracles of selective perception and moral judgment were also reported during the visit of a secular tour group whose otherwise ardently feminist members found the same Cuban nightclub performance praiseworthy. Ronald Radosh wrote: "When two of us term the contents [of the show] sexist and backward we are pounced upon: 'Sexist?' says one woman in our group. 'What's wrong with a woman showing her body and moving it on the stage?'" [Radosh 1976:64].

4. An American sociologist of religion reached diametrically opposed conclusions regarding the freedom of religion after her determined fact-finding efforts in Cuba [see Georgiana 1988].

5. They were: Alan McCoy, O.F.M., President of the Conference of Major Superiors of Men, USA, Oakland, Calif.; B. D. Napier, President, Pacific School of Religion, Berkeley, Calif.; Joy Napier of the Ecumenical Peace Institute, Berkeley; James Armstrong, Methodist Bishop of the Dakotas; Rev. Russell Dilley, Assistant to the Bishop of the Dakotas; Sydney Brown and Robert McAfee Brown of the Union Theological Seminary, New York.

6. Western visitors to Soviet camps and prisons also noted that the inmates engaged in various wholesome activities paid little attention to the visitors. Some of these Westerners learned later this was due to the simple fact that such visits were routine in these model establishments [Hollander 1988].

3

Higher Education: Reservoir of the Adversary Culture

In scenes reminiscent of the 60s, colleges are, once again, becoming a battle-ground . . . with radicals trampling the right of free expression and bullying those who do not share their zealotry . . .

William Simon, 1988

Never in American history have major universities been so dominated by an entire spectrum of radical ideologies as today.

Irving Kristol, 1986

In all too many instances, the American system of education now encourages the kind of self-doubt that . . . may seriously undermine democratic values and institutions.

Guenter Lewy, 1982

For more than a decade now, universities have been in full retreat from the minimal reforms instituted in the 1960s and early 70s. Black studies, women's studies and so on, have been cut back. Radicals and other nonestablishment scholars who did not manage to attain tenure by the early 70s have been purged.

Martin Oppenheimer, 1988

. . . the results of the conservative assault on the academy to date have been profound.

John W. Cole and Gerald F. Reid, 1986

How is it possible for people of intelligence and impressive educational credentials to disagree so profoundly about matters which are accessible to their day-to-day experience? Our times have been providing renewed accumulations of evidence that more, better, longer educational experience does not result in converging observations about the same phenomena, nor does it create a predisposition to a shared worldview. If in the 19th century it was widely believed that education will do wonders to remove prejudice, false beliefs, distorted perceptions, and assorted irrationalities, that it will inexorably propel people toward a shared, rational view of the world, only the most naïve or ignorant (of the attitudes of the highly educated) can continue to cherish this hope in this century.

A key to understanding the general problem (the conflicting judgments of intellectuals, in this case the conflicting interpretations of conditions on the campuses) is to be found in the observers' desires and expectations of *what the world ought to be like*. The latter determines what people consider normal or abnormal, reasonable or unreasonable, sufficient or excessive, too much or too little. These expectations create especially severe problems in intellectual discourse when, for example, polemicists can no longer agree even on what statements are normative or merely descriptive. It is not just particular arguments over specific issues which are on a collision course, but (as Mannheim noted with alarm over half a century ago) "fundamentally divergent thought-systems . . . widely differing modes of experience and interpretation . . . a systematic theoretical basis underlying the single judgement of the individual" [Mannheim 1936:57, 591]. The same phenomenon was also commented upon by Isaiah Berlin as he contrasted the role of rationality in political and philosophical affairs in the 19th and 20th centuries:

> Conservatives, liberals, radicals, socialists differed [in the 19th century, that is—P.H.] in their interpretation of historical change. They disagreed about what were the deepest needs, interests, ideals of human beings . . . They differed about the facts, they differed about ends and means . . . But what they had in common . . . was the belief that . . . social and political problems . . . could be solved only by the conscious application of truths upon which all men endowed with adequate mental powers could agree . . .
>
> This set of common assumptions . . . were, of course, deeply rationalistic. [Berlin 1968:13]

Berlin also observed of the major political-ideological movements of the 19th century that "Whatever their differences . . . they had this in common: they believed that the problems of both individuals and societies could be solved . . . that all clearly understood questions could be solved by human beings with the moral and intellectual resources at their disposal" [Ibid.:5].

It is precisely the agreement over a common access to shared truths, or a set of common assumptions, that is so acutely and obviously missing from the current political-intellectual discourse, as disagreement often arises at the very early stage of identifying the problems and agreeing on what the "clearly understood questions" are.

Shared understanding and communication is further impeded by the belief of many academic intellectuals that their particular view, or consciousness of reality (informed very often by some variety of Marxism), is the only correct one. As Stanley Rothman pointed out, "Many such teachers explicitly conceive of their mission as one of raising radical consciousness, for this consciousness is equated with a correct understanding of reality" [Rothman 1986:6; see also Lewy 1983 and Nettler 1973]. This being the case they have no reason to regard their activity as "indoctrination," or if so, "indoctrination" is transformed and elevated to "consciousness-level raising," which in turn becomes equated with truth seeking (and finding).

Disagreements over basic values or the urgency of supporting particularly cherished values create further difficulties in intellectual discourse, as they often lead toward semantic innovations and the attachment of new meanings to old concepts. For example, "racist" used to mean an attitude of hostile discrimination toward groups or individuals who belong to a particular "race" or ethnic group; whereas a "color blind" attitude was the praiseworthy antidote to such racism. More recently "racist" has meant the refusal to discriminate on the basis of race, in particular the disapproval of reverse or compensatory discrimination (or preferential treatment) based on race. Likewise almost any reservation about the conduct or performance of any member of certain minority groups calls forth the "racist" epithet. (Only "certain" because the concept of "minority" itself has undergone momentous transformations to include all women—half of the population—but it excludes groups such as Jews, who are no longer granted the victimized status which has become the foundation of a privileged one, the justification for compensatory discrimination.) It is now the governmentally certified claim of a victimized status that is the basis of the current usage of "minority."

The peculiarity of these current beliefs and policies is indicated by the fact that while the son of a wealthy black family belongs to a protected category claiming both preferential treatment and moral credit for past victimization, the son of a currently poor white family can do neither. Poverty by itself is not a sufficient ground for "affirmative action" or preferential treatment unless associated with particular minority status.

Problems of communication and of reaching consensus on the state of academia are exemplified by Professor Oppenheimer's observation (cited above). Whereas in his presumably considered judgment the academic reforms of the 1960s were "minimal," others quoted (and not quoted, including this author) see these reforms as quite substantial, indeed sweeping. Clearly these conflicting assessments have to do with both the evaluation of the reform (if one liked them, one would have liked to see more of them) and with that of the status quo the reforms were to correct. The more intensely one disliked the status quo, the more one wanted to change it, the more support for reforms. Conversely those basically satisfied with the status quo felt little urgency about change and their threshold of what was too much or too little (minimal or maximal) was quite different. Perceptions of what actually took place were thus decisively shaped by predispositions which in turn rested on deeper philosophical beliefs and political values. While all this is quite obvious and elementary it is useful to remind us of such determinants of our judgments at a time when these judgments are in sharp conflict.

Under these conditions it is difficult for the contending parties to reach agreement on whether or not the reforms of the 60s were "minimal" or far-reaching. It will be just as difficult for them to agree on the state of American higher education at the present time and the last quarter-century and especially on the influence of adversarial values on higher education.

For those who wanted to see the educational system radically transformed the changes of the 60s were long overdue and the reforms introduced still insufficient (minimal) given their vision of all that had to be changed. For those who felt otherwise these changes were excessive and destructive and it was the backlash against them that was minimal; for them, too many of these "reforms" survived and continued to undermine the integrity of higher education.

There is only one very general proposition about higher education that elicits agreement from groups and individuals located at different points of the political spectrum: it is that American higher education is deeply flawed. On this general proposition individuals as different in their educational (and political) philosophy as William Bennett (former secretary of education under Reagan) and Bartlett Giamatti (former president of Yale) can see eye to eye [Gutman 1988]. But when they come to the sources, remedies, or specifics of the deficiencies an instant gulf opens between such critics.

This author believes that the transformation of American higher education since the 1960s has been quite profound and on the whole not desirable. Undoubtedly this conclusion is based on a particular reading of the evidence, conditioned by a set of values, beliefs, standards. It is the message of this chapter that the institutions of higher education in America have since the 1960s become the major resources or reservoirs of the adversary culture, the setting in which its values and beliefs are most frequently elaborated and displayed in the most unqualified form. Several areas of academic life examined below testify to these developments. They include:

1) The erosion and decline of free expression leading to taboo topics and taboo speakers;

2) Extracurricular political activities on the campuses, or the public discourse and its increasingly monolithic character;

3) The curriculum, especially in the social sciences and humanities; and

4) Academic standards (including academic requirements, admissions, and the evaluation of students; the hiring, promotion, and retention of faculty).

These developments have taken place (or at any rate, solidified) against a background of a general shift in public opnion in a conservative or centrist direction, expressed most notably in the last three presidential elections. Moreover the changes here noted (and especially their political aspects) had very limited student support (except the relaxation of grading standards and academic requirements) and did not reflect majority student attitudes and preferences.

Paradoxically a left-of-center generation of faculty came into academic power and became "entrenched in positions of leadership" during the Reagan era [see also Cantor 1988 and Kimball 1990]. By the 1980s there was a marked divergence between the political beliefs and attitudes of students (undergraduates in particular) on the one hand and faculties and administrators on the other. In a revealing illustration of a new generation gap at Colby College in Maine it was the faculty not the students that voted to ban the CIA from recruiting on campus while the student government opposed such a ban ("Maine Faculty Votes CIA Ban" 1987). At Kenyon College in Ohio it was the administration not the students who favored the radical alteration of the curriculum and the introduction of women's studies [Lilla 1986]. Paradoxically

> Where the faculty of the sixties gratefully followed the students, the Left faculty today wishes to use the university to radicalize its students. The faculty is like Lenin looking at the working class, seeing a kind of natural trade unionism, and making a determination to bring revolutionary enlightenment from the outside, since the students are not spontaneously left-wing anymore. [Kors 1988:81]

Even if their following among students is limited, faculty influence extends beyond the campuses. A study of recent social movements concluded that "Radical academics have an increasing impact on many elites (journalists, bureaucrats, lawyers, artists, clergy) as they assume responsibility for certifying them and creating their intellectual resources" [Rosdil 1988:14].

The developments here discussed have largely been overlooked by the general public in part because they have been gradual and accomplished largely without violence or photogenic turmoil, unlike the campus disturbances of the 1960s.

The Faculty

How did so many of the campuses become the alleged strongholds of the adversary culture? Why did the movements and attitudes associated with the 1960s succeed in perpetuating themselves? How was a climate of opinion created that allowed, indeed encouraged, the persistence, the institutionalization* of these trends?

The key to these questions lies in the faculties which set the tone and determine the climate of opinion on most campuses. The faculties who were the most instrumental in the process here described represent a minority of the total teaching personnel, are concentrated in departments of social sciences and humanities, and are most numerous and vocal at elite institutions.

Two closely related circumstances help to explain these developments. To begin with it should be kept in mind that at least since the post-World War II period, faculties have been liberal or left-of-center as a matter of self-selection. Lipset and Ladd report for instance that a study of Berkeley undergraduates in 1959-61 (well before the era of student protest) found that 62% of those describing themselves as "socialist" considered becoming college professors, followed by 34% liberal Democrats and 20% liberal Republicans, but only 14% conservative Democrats and 15% conservative Republicans entertained academic careers. Another study found in 1964 (again capturing attitudes predating the 60s proper) that "77% of the sociologists . . . affirmed the need for 'basic change in structure and values' to accomplish necessary social reforms." On the basis of these and other studies Lipset and Ladd concluded that "academe as a profession has recruited heavily through the years from the more left-inclined undergraduates" [Lipset and Ladd 1972:90, 88].

The second circumstance that helps to explain the conditions here discussed is that a substantial number of 60s radical activists—at the time undergraduate or graduate students—chose to stay in or return to academic life. In the words of two observers of the process, "the Left in America sought sanctuary in the academy . . . [and] the academy provided a safe, even pleasant haven for ideological rest, recuperation and regrouping" [Balch and London 1986:42-43; see also Kimball 1990].

These were the people sharing the orientation of Anette Kolodny, dean of humanities at the University of Arizona, who told a reporter: "I see my scholarship as an extension of my political activism" [Sanoff 1989:54].

*Institutionalization is the right word when whole programs of instruction are established with the purpose of teaching and popularizing the political beliefs of an era; when new academic positions are created, such as affirmative action officers, to implement other values of the same period.

The better-known among former activists who became professors included Angela Davis (San Francisco State College), Todd Gitlin (University of California at Berkely), Eric Foner (Columbia University), Mark Rudd (University of New Mexico, Albuquerque), Richard Flacks, (University of California, Santa Barbara), Bruce Franklin (Rutgers University), Derek Shearer (Occidental College, Glendale, Calif.), and Allen Ginsberg, a more pacific protester (Brooklyn College in New York). Saul Landau, veteran promoter of Castro's Cuba, taught at the University of California, Davis and Santa Cruz campuses, and at the New School in New York (where he was listed in 1989 at the top of a full-page advertisement among the major attractions of the school). The respectability of former radical acitivists was also symbolized by Johnetta Cole's selection as president of Spelman College in Atlanta in 1987 [Collins 1987] and her being awarded an honorary degree by Princeton University in 1988. She used to be an organizer of the Venceremos Brigade (recruited from dedicated supporters of the Castro regime who volunteered to cut sugarcane in Cuba) in Amherst, Massachusetts, a professed admirer of Castro's Cuba, and sometime defender of the Soviet political system.[1]

As Theodore Draper described these conditons:

> A post-New Left professoriate has arisen out of the ashes of the New Left student movement of the 1960s . . . former activists and sympathizers chose to get advanced degrees and ascend the academic ladder . . . a good many have gained tenure and many more are on the way. The New Left is dead, and yet it is very much alive in the very places where it was born. [Draper 1987:29; see also Richardson 1982]

The moderate liberal majority had no objection to accommodating the younger generation of radical scholars; in fact it was generally sympathetic to these youthful idealists. Attraction to the spirit and ideals of the 1960s has also been nurtured by the simple fact that the tenured academics of today were much younger in that turbulent and colorful period, and that it became irresistible to link their own youth to the spirit of that era. The sympathy and nostalgia for the 1960s, even on the part of those who were mildly critical of its "excesses," became embedded in the wistful recollection and contemplation of one's youth.

It has been a recurring finding of opinion and attitude surveys that academics are substantially further to the left than the public at large. The 1975 Carnegie Commission study found that 49% of the academics surveyed identified themselves as liberal or left-wing [Brock 1985 December].

The 1989 Carnegie Report found that 25% identified themselves as liberal, 32% "moderately liberal" (total liberal: 57%) as opposed to 6%

conservative and 21% moderately conservative (total conservative: 27%). Not unexpectedly in the humanities and social sciences these disparities were much greater: a total of 70% were liberal in the humanities and exactly the same in the social sciences; only 18% in the humanities and 15% in the social sciences were of a professed conservative political orientation [*Condition of the Professoriate* 1989:143]. In the same survey a total of 63% of all faculty were "apprehensive about the future of this country" (73% in the humanities and 67% in the social sciences)—a sentiment that may be safely be considered a judgment over the Reagan era [Ibid.:138].

After reviewing the relevant research of several decades Lipset concluded that "faculty members have been disproportionately critical of society, and more disposed than other strata to support forces that reject the status quo," and especially those in the liberal arts (versus teachers in professional schools) [Lipset 1982:144]. High levels of achievement (reflected in employment at elite schools) were closely associated with left-wing social criticism.

Those in the vanguard of the changes in academic life sometimes described the process as "A Marxist cultural revolution . . . taking place today in American Universities . . . a peaceful and democratic revolution, fought chiefly with books and lectures . . ." [Ollman and Vernoff, eds. 1982:1]. Not everybody viewed these developments as either peaceful or democratic although reliance on overt violence was relatively rare and usually limited to silencing or deterring unwelcome outside speakers from appearing on the campuses.

At the same time Lipset argued that even if there were 10,000 Marxist teachers on the campuses (an estimate of the conservative Accuracy in Academia organization) this would represent only 2% of the total of 600,000 college teachers. Lipset regarded the gravitation of Marxists to the social sciences a long-standing phenomenon and little cause for alarm [Lipset 1986; see also Richardson 1982]. He did not however address (in the publication referred to) the question of the influence exerted by even such a minority over the more passive and apolitical majority, and over the political agenda and climate of opinion on the campuses.

The Marxist influences are also manifest in academic organizations (often prefaced by "Radical . . .") which claim a combined membership of some 12,000—again a small number in comparison with the total, but with a disproportionate impact since the members see themselves and act as a combative and committed vanguard. There are also at least two dozen Marxist journals and over 500 courses on the Marxist philosophy [Brock 1985 December] and countless others tinged or colored by a Marxist worldview that reveals itself in the critiques of contemporary American society.

How exactly did the radicals achieve a weight and influence out of proportion with their actual numbers? They accomplished this as all dedicated and commited minorities do: by persistence, hard work, and an abrasive and sometimes intimidating appeal to higher moral principles. Stanley Rothman provides an excellent summary of this process:

> Once radical teachers reach a critical mass [that can still be a minority—P.H.] in any department or institution, they often exercise an influence beyond their numbers. They can rely on the acquiescence of those who do not fully accept their views, but think that much of what they say is right. More importantly their conviction of their own virtue and rightness enables them to overwhelm traditional scholars who find it difficult to cope with their combativeness and the combativeness of their supporters. [Rothman 1986:6]

Most academics want "to do their work," that is, their research or class preparation. For the radicals "work" is more broadly defined; their work is also political and ideological and power-oriented within the institutional setting. Given their motivation they will attend many more meetings than their apolitical colleagues, and when both groups attend, the radicals usually outlast the moderates.

There is also an historical explanation for the trends here outlined. McCarthyism has enduringly discredited anticommunism and, by extension, most critiques of leftism among academic intellectuals. It has thus made (indirectly) procommunist, hard-left attitudes more acceptable as such acceptance or tolerance conveyed the rejection of McCarthyite "witch hunting" and "red-baiting" and solidarity with its potential or putative victims. In addition (as already noted) the eruptions and protests of the 1960s shifted the entire political spectrum to the left. In the light of the very radical positions then taken by many groups, "moderation," "the middle of the road," indeed the very notion of liberalism, have become redefined [Hollander 1988:Introduction]. When comparison of the United States to Nazi Germany and the CIA and FBI to the Gestapo represents a form of (admittedly extreme) social criticism, calling the United States merely rotten and corrupt (and the CIA and FBI merely lawless) becomes a form of moderation [see also Balch and London 1986:49].

Thus even hardcore radicals can secure a respectable place on the left-liberal political spectrum; they are not beyond the pale as often as even moderate conservatives are; they are far more acceptable and respectable to "right-thinking" liberals than their more moderate counterparts on the right.

Many liberals are not especially bothered by the attitudes and activism of their radical colleagues. Such centrist or mildy left-of-center liberals would not, for example, dream of organizing or participating in the disruption of speakers, even those they do not care for. On the other hand when such disruptions occur, aided or abetted by their radical colleagues, they are not *deeply* disturbed. They even rally to the support of the rare radical activist who may have to pay a price for partaking in such unseemly activites. This was the case of Barbara Foley at Northwestern University in Evanston, Illinois, who was refused tenure by the provost in part for leading the disruption of an invited speaker. As one of her colleagues observed," . . . if most members of faculty were outraged by the incidents . . . they managed to keep it to themselves." Among other expressions of campus support, a faculty meeting passed a resolution "by a vast majority" protesting her denial of tenure. At the meeting where it passed "people r[ose] to speak chiefly to show that their hearts were in the right place" [Epstein 1986:41, 47]. After her various appeals were turned down both by the president and the AAUP she took a position at the Newark campus of Rutgers University.

The changing composition and attitudes of faculties have been further influenced by yet another trend, the redefinition of academic freedom and the place of ideological commitment in the classroom since the 1960s. Whereas at earlier times it was thought desirable that professors resist the temptation to teach their political views to their students, of late "Not only is it considered a right but in many quarters, it is thought a fine thing. Thus . . . academic departments nowadays seek out feminists, Marxists and others in whom the political impulse runs stronger than any other . . . in the name of intellectual diversity" [Epstein 1986:39]. The quest for such diversity and for the honest ("upfront") display of political commitment does not extend to those who do not uphold the politically correct beliefs. It is hard to think of or imagine a single instance when members of a social science or humanities department came to the conclusion that it was time to hire a bona fide neoconservative or Republican in order to introduce some diversity into their predominantly liberal or left-of-center department.

It is an interesting question why professors in the humanities (and divinities) and the social sciences tend to gravitate to the left and are more prone to find fault with their society than those in the hard sciences and other more specialized fields. The most obvious and benign interpretation is that they are less immersed in their specialities, more cognizant of a wider range of social and political phenomena and the relationship among them, more alert to the deficiencies of their social environment, and, as noted earlier, selectively attracted to these fields in the first place, due to the political values already embraced. Moreover certain fields such as anthropology and sociology attract a breed of idealists who measure their society either against the standards of the bygone (or imaginary) harmony and contentment of small pre-literate groups or the quasi-uto-pian blueprints of the future. The moral indignation of anthropologists in particular also feeds on their subject matter, inhabitants of areas that used to be (or still are) colonized or dominated by Western capitalist nations—hence the perspective of victim and victimizer comes to them most readily. By extension the entire Third World is by now incorporated into the realm of innocent and virtuous victims, while the capitalist West (led by the United States) remains frozen into the role of ruthless and greedy exploiter-victimizer. It is then not surprising that some anthro-pologists believe that "the ultimate purpose of anthropology is . . . the revolutionary scrutiny of our own society" [Leacock in Ollman and Ver-noff eds. 1982:261].

The politics of sociologists follows similar patterns. Lipset found that in 1948 some 11% of them favored Henry Wallace and Norman Thomas in contrast with only 2% of the electorate; in 1968, 7% of sociologists reported voting for left-wing third-party candidates while less than half of 1% in the electorate at large did so. In the same year "a larger portion of sociologists than of any other discipline preferred [Eugene] McCarthy (66%) to Humphrey for the Democratic nomination."

On a five-point scale of self-identification ranging from "Left" to "Very conservative," 15% of anthropologists and social workers, 12% of sociologists, and 10% of all social scientists sampled opted for "left"; whereas only 2% of social workers, 1% of anthropologists, 3% of sociol-ogists, and 3% of all social scientists chose "very conservative" [Lipset and Ladd 1972:87, 91].

More recent qualitative assessment of the work of American sociolo-gists support these findings. Among the themes of their work Irving Louis Horowitz found "a revolt against cultural tradition," "the celebration of the political criminal," the belief that "welfare operates as a form of social control," and "the existence of conspiratorial elites a fixed point of faith"; indeed "American society [itself] is a cleverly rendered political conspiracy" whereas "Socialism as an ideal can never be sullied" regard-less the abundant historical experience of the failed attempts to create socialist societies—an attitude that survived their collapse in the late 1980s in Eastern Europe. But then these systems have rarely been given close scrutiny since doing so might lead to a more chastened comparative perspective that would undermine the anticapitalist impulse and rhetoric. In short much of the work of contemporary sociologists suggests that sociology has become a vehicle for an impassioned social criticism [Horo-witz 1987]. Nonetheless Lewis Coser, another sociologist, asserted that social criticism became virtually extinct: "Sociologists have forsaken social criticism and retreated to highly technical research . . . that sheds little light on the problems confronting society . . . [sociology] 'is in danger of abandoning its critical bite'" [Winkler 1988]. Presumably had his attention been drawn to examples of social criticism he would have dismissed them as too little or not hard-hitting enough—a phenomenon discussed at the beginning of this chapter.

Further evidence of the radicalization of faculties in these fields can be adduced from the activities of their professional associations. Anthropologists, sociologists, the Modern Language Association, Latin American Studies Association, and others routinely pass resolutions at their annual meetings denouncing American foreign (or domestic) policies and supporting various Third World dictatorships and undemocratic "national liberation" movements [for a thorough documentation of such activities see Washburn 1988]. For instance the American Anthropological Association (AAA) in 1982 expressed fervent support for the repressed peasants of Guatemala but refused to concern itself with the similarly cheerless condition of peasants in Vietnam, Laos, and Cambodia, or the Miskito Indians in Nicaragua [Washburn 1982]. On the same occasion the AAA condemned Israel for "a massive destruction of the Lebanese and Palestinian peoples and cultures" [Washburn 1984:2] and in 1983 "categorically condemned the U.S. invasion of Grenada" (a resolution opposed by one member of the association) [Washburn 1985:2].

The Modern Language Association (MLA) not only condemned "our government's unjust and frequently illegal assaults on the people and government of Nicaragua" but also "urge[d] our colleagues . . . to speak, educate and act against these policies . . ." [Neth 1987:13]. The MLA has long been a bastion of radical chic. Its president at the time, Louis Kampf (professor of literature at MIT), wrote that "the very concept of culture is rooted in elitism" and (not unlike Goebbels) felt at times it was "difficult not to gag on the word." These feelings help to understand the unusual but undeniably original measures he proposed: "The movement should have harassed Lincoln Center from the beginning. Not a performance should go without disruption. The fountains should be dried with calcium chloride, the statuary pissed on, the walls smeared with dirt" [Long ed. 1969:422, 420, 426]. Not without reason did James Atlas note that "In the late '60s the MLA was as insurrectionary as SDS" [Atlas 1987:13]. Apparently it has not changed a great deal in the intervening twenty years as was also illustrated by the topics and tone of its 1990 meetings at which "the words most commonly heard in the papers given . . . [were] 'empowerment,' 'patriarchal authority,' 'the dominant order' . . . 'discourses of emancipation,' 'marginalized subjects,' 'systems of stratification' . . ." [Bernstein 1990]. These concerns were ventilated at a meeting of professionals who used to be concerned with matters literary.

The Latin American Studies Association (LASA) went even beyond the recommendations of the MLA quoted above; it sent a delegation in

1984 to report on the probity of the elections in Nicaragua (described by the *New York Times* as a "sham") but perceived by the LASA Report as an exercise in "participatory democracy" [Report LASA 1984:4; for a critique of the Report see Cuzan 1985]. The authors of the Report were satisfied that whatever abuses or disruptions (of the electoral process) occurred (and they found few), they were not systemic. The LASA Report not only endorsed the elections but praised the Nicaraguan government and its various policies and took the opportunity to take an inventory of its accomplishments.

The attitudes discussed above were often shared by the college administrators who came from the ranks of the faculty. Administrators were, with few exceptions, even more anxious to respond to the demands of the radical minorities both among the faculty and students either out of conviction or for fear of embarrassing publicity which campus disturbances would create at a time when they were less common. As an editorial pointed out, "Today . . . it is college presidents, deans and faculties, not students—who are the zealots and chief enforcers of Political Correctness" ["Politically Correct" 1990].

Attitudes among the faculties and administrators and the climate of opinion they created had a considerable impact on academic standards, curriculum, extracurricular activities, and the new forms of political activism. A major outcome was the narrowing of the intellectual discourse and the rise of taboo topics.

The Decline of Free Expression and Political Activism
Although the political activism of students has generally diminished through the 1970s and 80s what there was usually originated with left-wing groups and often resulted in the constriction of free expression on the campuses. The American public is generally unaware of this state of affairs having been repeatedly assured by the media over the past fifteen to twenty years that today's students are interested only in grades and jobs. While this may be true for the majority (see Chapter 6) small but active pockets of radicalism have persisted and succeeded in monopolizing much of the public discourse and political agenda especially at major universities and elite institutions. Some observers reached the surprising conclusion that "Ivy League colleges have become perhaps the most narrow-minded and bigoted communities," and a former professor at one of them, James Q. Wilson, observed in 1972 that of all the institutions he had belonged to—among them the Catholic Church, the U.S. Navy, and a small college in California—Harvard might have been the least conducive to "free and uninhibited discussion" [Podhoretz 1986; see also Finn 1989]. Fifteen years later a Harvard Law School student noted that

"Conservatives here don't have the right to free speech" in the wake of the disruption of various events by radical groups [Nix 1987].

Much of this was accomplished quite peacefully, although the threat of violence did play a part. When disruptions occurred television cameras were not on hand to record the silencing of speakers who were verbally and sometimes physically assaulted, and prevented from making their presentation. Moreover these incidents had a halo effect: for every speaker thus silenced, dozens or possibly hundreds who might have received similar treatment were never given the chance to speak, and if invited many would decline. Hence most speakers appearing on major campuses were left-of-center. For example at the University of Colorado between 1981 and 1986, 82% of outside speakers (paid by student funds) "ranged from liberal to far left." They included Leonard Boudin, Alexander Cockburn, Noam Chomsky, Angela Davis, Seymour Hersh, Alger Hiss, George McGovern, and Michael Parenti. Student funds were also used to subsidize a "Central American Culture Week" organized by the Committee in Solidarity with the People of El Salvador (more below), a major supporter of communist guerilla movements (and governments) in Central America ["Righting the Leftist Tilt . . ." 1986; Csorba n.d.]. Such conditions were readily duplicated on other major campuses.

University or college administrators learned to either tacitly discourage the appearance of speakers likely to enrage the radicals (sometimes on the grounds of the cost of maintaining security), or would actually declare that they could not guarantee their safety, thus effectively barring them from appearing. A further, less discernible halo effect might have taken place in the classrooms. It is not too far-fetched to speculate that if certain individuals were, in effect, barred from the campuses, their ideas too were unwelcome and imprudent to entertain or disseminate. A former faculty member at Amherst College linked these developments as follows:

> The refusal to invite the most articulate opponents of the Left . . . be they anti-Communists of social-democratic hue, Republicans, old conservatives or neoconservatives, creates campus attitudes of intolerance toward this entire constituency. Their views are beyond the pale, not to be entertained . . . in a word, inadmissible.
>
> Should one really be surprised, therefore if violence is threatened when one of the "forbidden" persons is invited to speak . . .? Is there such a large step, conceptually, from keeping the articulate writing of Jeane Kirkpatrick out of courses on foreign policy, and the disposition of campus radicals to threaten "disturbances" when she is invited as a guest, causing cancellation, or if not, disruption, when she begins to speak? [Ryerson 1988:34]

These reflections were not merely based on general impressions of the life of the mind on the campuses but on a scrutiny of the offerings of college courses on U.S. foreign policy at institutions such as Clark University, Mount Holyoke College, Smith College, George Washington University, and Harvard University [see also Weissberg 1989]. (There is much supportive evidence elsewhere of such trends, which will be introduced later in the discussion of the curriculum.)

Although interference with free expression has not been a daily event, neither has it been a rare occasion, especially at some of the most distinguished institutions which used to be thought of as bastions of free expression and tolerance and marketplace of ideas. A sampling of such events will make the reader grasp that the phenomenon has been quite "systemic":

> In February 1983 . . . Jeane Kirkpatrick came to the Berkeley campus to deliver the Jefferson Lectures . . . As soon as [she] appeared . . . she became [the] target of loud heckling, jeering, and insults . . . Though the protest was well advertised . . . there was little security in the auditorium . . . Unable to make herself heard, Mrs. Kirkpatrick left the stage, returned to finish, then cancelled a speech scheduled for the next day after the Berkeley administration warned her that the next time it might be worse . . . [Brock 1985:36]

Nobody was arrested or disciplined by the university, and a week later the student senate "voted down a proposed apology to Mrs. Kirkpatrick 16 to 12" [Bunzel 1983].

In November 1983 Secretary of Defense Caspar Weinberg received similar treatment at Harvard. In April 1984 once more at Harvard ". . . the moderator of a panel sponsored by the Black Law Students Association . . . refused to allow members of the Jewish Law Students Association to question a representative of the Palestine Liberation Organization" [Brock 1985:37]. In May 1984 at the University of Colorado containers of blood were thrown at former Secretary of State Alexander Haig. In April 1984 Henry Kissinger, due to the threat of disruption, was forced to cancel his keynote address to the 50th anniversary commemoration at the Fletcher School of Diplomacy at Tufts University. The late U.S. Representative Larry McDonald of Georgia was prevented from speaking at American University in November 1982. Eldridge Cleaver, who renounced his radicalism, was prevented from speaking at Berkeley (among other places) in May 1982; in March 1983 he was disrupted during a speech at the University of Minnesota. Duane T. Gish, a proponent of creationism, "was shouted down by students and faculty members" in April 1982 at Berkeley. In April 1984 two representatives of the Nicaraguan resistance were prevented from speaking at the University of Massachusetts at Amherst and they cancelled their appearance at Amherst College the next day due to further threats of disruption. The same two representatives (Alvaro Montalvan and Alvaro Baldizon) were "spotted outside the auditorium [at the State University of New York in Albany] where they were to speak, and chased off by a small group of students who shouted, 'There is the CIA agent—let's hang him.'" In November 1983 Eden Pastora, who once fought Somoza and subsequently the communist government, tried but could not give a speech at Columbia University in New York. Phyllis Schafly, the antifeminist, got similar treatment at the University of Iowa in March 1983. In October 1984 students who were rescued by U.S. troops from Grenada were harassed and disrupted at Ithaca College. In December 1984 Brown University students disrupted a program presented by two CIA recruiters. Similar protests prevented CIA recruiters from giving presentations at Tufts, the University of Massachusetts at Amherst, and the University of Michigan at Ann Arbor [Brock 1985:36–38].

In the spring of 1980 William F. Buckley declined an invitation to speak at Vassar College "after he was warned that a large number of students and faculty did not support his invitation and that he would be shouted down and would risk personal injury" [Csorba n.d.:8–9]. In 1984 the UCLA Latin American Studies Department invited Colonel John Waghelstein to lecture on El Salvador. A group of students "jumped up and down yelling 'murderer' and 'assassin' . . . and that [he] . . . deserved to die like his colleague Commande Shaufelberger . . . murdered by the Marxist FMLN guerillas in 1983." In the spring of 1985 at the University of California at San Diego preacher Jed Smock, who "held a banner supporting President Botha's reforms in South Africa, was tackled, kicked and beaten by pro-divestment students." He also suffered a broken leg after being attacked by radicals at the University of Michigan. In 1985 at Northwestern University in Evanston, Adolfo Calero, a leader of the Nicaraguan resistance, attempted to speak but "As the speech was about to begin, students and faculty rushed the stage and threw red liquid on Mr. Calero . . . The microphone was seized by a Marxist English professor who was quoted as yelling: 'He has no right to speak . . . he will be lucky to get out of here alive.'"

In the fall of 1985 Paul Cameron, a critic of homosexuals, was disrupted and pelted with eggs at the University of Massachusetts; in October 1985 Arturo Cruz, the Nicaraguan opposition leader, tried but failed to speak at the University of California, San Diego campus. In the winter of 1985 at Berkeley an anti-abortion film ("Silent Scream") was interrupted when the showing was "stormed." In the spring of 1985 then Education Secretary William Bennett was supposed to give the commencement address at the University of the Pacific in California but was disinvited after threats from radical faculty and students. In October 1985 at the University of Colorado, Joseph Scheidler of the National Pro-Life Action League was abused as he tried to speak; subsequently the protesters blamed the conservative group which invited him for "provoking violence" by the invitation. Also at Northwestern University in January 1986, Reed Irvine, chairman of Accuracy in Media, was repeatedly interrupted. In the fall of 1985 nationally syndicated conservative columnist Allan Brownfeld was showered with insults at the University of Wisconsin at Madison campus.

In April 1986 Michael Waller of the Council for Inter-American Security and Jorge Rosales, a representative of the Nicaraguan resistance, attempted to speak at the University of Massachusetts at Amherst but could not, due to a highly organized disruption; eventually the campus security decided to end the meeting ahead of time due to what it perceived as a potentially violent situation. (This particular event was witnessed by this author, who can testify to the accuracy of the description here cited.) At Harvard University the same two would-be speakers "were hustled out of the hall just after they had arrived, as disrupters stormed the podium shouting 'death, death, death, death to fascists.' Rosales was hit in the eye by an egg and knocked to the ground. Waller was hit in the back with an unknown object." At Wellesley College the same two individuals "were met by disrupters who threw eggs and pig's blood at them. After five minutes of attempting to speak over loud chants and yells, Waller and Rosales were forced to walk out." According to one Wellesley official "the level of disruption was reasonable."

The incidents listed were recorded in "A Special Report on Campus Free Speech Abuses" and in turn based on various, usually locally published accounts of each incident [Csorba n.d.:8–15]. I did not cite every incident detailed in the report, nor does this report represent a comprehensive compilation of all such incidents.

The policy of not taking action against those disrupting speakers also extended to students who would occupy academic buildings and disrupt the academic enterprise in other ways. This too was reminiscent of the sixties when such sit-ins were daily occurrences around the country and the participants were routinely granted amnesty, whereas in the 70s and 80s such events were less frequent. But when they occurred administrators in the 1980s were just as reluctant (or impotent) to take action. Such policies were usually justified in the following manner: "'Most of the students who occupied the building were motivated by a genuine belief that immediate action was required to address the concerns of Penn State's black community,' the president, Dr. Bryce Jordan, said in granting amnesty to the protesters" ["Penn State Will Drop Charges Against

89 Students" 1988]. This time-honored rationalization would not have been put forth, one may suspect, if for example some other group of students motivated by a similarly "genuine belief" in the necessity of "immediate action" would have occupied a building in order to prevent Jesse Jackson or Louis Farrakhan from speaking.

More recently students who occupied a building of John Jay College in New York City were not only given amnesty but their demand that the school grant tenure to a Hispanic professor was also met as the president reversed his own earlier decision "under pressure from students occupying a campus building" [Weiss 1990; Terry 1990]. A building occupation at Sarah Lawrence College yielded commitments to increase minority faculty and "Afro-American and other multicultural offerings in the curriculum" [Feron 1989].

In the 1980s middle-of-the-road liberal faculties and administrators usually responded to disruptions by asserting that few occured, and those which did have been exaggerated. It was sometimes also claimed (as at Wellesley College) that the speakers could have persisted (since the level of disruption was not unreasonable) despite the "heckling." There has been a growing trend to blur the line between disruption and heckling, the latter elevated to a form of free expression also to be protected. Of late the Harvard Law School prepared a set of guidelines that sought to "balance the rights of speakers with the rights of people to protest and dissent." The guidelines permitted "chanting or making sustained or repeated noise" unless it "substantially interferes with the speaker's communication"—a situation which is likely to be judged differently by speaker and protester. Even the "vestigial loyalty to the old ideal of free speech . . . lurking timorously behind the cant about striking a balance . . . was however seriously flawed precisely by the idea that such a balance . . . between the 'right' to disrupt and the right to communicate and to hear undistrubed these communications—had to be struck" [Podhoretz 1988].

A letter of an MIT professor of political science to the *New York Times* is a fine specimen of the prevailing attitudes among faculties and administrators in such matters. To begin with the importance of such "episodes," as he put it, must be deflated. The writer prefers to call the incidents "unfortunate" rather than "deplorable" or "reprehensible," a choice of word that is not without significance. In this as in other instances the minimization of the seriousness and frequency of these incidents seems directly related to the observer's aversion to the views and policies upheld by the speakers who were silenced. Civil libertarian concerns fade and the threshold of tolerance for disruptions appears to rise when the ideas of the potential speakers are unwelcome. By contrast those who have more sympathy with the message of the speaker more readily uphold the principle of free speech.

Here then are excerpts from the letter criticizing former Secretary Bennett for his "recent charge that a significant body of opinion of college campuses openly 'rejects the democratic ethic' . . .":

> Mr. Bennett seems *fixated* on two *episodes* in which Caspar Weinberger and Jeane Kirkpatrick were hindered from speaking on campus. These were *unfortunate* occurrences, but such occurrences are also *exceedingly rare*. It is much more common for the appearance of a Weinberger or Kirkpatrick on campus to prompt demonstrations and *nondisruptive protest,* but protest and demonstration are more a part of democratic practice than a government official making a speech to a *passive audience.* Is Mr. Bennett distrubed that . . . people *express displeasure* with the policies of the Government of which he is a part? [Stewart 1986; all emphasis mine]

Informative semantic choices may be noted. "Fixated" intends to convey that Bennett's preoccupation with the repeated silencing of Kirkpatrick and Weinberger has a pathological, irrational quality, whereas the writer implies such "episodes" are not deserving of such excessive attention. "Expressing displeasure" is another revealing euphemism for characterizing the thuggish behavior here discussed. Presumably the more strongly such displeasure is felt, the more its expression is vindicated. (This was heard many times in mitigation of the destructive protests of the 1960s.) At last we have the remarkable concept of "a passive audience" the writer apparently disapproves of and contrasts with an active one which freely "expresses its displeasure" with certain speakers. But audiences interested in *listening* to and hearing any speaker—be it Ralph Nader, Jesse Jackson, Caspar Weinberger, or Jeane Kirkpatrick—are always "passive," they do not wish to shout down, chant insults, or throw things at the speaker they came to hear.

One would of course like to know *how* Professor Stewart reached the reassuring conclusion that such disruptions were "exceedingly rare." It is likely that in his case as in others (as was noted in the beginning of this chapter) what is "rare" or "common" rests on different thresholds of tolerance for certain events or phenomena. Professor Stewart's tolerance for the silencing of speakers whose beliefs and policies he finds abhorrent is probably quite high (although not unlimited) since he allows that such episodes are "unfortunate."

Campus disruptions and disturbances were sometimes replicated in high schools, as were some of the ostensible grievances precipating them. Thus in the fall of 1989,

Hundreds of black and Hispanic students, incensed by a history teacher's remark that they deemed racist, walked out of classes in a Brooklyn high school . . . smashing display cabinets and forcing the school to close early . . .

. . . The students were angry about a remark that Jeffrey Goldstein, a white social studies teacher, made during a discussion of South Africa . . . [he] told his students that American blacks were concerned about racism in South Africa but did not express the same concern about the subjugation of blacks in West African nations . . .

. . . Mr. Goldstein has been reassigned to the superintendent's office while officials investigate the students' allegations . . .

In a statement Mr. Goldstein said that in his lecture he described apartheid as a system that was unfair to blacks and then described how many black dictators in African nations had also committed atrocities on their people. [McKinley 1989; see also Navarro 1989]

The incident was an example of both the expanded use of the epithet "racist" and the risks teachers take in making a factually correct statement their audience would rather not hear.

Three groups have been particularly active in silencing speakers and thus representing the most active and militant elements of the adversary culture on the campuses: InCAR (International Committee on Racism), the Spartacus Youth League, and CISPES (Committee in Solidarity with the People of El Salvador).

InCAR, sometimes regarded as a descendant of SDS (Students for a Democratic Society, the major radical student organization of the 1960s subsequently giving rise to the Weathermen), was involved in the disruption already referred to at Northwestern University, among many others. Its activities were further exemplified by leaflets distributed on the campus of the City College of New York directed against a member of the faculty: "We need to expose this dog for the racist he is and have him kicked out of City"; "'This is a rabid CCNY racist . . . his bite is fatal!' [next to the photograph of the maligned professor]"; "Students . . . don't need this type of racist garbage teaching us." InCAR goes beyond verbal violence, as was the case at Northwestern University and also at UCLA when its members assaulted and injured a visiting professor in mathematics. Although active on the campuses InCAR is not campus-based ["InCAR—A Reincarnation of SDS?" 1987:2; see also Klehr 1988]. InCAR leaflets distributed on California campuses proposed that certain groups "must be stopped from spreading racist filth" and "Fascist groups . . . must be violently stopped." According to the California Department of Justice, InCAR members have been convicted of inciting to violence and riots, of assault, battery, and carrying concealed weapons [Csorba n.d.:20–21]. Barbara Foley, formerly of Northwestern University, was an active member and supporter of InCAR.

The Spartacus Youth League also played a leading part in many violent or semi-violent disruptions of speeches including those of Jeane Kirkpatrick at Berkeley and Caspar Weinberger at Harvard. Spartacus is distinguished by a pro-Soviet stance, including support for the Soviet invasion of Afghanistan, and is apparently regarded as truly extremist even by some other leftist groups [see Greene 1986; also Csorba n.d.:22–24; see also Klehr 1988].

CISPES, another major player in current campus activism, has a more moderate rhetoric, more congenial to the middle-of-the-road groups. Yet CISPES participated in many violent disruptions on several campuses involving Henry Kissinger, Jeane Kirkpatrick, and Alexander Haig, among others, and "At a January 1984 national conference it called for 'creative harassment' of supporters of President Reagan's Central American policies" [Csorba n.d.:24–26; Kleher 1988:140]. CISPES is said to be "probably the most well-organized and well-financed of the radical campus groups on the left" and it claims to have 350 to 400 local chapters mostly on campuses. It "has proclaimed that its goal . . . is to provide direct, concrete support for particular revolutonary movements" [Klehr 1988:136]. CISPES has been associated with both the Communist party of El Salvador and that of the United States [Klehr 1988:135–39] and has also been strongly anti-Israel.

Not unlike the relationship between moderate faculty and their radical colleagues, radical student groups too are, for the most part, tolerated by far more moderate students, some of them objecting more to their *tactics* than beliefs [Greene 1986]. And while students are far more conservative than faculties they are also more apolitical, often allowing small but vocal and well-organized radical-left groups (including those mentioned) to dominate the political life on the campuses. Such student apathy was exemplified by the student government elections at the University of Massachusetts at Amherst in 1988. Of some 20,000 undergraduates only 3000 bothered to vote, resulting in the election of a Young Communist League member to president of the student government; he received 1,454 votes, the runner-up 1,093 and a third contestant 492. ["Communist Heads UMass Student Body" 1988].

Special sections of the student newspaper *(The Massachusetts Daily Collegian)* entitled "Third World Affairs" and "Multicultural Affairs" provide further illustration of the prominence of student radicals and their privileged access to the major organ of student opinion on this large campus. A fall 1990 issue carried an article mourning the death of Che Guevara. The author wrote: "Che, your memory lives in me and in countless people throughtout the world. Your life and struggles were not in vain!" In the same issue in another article readers were assured (by the same writer) that "Cuba remains the leading mentor of revolutions of the oppressed people of the world today ..." [Monteverde 1990:7]. In a November issue of the same publication the readers were treated to a reverential biographical account of Saddam Hussein [Dastidar 1990:3]. Examples of this kind could be easily multiplied.

The censorship over the free circulation and exploration of ideas is not confined to the disruptions discussed above. There have also been various initiatives on numerous campuses to curtail types of research which appear to threaten particular values. For example believers in animal rights are opposed to all experiments on animals and exert increasing pressure to prevent them from being carried out, as was the case recently at Cornell University [Lyall 1988]. There also remains much hostility toward any research that would benefit the defense industries or the Department of Defense. Hampshire College president Adele Simmons advised that "... faculty should be careful about their research ... Research is sometimes manipulated by corporations and by the Defense Department and should be carefully monitored to ensure that research priorities are determined by academics" [McKay 1982:16]. It is not hard to imagine instances when Ms. Simmons might have been willing to depart from such standards and propose that academics should heed the suggestions (for research or teaching) emanating from non-academic sources. Indeed Hampshire College has prided itself among other things in its responsiveness to the needs of non-academic groups and in allowing itself to be guided by concerns and priorities far from purely academic. In the very same interview Ms. Simmons said, "I have little patience with the completely ivory tower view which says our job is to provide formal education and that's it" [Ibid.]. In short the "completely ivory tower view" may be embraced or rejected depending on the occasion.

Taboo research topics include investigations of the relationship between heredity and intelligence and the evaluation of the results of affirmative action programs [Rothman 1986; Beer 1987]. There was also widespread opposition to undertaking research on Third World countries for the Pentagon [Winkler 1985].

Campus activism in the 1980s was not limited to silencing speakers who challenged prevailing left-of-center orthodoxies or to discouraging research of the types noted above. Old and new causes of considerable variety continued to be championed. Among the new ones South Africa and divestment (or an economic blockade and boycott) was probably the most popular judged by the number of demonstrations it inspired. Not unlike the causes of the sixties, the passion South Africa unleased was closely related to an underlying animus toward American society. While

Vietnam used to symbolize for many activists the ultimate corruption of American society, now it was South Africa (apartheid, that is) that vindicated belief in the rottenness of "the system" and capitalism in particular. As a former student of the University of California at Berkeley (who returned to help "rekindle the movement") said:

> We are really looking to create a movement without the raw material of the 60's, the draft, civil rights, and we needed an issue. Nobody knew whether it would be Nicaragua, South Africa, El Salvador or what. To me South Africa is just as convenient issue that helps expose the system. By that I mean the whole system of corporate capitalism. [Lindsey 1987]

The old anticapitalist animus also survived (or revived) on Ivy League campuses such as Amherst College in Massachusetts, at any rate among a small number of activists no less hostile to the system than their predecessors were twenty years earlier. Thus reflected a student in the campus newspaper on the ties between his school and capitalism:

> . . . Amherst [College] is a class institution, and must . . . serve the interests of the American ruling class . . . Those interests include maintaining racism, sexism, a stratified class society and the barbaric, violent, exploitative system of property relations which constitutes advanced capitalism. But those interests also include covering up and mystifying the brutal, cynical principles which govern society . . . By presenting itself as a liberal, progressive, enlightened institution . . . the college cynically masks its true functions. ["Talk of the Campus" 1985]

The remarks of the Amherst College student echoed the argument of his elders who regularly warned about the ideals of academic freedom masking "academic repression" or "disguis[ing] and distort[ing] an essentially repressive practice." Professor Bertell Ollman—casting aside the skepticism reserved for American society—insisted that genuine academic freedom will flourish only "in a society that no longer needs its universities to reproduce and rationalize existing inequalities, that is, a socialist society" [Kaplan and Schrecker eds. 1983:54].

Besides the continued criticism of capitalism (with or without the issue of corporate responsibility for apartheid) other recent causes mobilizing the energies of left-wing activists were Central America, the various peace campaigns, and, on the domestic front, racism, sexism (to a lesser extent homophobia), and environmentalism.

The issues of racism and sexism exercised an especially powerful influence on campus life (as will also be noted under "curriculum" and "standards") because there was an obvious constituency, blacks and feminists, to promote them. In a unique demonstration of the susceptibility of academic institutions to such pressures Princeton University was considering in 1988 to require all incoming freshmen to take an oath avowing that they will abstain from sexist, racist, class discriminatory, or homophobic behavior [Whitmoyer 1988]. In a somewhat similar spirit, Smith College in Massachusetts—shaken by the findings of a methodologically dubious survey alleging omnipresent racism, sexism, and classism (discussed below)—was anxious lest its croquet court will be judged to be yet another manifestation of its elitism ["Smith College Croquet Court Elitist?" 1988].

Sometimes more transient causes would mobilize radical and left-of-center groups. Thus there were protest rallies against the U.S. invasion of Grenada in 1983 at the University of California in Berkeley and the University of Wisconsin in Madison (among other places) as the American assertion of power once more brought forth anger and a visceral revulsion among adversarial groups ["New Brand of Campus Activism" 1983]. At a teach-in at Mount Holyoke College in Massachusetts similar feelings were stimulated by the bombing of Libya:

> The speakers ranged from those ... passionately critical of the Reagan administration's decision ... to those who were only moderately disturbed by the action ... William McFeely ... Melon Professor in the humanities drew applause when he called on his listeners to "stop this hatred, stop this terrible love of war ... this lust of war." [Carlson 1986]

In the fall of 1980 at the University of Michigan at Ann Arbor a visit by CIA recruiters provided an opportunity to protest U.S. policies in Afghanistan. The recruiters "... were met by about fifty demonstrators. One carried a sign which read: 'Extend the Gains of the October Revolution to Afghanistan'" [Hewitt 1982:19].

The moral confusion (or double standards) of the new crop of activists was revealed in a conversation reported by Wilcomb Washburn, an anthropologist at the Smithsonian Institution:

> I twice met with students in the shanty built in 1986 in Harvard Yard ... I attempted to discuss with them the subject of "necklacing"—the practice of putting a rubber tire around the neck of someone suspected of being an informer ... filling it with petrol [gas] and burning the victim slowly to death ... I had not realised that most of the inhabitants of this pleasant shanty town ... were ignorant of these activities ... Nor did they have any idea of the number of blacks lynched in this fashion by fellow blacks ... One or two professed knowledge of the process but declined to express an attitude about it. Most of those who professed ignorance of the practice, after being informed of its character, refused to condemn it. Their argu-

ments took the following forms: 1) The real violence is apartheid . . . 2) Those lynched were "asking for it" . . . 3) "What about American support for the contras in Nicaragua?" . . . [Washburn 1988:408]

The spirit and substance of public discourse on the campuses is illuminatingly captured by a compilation[2] of campus activities during 1984–85 at the University of Massachusetts at Amherst (and some neighboring campuses) which could be readily duplicated on many other campuses.

For the school year 1984–1985 Latin America was the major preoccupation of the activists. Other issues, however, were not ignored as world hunger, nuclear arms and apartheid received their due share of attention. The events and groups listed below were advertised by posters and the campus newspaper.

For the student just arriving at the University, the American Friends Service Committee made available a mail-in pledge to protest U.S. military action in Central America. The pledge application provided a box where students could indicate if they wished to be contacted "concerning pre-invasion vigils."

On September 26th the UMass Friends of the Spartacus Youth League sponsor a Spartacus Youth League Film and Forum. The film is entitled "Labor's Turning Point" and the after-film discussion is led by Gene Herson, a former presidential candidate. Next day the Radical Student Union holds its introductory meeting for the Fall semester.

October's wealth of events start with thrice daily showings of Helen Caldicott's "If You Love This Planet" on the 9–12th. The film is sponsored by the UMass Peacemakers. On the 15th at nearby Elms College (in Chicopee, Mass.), Penny Lernoux (left-of-center investigative reporter and author of books on Latin America) speaks on "Human Rights: The Struggle in Latin America." On the 19th, Jim Stormes, a Jesuit priest, gives an early morning talk on "Liberation Theology." This serves to introduce a full week of talks and panel discussions entitled "Clouds of War, Winds of Change: U.S. and Revolution in Central America." The keynote address is given by Howard Zinn, the author of A People's History of the United States, well-known radical author and prominent anti-war activist of the Vietnam era. The week's events included films and videos, a panel discussion with Mel King (former mayoral candidate in Boston and leader of the Rainbow Coalition), Carol Bengelsdorf (Hampshire College) and John Childs (Amherst College); a lecture on "The Role of the Church in Central America" as well as one on the "History of U.S. Intervention in Central America" by Howard Zinn.

There was also a Rally for National Student Peace Day to express opposition to aid to El Salvador, protest illegal war in Nicaragua; "express outrage" at the Grenada Invasion of one year ago; support a nuclear freeze and eventually disarmament.

The "Militarization in Central America and the Caribbean" was discussed by Arthur Barisano (Lawyers' Committee Against Intervention in Central America), Karen Wanza (Grenada Foundation) and Doris Summers (Amherst College).

In November most of the activities centered around the presidential election. Other activities included a "Forum on Social Responsibility" on November 1, at Mount Holyoke College (on "Mt. Holyoke's Stock Investments") followed by a talk by two Vietnam veterans, Brian Wilson and Earl Williams, on the subject of "No More Vietnams." The next day a group called "Central America in Transition" presented a talk by Jose Luis Medal of the Central Bank of Nicaragua. The University radio station broadcast a program entitled "Ronald Reagan and the Prophecy of Armageddon." It purported to document how Reagan's "Christian fundamentalist belief in . . . Armageddon . . . threatens the world with Nuclear Holocaust."

December began with an appeal by the Western Massachusetts Latin American Solidarity Committee (WMLASC) for goods for the Nicaraguan peasants. The Nicaraguan Material Aid Campaign lasted from the 3rd till the 7th. One could also participate in a sit-in on the 9th protesting U.S. Militarism at Westover Air Force Base, the closest to provide such opportunity (also the setting for Vietnam era protests). Two days later one could listen to a talk sponsored, once again, by the UMmass Peacemakers. The speaker was the Reverend James P. Keller, and his speech was called "Nicaragua: A Fact Finding Mission."

The events of February included an introductory meeting for WMLASC offering a film and discussion afterwards and a "Women's Valentine Dance" sponsored by and a benefit for "Not in Our Name," a "women's resistance group."

On March 9, the UMass Peacemakers sponsored a coffeehouse to benefit the Trident II Plowshares (a protest against the Trident II submarine, an annual activity at Groton, Conn., shipyards spearheaded by the American Friends Service Committee). At this coffeehouse, peace activist and "plowshare" Leo Schiff was on hand to talk about this group and the future of the peace movement. Less than a week later Richard Falk (prominent social critic and professor at Princeton University), Joy Hackel (Institute for Policy Studies), Louis Wolf (editor of *Covert Action Information Bulletin*), and John Stockwell (former CIA agent and author of *In Search of Enemies*) were on hand for a discussion moderated by Francis Crowe (Western Massachusetts coordinator, leader of AFSC).

Another panel discussion followed on the 28th sponsored by the Five College Council on Investment Responsibility concerning "Divestment and Alternatives."

Shortly afterwards the Third World Women's Program, the Everywoman's Center, and the American Friends Service Committee of Northampton sponsored a talk by Minoru Yasui on "The American Concentration Camps: Wartime Necessity or Tragic Error?" Ms. Yasui is the attorney and chairperson of the National Redress Committee. On the 30th (of March) NECAN [New England Central America Network, evidently a kindred organization or offshoot of CISPES (listed on its stationary)] presented the play "La Ultima Banana en Managua," a "satire of U.S. policy towards Nicaragua as seen through . . . an American CIA agent."

April began with a four-day sit-in sponsored by the "April 1st Coalition." The Coalition protested a $171 increase in student fees and coupled this protest with a demand for divestment in South Africa. The connection was justified on the ground that "justice in South Africa starts with justice at home." One week later, TecNica (a Professionals' Brigade for Nicaragua) held a slide presentation co-sponsored by the "Coalition for the Responsible Use of Computer Science" and the Northampton Committee on Central America.

The very next day the "Women's Encampment for Peace and Justice" began. Sponsored by Mount Holyoke College Peace Through Disarmament Project, the MHC Women's Center, the Progressive Student Alliance, and the General Topic Committee, the encampment was a full, two-day event. It included "Opening and Sharing Herstories," Candlelight vigil and singing, "Despair and Empowerment Workshop," Anti-racism workshop, a discussion of connections between peace and social justice, among other activities.

The last week of April made extraordinary demands on an activist's time. The Western Mass. Central America Network (a collection of independent groups) called for a series of "vigils" every night from the 22nd to the 29th. Simultaneously, AHORA sponsored Latin America Week. Both of these groups' efforts were intended to stimulate opposition to the Congressional funding of the Nicaraguan resistance. The Western Mass. Central America Network's vigils were held every day in either Amherst, Northampton, Holyoke, Pittsfield, Springfield, or Greenfield.

Speakers during Latin America Week (April 22–28) featured a representative from the Nicaraguan embassy. A film on Guatemala, "When the Mountains Tremble," was shown; there was a talk on "Socialism in Cuba" by Tony Guglielmi, "Poetry and Prose of Central America," a dance with music by Concepto Latino, discussion on "The Guatemalean Tragedy and the Sanctuary Movement" and Chilean folk dancers.

April 29th was called "No Business as Usual Day," sponsored by the No Business as Usual Coalition. Teachers were urged to cancel their classes and students were asked to skip them if necessary in order to attend the day's events. This rally was organized to protest militarism, racism, and nuclear arms.

On May 3, a rally was organized to protest President Reagan's visit to the Bitburg Cemetery. On the 7th climaxing the year's events, Ernesto Cardenal (member of the Sandinista Directorate and described on the posters as Chancellor Duffy's Honored Guest) gave a poetry reading to a standing room only crowd. He received a standing ovation at the end of a poetry/question session that was frequently punctuated by applause. The very next day, perhaps stimulated by Padre Cardenal's visit, the Faculty for Peace in Central America held a teach-in entitled "Central America: What Can You Do About It." Their speakers included Eqbal Ahmad (Institute for Policy Studies and Hampshire College) and several faculty supporters of the Sandinistas.

It can be asserted with confidence that the type of political activities described above were not peculiar to the University of Massachusetts but could be encountered at all major universities and smaller elite institutions, private or public, in virtually identical form.

In the late 1980s the threats against free expression came not merely from the old-style activists but, more unexpectedly, from the administrators of colleges and universities. These threats took the form of campaigns and policies against what came to be called "harassment" and "insensitivity." The most notorious among such policies (subsequently found unconstitutional by a federal judge) was promulgated by the University of Michigan. According to a booklet published by the University, "discriminatory harassment" may include

> . . . comments and jokes . . . based on . . . many kinds of human differences. All members of the University community are subject to disciplinary action if their behavior threatens or interferes with another person's academic efforts, employment or participation in the University community or if it creates a hostile or demeaning environment.
> . . . Some examples are:
> . . . A male student makes remarks in class like "Women just aren't as good in this field as men," thus creating a hostile learning atmosphere for female classmates.
> Students in a residence hall have a floor party and invite everyone . . . except one person because they think she might be a lesbian.
> . . . Two men demand that their roommate in the residence hall move out and be tested for AIDS. [*What Students Should Know* n.d.]

A memorandum on the same topic provided this clarification:

> Certain types of behavior can create a discriminatory environment . . . [such as] comments that rely on stereotypic attitudes . . . the use of slang and epithets exhibiting a hostile or demeaning attitude . . . comments that rely on preconceived notions . . . about an individual's background, abilities or interests. [*Policy on Discrimination* 1989:1]

The memorandum listed eleven officials or official bodies designated to receive reports of such misbehavior, and the booklet quoted above listed eight additional or partially overlapping organizations or services on campus for advice on harassment.

Not only were these guidelines exceedingly vague and subject to the subjective interpretation of any aggrieved individual (as to what is demeaning, hostile, stereotypic, or offensive) but they were also selective in their inspiration as well as application: they condoned, for example, the hostile stereotyping of white males, who could be vilified and disparaged (at the University of Michigan as on most campuses) with total impunity.

The memorandum referred to above also declared that "even apparently consensual relationships often constitute sexual harassment" between people located on different rungs of one of the hierarchies at the University; hence the authorities reserved the right to investigate such relationships even when they were defined as consensual on the part of the participants [Ibid.:2].

If such invasions of privacy and violations of free expression had Orwellian undertones even more striking was the fact that the faculty of a law school, specifically that of the University of Buffalo in New York, would subscribe to similar constraints on free speech. It voted in 1987 unanimously in support of a "Statement Regarding Intellectual Freedom, Tolerance and Political Harassment" which proposed, among other things, that free speech within the law school "must become tempered by the responsibility to promote equality and justice" [Hentoff 1989:12] —another stunningly vague formulation admirably suited to justify a wide variety of restrictions on free speech that would have been joyfully endorsed by a Soviet censor in the old days.

In all such instances the obvious question arises: Who will be authorized to define what constitutes equality and justice and how they are best promoted? Alan Dershowitz, the legal scholar at Harvard Law School, wrote about what he called "speech crimes":

> On university campuses across the country efforts are under way to restrict speech that is deemed offensive to blacks, women, gays . . .
>
> If such paternalistic restrictions . . . had been advocated by members of the Moral Majority or the John Birch Society they would have been jeered off campus as crypto-fascist. But because current attempts to censor free speech are being pressed by some minority leaders . . . they are being seriously considered . . .
>
> Universities are training grounds for citizenship . . . Rules of free expression should not be different on and off campus. [Dershowitz 1989]

He also noted that these policies were designed not to interfere with "minority racists" like Louis Farrakhan, Al Sharpton, or Stokeley Carmichael, or "feminist sexists" like Andrea Dworkin; they allowed to censure or suppress right-wing publications but not left-wing ones. Commenting on such rules at the University of Wisconsin, Garry Wills also pointed out that "If a similar code were drawn up . . . banning unpatriotic, irreligious or sexually explicit expressions on campus—the people framing Wisconsin type rules would revert to their libertarian past" [Wills 1989:71]. But even the constitutional lawyers on the faculty went along with these rules.

Nat Hentoff's explanation of the acquiescence of faculties to these codes is persuasive:

> . . . it was more important to go on record as vigorously opposing racism and sexism than to expose oneself to charges of insensitivity to these malignancies.
> The pressures to have the "right" attitude—as proved by having the "right" language in and out of class—can be stifling. A student who opposes affirmative action, for instance, can be branded a racist. [Hentoff 1989:12]

Nor have these policies amounted to idle threats. University administrations have been quite zealously pursuing students violating their guidelines or displaying what they regarded as insensitivity toward selected groups. At Tufts University in Massachusetts a student was suspended for wearing a T-shirt that proclaimed preference for beer over women; at Yale and the University of Chicago students were suspended for putting up posters criticizing homosexuality while on the same campuses homosexuals were free to publicize in similar manner their own sexual preferences. At UCLA the editor of a student newspaper was suspended for publishing a "racially insensitive" cartoon that poked fun at affirmative action [Sowell 1989].

It needs to be stressed that solicitousness about the sensitivity of groups and individuals has been quite selective:

> At UCLA as elsewhere, the thought police are strictly one-sided. When a minority student newspaper at UCLA said that Europeans "do not possess the qualities of rational thought, generosity and magnanimity" nobody called that "racially insensitive" . . .
> Double standards are not simply racial but ideological. When a black student in a wheelchair was threatened by physical violence by another black student at Dartmouth, no one was suspended. The young man in the wheelchair was a reporter for the conservative *Dartmouth Review*. [Sowell 1989]

The sensitivity of those of European ancestry also remained unprotected at the City College of New York, where a black professor, Leonard

Jeffries, Jr., called them "the ice people . . . fundamentally materialistic, greedy, intent on domination" and contrasted them with people of African descent—"the sun people . . . essentially humanistic and communal." He also argued in booklets handed out to his students that "an abundance of the skin pigment melanin gives blacks intellectual and physical advantages over whites" [Berger 1990:B1]. Not incidentally Dr. Jeffries was "the leading author" of the report that urged sweeping curricular changes in the school system of New York State, discussed below.

Another academic observer of these trends provided a more comprehensive compilation of groups to which the new solicitousness did not extend and which, unprotected by elaborate guidelines against "discriminatory harassment," could be safely and heartily abused. They included the military establishment, the police, fundamentalist religious groups, the rich, big business, incumbent Republican presidents, and white males [Weissberg 1989–90].

The Curriculum
Not surprisingly the trends and tendencies discussed in the preceding had considerable impact on what is taught in the classrooms (in addition to constituting a "learning experience" by themselves). The influence of adversarial beliefs show up (a) in the new programs and courses designed to promote political-ideological messages and agendas (e.g., women studies, black studies, multicultural programs, gay studies, peace studies, and so on); (b) in the changing format and message of traditional courses; and (c) in the new textbooks. The "mainstreaming" of Marxism has accompanied these developments as many of its ideas and propositions acquired the status of conventional wisdom in the humanities and social sciences [see for example Barringer 1989; Burowoy 1982].

Three broad influences may be detected behind the rise of the curricular changes here discussed. The first is the entrenchment of a mentality, bequeathed by 1960s, that is sharply and reflexively critical of American society and institutions imparted foremost by the former 60s activists who entered the teaching profession. (As Roger Kimball noted, ". . . it is important to appreciate the extent to which the radical vision of the sixties has not so much been abandoned as internalized by many who came of age then and who now teach and administer our institutions of higher education" [Kimball 1990:xiv].) The second influence is exerted by a diffuse egalitarian impulse and the third is constituted by certain group interests and agendas.

The nature of the first factor is captured in a comment by Brigitte Berger, the sociologist:

> . . . what one finds widespread on the American campus today is a soft leftism . . . available for mobilization on behalf of a bewildering variety of

causes that have little in common except hostility to American society as it is. This "soft leftism" has several carriers: Environmentalism, Third Worldism, Peace Studies, remnant movements of the counterculture of the 60s (holistic medicine, alternative education etc.) and above all, feminism in its broadest definition. [Berger 1988:7]

This "soft leftism" does in fact permeate each new program of studies. It is a basic thrust of black (or Hispanic) studies to demonstrate the relationship between the injustices of American society and the hardships visited upon these minorities. Feminist studies focus on the sufferings borne by women in a patriarchal, capitalist society such as the United States. A similar perspective is no less congenial to gay studies. Nor do peace studies find it difficult to hold the United States responsible for global conflicts and tensions, while environmental studies are also quite capable of taking the same position regarding both the domestic and global deterioration of the environment. Latin American studies too are dedicated to the same proposition (perhaps the most zestfully) which is hardly surprising given the worldview of the Latin American Studies Association noted earlier. (At one of the major centers of such studies, the University of Texas at Austin, the brochure describing the Latin American Studies program begins by pointing out that "Understanding foreign areas and peoples is not a strong point of North Americans. The success of our continentwide conquest and our twentieth century free world leadership has further biased us to see the rest of the world in terms of our political and economic domination" [*Institute of Latin American Studies* 1986–87, p. 1].

It would not then be startling if the students exposed to and absorbing the messages of such programs emerge from them deeply shaken, angry, or sad and persuaded that their country has been guilty of an exceptionally wide range of misdeeds abroad and of perpetuating a uniquely unjust social-economic system at home. In most cases this is precisely the objective of the pedagogic project the instructors of such programs hope to accomplish.

Indeed a key characteristic of the new interdisciplinary programs mentioned is their frank disavowal of any degree of detachment or objectivity—even the possibility of disinterested curiosity is ruled out by the untroubled embrace of advocacy. It is not only the political commitment of those promoting these programs and courses that accounts for this but also the belief, with us since the 60s, that unique and distinctive perspectives are involved in teaching and studying certain groups which are not accessible to outsiders.

Women's studies (and feminist scholarship) has become "a theoretical approach exclusively anchored in gender subjectivity" [Berger 1988:12], its premise being that "gender is the root factor of existence, excluding all others (age, class, ethnicity, culture, belief, will, temperament and choice . . .)" [Ibid.:11]. That is to say, it is widely held among these academics that women, and especially the enlightened feminists among them, have a privileged access to truth and reality, as the proletariat used to have in Marxist epistemology, with the "redemptive role Marxists assign to the proletariat . . . now transferred to women" [Ibid.:13]. It has never been satisfactorily explained, neither by Marxists nor feminists, "how subjugation produces wider and clearer vision" [Levin 1988:101]—rather it is something taken for granted, perhaps a byproduct of the idealization of the authentic victim in Western social thought influenced by the Judeo-Christian ethic.

To be sure it is not easy to distinguish crude indoctrination and the attendant one-sidedness from the honest communication of the teacher's own values in a manner that allows students to choose among alternative interpretations. But it is clear that when a teacher is determined to pursue only a particular line of argument representing the only correct view of things (even if this is called consciousness-level raising), the line to indoctrination is crossed.

By now the issue of objectivity in the social sciences and humanities has largely been disposed of (by the new generation of radical scholars) as a sham, something both unattainable and unworthy of striving for. Nor is it any longer a generally accepted norm that the classroom is not the place for teachers to proselytize and to disseminate their political beliefs. On the contrary it is often claimed that allowing one's political beliefs to permeate what is taught is a sign of integrity and laudable candor. This has been increasingly the case in the humanities. John Searle observed, ". . . many members of the cultural left think that the primary function of teaching the humanities is political; they do not really believe that the humanities are valuable in their own right except as a means of achieving 'social transformation'" [Searle 1990:36].

It should be noted that those who openly advocate teaching as indoctrination (with the correct views and values) are fully persuaded that teaching *has always been* a tool of the ruling classes and an instrument of indoctrination. Ever since the 1960s social critics insisted that formal education was the main device for inculcating false consciousness into the masses, a point of view expressed not only by Bertell Ollman, quoted earlier, but also by Samuel Bowles and Herbert Gintis [see Bowles and Gintis 1976] and before them by Marcus Raskin, who perceived "the school . . . as the training instrument for the state . . . Children in a colonzied world [i.e., the United States] . . . are expected to be the tools of forces they cannot see, understand or control . . . the individual learns . . . to see himself functionally in the performance of a specialized series of tasks . . . In the Channeling Colony [Raskin's term for schools—P.H.]

students are essentially in the same position as the peasants of the Middle Ages" [Raskin 1971:111, 113, 118, 119].

It is not acknowledged in these circles that there may be a significant difference between the incomplete attainment of scholarly objectivity on the one hand, as opposed to on the other hand teaching or research directed at the attainment of specific political objectives or at proving preconceived ideological notions. "Commitment" and "advocacy" thus become not only acceptable but praiseworthy especially in the framework of programs—for example, black studies, women's studies—which emerged not in response to some deeply felt scholarly need but to promote an explicitly political-ideological agenda and serve the perceived interests of the groups which are the subject matter of these programs.

Thus spoke a professor active in women's studies:

> A very important aspect of women's studies is self-discovery and self-liberation . . . [students] begin to analyze their own lives in political terms as a natural result of the critical analysis of the distribution of power in society . . . The study of the ways in which power is distributed, including its distribution by sex, may lead to political commitment. [Lilla 1986:54]

A report produced in 1976 by the National Advisory Council on Women's Educational Programs declared that the classroom devoted to women's studies is "a place in which anyone may say anything, however private or political . . . both of intellect and feeling, qualitatively different from most college classrooms . . . mainly because of the reliance on a unique combination of scholarship and the experience of classroom participants" [Levin 1985:2]. The statement suggests that not only in such courses is the line crossed from what used to be considered teaching to indoctrination but therapy too has become part of them.

Advocates of women's studies make no bones about their desire to convert the classroom into a political platform. The University of Massachusetts Women's Studies Program says in its preamble: "Faculty members are active in current feminist research, scholarship and activism, and they bring this experience and background to the classroom and their advising" [Women's Studies Course Offerings 1987:n.p.]. The proposal for establishing a women's studies course at Kenyon College stated that "The course . . . will consider the issues of class, racism and homophobia as well as sexism . . . [and] consider the transformation needed to achieve a non-sexist society" [Lilla 1986:54].

Not all students are comfortable with these goals and points of view. A rare public account of such an undertaking was given by an unhappy male participant (in an introductory class in women's studies) at the University of Washington in Seattle who was dismissed from the course as a "disruptive influence":

> ... from the first day on they [the instructors] started in about how all men are wife-beaters and child-molestors and how the traditional American family ... doesn't work ... You read the course description and they say the class is supposed to foster "vigorous, open inquiry" into all issues regarding women but then they classified everything I had to say as racist or sexist. [Egan 1988:B8]

The "consciousness-level raising" associated with feminist (and similar) studies rests on the assumption that those taught and uplifted (to the level of the instructor) are neither aware of their true interests nor see the world as it is; nor do they fully or correctly understand their own condition and the nature of their oppression. Hence such studies have also been called, ironically but with good reason, "oppression studies" (a term that was introduced by Thomas Short but see also Goode [1988 December:47]).

Women's, black, Hispanic, and gay studies share a commitment to the elaboration and deepening of a sense of victimization; they also present a scheme of the victim-victimizer relationship that usually confers a sense of virtue and innocence upon the victim group finding its life entirely determined by circumstances beyond its control. As the title of the popular text in the early 70s implied, the victim must not be blamed. In this as in other respects the reigning assumptions in American society changed quite thoroughly as the pendulum swung from the past tendency to indeed blame the victims (e.g., the poor or incarcerated criminals) for their condition, to the current view that relieves them of *all* responsibility.

Each of the groups who support and staff these academic programs shares a firm commitment to their own victimized status and a belief that improvements in their condition are insignificant, more apparent than real. This belief seems to be bolstered by two circumstances. One is the institutionalized system of rewards which flow to certain victimized groups and is enshrined in legislation and academic policy. The more improvements are made and acknowledged the less justification for the continuation of the compensatory measures (affirmative action). The second basis for the denial of improvements is likely to be rooted in the personal and professional identities of the people involved. An acknowledgment of a substantial decline of their victimization would undermine huge intellectual and psychological investments and could also threaten thousands of jobs.

Black studies, the first of these new programs, preceded and paved the way to women's studies and similar enterprises. Its emergence was among the expressions of a striving for a new and stronger cultural and political identity; establishment of black studies programs was invariably among the demands black students made during sit-ins and protest demonstrations in the late 1960s. These programs, besides being symbolic affirmations of black identity, also helped to cushion the impact of what for many black students was an alien and difficult academic environment. ("By adopting the opinion that the standard curriculum is a cultural imposition, minority students can excuse their failures, actual or feared, and turn injured pride into principled defiance" [Short 1988 Summer: 14]. It was not unreasonable to expect that in such a program of study—where one's personal experiences and beliefs were in effect a part of the curriculum—it would be easier to do well than in other, more traditional disciplines and programs.

Since the mid-1980s there has emerged as a new focus of campus activism a demand for the establishment of "cultural diversity" or "multicultural" studies pressed primarily by black and Hispanic students already the putative beneficiaries of black or Hispanic study programs. These demands have also been supported by feminists and other radical groups, among both students and faculty. It is not easy to explain what precisely prompted the demand for and subsequent introduction of these new programs which to a considerable degree duplicate existing black, Hispanic, and feminist studies. The initiative for these new programs seems to have come primarily from black students and may in some measure reflect both their unhappiness with what has been sometimes called their "ghettoization" in black studies and their unhappiness with required survey courses in Western culture or civilization. These demands may also be a reflection of the desire to see some approximation of their ethnic studies be extended, in a mandatory manner, to the entire student population. The same may be said about the feminist constituency, equally anxious to see that its distinctive points of view be more widely disseminated and mandated.

It is important to make clear that the issue of "diversity" has been almost entirely spurious since Western civilization or culture courses have hardly been lacking in diversity, nor has the liberal arts curriculum as a whole. Thomas Short, a professor of philosophy, pointed out:

> The standard curriculum, remember, is in fact not a cultural imposition but imparts knowledge and skills that benefit anyone who receives them. . . . a diversity of perspective is already contained within "the western tradition." In addition the standard curriculum contains courses on other civilizations and on ethnic cultures . . .

> ... The liberal arts are nothing like an ethnic culture ... Greeks do not come to college knowing Plato, nor Italians Dante. Nor do Plato and Dante have much to do with Episcopalian Sunday School and country club culture of affluent WASPs. Plato, Dante, Milton, fugue and sonata forms, Latin, the Calculus, genetics, supply and demand curves, English constitutional history and Marxist theory ... ethnic background makes no difference to these studies ... The liberal arts are no one's ethnic culture. [Short 1988 Summer:14–15, 17, 10]

Irving Howe had equally compelling arguments in favor of the classics while drawing attention to the non-academic, non-intellectual pressures behind the new movement for "diversity":

> ... there was something wrong about the way the Stanford [University] decision was made, as a response to political pressures. This means that the basic humanities curriculum becomes subject to bargaining by "constituencies" ...
>
> Nor is there any strong reason for giving "substantial attention to issues of race, gender and class" in such courses. The Bible, Homer, Plato, Sophocles, Shakespeare are central to our culture; some knowledge of these or closely similar texts is part of any higher education worthy of the name ... And it ought to be part of any serious university education that students be encouraged to get past the provincialism of the contemporary. They go to college in order to learn something they cannot learn in the streets, on TV, or even a political rally. [Howe 1988:478–479]

Ever since the 1960s faculties have, for the most part, caved in to pressures to make their offerings more "relevant," that is to say, less foreign to the experience of students complaining that the classics did not address their experience. Howe asked: "Why should they? ... One (not the only) reason for reading the classics is that they widen and deepen our experience ..." [Ibid.:479].

A further irony that goes generally unrecognized by those attacking "Western culture," as both a course and a concept, is that it is only in Western culture that the idea of cultural relativity and ethnocentrism exist. Alan Bloom pointed out that

> if the students were really to learn something of ... these non-Western cultures ... they would find that each and every one of these cultures is ethnocentric. All of them think their way is the best way and all others are inferior ... Only in the Western nations ... is there some willingness to doubt the identification of good with one's own way. [Bloom 1987:36]

Rather than representing any genuine "cultural diversity" the new programs are best described as an effort to institute "affirmative action for ideas" [Himmelfarb 1988], a new quota system that seeks to ensure that certain ideas associated with authors of a particular race or ethnicity, "women, minorities and persons of color," will be represented in the curriculum. "Cultural diversity" studies represent a logical extension of existing affirmative action programs (which govern the hiring of faculty and admission of students).

An additional basis of the demand for such programs and the diversity they are supposed to promote is a contrived association of the traditional Western culture or civilization courses with racism, sexism, elitism, classism, and homophobia, and the claim that these courses, and Western culture itself, promote these dispositions.

As the foregoing makes clear, Western culture and its specific products are to be approached critically. But when it comes to the non-Western cultures cultural diversity programs seek to promote, the approach becomes strikingly different. At Stanford University, which was among the first to introduce cultural diversity programs, it was declared that

> Courses that fulfill the world cultures requirement "should study the history and culture of regions whose peoples are not of European descent" and "focus on these cultures in their own right, for their own sake and where appropriate, in their own terms" ["New Courses to Focus on Cultural Diversity" 1990]

Thus were students put on notice that these non-European cultures must *not* be studied in a detached, comparative, critical, or culturally relativizing manner! The quote captures what used to be meant by ethnocentrism. In fact the problem of the new "cultural diversity" or "multicultural" programs is that they do not broaden and enrich the intellectual diet of students but promote a non-intellectual, non-educational agenda, a new politically correct ethnocentrism. Arthur Schlesinger, Jr., wrote:

> Let us by all means teach women's history, black history, Hispanic history. But let us teach them as history, not as a means of promoting group self-esteem. . . .
> Novelists, moralists, politicians, fabulators can go beyond historical evidence to tell inspiring stories. But historians are custodians of professional standards. Their objective is critical analysis . . . not making people feel better about themselves. [Schlesinger 1990:12]

The hostility to Western culture courses is among the most powerful and strongly felt expressions of alienation from the dominant institutions of American society and the values supporting them; it is also a reflection of hostility to Western culture, or what is perceived as Western culture, rather than a manifestation of thirst for "diversity." It is not cultural or educational but political and ideological goals that are being pursued; those pressing for these courses do not clamor for Ibn Khaldun, the Upanishads, the works of Madame be Staël, the classics of Japanese or Chinese culture; nor are they anxious to immerse themselves in pre-Columbian art or religion. As a correspondent in the *New York Times* pointed out, proponents of these programs seek whatever is "trendy, contemporary and express all the right opinions . . . Rather than getting outside any Western cultural perspective all that this represents is contemporary American liberalism contemplating its own navel" [Tucker 1988].

Emerging contours of these programs indicate that what their advocates demand, under the pretense of "diversity," are source materials which will affirm their own hostility toward Western values and social systems. Not even race or gender is sufficient for inclusion: a Thomas Sowell or Glenn Loury, black social scientists, need not apply, since they are not of the proper left-of-center persuasion. Nor is it likely that feminist supporters of this undertaking will demand that the scholarly works of a woman such as Jeane Kirkpatrick be included. "Cultural diversity" programs seek, besides "affirmative action in ideas," a new dose of social criticism made compulsory instructional material for all students. Supporters of these programs seem to believe, as did participants of a symposium at Yale University (on "The Humanities and the Public Interest"), "that the function of education is not to impart knowledge but . . . to excite 'dissatisfaction'" [Kimball 1986:33]. The symposium and the attitudes it reflected (toward Western culture) have been among the phenomena which help to understand the ready acceptance of cultural diversity or multicultural programs among faculties. Again, as Thomas Short put it,

> The real objective of the "cultural diversity" movement is to swell the chorus of complaint against the supposed hegemony of Western civilization. This turns out to mean not Western civilization as a whole (which after all, includes Marxism) but the political, economic and social principles of liberal democracy.
>
> [Moreover] Amidst all the talk of a diversity of "lifestyles," of the "straight" and "gay," the alleged diversity of "values" of black Americans and white, the different ways in which men and women are said to "experience" the same objects . . . there is an unmistakable promise of an absolute uniformity of opinion: women's studies teaches that Western civilization is patriarchal and oppresses women . . . black studies teaches that racism and slavery were built into the very origins of Western philosophy . . . Third World studies shows how world hunger is induced by Western capitalism; and so on . . .

... The very nature of these courses as already taught should be warning enough about the political motives ... behind them ... [Short 1988 Summer:19]

That serious academic or intellectual purpose is not among the prime motives of those pressing for the new program was also indicated by the fact that at Stanford University "The task force, set up in 1986, after demands for change had been made by groups on campus ... rejected a proposal to turn the course into a world culture course favoring no single culture. This was seen as too 'textbooky' an approach ..." Equally revealing was a statement by Kennell Jackson, head of the university's African and Afro-American studies program, according to whom adding black authors such as Richard Wright, Ralph Ellison, and Toni Morrison is "little more than tokenism" since they are taught by "white males who sing praises of European culture," lacking in "passion for works by blacks." Thus the issue was no longer even the substance of the new course but who taught it and with what level of enthusiasm. In the same spirit the chairman of the Chicano student organization at Stanford observed that "The minority organizations regard this as a civil rights cause, to get our culture represented" [Goode 1988 March:59, 60]. It was also at Stanford that Jesse Jackson led the memorable demonstration and chant "Hey, hey, ho, ho, Western Culture's got to go."

Similar attitudes were in evidence elsewhere. A professor of English at Duke University

... talks about her work with a rhetorical intensity that reminded me of the fervent Students for Democratic Society types ... Like so many of those in the vanguard of the new canonical insurrection ["Canonical insurrection" refers to the replacement of the classics by new, allegedly more relevant and equally or more worthwhile readings] she is a child of the 60s and a dedicated feminist ... The writers offered up as classics didn't speak to Tompkins; they didn't address her own experience.

It was also observed in the same discussion that "The ideology behind these challenges to the canon is as unambiguous as the vanity plates on [Duke professor of English] Frank Letricchia's old Dodge: GO LEFT" [Atlas 1988:72-73].

Among the pressures leading to the acceptance of these cultural diversity programs, the instant accusations of racism (directed at those opposed to them) cannot be overlooked. The late Sidney Hook, a veteran of these controversies and close observer of the Stanford scene, pointed out that "The false charge of racism is simply a tactic to choke off rational discussion, a strategy of intimidation to silence expression of criticism of educationally dubious programs. It is based on a shrewd calculation of the moral cowardice of many faculty . . . fearful of becoming the target of such abuse . . ." [Hook 1988:4].

Nobody who taught at American colleges during the past two decades can in good faith dispute the power of the fear among white faculties and administrators of being charged with racism—a fear that also helps to explain other developments in academic life discussed below.

The pressure to introduce cultural diversity programs in colleges had its counterpart in secondary schools. The National Education Association, the largest union of teachers, also supported programs of cultural diversity ["Facing the Challenge of Cultural Diversity" 1990]. There seemed even less resistance to these programs in public secondary schools than in the colleges. One result was the rise of what came to be called "inspirational black history":

> Reaching for ways to inspire black students a growing number of educators are trying to tell them about their own ancestors, bringing tales of African kings and little-known black inventors, scientists and artists into the classrooms . . .
>
> [In] one school system [Indianapolis] using an Afrocentric approach . . . Pat Browne told a high school class that African people were "the first to show genius in art and architecture" . . . Africans had sailed to the Americas 2000 years before "anyone even heard of Columbus." And, she said, "it was a black man who had drawn up the plans for Bell's telephone." . . .[Daley 1990; see also Ravitch 1990 and Ricketts 1990]

A conference in Atlanta devoted to the diffusion of Afrocentric studies proclaimed belief in the superiority of black Africans and characterized much of Western culture as "vomit." There was much support for "the idea of teaching Egyptian hieroglyphs, cleansing rituals, numerology . . . As to the prospect of such children getting jobs, [Wade] Nobles [one of the speakers] replied, 'When we educate black man, we're not educating him for a job, we're educating him for eternity'" [Sullivan 1990:20].

The largely uncritical acceptance of these curricular innovations was usually based on the unexamined acceptance of various questionable claims. Foremost among them was the unverified assertion that the old curriculum, by giving insufficient attention to the contribution of non-whites, damaged them psychologically and undermined their academic performance. The "Curriculum of Inclusion," proposed for the school systems of New York State, was among the most ambitious of such undertakings. A report justifying the program stated that

African Americans, Asian Americans, Puerto Ricans/Latino and Native Americans have all been victims of an intellectual and educational oppression that has characterized the culture and institutions of the United States . . . for centuries. Negative characterizations or the absence of positive references have a terribly damaging effect on the psyche of young people of African, Asian, Latino and Native American descent . . . [these groups] . . . have all been the victims of a cultural oppression and stereotyping . . .

. . . These characterizations have contributed to intellectual victimization and miseducation . . . members of minority cultures are alienated and devalued, members of the majority culture are exclusionary and over-valued. . . . Continuing problems of high dropout rates, poor academic performance and ethnic friction in our schools and in our society at large have called into question whether the goals of curricular change have been met . . . the development of the United States is depicted from the dominant monocultural view of being the preserve of European Americans . . . The various contributions of the African Americans, the Asian Americans, the Puerto Ricans/Latinos and the Native Americans have been systematically distorted, marginalized or omitted.

. . . the current approach "turns off" the child who is not European American . . . Many young people leave the school system out of frustration and feelings of inadequacy or they are pushed out as non-achievers. . . . The failure of the educational system to meet the needs of . . . [these groups] . . . makes it imperative to re-examine and re-evaluate the total educational experience. [*Curriculum of Inclusion* 1989:iii, 6, 7, 12, 34, 35]

These arguments invite several questions. Is it true that at the present time minorities are demeaned in the curriculum? Is there an ascertainable relationship between a neglect (alleged or real) of the accomplishments of minorities in the curriculum and the academic performance of students belonging to such minorities? Can the claim be accepted that minority contributions to the essential character and basic institutions of American culture and society have in fact been as significant as those made by people of European descent? And finally it must also be asked if there is any evidence to show that negative self-conceptions or low self-esteem among minority children are in fact widespread and, if so, have they been created by the alleged deficiencies of the curriculum? And even if such a relationship could be established it still may not be clear how such self-conceptions interact with academic performance.

If these assertions were correct it would be difficult to answer the question "why do Asian-American children outperform every other group of the population, including white children?" asked by Diane Ravitch, a specialist of American education [Berger J. 1990 Feb. 27]. In turn the issue of low self-esteem as an explanation of educational underachievement among black children was called into question by a review of research which found it "questionable whether or not race and racial identification can be linked to perceptions of self-esteem in a meaningful way." It was also found that "the self-esteem of blacks was similar to that of whites yet the level of achievement was lower. . ."; even high aspirations among black students were found accompanied by low achievement [Powers et al. 1990:568, 571, 573].

Another curricular innovation, peace studies, was born during the early 1980s. While it did not arise to cater to a special constituency (as did black, ethnic, gay, and women's studies) it shares with them an interdisciplinary format and a social-critical disposition.

The rise of peace studies was associated with the growth of the peace movement and the new preoccupation with nuclear war and disaster that began in the 1980s. While no such programs existed in 1980, as of 1985 there were over a hundred of them [Greene 1985], and in 1987 fifty graduate programs were listed (not all of them in the United States) in a booklet advising those seeking further training in this field [Thomas 1987]. The directory of the Consortium on Peace Research, Education and Development (COPRED), located at the University of Illinois in Champaign, lists peace studies at 72 schools, many of them degree-granting programs [Smith 1985]. Peace studies have also become popular in secondary schools; at both the college and secondary level they have been governed by the same assumptions, assumptions virtually identical to those adopted by the peace movement. They may be summarized as follows:

> 1) Nuclear war would be the worst disaster that could befall mankind and everything must be done to avert it;
>
> 2) It follows that policies of deterrence are unsound and immoral (since they entertain the possible use of nuclear weapons) and should be dismantled beginning with a freeze on existing levels of nuclear weapons and culminating in the complete abolition of all nuclear weapons; the road to peace is disarmament, not deterrence or peace through strength;
>
> 3) There is no genuine conflict of interest between the U.S. and the Soviet Union that could not be resolved through goodwill and adequate communication; much of the tension has been caused by misunderstandings and mutual, mirror-image like, misperceptions (nonetheless the U.S. tends to be held primarily responsible for the Cold War);
>
> 4) The best way to achieve peace is for ordinary people to put pressure on their respective governments (especially since ordinary people, Soviet or American, are basically alike);
>
> 5) A moral equivalence prevails between the social-politial systems of the two superpowers but—it is sometimes implied sometimes asserted—

the Soviet desire for peace is deeper and its commitment to disarm more genuine than the American;

6) Domestic circumstances, in particular the military-industrial complex in the U.S., represent a major obstacle to achieving global peace and disarmament; and

7) Not only nuclear weapons but nuclear power for peaceful purposes is also dangerous and its uses to be avoided.

Peace studies, besides its social-critical undertones, also shares with the programs discussed above the consciousness-raising intent (". . . nationwide, professors of peace and nuclear war say that though they may have different views on specifics, most hope to reduce the arms race by increasing the awareness of all aspects of nuclear capability" [Green 1985:34]). In a guide to such programs it was also noted that "Most programs . . . encourage students to assume more active roles as citizens and political actors" [Thomas 1987:8]. Thus the consciousness-level-raising intent usually combines with the recommendation of political activism: those teaching these courses wish the students to apply what they learn and become active in the peace and disarmament movements. This was also seconded by Adele Simmons, while president of Hampshire College [Thomas 1987:3]. In turn the *Chronicle of Higher Education* reported that

> Several students [in these studies] say an important difference between the traditional academic disciplines and peace or nuclear-war studies is the latter's emphasis on the individual's ability to use what one learns to change society . . . Berkeley's Peace and Conflict Studies Program . . . goes as far as to require its majors to participate in an internship in an organization working for peace or justice, from a free health clinic to a nuclear-freeze group. [Greene 1985:34]

Thus many of these programs champion not only peace but also "justice"—an orientation that allows for an even more explicit social-critical stance. Often this shift of concern from international to domestic affairs or from peace to domestic social change is accomplished by the introduction of the concept of "positive peace." According to the guide already referred to

> The concept of positive peace emerges from the belief that mere intervals between outbreaks of warfare do not constitute the opposite of war or violence, and that a second approach to peace is therefore essential. It implies the eradication of *militarism* . . . and of *structural violence* (that is, the brutalizing and often lethal effects of oppressive social systems). Positive peace is generally understood to entail re-ordering of global priorities so as to promote social justice, economic development and participatory political processes. This attention to structural issues is motivated both by an under-

standing that poverty and oppression are a primary cause of overt violence and war, and by a desire to construct a more humane world future. [Thomas 1987:6–7]

It requires no great imagination to grasp that such a conceptualization of peace and war allows for, indeed merges with, a left-radical ideological agenda and worldview in which the United States, the West, and capitalism emerge as the major culprits promoting "structural violence" and other evils. Despite reference to "oppressive social systems," left-wing dictatorships are rarely if ever mentioned in the curriculum of these programs.

Peace studies may also be seen as part of the legacy of the 1960s. They strive for "relevance" by seeking to unite theory and practice, valuing knowledge less for its own sake, or its unspecified future benefits, than for its potential contribution to a particular vision of social change. The spirit of the 60s is also apparent in the diminished capacity for making (not so fine) distinctions; as may be recalled favored metaphors of the 60s included the equating of the United States and Nazi Germany, the campus police and the Gestapo, students and "niggers," and so on.

The character of peace studies has been influenced by the political disposition of the instructors attracted to them. It is hardly surprising that those with a strong adversarial bent will be attracted to a program that offers new opportunities for the critical scrutiny of American institutions and foreign policy.

The Five College Program in Peace and World Security Studies (begun in 1984 with a Ford Foundation grant and based at Hampshire College in Amherst, Mass.), was established and directed by Michael Klare, a former fellow and disarmament specialist of the Institute for Policy Studies, a major producer of the adversarial criticism of American society and foreign policy. He was enthusiastically endorsed by a similarly disposed Hampshire College faculty member: "We are very lucky to have him here . . . He has been out front in the peace movement since the 1960s" [Langfur 1984].

Peace studies also spread rapidly to high schools and elementary schools; there is even a peace curriculum for preschoolers. These peace or nuclear education programs (often part of social studies) closely resemble those taught in the colleges except for a greater emphasis on the vivid portrayal of the horrors of nuclear holocaust (described by Chester Finn and Joseph Adelson as "Terrorizing Children" [Finn and Adelson 1983]) and an even more simple-minded approach to issues of war and peace and human nature befitting the more impressionable audiences at which these messages are aimed. Forty-five major foundations provide support for "peace and social justice education efforts" [London 1987: ix].

In conclusion it should be pointed out that higher and secondary (and primary) systems of education are linked by the training which schoolteachers receive at colleges and universities. A generation of teachers currently staffing American schools was trained and certified between the late 1960s and mid-70s. It would be surprising if they did not absorb many of the beliefs and political values of the period. Many schools of education have been strongholds of the adversarial beliefs of the 60s and of educational innovations of dubious merit which survived and resurfaced decades later. Thus Bruce Goldberg, codirector of the American Federation of Teachers' Center for Restructuring, suggested that "We need to have children who are producers of knowledge instead of reproducers of knowledge." In turn Gary Watts, senior director for the Center for Innovation at the National Education Association, insisted that "it is most important not to divide students by academic ability but to assume all children can learn complex material if given proper motivation and support." There was also much enthusiasm among these experts for children "to work together to find answers and solutions cooperatively" ["Radical Changes in Schools Sought" 1990]. So there they were again, the major values of the 60s: opposition to hierarchy, differentiation, and knowledge-based authority; a visceral egalitariansism and collectivism; and belief in the limitless potential of all.

Even in the late 1980s the training of teachers showed more than a trace of the adversarial mindset. A widely used manual in the training of thousands of teachers in New York City was dedicated to the proposition that this is a thoroughly and hopelessly racist society, a belief these teachers were presumably expected to transmit to their pupils. The manual insisted that only whites can be racist, that they benefit from their racism, that in the struggle against racism good people must turn against established authority, and so on [McFadden 1987].

The left-of-center orientation also finds expression in the policies, publications, and public stands of the National Education Association. One of its curriculum guides wrote of the Ku Klux Klan: "Thus it is important to remember that the Klan is only the tip of the Iceberg, and the most visible and obvious manifestation of the entrenched racism in our society"—an assertion that was correctly described by a spokesman of the Anti-Defamation League as "turning the study of a violent and reprehensible aberration in our society into an indictment of that society as a whole" [Maeroff 1981].

The developments and attitudes discussed above suggest that the radical movements of the 1960s succeeded in transferring their agenda from the streets to the classrooms.

Textbooks

Textbooks, and especially those in the humanities and social sciences, codify cultural values and perspectives. They are also supposed to transmit major cultural values. At a time of rapid social cultural and political change—such as the past quarter-century—this cultural transmission function becomes increasingly problematic and comes directly under attack. Those who believe that the core values and practices of society are corrupt or unjust are not anxious to transmit these values to the younger generations; they find find fewer and fewer cultural values worth preserving and transmitting and they often link such transmission to the preservation of naked power. Robert Paul Wolff, the philosopher, suggested that "the call for return to the 'transmission of values' [in higher education] is a mask for the imposition of values by the right-wing establishment. It is . . . ultimately a call for orthodoxy and religious fundamentalism. Beneath this call for values is the message: 'Support your local police'" [Langiulli 1989–90:79].

Textbooks in colleges as in secondary and elementary schools are bound to reflect the changes in widely held American values and beliefs, or the growing uncertainty about these beliefs. If at earlier times school texts in both colleges and schools unself-consciously mirrored the prevailing cultural consensus it is not unreasonable to expect that in recent times they bear witness to the decline of that consensus and the ascendance of the adversarial ethos. As Frances Fitzgerald observed,

> In the space of a year or two, the political wind veered a hundred and eighty degrees . . . The system that ran so smoothly . . . is now a rattletrap affair . . . The word progress has been replaced by . . . "change" . . . The present, which was once portrayed . . . as a peaceful haven of scientific advances and Presidential inaugurations, is now a tangle of problems: race problems, urban problems, foreign-policy problems . . . pollution, poverty, energy depletion, youthful rebellion, assassination and drugs. [Fitzgerald 1979:38, 11]

It is arguable that these developments are part of a broader process (not limited to the United States) and one that does not necessarily originate with the protest movements of the 1960s. The author of a widely used text on the sociology of education wrote:

> Schools used to teach an authoritative body of truth and wisdom and a set of unquestioned values and ideals to their students. But the knowledge revolution and increasing cultural diversity have destroyed much of the consensus . . .

> For some decades now, modern Western societies have lost this con-
> viction of a body of enduring truth and wisdom that justified the traditional
> school of the past. Because of the explosion of knowledge in this century
> we are less sure than our ancestors about what particular things children
> should be taught . . . [Hurn 1985:204]

It is open to question how closely the trends here discussed are related
to the "knowledge explosion" and the attendant relativization of beliefs.
While it is doubtless true that modernization in itself undermines traditional values and certainties, the developments here noted cannot be subsumed under relativization since the old values have been replaced not
by a generally questioning, skeptical outlook but by an embrace of new
values and certainties, sometimes new orthodoxies. It is not so much that
(as Hurn put it) "in the last few decades . . . education has come to reflect
something of the competing ideals, values and ideological controversies
. . ." [Ibid.:206] but rather there has been a clearly focused attack on
some of the older values on behalf of new and different ones. For example
if the old certainties included the belief that men and women are fundamentally and irrevocably different and women's major, genetically
determined talent was child-raising and home-making, the new attitude
does not merely question this, but categorically introduces a new certainty, namely that women and men are no different and the former have
no genetically derived advantage in child-raising. Likewise if in the past
it was argued or implied that differences in levels of achievement among
different ethnic groups are due to heredity, today an equally dogmatic
certainty dictates that such differences (if acknowledged at all) can be
ascribed solely to the environment, or cultural conditioning. If textbooks
in the past neglected the victimization of minorities, the new ones over-
emphasize the victimization of some minorities [see also Glazer and Ueda
1983].

In short, new orthodoxies replaced the old ones. Peter Shaw in a more
general discussion of the intellectual climate summed it up: "In the typical manner of orthodoxies, these attitudes ceased being put forth as arguments: they had become unstated assumptions, grown so familiar as
hardly to merit comment" [Shaw 1989:xiii].

What has transpired is not so much a triumph of the view that "Education for a culturally diverse society . . . must involve full and open discussion of such issues as feminism, racism, sexuality and U.S. foreign
policy" or of the belief that "Students should not . . . be told what is the
correct or moral position on every issue but should learn to arrive at their
own considered moral choices and values" [Hurn:208]. Instead new
beliefs about the correct or desirable views of race, sex, or U.S. foreign
policy are encouraged by teachers and the texts they use. It is not quite

a moral free-for-all or trial-by-error in the classroom. Some of the new forms of moral indoctrination (e.g., "value clarification") are less heavy-handed but nonetheless discernible. The new texts have their messages just as the old ones did; enlightened tolerance has not necessarily triumphed over the obscurantism of the past. Actual and attempted censorship of school texts at the local level has actually increased rather than declined as have the levels of intolerance of certain political positions and individuals representing them.

According to the education correspondent of the *New York Times,* "Censorship of textbooks and school libraries has increased dramatically in the last five years . . . Objections have been raised against some 600 titles found in school libraries . . ." [Hechinger 1984]. It is true that a good deal of these pressures come from traditional religious groups and individuals offended by what they see as the pernicious immorality in contemporary fiction, including obscene words and explicit sex scenes. But a new wave of censorship has also been launched by left-of-center groups, offended by what they see as sexism or racism or an insufficiently critical attitude toward the United States, its history, and recent foreign policies. Thus a "peace activist" in Leverett, a small rural town in Massachusetts (inhabited however largely by members of the faculty of the nearby University of Massachusetts at Amherst), "spent considerable time and energy . . . opposing a junior high history textbook she claims omits some of the blunders in United States history." She also objected "to the book's treatment of the Cuban Missile crisis and its explanation of the Cold War" [Hill 1987]. The parents' group of which she was a member campaigned strenuously to have the text "pulled from use" while denying—as did the "education policy director" of the self-styled civil rights group People for the American Way —that this constituted a form of censorship and calling it instead "an attempt to expand the curriculum" [Gonzales 1988:9]. The "expansion" was to occur by replacing one book by another.

Self-censorship has also become an important factor in these developments as authors of textbooks learned what is acceptable and what is not, hence "avoidance of 'controversial' conservative materials is largely self-imposed . . . to give conservative writers, journals and research reports much beyond the most minimal recognition is to ask for trouble."

The worldview of those in the publishing industry provides a reliable barrier against ideas outside the left-of-center conventional wisdom. As experienced by an author in political science:

> Being a liberal democrat seems to be part of the job description of college
> textbook editor . . . among both editors and academic reviewers there seems

to be a much greater tolerance of weakly supported Left arguments. Such arguments seem self-evident. For example asserting that our economic system has failed millions of poor Americans is very likely to pass unchallenged into print. Imagine reaction to a manuscript that argues that laziness and immorality significantly contributed to poverty. The call for conclusive documentation would be loud and . . . unsatisfiable. Not surprisingly given such rules of evidence, left-wing texts far outnumber books with an acknowledged conservative bias . . .

Writing a respectable, authoritative and sound American government text meant accepting a largely "soft Left" interpretation of politics . . .

To members of the publishing and academic communities the final product appears to be politically neutral truth . . . [but school texts are products of] . . . a leftish vision, a vision so pervasive in publishing and leading departments that it is judged as politically neutral. [Weissberg 1989:101–3].

Highly patterned changes (rather than more diversity) in the character of school texts was found in a thorough anaysis of 90 widely used elementary social studies texts, high school history texts, and elementary readers. The study itself aroused considerable hostility. The author wrote: "Before I even began research on this project, I was surprised by the amount of partisan political opposition to its funding. . . . it was clear that the deeply entrenched liberal education establishment did not want to fund any research capable of challenging their views" [Vitz 1986:xiii].

The major finding of the study was that ". . . Religion, traditional family values, and conservative political and economic positions have been reliably excluded from children's textbooks."

Of particular interest for the purposes of this study is another conclusion Vitz drew: "In spite of the biases . . . there is no evidence of any kind of conscious conspiracy operating to censor textbooks. Instead, a very widespread secular and liberal mindset appears to be responsible" [Ibid.:1]. That is to say, we are once more confronting a series of cultural assumptions and beliefs widely and unself-consciously shared among those who produced these texts.

Considering that many of the textbooks in social studies were designed to introduce children to basic social institutions and social arrangements it is also among the striking findings of the study that "the words *marriage, wedding, husband, wife,* do not occur once in these books." It was also found that in books heavily involved in purveying "role models" to children "Not one contemporary role model is conservative and male, and no person from business since World War II was selected" [Ibid.:2].

In the social studies texts

> Political bias also shows in the reliable tendency of these books to char-
> acterize recent (and much of past) American history in terms of three
> issues or themes: minority rights, feminism, and ecological and environ-
> mental issues. In every case the *pro* position is presented as positive; the
> opposition is never given any serious treatment. There are no conservative
> positions identified or supported in any way in any of these books.
> [Ibid.:41]

The exclusion of religion from children's readers is equally striking:
"There is not one story or article in these books, in approximately nine
to ten thousand pages, in which the central motivation or major content
derives from Christianity or Judaism. Religious motivation is a significant,
although quite secondary concern in . . . less than 1% of the stories"
[Ibid.:65]. Other biases found in these children's readings—echoing
those in the social studies and high school history texts—are lack of patriotism and lack of support for business [Ibid.:70–71] while "By far the
most noticeable ideological position is the feminist one" [Ibid.:73].

These findings suggest—unlike the more optimistic explanations of
the curricular changes noted earlier—that diversity per se is not on the
rise in the schools. The author concluded that

> . . . public school textbooks commonly exclude the history, heritage,
> beliefs, and values of millions of Americans. Those who believe in the tra-
> ditional family are not represented. Those who believe in free enterprise
> are not represented. Those whose politics are conservative are not repre-
> sented . . . those who are committed to their religious tradition . . . are not
> represented . . . Even those who uphold the classic or republican virtues
> of discipline, public duty, hard work, patriotism, and concern for others
> are scarcely represented . . . Over and over, we have seen that liberal and
> secular bias is primarily accomplished by exclusion, by leaving out the
> opposing position. Such a bias is harder to observe than a positive vilifi-
> cation or direct criticism, but it is the essence of censorship. [Ibid.:77]

Vitz attributes this state of affairs to the worldview of the people
involved with the writing, editing, publishing, selecting, and using these
texts, that is, those "who control the schools of education, the publishers,
the federal and state education bureaucracies and the National Education
Association" [Ibid.:80].

It is also of some interest that although this was the first and only
systematic study of school texts, journals of education failed to review it
(as of December 1988), according to information I received from the
author.

The ascendance of what I prefer to call adversarial (rather then lib-
eral-secular) mindset in school texts has also been detected in other stud-

ies. An examination of "how the Cold War is taught" found, among other things, that

> none of the textbooks can be said to present an overly favorable view of U.S. foreign policy. On the contrary there is a tendency of several to give the Soviet Union greater benefit of doubt . . . [Moreover] the Russian perceptions of the West are better explained . . . than Western perceptions of a threat from the East.

It was also found that "several textbooks systematically glamorize the United Nations." Some of the textbooks examined "turn a blind eye toward human rights in Cuba and emphasize social and economic progress." There is also "a peculiar reluctance . . . to describe the Communist role in the Vietminh and the Vietcong . . ." The six major textbooks examined have in common a failure "to show how Western perceptions and policies were created by actions of the communist powers . . . in the post World War II period" [Herz 1978:72, 73, 74, 75].

A study of the economic content of leading high school texts in world and U.S. history, sociology, and government found an emphasis on the allegedly growing gap between rich and poor during the industrial revolution but "little appreciation . . . that in a market system, industrialists grow rich because they offer workers and consumers *better* terms of trade than they had before." Also revealing is the approach to "Prevailing wages and working conditions . . . viewed as largely the outcome of an ethical decision by the employer." It is hardly surprising then that "Capitalism is viewed as a wild beast . . . which must be 'tamed' so as to provide benefits to 'the people' rather than the owners of the factories" [Main 1978:116].

At the same time another study of "seventeen widely used United States history textbooks focusing on economic and labor history from the Civil War to World War I" found these books insufficiently critical of capitalism and capitalists (such as Andrew Carnegie) and "denying either subtly or overtly the legitimacy of more radical methods of change" as well as "unsympathetic to the more radical segments of the union movement" and favoring "the interests of the wealthy and powerful." The study concluded that "From its inception, the social studies curriculum provided ideological support for the industrial hierarchy . . ." [Anyon 1979:369, 373, 379, 381]. It is hard to know if the books found insufficiently adversarial in fact reflected an outlook sympathetic to capitalism that is no longer acceptable to the educators of the post-60s generation, or if they were groundlessly accused of such partiality due to the expectations of a critic intolerant of the slightest support school texts might provide for the status quo.

College texts in sociology and especially in one of its subdivisions, "social problems," provide particularly tempting opportunities for attacks on "the system" since these "problems" can be readily treated as "organic" products of the social order. They may be dealt with in a spirit of resigned acceptance or they can be examined in an indignantly critical spirit as proofs of the corruption, injustice, and irrationality prevailing in society. The latter is the approach more commonly taken. Even the non-Marxist functionalist perspective can be put to social-critical use since it tends to link the "problematic" with the "unproblematic" aspects of society. While this perspective has some relativizing implications it also conveys that society as a whole, its major institutions and values, generate the problems rather than particular sectors or groups which can thus be absolved of direct responsibility.

Social problem texts treat the problems selected as singular products of American society and capitalism and rarely if ever point to their presence in other contemporary societies, although there is frequent reference to the problems and misery of the Third World—for which usually the United States and other capitalist nations and the multinational corporations are held responsible.

Even the problems selected by these textbooks reveal the social critical intent and the underlying worldview. Stanley Eitzen's popular text, *Social Problems* (fourth edition), includes topics such as "Global Inequality: The Third World and the United States," "The Extent of Poverty in the United States," "The Reinforcement of Male Dominance," "the political economy of AIDS," "corporate fraud," and "discrimination against gay men and women." It promises to "demystify our complex social dilemmas with an exciting writing style and powerful examples that challenge students' basic beliefs" [Eitzen flyer for the fourth edition].

Jerome Skolnick's and Elliot Currie's *Crisis in American Institutions* (1985) was in its sixth edition at the time of this writing and it focuses "on five basic *systemic problems* in America today." It has chapters on "Corporate Power," "Economic Crises," "Inequality," "Racism," and "Sexism"; a part of the book entitled "Institutions in Crisis" takes on the family, the environment, the place of work, health and welfare, the criminal justice system, "the lawlessness of big companies," and so on [Skolnick and Currie flyer].

Charles Zastrow's *Social Problems* (1984, 1988) predictably enough includes racism, ethnocentrism, sexism, poverty, and even ageism. On its list of "troubled institutions" we find the family, health care, education, big business, technology, and work [Zastrow flyer].

Social Problems: Society in Crisis (1987) by Daniel Curran and Claire Renzetti is "written from a critical or conflict perspective" and includes chapters and sections on "Politics and Power: Problems of Government,"

"Social Class Inequality and Poverty," "Race and Ethnic Relations," "The Public as Victims of a Capitalist Society," "Multinationalization," "the military-industrial complex," and "Institutional Discrimination" among others. Remarkably enough, crime, which most Americans are likely to consider the major social problem, is not included (as is the case in other volumes), perhaps because many aspects of it conflict with the heavy institutional emphasis and because of the statistical over-representation of minority groups among its perpetrators (victims as well) [Curran and Renzetti flyer 1987].

Social Problems: A Critical Approach (1986, 1991) by Kenneth J. Neubeck includes "Exposing the Hunger of the World's Poor," "the effects of defense spending and nuclear war," "schooling and unequal opportunity," as well as sexism, racism, and ageism [Neubeck flyer 1986].

Ronald Pavalko's *Social Problems* (1986) treats poverty "as a consequence of economic stratification," whereas sexism and racism are treated "as a result of sex, race and ethnic stratification." Not unexpectedly "the problems of the elderly are seen as the consequences of age stratification" [Pavalko flyer]. Crime, mental illness, and drug abuse are treated as "nonconforming behaviors," and the book promises to explain how they "come to be defined as problems."

Social Problems and the Quality of Life (1978, 82, 86) by Robert H. Lauer features in its third edition marital rape, the arms race, the concept of "nuclear winter," comparable worth, and a "'What's to be done' section at the end of most chapters." It also promises to teach students "how the very structure and thinking of society perpetuates the problem" [Lauer flyer].

Popular texts in sociology also include *The New Class War—Reagan's Attack on the Welfare State and Its Consequences* by Frances Fox Piven and Richard A. Cloward (1985).

Sociology: A Liberating Perspective (1985) by Alexander Liazos offers "a deeply committed Marxist perspective" and promises to discuss all issues "emphasizing non-sexist language and concepts"; the advertisement assures the reader that "a consistent feminist perspective enhances and illustrates Liazos' commitment to social equality" [Liazos flyer].

The substance of these books confirms the intimations of their tables of contents and their descriptions in the advertisements. For example Eitzen's volume makes these points:

> Blacks and other minorities constitute another set of victims in American society . . . the institutional framework of society is the source of so many social problems (such as racism, pollution, unequal distribution of health care, poverty, war and economic cycles) . . . the economy is the force that determines the forms and substance of all other institutions—the church,

school, family and polity . . . The thesis of this book is that the problems of American society are the result of the distribution of power and the form of the economy . . . it takes money and a lot of it to be a successful politician . . . political leaders will be part of or beholden to the wealthy . . . The schools . . . consciously teach youth that capitalism is the only correct economic system . . . it is no accident that we tolerate millions of unemployed persons . . . racism has positive consequences for the maintenance of the status quo; it is one means by which the powerful remain in power . . . Sex inequality and male dominance are suited to the needs of the economy . . . If the U.S. and other developed nations do not take appropriate steps, human misery, acts of terror against affluent nations and the possibility of war—even nuclear war—will increase. . . . The sources of crime, poverty, drug addiction and racism are to be found in the laws, customs, quality of life, the maldistribution of wealth and power, and in the accepted practices of schools, governmental units and corporations. [Eitzen 1983: 10, 16, 17, 25, 42, 45, 56, 90, 165, 278, 389]

None of these quotes is "out of context" or represents views which are hard to come by in other textbooks; on the contrary each is central to the conventional wisdom found in these texts and much of the sociological profession.

Thus generally speaking the prevailing wisdom is that social problems are either the direct result of faulty social arrangements and institutions (and of the varieties of exploitation and repression which prevail in capitalist societies such as the American) or they are matters of arbitrary definitions (of nonconforming behavior) imposed by the rulers upon the masses.

While political science as a whole is not nearly as adversarial as sociology and anthropology some of its textbooks do reflect similar dispositions. Commenting on a major high school text on government (that apparently anticipated the far more explicit moral equivalence school) Jeane Kirkpatrick wrote: ". . . if students are taught to see everything as almost equally imperfect they are ill prepared to distinguish those areas which, in fact, constitute grounds for shame from those which are causes for legitimate pride" [Novak, Kirkpatrick, and Crutcher 1978:27].

Howard Zinn's popular *A People's History of the United States* (1980) goes well beyond attributions of imperfection; it presents the United States as the most depraved of all nations. Zinn's favorite decade in all of the history of mankind (observed a reviewer) is the 1960s. The reviewer expressed reservations about Zinn's neglect of religion and his simpleminded explanations of why the masses remain oppressed and the elites succeed in manipulating them time and again. The reviewer's comments capture the flavor of the book:

The book is clearly about the oppression of the people: there are eloquent renditions of the destruction of Indian culture and rich analyses of the torment of the slaves, their revolts and degradation . . . There are long explorations of the misery of the working class . . . Much time is also devoted to the study of left and radical politics . . . Zinn writes of the subjugation of women . . .

The book is actually a radical textbook history of the United States . . . designed to give the left a usable past and, I think, Zinn hopes, to inculcate into students a certain view of America. [Kuklick 1980: 634–35]

The inculcation of "a certain view of America" has been the apparent goal of many educators besides Zinn. Thus wrote Professor William Proefriedt in the *Harvard Educational Review*:

The Marxist paradigm permits the teacher to inquire into the mystifications that serve to rationalize the workings of our society, to break lose from the prison of our categories. Teachers, then no longer mirroring society or naively attempting to be neutral, would develop a theoretical perspective . . . Our recognition that the schools cannot be the primary vehicle in the achievement of social justice should not blind us to the possibility of the significant role that teachers may play. Teachers must see to it that their actions link up successfully with the efforts of others toward the creation of a just society. [Proefriedt 1980:478, 480]

Remarkable in this discussion is the serenely untroubled premise that this is a profoundly unjust society badly in need of major transformation and that all decent people, including teachers, share this premise. It is the type of assumption that once more justifies the appellation "cultural"—self-evidently true and no longer in need of proof.

A similar viewpoint permeates an article on teacher education by Professor Henry Giroux, who notes quite casually that ". . . teacher education programs and their respective schools of education provide the appearance of being neutral yet they operate within a social structure that . . . serves specific ruling interests." This author is among those who are unhappy with finding connections between curriculum and "cultural reproduction," which for social critics intent on ending such reproduction is highly undesirable. He is also troubled by what he believes to be the teachers' involvement in "legitimizing the categories and social practices of the dominant society." The article seeks to show, as if it were a dark secret at last revealed, that "Teacher education programs . . . function as agencies of social control" [Giroux 1980: 5, 10, 13, 20].

Undoubtedly teachers perform social controls; the very act of teaching basics and making children attend school and sit still (if indeed that can still be achieved) are forms of control (and quite universal at that). But the critics see a far more elaborate and expansive system of controls at work directly benefiting the rulers—a theme that also animates the Bowles and Gintis volume on American education [Bowles and Gintis 1976]. For the social critics even the minimal "cultural reproduction" the schools still perform is a reprehensible and sinister activity since it helps to perpetuate the status quo they find oppressive and unjust.

Yet another critique of American schools echoes the Marcusean view of the world (in fact, of the United States) in which education turns people into obedient automatons seduced by consumerism and unaware of their true interests: ". . . the technocratic ideology's promise of individual potency becomes a powerful source of deception in people's lives," and so on [Bowers 1977:46].

To be sure since the mid-1960s harsher things had been said about American schools which paved the way to the settled adversarial consensus that has prevailed in more recent times. Noam Chomsky for example wrote in 1966 that American

> schools are the first training ground for the troops that will enforce the muted, unending terror of the status quo in the coming years of a projected American century; for the technicians who will be developing the means for extension of American power; for the intellectuals who can be counted on . . . to provide the ideological justification for this particular form of barbarism . . . [Chomsky 1966:485]

The works of Jonathan Kozol provide similarly apocalyptic images of American schools. In 1976 he observed that

> the public schools are busily at work turning out another generation of self-serving experts in the arts of Needless Knowledge and Inert Ideas . . .
> . . . the research process, as now being sold to millions of young people in public schools, is no less venal, no less devious, no less corrupting . . . than those more subtle exercises of the research process . . . [at] such institutions as Harvard, Berkeley, Michigan and Brandeis.

That was not all. His investigations in the 1970s also convinced him that the unsavory activities of specialists and technocrats will continue far into the future "when the present generation of well-trained and learned exploitation experts finally set down their pens . . ." In conclusion he asked: "What did I expect to find here in this modern, antiseptic, subdivided, flagstone decorated prison of the soul?" [Kozol 1976].

In the light of such critiques (of both the schools and society at large) the adversarial citicism of the 1980s has been relatively restrained and civil.

Standards and Requirements

Academic standards and requirements during the past two decades have also been influenced by the values and beliefs that gained ground during the 1960s. We have already noted how specific concerns (such as women's rights, ethnic minorities, and fear of nuclear war) as well as a more generalized aversion toward American society influenced the curriculum and the faculties. In the following their impact on academic standards and requirements will be sketched.

Even educators sympathetic to the spirit of the 1960s have come to admit that academic standards have declined over the past quarter-century. Numerous indicators support this conclusion. Decline in test scores of scholastic aptitude tests is one of them. ("Between the early 1960s and the early 1980s, the national average of verbal SAT scores declined some fifty points" [Cheney 1988:9].) Widespread grade inflation is another. For example:

> Twenty years ago, graduating with honors from Yale University was a mark of distinction. Barely a quarter of . . . seniors qualified for honors. Fewer than 3% were awarded diplomas with . . . summa cum laude. This year however, with grade inflation, making an A is almost as common as getting a C once was. About half of the university's graduating class of 1300 will receive honors . . . 10% are expected to graduate summa cum laude. [Ravo 1988]

By the end of the 1980s at Smith College over 90% of all students got As and Bs, two-fifths of all students got As, the number of which tripled in the last 25 years [Grabar 1990]. Grade inflation, spreading since the late 1960s, has been nurtured by many sources, above all an egalitarian, anti-elitist ethos. The latter also led to new systems of student evaluation such as pass/fail (that usually meant pass/pass) and written evaluations that dispense with letter grades or numbers. The opposition to grades was also supported by an educational philosophy that emphasized the uniqueness of students and their performance, insisting that a simple letter grade is an unacceptably crude device for evaluating such performances and imposes an intolerable system of regimentation as did the traditional curriculum with its requirements.

There was also opposition to grading on the ground that it made students competitive and focused their attention on the grade rather than the pure experience of learning and intellectual enrichment. (As will be recalled the 1960s was a time when competition, competitiveness, acquisitiveness, materialism, and capitalism were all lumped together and rejected.) Those who rejected grades on the philosophical grounds noted above often sought to undermine the grading system by giving good grades to everybody. Grade inflation also coincided with the introduction of the students' evaluation of their teachers, which in turn had some bearing on promotion and merit increases. It rarely enhanced a teacher's popularity and ratings to be known widely as a strict grader—that too was a fact of life though indignantly denied by supporters of teacher evaluation. The anti-elitist, egalitarian impulse in particular stimulated opposition to grading perceived to be an instrument for making or furthering invidious, even harmful distinctions among students. Those among the faculty especially concerned with minority students—who often experienced academic difficulties—had additional motives for dismissing the importance of grades.

As the stormy 60s and their educational innovations and experimentation passed away the traditional grading system in most colleges survived or was reintroduced but the attitudes outlined above continued to be felt and chronic grade inflation was the result. Hostility to testing, including intelligence tests, has also been closely associated with the aversion to grading and for similar reasons, among them the poor performance of some minority groups on these tests [Snyderman and Rothman 1988].

A general decline of academic requirements was another outcome of the educational innovations of the 60s. Requirements, like grades, were declared stultifying and destructive of the creativity and the diverse, unique needs and potentials of individual students. Teachers were not supposed to impose a "lock step march" or educational "straitjacket" on students, who were the best judges of their own educational needs, of what, when, and how to study. Aversion to externally imposed demands, structures, and discipline and a strong aversion to authority were the major impulses behind these trends [for a succinct summary see Shils 1969].

Although many of these extreme views were abandoned by the 1980s the results endured. A 1985 Report of the American Association of Colleges found that "American colleges and universities have allowed their curriculum to slip into a state of 'disarray' and 'incoherence' . . . [and] adopted a 'misguided marketplace philosophy' . . . 'It is a supermarket where students are shoppers and professors are merchants of learning . . .'" Another study sponsored by the National Institute of Education reached similarly gloomy conclusions as did one undertaken by the National Endowment for the Humanities.

Evidence of decline in standards included "declining enrollment in foreign languages . . . a lack of science education for nonscientists, fuzzy curriculum requirements and lack of coherent rationale for degree requirements." The business community had trouble finding enough literate college graduates and "Remedial programs, designed to compensate

for lack of skill in using the English language, abound in colleges . . ."
[Fiske 1985]. In the early 1980s in the 17 units of the City University of
New York more than half of the 33,000 freshmen were required to take
at least one remedial courses and 17% of all courses were remedial.
Highly trained professors were used for remedial instruction [Maeroff
1981]. The difficulties the New York City colleges faced were particularly
severe and rooted in the policy of open admissions that began in the early
70s. Joseph Bensman, a teacher in City College, recalled that

> The next several years at City College were a total disaster . . . College
> admissions was redefined as a right, and that right existed apart from moti-
> vation and qualification. Some students were pushed into college to vali-
> date the principle of open enrollement . . . The clear if unstated demand
> they made was: "Entertain us. We are here to enjoy our rights." They did
> not recognize that a certain amount of work might be incumbent upon
> them. [Rosenberg and Goldstein 1982:383]

A survey revealed that among public school students

> . . . 45% of those polled thought that Karl Marx's phrase "from each
> according to his ability, to each according to his need" is in the U.S. Con-
> stitution . . . [and] more than two-thirds of the nation's seventeen-year-
> olds are unable to locate the Civil War within the correct half-century.
> More than two-thirds cannot identify the Reformation or *Magna Carta*. By
> vast majorities students demonstrate unfamiliarity with writers whose
> works are regarded as classics: Dante, Chaucer, Dostoevsky, Austen, Whit-
> man, Hawthorne, Melville and Cather. [Cheney 1988:5, 6]

In 1987 it was possible to graduate from Princeton University without
taking any courses

> in classical studies (history, philosophy, literature of the ancient world),
> medieval history, modern history or American history . . . hard science
> (physics, chemistry, biology, astronomy) . . . math . . . anthropology . . .
> economics . . . political science . . . world literature . . . American literature
> . . . geography . . . even [without] computer literacy.

The author of this compilation concluded that "if that adds up to a liberal
arts education from a place like Princeton, there is no longer any danger
that our society will ever suffer from elitism in any form" [Koppett
1987]. A professor of history at Mt. Holyoke College wrote:

> Reports from the classrooms are disturbing. Promising students asking why
> it's called World War II ("was there one before?") or searching for the

causes of the Great Depression in the 1820s instead of 10 decades later. In colleges across the country, including highly selective schools, most freshmen are products of social studies courses that focus on current events or on out-of-context comparisons, say, between Gothic buttresses and McDonald's arches . . . Chronological history is dead . . . The argument often hinted but almost never pursued, that chronology is . . . a weapon wielded by reactionaries to record the triumphal march of Western Progress. [Burns 1986]

Some of these developments have also been nourished by the laudable intention to rapidly expand educational opportunity for the underprivileged minority groups: black, Puerto Rican, Mexican-American. Open admissions, or the substantial lowering of standards to accommodate them, have added to the pressures to lower standards and requirements across the board, including curricular requirements and grading. For example at Harvard Medical School

Because black students experienced their greatest difficulty in basic science courses, it was suggested that the "long tradition of building on these courses as foundation for clinical training might have been wrong: perhaps one really did not need to be competent in science to be a good physician." Letter grading was replaced by . . . pass-fail . . . and incompletes were rendered invisible on students' records once the missing course work had been made up. Such changes made it easier for the dean to claim that performance records of minorities were indistinguishable from those of other gradutes. Departments were pressed to permit repeated re-examinations for failing students, and inevitably these examinations became less demanding. As a by-product, the standard for passing crept downward for all students. [Gordon 1988:85–86; the quotes in the above come from the book of Bernard D. Davis, professor at the Harvard Medical School, cited in References]

The threat to standards associated with these trends was also indicated by a proposal at Yale University (an outgrowth of concern with not having enough minorities on the faculty) "that non-academic figures be invited to teach seminars" ["Minority Hiring by Yale" 1989]. In a similar spirit David R. Jones, general director of the Community Service Society in New York City, "believes more stringent measures may be needed in New York to simplify the process of getting hired and then licensed as a teacher. He favors eliminating the Board of Examiners, which tests and licenses teachers and supervisors" [Berger 1990:B1].

At a conference entitled "From the Eurocentric University to the Multicultural University" held in Oakland, California, in 1989, the final speaker, Charles Willie, professor of education at Harvard, "began by saying that calls for increased excellence ... discriminate against minorities, since the criterion of excellence works to exclude minorities from the university. Standardized tests, he said, do likewise and should also be abolished. No matter whether these tests are biased or not, Willie argued, they should still be eliminated because they 'terrorize' minority students ... And when it comes to faculty hiring, we must also not pick the 'best,' but should rather give preference to minority candidates who fall within the range of adequacy, in order to achieve a more 'diverse' university" [Custred 1990:64].

There was an unmistakable relationship between the urgency of and pressures for preferential treatment and relaxing standards in regard to both student admissions and faculty recruitment, as most schools began to use different (that is, lower, or non-academic) standards to admit minorities [see for specifics Bunzel 1990; Hacker 1989; Thernstrom 1989]. Such preferential treatment sometimes encouraged "the special claims of ethnic groups that only they are able to understand and pass judgement on the merits of their groups" [Bunzel 1990:47]. Moreover

at the University of Michigan, the United Coalition Against Racism has demanded that all black professors be given immediate tenure and special pay incentives. [Bunzel 1990:47]

At Penn State a black student who maintains a grade average of C to C+ gets $550; for anything better the prize is $1000. At the Harvard Graduate School of Arts and Sciences, minorities are guaranteed full financial support regardless of need. [Thernstrom 1989:18]

Black faculty members are objects of "bidding wars," often inundated with offers extraordinary by prevailing standards. Ali A. Mazrui, a professor of political science, was in 1989 offered a salary of $105,000 at the State University of New York at Binghamton, plus various benefits and salaries for assistants amounting to a package costing over half a million dollars per year. This was taking place at a time when "SUNY Binghamton officials ... were talking of cutting staff and hocking the silverware from the campus dining rooms in order to remain afloat ... At one point [New York State Governor Mario] Cuomo himself urged him to accept the New York offer ... Mazrui ... currently holds simultanous appointments at three universities—Michigan, Cornell and one in Nigeria" [Rossie 1989; see also Begley 1990]. Mazrui was also the producer and narrator of a television program bitterly critical of Western societies and values and an admirer of Qadafi of Libya (see Chapter 4).

Examples of altering standards in support of affirmative action also abound outside academic life. The case of the black musician who was exempted from blind auditioning for the Detroit symphony orchestra was a notable example. In his case the usual form of auditioning was suspended, due to threats by black city council members that the orchestra funding would be cut unless it became integrated (reportedly the beneficiary of this action was quite unhappy with it) [Blanton 1989 and Wilkerson 1989]. More recently an art exhibit in Chicago was subject of "furious protest" since of "90 works selected [by a jury] only six were by minority artists . . . Although fewer than 100 of more than 1400 entries came from minority artists." But "a compromise was reached . . . Minority artists promised not to picket or boycott . . . In turn sponsors agreed that they would expand the exhibit, giving equal standing to 20 more minority artists, showing their works side by side with those picked by the jury" [Schmidt 1990:A10]. In other words admission standards were altered and minority works were accepted without being judged by a jury.

Defenders of affirmative action vigorously dispute that it has contributed to the lowering of standards and relaxing requirements. Sometimes it is argued that even if this is the case it is a price worth paying for righting the wrongs of the past—a proposition that has a certain appeal but is difficult to evaluate without knowing the short- and long-term effects—both intended and unintended—of these policies. Remarkably, enough, sociologists otherwise anxious to examine and evaluate a wide range of social programs and policies have shied away from examining the effects of affirmative action. What is beyond dispute is that over the past two decades these programs have become completely institutionalized, assimilated into the unquestioned, taken-for-granted aspects of the academic life. Yet as one sociologist pointed out

> Twenty years after the enactment of the Civil Rights Act of 1964 . . . there has been no systematic inquiry into the effects of affirmative action on American society, neither its costs to the nation's economy, nor its impact on our country's morale. In an age of program evaluation, when most other social experiments are studied almost to death, our profession has shown a resolute ignorance about an extraordinarily controversial policy that has been in place for over two decades. It is as if affirmative action has assumed the status of a religious article of faith, and professionals choose to avoid studying its effects for fear what they might find out. [Beer 1987:63; see also Beer 1988]

The reaction to the findings of James Coleman on busing in the 1970s helps to explain why sociologists have stayed away from such topics. Not only was Coleman subject to public vilification but the American Sociological Association sought to censure him "for research showing that city-wide busing had produced extensive white flight in cities where it had been used as a desegregation tool." Coleman noted that sociologists have been discouraged by their own discipline and its prevailing consensus from asking certain questions and that taboo topics exist, foremost among them "genetically-based differences . . . between the sexes or . . . between races" [Coleman 1989: 76, 77–78].

The unexamined issues surrounding affirmative action include the question of who precisely benefits from it and to what extent does membership in the minority groups selected for preferential treatment automatically translate into disadvantage? Many individuals who belong to these minorities are not necessarily underprivileged in socio-economic terms. *A Study of Race Relations at Harvard College* found that "Fully 70% of black undergraduates at Harvard come from professional or managerial families, compared with 86% of white undergraduates" [Skerry 1981:63].

On today's campuses mere reference to such findings is likely to elicit accusations of racism, as does any questioning or criticism of any aspect of existing affirmative action programs. There is much to suggest that the entrenchment of these programs has been aided by faculties and administrators apprehensive of being accused of racism. Truly, "'racist' has become the most abused term of abuse in American life" [Gordon 1988:88] and especially in academic settings. It is an accusation that rarely requires adequate proof or substantiation but is instantly accepted at face value and provides compelling pressure for the pursuit of remedies for its alleviation. Since the accusation is often unspecific it has also become fashionable to use terms such as "unconscious racism," "institutional racism" or "subtle racism" and most recently the most elusive— "insensitivity." (For example the high dropout rate of Hispanic students in Boston public schools was attributed to "insensitivity," which apparently meant the lack of special programs and personnel to help Hispanic students, and the lack of programs that "focus on Hispanic language, traditions and culture" ["Boston Schools Called Insensitive" 1988].)

Increasingly the term "racism" has acquired an aura similar to that of original sin: something pervasive and inescapable that should evoke profuse and repeated acknowledgments of guilt. Sometimes it is implied that racism is so deeply embedded in American culture that it is virtually ineradicable.

At a series of meetings and workshops at Harvard University the assertion that 85% of American whites "harbor some form of subtle racism while 15% are overt racists" went unchallenged. The gathering as a whole "resembled a religious revival meeting. Instead of the doctrine of Original Sin . . . we had the clinically proven fact of pandemic racism, manifest even among the well-intentioned . . . And like a religious congregation [the] . . . flock consisted entirely of the already converted . . ." The audience was encouraged to respond to racial insensitiviy in the classroom by: "Overreacting and being paranoid . . . the only way we can deal with this system . . . Never think that you imagined it [racial insensitivity] because chances are you didn't" [Detlefsen 1989:18, 19].

It is difficult to know why precisely the allegations of racism (in frequent combination with demands for divestment in South Africa and demands for cultural diversity programs) have increased since the mid-1980s, especially given the vast array of federally and judicially mandated programs of preferential treatment and those voluntarily established on the campuses [see also Thernstrom 1989]. The increase of racist incidents is said to be the explanation but keeping records of such incidents has not been systematic and it is not easy to know if such incidents have indeed increased or merely gained more publicity. Moreover many of these incidents have been relatively trivial, like racial epithets scrawled on walls or remarks made within someone's hearing range.

It is also conceivable that—as noted earlier in the discussion on campus activism—white radicals in search of a cause embraced racism (as they have South Africa) because it is a conveniently respectable issue helpful for raising the level of campus activism that has been low since the mid-70s. It is also possible that the cumulative effects of affirmative action include heightened levels of academic frustration among its beneficiaries contributing to a beleaguered outlook; correspondingly resentment has probably also risen among white students aware of the preferential treatment accorded to minorities, which in turn might have stimulated racial animosities.

It is paradoxical that by the mid-1980s something of a mild hysteria regarding the alleged new forms of racism has emerged on many campuses and especially at elite institutions which have made the most far-reaching efforts to introduce compensatory programs. Students, faculties, and administrators have been regularly engaged in identifying, tracking down, and rooting out racism and its cousin, elitism. As in the 60s endless meetings, rallies, and workshops have been devoted to uprooting racism and to earnest white self-flagellation. Smith College in Massachusetts, deeply involved in such activities and programs, provides an interesting illustration of the mindset of well-intentioned white liberals promoting these activities and programs. In 1986 there was a flurry of protests, buildings occupied and meetings occasioned by the issue of divestment. The response of a faculty member to these events captures the spirit here examined:

> "For Smith College this is unique," said Philip Green, a professor of government who has been at Smith for 20 years, referring to the events of the week and the trustees' agreement to talk to the students. "Smith is a different kind of campus now. It's a more colorful campus, more like being

in the Third World. It's an 'unSmith' and a really nice feeling." [Ellington 1986:7]

In 1987 Smith College commissioned a study to unearth racism, elitism, homophobia, classism, and elitism and the reasons why Smith College has not achieved the status of a "multicultural" institution.

The atmosphere surrounding this undertaking and some of the responses it generated are captured in comments such as the following made by "a white administrator":

> The way courses are taught . . . will have to be examined. Unfortunately students are not always aware of the subtler forms of oppression being "fed" to them by professors. (Probably a lot of professors do not know they are subtly passing oppressive views along.) [Equity Institute Report 1987:n.p.]

The report did not say who was to judge and what constituted these "subtler forms of oppression" promoted by the Smith professors. Nor was a definition or standard offered as to what constitutes "oppressive/discriminatory/insensitive behavior" although the survey was heavily weighted to capturing and cataloguing it.

One of the measures of racism (and other undesirable attitudes) was the following question (requiring agreement or disagreement):

> Specific things have happened to me at Smith which I have found oppressive, discriminatory or insensitive, related to any of the following issues of social identity (race, religion, class, sexual preference or orientation, ethnicity, gender, culture, age, size, physical ability).

The respondent was not requested to reveal *what* these "specific things" were.

Another question requiring agreement or disagreement was: "I have observed oppressive, discriminatory or insensitive behavior at Smith directed toward someone other than myself." Again the makers of the questionnaire showed no interest in finding out just what these forms of behavior consisted of. Apparently whatever the respondents considered such behavior or incidents was accepted at face value. This may explain for example that "One hundred percent of the staff who are racial minorities agreed that they had experienced racially oppressive/discriminatory/insensitive behavior directed at them" [Ibid.].

Although only 19% of those associated with the college bothered to respond (or 788 out of a total sample of 4,064, i.e., the entire college community), far-reaching conclusions were drawn from such a highly unrepresentative sample and from findings which were generated by what might have been an aggrieved minority anxious to ventilate its perceived grievances. "Insensitivity" was found everywhere: in relation to race, gender, sexual orientation, and religion. Among the findings of the study:

> Every staff member who belongs to a racial minority suffered racial discrimination . . . most women on the faculty, staff and administration have been targets of sexist insensitivity . . . Smith is still perceived as elitist by a large portion of its own staff and students . . . Almost three quarters . . . of the staff responding to the survey said they had been the target of classist discrimination . . . 61% of the students and 27% of the faculty also reported experiencing such behavior . . . 78% of minority students and 75% of minority faculty claimed to have been victims of discrimination based on race.

It was not made clear what the content or manifestation of such discrimination, insensitivity, or "classism" was [Elliot 1987; see also Equity Institute Report 1987].

On the basis of this exceedingly dubious survey the president and faculty of Smith College voted to introduce a new set of sweeping measures to raise the proportion of minorities among students, faculty, and administrators. Similar events took place on many other campuses [see for example Short 1988 August].

The atmosphere of hysteria and witch-hunt at Smith College that was fostered (among other things) by the survey described above continued to yield a rich harvest of accusations, suspiciousness, and combative self-righteousness. In December 1990

> After word came that a fellow resident had received unsigned racist notes this semester, the women of Smith College's Wilson House stopped talking to each other—except to accuse . . .
>
> Women were so afraid of being called racist . . . they pointed fingers at others. Relationships between floormates became so icy that many students left early for winter break . . .
>
> In the most recent reported incidents, a black woman told officials . . . she'd received four notes and a decapitated black doll earlier this semester . . . [It was also reported that she kept none of these—P.H.]
>
> When something racist does happen, people trip over themselves to show support for the victim . . . "By doing that you're showing you're not guilty."
>
> Some students say pressure against intolerance can be suffocating . . .
>
> [When] . . . students learned of the anonymous racism [the notes, etc.] against their black dorm-mate, the house held a meeting to talk about the issue, and 97 women showed up—the whole house minus two.

Those two—one a white women, one an Asian—had been in the library that night studying for exams.

. . . a group of white students decided the two absent students had committed the racist acts.

In the following days, the two had doors slammed in their faces, friends refused to talk to them and rumors spread about alleged atrocities they'd committed . . .

. . . no one was safe from accusations. [Grabar 1990:1, 10]

At nearby Mt. Holyoke College (in South Hadley, Mass.), an incident of a different character generated similar waves of collective soul-searching and breast-beating. Evidently a totally drunk male visitor urinated on the door of a room in one of the dormitories. Some of the reactions were captured in a newspaper report:

Led by the Association of Pan African Unity . . . several Mt. Holyoke student organizations joined with college administrators in a rally calling for the college to acknowledge that discrimination exists on campus and to combat it . . .

The rally was in response to an incident . . . in which a male Hispanic visitor in Mead dormitory urinated on the door of two black women. It is unclear whether the incident was a result of racism, sexism or was simply a drunken act . . .

Mead dormitory announced that it will conduct workshops . . . to deal with the issues raised by the incident. ["Mount Holyoke: Students Rally to Overcome Discrimination" 1990]

There was no subsequent information or clarification of the motives of the drunken individual and no evidence offered to suggest that his motives were either racist or sexist. Hopefully college administrators at the college have been at work developing guidelines on how to deal in the future with urination in public places as a presumed political statement.

Although well-intentioned white liberals on elite campuses (and the country at large) may be fully persuaded that expanding the meaning of, and endlessly dwelling on, racism is a service to blacks and other minorities this is by no means self-evident. The unintended result of these attitudes (and the policies inspired by them) is, in the words of the black author Shelby Steele,

[to] indirectly encourage blacks to exploit their own past victimization . . . [since] to receive the benefits of preferential treatment one must . . . become invested in the view of one's self as a victim. In this way affirmative action nurtures a victim-focused identity . . . [and] blacks are encouraged

to expand the boundaries of what qualifies as racial oppression. [Steele 1990:49]

While American society until the middle of this century was certainly racist there has been an enormous swing of the pendulum over the past quarter-century, and nowhere has it been more pronounced than on the campuses [see also Hacker 1990:23]. There has also been a vast array of laws and programs addressed to the elimination of racism and its many consequences. Nonetheless charges of racism not only persist but seem to be increasing, especially in academic institutions, and have become an essential and immutable part of the adversarial discourse and a powerful instrument of the delegitimation of the social system.

NOTES

1. The author is familiar with the political beliefs and activities of Dr. Cole as they used to be colleagues at the University of Massachusetts at Amherst, for a number of years and also because she and he had engaged in a public debate in 1982 on the topic of intellectuals and politics, moderated by Julius Lester.

2. The listing of political activities at the University of Massachusetts at Amherst was compiled by Mark Mensh, graduate student in history and research assistant of the author during the period.

4

The Mass Media: Popularizer of Social Criticism

... the world according to journalism. ... is a surpassingly bleak place. A Martian reading about it might ... suppose America to be composed entirely of abused minorities living in squalid and sadisticly-run state mental hospitals, except for a small elite of venal businessmen ... who are profiting from the unfortunates' misery.

Meg Greenfield, 1985

... anti-institutional themes reach the audience with one essential message: none of our national policies work, none of our institutions respond, none of our political organizations succeed.

Michael Robinson, 1976

The media have become the nation's critics, and as critics no political administration, regardless of how hard it tries, will satisfy them.

Roger Mudd, 1978

... television does not consciously pursue a liberal or left agenda ... This is because the point of view is fixed and in place, a part of the natural order.

John Corry, 1986

It will be shown below that the mass media* is among the institutions of American society that has come to play a major role in supporting adversarial values and role models, and it has significantly contributed to the reflexive denigration of American (and Western) institutions over the past quarter-century [see also Lasky 1985; Michaels 1986].

The press in particular was deeply affected by the adversarial ethos of the times. Michael Schudson believes that "The extent to which the press independently promoted an adversarial culture has been overemphasized, while the extent of the wider and growing adversarial culture's influence

*Following common usage I will refer to the media in the singular.

215

on the . . . press has perhaps not been emphasized enough" [Schudson 1978:181, 163].

Subsequently and more unexpectedly the media shed much of its iconoclastic incarnation and transformed itself into a new voice of conventional wisdom the adversarial outlook itself has become. Peter Collier remarked, "When I was growing up in the 1950s, the adversary culture was in an adversary position. Now it has triumphed; now it is the dominant culture, injecting leftist assumptions into our lives . . . it inculcates anti-American orthodoxies and enforces theories of our national guilt and irrationality" [Collier n.d.:3].

For some readers this will be a novel and implausible suggestion. At least since the early 1950s the mass media has been criticized for purveying worthless entertainment, providing harmful role models, trivializing important issues, distracting the citizen from matters of public concern, and contributing to the erosion of cultural and educational standards, as well as bolstering rather than subverting the status quo. (For such and other critiques see Howe and Macdonald in Rosenberg and White 1957.) In particular it used to be claimed, as in the case of formal education (by similarly disposed and often the same critics) that the mass media serves to prop up the System and helps to produce obedient cogs for the capitalist economy. It was said to play an equally or more insidious role as formal education implanting and bolstering the false consciousness of the masses [see, for example, Gitlin 1980; Parenti 1986; Herman and Chomsky 1988].

As was noted earlier, the attribution of false consciousness to ordinary people has become a staple of the critiques of American society and it functions as a powerful polemical rebuttal of any claim of consensus or legitimacy: whatever apparent degree of support there is for the social system it can always be dismissed and discredited by pointing out that it rests on delusions, misconceptions, or massive ignorance carefully nurtured by the powers that be.

Our social critics have for some time relied on the part played by the mass media to explain the acquiescence and even enthusiastic support the benighted masses and especially the working classes have given to the established institutions of society. According to Todd Gitlin, for example, "the mass media have become core systems for the distribution of ideology" [Gitlin 1980:2], by which he means the ideology of "hegemonic capitalism" or "corporate liberalism" and not an adversarial ideology. But Gitlin admits that the media can be helpful in promoting (what he regards as desirable) social change by publicizing adversarial social movements while treating them "with the customary mixture of undercoverage, trivialization, respect and disparagement" [Ibid.:288]. To be sure what for Gitlin is "undercoverage" is, for others—less sympathetic toward the movements in question—abundant coverage. I commented earlier (see Chapter 3) on this problem of the relationship between value, perception, and impressionistic quantification.

Although political conflicts intensified in the 1960s (presumably indicating that the masses, or portions of them, were no longer fully brainwashed) so have the critiques of the media. It was a time when virtually all institutions of American society came under attack. Herbert Marcuse and indeed the whole Frankfurt School (or what remained of it) were in the forefront of such critiques emphasizing the cultural, more than economic or political deformations of modern capitalist societies. The mass media was credited with helping to maintain the status quo not only by misinforming the public (of domestic or world developments) but also by diverting attention from the truly pressing social, political, and economic problems of their society through the provision of mindless, apolitical entertainments, by the trivialization of important issues and the inculcation of a consumer outlook.

The gradual but still not widely recognized drift of the media in the adversarial direction can be traced to the social and political protests of the 1960s. Perhaps the media became in some measure "radicalized" by the events it covered: the Vietnam war, the civil rights and antiwar protests, and Watergate. At the same time there has also been in American journalism a longstanding muckracking tradition, a propensity to exposure and sensationalism, associated with the passion for publicity and suspicion of the government and politicians. Edward Shils observed over thirty years ago that "American culture is a populistic culture. As such it seeks publicity as a good in itself. Extremely suspicious of anything which smacks of 'holding back,' it appreciates publicity . . . Favoring exposure of practically every aspect of life . . ." [Shils 1974:41]. While these traditions strengthened the recent revelatory tendencies in the media, the unmasking impulse used to be subject, in some measure, to political restraints and preferences. Thus, for example, the press refrained from exposing the the extramarital affairs of Presidents Roosevelt and Kennedy arguably because of its political sympathies.

Following Watergate in particular "Exposure became a sacred mission," as Elie Abel put it [Wattenberg 1984:405]. It stands to reason that the more estranged from the established institutions and political practices of society are the journalists, the more eager they will be to ventilate the perceived defects and shortcomings of the system. On the other hand many characteristics of the media and especially the news may be explained by the prominence of the entertainment function. If news originally served specific, practical needs, providing information about events beyond immediate, individual experience, increasingly in the United States it has turned into a peculiar kind of entertainment, full of melodramatic, horrifying, bizarre, or exotic events [Milgram 1977: 168–69].

Television intensified these trends by its natural affinity with whatever is visually striking. But more generally speaking the American media and not only television has a built-in, structural bias in favor of presenting bad news, defining as newsworthy whatever is disturbing or morbidly fascinating. Some of this tendency feeds on apolitical sources, such as competitive pressures to attract the attention of readers or viewers. Disasters, tragedies, lurid stories of violence and unusual tales of suffering, and those of colorful corruption in high places attract attention [see also Wattenberg 1984]. Attention-getting sensationalism is often also linked to public service and interest. Among the more distant roots of the more recent trends one may also include the nurturing of what Daniel Boorstin called "extravagant expectations"—an integral part of American culture [Boorstin 1961]. To the extent that the media reflected and catered to these expectations it was also bound to convey the disappointments their frustration creates.

These trends and traditions were given a new impetus in the 1960s when many of the currently familiar characteristics of the media emerged or solidified and the media increasingly assumed the social-critical coloration it has preserved up to the present. The adversarial politicization of the media reinforced the bad-news-is-news orientation by a renewed concern with the defects, problems, and inequities of the social order, by a pervasive preoccupation with the discrepancies between existing American society and its ideals. As a commentator of these trends put it: "Our television news programs . . . are concerned with what is wrong with our government structure, our leaders, our prisons, schools, roads, automobiles, race relations, traffic systems, pollution laws, every facet of our society" [Robinson 1976:428].

Not all students of the media reached the same conclusions. Herbert Gans, for one, using what he called an "impressionistic" methodology, found that

> the news contains many stories that are critical of domestic conditions, but these conditions are almost always treated as deviant cases . . . ; [atrocities committed by Americans in Vietnam] did not get into the news very often . . . The underlying posture of the news toward the economy resembles that taken toward the polity: an optimistic faith in the good society, businessmen and women will compete with each other in order to create prosperity for all but they will refrain from unreasonable profits . . . [Gans 1980:41, 42, 43, 46]

Again the question arises what "very often" means for Gans, and to what degree his conclusion, that these atrocities were not reported often enough, depended on his eagerness to see them reported, while other viewers or commentators might have found the reporting adequate or even excessive given their lesser desire to be provided with negative reports of the behavior of American troops.

With the mid-1960s the mass media increasingly moved from the role of more or less detached reporter and recorder of trends to that of the critic, judge, and self-appointed conscience of society. During the past two decades many journalists, in both print and television, have developed the belief that they are the major, if not only, guardians of public rectitude and as such entitled to influence on public affairs. Thus the older, apolitical muckraking impulse has fed on the newer conviction that journalists are the elite conscience of society, arbiters of public morality, and the only force that can save it from further corruption.

The importance of these developments cannot be overestimated. Even if one rejects the idea that people are "brainwashed" by the media it cannot be disputed that people are influenced by it. For most people whatever they know of the world outside the narrow boundaries of their personal experience comes from the media. The media sets the agenda of what is to be known about the world outside the personal domain. Exposure to a steady stream of unpleasant, shocking, or discouraging trends and events—such as American audiences experienced over the past quarter-century—makes it more difficult to take an optimistic, trusting, or confident view of the world, and especially of the character and direction of American society [see also Lerner and Rothman 1989]. The political scientist Austin Ranney observed that television in particular ". . . has altered the culture significantly by intensifying ordinary Americans' traditional low opinions of politics and politicians, by exacerbating the decline of their trust and confidence in their government and its institutions . . ." [Wattenberg 1984:338]. (This trend or tendency is hardly alleviated by the occasional "human interest story" designed to provide a contrast to the overall bleakness conveyed by the news.)

A relentlessly negative approach even without a particular political angle or agenda is bound to have an impact on the outlook of the audience. A study examining nightly network news coverage of public policy issues found that over a three-month period 17 positive, 14 neutral, and 126 negative features were telecast [Wattenberg 1984:373].

The part played by the media in implanting and perpetuating the adversarial worldview may also be brought into sharper focus by introducing the imprecise but suggestive concept of the "climate of opinion" (very similar to the concept of cultural belief). The climate of opinion is an aggregate of generally unquestioned, axiomatic beliefs often not precisely articulated, which are taken for granted, no longer in need of proof or rational defense. Apparently such "climates" become established after certain beliefs or positions have been argued at great length and with much intensity and without meeting strong opposition. Thus the climate of opinion is a diluted residue of beliefs that had earlier been expressed with great force and conviction which no longer stimulate controversy because they have become passively accepted and those opposed to them are apprehensive of making their opposition publicly known.

The German opinion researcher Elisabeth Noelle-Neumann's discussion of public opinion is close to the conception of the climate of opinion here entertained: "Public opinion inheres in those attitudes and models of behavior . . . which are adhered to with vigor; which, in any environment of established viewpoints, one must exhibit to avoid social isolation; and which . . . one can express without isolating oneself" [Noelle-Neumann 1984:110]. The writer John Updike—insufficiently "dovish" at the time—recalls such an isolated position: "It pained and embarrassed me to be out of step with my magazine and literary colleagues, with the bronzed and almost universally 'antiwar' summer denizens of Martha's Vineyard . . . and with many of my dearest friends . . ." [Updike 1989:124].

Nothing can compare with the effectiveness of the mass media in creating such a climate of opinion, that is, the impression that certain beliefs are both respectable and widely held. The media does so in part by the selective presentation of news and points of view, by the prestige, weight, and apparent authenticity it lends to almost any point of view it chooses to publicize in a positive or uncritical manner.

The climate of opinion surrounding the disease AIDS in the 1980s is a good example of this process. Not only has the media and especially television given huge coverage to AIDS [see, e.g., Holden 1990], it has also been instrumental in popularizing the vague belief that for some not clearly specified reason to suffer of AIDS is especially tragic and entitles the victim to greater solicitousness, social solidarity, and medical support than do the sufferings caused by other similarly lethal diseases. It is part of this climate of opinion that to think otherwise removes one from the company of compassionate or decent human beings. To ask why AIDS victims are deserving of special solicitousness—especially in view of the fact that much of the disease results from avoidable sexual or drug-related practices—invites indignant public rebuke and therefore rarely happens. The media contributes to this climate by the sympathetic presentation of AIDS victims or their distressed relatives or showing the spread and dreaded consequences of the disease; it rarely presents any comparison between the number of AIDS victims and those of other major diseases or critics of the ways of life which are associated with AIDS.

To sum up: the media sustains the adversarial worldview and climate of opinion in the following ways:

1. By providing space or time to social critics, both domestic and foreign (e.g., Soviet spokesmen; see Smith 1988);

2. By the ceaseless ventilation of the social problems and deficiencies of American society;

3. By constantly reminding it audience of the discrepancy between the ideal values and hopes of American society and its day-to-day practices which fall short of these ideals and by the associated emphasis on the gap between appearance and reality; and

4. By generally exposing the audience to a universe of bad news or negative information of a wide variety.

In the following I will examine in some detail the contributions of television, the film industry, and the alternative press to the conditions sketched above.

Television

Television has been the subject of endless criticism on grounds both cultural and political. For many social critics of varied ideological persuasion it has come to symbolize some of the worst aspects of modernity in general and those of contemporary American society and culture in particular.

Much of what has been said above about the part played by the mass media in disseminating and popularizing the adversarial outlook applies foremost to television, due to its reach. Richard Grenier noted, " . . . these days ideas and attitudes which have their origin in the estrangement of a quite small intellectual and artistic class come spewing out of every TV set" [Grenier 1991:xxi]. Most Americans spend more time watching television than doing anything else except work and sleep; television is also the single major source of information about the world outside—tens of millions of Americans rely on television news alone to learn about supposedly important events and developments in their country and to find out what kind of a world they live in. (Approximately 50 million people watch nightly one of the three evening news programs [Lichter, Rothman, Lichter 1986:11]. By selecting what is newsworthy television tells them what is and is not important, what problems of their society deserve or do not deserve attention, which countries and parts of the world matter, what events or groups of people merit compassionate concern and what may be relegated to benign neglect. As Noelle-Neumann put it, "What does not get reported does not exist, or . . . its chances of becoming part of . . . perceived reality are minimal" [Noelle-Neumann 1984:150].

Television coverage is not random, but guided by both values and the sought-for visual impact. Consequently, as John Corry observed, ". . . the news agenda is out of balance . . . A large part of the world is simply blocked from view" [Corry 1986:47–48]. This is in part because some parts of the world are inaccessible to American television reporters and in part because they are not interested in many parts of the world even if they were accessible to them.

Observations about the part played by television in conveying an adversarial worldview require qualifications. Much of television remains steadfastly apolitical and entertainment-oriented. But, as will be seen below, even television dramas carry socio-political messages with adversarial implications, for example the suggestion that most businessmen are dishonest [Theberge 1981]. The bulk of the adversarial-critical messages are conveyed on the news and documentaries or public affairs programs of the three major networks and national public television.

The adversarial message is rarely explicit, direct, or impassioned (except sometimes on public television); more often it is conveyed with detachment, and through selective emphasis or de-emphasis. But even a seemingly neutral or detached mode of reporting can have momentous consequences for the maintenance of social norms, as for instance in the coverage of riots, violent protest, or certain types of criminal conduct or political extremism. Again, as Noelle-Neumann observed, "To publicize behavior that violates norms without strongly disapproving of it makes it ... more acceptable. Everyone can see that engaging in this behavior no longer makes one isolated. Those who break social norms are often eager to receive ... sympathetic publicity ..." [Noelle-Neumann 1984:157]. This much television coverage has clearly accomplished: not only did it not convey disapproval of, say, urban riots and looting or street crime during the last decades, but it usually sought to present them as "understandable," thereby neutralizing the potential for disapproval.

It has been argued that a cultural relativism and determinism underlie the adversarial approaches here discussed. Cultural relativism can find support in a venerable journalistic tradition, namely the striving for objectivity. Thus paradoxically the adversarial approach often merges with the professed desire to avoid a judgmental stand, at least on certain issues. For example, Ted Smith writes, paraphrasing this approach, "Mr. Posner [the Soviet spokesman invited by ABC television to comment on President Reagan's speech] ... is not being deceitful, only telling the truth as he sees it. And his truth is every bit as valid as ours" [Smith 1988:43]. The president of NBC, Lawrence Grossman, supported ABC: "It is appropriate, when the President is accusing the Soviet Union of aggressive behavior, to get a perspective from the people on the other side" [Weinraub 1986].

Underlying this benign and seemingly detached relativism regarding the viewpoints represented by Mr. Posner and President Reagan is a cultural relativism and more specifically the moral equivalence theory of the

American and the Soviet political system already commented upon. But it is not just a matter of "moral equivalence" that is involved: since the late 1960s the gulf separating the Soviet critiques of the United States from the American critiques of American society has greatly narrowed, hence the Soviet critiques now appear less "foreign," less "strident," more familiar and acceptable and can more readily be assimilated into the "mainstream" discourse of American television. This may also explain the striking increase in the appearance of Soviet spokesmen on American television in the last few years.

Thus "from 1981 to 1985 there was a 550% increase in the number of times Soviet citizens appeared on American network evening news broadcasts," that is, the total number of network appearances by Soviet spokesmen increased from 50 in 1981 to 325 in 1985 [Smith 1988:1, 88], and that was a period of *preceding* the improvements in Soviet-American relations associated with greater Soviet openness and Gorbachev's reforms.

The cultural-relativist or nonjudgmental approach is selectively applied precisely because it is for the most part rooted in the adversarial mindset. Network reporters would not dream of taking a non-judgmental approach even by implication, toward, say, the grievances of racial minorities in the United States or apartheid in South Africa, or the plight of the poor in American society. No television reporter or anchorman would casually suggest that apartheid is one of many possible social arrangements for handling interaction among groups in a multiracial society and, although one may disapprove of it, others regard it as necessary and natural.

Cultural relativism and the associated air of impartiality tend to make their appearance only when those upholding it wish to avoid taking a stand in support of Western values (or American policies), when it becomes a device for bypassing identification with existing American society and institutions.

A social-cultural determinism often supplements such (selective) cultural relativism but in an equally inconsistent way. As I have written elsewhere [Hollander 1983:241–51] selective determinism enables one to take a judgmental stand in some cases but not others: it may thus be reported (in a gravely concerned and judgmental manner) that the contra guerillas in Nicaragua wantonly destroy nonmilitary installations and massacre civilians, whereas at another time it is suggested that the Marxist guerillas in El Salvador have no choice but to blow up buses and highways (together with their civilian users) given the nature of guerilla war and their understandable interest in weakening the infrastructure of the country. "Understandable" becomes a key phrase and code word in such discussions; things declared "understandable," such as "understandable frustration," are supposed to neutralize moral indignation; whenever a particular outrage is not presented as "understandable" we are free to wax judgmental. Needless to say, the wish to understand is itself selective and predetermined by the journalists' cultural beliefs and political sympathies.

South African mobs burning alive other blacks (accused of being government informants)—known as necklacing—are expressing their understandable frustration, so judgment on their behavior by comfortable American TV journalists would be out of place. South African policemen violently dispersing such crowds will not stimulate similar efforts at compassionate understanding (as if the policemen were under no situational, group, or political pressure); *their* behavior is freely chosen and consequently we are free to disapprove of it. In this frame of mind the American troops committing atrocities in Vietnam were also free agents, their behavior undetermined by the exigencies of the battle, whereas the Vietcong had no choice but to murder civilians working for the government given the nature of guerilla war. For that matter looting black youth in urban riots in the United States have yet to receive *critical* notice on television; they are merely responding to their hopeless existence by removing the goods from liquor or appliance stores.

On television as elsewhere it does not take much effort to discern the outlines of the adversarial, left-of-center sensibility in the allocation of the negative and positive roles in these deterministic schemes. Groups, individuals, nations, political movements, and so on viewed with sympathy and understanding are cast into the role of the victim-underdog, whose activities and attitudes are determined and overdetermined; by contrast those viewed with disfavor have virtually unlimited choice of action, we are free to judge them because nothing prevents them from acting in the right way.

The adversarial messages and allusions of television programs cover a wide spectrum and their presence can be both documented by rigorous content analysis and discerned by casual observation.

In an episode on the popular *Miami Vice* television show the producers combined critiques of both domestic aspects of American society and U.S. foreign policy. "Formidable looking men in business suits" brutalize the innocent and "assorted fictional Contra-supporting corporate and government leaders [are portrayed] as, at best, scheming liars." The thrust of the episode was to impress upon the viewers the moral degradation of both the American supporters of the contras and the contras themselves (". . . anti-Sandinista rebels slaughter the unarmed peasants . . ."; "There were no 'freedom fighters' in this scenario only . . . hired hands breaking the law. There was no high moral cause only blatant lying" [O'Connor 1986]).

Less surprisingly public television in its weekly documentary *Frontline* series portrayed the anti-communist guerillas and their American supporters in a similarly unflattering light: dominated by former henchmen of Somoza, "an ineffectual fighting force with 'a notoriously bad record on human rights' . . . the program reserves most of its scorn for Americans who support the contras . . ." The program was also marked by its selectivity: the anti-Somoza credentials of contra leaders go unmentioned, even Eden Pastora, a well-known former Sandinista leader, is overlooked; the appeal of the contras among dispossessed peasants goes unmentioned. In short the documentary presents what has become the conventional, left-of-center wisdom about the Nicaraguan resistance in the 1980s [Corry 1986 March].

A PBS documentary on Guatemala in similarly slanted socialist-realist style proposed that "The United States and the Guatemalan Army act in concert to murder innocent people; armed revolution is the only way to obtain justice . . . The soldiers, politicians and an archbishop speak in voices full of hypocrisy and general meanness; guerillas and other leftists sound like gentle saints [Corry 1986 January].

The same mindset was reflected in another documentary made for the occasion of the 25th anniversary of the Cuban Revolution, and transparently favorable to the Cuban political system. It "raise[d] criticisms . . . only to dispel them" and—in the spirit of selective cultural relativism noted above—withheld moral judgment in matters lending themselves to a criticism but was willing to make unverifiable assertions such as that "'the majority is quite happy with life in Cuba'" [Corry 1985 July]. It is precisely such assertions that would have come under skeptical scrutiny had they been made about, say, Chile, or Greece under the military regime. (Thus a selective credulousness, or selective skepticism, may be added to the characteristics of adversarial television journalism.) More recently National Public Television refused to air a documentary made by Cuban émigré film-makers, exposing human rights violations in Cuba, unless it was paired with a reverential program made by the venerable apologist of Castro and his system, Saul Landau [Weissberg 1990].

Political partisanship is also often reflected in the withholding of information, by what is left unsaid. In a program on the invasion of Grenada on national public television (telecast in Western Massachusetts on February 1, 1988) Seymour Hersh, the narrator, managed to avoid any reference to the existence or contents of the *Grenada Papers* (captured official documents providing much evidence of the pro-Soviet and pro-Cuban links and programs of the regime); he made no mention of the Grenadian popular support for the American invasion, nor did he note that the controversial airport built by Cuba was capable of handling both military aircraft and airliners carrying tourists. What he did stress and seek to convey was the alleged duplicitousness of the U. S. administration regarding the threat to the American students and the military uses of the airport. He also conveyed that the anti-communist policy pursued by the Reagan administration was both misguided and dangerous and that communist systems hardly ever represent a threat to the U.S.

An award-winning documentary produced by station WGBH in Boston entitled "Vietnam: A Television History" was another example of the extent to which the the adversarial assessment of the Vietnam war has been enshrined and legitimized by the media. In this program the United States alone was responsible for the horrors of war, including civilian casualties; the brutality and atrocities committed by the Vietcong and North Vietnamese went unmentioned. The producer did not interview former Vietcong fighters in the United States, not even such prominent individuals as Truong Nhu Tang, former Vietcong minister of justice available for such interviews (and author of a book entitled *A Viet Cong Memoir*). The program presented current and former North Vietnamese functionaries as totally credible sources of information [Chanoff 1985].

Selective coverage was also in evidence when the networks reported from Vietnam on the occasion of the 10th anniversary victory celebration. No reference was made to the fact that the camera crews could only cover what they were permitted to by the authorities. While reminiscing on the 1965 coverage of the burning of a village by the Marines it turned out that the district commander of the Vietcong was in fact hiding in the same village (earlier believed to be totally without military significance) and was interviewed on the same program [Corry 1985 May].

A critic of this program concluded that

> Once again as they did so often during the Vietnam war, Hanoi's tough and clever rulers have attempted to manipulate American public opinion . . . and they have skillfully sought to use American television for doing so. The parade they staged to mark their Saigon victory was pure show business . . . designed to dominate American television screens—which it did . . . No pictures did I see of those Vietnamese who dare to question the regime and who for such daring, have been tossed into work camps . . . of the thousands who are being held in "reeducation camps." The reason is simple: The Vietnamese . . . approved and disapproved what American television crews might film, they accompanied reporters on assignment . . . For all the promotional hullaballoo about the Vietnamese permitting live transmission from Ho Chi Minh City, the film we got came from cameras peeping through a keyhole only at what the Vietnamese wanted us to see. [Hughes 1985]

This also sums up the character of much of the Western reporting from other communist systems over the past decades. These tendencies intensified during the years of detente, in the 1970s, when for example ABC television featured programs of the Soviet Union characterized by "the systematic elimination of any references not likely to be acceptable to the prevailing authorities." It was "The first principle of detente, visiting-network style . . . to pretend that the police state all around just isn't there—and that life in Moscow is as free and easy, relaxed and happy as in some larger Stockholm." In the course of preparing its on-the-spot program, "The ABC people soon found out that government permission for every single camera setup had to be obtained before any film could roll." The agreement leading to this program was aptly characterized by a *New Yorker* staff writer as "docile accommodation to the Soviet propaganda establishment" [Whiteside 1975; see also Corry 1988] although as such by no means unusual in the annals of Western reporting from communist countries.

A program made by BBC and shown on American public television on religion in communist countries (entitled "Hammer and the Cross") proposed that the conflict between Marxist-Leninist systems and religion was more apparent than real, that "Communism and Christianity, rather than being in conflict, complement one another." Roman Catholics in Nicaragua in particular "are at a golden moment in history. The church . . . 'is in a unique position—in the vanguard of a Marxist revolution.'" (This was not nor has been the view of the Nicaraguan bishops but they were not consulted.) Tomas Borge, minister of interior (i.e., police) was depicted as "'uphold[ing] the moral principles of Christianity'" and it was also proposed that in Nicaragua "'. . . present day politics and the Christian faith are inseparable.'" This tender and sympathetic treatment of the Nicaraguan authorities was complemented by harsh references to the resistance movement and American interference. A community of Christians professing to feel free and happy and grateful to the government was also presented. Concluded the *New York Times* television critic, "We get the impression that the producers . . . visited Havana and Managua not so much to make a documentary report as to confirm a political faith . . . the Cuban and Nicaraguan authorities made this easy. Virtually everyone we see has official, semi-official or approved status" [Corry 1986 August 7 and 17].

A nine-part series on Africa shown in 1986 on public television (also offered as a course for college credit) illustrates another important attribute of the adversarial sensibility: the uncritical acceptance of the claim that the West and the United States in particular are responsible for all present-day problems of Third World countries. On this program, its single author and commentator, Ali A. Mazrui, was given full and unchallenged opportunity to denigrate Western democratic values, express support and admiration for authoritarian systems as can be found in Libya and Algeria, and suggest that "imperialism" (used interchangeably with capitalism and colonialism) is the singular sin of Western countries. Apparently the program was also sprinkled with a number of dubious factual assertions regarding the number of victims of Western colonialization [Corry 1986 October; also Grenier 1991:255–58].

Another British documentary shown on American television was devoted to "human rights," which in a similarly skewed fashion conveyed the message that "Communist governments may be heavy-handed, but real ferocity, systematized and calculated, is found only in the West or its dependents and in theocracies." The chief culprits emerging from the program included South Africa, Israel, Chile, and the British (in their treatment of the Irish Republican Army) although fleeting reference was also made to Cambodia. Perhaps given the British nationality of the producers it is not surprising that the single longest interview in the program was conducted with a man belonging to the IRA who claimed that he was tortured by the British (critics of social injustice usually reserve the greatest indignation to that found in their own society, regardless of its magnitude) [Corry 1985 October].

The political-cultural values shaping television programming are even more striking when, more unexpectedly, they make their presence felt in programs designed for what the producers conceive to be not public enlightenment or moral uplift but diversion or entertainment. That even such programs have highly patterned socio-political messages suggests how deeply embedded certain cultural and political attitudes have become, and how pervasive the influence of the adversarial outlook. To find uniformities reminiscent of Soviet socialist realism (of the old days) is all the more remarkable since there have been no authoritative American literary or media functionaries or organizations endeavoring (in the old Soviet mold) to instruct writers what kind of scripts they should produce for the good of the society. Nor have producers and writers gotten together to determine what social messages their programs should send to their audience, or which social types and groups are to be portrayed sympathetically or critically. Yet without such directives and mechanisms highly patterned images and themes populate television programs, a tribute to the power of cultural values and the prevailing climate of opinion.

The climate of opinion and cultural values are often tangibly reinforced by militant and vocal interest groups anxious to make sure that the producers of television programs define reality in a manner congruent with their own beliefs. These pressures usually crystallize in the demand that positive role models be presented of certain minorities and women. This helps to explain why, for example, we see few black criminals on television or women in traditional social roles. Robert Brustein said,

"Everybody is in the casting business . . . You have to cast a black woman in a law school as a law professor. You have to cast Asians, homosexuals, everyone, in order to get sufficiently diverse multicultural representation." And Richard Bernstein pointed out, "The quest for diversity can turn into its opposite, a conformity that masquerades as diversity, or just plain mediocrity. And given the sanctimonious current atmosphere that surrounds the issue of race and minorities, it seems possible that nobody will point the mediocrity out . . . What begins as rebellion often ends up as a new orthodoxy" [Bernstein 1990].

The idea of the "role model" is actually very similar to that of the "positive hero" in socialist-realist literature and art. Both are supposed to present people not the way they usually appear in life, but the way they should be or supposed to be according to ideological blueprints.

Soviet literature in the old days presented a parade of puritanical, class- and politically conscious, work-obsessed positive heroes not because this was a reflection of the actual attitudes and behavior of the vast majority of workers but because this was the embodiment of the allegedly emergent, ideal worker, what he was supposed to be or become. American television today must show women in unusual professional roles and with unusual professional accomplishments not because this is generally the case, but in order to encourage the movement of women into such professions and to stimulate their aspirations. The role models of today are the positive heroes of yesterday. Or, as a correspondent in the *New York Times* described this orientation: "films have a responsibility to portray role models who conform to current idealizations of women vetted and promulgated by their putative champions" [Legault 1989]. These comments were stimulated by an attack on the movie *Working Girl* by a professor of political science at Vassar College, who found it guilty of two major transgressions of feminist and radical socialist-realism. In the first place the movie portrayed a successful professional woman as an unpleasant individual, and, second, it presented another woman, acting in a more traditional way toward men, as more attractive and succeeding through sheer work and "gumption" thereby creating the impression that "We have no class injustice: anyone with gumption can make it" [Harrington 1989].

While women are to be presented in conformity with current feminist ideals, men, especially if white, can be portrayed in negative and stereotyped ways. Increasingly television commercials are populated by foolish, helpless, bumbling, and inept males and decisive, forceful, and professionally accomplished women. Bernard Goldberg wrote: "A colleague who writes about advertising and the media says advertisers are afraid to fool around with women's roles. They know, as she puts it, they'll 'set off the feminist emergency broadcast system' if they do. So, she concludes, men are fair game." He also observed, "In matters of gender discrimination, it has become part of the accepted orthodoxy . . . that only women have the right to complain" [Goldberg 1989].

Particular interest groups may also directly intervene in programming and demand that shows they find offensive or unfavorable to their interest be altered or removed. An interesting example of this was the protest launched and the actual (physical) interference with the NBC filming of *Midnight Caller*. Originally it featured a bisexual man aware of being infected with AIDS who continues to have sexual relations with large numbers of men and women. "In the original script one of the women he infected finally tracks him down and kills him." The reader may wonder why this plot aroused the protest and indignation of AIDS groups in San Francisco. The principles of socialist realism help to explain. AIDS carriers are not supposed to be irresponsible, they should be viewed with sympathy and compassion; those who thoughtlessly transmit the disease are difficult to regard with such sentiments. Although nobody knows what proportion of AIDS carriers act in a responsible or irresponsible way, television must not show the irresponsible ones—that would amount to the presentation of negative role models and it would be insensitive. This was the basic position of the protesters, although their criticism was couched in somewhat different terminology, calling the program "irresponsible" and perpetuating "ignorance about AIDS."

At the urging of the mayor of San Francisco (following the disruption of the filming) the producer agreed to meet with representatives of the AIDS coalition and "some changes were made in the script. Instead of the show ending with the AIDS carrier being killed, the hero saves his life and urges him to seek counseling. Dialogue was added to emphasize . . . that the AIDS carrier's [irresponsible] behavior is aberrant and not representative of homosexuals and bisexuals" [Farber 1988]. This however did not satisfy the AIDS coalition which continued to demand that the show be altogether withdrawn or changed even more drastically. The portrait of the "AIDS carrier as an irresponsible menace" was not to be countenanced (even in its watered-down form), even though at the end of the show it was didactically explained to the audience (in the best tradition of socialist realism) that "AIDS is a litmus test for all of us, a measure of our compassion . . ." [O'Connor 1988].

The ideologically inspired patterns and suggestions of television are especially striking when they patently conflict with reality. Thus few would have expected that "The American businessman has become television's most popular villain" [Basler 1987]. In the world outside television there is no evidence to show that businessmen commit the most crimes, especially violent crimes. But in the world of television they are the major group of criminals and not those, as in the real world, who commit most crimes, and especially violent ones: young, unskilled males, disproportionately of black and Hispanic background. Several carefully designed studies have established this unexpected finding.

In 1978 Ben Stein found in popular television programs a great deal of hostility toward businessmen (and the military) complemented by the idealization of the poor and minority groups rarely presented as participants in criminal activities. He noted that the poor (on television) ". . . are always either heroes or victims . . . [they] stand out . . . blameless and pure" [Stein 1979: 92–94].

A 1981 study based on the content analysis of 200 episodes from 50 major prime-time entertainment programs shown on the three major networks during the 1979–80 season confirmed and amplified Stein's findings and found that that "two of three businessmen are portrayed as criminal, evil, greedy or foolish; almost half of all work-related activities performed by businessmen involve illegal acts; most big businessmen are portrayed as criminals; and television almost never portrays business as a socially or economically useful activity" [Theberge 1981:vi]. Of further interest was the finding that "Big business gets the blackest eye of all. The top of the business ladder is populated . . . by ruthless criminals. *Over half* of all corporate heads on television do something illegal, ranging from fraud to murder [Ibid.:x].

It would be difficult to suggest that such portrayals are merely accidental. And while they do not result from a conspiratorial design either, thcy arc a rcflection of internalized, reflexive beliefs, in particular of a deep aversion toward capitalism, criticized by showing its embodiments as severely flawed human beings. The study cited [Theberge] also found that "The business world in general is portrayed in a rather curious light—as the embodiment of all that is wrong with American capitalism. Bosses reap major rewards at the expense of both their workers and the general public. The interests of busincss are unalterably opposed to those of working people and consumers" [Ibid.:32].

Outside pressures play a part in these portrayals. According to a network executive the skewed presentation of criminals reflects apprehension of complaints from minorities. "There is a tendency at the networks to say that you can't have the bad guy black or Chicano or Italian—so what does that leave you? . . . the networks [don't] care about middle-class men over the age of 30 because they don't write complaint letters" [Lacayo 1983]. Another producer said, "Blacks, women, Italians, Hispanics, everyone writes letters complaining how they are portrayed on television . . . we can't even use the word 'gypped' . . . anymore because it offended the Gypsies . . . That's why I love businessmen—they don't write letters" [Basler 1987].

The hostility toward capitalism these programs reflect is all the more ironic since the large corporations whose human representatives are caricatured sponsor these programs through their advertising. Equally par-

232 INSTITUTIONAL SETTINGS

adoxical of the antibusiness disposition of those who make these programs is that often they themselves are capitalist entrepreneurs commanding huge incomes. Again, after examining the presentation of crime in network dramas, adventure stories, and comedies Robert and Linda Lichter concluded that "businessmen, professionals and even police are portrayed as lawbreakers in numbers out of proportion to reality" [Lacayo 1983].

According to the producer of a documentary dealing with the presentation of businessmen on prime-time television, Michael Pack, "hard-line cynicism about business people [can be traced] to the Vietnam war and Watergate, when many lost faith in some of the country's key institutions . . . Today, he said, television reflects the general belief that the whole system is suspect and corrupt" [Basler 1987].

Sympathetic treatments of the critics of American society complement the critical view of the supporters of the system such as businessmen. The television documentary on Amiri Baraka, the black writer-activist and self-proclaimed revolutionary, is a case in point. Presented as a victim of police persecution he was arrested and convicted by a jury for assaulting his wife and resisting the police in 1979 (his wife subsequently denied this). While described by his wife as a "political prisoner" he was released a day after his sentencing pending his appeal "to attend a reception at the White House in honor of American poets." Mrs. Baraka said at a press conference held about the case that "Fascism is coming and soon the secret police will shoot our children down in the street." In turn Mr. Baraka dropped dark hints about "someone or something . . . still out to get him." The program aimed at and succeeded in presenting him as a man of integrity and sound judgment, innocently persecuted by the System [Corry 1983 June]. The political message was similar in another documentary about three imprisoned women (members of terrorist organizations according to the authorities) shown on several public television stations in 1990. They presented themselves as martyrs and political prisoners, a self-assessment eagerly accepted by the producer, according to the critic Walter Goodman. He also observed: "The ingenuous viewer may be left with the impression that the three women were not convicted for their connections with explosives or attempted prison breakouts or bank robberies . . . but because they happened to be attending a rally in Central Park" [Goodman 1990].

A sympathetic fictionalized portrait of a political activist-social critic was presented on a CBS special entitled "My Dissident Mom," which vigorously pressed the nuclear disarmament agenda of the unilateralist kind. The heroine seeking to save peace from the rapacious military-industrial complex observed: "Real strength comes from inside. People are like countries—the ones that are really strong don't have to threaten or bully anybody" [O'Connor 1987]. Translation: We will be truly secure when we provide a moral example for the world by disarming rather than when we try to protect ourselves by the force of arms.

A documentary presented on public television in Massachusetts entitled "Will Our Children Thank Us?" presented an almost identical non-fictionalized message and portrait of antinuclear activists and was narrated by Benjamin Spock, the venerable activist of the 1960s ["Documentary Discusses Social Change" 1985]. The military-industrial complex was also the culprit on a program shown on the Turner Broadcasting System entitled "Dark Circle," which conveyed that the arms race was the result of capitalistic greed exemplified by a convention of arms dealers and manufacturers in Washington [Corry 1986 December].

A docudrama on the Atlanta child murders sought to undermine public belief in the system of justice suggesting that Wayne Williams, the convicted murderer, was in fact innocent. The screenwriter-executive producer of the program, Abby Mann, expressed hope in an interview that

> "the film will raise larger social issues about poverty, racism and crime in this country." He also said, "If you're from a poor minority family and you're killed, it's treated one way, and if you're from a white-middle class family it's treated entirely differently. That's why these murders were ignored for so long. *The real murderers are greed and indifference which still rule the streets."* [Farber 1984; my emphasis]

John Erman, who directed the film (and had earlier directed *Roots,* observed that the docudrama " 'will disturb viewers in a way that television rarely does . . . We all like to think that the police and the Government are there to protect us, and that we are living in a safe society. I think one of the things this film says is that we are living in an unsafe society'" [Ibid.].

One may wonder if Mr. Erman is really among those who "like to think" that the police and government are benevolent, protective institutions; it is more plausible that he has long given up any such belief and regards the police and government as malevolent, threatening entities and accordingly produces programs which confirm such an outlook.

What the producers of "The Atlanta Child Murders" had to say conveys with exceptional clarity their adversarial sensibility and agenda. They sought to show that the system of justice miscarries and things are not what they are supposed to be; beyond the case in point they wished to indict the entire system by linking a specific case of (alleged) judicial wrongdoing to racism, greed, and poverty. (It was not made clear in the article what part greed was to play in the alleged miscarriage of justice.)

Even popular sitcoms may reflect social criticism. According to a sympathetic critic the program *Roseanne* portrayed both class conflict and a "proletarian feminism"; most welcome of all (according to the critic) it "leaves us hankering for a quality of change that goes beyond mere reform; for a world in which even the lowliest among us . . . will be recognized as the poet she truly is" [Ehrenreich 1990:31].

Adversarial values are not difficult to locate on television, which is not surprising given the personal beliefs of the journalists involved (discussed below). More difficult is to establish what has been the impact of being exposed to these values. What Noelle-Neumann observed about the mass media in general applies to television in particular:

> . . . fathoming the effects of the mass media is very hard. These effects do not come into being as a result of a single stimulus; they are as a rule cumulative, following the principle that "water dripping constantly wears away stone" . . . The media's effects are predominantly unconscious; people . . . mix their own direct perceptions and the perceptions filtered through the eyes of the media into an indivisible whole . . . [Noelle-Neumann 1984: 168–69]

Occasional empirical studies indicate that television also has a more direct influence on attitudes. A study entitled "Public Affairs Television and the Growth of Political Malaise: The Case of 'The Selling of the Pentagon'" found that

> exposure to public affairs television seemed to have a deleterious effect on one's sense of political self-esteem, [that] television journalism can foster social distrust . . . [and] Reliance on television . . . promotes images of society which are disproportionately sinister . . . [that] those who watch great amounts of television—entertainment and news alike—are more distrustful, cynical and misanthropic than those who watch little or no television . . .

The explanation of these attitudes was found in "the negativist emphasis of television news reports . . . the emphasis on conflict and violence . . . and the anti-institutional theme in network news programs" [Robinson 1976:419–20, 426].

Similar findings were presented in a study of "the impact of newspapers on public confidence." It established not only that by the end of 1974 "a majority of the adult population of the United States could be classified as politically disaffected" but also that media reporting of events (Vietnam, Watergate, urban riots) made a substantial contribution to the more general popular disaffection [Miller, Goldenberg, Erbring 1979].

At last conclusions reached by a team of liberal social scientists are also relevant here:

... broadcasters [of television] ... cast doubt on everything. Certainly they do not glorify "the power structure." Big business is not admirable; its leaders are frequently power-hungry bullies without any moral restraints ... Government is under a cloud of suspicion: politicians are crooks. Labor is badly tarnished: labor leaders are mobsters. The debunking that is characteristic of our intellectual culture is also characteristic of the mass media. While television does not preach it nevertheless presents a picture of reality that influences us more than an overt message would. [Bellah et al. 1985:279]

It is the contention of this study that while the sharp, clearly focused, and articulated discontent of the 60s and early 70s has declined, a low-grade, cultural variety of it has survived and remains incorporated into the adversarial mindset reflected and popularized by the mass media and television in particular.

The Film Industry
Given the trends found in the offerings of television it will not be surprising to come upon the traces of a similar outlook in the products of the film industry. (For case studies and a thorough examination of the political values in American and Western films see Grenier 1991.) Indeed the centers of film industry, Los Angeles and New York, overlap with those of television and are populated by people of similar background and worldview.

Sometimes the messages of television and the movies converge. A columnist for the *New York Times* recalled this experience:

> In the space of a couple of hours, I saw the demonization of a specific group of Americans in the movies, [and] a public relations version of Fidel Castro's Cuba on TV ... The most chilling thing about the movie is that it assumes that just as you don't have to explain being a member of the Gestapo was evil you don't have to explain about the CIA or ... Special Forces veterans. Kill, torture, maim they do in the service or out. [Rosenthal 1987]

On the television program referred to, *60 Minutes,* Morley Safer managed to conduct an interview with a Cuban ballerina which included comments about her past protests against Batista, but not a word about artistic freedom under Castro: ". . . not one question ... about how she feels about ... Mr. Castro's imprisonment of poets, painters and writers. An unquestioning plug for Mr. Castro and a rewriting of history by omission" [Ibid.].

Unlike the products of television which encompass documentaries and news programs, feature films usually do not make explicit political statements or transmit nakedly political messages—which of course does not mean that they are free of political suggestion. Feature films ostensibly serving the goals of diversion and entertainment may actually be more effective in dispensing the adversarial worldview since the latter is more likely to appear as background, or taken-for-granted assumption, wrapped into some absorbing plot or narrative and conveyed by glamorous stars. Sometimes the adversarial message and impact may not even be fully intended. Thus a member of the activist generation of the 60s, Todd Gitlin, is fully convinced that his alienation from American society was stimulated by apolitical movies as those which stared James Dean and Marlon Brando. He wrote

> The future New Left read David Riesman and C. Wright Mills and Albert Camus, and found in them warrants for estrangement, but nothing influenced me, or the baby-boom generation as a whole, as much as movies, music and comics did ... America was mass-producing images of white youth on the move yet nowhere to go. What moved the new sullen heroes was the famous rebellion without a cause ... [Gitlin 1987:31]

To be sure, as Gitlin also admits, "disaffiliation came first" and was followed by a search for justifications and role models which the media already in the early 1950s was ready to provide. In the 1960s "The myth of the doomed outsider surfaced again ... with Bonnie and Clyde and Easy Rider" [Ibid.:34]. Such anti-establishment heroes, especially "martyred" ones, like Bonnie and Clyde, not only suggested that robbing banks can be an innocent, youthful prank, but enshrined the authentic outlaw who challenged the establishment and bourgeois values for whatever reason (Norman Mailer's self-conscious veneration of violent criminals belongs to the same species). As Stanley Rothman described this trend, "The misfit became the new American hero and the forces of law (or convention) were pictured as either ludicrous or evil" [Rothman 1979:356]. As may be recalled the heroes in *Easy Rider* representing the new deviant cultural tastes and norms (drugs, long hair, motorbikes, and so on) also fall victim to the dehumanized authorities and get killed by the police. To be sure misfits have been American cultural heroes at earlier times as well but never in such abundance and in combination with such highly patterned political messages and explicit social criticism.

Anti-establishmentarian or adversarial films fall into several categories. One group addresses U.S. sins abroad with special reference to Vietnam and Central America. It includes films such as *Coming Home* (1978), *Apocalypse Now* (1979), *Full Metal Jacket* (1987), *Platoon* (1986), and *Born on the Fourth of July* (1989), dealing with the horrors of the Vietnam war and the seemingly exclusive American responsibility for it.

Even a movie like *The Killing Fields* (1984) which depicts the sufferings of the Cambodian people under the Pol Pot regime suggests that the United States had unleashed this outburst of murderousness by the heavy bombing of Cambodia which unhinged Pol Pot and his troops. *Missing* (1982) is an attack on alleged CIA involvement in the overthrow of Allende in Chile and the terrorism that accompanied it. *El Salvador* and *Under Fire* (1983) are critiques of American policy in Central America. The latter was described as "explicitly tak[ing] the side of the . . . Sandinistas and may be the only American movie in recent decades to side with a foreign government against which the United States has aligned itself" [Harmetz 1983]. Of *El Salvador* Walter Goodman of the *New York Times* has written that "One look at the youthful, idealistic guerillas, accompanied everywhere by folk music, and you know where Mr. Stone's [the director and author of the screenplay] heart lies." To make another point the American border patrolmen (arresting a Salvadorian heroine) "in their sunglasses bear a not strictly coincidental likeness to the paramilitary bully boys in El Salvador" [Goodman 1986]. *Air America* (1989) dealt with alleged CIA drug trafficking in Southeast Asia.

A second group of movies dwell on the corruption of American life and domestic institutions: corporations, law enforcement, the political process, and so on. For example, *All the President's Men* (1976) was a dramatization of Watergate; *Power* (1985) was "A study of corporate manipulations" involving a "ruthless media consultant working for politicians" [Video Home Entertainment Guide 1987:636]. *The China Syndrome* (1979) chronicled the dangers of nuclear energy and corporate corruption; *Silkwood* (1983) the ruthlessness of companies producing nuclear power who assassinate an activist ready to expose them. In *The Border* (1982) "A border guard [U.S.] faces corruption and violence within his department . . ." [*Video Guide* 1986:104]. In *Marie* (1985) " . . . an idealistic woman becomes the first female head of the Tennessee State Board of Paroles and uncovers a veritable nest of seething corruption" [Video Guide 1987:509]. In *The River* (1984) farmers fight foreclosures and the government attempt to build a destructive hydroelectric plant. Similarly in *Country* (1984) "A farm family's life starts to unravel when the government attempts to foreclose on their land" [*Video Guide:* 1984 edition].

The *King of Prussia* (1982) re-created the trial of the "Plowshares Eight" who destroyed missiles in a plant, featuring Daniel Berrigan; *Wall Street* (1987) dealt with Wall Street corruption; *Nine to Five* (1981) with sexism in the office; *Norma Rae* (1979) with heroic union organizers and corrupt bosses; *Mass Appeal* (1984) presented a sympathetic portrait of a young radical seminarian battling one of his complacent elders. *The Candidate* (1972) depicted abuses of the electoral process, *Three Days of the*

Condor (1975) exposed the CIA; *Parallax View* (1974) offered a conspiracy to cover up the assassination of a presidential candidate, with a heroic journalist seeking to uncover truth; *One Flew Over the Cuckoo's Nest* (1975) portrayed the repressiveness of mental institutions and by extension that of larger society. Even a science-fiction film like *E.T.* had social-critical implications: the creatures from outer space were decidedly superior to humans and their social arrangements prevailing in the United States. *Fat Man and Little Boy* (1989) indicted the United States for making the atom bomb and the American hunger for global power. *The Handmaid's Tale* (1990), based on a novel of the Canadian author Margaret Atwood and made into a screenplay by Harold Pinter, depicted a nightmarish future America controlled by fundamentalist fanatics with special emphasis on the oppression of women.

A third, more recent type of the adversarial movie seeks to romanticize and rehabilitate the 1960s, to provide retroactive idealization of the period, its movements, protagonists, and beliefs—they may be called the 60s nostalgia films. Such films include *The Big Chill* (1983); the *Secaucus 7* (1980), and more recently *1969* (1990) and *Running on Empty* (1988). The latter also happens to be a recent example of the idealization of the politicized outlaw and a classic of the adversarial mindset. *True Believer* (1989) features "a burned out lawyer of the 80s who rediscovers the principles that fueled him in the 60s" and whose "values have never changed" [Taitz 1989] but the film also manages to show the prevailing political corruption, expressed, among other things, in the government's interest in using the drug issue to curtail civil liberties [Szamuelly 1989].

Such movies, as much of the literature dealing with the 60s, intimate that although the people involved might have done some foolish things when they were young (blew up buildings, worshipped Castro or Stalin, and so on) they deserve our sympathy because they meant well. Occasionally not merely the adversarial groups and movements of the 1960s but the American communist movement too was given respectful and idealized treatment as in the movie *Reds* (1981) and *The Front* (1976).

Running on Empty deals with "a pair of campus radicals who blew up a building as an antiwar protest in 1971" and subsequently went underground and raised a loving family. It is a movie that, according to the *New York Times* critic, "asks viewers to empathize with leftists who turned to violence." One of the producers of the film, Amy Robinson, said, "We were dealing with people with whom we had an affinity . . . we decided we were going to do everything we could to portray these people sympathetically." The screenwriter Naomi Foner, who was a graduate student at Columbia in 1968, expressed admiration for the radicals who went underground and "were willing to give up everything for a cause." One of the actresses, Christine Lahti, had been a former participant in "the student unrest" at the University of Michigan, as the *Times* put it. The film's director Sidney Lumet had also made the movie *Daniel* (in 1983), based on E.L. Doctorow's novel, a fictionalized and idealized presentation of the Rosenbergs executed for spying for the Soviet Union [Kerr 1988; see also Maslin 1988].

1969 was another sixties nostalgia movie also addressing the effects of the Vietnam war in the United States. In it, as in many other products of American mass culture and entertainment (including television commercials), the old learn from the young: "a stiff-necked veteran of World War II and a cheerleader of the American effort in Vietnam comes to understand his son's refusal to fight and joins him in the march to Washington . . ." [Szamuely 1988]. Various forms of antiwar protest are glorified and the critique of U.S. involvement is unqualified. *Berkeley in the 60s* (1990), a documentary, conveyed among other things the "belief that those who led and participated in the movement were idealistic young people acting from belief in free speech, equality and justice. University administrators and politicians appear . . . as insensitive bureaucrats or buffoons . . . The police are seen only in their role as head-bashing blue meanies." The film also showed that "Many student radicals . . . today work as teachers, writers and community organizers, and still practice what they preached" [Bishop 1990].

It should be noted that in the 1980s the products of the film industry were not entirely homogeneous in their political orientation and a few movies with an anticommunist message were also made. It is also true enough that such films were met with great hostility by the critics and various adversarial groups. Among them the character "Rambo" (1982) became—in much of the media and liberal circles— a symbol and synonym of mindless American imperialism and militarism, an embodiment of distorted cultural and political values. *Red Dawn* (1989)—a film about youthful guerillas fighting Soviet and Cuban troops invading the southern United States—is another a case in point. Although criticized ostensibly on the grounds that it contained too much violence, it was the political message that irked the critics most, at a time when the peace movement had gone to great lengths to convince the American public that the U.S. had no enemies abroad and certainly not the Soviet Union or other communist states. According to a critic

"'Red Dawn' promotes intense hatred and open warfare against Russia, Cuba and Nicaragua," said coalition [National Coalition on Television Violence] chairman Dr. Thomas Radecki, a psychiatrist at the University of Illinois School of Medicine. "Movies like 'Red Dawn' are rapidly preparing America for World War III," Radecki said. "They are preparing the adult generation to financially support and the younger generation to be the cannon fodder for a war or series of wars . . . These movies teach a barbaric ethic of hate . . ." ["Group Criticizes Violence" 1984]

The Hanoi Hilton, depicting the mistreatment of captured American pilots by the North Vietnamese, received even harsher treatment. Two messages of the film in particular infuriated the critics. One was the rendering of the North Vietnamese authorities as inhuman and manipulative, and the second the suggestion that the antiwar or peace movement was used by them to further their political and military objectives.

As will be recalled a large (if unquantifiable) portion of the antiwar movement was not merely opposed to U.S. involvement on the ground that it was a distant, wasteful, and unwinnable war, but also because they held the officially designated enemies of the United States in high esteem [see for example Hollander 1981:267–75 and Hollander 1988:116–25]. The greater their sympathy was toward the Vietcong and North Vietnamese communist authorities, the more vehement their opposition to American involvement in the war. After all they wanted "the other side" (title of a relevant book by Tom Hayden and Staughton Lynd) to win. To the extent that the Vietcong and North Vietnamese were portrayed as inhumane, repressive, and manipulative, the case for American involvement was morally strengthened, both during the war and in the postmortems that followed its end.

For those who insisted on the moral and organizational autonomy and moral purity of the antiwar movement it was even more outrageous to suggest that it had been manipulated by the communist side. At last a film that glorified the heroism of American air force pilots was bound to be distasteful, to say the least, for those who harbored deep aversion toward the military establishment. No wonder then that the producer of the film, Lionel Chetwynd, was denounced as a "fascist pig," that movie critic Stanley Kauffmann called *The Hanoi Hilton* "filth," and the *LA Weekly* described it as a "one-sided, anti-red cheerleading session." Joel Siegal on *Good Morning America* put his finger on the source of the uproar, noting that the film was "political on the wrong side." Michael Medved, a former antiwar activist and one of the few writers sympathetic to the movie, observed—what has also been a theme of the entire discussion here—how pervasive and taken-for-granted these adversarial perspectives have become. The latter explains the intensity of the indignation that greeted a movie that represented a rare and unusual (and visual) challenge to these beliefs. Medved remarked: ". . . there is one established point of view that you must take, and if you depart from it, the flak is unbelievable" [Katz 1987].

Even a relatively apolitical and humorous movie, such as *Moscow on the Hudson,* about a Soviet defector in New York City, made its director

somewhat uneasy—after all he made a film about somebody who preferred to live in the United States (and took considerable risk to achieve
this goal). This called for a mildly apologetic comment. Paul Mazursky,
the movie's director, said:

> "Some people have trouble with the so-called patriotism in the film . . . I
> suppose they think a glib, cynical anti-Americanism would be more chic.
> We are working awfully hard at thinking the country stinks." The . . .
> director said that he was neither patriotic nor unpatriotic: "What I am
> saying is, in America it's possible for immigrants to be integrated into soci-
> ety and have a life." [Blau 1984]

It may also be noted here that the television mini-series *Amerika* elicited the same hostile reaction as had *Red Dawn* or *Hanoi Hilton* and on
precisely the same grounds. *Amerika* sought to envisage the conditions in
the United States after a Soviet victory and occupation. In presenting a
portrait of an imaginary, Sovietized United States the producers extrap-
olated quite realistically from aspects of life in Soviet or Soviet-controlled
systems, projecting them upon the U.S. Thus they had shown bleakness,
shortages, the privileges of the ruling elite, the surveillance of people,
massive attempts at political indoctrination. None of this was a fairy tale
or fantasy as far as such societies were concerned. Yet presenting a Sovietized United States along these lines turned out to be an unforgivable
sin, or profound lapse in taste in the eyes of the critics because it suggested that this was a better society than the Soviet and that we may
actually have something to lose in a conflict with the Soviet Union (other
than our lives in a nuclear exchange). Since the critics of the program
also tended to be critics of existing American society they were disturbed
by the suggestion that current institutions and ways of life in this country
were shown to be preferable to those which might be introduced if the
balance of power shifted drastically in favor of the Soviet Union.

But the main thrust of the objections voiced was that the mere presentation of the Soviet Union as a threat—an idea that peace movement
and its spokesmen worked hard to dispel—undermined Soviet-American
relations and peace efforts. Many of those most critical of *Amerika* were
the most enthusiastic boosters of another television program, *The Day
After*—a fantasy which showed in an equally if not more speculative fashion the horrors nuclear war would visit upon the United States. One fantasy scenario, the nuclear holocaust, was highly praised and recommended for all to watch, including school children, while the other, a
bloodless Soviet victory, was beyond the pale.

The outcry against *Amerika* might best be explained by the combination of the commitment to the denial that there was a Soviet threat and

a sense of the worthlessness of this society which may not deserve to be defended, neither morally nor by the force of arms. George Kennan expressed such feelings memorably:

> Show me first an America which has successfully coped with the problems of crime, drugs, deteriorating educational standards, urban decay, pornography and decadence of one sort or another—show me an America that . . . is what it ought to be, then I will tell you how we are going to defend ourselves from the Russians. [Kennan and His Critics 1978:32; see also Corry, 1983 November; Boyer 1986; Corry, 1987 January; O'Connor 1987]

The character of Hollywood movies is largely defined by their producers but their worldview is shared by many actors. The political activism of these celebrities has been quite longstanding and almost invariably left-of-center, as if the celebrity status mandated the belief that the society which lavished upon them fame and wealth was unjust and in need of drastic improvement [see for example Barnes 1989]. Even Castro's Cuba has retained its respectability among many of them, as indicated by the frequent visits of famous filmmakers and actors to Cuba such as Francis Coppola, Spike Lee, George Lucas, Sidney Pollack, Robert Redford, and Oliver Stone [Wolin 1990].

Another species of films carrying strongly critical and ideological messages, shown both on television and in some movie theaters, has been the social documentaries. Notable among them were those produced by Frederick Wiseman, which provided a panoramic portrait of the dreariness and inhumanity of life in various American institutional settings: prisons, mental hospitals, schools, juvenile courts, the military, police, welfare system, slaughterhouses, and so on. Wiseman's documentaries were by no means singular in depicting flawed or distasteful aspects of American life. A whole industry of such social-critical documentaries has developed since the 1960s to supply instructional materials for college and high school courses in history, the social sciences, and "social studies."

New Day Films in Wayne, New Jersey, for example, offered *Seeing Red—Stories of American Communists,* nominated for an Academy Award, which professor of sociology Richard Flacks (former SDS leader and social critic encountered earlier) warmly endorsed as "a rare glimpse at the meaning and reality of commitment to deeply held political values . . . [which] helped my students understand both the political significance and activism of an earlier generation." The film also received lavish praise from the Educational Film Library Association, Maurice Isserman (professor at Smith College), and Vicent Canby of the *New York Times*

[Advertisement n.d.] and won several awards. New Day Films also offered documentaries entitled *The Global Assembly Line* (an exposé of the multinationals and the exploitation of Third World workers) and *How to Prevent Nuclear War* (described in the promotional literature as "A refreshing upbeat and positive film about . . . activities . . . anyone can engage in to lessen the threat of nuclear war"), endorsed by Helen Caldicott, prominent advocate of unilateral disarmament.

The Downtown Community Television Center of New York offered documentaries on what is wrong with health care in the United States. A film raised the question, "Should any differences exist between the care of the rich and the poor?" To such and other questions it promised to provide "some disturbing answers." There were also two documentaries on Cuba *(Cuba: The People, Part I and II)* which included an exclusive interview with Castro and claimed to be "the most comprehensive view of Cuban life under socialism yet produced" with the camera crews "traveling all over the country" focusing "on the average people . . . fisherman, peasants, workers and housewives"; it also "graphically details how the Cuban revolution is trying to cope with the problems of housing, medical care and education—problems we increasingly must deal with in the United States." (The pamphlet shows a similing Castro with an "I Love New York" T-shirt.) A documentary of *Fidel Castro Comes to New York* was also available. Sympathetic views of communist Nicaragua were offered in two documentaries. Another pamphlet of the same organization also offered *Vietnam: Talking to the People* (including shots of "re-education camps" to which these camera crews were given access). *The Philippines: Life, Death and Revolution* was yet another offering ("with exclusive footage of the guerillas' daily lives"). The television critic of the *New York Times,* John O'Connor, commenting on the political slant of these documentaries, wrote that ". . . unflattering aspects of the overall picture can be curiously downplayed. In the documentary on Castro's Cuba, the fact of political prisoners tended to be ignored. The failures of the current Vietnamese Government were not dwelled upon" [O'Connor 1978:29].

The Downtown Community Television Center also advertised another series of documentary videotapes under the title "American survival." It included *Homeless in New York, Hunger in the Suburbs* ("In suburban towns all over the country we heard the same stories—husbands laid off, industrial accidents, benefits cut—and we found many middle-class people going hungry"); *Housing in America* ("for millions of Americans the endless struggle to obtain even the most basic shelter has turned the American dream into a nightmare"); *Junkie Junior—Life in the South Bronx* (". . . this shocking story happens everyday to thousands of people in the South Bronx . . ."); *Home on the Range* (". . . the story of a South

Dakota rancher and his battle against agrobusiness"); *South Dakota Gold Miners* (". . . a bitter history of labor unrest . . ."); *Toxic Waste in America* ("Are we slowly killing ourselves, poisoning this world beyond repair?") and *How to Make Community TV* ("So you want to be a TV reporter and fight for the downtrodden with your camera?"). We are also told that "segments of these documentaries have been broadcast on NBC TV's *Today Show* and have won numerous awards."

The Downtown Community Television Center—which must have a large mailing list—has been sending these pamphlets unsolicited to the author (who never used films in his classes) for years; it describes itself as a nonprofit organization "supported by the New York State Council on the Arts and the National Endowment for the Arts" even in the Reagan era of which these pamphlets date.

Many other organizations offered similar documentaries for teachers. Richter Productions also of New York offered *Hungry for Profit* (which "clearly makes the connection between first world corporate profit motive and Third World hunger") and came with the endorsement of the American Friends Service Committee. The Catticus Corporation of Berkeley, California (also nonprofit), distributed *America Against Itself,* a film about the disorders at the 1968 Democratic Convention in Chicago ("The sense of immediacy is sustained by the participants' urgent commentary"). This film too "raises a number of troubling . . . questions."

Films for the Humanities and Sciences (based in Princeton, N.J.) had an unusually long list of offerings for sociology courses. It included *Child Abuse, Abused Wives, Kids in Crisis, Runaways, Kids and Guns, Racism in America, Pockets of Hate* (of whites directed at minorities), *Sexual Harassment from 9 to 5,* and *Women and the Corporate Game* (". . . women are not only denied equal pay for equal work, but are denied the opportunity to show what they can do"). Three films were dedicated to the failings of the schools and to AIDS respectively and a multitude of other social problems were also targeted, all of them portrayed only in the United States.

Cine Research Associates of Boston offered several documnetaries on water pollution and shortages, on "the crisis of public housing," and on *The Collective: 15 Years Later* (". . . the story of one radical collective . . . focus[ing] on these activists' political ideals, and on how the decision to be 'revolutionaries' altered their lives . . .").

The documentary *America—From Hitler to MX* was not made primarily for classroom use but it "has been showing in theatres from Greenwich Village to Hyde Park and on public TV networks across Europe." Its promoters described it as ". . . An expose of America's top level corporate and banking links with fascism . . . It ties American bankers with our first strike policies . . . [and] indicts the United States as aggressor

. . ." ["First-Strike Chic" 1985]. It received numerous endorsements and commendations. George Wald, the famous biologist and Vietnam-era protester-social critic thought the film said "things that need to be said." The Educational Films Library Association endorsed it, as had the National Council of the Social Studies ("A hardhitting . . . powerful film useful in courses in Psychology, Social Issues, Foreign Policy Issues or American History Classes"). About 100 campuses arranged showings, as did many churches through the good offices of the Clergy and Laity Concerned and the Maryknoll Fathers ["First-Strike Chic" 1985].

First Run Features, also based in New York, offered in one of its pamphlets 33 films for classroom rental. They included *American Journey* (reporting the 1984 trip of a Witness for Peace group to Nicaragua); *Blood and Sand* (a film about the Polisario guerillas in the Western Sahara also purporting to show "how U.S. involvement . . . has escalated the war"), *End of Innocence* ("a poignant drama of a young Jewish boy's reaction" to the execution of the Rosenbergs for their "alleged" spying); *The Good Fight* (glorifying the communist-led Lincoln Brigade in the Spanish Civil War); *Nicaragua: Report from the Front* (another pro-Sandinista documentary exposing the contras which won the "Golden Dove" award at an East German film festival); *Until She Talks* (about the federal persecution of a moviemaker who made a film about the Weather Underground, called *Underground* [also included in the list]); *The War at Home* (about the Vietnam antiwar movement); and *Witness to War* ("a remarkable odyssey of conscience" about an American physician who decided to put his medical skills at the service of the communist guerillas in El Salvador).

As these examples have shown, the adversarial worldview has been disseminated through a wide variety of visual channels, often targeted at particular groups such as college students.

The Alternative Media
Some of the documentaries and their producers shade into the world of the alternative media that includes "alternative" newspapers, publishing houses, movie makers, and radio stations (especially those on campuses). The alternative media also overlaps in some measure, with public radio and public television.

As the "underground" newspapers of the 1960s merged into the "alternative" press of the 1970s it has become more difficult to draw the line—in content if not form—between the regular or mainstream and the alternative media, as the mainstream media gradually absorbed many of the values and beliefs of the underground-alternative publications. At least the avowed rejection of objectivity has been retained as a defining characteristic of the alternative press, according to Robert Roth, president of the Association of Alternative Newsweeklies [Friendly 1984].

The declining difference between the messages and taken-for-granted beliefs of the alternative and regular media has been a reflection of the gradual absorption of the adversarial outlook into mainstream, attitudes, and institutions. There has also been a movement of journalists from the alternative to mainstream publications, some of them publishing in both. Differences remain but are more in format and the numbers of readers reached than in substance or spirit.

An unusual example of "a radical in the mainstream press" was provided by the case of Kent MacDougall, self-proclaimed socialist, who worked for "the capitalist press [mostly the *Wall Street Journal* and *Los Angeles Times*] for nearly twenty five years" fully disguising his values and loyalties. Subsequently he joined the Graduate School of Journalism at the University of California at Berkeley as a tenured professor—a move that gave him "the luxury of coming out of the ideological closet at last" [MacDougall 1989].

The producers of the alternative media are persuaded of the existence of a clear dividing line between their work and the regular media. The introduction to a massive collection of "alternative papers" (culled from about one hundered alternative publications) proclaims that such writings "offer a view of reality that differs both in scope and emphasis from that presented by the corporate media . . . [which] present a version of reality designed to reenforce rather than challenge the social and political consensus" [Shore et al. eds. 1982:1]. Yet the convergence between the two types of media is suggested by both the topics addressed and the beliefs associated with the coverage.

According to an authority on the alternative media the core beliefs of its contributors included the following:

> . . . nuclear power is an inefficient and dangerous source of energy; our lives are threatened by increasing corporate power; nonhierarchical structures should prevail in government, the workplace and personal life . . . American society [is] racist, sexist and violent . . ." [Ibid.:4]

As will be shown below such beliefs barely differentiate those who produce the alternative media from those working for major newspapers, magazines, and television networks. Many of the favorite topics of the alternative media such as "alternative energy sources, apartheid, violence against women, institutional racism, multinational corporations, union-busting and the anti-draft movement" [Ibid.] are far from foreign to the maninstream media. By the same token a characterization of American

journalism in general certainly applies to its alternative variety: "...
whereas journalism was always distrustful of all public officials, it is now
distrustful of all public authority: the corrupt official has been replaced
by the corrupt institution as journalism's natural enemy" [Kristol
1978:40].

The nature of television as the trend-setting medium of communications in our times added further pressures to slant coverage to situations
which represent challenges to authority. Edward Epstein argued that stories involving defiance of authority are more dramatic and easier to convey. "By comparison, the legitimizing myths of authority, which depend
on complex historical analogies and cannot be easily be illustrated by current news happenings suffer ... the need for visual images of action
makes network news oriented toward the most immediate aspects of an
event" [Epstein 1973:266].

Certainly the social-critical intent is far more openly expressed in the
alternative than in the regular media, conveyed in more colorful and
impassioned manner, whereas the adversarial message in the regular
media tends to be more restrained and understated, sometimes merely
implied or conveyed by selective coverage of events.

There are also differences in circulation, in the size of audiences
reached. For instance radical-left publishing houses such as Pathfinder
and Monthly Review Press in New York, South End Press in Boston (the
regular publisher of Noam Chomsky), and the Revolutionary Communist
Party publisher in Chicago have print runs averaging 5000. (But academic publishers often print far fewer copies of their books.) They dog-
gedly print and reprint the "classics"—Marx, Engels, Lenin, and Mao
and less familiar authors such as Thomas Sankara, late president of the
West African nation, Burkina Faso, and Jim Cannon, an early leader of
the U.S. Communist Party. (Among their publications one may also discover the wisdom of Enver Hodza, late leader of Albania, and possibly
Kim Il Sung, head of North Korea.) Significantly the bulk of sales of such
publishers are required readings in college courses (40% of South End
Press sales and 70% of Monthly Review Press sales consist of course readings). Pathfinder Press had a network of 35 stores around the country;
the Revolutionary Communist Party publisher had 12 [Goode 1988].

The alternative media as a whole adds up to a huge undertaking; the
alternative press probably has a combined national readership of several
million. A major reference work on the subject *(Alternatives in Print)*
listed 1400 periodicals [Shore et al. eds. 1982:3]. These publications
range from obscure sectarian, political tracts like, say, *Workers Vanguard*
of the Spartacus League or the *Philadelphia Solidarity,* to slick large-cir-
culation magazines such as *Mother Jones* or *Rolling Stone* and the well-
established *Village Voice,* as well as religious publications embracing the

radical-left agenda such as *Sojourners*. A publication such as *The Nation*, wholeheartedly devoted to a radical-left agenda but by no means a descendant of the underground press of the 1960s, is neither "alternative" nor mainstream. Several important alternative publications have been launched or sponsored by or remain associated in various ways with the Institute for Policy Studies, such as *Mother Jones*, *In These Times*, and *Sojourners*. The growth, and staying power, of the alternative press is also suggested by the fact that a bimonthly publication, *The Utne Reader*, exists solely to reprint selections from it.

The circulation of alternative publications may range from two thousand to two hundred thousand and they can be found in all major cities and campuses of the country [Watson 1979:16–17]. Probably the majority of college newspapers, especially on major campuses, remain controlled by the left and may thus be added to the ranks of the "alternative" or outspokenly adversarial publications. It is in fact quite possible for college students living on many campuses to remain completely immersed in an adversarial communications environment composed of teachings and course readings in the humanities and social sciences, the campus newspaper, radio, and alternative publications, and visiting lecturers whose worldview supplements the prevalent left-of-center conventional wisdom.

The Media People

An examination of the adversarial characteristics of the media would be incomplete without a discussion of the people who produce what the media disseminates. Like so much of the phenomena discussed in this book the transformation of attitudes associated with the adversarial qualities of the media began in the 1960s. In those years the social background of journalists also began to change as more and more idealistic members of the middle and upper-middle class were attracted to the profession. Journalism (and especially its electronic divisions) offered a welcome combination of fame, or at least a measure of visibility, a good income (and possibilities of very high income), and a chance to do something worthwhile for society, a service to public interest.

Sometimes the family background of journalists was among the influences on their work and outlook. Thus while the parents of Carl Bernstein did not pass on to their famous son their loyalty to the American communist movement, he did turn out to be an important social critic suspicious and critical of American institutions and policies, not unlike his parents [Bernstein 1989]. Kent MacDougall, a radical journalist mentioned earlier, wrote that "I simply followed my father's lead"—his father was also a left-wing journalist [MacDougall 1989:36].

Writing about network correspondents in the early 1970s Jay Epstein found that they were ". . . upwardly mobile . . . [typically] born in the Depression in a small Midwestern city, attended a non-Ivy League college . . . moved East and rapidly ascended the ladder of success, surpassing the income and educational level reached by his parents . . . most correspondents maintained that they . . . had no religious affiliations." By contrast Epstein found that "Most network producers and news editors come from . . . a cosmopolitan environment . . . New York City or Chicago and . . . other large metropolitan areas . . . A majority came from middle or upper middle class families . . . Twenty-one were of Jewish descent [out of a group of thirty-six] . . . two thirds attended . . . competitive city colleges . . ." [Epstein 1973: 222–23].

While the more recent generation of "the media elite" had more privileged backgrounds (as will be seen below) the groups studied by Jay Epstein as well as Robert and Linda Lichter and Stanley Rothman shared certain basic attitudes. [See Lichter, Rothman, and Lichter 1986] Epstein wrote:

> Privately almost all network correspondents expressed a strong belief in their ability to effect change in public policy through their work . . . In this view government officials are presumed to continue in their inertial rut until confronted with the glare of public exposure . . . Needed change is thus seen as depending not on politicians or bureaucrats but on the . . . national press. [Epstein 1973:205–6, 222–23]

The Lichters and Rothman, commenting on the link between the sense of mission and personality disposition, wrote: ". . . the journalists' self-image as public tribunes serves important psychological functions. It permits them to engage in power strivings without having to acknowledge the nature of the striving" [Lichter et al. 1986:118]. Another recent study of the press observed, "Scratch a journalist, and . . . you will find someone who considers himself at least as important to the survival of the American republic as a congressman or senator" [Stoler 1986:1–2]. They may also be described as belonging to the "class of people who have a high opinion of themselves . . . but think the society from which they emerged contemptible. They find this society morally wretched . . . lacking in the shining values that give life meaning" [Grenier 1991:xxii].

Network television anchormen in particular developed a great sense of importance that has also been nurtured by the print media, which treats them as combination of statesman and celebrity. The *New York Times Magazine* would run lengthy, highly personalized feature articles on Dan Rather and Ted Koppel, describing them in hushed tones of reverence as if they were towering public figures of unique talents and profound minds. Ted Koppel had "millions of Americans examining their consciences and those of their leaders at the end of the day" (perhaps the modern equivalent of leading them to prayer? The article actually called him a "television priest"). Evidently it was not easy for the author of the article to absorb the complexities of Koppel's character: ". . . I grasp the duality of the man. He is powerful but alone . . . He appears smooth but he is rough." There is serious reference to "Koppel's growing marble monument," that is, some of his programs. The reverential piece concludes with the observation that Koppel "must resign himself to being not Moses but a television priest. That is why he is tough and smooth, principled and self-effacing, restless and content, successful and dissatisfied."

No wonder that being taken so seriously people like Koppel develop an inflated sense of self-importance and regard it natural to be in demand as commencement speaker and font of wisdom. No wonder either that Koppel did not flinch from comparing himself with Moses (in an address at Duke University) warning against the "false gods of material success and shallow fame" of both of which he has been an eager recipient [Blonsky 1988:15, 30, 32, 60]. In the same spirit as commencement speaker at Stanford University, Koppel berated the "electronic voyeurs" (upon whom his fame and fortune depend) and bemoaned the excesses of public communications he has been contributing to so generously every night [Koppel 1986]. To be sure, "If society treats newscasters as more important than senators, it is unrealisic to expect the newscasters to reject society's opinion . . . In keeping with their newfound status, leading journalists are increasingly likely to see themselves as professionals who translate the news rather than craftsmen who merely transmit it" [Lichter et al. 1986:27].

A similar but more understated sense of self-importance has also been radiating from Walter Cronkite, celebrated in another reverential article in the *New York Times* for "speaking his mind." Cronkite's reaffirmation of his liberal values was presented as an instance of being daringly outspoken and iconoclastic—it amounted to an expression of support for well-worn left-of-center political attitudes (e.g., disapproval of military action in Grenada and Tripoli, objection to Star Wars, a warning that "the real threat to democracy is . . . poverty," and soon [Gerard 1989]).

Cronkite's pronouncements also illustrate the ways in which the left-of-center conventional wisdom became grafted upon the belief that the media people are the guardians of public rectitude. In a *Playboy* interview he said, "As far as the leftist thing is concerned, that I think is something that comes from the nature of the journalists' work . . . I think they're inclined to side with humanity rather than with authority and institutions" [Rothman 1979:364]. Thus Cronkite combined the exaltation of the journalist's public role with a questionable equation of "the left" with opposition to authority and established institutions.

A more realistic view of the journalist's calling and the risks associated with it was voiced by Daniel Schorr, former CBS correspondent, at the time of this writing working for the National Public Radio. Schorr observed:

> ... If something happens to you so as to single you out ... it helps to make you more salable. I've calculated that the FBI investigation of me, together with my being put on the Administration enemies list, has been worth a hundred thousand dollars to me, through lecture fees ... People would say "you're very brave" and I don't know what they were talking about ... I was not in any imminent danger of anything, and I had a big corporation behind me. [Tyrmand 1975–76:23]

The most systematic and comprehensive examination of what was called "the media elite" (journalists working for the *New York Times, Washington Post, Wall Street Journal, Newsweek, Time, U.S. News and World Report,* and the television networks CBS, NBC, ABC, and PBS) was carried out by Robert and Linda Richter and Stanley Rothman. They interviewed 238 journalists randomly selected from the news staff and upper echelons of the outlets listed above. Unlike Epstein's study quoted earlier they found that these media people were generally raised in upper-middle-class homes, were highly educated (often in elite schools) and generally enjoyed upper-middle-class incomes. They differed in a variety of attitudes from both business elites and the general public, especially in being nonreligious, urban, and left-of-center.

The survey established that "the proportion of leading journalists who supported the Democratic candidate [in presidential elections] never drops below 80%. In 1972 when more than 60% of all voters chose Nixon, over 80% among the media elite voted for McGovern." Some 68% believed that "The Government should reduce the income gap"; 49% that society is alienating; 80% favored strong affirmative action for blacks; 56% believed that the American exploitation of the Third World is the cause of poverty; and 57% that the United States' use of resources is immoral. Five out of the six respondents believe that the legal system favors the rich. Media leaders also perceive business leaders "as the most influential group and would ... strip away most of their influence."

Dividing the sample into old guard (over 50 years old), mid-career group (between 35 and 50), and the younger generation, who joined the profession after Watergate, it was found that among the old guard 43% place themselves left-of-center, in the mid-career group 52%, whereas in the post-Watergate generation 70% see themselves as being on the left. Left-of-center attitudes were found especially pronounced among journalism students at one of the most prestigious (graduate) schools of journalism, that of Columbia University. Among them belief in society's alienating attributes rose to 71%; 50% believed in the need to overhaul major institutions; 82% favored the government reducing the income gap; 75% held the United States reponsible for Third World poverty, and 74% for the immoral use of resources. Some 79% saw the U.S. foreign policy serving American business interests; 85% described themselves as political liberals.

Individuals most positively rated by this group were Ralph Nader, Gloria Steinem, Edward Kennedy, Andrew Young, and John Kenneth Galbraith. Most negatively rated were President Reagan (78%), Jeane Kirkpatrick, and Margaret Thatcher. Fidel Castro was far more popular than Reagan. Among journals of opinion *Commentary* and the *National Review* got the lowest rating [Lichter et al. 1986:28, 29, 31, 38, 45, 47, 49, 50].

Findings of a study of the "motion picture elite" had very similar results, with 60% of those interviewed locating the source of alienation in the very structure of American society, half of them believing that American institutions need complete overhaul, seven out ten convinced that public officials don't care about ordinary people, and so on [Rothman 1987:3].

Attitudes in the publishing industry were similar:

> . . . editors, regardless of the type of house, tend overwhelmingly to be liberals. Fewer than 20% classifed themselves as moderates or conservatives. Slightly fewer than half said they were liberal, while one third checked "strong liberal" or "radical." Seventy percent of the men and 90 percent of the women editors said their political affiliation was Democrat (these declarations were made in 1977 and 1978). [Coser et al. 1982:113]

Not surprisingly the findings of the studies of Rothman and the Lichters were not readily accepted. While the critics reluctantly conceded that elite journalists may indeed be liberal, they questioned the impact of these beliefs on their work [Gans 1985; also Kowet 1985], maintaining that professional standards prevent personal values from having an impact on the work. Gans criticized these authors for not proclaiming their own conservative bias without informing the readers of his own left-of-center disposition. It is unlikely that his own views of the "media elite" (and the study here discussed) were unaffected by his sympathy with liberal values. While he insisted that such values have no bearing on the work of journalists it is unlikely that spotting their intrusion would have greatly disturbed him.

Gans wrote, "Personal political beliefs are left at home, not only because journalists are trained to be objective and detached, but also because their credibility and their paychecks depend on their remaining detached" [Gans 1985:32]. But it is by no means necessarily true that in recent decades journalists were trained to be objective and still more questionable why they would be penalized (and by whom?) for selecting and reporting the news in ways congruent with their (left-of-center) values when media organizations are headed by people of similar persuasion. Gans seems to have forgotten that since the 1960s "'objectivity' became a term of abuse . . . objectivity in journalism, . . . as an antidote to bias, came to be looked upon as the most insidious bias of all. For 'objective' reporting reproduced a vision of social reality which refused to examine the basic structures of power and privilege" [Schudson 1978:160]. This at any rate was the received wisdom of the times which did not altogether disappear in the course of the 1980s, although it came to be asserted less vocally—or again as Schudson put it, "a simmering disaffection with objective reporting" survived [Ibid.:193].

It is not suggested here that journalists deliberately misrepresent trends or events. Rather, they unself-consciously select what they regard to be important and relevant, politically as well as morally. But judgments of what is important and morally relevant are guided by basic values. Thus for example a survey found that ". . . the *New York Times* and the *Washington Post* together mentioned human rights violations in Southeast Asia only 13 times in 1976 at the height of the bloodletting [associated with Pol Pot]. By comparison they had 124 stories on human rights abuse in Chile and 85 such stories on South Korea" [D'Souza 1984:23]. Two detailed studies demonstrated similarly skewed coverage of political violence in Nicaragua involving and following the 1979 revolution [Christian 1982; Muravchik 1988].

Case studies of the media treatment of domestic topics show a similar trend. The Lichters and Rothman found, for instance, a wide discrepancy between the perception of reporters (science journalists in this case) and experts (nuclear scientists and engineers) of the dangers associated with nuclear energy. While 70% of engineers and 82% of scientists in the sample favored the rapid development of nuclear energy only 24% of the journalists did so. Given these attitudes it is not surprising that negative stories about nuclear energy were approximately double those favorable in magazines and on television. The media also tended to cite experts most critical of nuclear energy.

In another case study the Lichters and Rothman examined reporting of busing. Pro-busing coverage dominated over stories which noted negative aspects of busing. In this instance the

> pattern of coverage runs counter to another widespread explanation of media behavior—the bad news bias. We found that the major media often

> dismissed or reinterpreted the so-called bad news about busing. In both
> the political arena and the classrooms, they emphasized order rather than
> disorder . . . and the importance of the end goal (integration) rather than
> the weakness of the means (busing) . . . As the adverse comments of busing
> continued to escalate . . . the coverage fell off dramatically . . . [Lichter et
> al. 1986:179, 205, 215–17, 251–52]

Thus even the preference for bad news is subject to the political disposition of journalists, who play down such news when it conflicts with
their political values and would undermine support for the social policies
they favor.

Snyderman and Rothman found similarly clear-cut bias in the media
against intelligence, or IQ, testing, totally at odds with the judgment of
experts regarding the value and validity of such tests [for example Snyderman and Rothman 1988:247]. The media's tendency to debunk testing corresponded to changes in the climate of liberal public opinion
regarding intelligence, its measurement, and genetic components.
Reflecting the political agenda of the 60s there has been a major shift
toward environmental explanations of differences in intelligence since
only such explanations would vindicate the social policies designed to
reduce differences in educational and occupational achievement between
ethnic groups. Academic intellectuals (though not necessarily those most
knowledgeable of testing) were in the forefront of this new environmentalism. Tests became "an easy target for the rejected, and for those,
including the news media, who seem themselves as champions of the
oppressed" [Ibid.:248]. The liberal aversion to such tests was motivated
by concern with the poor performance of minority groups on IQ and
other tests, including those designed to predict performance for policemen, firemen, and others. Frequently the poor performance by the
minority groups was regarded as self-evident proof of cultural bias or
other defects of the tests which were then repeatedly revised to assure
better results.

In the final analysis the criticism of testing was a byproduct of the
egalitarian beliefs of media elites and academic intellectuals. The rise and
dominance of such beliefs was a major outcome of the 60s that outlived
the period and found a variety of institutional expressions besides those
in the media.

Prevalent attitudes in the media were also reflected in two widely
publicized controversies involving journalists and the institutional
response to their views which violated a tacit consensus. In one instance
an editorial writer in the *Philadelphia Inquirer* "expressed concern about
the growing poverty of blacks and suggested that it might be wise to offer
welfare mothers incentives to use Norplant, a new contraceptive . . .

implanted under a woman's skin . . ." Although the difficulties associated with large, single-mother-headed welfare families are well documented and widely acknowledged, the editorial suggestion was denounced as racist, its author compared to a former Ku Klux Klan leader, and his editorial assailed (by the president of the Philadelphia chapter of the National Association of Black Journalists) as "'tacit endorsmement of slow genocide.'" The paper published another editorial rebutting the offending one and apologizing for it [Jones 1990].

In a somewhat similar incident Cuban-American television commentator Carlos Alberto Montaner pointed out on the largest Spanish-language television network in the U.S. that there is "a grave family problem in the Puerto Rican ghettos of the United States" associated with female-headed families and connected with the attempts of young, single Puerto Rican mothers to "try to escape poverty through welfare or through new partners who then leave and leave behind other children to worsen the problem." This observation led to a storm of protest, pressures for terminating Montaner's program, and his being branded as a sexist and racist who insulted the Puerto Rican community [Navarro 1990; for a rejoinder, see Montaner 1991].

At last the question may be raised of how much the social-critical disposition of journalists matters, especially if it represents attitudes far removed from those of the general public (as was found by both Lichter and Rothman and other studies), and if the public has come to distrust the media [see for example Gergen 1984]. Can the media have a significant impact under these circumstances?

Even as an increasing number of Americans became skeptical of the media in the past decades, it has had an impact. It has been said that "*The New York Times* editorial page can't swing even 100,000 votes in any New York City election. But it affects the thinking of all executive, intellectual and communications leadership. And ten years hence this thinking does shape elections . . ." [White 1969–70:9]. Even when some or many of its specific assertions are called into question, the media has molded the worldview of Americans by selectively questioning (or not questioning) aspects of the social-political world, by creating a semblance of public opinion or climate of opinion regarding matters most people cannot directly experience, and by creating public agendas reflecting particular beliefs, many of them adversarial.

PART II

RESULTS AT HOME

5

The Pilgrimage
to Nicaragua

I

There are few phenomena which better illustrate the survival of the adversarial outlook into the 1980s than the political pilgrimages to Nicaragua undertaken by Americans (as well as Western Europeans). Although this author has written extensively on the topic of such pilgrimages and their various settings [Hollander 1981, 1983, 1985, 1986, 1987], its latest manifestation justifies further comment since it is closely related to the central themes of this study. (According to an English writer, "Anti-Americanism is part of . . . the feeling that here was a deserving little country being cruelly bullied by . . . America . . ." [Stone 1990: C16].)

"Political tourism" may be a more appropriate term for the phenomenon here examined since the trips to Nicaragua rapidly evolved into mass tourism involving numerous tour operators, highly standardized formats and itineraries, and hundreds of thousands of tourists. According to a Nicaraguan official in charge of tourism, 100,000 tourists visited the country in a single year (1985), of whom 40% were Americans [Miller 1986]. Even if conservatively generalized over a ten-year period (allowing for fewer visitors in the early years and in the most recent ones, as well as some repeaters) we would still end up with approximately 30,000 Americans visiting each year. That means that at least a quarter-million U.S. citizens visited over the decade.

There has also been a resident contingent of especially strongly committed American (and other foreign) supporters, the so-called "internacionalistas"; the Americans among them have been variously estimated to number between 1500 and several thousand at any given time. Reportedly between 1979 and 1987 "about 40,000 Americans have gone to Nicaragua for political or humanitarian work" [Sullivan 1987:4; see also Garvin 1986:34].

The "internacionalistas" worked for the local authorities in various capacities:

The U.S. internationalists . . . were there to participate . . . in the struggle for Nicaragua to survive—planting trees, programming computers, experimenting with . . . environmentally sound methods of pest control, coordinating seminars on workplace health and safety, or trying to cover news stories routinely . . . distorted by the mainstream press. [Ozer 1986:51]

The "internacionalistas" were also said to be found ". . . on farms, in hospitals, in schools, in government ministries . . . One of them, Howard Heiner, a forestry worker, said . . . : 'The only hope is that we can convince the American public that an invasion shouldn't happen. So we entertain a lot of reporters and visitors'" [Williams 1984].

Participants in the tours of Nicaragua were somewhat different from those of earlier pilgrimages, as most of them were anxious not merely to behold a putatively more advanced social system but also to make a political statement of their own by being there. There seem to have been fewer well-known, elite intellectuals and artists among them but far more left-of-center or liberal professional groups and church people (many tours were organized by churches), including teachers, college students, social workers, politicians, and entertainers. Hollywood was especially well represented among the supporters of Nicaragua [for a detailed examination of such celebrity support see Oney 1984], which is not surprising given other indications of the political values prevalent in the entertainment industry discussed earlier. The actor and singer Kris Kristofferson, for example, used the counter-inaugural celebration (paralleling the inauguration of President Bush in 1989) to sing a ballad to the Sandinistas which included "Sandaynistaaah! You have lived up to your name . . . May your spirit never die! Hold a candle to the darkness! You're the keeper of the flame!" [Heard 1989:14]

More generally speaking

Many of the most visible critics of U.S. policy [toward Nicaragua] come from Hollywood—celebrities like Ed Asner, Mike Douglas and Susan Anspach.

Much of the Hollywood interest in Nicargua can be traced back to Blase Bonpane, who helped organize a nine-city U.S. tour with singer Jackson Browne, actors Mike Farrell and Diane Ladd, former Georgia State Senator Julian Bond and others.

[Mr. Bonpane was described as] . . . a former Maryknoll priest and professor of Latin American history at the University of California at Los Angeles . . . a liberation theologian sympathetic to the Sandinistas. He understood . . . the impact Hollywood stars could have on American public opinion. [Ingwerson 1984]

He was in turn approached by Rosario Murillo, wife of Daniel Ortega, "to organize delegations of prominent American celebrities to Nicaragua" [Ibid.]. Ms. Murillo also extended her personal invitation to Norman Mailer when she visited New York City and promised that "You will be my very special guest" [Grove 1986:60].

Mr. Bonpane made good use of his frequent visits to Nicaragua and was ready to defend its government even against the mild criticism he encountered in the *New York Times*. As "eyewitness to events in Nicaragua several times a year for the last nine years," he assured readers that "The Sandinistas are not dictators nor do they look like dictators. On the contrary they are a beacon for third world countries and a model of self-determination" [Bonpane 1988].

The convictions of Mr. Bonpane were shared by other tour organizers. In fact the highly political character of the tours was never in doubt as time and again their stated objectives were made clear by both the organizers in the United States and the authorities in Nicaragua. Most authoritatively Tomas Borge, Nicaragua's minister of police, advised that "Nicaragua's most important war is the one fought inside the United States . . . The battlefield will be the American conscience . . . When they [the visitors] return to the United States they have a multiplier effect on the public opinion of your country . . ." Borge correctly sensed the disposition of these visitors as reflected in a question addressed to him by a nun from Wisconsin: "'What can we do to help your country, commandante?' Borge was ready. 'Go back to your country and tell the truth about Nicaragua . . .'" [Tamayo 1983]. The head of Nicaraguan tourism, Herty Lewites, was also aware that "Most of the foreigners who visit . . . come not to see the natural beauty, but to get a look at the . . . revolution. Most of them, Lewites said, are connected with churches, unions and universities, groups generally sympathetic to the Sandinistas . . ." [Miller 1986].

An American working for the Nicaragua Information Center in San Francisco seconded Borge's approach: "It [the tour] is really part of the Nicaraguan foreign policy . . . They trust that when people travel to Nicaragua, they will see a different story . . . and that they will have a significant influence (on American public opinion)" [Foley 1984]. The same desire was also echoed by an American activist of impeccable radical credentials, Stuart Ozer (who organized work brigades to Nicaragua, was business manager of the North American Congress on Latin America, a major pro-Sandinista lobby, and wrote for the radical *Guardian*). He advised:

> Our principal goal must be to reach mainstream America, and make the issue of revolutionary social change in Latin America a matter of general interest, concern and support . . . we ought to be describing and defending wherever possible within mainstream institutions, the goals and projects of revolutionary movements and governments in the region. [Ozer 1986:53]

He was not the only one to urge such actions:

> The 75 solidarity organizations linked to the National Network in Washington, D.C. . . . encourage returnees to become acivists. Most do . . . by giving slide shows to church and civic groups, by raising money for medical supplies or day care centers in Nicaragua, by helping to organize sister-city programs . . . and by writing to their representatives in Washington. [Foley 1984]

Jody Williams, coordinator of the Nicaragua-Honduras Education Project in Washington, D.C. (which specialized in tours for "members of Congress, state and local officials and other community leaders") "acknowledged that many other private groups running private ventures to Nicaragua . . . do so out of a sense of 'ideological solidarity' with the Sandinista government" ["On Traveling to Nicaragua" 1986].

The elaborate organization and itinerary of the tours (discussed below) certainly support these claims and provide further evidence of their political nature. A study group program by Marazul Tours of New York City illustrates the magnitude of the effort to cater to a remarkably wide variety of interests and groups. A listing from 1984–85 included the following tour groups and conferences: Pan American Nurses Conference, New Orleans Study Tour, Boston Nicaragua Study Tour, Christian Theological Seminary, Teachers College Study Group, OXFAM America Group, Bengis Social Service Group, Vassar College Study Group, Marazul Study Tour, Militant/Perspective Mundial Tour, several Witness for Peace Tours (from various locations), and several Harvest Brigade tours [Marazul Tours . . . 1983].

In a covering letter the Marazul tour organizers also informed the prospective visitor that

> this type of program requires meeting with experts in the field as well as persons playing a leading role in government and political affairs. You will learn about the revolutionary process, the forces which oppose it, and the role of the United States, in a way not afforded by the usual media accounts. [Marazul Tours . . . 1983]

Participants in the tours also made clear, indeed proudly proclaimed, the political purpose of their trip and in doing so revealed their own well-defined predispositions. A *Washington Post* correspondent noted that "For many, traveling here confirms an already solid belief in what the Sandinistas are trying to do" [Cody 1985]. Jaime Chamorro, editor of the opposition newspaper *La Prensa,* concluded that "most come to confirm what they already believe" [Kinzer 1985 July]. Such visitors were anxious to demonstrate their solidarity with the Nicaraguan political system and their corresponding opposition to the policies of the U.S. government toward Nicaragua. Jennifer Dohrn, a visiting nurse-midwife (any relation to Bernardine, sometime Weather Underground activist?), said in Managua that "Our presence here is a sign of solidarity with what is going on in Nicaragua . . . This experience is going to help us organize health workers in the States in opposition to what Reagan is doing" [Kinzer 1985 July].

Mrs. Burlingame of Berkeley, California, a member of a senior citizen coffee-picking brigade, explained her motives for being there:

> . . . it's a privilege, an invigorating, rewarding experience . . . a joy to be doing something worthwhile . . . I came out of a need to do what was most effective . . . To do what one person could to intervene between the Reagan administration and its dastardly deeds. ["Americans Work for Free" 1985 July].

A member of a women's construction brigade from Northampton, Mass., "'was drawn to Nicaragua as one is drawn to the eye of a hurricane . . . At a time when the U.S. government is putting a tight squeeze on the country our work represents a show of faith . . . that Nicaragua will continue . . . to show strength. That's one of the things that's very inspiring about this'" [Decker 1987]. According to a brochure put out by this brigade "Going to Nicaragua is a direct act of conscience in opposition to our government's aggression and in solidarity with the Nicaraguan people" [Lobenstein 1987:1]. Another visitor appreciated that "We got a chance to be with Nicaraguan campesinos and to see the revolution for ourselves" [Miller 1986].

For Ben Linder, an "internacionalista" who was killed in the fighting, "No other choice [than working in Nicaragua—P.H.] could have fulfilled him more . . . What on earth could he be doing in the United States or anywhere that would have made him so uncompromisingly happy?" asked the *Village Voice* obituary ["Ben Linder" 1987:23].

A former Peace Corps member, a college professor on leave to teach in Nicaragua, wanted his thirteen-year-old son

> to see a country that is truly dedicated to human rights, that believes that everyone should be able to eat, receive health care and education. My shame for the actions of my country is heightened by my fear that my son's generation is being threatened by horrors like the horror that Vietnam was . . . [Woodhull 1988]

As such and other testimonies indicate, for many visitors this was indeed a pilgrimage, reverently undertaken to a new political shrine. A

Lutheran Church official observed that many Americans journey to Nicaragua "as a matter of faith" [Foley 1984]. Or as a tour organizer put it: ". . . the stream of travelers is a spontaneous grass-roots movement dedicated to humanity . . . it springs from an American desire to fight injustice and poverty and to halt what they see as an ominous U.S. involvement in Nicaraguan affairs" [Foley 1984]. Others, according to Sergio Ramirez, member of the ruling junta, "come to resolve their doubts" ["The 'Other Side'" 1983].

The tours were a symbolic reaffirmation of the continued commitment to the values bequeathed by the 60s and a reflection of yearnings for ways of life contemporary American society could not gratify. A contributor to the *Village Voice* summed it up rather well:

> . . . these volunteers [to Nicaragua] . . . They're just fed up—not only with the societies where they felt shitty waking up every morning, but with the whole postcountercultural web of second thoughts and rationalizations . . . for many of the North Americans and Europeans alike, coming here has turned out to be the beginning of the long way back from 20 years of lockstep faith that nobody can ever really do anything anyway, and nothing good can last.
>
> . . . Nicaragua has become the crossroads. So many desires, so many *themes,* have converged here . . . The worldwide face-off . . . between the have-not nations and the haves. A renewal of belief in the possibility of a revolution . . . [Carson 1987:5, 6–7]

That was indeed for many the key attraction: "a renewal of belief in the possibility of a revolution"—somehow, somewhere. As such desires make clear, the estrangement of a large contingent of activists and social critics did not abate in the aftermath of the Vietnam war. This was also apparent from the support—symbolic or tangible—many well-known protesters and activitists of the 60s have given the government of Nicaragua. They included the Berrigan brothers, Julian Bond, Noam Chomsky, Ramsey Clark, William Sloan Coffin, Harvey Cox, David Dellinger, Richard Falk, Alan Ginsberg, Bianca Jagger, Staughton Lynd, Jessica Mitford, Linus Pauling, Adrienne Rich (the radical feminist poet), Bernard Sanders (the former socialist mayor of Burlington, Vt., elected to the House of Representatives in 1990), Dr. Spock, George Wald, and the entire Institute for Policy Studies, among others.

Most visitors went to Nicaragua in search of vindication of their critiques of the American political and social system—a desire which, as had been the case before, was combined with the hope of finding a new and authentic expression of socialist values, free of the taints and errors of other similar, by now discredited system. As Martin Peretz put it, "Nicaragua remains the revolutionary idyll, filling the vast emotional void created by the sequential disenchantments with the Soviet Union . . . China . . . Cuba and . . . Vietnam" [Peretz 1986].

Many of the veterans of the protest movements and political activism of the 1960s rushed to Nicaragua to fill precisely this void. According to Paul Berman (himself a descendant of the New Left),

> Backwater Nicaragua was the world center of the New Left . . . Fantasy elsewhere was realism in Nicaragua . . . everyone who went through our own North American New Left, or who identifies with it after the fact, finds the Sandinistas so appealing . . . it's so natural for us to look at them and explain, "Hey, those are our guys down there" . . . we feel a natural solidarity. [Berman 1986:20, 22]

According to Berman, Nicaraguan leaders exercised this attraction because they were young, opposed to the Old Left, part of a generational revolt, and of middle-class student background; they really picked up the gun while American students merely fantasized about it.

As another observer saw it, ". . . Nicaragua seems to be a way station on a trip back through the 1960s" [Cody 1985]. Abbie Hoffman was among the tour leaders ["Washington Talk" 1984]. Journalist Claudia Dreifus reported:

> To be in Managua was like being in a time machine. Here was a place seemingly run by the kind of people who were Sixties radicals. Wherever one went, people were young, singing political folk songs and chanting "Power to the People." One night there was even a Pete Seeger concert in town! [Dreifus 1983:58]

According to a contributor to *Socialist Review*, "In an odd sort of way, the streets of Managua last summer looked a bit like Manhattan's Lower East Side . . . I would run into a dozen acquaintances from the movement each day. There were several street corners filled with more North Americans than Nicas. It was almost surreal: 'The left takes a holiday in Managua'" [Ozer 1986:51].

The mindset of these visitors was virtually identical to those who in the 1930s went to pilgrimages to the Soviet Union, who in the 60s and 70s to China or Cuba, and who gave their benediction to communist Vietnam during the war. Accounts of the tours of Nicaragua and what impressed their authors incorporate every single theme and appeal of past political pilgrimages.

Each successive political pilgrimage compounded the irrationality of the phenomenon. Misreading the nature of the Soviet system under Stalin was somewhat more understandable since the Soviet system and its techniques of hospitality represented an unprecedented experience. The Soviet Union was the first putatively socialist system with several historically unique or unusual features (e.g., central planning, collectivization of agriculture, show trials, a secular "cult of personality," vast political police and propaganda apparatus); it was also the first of several 20th-century political systems characterized by forms of political brutality it succeeded in concealing for decades. There was at the time (in the 1930s) no historical experience or precedent for interpreting such a system. It was also the first modern state that made a systematic effort through its conducted tours to purposefully and routinely deceive favorably disposed visitors.

When the time came between the 1950s and early 70s for the same illusions to be grafted upon Mao's China—by a new generation of sympathetically disposed Western visitors—there was a fund of historical experience, that of the Soviet system and its colossal deceptions, to draw upon. But the new political pilgrims were incapable or unwilling to do so. When in turn Mao's China was discredited—with the help of the leaders who succeeded him—there was still less excuse to entertain similar illusions about yet another set of communist states such as Cuba or Vietnam; nonetheless once more there was a surge of illusions about them, and the lessons of China were ignored just as were the lessons of the Soviet Union by the admirers of Mao's China.

By the time Nicaragua came along there was more than half a century of experience of both political tourism (i.e., the systematic manipulation of favorably disposed visitors) and of the characteristic flaws and failed promises of political systems which have been legitimating themselves by the ideals of Marxism-Leninism. There was also a vast amount of critical literature about these systems, much of it produced by their former citizens following their escape. Critiques also began to mount inside several of these subsequently liberalized countries such as Hungary, Poland, and the Soviet Union, and most recently East Germany, Czechoslovakia, Bulgaria, and Rumania.

Every single communist system idealized by Westerners in this century produced a massive outpouring of its discontented citizens when circumstances allowed such exodus to take place. Nicaragua has been no exception: "the most frequently cited figure" of the number who left is half a million, or some 15% of its population [Berman 1989:43]. According to the leader of the Nicaraguan opposition the exodus amounted to a fifth of the population [Chamorro 1989:A23]. But that need not have proved anything as far as the sympathizers were concerned: have we not been told before that people leaving socialist countries are mostly members of the former ruling classes, or those of questionable moral character, or else they suffer of false consciousnesss, unwilling to undertake the necessary and reasonable sacrifices which the building of a just social system demands?

In the light of these circumstances the political illusions associated with Nicaragua were perhaps that most remarkable in our times, representing the most adamant refusal to learn from history, the most spectacular case of the suspension of disbelief, an extraordinary determination to ignore or suppress whatever detracts from an idealized view of a political system. The idealizations of the Nicaraguan political system also represent a renewed triumph of wishful thinking and the reflexive support of the enemy of one's enemy.

Perhaps the most important factor in these developments was that by the early 1980s few destinations besides Nicaragua remained for those who sought a setting where the true values of socialism were being realized or their realization attempted. The reasons were obvious: the Soviet Union (the other superpower, by now morally equivalent to the United States) has long lost its attractions; China, now embracing forms of capitalism and having earlier welcomed Nixon also has shed its revolutionary glow; the boat people have made the admiration of Vietnam more difficult; and Cuba too has produced a continuing stream of refugees and its repression of homosexuals and intellectuals gave pause to many erstwhile admirers, although with charismatic Castro still at the helm disillusionment was moderated. While the Third World in general remained an appealing idea, particular embodiments of Third World virtues were difficult to find. Under these circumstances the 1979 revolution in Nicaragua was a providential event offering a haven for the free-floating impulses looking for a new focus of loyalty. It is thus also understandable that American leftists were anxious about the purity of this latest "socialist" revolution. Lenin would have heartily endorsed the concerns of a writer in *Monthly Review* about the course of the Nicaraguan revolution:

> Another key factor in the struggle for a socialist society is the forging of a proletarian ideology ... much remains to be done. A socialist consciousness still hasn't permeated all sectors of the mass organizations in Nicaragua. For some workers "socialism" means little more than a society similar to Costa Rica ... To develop a true socialist perspective the Sandinista Front will have to deepen the process of political education and publicly enunciate a socialist ideology that calls for workers and peasants to assume complete control of the means of production and the state apparatus. Until this happens ... the revolutionary process could falter ... [and] a social democratic or reformist approach could gain ascendancy in Nicaragua. [Burbach 1980:38]

Thus there emerged a symbiotic relationship between the American left and the rulers of Nicaragua, each needing the other for different purposes. The Nicaraguan rulers desperately needed the legitimacy, the moral and material support their American supporters provided, and their assistance in reducing and finally halting all help to the anticommunist guerillas. In turn for the American left Nicaragua was the latest, badly needed promise of an authentic socialist system. As Robert Leiken put it:

> The American Left has been of enormous importance to the Sandinistas' effort to consolidate . . . their domination over the Nicaraguan people and undermine their resistance, but the Sandinistas have been just as important to the American Left. They have revived the notion of American imperialism on which the Left nourished itself, and provided new heroes . . . they have renewed the faith. [Collier and Horowitz, eds. 1989:129]

Besides a general desire to locate somewhere an authentic socialist system, there were also some specific factors which made Nicaragua a particularly suitable object of admiration and idealization among those disposed to reject their own society.

Quite possibly the single major reason for the surge of affection for the communist government of Nicaragua was the hostility shown toward it by the Reagan administration. Given the unpopularity of Reagan in the adversary culture it was axiomatic that whatever or whoever he opposed was deserving of support. Nicaragua came to benefit from the irresistible emotional logic of the impulse to treat the enemies of one's enemies as friends. Anthony Lewis, among others, believed that Reagan was "obsessed" with the Sandinistas, as part of a more general and even more destructive obsession with communism [Lewis 1986]. Supporting the Sandinistas was both a practical and symbolic declaration of hostility to Reagan and as such was embraced with great enthusiasm.

Not all supporters of the Sandinistas visited Nicaragua, but there was room for supportive activism within the United States. The Nicaragua lobby grew into a powerful political force and was instrumental in reducing, suspending, and finally ending government aid to the anticommunist guerillas [see, for example, Barnes 1986]. This is not to say that all those opposed to such assistance were friends of the Sandinistas, but the most vocal and dedicated opponents of military assistance certainly were, as was also the case during the Vietnam war when sympathy for the Vietcong and opposition to American military involvement and assistance to the anticommunist side were similarly linked.

But a deeper antagonism toward American society and culture (which went beyond the visceral aversion to Reagan) was also part of the critiques of U.S. policy toward Nicaragua. American policies toward that country were, in this view, not merely irrational but also inextricably tied to domestic politics, to American culture (as was the intervention in Vietnam supposed to be). Alexander Cockburn, the veteran *Nation* columnist, wrote on the editorial page of the *Wall Street Journal:*

> Goetz today, Nicaragua tomorrow; the public is on a euphoric high about punitive action . . . [He quoted psychohistorian Lloyd de Mause]: "We want Reagan to find a pretext to get into war, and down there is Nicaragua. There we have an enemy we can punish for our guilt about our greed and prosperity . . . We'll punish them, our boys will be sacrificed, and we'll feel so good that the Dow will go right through the roof." [Cockburn 1985]

Sympathy toward Nicaragua also had much to do with guilt over past American domination of that country and region and especially past American support for Somoza. Nicaragua was a plausible victim of the United States: a small, poor country economically exploited and politically dominated. It was also plausibly perceived as a small country under attack by overwhelming force, although upon closer inspection it was a badly organized, poorly financed, and hesitant attack. Still, it was tempting to connect victimization of the past with aggression in the present. According to David Wald ("a socialist and three-time Peace and Freedom candidate for the U.S. Senate"), many people visit Nicaragua because they see it as "the victim of a bully being set upon and the tendency of any decent citizen is to come to the aid of the victim" [Foley 1984]. It was also axiomatic among the supporters of Nicaragua that the United States was responsible for its poverty and the corruption and abuse of power of its previous governments.

The small size and population of the country were among the outstanding attractions of Nicaragua, possibly in part because of the general appeals of smallness ("small is beautiful" is among the legacies of the 60s), and because smallness made it a better candidate for the victim role. "Smallness" was endlessly invoked to ridicule American concern with Sandinista support for communist guerillas in the area (and especially in El Salvador) and with the Cuban and Soviet presence in Nicaragua.

A professor of philosophy at the University of Massachusetts at Amherst wrote:

> The little country of Nicaragua, whose population is the size of metropolitan Boston, is a threat to Reagan only because it has declared independence from the U.S. and instituted programs of democracy and social reform that recognize the validity of certain socialist ideas: farm cooperatives, free education, and health care, universal literacy, and planned eco-

nomic development . . . They are honestly committed to the poor and
could be a model of other Latin American countries . . . they give priority
to the needs of their own people, instead of U.S. corporations . . . [Brent-
linger 1985]

When Ortega unilaterally ended the cease-fire with the guerillas in
November 1989 Anthony Lewis pleaded on somewhat similar grounds
for understanding—an effort he was not in the habit of making on behalf
of those opposed to the Nicaraguan political system, including the peasants and Indians who joined the guerilla forces:

If we want to understand why Mr. Ortega did what he did, we should begin
by trying to imagine ourselves in his circumstances . . . Nicaragua is a tiny
country, population 3.7 million, and one of the poorest on earth. For the
last eight years a superpower with 70 times its population has been trying
to overthrow its Government by subversion, economic warfare and military
attack. [Lewis 1989]

Lewis, as other sympathizers, failed to note and concede that this
small country created (with Soviet and Cuban help) the largest and best
equipped armed forces in Central America, while the United States, notwithstanding its superpower status, provided, on and off, limited military
supplies to the guerillas.

Opposition to the American support for the guerillas—when not
based on the openly expressed sympathy toward the Sandinistas—was
often justified by the assertion that the government they battled was not
and could not possibly become a threat to the United States. It was even
argued (by a director of a foreign affairs program of the Carnegie Endowment for International Peace) that if it were a threat, "the [Reagan]
Administration would already have invaded Nicaragua" [Kramer 1987].
It is most doubtful however that Mr. Kramer would have accepted such
invasion, had it occurred, as proof that Nicaragua was a threat.

The appeals of Marxist-Leninist Nicaragua were also associated, as in
the case of similar systems in the past, with the idea that this was a "revolutionary" society to be judged as much on the basis of the stated (or
imputed) intentions of its founders and rulers as on those of its actual
accomplishments. If so, it was again axiomatic that "nothing the revolutionaries do could possibly be worse than what we do," as Martin Peretz
put it. He also wrote:

. . . there is already a richly elaborated romanticization of the Sandinistas,
much like the romanticization of the Vietnamese and Cambodian Communists. Some of the romanticists are the same, or are their spiritual chil-

dren . . . They tell us about happy and determined peasants, always with a rising literacy rate. We are given the same breathless tour reports from the front of nobility and simplicity and sacrifice. ["The Myth of Revolution" 1985]

Such admonitions made little impact on those persuaded of the virtues of this new revolutionary government. One of them, Ron Kovic (the Vietnam veteran portrayed in the film *Born on the Fourth of July*), assured Daniel Ortega on one of his visits in New York: "We know your revolution is a revolution of concern, of caring, of sensitivity" [Rohter 1985 October].

Champions of Nicaragua argued that it was different from and superior to the other discredited state socialist systems, and in any event, its blemishes were caused by American pressure and intervention, by the guerilla war and economic blockade. While these are disputable claims (and more will be said about them below), what is beyond dispute is that the attractions of Nicaragua replicated precisely the attractions of other communist systems in the past.

Another factor in the popularity of touring Nicaragua was geographic: it was easy to get to and travel expenses (and those of the package tours) were affordable for middle- and upper-middle-class Americans. Moreover the U.S. government put no obstacles in the way of such visits (unlike its earlier policy regarding Cuba), and the Nicaraguan government did not even require visas for U.S. citizens.

It should also be noted here that the sympathies of one group of visitors were especially consequential in creating a favorable image of the authorities in Nicaragua among the American public at large—the journalists. Most of them, even if not highly committed advocates of the Sandinistas, gave them the benefit of doubt and were invariably critical of U.S. policy, which reminded them of Vietnam. Hence the reports coming out of Nicaragua tended to reinforce the predisposition of the tourists and potential tourists. Shirley Christian, one of the few "deviant" journalists, wrote of the coverage of the insurrection which set the tone of much later reporting:

> Probably not since Spain has there been a more open love affair between the foreign press and one of the belligerents in a civil war . . . There were almost no reports by the *Post, Times* and CBS of . . . noncombat brutality by Sandinista forces . . . The American media, like most of the United States, went on a guilt trip in Nicaragua. [Christian 1987:34, 37, 38; on the media coverage see also Muravchik 1988 and Moore 1986]

For all these reasons the political tour of Nicaragua became during the 1980s the major political statement conveying both a durable estrangement from American society and an affirmation of the adversarial values of the 60s many tourists hoped to be realized in Nicaragua.

II

Even in comparison with such pioneers of conducted political tours as the Soviet Union under Stalin, China during Mao, and Castro's Cuba, the efforts of the Nicaraguan authorities stand out in both their scope and impact. The talent for these manipulations was honed in the political struggles antedating the seizure of power; the conducted tours may be viewed as part of a more ambitious agenda of ". . . *manto* or cover, which means appearing and behaving in a manner that will conceal your true nature and your real agenda." While such deviousness is often part of political warfare wherever it is conducted, communist movements inspired by Lenin excelled in it: "Stalin's abolition of the Comintern in 1943 . . . Castro's donning of rosary beads for the drive down from the Sierra Maestra was *manto*" [Payne 1985:2].

The organization and encouragement of the political tours and the images they sought to convey may indeed be viewed as an integral part of "a succesion of *mantos* to mask a determined drive to achieve goals founded in [Marxist-Leninist] ideology" [Ibid.].

The Nicaraguan leaders, partly because several of them were familiar with American cultural attitudes and values (having lived or studied in this country), were exceptionally gifted in manipulating American public opinion. The tours were a major but not the only instrument they used. As Mark Falcoff observed,

> . . . unique among Marxist revolutionary cadres around the world, the San-dinistas have a deep understanding of the peculiar vulnerabilities of American culture and the American political system . . . they appreciate the deep strains of isolationism that pervade the national character and restrain the international conduct of all administrations. They also understand . . . the deep sense of guilt, shame and even self-hatred that plagues . . . sectors of the intellectural class. [Falcoff 1986:7]

They also learned from Vietnam that public opinion plays a major role in shaping American foreign policy.

At the same time, as had been the case in the past, there was once more a large number of Americans ready to be favorably impressed by yet another (putatively) socialist country, and a huge network of supportive organizations in the United States emerged to lobby on behalf of the government of Nicaragua. There were dozens of organizations with hundreds of chapters and tens of thousands of activists ready to proselytize, protest, demonstrate, and lobby. There were well-paid professional lobbyists such as the law firm of Reichler and Applebaum in Washington, D.C., retained for an annual fee of $320,000 [Denton 1985]; there were also many "sister city" programs which often led to more than symbolic support:

> ... since ... 1979 ... private groups and sister city projects in more than 30 cities have sent more than $20 million in aid ... The [Nicaraguan] embassy said that 37 American cities are twinned and 12 more are in the process of establishing ties. [Chavez 1987]

> ... Supplies and labor worth $40 million ... [were donated] since July 1986, according to Sister Maureen Fiedler of the Quixote Center in Maryland ... In its national campaign ... the center hopes to collect another $60 million worth of donations by the fall—to match the $100 million Congress is sending to contras. [Sullivan 1987]

> ... At least 800 to 1000 organizations across the United States are involved on a regular basis with relief efforts in Nicaragua ... Countless other groups, like churches and schools, have provided ... occasional help, *Mother Jones* reported. [Berman 1986:24]

Academic communities such as Berkeley, California; Ann Arbor, Michigan; and Burlington, Vermont, were in the forefront of such efforts. A former member of the Lincoln Brigade (procommunist volunteers fighting in the Spanish Civil War against Franco) solicited funds for ambulances to Nicaragua ("What better symbol of our opposition to U.S. policy in Nicaragua could there be ..." [Ambulances for Nicaragua n.d.]).

In 1988 "The Boston City Council proclaimed November 3 'Ernesto Cardenal Day'" to honor a member of the Nicaraguan ruling group and minister of culture who declared in one of his writings that "'A Christian should embrace Marxism if he wants to be with God and all men'" ["Sandinista Holiday" 1988:9].

At the 1986 PEN Club Congress in New York, "Omar Cabezas, the Nicaraguan Deputy Minister of the Interior [police, that is] ha[d] been invited as a guest of honor ..." [McDowell 1986]; he was "lustily applauded having just conceded that his Government censors writers" [Ozick 1986]. Another observer noted that "The most popular statement [at the Congress] expressed 'acute distress at U.S. Government intervention in Nicaragua' and attributed to that intervention the restriction of civil liberties by the Sandinistas ..." [Goodman 1986]. The mood of these writers was further illustrated by "... a petition in support of Nicaraguan positions [which] was openly encouraged from the podium by PEN president Norman Mailer ..." [Ozick 1986].

In the U.S. Congress, Senators Tom Harkin of Iowa, John Kerry of Massachusetts, and Christopher Dodd of Connecticut led the charge against military assistance to the guerillas, and in the House, Congressmen David Bonoir, George Crocket, and George Miller were among those similarly distinguished. House Speaker Thomas O'Neill, influenced by Maryknoll nuns, reached the conclusion that withdrawal of support for the guerillas would "... allow [the Nicaraguan people] to make their own free choice of government" [Swaim 1985; see also Shapiro 1985]. Even more committed champions of the Sandinistas in the U.S. House of Representatives were

> ... Ron Dellums and John Conyers [who] argue that Detroit could use a literacy program as successful as the Nicaraguan government's; that a popular democracy *was* being built by the Sandinistas, grounded in a program for health, education and social opportunities for the vast majority of the Nicaraguan people; that Americans should support the accomplishments of this young revolution ... [Ozer 1986:57–58]

The actual techniques of hospitality the Nicaraguan authorities employed were similar, in most respects, to those of their predecessors in the Soviet Union, China, and especially Cuba, but there were some differences at least in emphasis.

These techniques crystallize around two simple principles. The first is to expose the tourists to pleasant or uplifting sights and friendly people and to prevent them from seeing what is ugly or dispiriting and from meeting people who do not see things the way the authorities do. Designers of these tours also find it expedient to include sights or experiences which combine the political message with aesthetic pleasures and entertainment—fiestas, festivities, and especially folk dances—performed preferably by peasants or factory workers, who supposedly were not able to indulge in these forms of artistic self-expression in the past.

The second principle is to make the political tourist or pilgrim feel good in more personal ways: by catering to creature comforts (regarding accommodations, food, transportation, and so on) and by making him feel important usually through meeting the leading representatives of the political system.

It is then not surprising that in Nicaragua too visitors were taken to all the institutions and physical creations of the regime which were supposed to testify to its humane policies: new schools, kindergartens, clinics, rural cooperatives, factories, cultural and recreational centers, housing projects, a center for rehabilitating prostitutes, nonpunitive correctional institutions, and so on. The tourists met ordinary citizens who would assure them of the beneficial changes in their personal lives thanks to the policies of the government, as well as intellectuals, artists, and wise planners who represented the enlightened elite presiding over these vast improvements. They were also taken on sightseeing tours in pleasant natural settings lacking in political but not psychological significance (e.g., a "cruise on the Escondido river, through the tropical jungle," or on Lake Nicaragua).

In one crucial regard the Nicaraguan hosts differed from those in other communist countries. The Nicaraguan authorities did not attempt to shield the tourists from mass poverty. Quite to the contrary they made good use of the spectacle of poverty which in any event would have been difficult to conceal. Exposing the tourists who in their own countries enjoyed a high standard of living to the images of dire provety served several purposes. The visitors were told, time and again, that they could see for themselves that Nicaragua was a small and poor country—how could it possibly threaten the United States? How could it not desire peace in order to put its resources into civilian projects? It was endlessly pointed out to the visitors (ready for this message, in any event) that the government of the United States was responsible for the wretched conditions: in the past it supported the corrupt Somoza oligarchy, in the present the guerilla war which alone prevented the government from devoting all its resources and energy to raising the standard of living of the people.

The suggested proper approach to this poverty was captured in the comments of one of the few skeptical visitors:

> That afternoon we take a brief walking tour [in Managua] . . . we encounter a few dilapidated barrio dwellings similar to the ones we'd deplored in Mexico and Salvador. Now, responding to our guide's enthusiasm, we almost feel the shack's allure of revolutionary austerity, defiant in the face of the U.S. inspired dependency that plagues the region. We have not been here for twenty-four hours and already we sense that the Sandinista's achievements must be measured by different, perhaps metaphysical standards. [Frawley 1985]

Also, to the extent that the American sympathizers were estranged from their own society and its "empty affluence," the privations and austerity in Nicaragua were not necessarily a liability. An American "internacionalista" said: "Material goods are not important to me . . . I don't want my children to develop consumer values. I find it overwhelming to go into a supermarket and have 15 different brands of breakfast food . . . I want my children . . . not be forced to adopt false needs" [Riderour 1986:28].

The appeal of or (for some) the romance of poverty was also utilized on the occasions when pampered Americans were exposed to the adventure of "roughing it" in primitive rural areas (e.g., those going on coffee-bean picking expeditions) or when visiting dignitaries were pointedly *not* taken to good restaurants but to authentic local spots frequented by the toilers. Thus when Senator Moynihan "suggested a *tipico* lunch commandante Borge [always available to chaperon-important visitors—P.H.] swept him along . . . to a *comedor popular*—a workers' hash house in the grimy Managua slum of Ciudad Sandino" [Tamayo 1983].

The impact of the exposure to poverty and the corresponding feelings of guilt could predictably be intensified when the visitors were taken to the war zone where poverty and destruction could be more plausibly blamed on the United States and its support for the guerillas. It was a strategy that rarely failed. A member of a Witness for Peace delegation (one of the most unabashedly pro-Sandinista groups) wrote: "To be an American in this war zone is both frightening and inspiring. To witness daily destruction committed by the U.S. government with U.S. tax dollars, to be responsible for murders of innocent people, is to feel shame and rage" [Miller 1987:13].

The Nicaraguan techniques of political hospitality differed from those in other communist states insofar as in Nicaragua it was sometimes arranged for the tourists to meet with opposition groups and an editor of the opposition newspaper *La Prensa*. Rarely did the visitors realize that the contents of the paper were severely and frequently censored and its publication suspended from time to time [Chamorro 1988:99–101] or that opposition parties could barely function due to intimidation and various restrictions on their activities.

Encounters between the American supporters of the regime and opposition figures posed little risk for the authorities since the vast majority of the visitors were, in any event, suspicious of and unsympathetic toward the critics of the system. For example Jaime Chamorro, an editor of *La Prensa*, wrote that when one of the opposition politicians, Virgilio Godoy (himself a former member of the Sandinista government), told a visiting group that "the Sandinista TV show '*De Cara al Pueblo,*' in which ordinary citizens supposedly get to ask questions of Sandinista leaders, was arranged beforehand, a newly arrived North American tourist angrily stood up and shouted, 'That's a lie!'" [Chamorro 1988:100]. A similar attitude was taken by Professor Richard Falk of Princeton University, who suggested that ". . . it seems imprudent for a progressive interpreter of Central America to dwell on the deficiencies of the Nicaraguan revolution . . ." [Falk 1985:456, 458]. A similarly protective attitude was displayed by Richard Barnet of the Institute for Policy Studies, who proposed that "To defend the right of the Nicaraguan people to conduct their experiment . . . is . . . an obligation of U.S. citizenship" [Barnet 1985:456, 458].

While in all communist systems the more important visitors were given the chance to meet high-ranking officials, sometimes even the supreme leader, the Nicaraguan authorities went further than any other of these systems. According to one account,

> Almost any visiting American official, no matter how low his rank, can now expect to meet with at least two of the nine commandantes in the Sandinista National Directorate, the apex of power . . . Nonofficial American visitors . . . can count on at least one commandante and a well-worn tour of revolutionary highlights. [Tamayo 1983]

A visitor's experience of meeting Ernesto Cardenal, minister of culture (and member of the directorate), further underlined the leaders' personal involvement with hospitality:

> A few days into the stay, guide Jorge announces that it is possible to meet with Ernesto Cardenal. The group hurriedly composes a song to perform as a gift to Cardenal at their meeting. He enters dazed. One has the impression this is the fifteenth delegation he has greeted in so many minutes. One wonders how the Sandinistas' need and willingness to attend to such visitors has impeded the working of the government. [Smith 1987]

The leaders also generously made themselves available to a *Playboy* reporter: "After the interviews were under way, some of the Nicaraguan leaders began inviting Marcelo [the photographer?] and me to . . . hang out with them. Things we did in Managua: go with Borge to a prison farm . . . watch Father Cardenal put on an all-day Latin-American song festival . . . take seven uninvited people to dinner at Ramirez' house [another junta member]" [Dreifus 1983:58].

A similar division of labor was in evidence during the visit of two important American writers, William Styron and Carlos Fuentes:

> Interior Minister Tomas Borge took the visitors to coffee-growing Matagalpa Province, and Minister of Agrarian Reform Jaime Wheelock showed them rural cooperatives. The Minister of Health, Dora Maria Tellez, took them to a hospital to see children, some without limbs who were wounded in a recent raid by United States-backed guerillas.
>
> On Thursday diplomats and senior government officials converged at what was once the Managua Country Club to watch Mr. Ortega bestow the Ruben Dario Cultural Independence Order on Mr. Fuentes. . . . Other recipients . . . have included Graham Greene and Gabriel Gracia Marquez. [Kinzer 1988 January]

Borge, as already noted, played a key role in political hospitality, especially as extended to important visitors. He had a special appeal on account of his past sufferings and his credentials as poet and author of the official anthem, which includes the line "We fight against the Yankee, enemy of humanity." Reportedly ". . . he considers himself to be, in the phrase he has had painted on the front of the Interior [police] Ministry building, 'Sentinel of the People's Happiness.' Borge also established a film-making unit within the Interior Ministry, and as one of its first tasks, he assigned the unit to film a dramatization of how he was tortured in jail. He shows the film to visitors on request" [Kinzer 1985 Sept.].

Borge took the famous German writer Gunter Grass on a tour of one of the enlightened prisons. Suitably impressed, he concluded from the prison visit that ". . . in this tiny, sparsely populated land . . . Christ's words are taken literally" [Diskin ed. 1983:247]. Grass also happens to be one of the most impassioned critics of the injustices of American society; while attending the PEN Club conference in New York in 1986 he enriched these critical views by exploring the slums of the Bronx.

Borge was not always so forthcoming in the matter of prison visits. In 1985 "Representatives [of the Lawyers Committee for International Human Rights] were refused permission to visit El Chipote, the main security police detention center in Managua . . . 'Minister Borge explained that the presence of a stranger could interrupt the process of interrogation and persuasion'" [Christian 1985]—a proposition nobody would take issue with. In 1987 Borge provided access to two American senators to the same prison; they found it "empty and undergoing renovations." But "No representative of Nicaragua's non-governmental Permanent Commission for Human Rights was invited," and its head, Lino Fernandez, ventured to suggest that "he was uncertain that what the [American] visitors had seen was a good indication of what the prison had been like. 'Past experience tells us that when foreigners come on missions like this, things are arranged for them in advance'" [Kinzer 1987 December:A11].

A former supporter of the Sandinista government reached similar conclusions:

> Many visitors . . . are misled in regards to human rights by a model prison, the "Open Farm" fourteen miles from Managua, where the inmates can be seen working the . . . farmland and enjoying a most benign penal regimen . . . Although this prison . . . only houses a fraction of the total inmate population . . . many visitors mistake it for a representative sample of the entire correctional system. They are seldom taken to the "Zona Franca," the huge master prison where thousands of inmates are crammed into filthy cells. [Belli 1985:127]

The novelist Mario Vargas Llosa requested and was promised permission by Borge to visit Zona Franca but the permission never arrived [Ibid.].

The Nicaraguan Permanent Commission on Human Rights had this to say about model prisons:

> What are called *Granjas de Regimen Abierto,* or "Open Rule Farms," in reality are prisons for display purposes, where a limited number of prisoners ... enjoy really positive conditions. The majority ... have been transferred to these prisons as a prize for having stood out as "informers" for State Security in other prisons ... The international delegations taken to these centers normally find prisoners "happy and grateful" to be in the prisons, and in some cases they even put on "cultural shows" in which the prisoners sing and dance for the visitors.
>
> But there is another type of prison in Nicaragua where no international organizations are allowed to enter ... these are the State Security jails that are ... some of the worst jails in Latin America ... These prisoners are usually kept incommunicado, completely isolated, in totally dark cells; both food and water are given out at irregular intervals depending on the "cooperation" of the prisoners ... physical and psychological tortures, and the use of drugs during interrogations are all everyday events in these prisons ... [*Statement Regarding the Prison Situation* 1986:1]

Such model prisons were not the only devices with which to impress the foreign visitors. Borge's two offices were among the most inventive measures in the line of political hospitality. According to a former employee of his, Alvaro Jose Baldizon, who used to be chief investigator within the Special Investigation Commission of the Ministry of Interior (and who defected to the U.S. in 1985):

> ... Borge has two offices. One ... is located in the Silvio Mayorga building where he meets with religious delegations and delegations from democratic political parties. In this office Borge has photographs of children, gilded carved crucifixes and a Bible or two. Before Borge meets with religious delegations he usually memorizes Bible passages which he can quote ... Borge's real office where he fulfills his duties as Interior Minister is located where he lives in Bello Horizonte in Managua. In that office there are no crucifixes or Bibles—only Marxist literature and posters of Marx, Engels and Lenin. [Baldizon 1985:2]

The deceptions associated with impressing visitors from abroad were not limited to the two offices of Borge. Baldizon also reported that

> The Sandinista Front ... has at its disposal many different mechanisms to project an image that it wishes a foreign delegation to perceive. Members of the Sandinistas' army dress as civilians, follow each delegation and are always present when the Nicaraguan people speak with members of the delegations ... therefore very few people dare to speak ill of the Sandinista

regime. The Sandinistas prepare the terrain before the arrival of a delegation through what they call "preparacion defensiva" . . . This consists of visiting the homes of opponents and threatening them. Every opponent is put under surveillance, has a file called the "potential enemy file" and receives periodic "preventive visits" from State Security officers. [Baldizon 1985:3]

Baldizon explained that when the Nicaraguan government learns that a foreign delegation wants to visit certain areas . . . MINT [Ministry of Interior] officials are sent out to prepare the way. People who appear on MINT's list of "potential enemies" receive visits by the officials and are told to stay away from the visiting delegation. Other "potential enemies" are locked up during the visit . . . Security agents pretending to be photographers, journalists or relatives of people in the region to be visited frequently join the delegations . . . on their trips . . . Borge sends teams of people to be on the routes used and in the localities visited. These are called "causal encounter" teams and when a delegation arrives at a location MINT personnel pretending to be local residents . . . [are] . . . available to talk with the delegation . . . They describe alleged contra atrocities and the benefits of the Sandinista revolution for Nicaragua's peasants and workers. [Nicaraguan Defector . . . 1985:6]

Baldizon also related how Borge arranged "other apparently spontaneous events" for the benefit of foreign delegations:

In January 1985 Tomas Borge ordered Baldizon's office to . . . provide him with names of persons in dire economic straits or serious health problems . . . Minister Borge arranged his reception of these unfortunate or needy persons to coincide with the arrival in his office of a foreign delegation . . . the ministry TV film crew was on hand to record the apparently spontaneous event. As the foreign delegation was ushered in, Borge would be seen engaged in earnest conversation with one of the needy or handicapped persons, promising help . . . In May 1985 such a show was staged for a visiting delegation of West German Christian Democratic Union/Christian Social Union. In this show a blind man who had earlier requested an accordion so he could entertain to earn his living was presented with the instrument. He thereupon entertained the German guests . . . The instrument was repossessed from the blind man after his show . . . [Baldizon 1986:12]

If skeptics find such stories far-fetched or implausible they should recall that similarly colorful and well-documented deceptions were part of political hospitality in other communist systems as well [Hollander 1981:347–99].

It should be noted that Americans sympathetic to the Nicaraguan authorities made considerable efforts to discredit Mr. Baldizon. These efforts followed the same pattern as those elicited by earlier defectors from communist systems (or movements), although subsequent information invariably confirmed their "lurid" accounts. Thus Aryeh Neier, noted civil libertarian and vice chairman of Americas Watch, a human rights organization, wrote that

> In the 1950s, those who saw a conspiracy to destroy America from within . . . esteemed the lurid revelations of defectors from the enemy cause— former American communists such as Elizabeth Bentley, Louis Budenz and Harvey Matusow. In the same way today an Administration . . . is touting the revelations of defectors from the Sandinistas. Currently the most prized defector is Alvaro Baldizon . . . [Neier 1986]

Mr. Neier gave no persuasive reason why Baldizon was not to be believed, nor did he tell which of the revelations of former American communists such as he mentioned were untrue—although he intimated that they were not to be trusted. Least of all did he allow that there are differences between defectors from Western communist parties and from communist countries and that much of the valid information about the latter first reached us from such defectors.

Baldizon was not the only defector providing information about Nicaraguan political hospitality. Alberto Gamez Ortega, a former prosecutor and vice minister of justice, related that

> Visits of human rights groups are "scheduled for selected places such as the Open Structure Penitentiary System . . . or to certain prisons which show only what they wish to be known. Visitors are not shown El Chipote, the punishment cells or the clandestine cells." . . . Another defector, Mateo Jose Guerrero, who served as director of the Sandinista human rights organization, said that he was ordered to "take charge" of Mr. Mendez [director of Americas Watch, on a fact-finding visit to investigate human rights abuses—P.H.] "providing him with a car and arranging his interviews with government entities." [Morrison 1986]

Another "regular" deeply involved in interpreting local conditions for the benefit of American visitors was Sister Mary Hartman, an American nun and longtime resident of Nicaragua, coincidentally a representative of the government's human rights commission (that could only discover human rights violations committed by the contras). She assured one group of visitors that ". . . some Nicaraguans . . . are unhappy with the revolution, but that's because they don't live the Gospel and so can't adjust to the new Nicaragua. 'Sharing isn't easy,' she explains. 'It requires conversion'" [Frawley 1985]. Another skeptical tourist described the following encounter:

One of the StaffDel [congressional staff delegation] members asked Sister Mary about the unusually high rate of confessions among Nicaragua's political prisoners. "I don't find that surprising," she said, "because they were captured . . ."

"This afternoon," Jim Denton said to Sister Mary, "we're going to talk to a group called Mothers of Political Prisoners."

Sister Mary had little use for the mothers. They were not people of good character, she said. And they had been funded by the U.S., bribed "with things like Camel cigarettes, huh?"

"Could you give us specific cases where the mothers had been bribed or were otherwise found untrustworthy?" Denton asked.

Mary Hartman said she could, she certainly could.

"Well . . . ," said Denton.

"I don't have the files right with me, huh?" [O'Rourke 1987:38]

Further light was shed on political hospitality by two disillusioned participants of one such tour (that also included Mexico and El Salvador), organized by the Center for Global Service and Education of Augsburg College, Minneapolis, and sponsored by the American Lutheran Church Women. They reported

During the two week period our group was subject to incessant thinly disguised indoctrination. The root cause of poverty in Central America was the United States and its evil capitalistic system. The socio-political system which would rescue the area would come from the Marxist revolution as exemplified by the Sandinistas and validated by Christianity as defined by Liberation Theology . . . The Center organized full itineraries for each country which allowed only short periods of time on our own. However the language barrier and unfamiliar environments still kept us dependent on the staff.

A technique throughout the trip was incessant anti-U.S. rhetoric . . . One . . . poster depicted U.S. helicopters carrying bombs with the caption, "Herod searches for the baby Jesus to kill." Ronald Reagan was equated with Herod several times during the trip . . .

We found that it is extremely difficult to maintain a balanced perspective after being exposed to these . . . techniques for . . . two weeks. If we had not had each other [the two people who provided this account— P.H.] to talk to we might have begun to question our own position . . .

. . . [Minister of Education Ernesto] Cardinal told us he sometimes spoke to groups like ours two or three times a day and nine out of ten of them represented protestant churches . . . [Report on Travel Seminar . . . Congressional Record 1985:H2043–46]

Such responses to political hospitality were rare; most of the tourists did not react unfavorably to either the anti-American rhetoric or to thinly disguised Marxist-Leninist propaganda; rather, they welcomed the opportunity to find confirmation for their beliefs and predisposition. An unusually independent-minded member of one of the Witness for Peace tour groups noted, "Public apologies for the United States and presumably for our being American citizens became one of the most exasperating features of our numerous prayer vigils and public meetings along with the eagerness of some delegates to condemn their own country" [Lanier 1984:261].

At last it should also be pointed out that many Nicaraguan citizens were restrained from enlightening American visitors about the true state of affairs (and their feelings) by the possible consequences of such actions. One of them, "a former university professor and life long opponent of the Somoza dictatorship," wrote:

> A good number of . . . visitors do not see our own reality because they do not want to: "Leftist" political experiments cannot by definition suffer from the ills that we are suffering . . . For a question to have meaning it must be asked in circumstances that make possible an honest answer. To ask in Nicaragua whether the Revolution benefits the people; whether one is in favor or against the Revolution . . . without taking into account the circumstances, the place where one is asking, who is present, the degree of trust that the person being interviewed has in the interviewer, is tantamount . . . to not being interested in an honest answer. ["Letter from Nicaragua" 1984:7]

III

What precisely were the attractions of the political system in Nicaragua, and in what way did these attractions replicate those of other, earlier communist systems?

The appeals of Nicaragua were hard to separate from the aversion to American society and U.S. foreign policy. The more critical the tourists were of the United States, the more congenial a benefit-of-doubt posture became. The late Michael Harrington, famous socialist author and organizer, "came back [from a trip to Nicaragua] more ashamed of my country than at any time since the Vietnam war. The Nicaraguans are a generous people, a poor and hungry people who want to make a truly democratic revolution and it is we who subvert their decency . . ." [Harrington 1981]. Noam Chomsky linked the efforts of Nicaragua to "devote its meager resources to the need of the poor and deprived" to "U.S. savagery," the response to such efforts [Chomsky 1987:90].

For some visitors coming into contact with Nicaragua was a profoundly transforming experience that changed their outlook, sometimes even their sense of identity (just as Shirley MacLaine reported upon her return from Mao's China that it was a spiritual transformation so profound that she even stopped biting her nails, picking her fingers, and smoking). An "internacionalista" revealed that "Nicaragua has changed my life drastically . . . These people have a solid sense of community, something the vast majority of Americans lack. So many of us live lives of despair and impotence. Here, one is alive with a sense of purpose" [Riderour 1986:153]. Mrs. Rose Markham, a retired social worker, from Northampton, Massachusetts, reported that "You know, it [the visit to Nicaragua] changed me. I didn't come back the same person I went as . . ." [Lyons 1983:3]. An American "internacionalista" observed that ". . . Jesus would be very happy with Nicaragua today . . . I feel like there is no place on earth like Nicaragua right now . . . Things are happening here now have never happened before and may never happen again" [Riderour 1986:98, 90].

Conor Cruise O'Brien was similarly impressed: "You can actually feel around you in Nicaragua something going on that you know can't be switched off . . . that most intractable thing, a new kind of faith" [O'Brien 1986:55]. In *Sojourners* magazine two visitors wrote: "We believe that something unprecedented in Central America is happening in Nicaragua" [Hollyday and Wallis 1983:13]. An attorney from Harrisonburg, Virginia, reported that "there was an exciting and vibrant spirit of independence of a people finding a new way . . . [he found] the commitment of the people to the revolution . . . firm . . ." The remaining problems, such as a mosquito infestation, were blamed on the CIA by residents he spoke to [Hoover 1986].

An English teacher from Green Bay, Wisconsin, concluded upon his return that "The people were so repressed [before 1979] they see the revolution as a Godsend" [Fehrenbach 1984]. A retired minister from Atlanta, Georgia, said:

> As a person who likes to know the truth, I felt a need to go. I also heard wonderful things about the Nicaraguan people—their hopefulness . . . their forgiveness of their enemies. I wanted to see that . . . What I found is that they [the Sandinista government] have done some things that as a Christian I value highly.

He was also impressed by children in a poor village "dressed in bright colors, like flowers blooming out of nothing. They were singing and dancing" [Donziger 1988:99]. As this citation suggests political pilgrims and tourists—in the past as in the present—frequently confused and conflated the virtues and aesthetic appeals of pre-modern life with those supposedly conferred by the new political authorities: happy children in a poor village bestowed legitimacy upon the government. Equally wide-spread was the insistence that these supposedly atheistic systems were in fact realizing the true values of Christianity; in Nicaragua this was made more plausible by the prominence of liberation theology and the presence of several Roman Catholic priests, or former priests, among high-ranking officials.

A reporter who toured the country in the company of Abbie Hoffman, Betty Friedan, and other luminaries (altogether "64 writers, film producers, professors, politicians and doctors") pointed out that "Certainly this state is not Godless. It is the first revolutionary government to be propelled by the theology-of-liberation movement. There are more Catholics in charge than Marxists. Four of the government's ministers are Roman Catholic priests . . ." [Nielson 1985:9A]. The authors in the *Sojourner* too assured their readers that "Jesus Christ has had the far greater influence" than Marx [Hollyday and Wallis 1983:12].

Gunter Grass was not alone in discerning a religious inspiration behind the correctional system of Nicaragua. A political tourist from Massachusetts was persuaded that "One of the clearest indicators of the religious-based nature of Nicaragua's revolutionary government is its criminal justice and prison system" [Markham 1987]. Benedict Alper, a professor of criminology at Boston College, was especially anxious to learn about (what he, one may suspect, expected to be) an exceptionally progressive penal system, and upon his return suggested that

> . . . prison officials in the United States should adopt some of the Nicaraguans' methods of rehabilitating and treating prisoners . . .
>
> He returned . . . from a three-week tour of Nicaragua's prisons because he had heard that inmates were subjected to inhumane conditions.
>
> "I went down myself to see what it was all about," he explained . . . He was allowed to speak with government ministers, . . . prison officials as well as imprisoned Contras.
>
> . . . Alper said he was surprised by what he saw in Nicaraguan prisons.
>
> "One of the things that really got to me was the amount of compassion they have," Alper said. [Stone 1987]

Another visitor, sent to Nicaragua by the United Church in Washington, D.C., wrote: "The visit to the prison [in Esteli] was surprising. It is a very enlightened prison system, but of course it isn't overloaded like ours is. What struck me about it was the politeness and calm behavior of the prisoners . . . The idea is definitely rehabilitation rather than restitution" [Uncapher 1987:17].

As may be recalled Western visitors of yesteryear also found the Soviet correctional authorities in the days of Stalin impressively compassionate and their policies humane [Hollander 1981:140–60]. In point of fact communist prisons had been lavishly praised by Western tourists everywhere they were made part of the conducted tours [Hollander 1987].

Not only was Nicaragua a good place to be a prison inmate, it was also, according to the Pulitzer Prize-winning writer Alice Walker, "a writer's paradise." She also said, "Not since I was a child growing up in the South have I seen such a love of books and learning" [Rohmer 1987:19]. It is unlikely that she knew about the books that could *not* be published or distributed. Adrienne Rich, the radical feminist poet, described revolutionary Nicaragua as a "society that took poets seriously" and approvingly quoted someone who told her that "You'll love Nicaragua. Everyone there is a poet" [Driscoll 1983]. A writer for *In These Times* pronounced Nicaragua "the land of poets" [Burns 1983:16].

The literacy campaign of the government was among the most frequently cited accomplishments of the system, but few of its admirers entertained the possibility that the newly literate masses might be nourished on a limited diet of permissible reading materials, or reflected on the extent to which the campaign served purposes of political indoctrination rather than general enlightenment. That the former was the case is suggested even by some of the admirers. Thus a sympathetic correspondent of the *Village Voice* quoted a Jesuit engaged in the literacy project he modestly called

> "a gigantic act of love for all the people of Nicaragua . . . who have lacked everything." The basic point of the Freire method [used in the campaign], Cardenal explained, "is that you not only learn to read, you learn to identify and understand the reality you live in and your own history so that you can become an agent of history." [Singer 1980]

The authorities' interpretation of history and reality as part of the literacy campaign presumably allowed for a comfortable margin of political indoctrination. Elsewhere the general coordinator of the campaign, Fr. Fernando Cardenal, pointed out that "We do not pretend to teach only how to read, write . . . we also have as key goals the consciousness raising and politicization of the illiterates . . ." [Belli 1985:102].

There was near unanimity among the political tourists about the state of mind of the natives. While grumbling about shortages was occasionally reported the visitors believed that the people of Nicaragua were generally happy with the new political systems and appreciative of the blessings it brought to them: "they exuded a new pride and displayed a lively confidence. The revolution had touched every life," was how one visitor put it [Burns 1983:16]. A senior at the University of Massachusetts at

Amherst and beneficiary of a week-long trip "to learn about the revolution" found "Nicaragua to be a happy, hospitable country, its people filled with hope for the future" ["Two Return from Trips to Nicaragua" 1984–85]. An interpreter for a work brigade sponsored by the United Methodist Church discovered that "Nicaraguans who were very poor prior to the revolution are happy now because they are living better . . ." He also reported that "I never heard anyone blame the government . . . They blame the Contra war for their drained resources" [Livingston 1987]. Members of the Witness for Peace group from Arizona were satisfied ". . . that the overwhelming majority of Nicaraguans support—and are ready to defend with their lives—the Sandinista regime that . . . restored the rule of law, a sense of personal dignity, and a respect for human rights" [Johns 1987:62]. More than that: "Nicaraguans are building a society which may become a model for poverty-ridden countries," another tourist wrote in Austin, Texas [Rodriguez 1984:A11].

There was no malnutrition or begging to be found, or at any rate James Harrington, legal director of the Texas Civil Liberties Union, wrote that "We did not see begging or malnutrition in Nicaragua" [Harrington 1984:17] and he did not mean to convey that though he did not see any, he might have missed some. (At the height of the Soviet famine in the early 1930s, G. B. Shaw remarked, looking around in a well-provisioned restaurant in Moscow, that food shortages seemed rather implausible [Hollander 1981:118], and John Kenneth Galbraith, the famous economist, concluded after he was shown the kitchen of a plant in Peking that "if there was any shortage of food it was not evident in the kitchen" [Ibid.:350]—a remark clearly *not* calculated to suggest that the favorable conditions were limited to the kitchen he happened to inspect.) In the same spirit an Amherst College student and his father on an "intensive two week study trip" noted that "As for Soviet dominance, in all our travels we saw only two Russian appearing civilian men" [Shepherd and Shepherd 1984:20]—as if such sightings could be taken as indications of the total absence of the phenomena in question, be they beggars, Soviet soldiers, or food shortages. In each of these instances the visitors sought to suggest that generalizing from their observation was a reasonable procedure.

As in the past admiration of the political systems was greatly enhanced by the tourists' favorable impression of its leaders. The rulers of Nicaragua, as noted earlier, made a special effort to encourage these attitudes. Two visitors wrote:

> . . . All Nicaraguans have a great deal of access to the Sandinista leaders. We were convinced of this the evening we met Daniel Ortega. After each member of our delegation had stepped forward to shake the hand of the

chief of state and the television cameras had stopped rolling, Gillberto Aguirre of CEPAD (the Evangelical Committee for Aid and Development) stepped up smiling and said "Daniel!" and the two embraced. We explained that we do not have such a relationship to Ronald Reagan. [Hollyday and Wallis 1983:12]

So strong was the favorable predisposition and so limited their exposure to conflicting realities that these tourists remained totally unaware of the privileged life of the ruling elites. Instead they saw them as a selfless, beleaguered group of enlightened men and women tirelessly struggling to uplift their people. Thus Richard Falk thought that these leaders "may be brutal, they may be imprudent in certain ways, but I think they are basically trying to create a much fairer social and economic order for their people. They have done wonderful things in education, extraordinary things . . ." [Falk 1983:9].

Richard Falk was not the only commentator with ties to the Institute for Policy Studies who took a charitable view of the Sandinistas. Key institute members maintained warm relations with and were actively helping the Nicaraguan authorities. Thus for example when

Robert Borosage, Saul Landau, Richard Barnet, Peter Kornbluh and Cora Weiss . . . travelled to Nicaragua in 1983, 1984 and 1985 they were warmly embraced by the top Sandinista leadership—Tomas Borge, Daniel Ortega, and Sergio Ramirez . . . after returning to the United States Borosage and Landau reported that they had gone there to "make sure that the eight [Sandinista] ministries . . . had their projects in order" so that European support . . . would continue "to keep Nicaragua from being isolated politically and economically." When . . . Ortega came to New York in November 1985 and in July 1986 . . . he paid a personal visit to Rev. William Sloane Coffin and Cora and Peter Weiss at the Riverside Church. [Powell 1987:79]

As in other communist systems in the past the appeals of these leaders were greatly enhanced by their putative intellectual-artistic credentials and accomplishments. Stalin used to bask in the reputation of all-around genius deeply involved in literary criticism, economics, linguistics, and Marxist theory; both Mao and Ho Chi Minh wrote poetry; Castro too was perceived as all-around genius, voracious reader, and deep thinker ready to discourse on weighty topics with Sartre or C. Wright Mills; virtually all communist leaders from Kim Il Sung to Enver Hodza claimed to make creative contributions to Marxist-Leninist theory and published them in thick volumes with huge printings.

Several Nicaraguan leaders claimed or possessed literary credentials. Sergio Ramirez (vice president)

> had a reputation as one of Latin America's promising young writers . . . [and] . . . personif[ied] the hope that Nicaragua might one day evolve into a stable society representative of that often-sought political "missing link," socialism with a human face. But he is not the only politically powerful writer in Nicaragua today . . . there is Ernesto Cardenal, the famous poet-priest and current Minister of Culture; the poet Rosario Murillo, wife of President Ortega and head of the powerful Sandinista Association of Cultural Workers, and a Sandinista commander Omar Cabezas . . . [Goldman 1987:45–46]

Rosario Murillo also made a deep impression on a reporter for *Vanity Fair*, who described her as "the First Lady of the Republic of Nicaragua . . . Her charm is the charm of the revolution peopled by the young, the brave, and the good-looking . . . halfway between La Pasionaria and Bianca Jagger" [Grove 1986:58, 59]. On top of it she attended both a Franciscan convent school in England and a finishing school in Switzerland. Her visit to Hollywood in 1983 was celebrated "at an elegant private dinner party given at Trumps" [a restaurant]. Those invited included Warren Beatty, Gary Hart, Orion Pictures President Michael Medavoy, *Los Angeles Times* writers Charles Champlin and Robert Scheer, *LA Weekly* publisher Jay Levin, and Joan Keller Selznick who was host. Ms. Murillo was "intoxicating everyone with tales of revolution and pleas of help . . . [she] mesmerised Ed Asner and then Huey Newton . . . At a genteel old mansion . . . she held a group of several hundred spellbound for an hour as she described the beauty of the revolution." She also met Tom Hayden and Jane Fonda [Oney 1984:74].

Nora Astorga was another heroine of the Nicaraguan revolution much admired in the United States. The *Washington Post* in a portrait of her noted that "She walks down the stairs in Gloria Vanderbilt jeans and a green cashmere sweater . . . Her nails are lacquered pearl and her voice is husky from inhaling too many Marlboros and exhaling revolution." According to Susan Horowitz, "a political activist who champions liberal causes," Astorga was "an inspiration for the New Woman. 'She is the most exciting modern female revolutionary around'" [Harris 1984:B1, B8].

The male members of the ruling group too had their admirers. Daniel Ortega was said to be "known by the people as brilliant and dedicated . . . a truly organic leader," according to an American volunteer [Thatcher 1984:3]. Borge, it was reported by a member of a Witness for Peace

Group, "charmed his fellow Nicaraguans as well as the entire U.S. delegation. The only English he used was his conclusion when he said 'We
love you,' and we knew he meant it" [Johns 1987:62].

The youthfulness of the leaders was another attraction since Americans are inclined to associate youth with purity, idealism, and noble aspirations. As one visitor put it: ". . . the Sandinista leaders are young, intelligent, energetic and practical and they mingle with the people in a
responsive fashion" [Shepherd and Shepherd 1984:18]. The reporter of
an "alternative" newspaper characterized them as "Rock 'n' Roll Rebels
. . . The president is 39. The general is 26. The police chief is 19. They're
into basefull, beer and Bruce Springsteen" [Nielson 1985:1].

But time and again the appeals of Nicaragua were intertwined with and
inextricably embedded in the revulsion which the United States and its
policies inspired. Noam Chomsky wrote:

> If peasants starving to death in Honduras can look across the borders [to
> Nicaragua, that is] and see health clinics, land reform, literacy programs,
> improvements in subsistence agriculture . . . in a country no better
> endowed than their own, the rot may spread; and it may spread still far-
> ther, perhaps even to the United States, where the many people suffering
> from malnutrition or the homeless in the streets of the world's richest
> country may begin to ask some questions. It is necessary to destroy the
> rotten apple before the rot spreads through the barrel. [Quoted in Collier
> and Horowitz 1989:237; see also Chomsky 1987:38–39]

Thus Chomsky believed that the accomplishments of Nicaragua provided a countermodel to the dire conditions prevailing both among its
neighbors *and* the United States, which in turn explained the relentless
hostility of the government of the United States.

Those who praised the authorities in Nicaragua were also ready to
defend them against criticism and to overlook the "blemishes" of the new
social system. Penny Lernoux, a reporter and energetic supporter of the
Sandinistas, suggested that "Americans re-evaluate their ideas about
democracy and imperialism in Central America before criticizing revolutionary movements there" [Lindauer 1984:4]. Staughton Lynd, the
prominent 60s activist, was convinced that the suspension of civil liberties by the Nicaraguan government was a policy reluctantly undertaken
under the pressure of the war "masterminded and financed by the United
States." Moreover the Sandinista "leadership was merciful to National
Guardsmen captured during the insurrection. It abolished the death pen-
alty and has not reinstated it." Once the "external harassment" by the

U.S. government was removed he was confident that they would act as true democrats [Lynd 1985].

Noam Chomsky was also ready to justify the censorship with gusto: "Naturally if the U.S. were being attacked by a state of unimaginable power, we would not impose censorship on a journal that offered them support and that received a $100,00 grant from the aggressor; that is in fact correct, since the editors . . . would be in concentration camps; recall the fate of the Japanese during World War II" [Chomsky 1985:73]. But Chomsky did not tell his readers which journals in the United States were banned during World War II and which editors of such journals were imprisoned, nor did he say in what way the "unimaginable power" of the United States was brought to bear on the conflict in Nicaragua since the guerillas were given halting and limited support (which was finally terminated) and all along faced a huge and lavishly supplied military force equipped with every modern weapon usable in guerilla war (and some that are not).

Even a friendly observer of Nicaragua noted that "government censorship in Nicaragua routinely exceeds the requirement of national security" [Massing 1985:397]. But many supporters of the regime took the position that "even if they [the criticisms] were true, it would still be decent and intellectually defensible to insist that wartime is not the time to highlight them or to equate them with the abuses of the [U.S.] Administration" [the authors of this communication identified themselves as associates of the Covert Action Information Bulletin; see Ray et al. 1985:482].

External (or internal) threats have been a time-honored justification for restricting or altogether abolishing civil rights and political freedoms in virtually every police state in our times and especially those of a Marxist-Leninist inspiration. It should also be noted that these restrictions began in Nicaragua well before the guerilla war and they did not end when the guerillas were reduced to virtual impotence due to the U.S. ending their military support.

To sum up: the attractions of Nicaragua under the Sandinistas were no different from the appeals of other state socialist systems of the past. As its American supporters saw it, Nicaragua was attempting to establish an egalitarian society, implement social justice, uplift the poor, overcome backwardness, create a moral community, encourage genuine political participation, and restore the increasingly discredited doctrines of socialism. As such it was, in the eyes of these beholders, diametrically opposed to everything they rejected in their own society; its alleged victimization by the United States helped to prove and reaffirm their beliefs in the incorrigible flaws of American society and culture. Support for Nicaragua thus became an essential part of the critique of the United States.

IV

The highly favorable perceptions and assessments of the Nicaraguan political systems sampled above were projections and products of wishful thinking, outgrowth of fervent idealization reflecting more the inner needs of the observers than existing realities.

This assertion rests in part on precedent, on historical analogy: the favorable perceptions of Nicaragua were strikingly similar, often identical in substance to those of other communist systems, which were subsequently found to have no objective basis. The yawning gap between the idealized portraits and the realities of life in the Soviet Union under Stalin, in China under Mao, in Cuba under Castro, and in various East European countries under Soviet domination has been well established.

It would have been remarkable if things were different in Nicaragua in the light of these precedents, but the precedents by themselves are not conclusive evidence of the misperceptions and misjudgments. One cannot insist that just because the Soviet, Chinese, Cuban, Vietnamese, Polish, Hungarian, and so on experiments in building a better society inspired by Marxism-Leninism failed, such attempts must fail everywhere and have in fact failed in Nicaragua too.

One need not rely on the historical analogies and parallels alone to question the naïve visions of communist Nicaragua. There is a substantial body of evidence pertaining to the Nicaraguan case which thoroughly undermines the rosy-colored pictures. While the favorable depictions of the Nicaraguan system vastly outnumber the critical ones—just as the numbers of favorably disposed tourists dwarf those critically minded— the critical accounts and analyses of conditions in Nicaragua deserve serious attention. They are especially persuasive when they originate with former admirers of the system who had been predisposed to be sympathetic but changed their mind under the weight of evidence and experience. (It is difficult to think of any other motive: the vocal critics of the Sandinistas were not given endowed chairs at universities or rewarded in any discernible way by the Reagan administration, nor did they receive social acclaim; quite the opposite, they became targets of freely expressed hostility, as will be shown below.)

It may be asked why only a few of the sympathizers changed their mind (at least in public) under the weight of evidence. It is not hard to explain. In the first place it is both psychologically and socially inconvenient, indeed painful, to undertake a radical and wrenching revision of deeply held beliefs and values. More specifically the American supporters of Nicaragua nurtured by the values and attitudes of the 60s represent a massive and fairly cohesive subculture that has demanded conformity with its major beliefs. The break with these beliefs, especially in public, elicits ostracism or virtual excommunication from this political and cultural community. It is easy to be accused of selling out, being coopted, or becoming morally corrupted—all of which happened to the few visible critics of Nicaragua on the left who had earlier been sympathizers.

The case of Robert Leiken—one of these visible critics, formerly a left-of-center liberal in good standing—is particularly instructive. Following his unexpected exposé of conditions in Nicaragua (in the *New Republic* in 1984) he became subject of vicious attacks on the pages of *The Nation* and the *New York Review of Books,* among other places, and he "found himself something of a pariah" [Smolowe 1986; West 1986:16]. In his own words he became

> . . . a household oath in those homes which subscribed to publications like *The Nation, In These Times, The Village Voice* and *The Guardian* or who tuned into Pacifica radio . . . I was "a propagandist for the Reagan administration" . . . The former Central American correspondent of the *New York Times,* Ray Bonner . . . spread the word that I had obtained all my information from the U.S. Embassy [in Managua], had refused to meet with Sandinistas . . . Representative George Miller of California . . . accused me of employing "innuendo" . . . Witness for Peace said that my article was a bunch of "rumors, smears and cheap shots" and Noam Chomsky compared me unfavorably to Abu Nidal. [Collier and Horowitz, eds. 1989:127]

Criticism of the "new socialist experiment" was made especially difficult by the fact that it automatically linked the critic to despised symbols and figures at the other end of the political spectrum.

Defectors from the Sandinista side were just as readily dismissed as renegades, stooges of the CIA, or unstable converts—as was noted earlier in the case of Baldizon. (Eden Pastora was widely rumored to be unstable, indeed megalomaniac.)

Fortunately for the case being made here some of the evidence useful in a critical evaluation of the chorus of praise (lavished on the Sandinista government) comes from official Nicaraguan sources themselves. But in the final analysis no amount of evidence will convince the true believer, or not in the short run.

We may begin by examining the ceaselessly repeated assertion that the rulers of Nicaragua were true democrats, neither Marxist-Leninists nor pro-Soviet (or pro-Castro); if they came to depend on the Soviet Union (or Cuba) it was entirely the fault of the United States which by its relentless hostility pushed them into Soviet arms (this was also said of Castro).

Susan Kauffman Purcell, director of the Latin American Program at the Council on Foreign Relations, wrote:

Miss Christian's . . . account [that is, the book entitled *Revolution in the Family*] provides convincing evidence that the Sandinistas "intended to establish a Leninist system from the day they marched into Managua" . . . The idea that the Sandinistas were pushed toward radicalism ignores the early sequence of events . . . the foundations of the current system were laid while Jimmy Carter was still President, before Ronald Reagan was even nominated and well before President Reagan authorized CIA backing for the . . . contras. The Sandinistas almost immediately took control of and expanded military and security functions with the help of Cuban advisers. The Cubans also helped them create a network of mass organizations characteristic of Marxist dictatorships and to reshape Nicaragua's education system. Internationally, the Sandinistas aligned themselves with Cuba and the Soviet Union. [Purcell 1985]

By late 1989, Paul Berman, a friend of the Nicaraguan revolution, reached similar conclusions:

They [the Sandinista leaders] decided [in September 1979] to push aside the other anti-Somocista forces to take all power into their hands, and go ahead with their Sandinista "New Nicaragua" . . . during 17 years in the mountains and 10 years in power their understanding of Nicaragua has pretty much run along the same track, and the moral belief has always, with occasional tactical retreats and even some strategic ones, pointed in a single direction to all the crucial questions, toward the giant party-state of the communist imagination. [Berman 1989:34]

Foreign Minister Miguel D'Escoto's remarks (made in 1987 while in Moscow accepting the Lenin Prize) were consonant with such assessments:

I believe that the Soviet Union is a great torch which emits hope for the preservation of peace on our planet. Always in the vanguard of the . . . struggle for peace, the Soviet Union has become the personification of ethical and moral norms in international relations. I admire the revolutionary principles and consistency of the foreign policy of the Communist Party of the fraternal Soviet Union. [Quoted in *Nicaragua in Focus* 1987:29]

Of course D'Escoto might have said such things to convey gratitude for Soviet assistance, not because he really believed them, once his government was pushed into Soviet arms by the United States. But this could hardly be said of one of the great underground heroes and founders of the Sandinista movement, Carlos Fonseca, who already in 1958 sang the praise of the Soviet system in a book entitled *A Nicaraguan in Moscow,* based on his experiences in the Soviet Union (e.g., Berman 1986:22–23].

The closeness of these ties was also conveyed by the support the Nicaraguan government gave to the Soviet Union in the United Nations especially in the matter of Afghanistan. Sergio Ramirez explained: "Our sense of decency prevented us from joining those who voted for the United States against the Soviet Union" [condemning the Soviet invasion of Afghanistan, that is] ["The Meaning and Destiny" 1987].

The importance of Marxism-Leninism and the close ties to both Cuba and the Soviet Union were also conveyed in Humberto Ortega's (minister of defense, brother of Daniel Ortega) speech to a gathering of "army specialists" in 1981 [Leiken and Rubin eds. 1987:684–87, see also 674–76].

American supporters of the government of Nicaragua unhesitatingly affirmed its commitment to political democracy and pluralism.

By contrast Bayardo Arce, one of the nine commandantes, articulated the Sandinista view of elections and their utility as of 1985 as follows:

> Of course if we did not have the war situation imposed on us by the United States, the electoral problem would be totally out of place in terms of its usefulness . . .
>
> For us, the elections . . . are a nuisance . . .
>
> We believe that the elections should be used . . . to vote for Sandinismo . . . in order to be able to demonstrate that . . . the Nicaraguan people are for Marxism-Leninism . . .
>
> We have not declared ourselves Marxist-Leninist publicly and officially, we get along without definition . . .
>
> We see the elections as one more weapon of the revolution to bring its historical objectives gradually into reality. [Arce 1985:4–5, 6–7]

Arce also disclosed in the same speech that his party (the FSLN) encouraged the participation of small parties in the election "To show there was pluralism; that is one factor that has been useful until now—to be able to say there are 11 parties here" [Ibid.:5].

The reluctance to share power on the part of the rulers of Nicaragua is further suggested by their collective self-conception, as articulated by Borge:

> It was the Sandinista National Liberation Front [FSLN] . . . that knew how to apply the theory of revolution to the concrete reality of Nicaragua . . . The Sandinista Front is the living instrument of the revolutionary classes, it is the guide leading toward a new society . . . It has the wisdom

and courage ... It knew, and it will know, the role of the revolutionary
classes ... [in Radu ed. 1988:121]

To be sure in the end these views did not prevail as the commandantes decided to hold elections in February 1990 in the confident expectation that they would overwhelmingly win. They did not.

One of the least-known flaws of the Nicaraguan political system was the
privileges of the rulers, also a most telling illustration of the gap between
theory and practice found in all communist systems, overlooked by their
admirers in the past as it was by the political tourists in Nicaragua. Robert
Leiken was the first to draw attention to these privileges:

> Party members shop at hard currency stores, dine at luxury restaurants
> restricted to party officials and vacation in the mansions of the Somoza
> dynasty, labeled "protocol houses" [a terminology apparently borrowed
> from Cuba—P.H.]. Vans pull up daily at government and party offices to
> deliver ... delicacies unavailable elsewhere. In a private state dining room,
> I ate a sumptuous meal with a commandante at a long table attended by
> five servants ...
>   One of the most depressing aspects of our trip was to hear from so
> many that their lives are worse today than they were at the time of Somoza
> ... consumer goods available to the masses in other Central American
> countries are no longer obtainable ... [Leiken 1984:17, 16]

The shortages have also been also used to exert political leverage as
participants of the well-attended political rallies and meetings (which so
impressed the political tourists) were often recruited under duress: Leiken
reported that "ration cards are confiscated for nonattendance at Sandinista meetings" [Ibid.:19]. The committees involved in such activities and
"adored by revolutionary tourists as examples of participatory democracy
... were in fact a much-hated Cuban-style effort to establish total party
control," Paul Berman reported five years later [Berman 1989:34].
    The distribution of housing too was influenced by political criteria, as
it has been in all communist states:

> Many settlers [in Managua] feel they are being passed over in favor of
> Sandinista activists. In particular their complaints are directed toward a
> housing project in a barrio called Batahola Sur ... There 860 new houses
> have been built and occupied by families chosen through a system in
> which, say the residents of the model project, political loyalties were one
> of the principal criteria. "Ninety percent of the residents ... are people
> who are active in mass organizations," ... said ... a neighborhood offi-

cial . . ." All of us have been working with the mass groups . . . The revolution has been very generous to us." [Rohter 1985 February]

A *New York Times* reporter also commented on the inequalities:

> . . . the most striking is the emergence of what one diplomat here calls "the Sandinista nomenklatura"—a new revolutionary bureaucratic elite of commandantes and other high officials insulated from the hardships and privations endured by the rest of the population.
> They live in homes expropriated from the old bourgeoisie in comfortable suburbs . . . They can shop at a special "dollar store" reserved for diplomats and enjoy privileges ranging from reserved box seats at the baseball stadium to unlimited supplies of rationed gasoline and water. [Rother 1985 March]

Humberto Belli, a former Sandinista, pointed out that the new leaders

> started to ride in Mercedes Benzes . . . They . . . took over the best neighborhoods . . . They have private swimming pools, tennis courts and bars . . . They are constantly asking people to make sacrifices but not sharing them. There are special sectors in the military hospital where Sandinistas members can go for special treatment, while the average Nicaraguan will wait in line for hours. [Belli 1982:7]

The system of such special privileges was also observed by a German visitor:

> Only reliable Party members climb to . . . the upper reaches of the salary scale, where earnings are three times the average income or six times as much as a farm labourer. Such privileged officials also receive an income supplement of U.S. $300 per month and a special card entitling them to buy goods at the dollar shop . . . Everything which is denied to the Nicaraguan people can be obtained here . . . [Kriele 1985:46]

The social background of the new leaders probably had some bearing on these developments. Michael Radu, a Latin American specialist, wrote:

> Nowhere is the elitist background and self-limited origin of the revolutionary leadership in Latin America clearer than in the corridors of power in Managua . . . middle-class professional revolutionaries . . . share power with the rebellious scions of the aristocratic families . . . marry their daughters and adopt their claims to intellectual accomplishments as well as their taste for Gucci eyeglasses. [Radu 1988:9—10]

The 1990 electoral defeat of the government was also in part a result of popular awareness of such privileges: "'All the top people got themselves a house, a car, shopping privileges in the dollar store, and free electricity and water,' a Sandinista army officer said. 'The people knew that and they resented it because they were suffering and had nothing'" [Rother 1990]. A former Sandinista mayor of Managua who broke with the FSLN in 1988 noted of the commandantes that they "'have lived a life of luxury, and they continue to live it'" ["Nicaraguans Want Property Back" 1990].

None of this was unusual by the standards of other Marxist-Leninist systems but it all eluded the visitors who were fully persuaded that an idealistic, self-sacrificing group of men and women were running Nicaragua in the best interests of the masses. Few visitors saw "D'Escoto's stately home . . . and its adjacent parkland surrounded by a high wall . . ." in the former millionaires' district [Kriele 1985:110], and those who did presumably were not disturbed by the luxuries enjoyed by a deserving leader of the revolution. The only widely publicized incident shedding light on the life-style of the new leaders was the Ortega couple's purchase of designer glasses in New York to the tune of $3500 [Dowd 1985]. But revealing the mentality of their American friends, there were "hisses from the audience" when somebody asked Ortega "about the propriety" of this purchase [Rohter 1985 October].

The same blindness to the inequalities and sufferings of ordinary people prevented American sympathizers from facing the fact, and its deeper implications, that much of the contra army, and certainly the vast majority of ordinary fighters, was made up of peasants who should have, in theory, been beneficiaries and supporters of the Sandinistas [see also Llosa 1985:41].

While the discrepancy between illusions and reality in the matter of inequalities and elite privilege was rarely commented upon, the human and civil rights record of the Sandinistas was more controversial. Not surprisingly their supporters were always ready to justify infringements by the emergency created by the guerilla war. More generally the besieged nature of the country and American hostility threatening the survival of its government were invoked to justify restrictions of political freedoms and human rights abuses (if they were acknowledged at all). Rarely was the full magnitude of human rights violations confronted by the apologists because this would have made it far more difficult to justify the policies of the government.

The view taken of human rights violations in Nicaragua (as elsewhere) depends largely on the predisposition of those contemplating such matters and especially on their choice of what sources of information are deemed credible. Sympathizers did not doubt the veracity of the information provided by the Nicaraguan government and the organizations associated with or influenced by it such as the human rights group Nicaraguan National Commission for the Promotion and Protection of Human Rights. But the realities were different, as was described by a representative of an American human rights organization, the Puebla Institute:

> Under the guise of adjudicating national security cases, the popular tribunals have become a principal Sandinista instrument for repressing the peaceful democratic opposition . . . many defendants have been involved solely in nonviolent political activity. They are arrested on vaguely worded charges . . . And they are judged by party hacks . . . Independent labor unionists, opposition party activists, journalists . . . have been proclaimed "counter-revolutionaries" and given stiff jail terms . . . Mauricio Membreno, an 18 year old president of the Social Democratic Youth, is serving an 11 year sentence on trumped up charges. Luis Mora, the former head of La Prensa's journalists' union, was . . . convicted of "disseminating information prejudicial for national security" after he criticized the Sandinistas on Costa Rican radio . . . The common experience of political defendants is arrest without warrant and incommunicado detention . . . The trial is normally closed to the public . . . Appeals cannot be taken to the Nicaraguan Supreme Court but are heard solely by the revolutionary panels. Sentences have been known to increase by 10 years on appeal . . . several lawyers have been imprisoned for too vigorously defending political clients. [Shea 1986]

Not only have the sentencing procedures been arbitrary, conditions within prisons have been correspondingly inhumane. A former prisoner who suffered back injuries when his plane crashed (he flew supply planes to the contras) and was released under the cease-fire agreement in March 1988 told a *New York Times* reporter:

> "Medical attention in Nicaraguan jails is virtually non-existent except for those who are part of the Sandinista 'rehabilitation program' . . ." To make him talk . . . the Sandinistas kept him in isolation in a small cell . . . For more than a year . . . he was not allowed outside the Chipote jail building . . . Before his release . . . he was warned not to talk about the situation in Nicaraguan jails by prison officials who told him "the arms of the revolution are very long." [Volsky 1988]

The mistreatment of the Indian minorities and the Miskitos in particular was among the major forms of political violence to which the authorities resorted. These actions led to the criticism of former sympathizers such as Werner Herzog, the German film-maker, who, after making a documentary movie about the Indians, reported their situation "appalling": "For quite some time I was intrigued by the Sandinista struggle ... From Europe it looked particularly interesting ... the Sandinistas tried to bring 'scientific socialism' to the Miskitos ... The story instead is one of deportation and concentration camps ..." [Vinocur 1984]. (He was duly denounced by the large contingents of pro-Sandinista intellectuals and journalists in his native country [Kriele 1985:74–76].)

Senator Edward Kennedy wrote that

> ... the Sandinistas' treatment of the Indians continues to be unconscionable. One-third to one-half of the 90,000 Indians on the coast have been displaced. Some 20,000 fled to Honduras to escape the Sandinistas' scorched-earth polIcty ... and 10,000 are confined in resettlement camps ... Most disturbing of all, 3000 to 5000 have lived for two years in intolerable conditions in forced-labor camps—which resemble concentration camps ... [Kennedy 1984]

A 209-page report on human rights in Nicaragua prepared by the International League for Human Rights left no doubt about the wide scope of such violations extending over the treatment of the accused, conditions of imprisonment, judical proceedings, restrictions on free expression, and the overall repressiveness of political life under the Sandinistas [*Report on Human Rights* 1986].

With a thoroughness characteristic of communist police states the authorities' mistreatment extended to the relatives of prisoners who tried to organize a prisoners' rights group. Minister Borge explained that such people suffered from false consciousness: "At a news conference today ... Borge said the new movement 'does not represent the will of family members.' He said most relatives of prisoners considered the Sandinista Government to be a protector, not an adversary" [Kinzer 1987 April].

Again, as in other communist police states before, definitions of what constitutes a "state secret" (as those of political crimes) were greatly expanded. In 1988 "Two Nicaraguan economists have been sentenced to 16 year jail terms for possession of state secrets. The secrets are economic projections, estimates of grain production, export figures and other data that are public information in most countries" [Kinzer 1988 October].

While not formally banning opposition groups (in order to create a more favorable image for the Western public) the Sandinista government had devised ways to harass and intimidate them and circumscribe their activities. Robert Leiken pointed out that "Opposition groups had been forbidden to hold outdoor rallies since early 1981; political and trade union activists were frequently detained and imprisoned, and opposition offices were attacked by Sandinista mobs called *turbas* ..." [Leiken 1985:57].

In 1988 Michael Massing, although far more friendly toward the Sandinistas than Leiken, noted

> ... the *turbas* were again called into action ... with the lifting of the state of emergency and the resumption of opposition meetings, the *turbas* had reemerged, setting upon demonstrators with threats, sticks and stones. For instance, days after the emergency ended, the Democratic Coordinating Group—a conservative coalition of 6 opposition parties, 2 trade unions and a business association—tested the climate by holding an indoor meeting in Managua; the gathering was broken up by a gang of rock-throwing Sandinista militants. [Massing 1988:51]

Meetings of the Mothers of Political Prisoners were also broken up by similar mobs in 1988, as were other attempts by opposition groups to meet or march in public [Berman 1989:37].

American admirers of the government claimed to be either unaware of such events or uncertain as to who initiated the violence, or would plead that while they did not condone violence they could "understand" how in an atmosphere of American threats and civil war (which may yet erupt again, even after the cease-fire) such excesses *might* occur; if they did occur, they were surely not sanctioned by the government, but in any event they were no worse than American intervention in Vietnam, Grenada, or Panama, and in any case who are we to lecture the Nicaraguans on how to run their government given the number of homeless people in American cities?

But as Berman saw it, "... a good many repressive actions that are chalked up to the war are actually due to economic catastrophe and the government's inability to win the support of large parts of the working class" [Berman 1986:53].

The type of political control and coerciveness the Sandinistas developed were not visible to the naked eye and certainly not to those who happily followed their tour leaders on carefully planned visits and meetings. But some visitors made an effort to learn more about the way people lived. Paul Berman was one of this handful. His account of the treatment of shoemakers in a provincial town illuminates both the forms of political control used and sources of the economic malfunctioning of the system:

> The Sandinistas called rallies every February in the rough baseball field at Masaya ... and the shoemakers had to go. A Sandinista official accompanied them to the field with a pad and pencil, marking down who was there and whether they stayed to the end. Anyone who didn't attend was threatened with loss of one month's access to leather and raw materials from the Sandinista monopoly ...

> The Sandinistas ordered the shoemakers to chant Sandinista slogans
> . . . [they] stood in the sun and chanted. The Sandinistas instructed them
> to donate "voluntary" labor . . .
>
> . . . what happened to the shoemakers was happening to all of the arti-
> san trades in Masaya . . . These artisan workers had been ruined econom-
> ically, deceived politically, stripped of their autonomy, deprived of their
> rights as workers, reduced to forced labor, and turned into puppets who
> had no choice but shout slogans . . . [Berman 1989:36]

Another of the less visible adjuncts of the police state were the Sandinista Defense Committees (CDS) modeled after those in Cuba. In the
eyes of the visitors they were benign neighborhood groups helping wid-
ows and planting flowers in parks; in reality they were assisting the
authorities in the surveillance of the population. A German traveler compared them to similar groups in Nazi Germany:

> . . . the power of the CDS extends far beyond that once held by block
> overseers in Nazi Germany. The CDS issue letters of recommendation for
> local residents, documents which have to accompany any application to a
> government authority . . . for obtaining a driving license, a trading license,
> a permit to employ staff, a work permit, obtaining a loan, matriculation in
> higher education establishments, obtaining a student grant, a certificate of
> good conduct from the police . . . Unofficially it is also a prerequisite for
> obtaining food cards [ration cards] and medical care. [Kriele 1985:42]

Such observations were corroborated, among others, by Paul Berman,
who was informed by "a small businessman in Managua [that he] . . .
could no longer buy soap after he declined to spy on his next-door neighbor for the Sandinista neighborhood committee" [Berman 1986:53].

Perhaps all this could have been redeemed by the social policies of
the government. According to the apologists, unheard-of advances were
made in extending literacy, in health care, and in education. Here again
the assessments will depend on which source of information is deemed
more credible. Gains in lowering infant mortality rates were said to be
among the achievements. But according to Norman Luxemburg, of the
University of Iowa, the gains regarded as spectacular were based on comparisons with greatly inflated pre-revolutionary rates and especially the
rates in 1979—a highly atypical year of the culmination of the civil war.
In any case similar gains in the lowering of infant mortality were also
made in other countries without provoking the exultation that was elicited by those in Nicaragua [Luxemburg 1984].

The shortages were more readily admitted but shrugged off as a result
of the war, U.S. trade restrictions, the legacy of the Somoza era—everything but the policies of the rulers was held responsible for them. What

made the presence of shortages and material deprivations still easier to accept as morally defensible was the mistaken belief that they were equally shared.

It was generally forgotten (or never learned) that even if the shortages were caused by the war there was also enormous economic and military assistance pouring into the country not only from the Soviet bloc but also from Western Europe, and in the beginning even from the United States under Carter. But as in other communist systems, the major cause of economic difficulties was a doctrinaire misconception of reality (i.e., that nationalizing property and means of production is the right and necessary thing to do), the resulting bureaucracy, decline of incentive, and the associated repression to keep the system going.

Most difficult for the sympathizers to believe was that this became a political system with little legitimacy and support among its own people and that the spirit of community they projected upon Nicaragua was largely a fantasy. As an aging onion farmer put it: "They [the Sandinistas] live by distrust. They never taught us to be sincere with each other, or to live side by side accepting one another" [Preston 1990:25].

Such a possibility was not to be entertained, as it would have made mockery of the political tourists' key beliefs. Their admiration for the political system—as that of earlier generations of tourists of other communist countries—was based on the premise that these governments were doing wonders for their own people and the people were deeply appreciative. Few of these visitors would realize, for example, that they themselves were held in contempt by the native Nicaraguans just as similarly benighted visitors were scorned and despised by citizens of other communist countries. A German visitor to Nicaragua (already quoted) recalled:

> From the very first evening I tried to make contact with ordinary people and hear their views. At first, people were mistrustful, reticent. But I was not long in discovering a method of gaining their confidence ... They always asked whether I came from East or West Germany. When answering all I had to do was to add that I was not one of the "internacionalistas," if possible throwing in a sarcastic remark. This provoked relieved laughter and was almost always followed by the whispered comment: our situation is very, very grave ... they would begin to talk.
>
> "Internacionalistas" is used as a term of abuse. ... [it] has connotations of social leprosy. Hatred of internacionalistas is so strong that the "Nicas" have thought up a particularly disgusting name for them: "pacusos" ... [Kriele 1985:17–18]

There is more than anecdotal evidence indicating that by the late 1980s the popular support for the authorities has drastically decreased (if it was ever high) and that they, and not the United States or the guerillas, were held responsible for the scarcities, poverty, and political repression. Paul Berman reported after a visit in 1989:

> The poor and the working class have mostly turned away from the Sandinistas. In one of the university polls, people who were illiterate, which is to say, the very poor, supported the Front at a rate of 16.9% . . . an illiterate impoverished woman is . . . the least likely to approve of the Sandinistas . . . Support for the Sandinistas among all social classes . . . dwindled to as low as 20% in a recent Prensa poll, or 25% in a university poll . . . The highest figure I have seen is a *Cronica* poll . . . which gave the Sandinistas 38% support nationwide. [Berman 1989:40–41]

The 1990 elections vindicated these estimates.

V

The reactions of the American supporters of the Sandinistas following their electoral defeat displayed the continuity of belief. The electoral expression of massive popular discontent was treated as a phenomenon in no way relevant to the character of the political system rejected by the voters and even less relevant to the commitment of the American sympathizers. The defeat of the rulers they admired was met with a series of rationalizations designed to salvage these deeply held beliefs.

It should be recalled that not only the supporters but the media in general (including television pundits) unhesitatingly predicted a Sandinista victory and by a large margin. One supporter wrote in a letter to the *New Republic:*

> As a Quaker and a journalist . . . I am appalled with what must be your ignorance, irresponsibility or plain outright propaganda regarding the upcoming elections in Nicaragua . . .
> Your thinking that anybody but Daniel Ortega will win . . . is like believing that Americans would have voted for a British candidate for the American presidency after George Washington . . . had won the American Revolution.
> Everywhere in Nicaragua . . . if you care to visit, you will see signs, "They shall not pass!," "There will be no surrender!" . . . You should be ashamed of yourselves. [Copeland 1990:21]

An article in *The Nation* written shortly before the election noted that "the Sandinistas have no credible opposition," their "campaign seeds are falling on fertile ground," and that "As the campaign moved . . . into 1990 it became increasingly obvious that they couldn't lose." The only question left to ponder was "How the Bush Administration will greet a Sandinista victory . . ." [Bensky 1990:302–5]. Another *Nation* correspondent wrote: "Daniel Ortega will be re-elected President of Nicaragua and his ruling Sandinista National Liberation Front is likely to win a majority of seats in the new National Assembly . . . That's not left-wing wishful thinking . . . The political opposition to the Sandinistas is morally and ideologically corrupt . . . [it] does not offer credible alternative to the FSLN . . ." [Jenkins 1990:269].

More specifically the rulers were supposed to win because—so the theory went—the opposition was viewed as American puppets and hence widely despised; anti-Americanism reached a new intensity due to American intervention in Panama; the Sandinistas developed superb campaign skills to win over the masses; and the masses were, despite their grumbling, deeply loyal to the government and grateful for the improvements in their standard of living and sense of national dignity.

The government was certainly successful assembling huge mass rallies which many observers took to be authentic expressions of popular support—as if communist systems had not in the past been equally skilled in organizing such spectacles. Most opinion polls showed support for the FSLN, but again few among those commenting on these polls gave any thought to the possibility that those polled might not have been anxious to reveal their real political preferences. American observers were also impressed by the multitude of Nicaraguans wearing FSLN T-shirts and other paraphernalia, but again it did not occur to them that, as a native put it, "Anybody can wear one of those . . . But we keep our feelings hidden" [Preston 1990:26].

The most popular response to the loss of the election in the adversary culture was that it "should not be mistaken as a vote against the Sandinistas or the goals of the revolution" [Sanders 1990:91]; this was pointed out by a member of the Western Massachusetts observer team of the elections who evidently divined the deeper motives of the voters concealed by their actual behavior. The faithful also argued that the Sandinistas lost because the United States succeeded in intimidating the masses by its support of the guerillas and the economic blockade which created unbearable conditions, hence people were willing to vote for any party whose victory held a promise of an end to the economic blockade and the guerilla war. As a bitter *Nation* editorial put it:

> The defeat of Daniel Ortega by Violeta . . . Chamorro shows that the imperial monarchs of Washington still have more weapons at their disposal . . . than we . . . had suspected . . .

... a few Nicaraguans will again enjoy the freedom of the shopping mall ...
... Nicaraguan voters have done what they have been bludgeoned, starved and blockaded into doing. ["Spoils of War" 1990:367–68]

Thus the United States at last succeeded in diverting people from higher principles for mere material advantage ("They voted with their pocketbooks ... but their hearts are still with the revolution" [Sanders 1990].

For the most committed supporters, those belonging to the "solidarity groups" (or "internacionalistas"), there remained the conviction that "despite the results of the ... vote, the Sandinistas and not Mrs. Chamorro represent the Nicaraguan people" [Rohter 1990 March 13]. Such a conclusion was presumably based on two beliefs: that people did not vote their true convictions, but compromised or acquiesced; and, that the Sandinistas represent the people in some deeper, more essential way that transcends prosaic and crude measurements of public opinion provided by elections.

Only one possibility had stubbornly eluded the supporters of the Sandinistas: that they were voted out of office on the first occasion when this was possible because the majority were repelled by their performance and policies. As a Nicaraguan voter said in a former stronghold of the Sandinistas: "It was all lies, what they promised us" [Rohter 1990 March 5]

6

The Worldview of College Students

In examining the rejections or harsh critiques of American society two questions are of special interest and importance: first, are these attitudes relatively isolated, confined to the elite groups, and second, to what extent are they a generational phenomenon?

The previous chapters sought to identify and examine the critiques of American society found among elite groups such as academic intellectuals, church people, and journalists. Assuming that elite groups critical of American society exert influence on popular attitudes one would expect to find echoes of their beliefs in other strata of society. College students would be the most obviously affected since they are exposed directly and for extended periods of time to the views of those highly critical of American society—many of their teachers and the authors of books they read in their social science and humanities courses.

It also used to be an article of faith that the young are by nature more idealistic and more capable of discerning the gaps between social ideals and realities, hence more disposed to be critical of existing institutional arrangements. But if the social protest and activism of the 1960s was in large measure a generational phenomenon, undergraduate students in the mid-1980s are a different generation from those of their peers in the 60s and early 70s and the society around them has also changed in some ways. It is in fact very plausible that as of the late 1980s those most critical of American society are people in their forties and early fifties who had belonged to the activist generation of the 60s rather than those born in the 60s.

While this author is satisfied that there is ample evidence of intensely critical attitudes among the elites discussed (as was shown in previous chapters), the questions remain: How far do these attitudes extend? How wide an influence do they exert on the general population? and Are they age related? Members of the elite groups discussed earlier are, by definition, not especially young as it takes time to attain elite status (except possibly in entertainment and sports). The well-known social critics cited or referred to earlier are overwhelmingly middle-aged. While in the 60s and early 70s there were social critics and activists who achieved prominence at an early age, thanks in large measure to the media, in the 1980s such rise to prominence of young social critics has not occurred.

Examining the political attitudes of present-day college students is of further interest since they provide the reservoir from which the successors of the current elites will be drawn. Looking at their beliefs in the 1980s will help to answer the questions to what degree has the adversary culture been a generational phenomenon (rooted in the collective experiences of the 1960s) and how strong have been the influences of the campus setting examined earlier.

There has been a fair amount of public discussion of the political attitudes of college students in the 1970s and 80s, much of it lamenting the decline of idealistic activism among them and suggesting that the more recent generation of college students are far more apolitical and materialistic than was the heroic generation of the 60s. In the words of a syndicated journalist reflecting on the 20th anniversary of the killing of four students at Kent State: "From being involved in causes, young Americans placed increasingly greater premium on materialism and making money" [Johnson 1990]. A self-identified socialist, at the time of his writing professor in the graduate school of journalism at the University of California at Berkeley, observed:

> ... the sense of outrage at the injustices and excesses of the system that is essential to a radical perspective cannot be taught. It would be nice if now and then a student showed a disposition to follow my lead in covering capitalism critically. But in three years of part-time and five years of full-time teaching at three universities, the only identifiable radical student of the several hundred I have taught was an Ethiopian. My American students seem less eager to alter the system than to find a secure niche within it. [MacDougall 1989:41]

We cannot be sure to what degree the expectations of Mr. Mac-Dougall led to his conclusions; quite possibly a conservative observer of the same students might have reached different conclusions and found more radicalism among them given his different views of what constitutes radicalism or a critical attitude toward capitalism.

The views about the more recent student generation cited above have certainly been widespread and paralleled the broader conventional wisdom (commented upon in the first chapter), according to which there has been a far-reaching swing of the pendulum from the public-spirited, political sixties to the self-centered 70s and 80s, from a left-liberal ethos to a right-wing Republican one symbolized by the presidencies of Ronald Reagan.

While I have been generally skeptical of this point of view I was less certain in what measure it would apply to college students, in particular the undergraduates born in the 1960s. I wanted to find out if indeed they were apolitical, or possibly even conservative rather than adversarial. In seeking information about their attitudes I was not guided by any particular hypothesis and my own experience as a teacher of undergraduates at a large state university has failed to provide me with intuitive insights. I was mainly interested in the extent to which undergraduate students shared or rejected the stereotyped critiques of American society and its various institutions which have been with us since the 60s and have become part of the conventional wisdom discussed earlier. I was also interested in what way might contemporary college students be considered "alienated," how they themselves perceive their own political attitudes, and how a negative view of American society may be associated with a more positive attitude toward political systems which used to claim socialist credentials and insist on being free of the inequities critics find in such abundance in the United States. (The investigation of these and related matters was carried out in 1984–86, well before the dramatic changes began to unfold in Eastern Europe and the Soviet Union.) I was also interested in the usual variables social scientists examine when they seek to explain political attitudes, such as social class, ethnicity, religion, education, and so on, and some less usual ones such as the connection between an optimistic or pessimistic expectations (of future) and the critical, disillusioned disposition toward society.

Since this author did not have the resources to undertake a full-scale representative survey of the student population of the United States and since existing studies do not necessarily address precisely the same issues and attitudes I was interested in, I decided to undertake a more limited survery of college students which, while not representative of the entire student population of the United States, would nonetheless offer some useful information that could be compared with the findings of some national surveys and other studies of attitudes among the young.

In my limited sample the academic institutions were chosen on the basis of personal contact. I asked college teachers I knew around the country to distribute questionnaires in their classes. While purists may argue that this choice of schools hopelessly biased the sample, brief reflection on the matter suggests that this need not be the case. First of all the people I knew represented varied political attitudes and beliefs, in many instances quite different from my own. Second, even if they had uniformly and rigidly shared my political beliefs it is far from self-evident how this would have translated into influencing the responses of their students unless we assume that these students knew ahead of time the political philosophy of their teachers and selected their classes accordingly; or else they became converted to their instructors' worldview in their classes if they entered them innocent of any expectation.

In fact most undergraduate students select their classes for reasons other than the perceived political beliefs of their instructors, which in most cases are not generally known, nor are they matters of interest for most students. Far more typically, the reasons for choosing a particular course include the convenience of timing, the title of the course, its requirements, whether or not the course itself is required to satisfy a distribution requirement or that of a major, the reputation of the personality and style of teaching of the instructor (rather than his politics), and that of his manner of grading. Nor is it clearly established that the political beliefs of teachers, even when freely communicated in their courses, leave a decisive imprint on their students although this certainly is a possibility.

The unrepresentativeness of the sample described below is in any event mitigated by the diversity in the character of the schools where the questionnaires were distributed. They included both private and public, small and large, elite and non-elite, denominational and nondenominational institutions in different parts of the country. They were located in the East, Midwest, and West. The South was poorly represented (only by one school in Florida) and the numbers of questionnaires from the West was also small. None came from the Northwest and only one school from the Mountain States was included.

Students from the following colleges participated in the survey; Amherst College, Boston University, Boston College, University of California at La Jolla, University of California at Los Angeles, State University of California at Hayward, Colorado College, Harvard Law School (first-year students), James Madison University (Harrisonburg, Va.), John Jay College in New York City, University of Maryland at College Park, University of Massachusetts at Amherst, Miami-Dade Community College (Miami, Fla.), Pittsburgh University, Roosevelt University (Chicago), Smith College (Northampton, Mass.), St. Meinrad College (Indiana), and Washington University (St. Louis). The number of respondents from each institution averaged between 40 and 50 students depending on the size of the class where the questionnaire was distributed, and in some instances, whether or not it was completed in class or taken home and returned later.

The total number of responses was 875 out of 1,296 questionnaires sent out. All questionnaires were anonymous. Some 46% of the respondents were male, 49% female (the missing percentage did not respond to the question); 47% of the students were Catholic, 28% Protestant, and 12% Jewish.

The questionnaires were distributed to students taking courses in the humanities and social sciences, many of them introductory and required, thereby assuring a broader distribution of students in different majors.

The principal categories of academic majors were as follows: (percentages always rounded up or down, except for 0.5)

> Social sciences 29%
> Humanities 20%
> Business School 14%
> Physical sciences (incl. computer sciences) 10%
> Engineering 6%
> Visual and performing arts 3%
> Law 5%

A sample of all entering freshmen at the University of Massachusetts in Fall 1988 found the following probable majors: social science 16%, humanities 15%, business school 20%, engineering 12% [Barrow and Lam 1988:2]. These findings, among others, suggest the likelihood that my sample had a higher proportion of social science and humanities majors than is likely to be the case nationally. Thus my sample over-represents social science and humanities majors, who tend to be more liberal, or left-of-center. Consequently there is a probability that my sample is generally more liberal than a corresponding national sample would be. This is all the more likely since I have only a small contingent from the South where traditionally attitudes are more conservative.

Perhaps the best way to sum up the political attitudes of the students in my survey is to report their political self-identification based on the options provided:

> Radical 1%
> Radical-liberal 9%
> Liberal-moderate 35%
> Liberal-conservative 35%
> Conservative-neoconservative 13%

I felt it necessary to divide mainstream liberal into the two categories (moderate and conservative) in view of the difference between the conventional meaning and more recent reinterpretations of the concept discussed earlier, which increasingly means different things to different people. "Radical liberal" was introduced to provide an option for radicals to identify their political outlook without placing themselves at the extremity of the political spectrum (an unattractive option for most people) in the context of these labels. Unhappily other student surveys (see below) make no similar distinctions and further complicate matters by using the "middle-of-the-road" designation which is open to various interpretations and seems to lack any clear political or ideological content.

It seems safe to assume that the first two categories in my survey—radical and radical-liberal—could be considered "left," "left-of-center," or even "radical-left," especially in the light of the other options provided, whereas the two other liberal categories (liberal-moderate and liberal-conservative) could both be regarded as moderate or middle-of-the-road. At the other end of the spectrum the conservative-neoconservative group could also be regarded as the "right," perhaps extreme right, again in the context of other options available in the questionnaire.

The self-identified hard-core leftists ("radical," "radical-liberal") comprising approximately 10% of the sample showed up with great regularity in the answers to specific questions, consistently taking the most leftist position on various issues, as will be shown below.

The moderate (in the context of the options provided) majority, 70%, was comprised in equal measure of self-identified moderate liberals and moderate conservatives who might show up in other surveys under "middle-of-the-road"—except for the problem of how to interpret "liberal" when a "middle-of-the-road" option is also available.

The representativeness of the attitudes found in my survey may be assessed in some measure by comparing them (when possible) with those of other surveys of student attitudes.

A national survey of undergraduates by the Carnegie Foundation found in 1984 the following distribution of political attitudes: Left 2%, Liberal 23%, Middle-of-the road 39%, Moderately conservative 31%, Strongly conservative 5% [Boyer 1987:189]. Another survey [Students' Views 1986:28] found the following distribution: Left 2%, Liberal 21%, Middle-of-the-road 38%, Moderate conservative 32%, Strongly conservative 6%. It may be noted that in this survey the percentage of "moderate conservative" (32%) came very close to my "liberal conservative" category (35%), although the "strongly conservative" group was less than half of my "conservative-neoconservative" category.

A comparable political attitude survey of a representative sample of all undergraduates at the University of Massachusetts (Amherst campus) in 1986 yielded these results: Far left 4.8%, Liberal 39.8%, Middle of the road 37.5%, Conservative 16.7%, Far right 1.2% ["Political Attitude Survey" 1986:6].

One may theorize that in the latter survey some of those opting for "liberal" would have identified themselves—in terms of my categories—as "radical-liberal," and in turn the "middle-of-the-road" group undoubtedly included an even larger portion of those who in my survey chose the liberal-conservative designation. Also of some interest is that the "far left" contingent exceeded by more than threefold the "far right."

A national survey of 23 public universities defined as "highly selective" was compared with the U. Mass. sample:

	U. Mass.	National
Liberal or far left	33.5%	30.4%
Middle-of-the-road	52.2%	46.8%
Conservative or far right	14.3%	22.8%
[Barrow 1989:28]		

In light of the national sample the student population at U. Mass. is clearly more to the left, and U. Mass. has far fewer self-declared conservatives than is the case nationwide. In both surveys "liberal or far left" identifications significantly exceed the conservative ones. To be sure these findings are marred by combining "liberal" and "far left," traditionally perceived as not merely different but antithetical, and the same goes for "conservative" and "far right." Putting these attributes together may be viewed as a form of political illiteracy. It also illustrates the process of redefinition of the political spectrum (to which reference has already been made in this study) which obliterates distinctions which used to be considered important at earlier times. Presumably when "liberal" and "far left" are merged in the same category, the liberalism involved is what Shils called "collectivist," which "parted from the great tradition of individualistic constitutional and conservative liberalism ... The critical function of public liberties is seen by collectivist liberals to be, not the limitation in the powers of the government, but rather its extension, so as to enable it to 'solve' all social problems, to realize and fulfill its obligation to cure every deficiency of human life" [Shils 1989:13].

In all these surveys the major difficulty is presented by interpreting the "middle of the road" category and also that of the relationship between "liberal" and "left." It appears that for many respondents (as well as for those who devised these ratings) "liberal" has come to mean "moderate left," "left-of-center," or what Shils called "collectivist liberalism." But there was a time when "liberal" was understood to be a middle-of-the-road position between the extremes of right and left. Of late "liberal" has increasingly carried, in the United States, a burden of association with "left" (as was also discussed in Chapter 1), which may explain the terminology of these surveys. When "liberal" is set apart from a centrist (or "middle-of-the-road") position—as was the case in the surveys noted above—it is not unreasonable to suspect that it is seen by many respondents as a milder form of leftism, whereas "left" would be construed in the context of the options available as a more extreme, radical position. Hence one may also assume that most of those identifying themselves as "liberal" meant "left" or left-of-center.

The two distributions (in the national and in my survey) resemble one another as far as the proportion of moderate attitudes are concerned: the self-described "middle-of-the-road" group is likely to display liberal attitudes on many specific issues as might the "moderate conservative." My radical-liberal category might have included many of those who in the national sample defined themselves as liberal or left, in the absence of a choice between the two types of liberalism I offered.

In the survey I devised I also sought to probe what may be called the psychological underpinnings of political attitudes, in the question asking students about their self-assessed level of alienation. Although it was left to the respondents to define for themselves what "alienation" meant, it is most likely that they interpreted alienation (which was contrasted with "adjustment" among other options) as the term is generally used, that is, of not being a part of society, of being marginal, withdrawn, unintegrated, disillusioned, and dissatisfied.

These were the responses: Quite alienated 2%, Somewhat alienated 14.5%, Reasonably well-adjusted 42.5%, Well-adjusted 41%. The students were also asked how they perceived alienation in others of their generation: Quite alienated 2%, Somewhat alienated 9%, Reasonably well-adjusted 56%, Well-adjusted 31%.

As will be seen below the proportion of quite or somewhat alienated was between 10% and 15% in both groups, which was also the recurring proportion of those who displayed the most radically critical attitude toward American society and whom I came to refer to as "the radical minority."

Another basic test of alienation or negativity toward one's society is the willingness to "vote with one's feet" and leave the country, as happened so often in this century in different parts of the world when the opportunity presented itself. Since all students in my sample lived in this country and since there has been no politically or otherwise motivated migration since the Vietnam war (such as the fear of draft), all I could do was to ask if they could *conceive of* leaving the United States and under what conditions.

The statement to which these responses were sought was one of several in a group of statements of hypothetical conditions prefaced by the question, "Which of the following possibilities can you imagine coming true?" These questions were designed to probe degrees of general optimism or pessimism in ways which linked personal fortunes to matters social-political. The question addressed to the willingness to leave this country was phrased as follows: "I will find life in the U.S. so disagreeable (for political, economic or other reasons) that I will emigrate to some other country." Precoded responses ranged from "could very easily happen," "could possibly happen," "not sure," "probably could not happen," and "could in no way happen." Some 14% could envisage this possibility (again roughly corresponding to the group I called the "radical minority"); 8% were unsure; and 78% ruled it out.

In another question that probed political estrangement respondents were to entertain the possibility of being jailed for political reasons. This is how the question was phrased (among the possibilities coming true): "I will be sent to jail for my political beliefs or activities." This statement was regarded as a possibility by 8% of the respondents, clearly among the most radical both for attributing to the American political system the jailing of people for political beliefs and for regarding their own as important enough to warrant such punishment. Some 5% were not sure and 86.5% ruled out the possibility.

The same basic attitudes were tested in responses to the statement "Despite some serious flaws the U.S. is the best country in the world to live in": 11% disagreed, 17% were not sure, and 72% agreed.

Such attitudes confirm the impression that approximately 75 to 80% of the respondents were moderate in their political beliefs and attitudes, not alienated in any sense of the word, and generally satisfied with the political system of their country and with life in it. They certainly differed from their peers of an earlier generation in elite schools such as Harvard, whose attitudes Daniel Patrick Moynihan found disturbing in 1975 noting that "The condition of democratic belief among the students was unnerving. The youth had learned to hate and fear their own government, and had almost no standards by which to measure other regimes" [Moynihan 1975:46].

Among the more interesting findings of this survey was the lack of integration of many attitudes. Thus for example the same respondent (0040) who considered himself "well-adjusted to American society," who professed to admire the American political system, and who identified himself as a conservative and right-winger offered the following response to the (open-ended) question, "What in your own words is wrong with American society?": "American society caters to the needs of the rich rather than the plight of the poor and oppressed. America should, through its political leaders (most of whom are rich), concentrate on raising its standards of living and its morals."

The same respondent also agreed strongly with the statement that "It is difficult to realize one's full potentials in American society" and agreed that "big corporations, esp. multinationals, are today the prime enemies of freedom and social justice around the world"; he also agreed that Soviet leaders "are committed to abolishing material inequalities and to improving the life of their people." Such inconsistencies were not unusual.

That a strongly critical stance toward capitalism and certain aspects of American society was felt to be compatible with a self-declared conservative outlook is a finding suggestive of the varied uses people make of these designations; these responses also raise the possibility that sympathy with capitalism need not be felt to be part of the conservative outlook. The combination of these responses also leads one to wonder how an individual can claim to be well-adjusted to a system he perceives as neglecting or mistreating the poor, dominated by the rich, and which makes self-realization difficult? What did he or she mean by being well-adjusted?

Some of these conflicting or contradictory attitudes were most pronounced in matters regarding the military, its uses, and costs. (It should be recalled once more that this survey was conducted before the collapse of the Soviet empire in Eastern Europe and the disarray within the Soviet Union produced by ethnic conflict and economic decline which provided new and more solid grounds for reducing military expenditures and preparedness on the part of the United States.)

Over 61% of the respondents agreed (strongly or otherwise) that "current military expenditures in the U.S. are excessive"; 14% were not sure; and only 24% disagreed, that is to say supported the current levels of military expenditures. (A very similar percentage, 57%, in the Carnegie survey believed that "The United States is spending too much on national defense" [Boyer 1987:190].)

At the same time the statement "The military power of the U.S. is the major obstacle to the further extension of Soviet power and influence in many parts of the world" was endorsed by 56.5%; 16% were not sure; and only 27% disagreed. It may be wondered how American military expenditures could be viewed as excessive if they achieve their purpose, that is, to deter Soviet expansion.

It was also noteworthy that although close to two-thirds of the respondents regarded military expenditures to be excessive, a majority did not take the corresponding prototypical left-of-center view that foreign threats to the United States are negligible. This was indicated by the responses to the statement "The only threat facing the U.S. comes from its unresolved social problems." Only 12% agreed, 13% were not sure; and 76% rejected the idea—a surprisingly large portion given the public popularity of this belief on the campuses and its status as a major article of faith in social science courses.

Regarding willingness to serve in the military (which I took to be an important indicator of support for or estrangement from the political system) the findings reflect a wide range of attitudes including a reluctance to undertake this obligation on the part of a substantial minority. Some 64% agreed that draft registration "is a reasonable requirement"; 10%

were not sure; and 25% disagreed (9% very strongly). Considering how minimal a requirement or encroachment on personal freedom draft registration represents, the quarter of respondents rejecting it, plus the 10% who were not sure if it was reasonable, is a high proportion of young Americans reluctant to meet such a modest obligation.

Less surprisingly, there was strong opposition to the idea of compulsory military service as indicated by the responses to the statement "Universal compulsory military draft should replace the current system of a volunteer army." This idea was rejected by 72%; 13% were not sure; and only 15% were in favor.

The statement "I would not serve in the military under any conditions" found favor with 18%, prompted "not sure" by 14%, and was rejected by 68%. Again, 18% is a substantial minority for such an unqualified refusal to entertain the sacrifice military service entails. It is a position that obviously reflects alienation from American society. This group evidently finds nothing worth defending, or possibly believes that any involvement with the military amounts to an endorsement of using nuclear weapons and thus complicity in a nuclear holocaust. In some cases this attitude may also reflect a principled pacifism.

A highly qualified willingness to serve in the armed forces was also revealed in the responses to the statement "I would not serve in the miliary unless there is an attack to the continental United States." Some 40.5% agreed that they would only serve under these severely limited circumstances; 19% were undecided; and another 40% disagreed, meaning that they would be willing to serve even short of such an attack.

Students were also asked if they would serve in the military if it would be used to assist national liberation movements as for example those in South Africa. Given the different meanings that can be attached to the concept of "national liberation movements," the example of South Africa served to reduce ambiguity by focusing on what most students would regard a just cause. At the same time the concept of "national liberation movement" is colored by left-wing associations. Of those responding, 18% agreed to serve under such conditions, 34% were not sure, and almost half of the sample rejected the idea, possibly because of the ambiguity of the concept of "national liberation movements," which for some represent primarily Marxist-Leninist groups while for others may include the Afghan guerillas and the contras of Nicaragua. It is most likely that the 18% in favor responded to the South African example and were among the more leftist students in the group.

The highly qualified willingness to serve in the armed forces was also reflected in the response to the statement "I would serve in the military if the U.S. goes to war to help one of its allies." Some 27% would not, 30% were not sure, and only 43% would. Again it should be stressed that all these questions including those regarding military service were raised at a time when the international environment was more threatening and the cold war by no means over.

The post-Vietnam isolationism may have been among the factors predisposing to these attitudes. The latter may also be detected in the replies regarding the issue of help to anti-Soviet guerillas such as those in Afghanistan. Since personal risk and sacrifice were not involved in American military assistance (specified as "weapons, supplies") to the guerillas in Afghanistan it is significant that only 34% favored such support, 27% were not sure, and almost 40% objected. It should be noted that these questions were asked several years before the Soviet withdrawal from Afghanistan and before indications of the disunity in the resistance movement, and at a time when the American mass media and the overwhelming majority of Congress still supported generous assistance to the guerillas.

In a similar question regarding military assistance to the "anti-Marxist, anti-Cuban guerillas in Angola" there was even less support and somewhat greater uncertainty. Those in favor of such aid totaled 24%; 36% were undecided; and 40% were opposed. In this and other responses an instinctive isolationist sentiment appeared to assert itself.

Asked to indicate their attitude toward the invasion of Grenada, 43% found it "justified," 32.5% found it unjustified, and 25% were not sure. (According to a *New York Times*/CBS poll 51% of the public at large approved of the invasion shortly after it took place [Shribman 1983].) Once more the modest support given to what the media generally presented as justified intervention and what most lawmakers endorsed can be taken as evidence of the survival or revival of a significant isolationist or anti-interventionist sentiment among students. It should also be remembered that the intervention in Grenada was in large measure validated by the official concern for the safety of American medical students on the island rather than merely by the desirability of removing a pro-Soviet and pro-Castro dictatorship close to the United States. Either the students responding unfavorably did not believe the administration's justification of the invasion or they found the fate of their fellow students insufficient justification to intervene.

If most students were at least ambivalent about the invasion of Grenada this attitude somewhat perplexingly contrasted with their perception of the Soviet threat in the Caribbean. Responding to the statement "Soviet military bases in the Caribbean or Central America are no threat to the U.S." 81% disagreed, 11% were not sure, and only 7% regarded such presence as nonthreatening. To be sure many of those lukewarm about the invasion of Grenada need not have regarded it as an actual or potential Soviet base. (It is of some interest to note here that in the 1984

Carnegie survey 54% of the students agreed to a statement that by implication minimizes Soviet or other external involvement in Central America, namely, that "Current unrest in Central America is caused by internal poverty and injustice rather than external political interaction" [Boyer 1987:190]. This of course is the left-of-center conventional wisdom in such matters and the basis for the rejection of American military assistance to anticommunist governments or movements.)

Whatever the degree of isolationism displayed it appeared compatible for the majority with a generally favorable view of the United States—an attitude different from that of the adversarial social critics discussed earlier. The latter, as may be recalled, typically combined adamant opposition to American intervention anywhere in the world with an exceedingly negative view of the domestic institutions of the United States. Such a perception of the United States as the repository of malign influences (which ought not to be allowed to spread) was central to the isolationism of the social critics, though apparently not of that of the students surveyed.

That the majority (in the student survey) entertained generally favorable views of the United States was indicated in the response to a series of questions designed to probe these attitudes. At the same time, as the responses below indicate, in almost every instance a substantial minority ranging from approximately 10 to 25% inclined to take a highly critical position of various aspects of American society and its major institutions.

Responding to the first statement in the questionnaire 20.5% agreed that "American society, more than most others, has failed to live up to its own ideals"; 12% were not sure; and a total of 68% disagreed (10% of them strongly). Thus a substantial minority (20%) was willing to associate itself with the belief—the centerpiece of social criticism since the 1960s—that this country or its social-political systems betrayed or abandoned its ideals.

The statement "It is difficult to realize one's full potential in American society" also addresses critical sentiments associated with preoccupation with such potentials and their realization, which became widespread since the later 1960s. Once more a similar proportion, 21%, agreed with the highly critical statement (though it may be noted only 2% "very strongly"); 12% were not sure; and a total of 67% disagreed.

The responses to the following statement also revealed highly critical attitudes or the reflexive acceptance of a well-worn stereotype: "American culture and society, dedicated to competitiveness and material gain, nurture indifference to one's fellow human beings." Almost half, or 48%, agreed; 17% were not sure; and 35% disagreed. This was certainly among the responses which indicate the contradictory nature of the attitudes toward American society. Half of the students shared this severe indictment of American society, which is not easy to square with other, more favorable attitudes (see above and below). The conflicting assessment might exemplify the capacity for compartmentalization or else support the hypothesis put forward above, namely, that agreement to such a statement is among the widely accepted pieties of our times, absentmindedly absorbed while in college and accepted perhaps because agreement with these sentiments came to signify high moral-ethical standards.

Such and other critical sentiments however did not carry over into an undiscriminating "blame America first" attitude. Thus for instance the majority of students resisted the fashionable notion that "It is the U.S. and the [Vietnam] war that bear the responsibility for the exodus of refugees from Indochina and not the political system prevailing since the end of the war." Only 11%, the radical minority, agreed to this idea; but 47% were not sure who bears the responsibility, and 41% rejected the proposition, blaming presumably the communist system for the rise of the boat people. In a complementary question it was proposed that "It is the political system prevailing in Indochina since the end of the war that is responsible for the outpouring of the boat people." The attitudes revealed were strikingly similar: 44% agreed; 46% were not sure; and 10% disagreed, holding the U.S. responsible. What was interesting in both responses was the high proportion, almost half, of the students who were not sure how to account for the phenomenon.

While still a minority, the proportion of students critical of the United States rose rapidly among those ascribing to the notion that "The U.S. bears responsibility for much of the suffering and deprivation in the Third World." Some 26% agreed—double the usual proportion of the "hardcore radical minority"; 17% were unsure; and 57% disagreed.

Even more spectacular was the increase in critical attitudes in response to the simple question: "Do you think the U.S. is responsible for any/many of the world's problems?"—66% thought so and 33% did not. The high level of agreement may once more be interpreted as a semi-automatic or conditioned reflex resulting from prevailing conventional wisdom on the campuses (and to some degree in the media) and from a tendency among many educated, middle-class Americans to feel uneasy about their affluence when contrasted with the misery in much of the world. In open-ended questions students were also asked for what problems they held the U.S. responsible. Significant minorities found the United States responsible for third world problems (22%), for the arms race (22%), for contributing to an unstable political situation in the world (17%), and for the problems of Central America (6%).

The social-critical sentiment emerged in similar proportions in response to the statement "Big corporations, especially the multinationals, are today the prime enemies of freedom and social justice around the world": 26% agreed, 27% were not sure, and 47% rejected the idea. That is to say, half of the students entertained the idea with various degrees of conviction that capitalism is the source of major evils in the world today, a belief likely to be associated with a taken-for-granted anticapitalism that is part of the values of the 1960s which continue to be transmitted to the young on many campuses.

Attitudes toward capitalism were further probed by means of the statement "Criticism of the big corporations has been exaggerated and their political influence overdrawn." The responses further confirm the anticapitalist sentiment among a large proportion of respondents: only 23% agreed, 27% were not sure, but slightly over 50% disagreed, finding the critiques of big corporations justified.

The conventional leftist wisdom on the connection between wealth and political power was suggested by the statement "In the U.S. there is no political democracy since the political process is dominated by the rich"—23% agreed, 12% were not sure, and 65% rejected the idea.

The conventional left-wing view of the mass media under capitalism was shared by a similar proportion of students. The statement eliciting such beliefs went as follows: "The mass media is a servant of the status quo as it seeks to divert attention from pressing social-political problems." While the first part of the statement is at least debatable, the second, suggesting that the media seeks to divert attention from pressing social-political problems, is quite incorrect considering the obsessive preoccupation of the media with social and political problems, be they the drug epidemic, teenage pregnancy, AIDS, crime, homelessness, unemployment, pollution, or political corruption. Nonetheless, 27.5% of the respondents agreed to this slanted view of the media; 13% were unsure; and 60% disagreed.

Attitudes toward the media were also probed by proposing the opposite view: "The American mass media in recent times has been the voice of social criticism." Some 20% disagreed, presumably not finding the media critical enough; 18.5% were not sure; and 62%, again the moderate majority, agreed.

Attributions of sexual and racial discrimination have for the past quarter-century been central to the critiques of American society. Those entertaining a more favorable view of American society find these critiques exaggerated, while the critics do not. The statement seeking to probe these attitudes was the following: "The persistence of racism and sexism in the U.S. has been greatly exaggerated." Only 24% agreed to this proposition; 16% were not sure; and 60% disagreed, that is, believed that assertions about the prevalence of sexism and racism are *not* overdrawn, but valid, thereby accepting another important critique of American society. Unfortunately having combined these two attributes in the same statement we do not know if the respondents felt the same way about each. Arguably many might have felt more strongly about the persistence of racism than sexism (or vice versa), or might have regarded racism a more serious evil than sexism. It is also possible though less likely that some of these students might not have regarded sexism and racism to be self-evidently deplorable attitudes and therefore their agreement over their persistence was not necessarily a form of social criticism, they were merely registering a fact dispassionately and without disapproval. Supporting this theory is that in another question ("American society may be described as . . .") "racist" and "sexist" were chosen only by 8% and 7% respectively—a finding that perplexingly conflicts with the stated belief of 60% that these attributions are *not* exaggerated.

Another statement designed to test the degree of the radical rejection of American society proposed that "Only revolutionary change can remedy the ills of American society." Once more the radical minority showed up with 10% agreeing, 12.5% not sure, and 77% disagreeing.

Attitudes toward the United States were also probed by presenting a list of attributes following the question "How do you think the U.S. is regarded today by most people in the world?" Of this a list of the following choices were made: with criticism 23%, envy 18%, admiration 15%, hatred 13%, curiosity 11%, ambivalence 7%.

In a similar question respondents were asked how *they felt* about being American and were once more given a list of attitudes such as: lucky 26%, proud 25%, happy 16%, good 10%. Thus over three-quarters chose highly positive sentiments. Only 7% selected "ashamed" and "guilty," again a somewhat puzzling finding given some of the severely critical propositions which were embraced by far greater numbers, as shown earlier.

A third question aimed at learning more of the same attitudes provided a list of attributes with which to describe American society: one of the few free and materially prosperous countries in the world 19%, allows much personal freedom 18%, provides both free expression and decent living standards 18%, no worse than most other societies 10%, racist 8% , exploitative 8%, sexist 7%, cold, impersonal 5%. Only 1.5% chose "basically flawed" and an identical 1.5% "unjust and oppressive."

Thus responses to listings of attributes of American society proved far more positive than responses to longer statements regarding characteristics of the same society (such as its competitiveness, lack of realization of its ideals, and so on).

Attitudes toward American society are not independent of the assessment of other countries and especially those of its rivals or adversaries. A series of statements tested these attitudes beginning with the generalized left-wing proposition that "The ideals of socialism offer the best hope for peace and social justice in the world." Some 20.5% agreed (but only 3% very strongly); 24% were not sure; and 55% disagreed. The number agreeing was double that of the radical minority, suggesting that many who might be called "soft leftists" also find these ideals attractive in the abstract. (Whether or not the events of 1989 in Eastern Europe would have made a difference to the attraction of these ideals we do not know, although it is possible that the massive rejection of the attempted realization of these ideals might have raised more questions about the ideals themselves.)

Students were also asked to respond to the statement "Although many socialist countries are poor, they are morally superior to the capitalist ones, including the U.S.": 12% agreed; 20% were not sure; and 68% disagreed.

The statement "Soviet foreign policy is more peaceful than the American" found agreement with only 4% of the respondents; 16% were unsure, and 80% disagreed, showing that illusions about the Soviet Union were not among the attributes of this group of students, including most of the radicals. But a more favorable view of the domestic aspects of the Soviet system was apparent in the responses to the statement "Whatever the shortcomings of the Soviet political system, at least one knows that its leaders are committed to abolishing material inequalities and to improving the life of their people": 13% agreed; 20% were not sure; and 67% rejected this point of view. Thus there were three times as many favorable views of the domestic as opposed to the foreign policies of the Soviet Union at a time before a highly favorable American media coverage of the Gorbachev reforms began.

There was a series of questions about repression in the Soviet Union, China, and Cuba provided by the statement: "Western reports of repression in . . . are greatly exaggerated." Almost identical percentages agreed that this was the case: 13% for the Soviet Union, 13% for China, and 11% for Cuba. Of those unsure, 37% were regarding the Soviet case, 50% the Chinese, and 44% the Cuban. Some 53.5% did not find such reports exaggerated in the Soviet case (i.e., believed that there was substantial repression), 38% in the Chinese, and 44% in the Cuban case. Notable again were the large percentages of those undecided in these matters. Once more the "radical minority" was reluctant to believe that repression was correctly attributed to these systems. It was presumably the same minority that disagreed (12%) with the statement "There is more freedom of expression in the U.S. than any country past or present"; 20% were not sure and 67% agreed.

If many students had illusions about the political system prevailing in Nicaragua, it was not apparent from their responses to the statement "Nicaragua has emerged as the most authentic socialist regime in the world today." Only 8% agreed; but a majority of 57% were unsure and 34% disagreed.

A further attempt was made to learn about the political values of the students by asking them to name (in an open-ended question) contemporary political leaders they admired most and least. Among the most admired, 15% named John F. Kennedy, 10% Ronald Reagan, 7% F. D. Roosevelt, 7% Gandhi, 6% Margaret Thatcher, 5% Sadat and Martin Luther King, Jr., 4% Churchill, 3% Nixon. (Other choices were too small to tabulate.)

While these responses were not astonishing—especially given the mythology of John F. Kennedy associated with his assassination and the fact that a sizable minority in the sample came from (or attended college in) his home state, Massachusetts—the choices in the following questions were more surprising and provided a clearer indication of the influences of the adversarial ethos of the campuses.

Regarding the least admired political leader, the results are as follows: Hitler 13%, Reagan 9%; Stalin 9%; Qadafi 9%, Khomeni 9%, Castro 8%; Nixon 6%, Carter 4%, Idi Amin 4%.

While it is astonishing enough that Reagan directly followed Hitler as the second most unappealing political leader, it is of further interest that he was actually named as such by more students than was Stalin. Given the practice of rounding up or down the fractional percentages it should be noted here that 9.4% found Reagan the most unappealing politician, as opposed to 8.9% placing Stalin into this category. Equally remarkable that Reagan was rated comparable with Qadafi and Khomeni, while Castro was actually given a slightly better rating than Reagan (8.4% vs. Reagan's 9.4%).

These findings are certainly part of the inconsistencies referred to earlier, and they conflict with the overall impression of moderation many of the other answers reflected. To say the least, the choices described above indicate a striking inability to differentiate between a democratic politician of questionable personal qualities and debatable accomplishments such as Reagan, on the one hand, and heads of police states with impressive records of bloodshed and repression, on the other.

In the final attempt to learn more about the impact of the political culture and higher education the respondents were asked to name "the most shocking political-historical event of our times." Here are the results: the Holocaust 14%, Vietnam war 14%, World War II 10%, bombing of Japan 6%, World War I 5%, Hostages taken by Iran 5%, Watergate 5%, Kennedy's assassination 4%, the Russian Revolution 3%, exterminations by Stalin 3%, the cold war 3%.

These too are remarkable responses based presumably on a combination of a modest knowledge of history, an impaired capacity to differentiate, and the influence of the political culture of academia. The answers probably also reflect the impact of the media and the political culture as a whole. It is for example plausible enough that if a young person sees more references in the media or in his college courses to Vietnam than to the slaughters of Stalin he is likely to conclude that the former must have been a more shocking episode in history than the latter. The same may be said about Watergate and the Iranian hostage-taking overshadowing other far more monumental and consequential historical outrages, some of which never even got mentioned, as for example the genocide of Armenians or more recently the bloodletting associated with Pol Pot of Cambodia, the Soviet collectivization in the early 1930s, the Purge Trials, the Nazi-Soviet Pact of 1939, the Chinese Cultural Revolution, the fate of political refugees such as the boat people, and others.

Equally revealing of the mentality (or level of information here pondered) is the equation of the Holocaust and Vietnam, another form of moral equivalence.

Attitudes toward free expression were probed in a question which asked "Which of the following organizations/employers should *not* be allowed to recruit on campus?" Commendably enough 78% chose the option "all should be allowed"; 6% chose "none of the above should be allowed" (those listed "above" were the CIA, Department of Defense, Dept. of State, Exxon, IBM); 9% would have barred the Dept. of Defense; and 5% the CIA—again the radical core showing up.

In a similar question students were asked "Which of the following groups should be discouraged from engaging in political activity on campus (such as recruiting, distributing literature, holding public meetings)?" In a significant departure from the attitude noted above (which presumably had been influenced by the evident connection between recruitment and employment opportunities) only 24% opposed all such bans on *political organizations*. Some 63% favored barring the KKK; 10.5% would have discouraged all groups listed. They included the Pro-Castro Venceremos Brigade, Jewish Defense League, Revolutionary Communist Party, and the (imaginary) "National Association for the Protection of Minorities."

An attempt was also made to learn about the apolitical aspects of the outlook of the students and in particular about the degree of optimism or pessimism characterizing their expectations.

These questions were put in the form of predictions, and respondents were asked "Which of the following possibilities can you imagine coming true?" They could choose "could very easily happen," "could in no way happen," or three more intermediate positions between these extremes.

The first statement was "I will not find any job and will lead a life of poverty with or without welfare assistance": 88% ruled out this prospect; 8% regarded it a possibility; and 4.5% were not sure (again the latter percentages correspond to those who expressed the most radical views and political matters).

The next statement in this series was "I will not find a job appropriate to my training and education and only obtain odd jobs or manual labor": 75% ruled this out; 17% thought it might happen; and 8% were not sure.

"I will not be able to afford to own a car" was the next statement rejected by 77%; 14% considered it a possibility; and 9.5% were not sure.

Next came "I will not be able to own my own house ten years or more from now": 30% thought this was quite possible; 21% were not sure; and 49.5% disagreed with such a gloomy prospect.

It was also suggested that "I will be drafted and sent to fight another unpopular war like Vietnam": 25% considered this a possibility; 17% were not sure; and 58% ruled it out.

Two more questions regarding expectations of a less personal character were put before the students. The first stated "The U.S. is attacked by nuclear weapons." An astonishing 72% thought this *could* happen; (for 55% "could possibly happen" and only for 17% "could easily happen"). Only 17% rejected this possibility without qualification and 10% were not sure. It may be recalled that the mid-1980s (when this survey was made) was a period of the resurgence of the peace and antinuclear movements which sharply increased awareness and apprehension about the prospects of nuclear holocaust; these movements were active on the campuses where "peace studies" (usually concerned with nuclear war) often also flourished.

The second question concerned with matters nuclear proposed that "A dreadful accident occurs in the U.S. involving either nuclear power plants or weapons." The proportion of those regarding such an event plausible rose to 79%, with only 12% regarding it unlikely and 9% unsure. It is notable that whereas in the realm of personal expectations the majority was optimistic, the nuclear menace was readily accepted by a similar or even greater majority.

One more question is worth reporting in part as a measure of change; by 1990 (when this is being written) the issue of communist advances in Central America has become quite anachronistic. But in the mid-1980s it was not totally fantastic to propose that "Central America as a whole, including Mexico, comes to be controlled by Marxist governments similar to the Cuban system and friendly to the Soviet Union." Some 50% thought this to be possible; 22% were unsure; and 28% ruled it out.

No attempt was made in this survey to correlate background variables with political attitudes. Thus we do not know if the students of particular ethnic, religious, or social background were more or less likely to express certain political attitudes; if science majors were more conservative than those in sociology or English; or if there is any pattern related to the college attended and the political beliefs displayed. Nor were personal expectations of the future linked to political attitudes. It is plausible enough that those more pessimistic would more likely be alienated and politically radical, but no data analysis has been performed to substantiate this assumption. Such cross-tabulations will have to await another study. There is however one piece of information of some interst, although its influence can only be a matter of speculation. Students were asked if they had ever read anything by Marx, Engels, Lenin, or their followers. Some 79% did and 19% did not. They were also asked "Did any of your high school or college teachers present the ideas of Marxism as part of a course?" Once more 79% replied in the affirmative. While no obvious interpretation can be attached to this finding it is apparent that some degree of exposure to Marxism has become a part of college (perhaps even high school) education and part of the fund of ideas students can draw from and associate with the prevalent conventional wisdom passed on by schools.

The information presented above demonstrates that contrary to much popular theorizing, a spectacular swing to conservative attitudes among students has not occurred and "the new conservatism on campus" is neither deep nor widespread. It seems that one basis of this belief has been the identification of greater materialism with conservativism, as an article in the *Chronicle of Higher Education* put it [Meyer 1985]. While there has been evidence of a greater concern on the part of students with grades, jobs, and money such concerns have coexisted with numerous left-of-center attitudes (or pieties?). I would hazard the guess that for students as for the adults (touched by the 60s) it has become of some importance to think of themselves as "idealistic," at least in their value orientation if not day-to-day behavior. And even if "students voted for Ronald Reagan by the same 3-2 margin as the rest of the nation" [Karlen et al. 1985] their worldview is far from consistently conservative or right-of-center. At the same time most of them do not seem to have been "imprinted" with the intensely critical attitudes of the earlier generation of students, nor do they echo the reflexive left-of-centrism of their teachers (in the humanities and social sciences), especially as regards their basic attitudes toward American society.

The relative stability of the political attitudes of college students and especially the modest rise of conservative attitudes among them was shown in a twenty-year trend report published by the Higher Education Research Institute at the University of California at Los Angeles. It found that while the number of students who identify themselves as liberal has shrunk by a third from the number in 1970, the total who define themselves as conservatives has held relatively steady: 15% to 20%, with a net gain of 2.4% since 1970. . . . The number of freshmen describing themselves as political centrists has increased about 11%, from 45.4% in 1970 to 56.7% last year [1985]. [Survey Finds No Big College Swing to Right 1986]

It was also noted by a specialist engaged in long-term observation of student attitudes that "Our data . . . very clearly show that students are as, if not more, supportive of liberal issues than they have been at any time in the 20-year history of the survey . . . in terms of self-assessment . . . [it] has not been from left to right, but rather . . . from liberal to a middle-of-the-road or moderate position" [Landers 1986]. This comment lends support to an earlier proposition of this study, namely that the whole political spectrum has shifted and in the light of the extremes embraced during the 1960s and early 70s moderation has acquired new meaning (as had liberalism). But this new moderation is also compatible with attitudes and values which at earlier times would have been classified as left-of-center. Apparently the moderate or centrist self-perception frequently coexists with the acceptance of political verities bequeathed by the 60s—as was also indicated in several specific attitudes uncovered by this survey. Although generally speaking the student group here discussed may best be characterized as moderate in its political attitudes, it also displayed, as we have seen, dispositions and beliefs which conflict with the generalized picture of moderation and reflect the survival or revival of certain values and beliefs associated with the adversarial ethos of the 60s. Also of some interest is that evidently self-identification in terms of various political labels has become compatible, in a somewhat unpredictable pattern, with a wide range of views on specific matters. (Or, as an article in Newsweek magazine put it, "When it comes to politics, this year's freshmen have opinions all over the map" [Karlen et al. 1986:9].)

The adversarial attitudes and values found the clearest reflection in the responses regarding the U.S. military and capitalism. There was also a minority (approx. 10%) of hardcore radicals who consistently gave extremely negative assessments of every aspect of American society and displayed highly favorable attitudes toward left-wing ideas, movements, or political systems. It is presumably this group, inclined to political activism, which, together with the similarly disposed members of faculties, sets the tone of the political discourse on major campuses and especially the elite ones, as had been discussed earlier.

It was also found that the percentage of self-identified radicals and radical-liberals corresponds to the percentage of those giving the most radical or adversarial responses to specific questions, while the proportion of those putting themselves in the two centrist, moderate categories corresponds in most instances to the percentage of moderate responses to specific questions.

Given the inconsistencies found in the responses these findings support neither the view that most students since the mid-1970s have become largely apolitical or avid conservatives, nor the opposite belief that their worldview has been decisively molded by the left-of-center conventional wisdom that has become established in major academic settings over the past quarter-century. Rather, it would seem that most college students have absorbed some of the adversarial views but not others, and their critiques of aspects of American society or their doubts about capitalism did not create a generally adversarial or alienated disposition. The information presented in this chapter suggests that a gap has opened, in the course of the past two decades, between the majority of moderate students and the left-of-center faculties which have retained and replenished their estrangement from American society over these decades. It may thus not be ruled out that in an ironic reversal of the conventional wisdom of the 60s, an intensely social-critical disposition is now more a function of the discontents of ripe middle age than of youthful impatience.

PART III

CRITIQUES ABROAD

7

The Third World

> . . . at the root of all anti-Americanism . . . is both the understanding that the world is being Americanized and a fear of the process.
>
> *Henry Fairlie, 1975*

> . . . anti-Americanism should not be confused with criticism of America . . . [it] is first and foremost a disease of the intellectuals and as such . . . a symptom of a far more serious ailment . . .: their revulsion against Western society as we know it.
>
> *Jan van Houten, 1983*

> It is Americans themselves who supply most of the materials of anti-Americanism.
>
> *Kenneth Minogoe, 1986*

In the second half of the 20th century the United States emerged in many parts of the world as a readily available symbol of political evil and irresponsibility, social injustice and cultural corruption; it became subject of a reflexive disparagement and vilification. A dark suspicion toward the United States and readiness to believe the worst about it are among the key characteristics of the attitude designated as anti-Americanism. It is, as admitted earlier, a vague concept with a variety of possible meanings, yet it captures attitudes much in evidence.

The more one learns about the hostility toward the United States the more difficult it becomes to make an unambiguous assessment of the phenomenon. On the one hand there is the puzzle: why has the United States—a generous, friendly country, which millions of people around the globe continually seek to enter, a democratic and open society—become the recipient of so much abuse? On the other hand, after looking at some historical facts one may also conclude that anti-Americanism is a natural development given certain attributes of the United States, the condition of various nations, and human nature in general. Indeed some observers believe that anti-Americanism is hardly surprising: "The world's most powerful nation, whose economic, military and cultural reach touches every region, is bound to be the target of considerable criticism from many quarters . . . The United States will always be subject to criticism, whether it is deserved or not" [Luck and Fromuth in Rubinstein and Smith 1985:219, 220].

The essence of anti-Americanism is often obscured not only by the different meanings associated with the concept but also by the frequent disavowal of those who display it. On a *Firing Line* television program William F. Buckley and Robert Scheer, a radical social critic, predictably enough, disagreed about the meaning of the concept. Scheer argued that as long as people like him and Buckley had different ideas as to "what the core of being an American is" one could not define what anti-American was [Buckley 1989:28–31]. Scheer was among many intensely critical commentators (domestic and foreign) who felt compelled to disclaim hostility toward the United States.

E. P. Thompson, a prominent English critic of the United States, begins an essay (consisting largely of critiques of the United States) by declaring, "I don't think that I can be accused of being anti-American. It would be strange if I were, for I am ethnically half-American myself"—a point of grotesque irrelevance suggesting that American blood prevents people from becoming vitriolic critics of the United States. He goes on to claim that he is not anti- but pro-American and favors the survival of American civilization [Thompson and Smith, eds. 1981:3, 6].

For the late Sukarno of Indonesia not even the burning of American libraries amounted to such attitudes. He said

> We Indonesians were angry and felt insulted by the American senator who, after the burning of books in the American library in Jakarta, scolded us for being uncivilized because we burnt books. That man could not understand that this was an explosion of dislike for American policy. Moreover, what was burnt was not the books, but the spirit of the books . . . [Morgan 1967:115–16]

Andreas Papandreou, former prime minister of Greece, also made a point of denying that he was anti-American, although he made anti-American rhetoric a cornerstone of his domestic policies and has written that ". . . American imperialism . . . constitutes a global threat not only to the independence of nations and the dignity of life, but a direct and immediate threat to human survival" [Kamm 1985:21, 46].

Despite such obfuscations and denials anti-Americanism is an identifiable attitude and a concept hardly more elusive than many others employed to designate attitudes of diffuse hostility toward various groups of people, countries, movements, or ideas. Anti-Americanism may be defined as an unfocused and largely irrational, often visceral aversion toward the United States, its government, domestic institutions, foreign policies, prevailing values, culture, and people. It appears to be born out of a scapegoating impulse fueled by a wide variety of frustrations and grievances; as such it has much in common with chauvinistic nationalism that seeks to bolster collective self-esteem by the denigration of other nations, preferably those close by. Anti-Americanism may also refer to the resentment which the presence and policies of a great power arouse among those it comes in contact with. It may be a calculated policy or a spontaneous outburst of emotions. It may also be thought of as originating in the justified grievances of nations, groups, or individuals who have over time been victimized or harmed by the United States or offended by what is seen as its inhumane policies and unjust social order. (But the grievances of the past may be used to justify hostility that no longer has a rational basis.)

Anti-Americanism is not to be confused with opposition to particular policies of the United States and with desires for national independence and self-determination [Haseler 1985], although such opposition and such desires may be colored by it. A memorandum of the U.S. Information Agency (that has for decades monitored these attitudes around the world) also emphasized this point: "It is important to distinguish anti-Americanism from criticism of U.S. foreign policies . . . there is considerably more of the latter than the former . . . people can be critical of U.S. policies without being basically unfavorable in their opinion of the U.S." [Crespi 1979:1].

It is the nonrational aspects of anti-Americanism, the idea of a largely groundless hostility, that is its most intriguing and characteristic ingredient. Anti-Americanism would not stimulate curiosity and warrant inquiry if it were totally rational. Since Nazism is universally perceived as self-evidently evil, nobody is seeking a better understanding of anti-Nazi sentiments in the post-World War II period. By contrast, racism, sexism, and ethnic prejudice continue to stimulate interest and research not only because of their devastating consequences but also because of the irrational aspects of the sentiments and attitudes involved. Anticommunism, a far more controversial phenomenon in the West, has also inspired a fair amount of published reflection on the part of those who regard it as both dangerous and irrational [see, for example, Parenti 1969 and "Anti-Communism and the U.S." Conference 1988].

Unlike investigations of racism, ethnic prejudice, and more recently of sexism, the literature on anti-Americanism is surprisingly meager and largely impressionistic despite the many puzzling aspects of the phenomenon and its connections with issues of national interest and self-respect. Given the national concern with how Americans are perceived around the world (as well as at home in various social settings) and the national interest in being liked (associated with the historical problems of the national and cultural identity of a new nation [see also Scott in Thornton 1988:21]) one would expect a greater interest in understanding the animosity directed at the United States.

Jacques Barzun observed almost a quarter-century ago that "As a nation whose citizens seek popularity more than any other kind of success it is galling (and inexplicable) that we, the United States, are so extensively unpopular" [Barzun 1965]. Two decades later a British visitor made similar comments:

> Why, Americans ask, are our achievements not universally recognised and admired? Why does American generosity not evoke more gratitude? Why have American economic power and military strength not brought more influence in the world? Why are small countries in Southeast Asia and the Middle East able to defy the United States, and to gain such widespread support when they do? Why is the United States always in a minority at the United Nations, which it did so much to create and still does so much to sustain? [Howard 1985:55]

Solzhenitsyn too was puzzled:

> The United States has long shown itself to be the most magnanimous, the most generous country in the world. Wherever there is a flood, an earthquake, a fire, a natural disaster, disease who is the first to help? The United States . . . And what do we hear in reply? Reproaches, curses . . . American cultural centers are burned, and the representatives of the Third World jump on tables to vote against the United States. [Quoted in Moynihan 1978:76]

Another Soviet writer, Vassily Aksyonov, who also emigrated to this country, was similarly bewildered: "Even now, after living in America for more than five years, I keep wondering what provokes so many people in Latin America, Russia and Europe to anti-American sentiment of such intensity that it can only be called hatred. There is something oddly hysterical about it all . . ." [Aksyonov 1985:7].

Despite such well-founded questions and concerns few attempts have been made either to explain the phenomenon or to challenge the beliefs in which it is rooted. Several explanations may be suggested. One is the possibility that for many Americans anti-Americanism and the hostile feelings and actions it entails may be too disturbing to be confronted and analyzed; second, many of those professionally most qualified to investigate it may accept the phenomenon as normal, self-evidently justified, and thus not worth studying; at last there are undoubtedly those who regard the concept too vague and value-laden to stimulate serious inquiry.

Anti-Americanism abroad is consequential and widespread enough to merit thorough examination, even if the concept is imprecise and coexists with the manifest desire of millions of people all over the world to gain entry into this much vilified country, and even if it is paralleled in many parts of the world by goodwill and sympathy toward the United States. Like the reflexive rejection of American institutions at home, anti-Americanism abroad too is an attitude of minorities (numerically speaking), usually of elite groups. Indeed the U.S. Information Agency investigating these attitudes concluded that

> pro-American orientations for the most part continue to prevail . . . [and] . . . in a quarter-century of surveys in over 50 countries . . . it has been a very rare exception to find the extent of unfavorable opinion of the U.S. equaling or exceeding the extent of favorable sentiment. That a large reservoir of good opinion toward the U.S. exists abroad has been repeatedly confirmed . . . [Crespi 1981]

As is the case with other consequential beliefs and attitudes, the significance of anti-Americanism is not determined by the numbers of people displaying it.

Anti-Americanism has less to do with the policies and actions of the United States and more with what the United States is or what it stands for. Anti-Americanism originates as much or more in the circumstances of those beholden to it as in the attributes of American culture, society, or foreign policy. Likewise theories of antisemitism, racism, sexism or other discredited beliefs routinely prompt the investigator to ask why people hold such questionable beliefs and what service they perform for those holding them.

The component of irrational hostility toward things American links anti-Americanism to other irrational aversions such as those elicited by racial, ethnic, or gender differences, or those having to do with more unusual sexual preferences [see also Minogue 1986]. Andre Glucksman, the French philosopher, believes that ". . . anti-Americanism now has the contours of classic anti-Semitism—power unseen; dark, violent forces beyond all control. The reproaches are the same . . . Einstein, Freud, Rothschild. The words are just different. 'They're everywhere. They are behind everything'" [Vinocur 1984:74].

Attribution of conspiratorial intent was also reported from the Philippines:

> It probably hasn't occurred to many Americans that the United States might be contemplating an invasion of the Philippines. But anyone who has grazed through an armful of Manila's more than thirty daily papers

knows that conspiracies involving the United States are a staple of this city's political culture . . . Filippinos are perceived as powerless and Americans as larger than life. (The most insignificant dunderhead from a U.S. congressional subcommittee becomes "powerful" and "influential" upon arrival in Manila.) [Berlow 1990:19]

To be sure, the American military presence in the Philippines is a powerful stimulant of such sentiments and an affront to national pride; the military bases are "a veritable obsession of the country's educated elite" [Ibid.]. American military presence may also be a major explanation of an even more intense anti-American disposition among South Korean intellectuals and especially university students [see, for example, "Korean Students Attack U.S. Site" 1990].

It is a presupposition of this study that much of the highly patterned and sweeping rejection of the United States cannot be adequately explained on the basis of the observable flaws of American society, culture, and foreign policy; that, as another writer asserted, "Most of the sources of anti-Americanism . . . are not based upon antagonism toward specific policies" [Bissell in Rubinstein and Smith, eds. 1985:255]. This was also the conclusion of Joseph Godson, the political scientist: "The roots of . . . anti-Americanism run deep and have little to do with anything we actually do in the world" [Godson 1986]. If so it would also be futile to expect that knowing more about the United States will remedy these matters. In fact the opposite may be the case, because much of the information most readily available is disseminated by American sources themselves either outright negative or lending themselves to negative interpretation. In any event information is absorbed selectively and can be assimilated into a hostile predisposition. This was also the belief of a foreign critic of the United States who noted that ". . . increased exposure to and knowledge of U.S. culture and politics tend to arouse antipathy not sympathy, while the relative lack of knowledge of the Soviet Union leaves untarnished the appealing ideology with which the educated elite [in the Third World] is familiar" [Hamid in Rubinstein and Smith 1985:89].

Indeed the irrational components of anti-Americanism are especially striking when, over a period of time, one compares attitudes toward the United States and the Soviet Union—another global power of equally if not far more pronounced imperial aspirations and policies and far more deformed domestic institutions. Theodore Draper, in his discussion of what he called "the deafening anti-Americanism of European intellectuals," observed that "this type of European anti-Americanism struck even a critical American as obsessive and repetitive to the point of psychopathology, especially when countries and systems deserving of far more strident criticism were let off with threadbare alibis and tattered apologies" [Draper in Laqueur and Hunter, eds. 1985:103].

Besides establishing more precisely what attitudes the concept covers and what critiques it entails, the most intriguing question is why the United States, following World War II, has become such an inviting target for an unusually wide range of grievances and resentments, why it has become such a popular symbol of evil, corruption, and injustice in so many parts of the world, in countries of diverse political systems, cultural traditions, and levels of economic development.

Other matters of special interest will be the relationship between the domestic critiques of the United States and those prevalent abroad; how they influence or stimulate one another; and how their specific themes differ from or resemble one another.

Other topics of interest associated with anti-Americanism include its fluctuations over time, regional varieties, real and apparent sources, its connections with social criticism directed at the country where it arises, and the groups of people who most typically embrace and express these sentiments.

Anti-Americanism is *a predisposition to hostility* toward the United States and American society, a relentlessly critical impulse toward American social, economic, and political institutions, traditions, and values; it entails an aversion to American culture in particular and its influence abroad, often also contempt for the American national character (or what is presumed to be such a character) and dislike of American people, manners, behavior, dress, and so on; rejection of American foreign policy and a firm belief in the malignity of American influence and presence anywhere in the world. Frequently anti-Americanism is a form of anticapitalism, when the United States is thought to be a repository of social injustice as the major capitalist nation in the world and defender of other capitalist nations.

Rubinstein and Smith see anti-Americanism "as any hostile action or expression that becomes part and parcel of an *undifferentiated* attack on the foreign policy, society, culture and values of the United States" [Rubinstein and Smith in Thornton ed. 1988:36; my emphasis].

Domestic critiques and denunciations of American society often as intense and vitriolic as those abroad have not, as a rule, been designated as anti-Americanism, a term reserved to foreign critiques or expressions of hostility. "Un-American" has been used—as in the designation of a congressional subcommittee in the late 1940s and early 50s set up to investigate acts of "subversion"—but not "anti-American." Perhaps this usage reflects the unstated premise that an American could not be "anti-American," hence the concept came to be largely reserved to foreigners hostile toward the United States. (A French commentator noted that "There is no nation but the United States where . . . external hostility is called anti-American and internal hostility called un-American" [Toinet in Thornton 1988:137]. But other writers abroad refer with little hesitation to a domestic anti-Americanism as for example Mohammad Beshir Hamid, who observed that "nowhere was anti-Americanism so clearly and vehemently manifested than in the United States itself during the . . . 1960s" [Hamid in Rubinstein and Smith 1985:87].

It may be argued that there is no good reason aside from custom for designating foreign critiques of questionable rationality as manifestations of anti-Americanism without doing the same to their domestic counterparts. We may call "anti-American" domestic and foreign critiques alike if they meet certain standards of irrational, virulent hostility.

It is not easy to establish to everybody's satisfaction what constitute *irrational* critiques of, or *groundless* hostility toward the United States, but attempts will be made to do so in the following pages. On the other hand it will not be widely disputed that there has been much hostility toward the United States since the end of World War II. No country had more hostile demonstrations in front of its embassies, more of its flags burned, cultural missions ransacked, diplomats killed or kidnapped, policies routinely denounced in the United Nations and other international organizations. Nor could we avoid learning of such events, as the mass media at home and abroad has been eager to present them and the associated images of hate, contempt, anger, and bitterness directed at this country. More often than not, the media conveyed that these expressions of hostility are well founded and warrant serious collective self-scrutiny on the part of Americans and their leaders (see Chapter 4).

Hostility toward the United States has other, less dramatic expressions as well. It unfolds in massive propaganda campaigns lavishly funded by many governments, in votes taken in the United Nations, sometimes in the opinion polls of various countries, the writings of intellectuals, occasionally even in works of fiction. (For instance, "a popular novel in Sweden, *Journal to the Earth,* portrays a drunken 'President Raygun' sitting in the White House in 2017 with his fingers on the nuclear button" [Powell 1985:30].) Even when such attitudes have been displayed only by vocal minorities, or artificially stirred up by well-oiled propaganda machines, they have been sufficient to impress upon Americans that there is much hostility and resentment floating around the world that is aimed at their country, and if it is so often expressed, some of it must be justified.

Even when it is recognized that anti-Americanism is widespread and multifaceted it is not easy to determine its effects: in what way it might have hurt national interest or national self-esteem; whether or not it has contributed to a decline of the political, cultural, and social influences of the country around the world. Anti-Americanism may find consequential expression in the policies which countries hostile to the United States pursue in the United Nations, in the closing of American military bases abroad, in physical attacks on American officials or civilians abroad, in restrictions on the flow of American cultural products, in the expulsion of American journalists or businesses, and so on. To be sure it may also be argued, as many do, that such actions are merely the result of the misguided policies of the United States and have nothing to do with anti-Americanism as the term is used here.

Anti-Americanism may be classified in various ways. There is, first of all, the anti-Americanism of Americans (discussed in the earlier parts of this book) and of those abroad; there is anti-Americanism as an elite as distinct from mass phenomenon; anti-Americanism as part and product of official propaganda campaigns or spontaneous grass-roots sentiment independent of institutional encouragement and support; and apolitical or largely apolitical anti-Americanism, that is, the cultural and social variety.

One of the few studies of anti-Americanism (limited to its Third World variants) proposes a typology consisting of 1) issue-oriented anti-Americanism (i.e., specific, having to do with policy disagreements between governments); 2) ideological (rooted in belief systems such as nationalism, Marxism, or Islamic fundamentalism); 3) instrumental (deliberately generated and manipulatively used for domestic political purposes); and 4) revolutionary (which emerges from the ideological variant and becomes a central form of legitimation after a revolutionary seizure of power) [Rubinstein and Smith 1985:19–28].

A broad geographic classification suggests three major types:

1) Third World anti-Americanism, perhaps the richest in substantive themes and the most intense. It combines political, economic, and cultural critiques. Third World anti-Americanism may be further subdivided into Latin American, Middle Eastern (or Arab), African, and Asian varieties.

2) Western European anti-Americanism: Of a lesser intensity, which tends to be more cultural than political, but also feeds on American military presence.

3) Official, state-sponsored, Soviet-bloc and Chinese anti-Americanism resting on little popular support but representing a highly organized propaganda effort. Official Soviet and Third World anti-Americanism may overlap, as in the case of Cuba where the Third World aspects and Marxist-Leninist ideology reinforce one another leading to an exceptionally virulent blend that becomes a major determinant of Cuban policies. (The question was raised: "Can a nation subsist on anti-Americanism

alone? Castro's Cuba seems determined to test the proposition to the limits of its most grotesque possibilities" [Falcoff 1989:41].)

Communist state-sponsored anti-Americanism has diminished in the Gorbachev era as a component of Soviet domestic propaganda, but Soviet agencies continue to support anti-American sentiment in Third World countries, perhaps a reflection of the greater stability of Soviet policies in the Third World than in the domestic and European sphere [see also Fairbanks 1990]. While it is difficult to estimate the contribution the Soviet and other communist state propaganda and disinformation agencies have made to anti-Americanism around the world, the effort and the resources devoted to these activities have been substantial and endured through much of the period surveyed in this study. A former agent of the Czech communist intelligence service wrote:

> Anti-American propaganda campaigns are the easiest to carry out. A single press article containing sensational facts of a "new American conspiracy" may be sufficient. Other papers become interested, the public is shocked, and government authorities in developing countries have a fresh opportunity to clamor against the imperialists while demonstrators hasten to break American embassy windows . . .
> . . . To what extent, then, is contemporary anti-Americanism the result of special operations? Anti-American agitation, demonstration and riots became a commonplace phenomenon in the second half of the 1960s . . . Less than twenty years before the United States had been considered a model society by the majority of its own citizens and many abroad as well . . . The sixties altered this viewpoint in the United States itself . . .
> . . . Foreign and domestic problems, of which the American public had previously been unaware, appeared in new forms, sometimes resulting in feelings of guilt and self-hatred. It has become fashionable among certain American intellectuals to be extremely critical of the existing "establishment" . . . These views, disseminated worldwide by mass media . . . are interpreted by many non-Communist peoples as reflecting an objective, overall picture of American reality. Thus one source of contemporary anti-Americanism is the United States herself . . .
> . . . . Anti-Americanism induced by the intelligence centers of the Soviet bloc is only a secondary phenomenon encouraged by the economic, political and social problems of the non-Communist world. [Bittman 1972:23, 233–35]

State sponsored anti-Americanism in China intensified following the repression of 1989. Arguably official Chinese anti-Americanism equals the most scurrilous Stalinist or Maoist types of the past. As reported from Beijing the Chinese press treats its readers to the kind of information sampled below:

"In capitalist countries, people periodically kill their relatives for the insurance profit," the official Guangming Daily reported . . .

These were among other recent headlines in People's Daily: "The American Way of Life Leads to Drugs," "Gambling: Another Form of Pollution in the United States," "The Forgotten Child Laborers of the United States" . . . The only two recent news items from New York that many Chinese seem to have remembered are the fire in a Bronx social club . . . and the slaying . . . of a 31-year old Chinese student in the subway. [Kristof 1990]

What holds together the varieties of anti-Americanism is a sense of grievance and the compelling need to find some clear-cut and morally satisfying explanation for a wide range of unwelcome circumstances associated with either actual states or feelings of backwardness, inferiority, weakness, diminished competitiveness, or a loss of coherence and stability in the life of a nation, group, or individual.

None of this means that anti-Americanism is totally unrelated to the actions, policies, cultural and institutional characteristics of the United States, or the economic forces associated with it. Rather it means that many of the objective grounds for hostility toward the United States are exaggerated and historical, that is, rooted in the past, in collective memories of humiliation and exploitation (as for example in Latin America), and that the present-day responsibility of the United States for the problems of various countries or groups is often vastly overstated for political, ideological, or social-psychological reasons. As an observer of such attitudes in one major setting of anti-Americanism, the United Nations, put it, "No change of policy in Washington is likely to make the United Nations friendlier to the values and interests of the United States" [Bernstein 1984 January:22]. A student of Latin American anti-Americanism likewise concluded that "whether the United States interests suffer defeat in Nicaragua or victory in Grenada, anti-Americanism is constant" [Horowitz in Rubinstein and Smith 1985:63]. Hence the scapegoating aspects of anti-Americanism are extremely important, making it possible to entertain animosity both when the United States throws its weight around and when it suffers reverses. Presumably in the first situation it is the exercise of power that arouses nationalistic resentment while in the second it is contempt for the weakness and rejoicing over the defeat of the United States that animates anti-Americanism.

The United Nations and Third World Anti-Americanism

The anti-Americanism found in the United Nations is one of its most clear-cut and paradigmatic species, rich in symbolic as well as substantive content. It may be gauged both in actions, in the votes taken and policies adopted, and in the huge volume of rhetoric produced. Given the global character of the U.N. the expressions of anti-Americanism found in its transactions graphically illustrate its geographic distribution.

The anti-Americanism of the U.N. belongs to one of its well-defined varieties: the official, or governmental one, or that of the governing elite. By the same token the sentiments voiced by U.N. delegates tell us little about prevailing levels of popular anti-Americanism in their countries since these delegates represent for the most part undemocratic, authoritarian states. It is a type of anti-Americanism that is largely unspontaneous and instrumental although not without expressive pleasure and relief for those indulging in it. For example in 1983

> when the United States failed in its challenge to the credentials of a delegate from Grenada, the General Assembly burst into what seemed a kind of gleeful, derisive, anti-American applause. The incident reminded some delegates of other such outbursts—including dancing in the aisles—that apparently showed general pleasure at American embarrassments, such as the time in 1974 when Yasir Arafat . . . was allowed to address the Assembly and the vote in 1980 electing Nicaragua to the Security Council. [Bernstein 1983]

Anti-Americanism in the U.N. is especially rich in moralizing and scapegoating themes. For example at the 1974 World Food Conference in Rome ". . . the scene grew orgiastic as speakers competed in their denunciation of the country that had called the conference, mostly to discuss giving away its own wheat, as ours was the only country at the time that had any to give away" [Moynihan 1978:32; see also Pilon 1982:12]. In the annual report of the U.N. Decolonization Committee, "United States military forces on the Virgin Islands were described as a threat to peace of the region" although they consisted of "fourteen Coast Guardsmen, one shotgun, one pistol and an 82-foot vessel used for emergency rescue . . ." [Moynihan 1978:253].

The anti-Americanism in the U.N. may to some degree also be classified as the anti-Americanism of intellectuals insofar as U.N. delegates, or some of them, may be considered intellectuals or former intellectuals (or perhaps quasi-intellectuals). Many of them imbibed Western ideas in particular those of British socialism at Western universities [Moynihan 1975]. This connection is also suggested by the even more virulent anti-Americanism found in UNESCO, an organization more clearly dominated by intellectuals (former or quasi-intellectuals). UNESCO was described by one of its critics as

> a thoroughly politicized institution dedicated to attacking fundamental Western values, interests and institutions. It attacks and seeks to circum-

scribe the free Western press. It characterizes Western culture as an "imperialist" threat to the identity of other peoples. It attacks the free-market economy ... It seeks to downgrade individual human rights in favor of nebulous ... "rights of peoples" ... mostly silent about the sins of totalitarian regimes and repressive third world countries. [Harries 1983]

As such comments suggest, in UNESCO activities, as in those of its mother organization, the U.N., anti-Americanism and a broader, visceral anti-Western disposition merge. Both attitudes include an aversion to political democracy, liberalism, and capitalism and a more diffuse rejection of Western culture associated with racism, past claims of Western cultural superiority, and imposition of cultural patterns of the colonial era. Anti-Americanism in UNESCO, not unlike in the U.N., is also strengthened by persistent and energetic Soviet block efforts which cultivate and support these attitudes and policies [see for example Dionne 1983].

Anti-Americanism in the U.N. is most clearly revealed in its voting patterns which acquired the anti-American coloration as the number of Third World nations increased and their voting record become similar to that of the Soviet bloc. For example in 1983 in the General Assembly "the overall degree of support [for the United States] shown by all countries was 25.5% ... Only the Western European countries and Israel voted more than half time on the same side as the United States." A striking counterpart to these attitudes was the support for Soviet positions, which among "the countries professing non-alignment ... was about 80%, compared with 20% for the United States" [Bernstein 1984 March]. According to a more recent report, voting patterns showed in 1989 "that a majority of U.N. members supported the United States on only 15.4% of resolutions put to a yes-or-no vote ..." In 1987 it was 18.5%; in 1986, 23.7%; in 1985, 22.5%; in 1984, 21%; and in 1983, 25.5% [Lewis 1989].

More recently (as of spring 1990) the State Department discerned some improvement in such voting records. An analysis of voting patterns on 16 issues of importance to the U.S. revealed that Assembly members sided with the U.S. in 23.3% of the cases compared with 16.9% support for the American position that was found in all General Assembly votes [Lewis 1990].

U.N. anti-Americanism also manifests itself in double standards of judgment when the United States (and Israel) are singled out for criticism for actions or policies other countries also engage in, or when the United States is criticized for aggression or human rights violations, although most critics are far worse offenders. Thus the United States is often chastised for trade and economic relations with South Africa, although most

European and many African countries have similar ties [Bernstein 1984 January]. Likewise, for the so-called "non-aligned" nations (numbering close to a hundred) it was only the United States that represented a threat to world peace as indicated by a document prepared in 1981. The charges included the downing of two Libyan planes (according to the United States, Libya attacked American planes over international waters), responsibility for the Palestinians' plight, refusal to grant independence to Puerto Rico (although in several referenda the vast majority voted against independence), American involvement in the arms race, and so on. The Soviet Union and its allies were never even mentioned, "save as victims." By contrast the Soviet Union has been widely perceived, in the words of the permanent representative of India, as ". . . deeply understand[ing] and share[ing] the aspirations of the Third World" [Moynihan 1975:35]. The disparity between Indian attitudes toward the United States and the Soviet Union is also revealed in the existence of 1500 Indo-Soviet Friendship Societies versus two Indo-American Friendship Societies [Embree in Rubinstein and Smith eds. 1985:138].

Solicitousness toward the Soviet Union and its allies was further expressed over the years in reference to "foreign forces" in Afghanistan (rather than Soviet troops) and, in deference to communist Vietnam, to foreign forces in Cambodia (rather than Vietnamese) [Nossiter 1981]. Similar double standards were even more strikingly shown by the fact that "Human rights violations in Communist countries . . . have never been placed on the agenda of the General Assembly or any of its committees . . ." [Bernstein 1984 January:24, 26]. Anti-Americanism and the associated double standards were also apparent in another international organization, the PEN club, which at its 1986 Congress passionately protested American intervention in Central America, while "no similar petition opposing Soviet presence in the region has emerged," as was pointed out by Aksyonov, the Soviet émigré writer [Freedman 1986].

Thus in the U.N. sympathy toward the Soviet Union complemented hostility toward the United States just as similar attitudes could often be found among the American critics of the United States. In the U.N. the Soviet Union was supported as a counterweight to the perceived aggressiveness and irresponsible power of the United States and, more generally, because the hostility toward the United States on the part of Third World elites found a natural ally in the hostility of the Soviet Union (once more the venerable principle "my enemies' enemies are my friends" was operating in both cases). Furthermore, as Michael Howard observed, "In many Third World countries there is clearly an instinctive sympathy with the Soviet Union, whose modern problems and experiences—its underdevelopment, its inefficiency, and its endemic corruption—are not entirely remote from their own" [Howard 1985:59].

Third World countries were also sympathetic toward the Soviet Union because it offered useful lessons (and often tangible assistance) in how to build durable police states without popular support ("'the export of revolution' means largely the export of the oppressive technology of government perfected by the Soviet apparatus, which certain local power elites are only too eager to take over" [Feher et al. 1983:274].

Third World elites also felt an affinity toward the Soviet Union on account of their belief in state socialism, often acquired during their youth while studying at Western universities and coming in contact with left-wing movements and ideas [see for example Handlin 1981:70–71]. Or, as Moynihan pointed out—referring in part to the influence of British socialism—"the new nations . . . adapted their international politics to the modes of the upper-class theorists and working class parties of their former masters" [Moynihan 1978:35]. Until recently many of the same Third World elites also had hoped that rapid modernization would be easier to achieve by following the Soviet model of industrialization. As of 1990 the leadership of the South African African National Congress movement continues to believe, with few reservations, in state ownership of industry.

But the major source of anti-Americanism in the U.N. has been less political or practical than ideological and psychological: it rests on a rejection of Western values and beliefs, on attributions of racism, colonialism, and neocolonialism. American (and Western) values as much as specific policies are under attack.

There is also a conviction among the Third World delegates ". . . that their own poverty is an outgrowth of their earlier domination by Western colonialism, and a suspicion of free institutions as both harmful to their own power and unsuitable to their . . . circumstances" [Bernstein 1984 January:22]. It is this sense of victimization which is the most potent factor in the generation and maintenance of anti-Americanism in the U.N. and the Third World at large; it also is the most effective stimulant and major component of nationalism. As Oscar Handlin noted, "Again and again stoked-up nationalism compensated for intolerable social deficiencies, enabling men and women to explain the difficulties of the present by the past sins of outsiders" [Handlin 1981:73].

Since the United States has not been a colonial power for a long time and since its support for decolonialization after World War II has been strong and public it is not self-evident why such a sense of victimization led to the inclusion of the United States among the victimizers.

Several explanations may be suggested. The United States has been associated and allied with Western countries which had been colonial powers; it also shares with them a cultural and political-institutional heritage and economic system, that is, capitalism. Most important, the

United States is the most powerful among Western nations, hence, in the eyes of Third World ideologues, the major repository of all sins of the West and protector of Western interests, economic and political. Yet anti-Americanism and anticolonialism—aroused by British, French, Dutch, or Portuguese colonialism—cannot be equated and must not be confused; the targets of anticolonialism were far more specific and clear-cut. The sense of victimization that is an integral part of Third World anti-Americanism feeds on grievances deeper and less easily remedied than the sins of colonialism. (The introduction of the concept of neocolonialism represents an effort to retain colonialism as a scapegoat for Third World difficulties even after colonialism proper passed away.)

The connections between Third World anti-Americanism and Third World nationalism explain why the U.N. has become such an important institutional forum for the articulation and venting of hostility toward the United States. In the first place the U.N. has become, paradoxically enough, and contrary to its original purposes, a major setting for the display and protection of nationalism, "national dignity," and national interest. Each nation, no matter how small, new, or powerless, was given a voice (and vote) in the U.N. and its representative could insist on being heard. A sense of national identity, often shallow and not rooted in historical continuity, could thus be sustained from the very fact of U.N. representation and participation.

For the many new nations which joined the U.N. an officially inculcated and inflamed nationalism became a vital means of attaining a measure of collective identity and social cohesion. Unlike the older nations in other parts of the world, many of those in the Third World were artificial, administrative creations with boundaries derived from those of former colonies, often without ethnic or linguistic homogeneity, countries with weak economies and untried political institutions. The notion of a national identity did not come readily and therefore required much symbolic reinforcement, mobilization, and prodding. As is always the case, social cohesion, a sense of community and unity, or group solidarity, could be forged more readily in opposition to something. The kinds of national bonds Isaiah Berlin best described often were simply not there: ". . . the conviction . . . that men belong to a particular human group, and that their way of life differs from that of others; that the characters of the individuals who compose the group are . . . defined in terms of common territory, customs, law, memories, beliefs, language, artistic and religious expression, social institutions, ways of life . . ." A further component of nationalism also needed strengthening, the belief that "the essential human unit in which man's nature is fully realised is not the individual, or a voluntary association . . . but the nation . . ." [Berlin 1979:345, 346]. All these components of nationalism tend to become more virulent when new nations seek to establish their identity and assert it publicly and globally, as they have done in the U.N.

It is a matter of historical record that the most intense modes of collective identification entailed in nationalism develop out of shared humiliation, deprivation, or oppression which a group of people suffer at the hands of some alien group or foreign power. It is out of such collective experiences, and its byproduct, a sense of victimization, that intense nationalism develops. Colonialism was an obvious source and form of such victimization as has been the poverty associated with colonialism, although poverty has persisted well after colonial rule and could not be blamed fully (if at all) on colonialism. (P. T. Bauer marshals many arguments indicating that Western responsibility and guilt for Third World poverty are largely groundless. [See for example Bauer 1976]).

It was not difficult for the new rulers of former colonies to realize that the persisting economic and political difficulties of their countries could be given explanations more satisfactory than those found in concepts such as levels of economic development, lack of capital formation, or traditional work ethics not especially conducive to rapid economic growth. For these elites of dubious legitimacy (most neither were elected nor gained power through some traditional selection process) "the ability to explain the persistence of slow development and poverty by external factors provides an important legitimizing function" [Luck and Fromuth in Rubinstein and Smith 1985:253]. The United States had become such an "external factor." In the words of Irving Louis Horowitz, anti-Americanism "provides an organizing and mobilizing force that serves a variety of purposes, not the least of which is the refusal of these nations to explain poor economic performance or political repression self-critically" [Horowitz in Rubinstein and Smith 1985:631]. Or, as Carlos Rangel, the Venezuelan sociologist, put it, "Countries frustrated by their lack of real power find in rhetoric a form of compensation that satisfies those who practice it and those who listen to them" [Rangel 1977:228–29].

A confluence of such scapegoating rhetoric (utilizing a sense of grievance) and an anti-capitalist conviction has come to provide an unusually potent form of nationalism. Again, as Berlin points out,

> ... even though nationalism seems ... a response to a wound inflicted upon a society, this, although it is a necessary, is not a sufficient cause of national self-assertion ... For that, something more is needed—namely a new vision of life with which the wounded society ... can identify themselves, around which they can gather and attempt to restore their collective life. [Berlin 1979:352–53]

This "new vision of life" coalesced around versions of Marxism-Leninism and especially the appeals of state socialism adapted to local conditions; it was bolstered by a glorification of the accomplishments and sufferings of the past vindicating the new national unity being pursued.

Third World nationalism has also been bolstered by its Western support and sympathetic understanding—a curious development since in the West the nationalism of Western nations has been in disrepute given its contribution to two world wars. Yet in a mixture of humility and condescension (such as also found on American campuses where discrimination by whites against blacks is not tolerated but black separatism is condoned and catered to) the nationalism of Third World nations is encouraged or at least treated with a good-natured tolerance by the Western powers. (Daniel Moynihan, one of the few American representatives in the U.N. who did not subscribe to these attitudes, advised that "It is time we grew out of our initial—not a little condescending—supersensitivity about the feelings of new nations" [Moynihan 1978:36]. George F. Kennan in turn was credited with the view that

> the new nations were of no consequence, and disagreeable as well . . . such that, as he once put it, quite the best policy toward the new nations would be to pay them no attention of any kind for three to four decades, after which they could be told that if they were ready to behave like grown-up countries they would be admitted to grown-up society. [Moynihan 1978:239]

Supersensitivity and solicitousness toward the new nations has not only been the fruit of Western guilt for the misdeeds of the past but also a reflection of Western interest in and nostalgia for what appears to many Westerners (and especially intellectuals) a form of authenticity and spiritual superiority possessed by the more traditional and impoverished societies of the Third World. Pascal Bruckner, the French author, wrote: "The developed countries . . . suspect that something they are eager to rediscover has been irrevocably lost. . . . [hence there is] a romantic flight to societies that had remained pure" and the hope that the Third World may offer some guidance to renewal. To be sure these attitudes predate the rise of Third World nationalism and the U.N.; they have been present in Western societies for a long time especially among members of the upper classes. They intensified and spread as have the discontents with the unanticipated byproducts of modernity. The gradual intensification of such sentiments over the last century has been testified to, among other things, by the rise of anthropology and a new respect for primitive art. Already at the beginning of this century the savage "became the original man, man without sin, and the West was called to renew itself through contact with him" [Bruckner 1986:85, 100, 101; see also Berger 1976:17].

The symbiotic relationship between Third World nationalism, anti-Western and anti-American attitudes on the one hand and Western encouragement of these attitudes on the other has also been nurtured by the anti-technological, anti-industrial elements in Western thought. If Third World countries were industrially, technologically underdeveloped and "unmodernized" perhaps it was for the better. Thus "a modern form of an ancient idea—the idea of Natural Man . . ." made its appearance once more, observed Walter Laqueur, reflecting on "third worldism" [Laqueur 1980:193].

The more the discontents of modernity spread (along with the continued discomfort over the sins of colonialization) the more the attitudes here sketched have contributed to both Third World anti-Westernism and nationalism (". . . the value attached to other cultures is in proportion to the disdain for our own . . ." [Bruckner 1986:147]).

A curiously ambivalent attitude toward poverty became incorporated into Third World nationalism that also fed into anti-Western and anti-American attitudes. On the one hand poverty was of course an affliction, bitterly resented and blamed on the West (". . . it was excessive consumption in the developed economies which was the true source of the problems of the underdeveloped nations . . ." [Moynihan 1975:36]). But on the other hand there has been a rediscovery of the notion of virtuous poverty and some sort of spiritual superiority associated with it. This too was an idea with ancient Western roots which met a renewed Western receptivity as the spiritual malaise of consumer societies unfolded. The rewards of virtuous poverty were seen as a simple life, unencumbered and uncorrupted by material possessions and aspirations and fortified by wholesome traditions; even an aesthetic superiority was sometimes ascribed to poverty. Gunter Grass, the famous German author and impassioned critic of the United States, provides graphic illustrations of these attitudes. Contemplating the streets of Calcutta, he wrote:

> If . . . you replaced that granite celebrating its flawless self, and set down instead one single slum hovel, as authentic as want has made it, right next to the glassy arrogance of the Deutsche Bank, beauty would at once be on the side of the hovel, and truth too . . . The mirrored art of all those palaces consecrated to money would fall to its knees, because the slum hovel . . . belongs to tomorrow. [Grass 1989:21]

Similar though less pronounced attitudes came to be associated with power; while its absence was decried and the new states strained to acquire some (by building up their military forces far beyond their means), powerlessness too, like poverty, was linked to innocence and virtue. Thus the Archbishop of Recife (Brazil) Dom Helder Camara spoke of ". . . Asia, Africa and Latin America represent[ing] a moral power without weapons" [Mead 1974:327]. Many of his successors and contemporaries embracing liberation theology were less certain about "moral power without weapons" as they rallied to the support of guerilla movements seeking social justice through violent means. On the other hand Dom Helder expressed mainstream Third World sentiments blaming the United States and its anticommunist policies for its own unpopularity and holding the U.S. responsible for Third World poverty and leftist radicalism. Thus

> Fidelismo . . . is the result of the want of understanding and sensibility on the part of the United States facing the struggle against underdevelopment and misery. And so is Catholic Marxism among Brazilian students. They are the creation of your anticommunism which is unable to understand our hunger and thirst for justice . . . I don't think Castro was a communist until he was made desperate. [Morgan 1967:26]

Since the West and the United States in particular are rich, and formerly in control of the areas involved, it takes little effort or imagination to hold them responsible for the low living standards and other afflictions of much of the Third World. (This simple idea was given more sophisticated expression in the "dependency theories" developed by Western critics of the West and the United States.) Third World spokesmen, not unlike those of some minority groups in the United States, became quite adept at making Western elites and public opinion feel guilty for the sins of the past and the poverty of the present. Bertrand Russell, among others, came to subscribe to this position, observing that "If today we are not hungry because the peoples of Africa, Asia, and Latin America die daily to keep us fed, we are degraded and corrupted by that unworthy plenty . . . a high standard of living in the West . . . is inexorably derived from brutality and exploitation . . ." [Russell 1967:114].

The contemporary efforts to rejuvenate Marxism have also sustained the notion of virtuous victim now incarnated in the poverty-stricken masses of the Third World: "The elevation of poor nations to the status of proletarians gave new life to a revolutionary principle . . . the simple fact of being poor was supposed to make particular peoples the carriers of progress" [Bruckner 1986:13]. While these ideas are easily traced to their Western roots and promoters, they were eagerly embraced by Third World elites and contributed to the forms of Third World nationalism (and anti-Americanism) here discussed. These ideas, and in particular the notion of the virtuous victim, have provided justification for the periodic demands in the U.N. for a global income redistribution involving the transfer of wealth from the West to the Third World.

The persistence of Third World nationalism, incorporating anti-Western and anti-American themes, can thus be explained by many circumstances. Among them is the very existence of the U.N. and other associated international organizations which provide a permanent forum and institutional invitation and incentive for venting these attitudes. A content analysis of U.N. speeches and documents would probably show that a large proportion of them consists of anti-Western rhetoric. The relationship between anti-Americanism and the U.N. may also be seen as an example of the connection between large bureaucracies and the perpetuation of political values and attitudes. (The National, as well as the World Council of Churches, discussed earlier, may be considered among such bureaucracies perpetuating many political attitudes for which mass support has declined.) It is probable that the anti-Americanism the U.N. continues to churn out is in part a function of its bureaucratic inertia: the perpetuation of anti-American rhetoric and resolutions has, for many delegates and employees, become a part of the occupational role. It should also be noted here that some authors believe that anti-Americanism in the U.N. is more prevalent in the General Assembly than in the Secretariat and the more functional and specialized agencies; they also find the anti-U.S. voting pattern not necessarily an expression of anti-Americanism but opposition to particular American policies [Luck and Fromuth 1985:240–41].

Third World nationalism and the associated anti-Western and anti-American attitudes also persist because the indigenous roots and grievances sustaining them remain largely intact; that is, economic, social, and political conditions in most Third World countries remain bleak and need continued explanation and rationalization. These attitudes are nurtured by the Western receptivity to them, in particular by an enduring legacy of guilt, replenished by the efforts of Western social critics. "The old relationship between colonizer and colonized is endlessly atoned for, and we search for after effects of imperialism everywhere" [Bruckner 1986:66; see also 67–70]. Carlos Rangel also noted:

> An astonishing number of Western opinion makers . . . are . . . persuaded that they and their fellow citizens owe their relative well-being to shameful abuses committed by their countries against the Third World. They also seem to feel that as a consequence, Western civilization is disqualified, fundamentally inhuman and corrupt; deserves to be punished . . . and . . . it cannot regain (or acquire for the first time) true humanity unless it surrenders politically and psychologically to the values and supposedly superior worldview of the "oppressed countries," exactly in the way that the bourgeoisie was to be saved by the proletariat in the Marxist morality play. [Rangel 1986:59–60]

Similar attitudes are in evidence on American campuses among those most vocal in their demand to abolish or dilute Western civilization or culture courses, as was discussed in Chapter 3.

The Western attitudes of cultural relativism enriched by such guilt also help to perpetuate Third World hostility by regarding it with bemused tolerance: "Our historical and relativist approach to alien cultures tempts us into an effort of comprehension which disarms our objections to what we believe we have understood" [Hartley 1989:75]. How far and wide these attitudes have spread is illustrated by the comments of two teachers in a small town in western Massachusetts back from two years of living in Lima, Peru: "The two say that the most important lesson they have learned . . . and will try to communicate to their students here, is that there is no better or worse from one country to another, just difference" [Reid 1989:12].

Third World resentment of the United States shows no signs of being assuaged by aid; in fact such aid is transformed into entitlement which allows the recipient to continue harboring hostility and avoiding gratitude.

Anti-Americanism in the U.N. has, curiously enough, much in common with the adversarial ethos that is found on many campuses in the United States. In both settings such an ethos has become entrenched, part of the dominant climate of opinion which is infrequently challenged and largely taken for granted. On the campuses as in the U.N. the rhetorical excesses have shifted the boundaries of what constitutes extremism and moderation, redefining the whole political spectrum and altering the quality of public discourse. Those unhappy with this state of affairs but disinclined to defy it publicly take comfort in dismissing it as mere "rhetoric." Daniel Moynihan, former U.N. delegate of the U.S., noted that often ". . . the disposition in Washington . . . was to dismiss exchanges in the General Assembly as 'mere words'" [Moynihan 1978:30]. He also observed that "three decades of habit and incentive created patterns of appeasement so profound as to seem wholly normal" [Moynihan 1975:43]. William F. Buckley, Jr., who in the early 1970s was a public member of the American delegation called "The U.N. . . . the most concentrated assault on moral reality in the history of free institutions, and it does not do to ignore that fact, or worse, to get used to it" [Quoted in Moynihan 1978:29].

Much of the anti-Western rhetoric in the U.N. rests on a tacit acceptance of Third World (and Soviet bloc) definitions of global victims and victimizers, not unlike much of campus discourse which rests on similarly questionable assumptions regarding the identity and attributes of victim and victimizer in the current domestic American context. Like the demands and complaints of minority groups on campuses, those put forth

by the Third World nations in the U.N. are treated with bemused tolerance and indulgence by the representatives of Western nations who are
at once demoralized and used to being ritualistically denounced.

It should be noted here that the U.N. is not the only international
organization permeated by aversion toward the United States and Western political and cultural values. The World Council of Churches
(WCC) equals and possibly exceeds the U.N. as a forum generating anti-
American rhetoric and resolutions. Like the U.N. its voting patterns are
strongly influenced by its Third World members and by the sympathy of
many Western delegations for such countries. More strongly than the
U.N., the WCC has also embraced anticapitalism and like the U.N. displays double standards regarding human rights violations in countries it
favors as opposed to countries it generally regards with disfavor and criticism [for documentation of such policies and attitudes see Lefever 1987
and Vermaat 1989].

Latin America

As noted earlier Third World anti-Americanism may be subdivided into
several regional or geographical varieties. Two of these, the Latin American and Arab, will be addressed below given their intensity and prominence.

Latin American anti-Americanism has the deepest historical roots as
it represents a response to past—and in some measure continued—American domination and influence of the region. As such it exemplifies
the "bent twig" model of nationalism proposed by Isaiah Berlin [Berlin
1972]. As the metaphor has it, such nationalism represents a violent reaction, or "lashing back," against collective humiliation, exploitation, and
mistreatment by a smaller or weaker country against this powerful, over-
bearing nation at whose hands the humiliations were suffered. American
military interventions (as in Cuba, the Dominican Republic, Grenada,
Guatemala, Mexico, Nicaragua, and Panama), economic dominance,
and, of late, cultural penetration provide the background against which
these sentiments developed. (Between 1905 and 1965 the U.S. Marines
landed twenty times in Caribbean countries [Rangel 1977:37].) As of
1967 the United States was still seen as "the single most powerful influence in Latin America" [West 1967:12]; by the late 1980s the same proposition has become far more questionable.

Thus it is hard to separate this variety of anti-Americanism from
nationalism and nationalistic self-assertion. As is the case with other
forms of nationalism not only the humiliations but the glories of the
past—real or imagined—play an important part, bolstering a sense of
national dignity and legitimacy, compensating for the deficiencies of the
present. This interpretation "sees our history since the Conquest as a

story of steady deterioration due to the intrusion of imperialism . . . It claims that our situation once supposedly authentic, autochthonous, happy and free, has since become false, alienated, unhappy and dependent. This is the myth of the Fall (of the noble savage) which can be reversed and avenged only by the virtuous revolutionary" [Rangel 1977:175].

Latin American anti-Americanism is also a classic example of the self-serving functions of these attitudes:

> There is an almost general belief in Latin America today that the United States has siphoned off the wealth which could have led to the Southern Hemisphere's development. *"They* are rich because *we* are poor; *we* are poor because *they* are rich." [Rangel 1977:44]

Such are the rudiments of the "dependency theory" popular with American social critics and students of Latin American affairs.

Latin American anti-Americanism is also of special interest because it mirrors, with special clarity, the attitudes of American academic intellectuals and specialists on Latin America and others who have been in the forefront of domestic academic criticism of the United States. At its annual meetings the Latin American Studies Association (LASA) regularly passes resolutions condemning U.S. foreign policy and supporting Marxist-Leninist guerillas in Latin America and governments such as those of Cuba and Sandinista Nicaragua; it even sent a suitably predisposed delegation to certify the probity of elections in Nicaragua [Cuzan 1985; Payne 1988].

Riordan Roett, director of Latin American Studies at Johns Hopkins University was persuaded that "No image—the big stick, big brother, banana republic—that has emerged from the critical literature can capture the enormity of American malevolence in that region" (the Caribbean and Central America, that is) [Roett in Thornton ed. 1988:71].

According to Irving Louis Horowitz, the influence of such voices has been crucial:

> It is dangerous and erroneous to view anti-Americanism as an indigenous phenomenon within Latin America. The broad masses of the region have shown little inclination to follow its Marxist intellectuals down such a primrose path. Present day anti-Americanism is ironically an attribute much more likely to be found and celebrated in elite intellectual circles of North America than in the hovels of Latin America. [Horowitz in Rubinstein and Smith 1985:56–57]

Robert Leiken's experiences led to the same conclusion: "Contrary to my expectations, workers and peasants in Latin America had little of the anti-Americanism of their mentors" [Collier and Horowitz, eds. 1989:30].

The issue of the relationship between the anti-Americanism of Americans and those abroad is not limited to Latin America; likewise the question of whether or not anti-Americanism on closer inspection reduces to an attitude concentrated among intellectuals is also of global relevance. It is not easy to trace precisely the transmission of ideas from one country or group to another, hence it would be difficult to establish conclusively that anti-Americanism in Latin America has arrived from the north and continues to be sustained by such transmissions. It is safer to suggest that the northern varieties have stimulated and fertilized an indigenous receptivity produced by the historical conditions noted above; in turn American social critics have been heartened by finding confirmation of their own critical views of their country in certain conditions and criticisms in Latin America.

Latin American anti-Americanism exemplifies the centrality of intellectuals. Probably more so than in most other regions anti-Americanism in Latin America is most fervently embraced by academic intellectuals and intertwined with not only nationalism but also Marxist-Leninist beliefs and more recently liberation theology.

Alan Riding defines the intellectual in Mexico as ". . . someone who signs anti-American protests, writes a weekly column in a newspaper and dreams of becoming an ambassador"—a definition that may also apply outside Mexico [Riding 1985:295–96]. Latin American universities, where subcultures of vocally alienated young people have flourished, have been the breeding ground of these attitudes. A six-country (Argentina, Brazil, Colombia, Ecuador, Mexico, and Venezuela) opinion survey from the early 70s found that "In all [these] countries, university students are least favorably inclined toward the United States" ["Image of the U.S." 1972:II].

Latin American universities have been characterized by an

> extremely low academic effectiveness, even as measured by the elementary yardsticks of actual teaching hours, total class attendance, the number of B.A.s or Ph.D.s in relation to enrollment, or . . . the number of graduate degrees granted in disciplines for which society has a real need and in which there are suitable employment opportunities. [Rangel 1977:211]

The influence of these intellectuals on public opinion and political life is greatly enhanced by the Latin American custom of giving intellectuals high positions in various government bureaucracies, including the foreign service.

There have been other indications that negative attitudes toward the United States in Latin America are not nearly as widespread as is often believed, despite the vocal and conspicuous expression of such sentiments among those who hold them. Thus for example one survey found that majorities ranging from 55 to 80% in Brazil, Colombia, Ecuador, Mexico, and Venezuela "expressed very much respect for the United States" ["Image of the U.S. . . ." 1972:32]. But as with domestic rejections of American society it may also be true in Latin America that what matters is not how many people hold these views but who they are. Even if majorities do not entertain negative conceptions of the United States, if important elite groups do, such perceptions and attitudes are more consequential.

Among the Latin American varieties *Mexican anti-Americanism* has been the most virulent and paradigmatic, encapsulating the attributes of the phenomenon over the whole region. (See also Chapter 9, a case study of such attitudes among academic intellectuals.) The intensity of Mexican anti-Americanism has obvious explanations including the spectacular asymmetry between the power, wealth, and global weight of these neighboring countries. Being neighbors provides endless opportunities for interaction and friction. The other seemingly inexhaustible source of resentment is historical: the United States fought several wars with Mexico, inflicted military defeat on it, and took half of its land. Nothing is more conducive to durable nationalistic resentment than military defeat and loss of territory especially when such defeat is not followed by rapid economic recovery and material prosperity, as was the case in Germany and Japan after World War II, both of whom suffered military defeat, lost territory, yet did not respond by an upsurge of nationalistic hostility. In those instances the blow to national pride and integrity was balanced by material prosperity and democratic political institutions successfully established after the war. Nationalism tends to flourish in countries which are undemocratic both institutionally and in their political culture.

As Alan Riding observed, Mexicans expect to be treated unfairly by the United States but they also feel that "Mexico is owed a historical debt by the United States which allows it to ignore American 'favors' and to rage against American offenses without costly reprisals" [Riding 1985:317].

Anti-Americanism in Mexico has become incorporated into the political culture, turned into a major source of legitimacy of the political system and a key component of national pride and identity. It is disseminated by the schools, politicians, and mass media. "Mexico's younger generation . . . learn almost as soon as they can read that the United States has actively interfered in Mexican affairs, not only in the nineteenth century but also as recently as the Revolution." Moreover, "the picture Mexican schoolchildren perceive is that the United States intrudes in matters which are none of its business and does so on the wrong side" [Pastor and Castaneda 1988:29, 30].

The authorities keep alive Mexican nationalism and the threats to it from the north by reminding the population of past indignities, for example by maintaining a National Museum of Interventions (it opened in 1981 in what used to be a Catholic monastery in Mexico City). Because of its deep roots in historical humiliation and loss Mexican anti-Americanism continues to operate as a major political myth and scapegoating mechanism.

The geographic proximity combined with the discrepancy between the power of the two nations exacerbates these attitudes. Octavio Paz revealingly described the Mexican view of the United States that so easily shades into anti-Americanism: ". . . the United States is a modern culture while we are still struggling with our past . . . the United States is the image of everything we are not . . . [it] is always present in our midst . . . its shadow falls on the whole continent. It is the shadow of a giant" [Paz 1972:67]. A former president of Mexico, Jose Lopez Portillo, said less charitably that Mexico "cannot work and be organized only to have its life blood drained off by the gravitational pull of the colossus of the North" [Grayson in Rubinstein and Smith 1985:41]. More matter of fact, Jorge Castaneda, the Mexican author and specialist on U.S.-Mexican relations, wrote:

> The United States plays too large a role in my country's life, domestic and international. In economic matters, in cultural and psychological terms and even in . . . foreign policy, the American presence is overwhelming. It obsesses Mexico, drives us to distraction . . . [Pastor and Castaneda 1988:13]

The Mexican hostility and resentment are colored and complicated by ambivalence and envy; again as Paz put it, "the titan had become the enemy of our identity and the secret model of what we wanted to be" [Paz 1972:68]. Such ambivalence is not unique to Mexico but it is more pronounced there for the historical and geographic reasons noted above; in other Third World countries too contempt and envy, feelings of superiority and inferiority alternate. This ambivalence finds characteristic expression in the rejection and ridicule of American materialism, depersonalization, competitiveness, individualism, and coldness that combines with a furtive or open admiration of American power, prosperity, knowhow, efficiency, and consumer goods. The Mexican middle classes in particular have become devotees of American styles of consumption, recreational activities, and mass media. American-type shopping centers, suburbs, amusement parks, fast-food chains, advertising, and television programs have become hugely popular, stimulating in turn more protest against such influences on the part of the guardians of Mexican tradition and culture. A telling illustration of such American influences has been the fact that of some 20,000 movies shown in Mexico between 1930 and 1985, 53% were American, 27% from other countries, and only 20% Mexican [Pastor and Castaneda 1988:339].

Mexican critics of the American cultural penetration would agree with a Chilean commentator who claimed that "The content of almost all these [television] programs is meant to stupefy our people, to keep them within the imperialistic framework, to make them consumers" [Humbert 1970:39]. Perhaps more typically, resentment and apprehension in Latin America are aroused not so much by belief in such outright conspiratorial designs (carried by cultural penetration or infiltration) but more by the idea of homogenization synonymous with Americanization. A columnist in Venezuela wrote:

> Americans indeed have a mania for uniformity . . . Everywhere are the same gas stations, the same supermarkets, the same food, the same churches, the same press, the same people. The American cultural mosaic is in fact a monolith, a monochrome, a monotone. All flat and of one piece. . . . Little by little all the nations of the world . . . are becoming more like one another in their Americanization. The Pepsi Cola plant . . . is no less than a great cultural outpost, a contemporary frontier abbey converting the barbarians . . .
> . . . Yet this Yankee might does not represent colonization by force but voluntary subjugation . . . [Montaner 1976:39]

A Mexican survey found that "85% of children questioned recognized the trademark of a brand of potato chips but only 65% identified Mexico's national emblem. In another poll only 14% recognized the Monument to the Revolution in Mexico City, but 70% identified a brand of cornflakes" [Riding 1982]—findings that cannot but inflame nationalistic anger and indignation, especially among the educated.

Significantly, Jorge Castaneda argues that "Even the modern Mexican middle classes continue to harbor deep feelings of resentment and even anger at the United States. Their penchant for American lifestyles and products should not be mistaken for an ebbing of traditional suspicion and hostility toward the United States" [Pastor and Castaneda 1988:16]. It is of some interest that Castaneda (the Mexican author of parts of the volume) believes that his American co-author, Pastor, underestimates the intensity of anti-Americanism in Mexico. If so it would not be the first time that American authors played down this unpleasant phenomenon.

The coexistence of conflicting attitudes toward the United States is even more clearly indicated by the huge number of Mexicans anxious to live or work here and the millions who have done so already. A national survey conducted in Mexico in 1986 by the *New York Times* found that 40% of the respondents would live in the United States given the opportunity. Half of them had a close relative who moved to the United States and 34% had visited the United States for various reasons. Some 48% of those questioned held a favorable view of the government of the United States; 27% unfavorable; 25% had no opinion; 59% perceived the relations between Mexico and the U.S. as "friendly," 7% "very friendly," 30% as "unfriendly," and 3% "very unfriendly" [Stockton 1988:A8]. Such findings suggest that anti-Americanism, or certain dimensions of it, is not a majority attitude.

Feelings of ambivalence also exist in the smaller countries of Central America, indeed much of Latin America. It was noted for instance that "Anti-Americanism has been and will remain a feature of Central American life, yet it has always coexisted with profound admiration and respect for the United States and a partiality for the American life-style" [Langley in Thornton ed. 1988:78]. Such partiality however is unlikely to translate into pro-American politics [Ibid.:87].

A survey conducted in 1983 in Mexico City commissioned by the U.S. Information Agency also documents the ambivalence noted above. Only 18% of the respondents defined "dependency on the U.S." among the most pressing problems of Mexico; 70% had a favorable opinion of the U.S.; it was also at the top among the countries "with which Mexico should work most closely for economic reasons," chosen by 68%; it was at the top (56%) among the countries with which Mexico "should develop the closest political relationship" (Cuba was chosen by a mere 5%; the Soviet Union by 23%); the U.S. followed Japan as the second preferred source of foreign investment in Mexico (54% and 40%). At the same time 66% believed that Mexico was treated unfairly by the United States and 55% that the economic policies of the U.S. hurt Mexico ["The Climate of Opinion in Mexico City" 1983]. More negative attitudes were found in another opinion poll reported by the Mexican newspaper *Excelsior* in 1986, which showed ". . . a high degree of anti-Americanism among those questioned: 47% said their opinion of the United States had worsened over the past five years; 60% felt that the United States was a disagreeable or unpleasant neighbor and 59% considered it to be 'an enemy country.'" Another poll by *Excelsior* found that 84% of the respondents deemed a U.S. Senate hearing on Mexican-American relations a form of interference in Mexican domestic affairs; 86% believed its goal was "to subjugate the government of Mexico even more to the interests of the United States" [Pastor and Castaneda 1988:37–38, 72].

It is thus not surprising that an extreme sensitivity to perceived slights to national honor and dignity often calls forth strong anti-American sentiment. In the mid-1960s "the Mexican government banned Mr. Frank

Sinatra from going there on a holiday ... He had appeared in a film called *Marriage on the Rocks* which, according to the government, 'presented a false image of a filthy Mexican border town where quickie divorces and marriages are performed by a shabby mayor'" [West 1967:262]. More recently Mexican politicians and intellectuals called "hostile and insulting" a drainage ditch project on the border near San Diego that was designed both to handle toxic wastes and to deter illegal immigrants and drug traffickers, and demanded that the project be halted [Rohter 1989]. Mexican national dignity was still more seriously offended when the CIA director described Mexico City as the world's espionage capital and called the Mexican republic "fragile." In an indignant response the Mexican newspaper *El Dia* noted that if so, most spies were American, and if Mexico was fragile it "is due completely to our creditors mostly from the U.S.—and the economic policy of the U.S. ... " The paper averred that "Foreign powers have invaded us many times and have stolen more than half our territory, but they have never been able to take away our pride and dignity" ["CIA Chief's Phrases" 1989:31].

When the Carter administration decided against buying Mexican natural gas in 1977 "for the mundane reason of overpricing," this too was defined as a personal humiliation by the president of Mexico. And when an American ambassador quoted a Mexican author to the effect that the Mexican political system resembled in some respects a monarchy, it provoked "collective indignation" and was said to constitute "'apparent efforts to destabilize Mexico through mocking criticism,'" according to the then presidential candidate Lopez Portillo [Riding 1985:320, 325].

There was also a widespread feeling that Mexico was insulted when its President De la Madrid in 1984 was not met on arrival to the United States by the Secretary of State, although the State Department, mindful of Mexican sensitivity, "prepared a list of all those leaders which had been met at the airport by the Deputy Secretary of State, including the British and West German Prime Ministers" [Pastor and Castaneda 1988:80; also 63–64]. Mexicans also tend to attribute sinister significance to the size of the United States diplomatic mission in Mexico (the largest embassy staff in the world supplemented by four major and four smaller consular offices) whereas it could also be seen as an expression of American interest in U.S.-Mexican relations.

Mexican sensitivity to foreign criticism was also eloquently conveyed in a taped discussion this author had with a group of Mexican intellectuals in Mexico City in 1984. One of them offered this metaphor regarding the issue of foreign criticism: "I know that I have a retarded child but you cannot say that I have a retarded child" [Hollander 1984]. Generally speaking, Mexicans often become offended when foreigners hold opinions about matters Mexican and find it hard to separate such expressions of opinion from interference in Mexican affairs [see also Pastor and Castenada 1988:73, 75].

Not only do many Mexicans (especially intellectuals and politicians) blame the United States for past military aggression, continued economic exploitation, cultural subversion, and other forms of interventions in its affairs, the United States was also blamed for the drought in 1980. According to Mexican sources, American aircraft diverted hurricanes from the Mexican shore "thereby contributing to the country's worst drought in 20 years" [Grayson in Rubinstein and Smith 1985:41]. For three weeks Mexican newspapers reported in front-page headlines this new American interference in Mexican internal affairs, one of them suggesting that the hurricanes were diverted to protect Florida's tourism [Pastor and Castaneda 1988:91]. Almost equally startling was the response of President Echeverria to students demonstrating against him at the Autonomous University of Mexico in 1975: "Echeverria responded by shaking his fist at the students and shouting at them the darkest accusation in the repertoire of Latin-American politicians today: 'Youngsters manipulated by the CIA!'" [Rangel 1977:59]. (In Panama it was believed that the United States had assassinated General Torrijos. Graham Greene reported that a Panamanian official included in the evidence for this supposition "two articles . . . containing attacks on Omar [Torrijos] by President Reagan." Even for Greene, himself inclined to this belief, "it seemed flimsy evidence" [Greene 1984:213].)

More recently an American correspondent in Mexico

> began to notice a scattering of bizarre stories in the respectable press. It was reported that Mexican children routinely were being kidnapped, spirited across the U.S. border, and murdered for their vital organs, which were then transplanted into sick American children with rich parents . . . The dead babies story has been traveling the globe for almost four years. Regional versions have materialized in at least fifty countries . . . Millions of educated and uneducated people—particularly in Latin America—firmly believe that the United States has created, in essence, an international network of child murderers, backed by gruesome teams of medical butchers. [Schrieberg 1990:12]

It should be noted that in this instance the Soviet Union in 1987 also joined in "pushing the story, promoting it in Soviet and East bloc newspapers and magazines as well as in Communist media outlets around the world" [Ibid.]. It certainly went well with earlier Soviet disinformation campaigns asserting that "the American military created the AIDS virus and is working on an 'ethnic weapon' to kill non-whites" [Ibid.].

Thus the baby kidnapping myths fed on several sources especially in Latin America: the traditional suspicion toward the United States and readiness to believe that it would murderously exploit Latin American people; the old tradition of child murder used in inter-group hate-mongering (as in the accusation of Jews killing gentile children for religious reasons); the suspicion toward modern science (organ transplants); and, in this case, the organized Soviet contribution.

Mexicans tend equate American presence with influence and interference; they also find the American readiness to propose various remedies to Mexican problems irritating and condescending [Pastor and Castaneda 1988:61–62, 83, 195–96].

Although greatly sharpened by the historical and geographic circumstances noted above, the major accusations entailed in Mexican anti-Americanism are similar to those found in all Latin American anti-Americanism, or for that matter in corresponding sentiments throughout the Third World. It is not only that the United States is an economically predatory, imperialistic nation but it is also ready to export, indeed impose its own values—along with its consumer goods—on other nations. Mexican anti-Americanism is prototypical of all such attitudes, being rooted in a sense of injured national dignity, weakness, and a durable sense of historical victimization.

The Middle East

Anti-Americanism in Arab countries is comparable in intensity and virulence to that found in Latin America, including Mexico. Its sources are different through, since the United States, thousands of miles distant, was hardly a major presence and did not historically dominate Arab countries. The chief and most tangible source of Arab hostility to the United States is due to the existence of Israel, which the United States helped to create and has continued to support militarily, economically, and politically ever since. Thus to a large degree anti-Americanism represents a transfer of hatred from Israel to the United States since these two countries are closely allied and identified with one another [see also Hameed 1984]. Another source of friction peculiar to Arab countries is the presence and position of American oil companies involved in oil production.

More recently, roughly since the 1970s, the hostility to the United States was given new impetus by the Islamic revival, a countermodernizing force *par excellence*. This new type of anti-Americanism goes beyond the protective attitudes toward an indigenous culture or way of life threatened by modernity; this is anti-Americanism that is religiously grounded and legitimated, the only type of anti-Americanism nurtured by religious values and motives.

Anti-Americanism in Arab countries is also stimulated by the more universal attitudes noted earlier: the need for nationalistic cohesion most readily provided by the image of a powerful external enemy, a "Great

Satan" as the United States has come to be called more recently and most frequently by the late Ayatollah Khomeni of Iran. Arab countries, constantly at odds with each other, ruled by elites of shaky legitimacy, most of them recent creations of their former Western colonial masters (Britain and France) or the United Nations, also needed the type of political cohesion which the existence of an endlessly denounced alien, intrusive force can provide. Moreover several of these countries could dwell nostalgically on a great past but point to few achievements in the present or recent past. Such contrasts between the glories of the past and the underachievement and weakness of the present provide the best conditions for an impassioned nationalism to germinate.

Arab nationalism and anti-Americanism sometimes exceeds even its Latin American counterparts in its preoccupation with national dignity and sensitivity to insult to national dignity or what is perceived as such. Hence the inimitable quality of Arab political rhetoric:

> hurling insults at the once invincible and powerful was as good as defeating them militarily or overhauling them intellectually. Why should they not dance in the streets deliriously when they hear the young leader of Arab nationalism publicly tell mighty America: "We shall cut the tongue of anyone who dares to insult us . . . we do not accept humiliation. We are people whose dignity cannot be sacrificed." [Dawisha in Rubinstein and Smith 1985:77]

The popularity of Saddam Hussein in the Arab world since his occupation of Kuwait in August 1990 is also closely related to anti-American and anti-Western sentiments and the preoccupation with dignity. A visitor to the Middle East wrote:

> The dominant impression . . . is of an Arab world seething with resentment against the U.S., barely able to contain its glee at the prospect of an Arab leader bold enough to defy the greatest power on earth . . .
> Arab intellectuals . . . are still rooting for him to succeed in his Kuwait campaign at least to the point of humbling the colossus that now confronts him . . .
> . . . today's Arabs yearn desperately for the dignity and vindication that a Saddam Hussein seems to offer. [Goldin 1990]

These sources of Hussein's popularity are very similar to those Castro used to enjoy among Latin American intellectuals and critics of the United States; he too was credited with "standing up" to the colossus (see also Chapter 9).

Another result of the nationalistic preoccupation with dignity, strength, and respect is that the weakness or perceived weakness of the adversary fuels and further vindicates hostility toward it. Hence the United States inspires hostility not only when it occupies the powerful position of the "Great Satan" but also when it displays weakness or hesitation. According to an American observer of these Arab attitudes,

> Anti-Americanism results from, among other things, lack of respect. Defeat is an orphan, and American bumbling and inability to stay the course in Lebanon have reflected severely on American prestige and popularity. That makes it easier to be anti-American and to act out one's hostility. [Parker in Thornton ed. 1988:52]

The point is more generally applicable: a global anti-Americanism stimulated by destructive American interference in Vietnam was greatly intensified by the ultimate failure of the United States to accomplish its political and military objectives.

By contrast, the Soviet Union did not project an image of hesitation and weakness (at least until the late 1980s) and its interference into the affairs of other nations was determined and successful. Hardly ever have Soviet citizens been taken hostage and on the rare occasion when they were, they were speedily released due to forceful Soviet response and a clear determination not to be influenced by concern for the lives of a few hostages. Correspondingly the Soviet Union did not inspire the type of hostility gleefully reserved for the United States for its failures to act as a great power. Indeed a major difference in Third World attitudes toward the United States and the Soviet Union has been the lack of respect toward the United States and respect toward the Soviet Union.

It has also been suggested that Arab anti-Americanism is a response not merely to the grievances noted above (the pro-Israeli policies of the United States and its role as a general modernizing agent) but specifically to anti-Arab attitudes and stereotypes in the United States including "the dehumanization of the Arabs and Muslims in general . . . more often than not, intentionally propagated by the U.S. mass media, U.S. public figures and U.S. scholars" [Hamid in Rubinstein and Smith 1985:110, see also 112–13].

Anti-American sentiments are likely to persist in the foreseeable future in much of the Third World and especially in Latin America and the Middle East. Both are areas seething with nationalistic grievances, both are exposed in different ways to American power and influence, and both are grappling with the very mixed blessings of the uneven penetration of modernity.

8
Western Europe

I am one of the rare European intellectuals who has never been anti-American.
Eugene Ionescu, 1985

I

European anti-Americanism has so far been limited to the Western half of Europe, to the countries outside what used to be the Soviet bloc. The absence of these attitudes in Eastern Europe helps us to understand their presence elsewhere.

The nationalism of Eastern European nations, although quite intense, has never been nurtured by a threatening image of the United States and thus could not stimulate anti-Americanism. The anticapitalistic ingredients of anti-Americanism have been similarly absent: Eastern Europeans—intellectuals and non-intellectuals—having been subjected to an official anticapitalism since the end of World War II (when the Soviet Union gained political control of the region) harbor no such sentiments. At last and most important the United States and "the West" are for the most part inseparable entities and held in high esteem by those who sought to cast off Soviet political, economic, and cultural influences.

If and insofar as East Europeans need scapegoats and simple explanations for their frustrations and collective misfortunes, it is, for obvious reasons, the Soviet Union and their own former pro-Soviet leaders which are the most inviting targets.

To be sure there has been official anti-Americanism in the region promoted by the local agit-prop institutions but—not unlike other forms of official propaganda—it had little impact on the popular attitudes. While East Europeans have been critical of specific American policies (or the lack of them) and in particular of insufficient American assertiveness in global politics and hesitation in confronting the Soviet Union, on the whole the United States, its political system, standard of living, and technological and scientific accomplishments have been widely and steadfastly admired.

By the mid-1980s there had been minor stirrings of the moral equivalence attitude in Eastern Europe as well. To the citizens of these small nations the imagery of "superpowers" had particular meaning since East Europeans could justifiably feel victimized by one (the USSR) and abandoned by the other (the U.S.). The moral equivalence approach also allowed East European intellectuals to see themselves as more autonomous and independent of each power bloc. George Konrad of Hungary has been among those occasionally expressing the East European version of moral equivalence [Konrad 1984]. Vaclav Havel of Czechoslovakia came close to the same outlook when he said that ". . . Soviet totalitarianism is an extreme manifestation—a strange, cruel and dangerous species—of a deep-seated problem that finds equal expression in advanced Western society. It is a trend toward impersonal power and rule by megamachines that escape human control" [Havel 1987:24].

Following the sweeping political changes of 1989–90 anti-Americanism may yet arise and intensify in Eastern Europe as the American cultural and economic penetration of the region gets under way and as the first halting steps reintroducing capitalism are unlikely to resolve rapidly the difficulties of these economies. Learning from more reliable sources about the social and cultural problems of the United States may also prepare the ground for at least milder forms of anti-Americanism. But it has also been argued that these processes will have a more limited impact in the former communist states. Martin Esslin wrote:

> . . . the pop culture of the West, in all its manifestations, has attained an immense interest and popularity . . . among the broad masses of the Eastern-bloc countries. . . . This may be depressing to a Western intellectual. But the fact [is] that American pop culture, the product of the market economy in the field of entertainment—and thus, like it or not, a truly democratic expression of popular taste—has conquered the world . . .
>
> . . . That the Western world is in the grip of spiritual malaise, expressed in drug culture, alcoholism, crime and mental *accidie* is a much more serious problem for the Eastern intellectuals to come to grips with . . . The [Eastern] intellectual elites will . . . have to come to terms with the fading of their over-idealized picture of the West—in so far as they entertained such an image. [Esslin 1990:59–60; see also Urban 1989]

Unlike East Europeans, those in the western half of Europe did not have the kind of historical experiences (including the presence of Soviet troops) that would have predisposed them to sympathize with the major global adversary of the Soviet Union, the United States. Western Europe since World War II—and in the course of the establishment of NATO— has come under American military, political, and cultural influence. On the other hand, unlike Mexico and some other Latin American countries,

Western Europe has not been mistreated, humiliated, or exploited by the United States in the course of this relationship. (To be sure, some Western European critics would reject this proposition, as will be seen below.) And although the United States through the Marshall Plan and other aid programs provided substantial economic assistance to Western Europe, such aid did not become a source of resentment as it had in some Third World countries. Nor has Western European nationalism been as intense as corresponding attitudes in much of the Third World; the nations of Western Europe did not have to establish a sense of national identity by stressing what separated them from another nation, by cultivating the virtuous victim image. Conditions in Western Europe were far from wretched and did not call for a scapegoating mythology, of external explanations of collective misfortunes. Thus at first glance conditions for the development of anti-Americanism have not been especially auspicious in Western Europe. Nonetheless, as Paul Theroux, the American writer living in London, observed, the Europeans "feel put upon. There is a tremendous amount of anti-Americanism in Europe. There is a sense that they are in the front lines of a war that doesn't have to be fought" [Welles 1986].

Such assessments notwithstanding it has to be noted at the outset that the anti-Americanism in Western Europe, as in Latin America, has not been, generally speaking, the attitude of majorities but rather of substantial minorities and especially of important elite groups. A U.S. Information Agency Report examining "long-term trends" in these matters concluded in 1983 that ". . . favorable general opinion of the U.S. continued to outweigh unfavorable sentiment by considerable margins . . . [and] expressions of avowed anti-Americanism . . . ranged from only 14% in West Germany to 23% in Great Britain [Crespi 1983:1].

Anti-Americanism is a response to a variety of circumstances which need not include gross insults to national dignity, bullying by American corporations, or the presence of restless and impoverished masses. In Western Europe anti-Americanism arose as a blend of envy of American power, contempt for American culture, and apprehension about American military might and presence. As in other parts of the world the anti-capitalism of intellectuals has also been a steady contributing factor. Former Prime Minister Papandreou of Greece, mentioned earlier, is an exemplar of an intellectual (college professor) turned into anti-American politician animated by a sturdy anticapitalism. It was his belief that "On a global scale, capitalism has to be held responsible for the more nefarious ills of human existence" [Papandreou 1987:52]. Having spent decades of his life in the United States in academic settings such as Harvard and Berkeley, Papandreou personifies the cross-fertilization and confluence of the domestic and foreign critiques of the United States.

A perception of the United States as a custodian of immensely destructive nuclear weapons and a conception of cultural immaturity and political irresponsibility were the major ingredients of Western European anti-Americanism. In the early and mid-1980s in particular "fear rather than resentment . . . generated by apocalyptic visions of nuclear disaster" [Godson 1986] became a major factor in the hostility toward the United States. According to a British observer, "the American as a philistine has been supplanted by the image of the American as a monster" who threatens world peace [Walden 1989]. President Reagan and his symbolic identification with the wild West and cowboys has made a substantial contribution to such conceptions of the United States ["We Love You, We Love You Not" [1986].

For such reasons since the early 1980s anti-Americanism and a professed dread of nuclear weapons and war have become virtually inseparable in Western Europe. The peace movements have been important agents of anti-Americanism attracting both those fearful of nuclear war and others unfavorably predisposed toward the United States (as well as their own social systems) on other grounds as well. Data collected by the British sociologist Frank Parkin in the mid-1960s make clear, for example, that the majority of the supporters of the British Campaign for Nuclear Disarmament (CND) were highly critical of existing social arrangements and institutions in Britain, indeed estranged from dominant social values. These "middle-class radicals" found in the peace movement a new vehicle for criticizing and indicting their social system. The very possession of nuclear weapons and the apparent willingness to use them (embodied in the doctrine of deterrence) provided vindication of their hostility and mistrust of their political system, the military policies of NATO, and by implication the United States. Most of these early CND supporters were also supporters of the Labor Party and state socialism [Parkin 1968].

A wishful thinking about the Soviet Union and determination to avert one's eyes from its contribution to the arms race and potential nuclear conflict were among the characteristics of these movements. Thirteen years after Parkin's book appeared an American observer of the British political scene noted that "the 'better-red-than-dead' argument is being put forward again with the same naivete and relentlessness that marked its use 20 years ago . . . like the feelings then, anti-nuclear sentiment today is heavily tinged with anti-Americanism" [Gelb 1981:4].

Highly moralistic movements such as the peace and antinuclear movements of Western Europe (and for that matter their American counterparts) need a symbol of evil (or the profane) to juxtapose to their lofty moral strivings; the United States came to meet this need for reasons already alluded to and further examined below.

II

An article on American air bases in Britain published in *Sanity,* a publication of the British Campaign for Nuclear Disarmament, displays the characteristic components of anti-Americanism in Britain and in Western Europe as a whole:

> To the observer outside the fences, a major U.S. airbase is a strange, different, alien and menacing world . . . [unlike other military bases presumably warm, friendly and inviting?—P.H.]
>
> In the officer's mess at Mildenhall, a champagne brunch is laid on . . . a young pilot clad in a very zippy flying suit festooned with bright badges, flashes, emblems, decals, numbers and bars, sits at a table covered with fine linen eating a giant cream puff with a silver fork. He has champagne there and three other types of cream cake and, as he quaffs away at both, he is deeply absorbed in the pages of a child's comic. [Campbell 1984:16]

This little sketch of the American barbarian is almost a classic of the genre. There he is, the uncouth American oblivious to fine linen and silver fork, in the heart of Britain where he clearly doesn't belong. He is the stereotypical childlike American absorbed in comics and dressed in an equally childlike manner. Not only does he offend good taste but this immature creature wields awesome power: he flies the machines of destruction. The article also informs the reader that U.S. military personnel are beyond the reach of British law, that life on the U.S. bases is not unlike life "in the middle of Kansas" except for the abundance of cheap luxuries available in Britain for the Americans. It is, in short, a depiction of American presence in England calculated to provoke both nationalistic indignation about the overfed barbarians luxuriating on British soil and apprehension about their power.

From the pamphlet entitled "Greenham Women Against Cruise Missiles" (published in the United States by the Center for Constitutional Rights, set up by the well-known American radical social critics William Kunstler and Peter Weiss [see also Collier and Horowitz 1989:182]), we learn that "Britain was becoming a nuclear dump for a foreign power," that inside the base at Greenham Common

> is a small American town in which the U.S. dollar is the currency and British criminal law counts for little," [that U.S. troops] intervene around the world . . . stifling . . . the rights of people to determine their own destinies. In a world armed for nuclear war this tendency to intervention has an added sinister dimension. . . . The U.S. policy of developing and deploying more and more sophisticated nuclear weapons feeds the atmosphere of confrontation and distrust.

The vast increases in American military expenditures between 1982 and 1987, we are told, were taking place against a background of growing unemployment ("highest since the Great Depression") and drastic cuts in vital services ["Greenham Women" n.d.:4, 9, 10]. Illustrative of the survival of the spirit of the protest movements of the 1960s "in spring of 1983 . . . 20 women climbed on to the base dressed in teddy bear outfits and coated with honey . . ." [Ibid.:6]. These protests also had in common with similar events in the 1960s an air of festive exuberance, a quest for community and new spiritual values unrelated to the manifest purpose of the specific event [see also Bethel 1983].

While the appeals of such offended nationalism were put to good use by left-wing groups, injured national pride has a broad constituency in Britain as elsewhere. According to an American observer these attitudes are linked to "nationalist fears that this former imperial power is in danger of becoming a client state to a superpower and envy stemming from the unmistakable decline of British power and influence. Both the nationalistic fears and envy contribute to a general sense that Washington rides roughshod over British concerns and interests . . ." [Lelyveld 1986].

Such concerns and an image of the trigger-happy irresponsibility of the United States help to explain the outburst of protest and criticism that followed the American bombing of Libya in 1986 in which British air bases were used. (There is a great similarity between the foreign sensitivity to the use of American power and the outrage of domestic social critics when such power is used.) The incident inflamed nationalistic passion and anti-American rhetoric: ". . . opinion polls . . . have consistently shown that a high proportion of Britons have come to believe that the United States in general and President Reagan in particular are inclined to the reckless use of military power." Such suspicions of the United States and especially of its military forces and intelligence gathering agencies were also strikingly expressed in the conspiratorial theory of a Fellow of Magdalen College at Oxford who proposed on the basis of a highly speculative scenario that "the U.S. bears the major responsibility for putting KAL 007 [the Korean airliner downed by Soviet planes in 1983] at risk and thus for the deaths of its passengers" [Johnson 1984:26]. As noted earlier this was also a belief readily adopted by American social critics.

Moreover "mistrust of the United States [in Britain] has remained almost constant . . ." A Gallup poll of January 1983 found that "70% of those questioned had little, very little, or no confidence at all 'in the ability of the United States to deal wisely with present day problems.'" A survey taken a few months before the Libyan raid found that "54% of those questioned could agree to the propostion that the United States was either as great a threat to world peace as the Soviet Union or a worse threat" [Lelyveld 1986].

According to the *Sunday Times* of London, "Anti-Americanism has become strongly rooted in British attitudes . . ." A poll taken for the same newspaper found that "most British people resent the extent of American influence on British industry, the economy, defense policy and television . . ." There were also other findings similar to those cited above concerning American indifference to British interests and the dubious qualifications of President Reagan ["British Anti-Americanism" 1986].

English anti-Americanism has other roots as well, as it feeds on historical resentment especially among the upper classes and intellectuals including figures such as Bertrand Russell, Graham Greene, and E. P. Thompson, each of whom illustrates types of aversion to the United States and American culture. In the case of Russell, personal grievance (the loss of an appointment at City College in New York in 1940 due to political pressure) combined with other objections to American policies.

Russell, who after World War II favored American nuclear blackmail of the Soviet Union, first moved to a moral equivalence position that was followed by a most embittered hostility to the United States. Russell's anti-Americanism illuminates the affinity between hostility to the United States and the moral equivalence approach; Russell, as many other critics of the United States, began with a seemingly dispassionate equation of the two superpowers which gave way to a strongly felt condemnation of the Untied States. He held the United States responsible for an impending nuclear holocaust and became one of the most impassioned critics of the American role in the Vietnam war. (These attitudes might have been inflamed by Ralph Schoeneman, an unusually estranged American in his entourage.) Late in life Russell reached the conclusion that "the American government was genocidal, the police efforts pretty much on par with the camp guards at Auschwitz and black rioting a justified response to a campaign of extermination" [Goodman 1988]. His inclination to compare the United States or aspects of American life with those of Nazi Germany was longstanding. Thus in 1939 the faculty meetings at the University of California in Los Angeles and the behavior of the president of that institution "reminded [him] of a meeting of the Reichstag under Hitler [Russell 1968:218]. In 1951, well before the Vietnam war, he wrote in the *Manchester Guardian* that the United States was as much a police state as Germany under Hitler and the Soviet Union under Stalin, and that in the United States as in those countries

> nobody ventured to pass a political remark without first looking behind the door to make sure no one was listening . . . if by some misfortune you were

to quote with approval some remark by Jefferson you would probably lose your job and perhaps find yourself behind the bars. . . . Any Englishman going to America at the present time has the strange experience of a population subjected to a reign of terror and always obliged to think twice before giving utterance to any serious conviction. [Russell 1951]

He also bet Malcolm Muggeridge five pounds that Senator Joe McCarthy would become president of the United States [Hook 1987:367]. During the Korean war he came to accept that the United States waged germ warfare [Hook 1987:368]. He averred that "On a purely statistical basis, [Prime Minister Harold] Macmillan and [John F.] Kennedy are about fifty times as wicked as Hitler" [Johnson 1988:209].

In a preface to a book by Corliss Lamont (a vehement critic of the United States and lifelong admirer of the Soviet Union [see Hollander 1988:97–101], Russell wrote: "Anybody who goes so far as to support equal rights to colored people, or to say good word for the U.N. is liable to a visit by officers of the FBI and threatened with blacklisting and consequent inability to earn a living." Elsewhere he explained these developments by noting that "The object of this persecution has been to impose upon the United States an acceptance of capitalism . . . After a time . . . the persecution of dissidents . . . became a career in itself and more and more victims were necessary to feed the inquisition and its victim-hungry administrators." He also pointed out that "There are now [in 1965] . . . autonomous armies within the United States, armed to [the] teeth to fight anyone who shows any tendency to differ with them politically." Unhappily, as he saw it, "irrational Americans are armed and rational Americans are not." Capitalism was to blame for both domestic repression and the involvement in Vietman: "Every food store and every petrol station in America requires, under capitalism, the perpetuation of war production." American soldiers were sent to Vietnam "to protect the riches of a few men in the United States . . ." Addressing the G.I.s on a Hanoi ("National Liberation Front") broadcast in 1966 he continued: "You are being used to enrich a few industrialists whose profits depend on taking the natural resources from other countries . . ." [Feinberg and Kasrils eds. 1983:339, 356, 358, 387, 389, 396, 400, 401].

During the Vietnam war his anti-Americanism rose to a paroxysm prompting him to assert that the United States waged war in Vietnam in a manner indistinguishable from that of the Nazis in Eastern Europe and that

The United States today is a force for suffering, reaction and counter-revolution the world over. Wherever people are hungry and exploited, wherever they are oppressed and humiliated, the agency of this evil exists with the support and approval of the United States . . . [The U.S. intervened in Vietnam] . . . to protect the continued control over the wealth of the region by American capitalists . . . . . . people have come to see the men who control the United States Government as brutal bullies, acting in their own economic interests and exterminating any people foolhardy enough to struggle against this naked exploitation and aggression. [Russell 1967:112, 117, 118]

Russell's anti-Americanism belongs to the most extreme, bizarre, and irrational type and unexpectedly enough appears to be fueled by the same kind of raging scapegoating impulses which make Mexicans believe that the United States was responsible for drought by manipulating clouds. Astonishingly in Russell's case the scapegoating impulse overwhelms an exceptional intellect and concern for precise language. On the other hand, if Orwell was right, intellectuals are no more immune to absurd beliefs than others and may even be more susceptible given a certain deficit of common sense. Perhaps Russell's attitudes—as those of many other intellectuals—were best explained by Paul Johnson: "When his sense of justice was outraged and his emotions aroused, his respect for accuracy collapsed" [Johnson 1988:203]. In short Russell's anti-Americanism illustrates the compatibility of these attitudes—in their purest, most extreme form—with an otherwise highly rational disposition.

The manifest justification of Russell's anti-Americanism was the conviction that the United States and its aggressive, irresponsible leaders were poised to destroy the world. During the Cuban missile crisis in 1962 he said, "It seems likely that within a week you will all be dead to please American madmen . . ." [Johnson 1988:212]. Unlike other embittered critics of the United States, Russell was not anti-Western, or especially preoccupied with capitalism (although he was contemptuous of commerce and business as one would expect given his social background). He could not be classified as an "estranged intellectual" in his own society or accused of being resentful for lacking in recognition—his anti-Americanism was not an extension of either of these attitudes. Instead, according to Paul Johnson, Russell's anti-Americanism "was propelled by old-fashioned British pride and patriotism of an upper-class kind, contempt for upstarts and counter-jumpers, as well as liberal-progressive hatred for the world's largest capitalist state" [Johnson 1988:210].

Graham Greene's anti-Americanism was equally robust if less shrill, also rooted in some measure in an English upper-class background but more discernibly nurtured by an idiosyncratic sympathy for certain embodiments of the victim-underdog (which included at different times the communist guerillas in Malaya, Castro's Cuba, communist Vietnam, General Omar Torrijos of Panama, the Irish Republican Army, and most recently communist Nicaragua). Unlike Russell, who was capable of scathing criticism of the Soviet system, Greene rarely displayed critical sentiment in that direction. Greene even managed to admire Kim Philby, the master spy who found refuge in the Soviet Union [Pryce-Jones 1989]. In a letter to the *London Times* critical of the Soviet treatment of writers Yuli Daniel and Andrei Sinyavsky, Greene felt compelled to make the point that:

> If I had to choose between life in the Soviet Union and life in the United States I would certainly choose the Soviet Union, just as I would choose life in Cuba to life in those southern American republics . . . dominated by their northern neighbor, or life in North Vietnam to life in South Vietnam. But the greater affection one feels for any country the more one is driven to protest against any failure of justice there. [Greene 1967]

The latter point was made to explain his criticism of the treatment of these writers.

Greene's anti-Americanism (like Russell's) had a pronounced social-cultural thrust; he disliked not merely the policies of the United States but also Americans as a group; he regarded them as crude, coarse, undignified, and materialistic [Pryce-Jones 1989] and was contemptuous of what he took to be the American national character [Greene 1955]. He was appalled by Donald Duck figures in Panamanian villages and wished for their destruction [Greene 1984:93].

Earlier in his life as film critic he made reference to "the eternal adolescence of the American mind, to which . . . morality means keeping Mother's Day and looking after the kid sister's purity . . . the same adolescent features, plump, smug, sentimental, ready for easy tear and hearty laugh and the fraternity yell. What use in pretending that with these allies it was ever possible to fight for civilization?" On his first visit to the United States he was oppressed by "the terrifying weight of this consumer society" [Finn 1990:25]. Given his estrangement from English society, his disposition to a romantic view of non-industrial people, and his selective identification with victim groups, Greene's anti-Americanism was a more or less natural development, counterpart and complement of his attraction to colorful Third World countries and the spirit of adventure he associated with them.

More unexpectedly, Greene—unlike other Western social critics harboring similar political attitudes—included Panama among the countries he embraced among those victimized by the United States. His love affair with Panama and friendship with the late General Torrijos, its leader, unfolded against the background of a matter-of-course anti-Americanism. An all-too-discernible element in Greene's attitudes was his hero-worship of the general—a disposition with ample precedent among Western intellectuals similarly impressed by other powerful leaders and their way of life, as for example George Bernard Shaw was by Stalin, Edgar Snow by Mao, Sartre by Castro, and Gunter Grass by Tomas Borge of Nicaragua, among others. Although Torrijos was Greene's particular favorite, he also revered and considered among his friends a variety of Marxist guerilla leaders in Central America, including Borge and Salvador Cayetano of El Salvador, and he also maintained cordial personal relations with Castro [Greene 1984:154, 158, 181–82, 191, 221, 236].

In the case of E. P. Thompson, the British historian and guru of anti-nuclear movements, the anti-American impulse was more controlled, indeed masked. As noted earlier Thompson insisted on being a friend of the United States and fondly recalled his American visits and academic connections. Nonetheless his writings make clear that he regards the United States as the major culprit for the perilous state of the world and especially the menace of nuclear war. He wrote:

> The United States seems to me to be more dangerous and provocative in its general military and diplomatic strategies, which press around the Soviet Union with menancing bases. It is in Washington, rather than Moscow, that scenarios are dreamed up for theater wars; and it is in America that the alchemists of superkill, the clever technologists of . . . ultimate weapons, press forward . . . [Thompson and Smith 1981:40]

Unlike Russell or Greene, Thompson regards himself as a Marxist, hence his anti-Americanism is also reliably nurtured and reinforced by an abiding concern with the ineradicable evils of capitalism (". . . I know that the beast [capitalism] is not changed: it is held in the fragile but well-tempered chains of our own watchfulness and actions" [Thompson 1978:392]).

A fairly typical British, indeed more generally Western European cultural anti-Americanism, is also captured in the musings of a fictional English character, a journalist living in New York: "Like more than one Englishman in New York, he looked upon Americans as hopeless children whom Providence had perversely provided with this great swollen fat fowl of a Continent. Any way to relieve them of their riches . . . was sporting . . . since they would only squander it in some tasteless and useless fashion . . ." [Wolfe 1987:164].

III

West German anti-Americanism is a richer and more complex variety than the British and a more integral part of a far more profoundly critical view of Western values and institutions. It is probably also more wide-spread and probably more deeply and uniformly entrenched among intellectuals than is the case in Britain.

The intensity of West German anti-Americanism derives from several sources. Its most proximate cause is probably the overwhelming and long-standing American presence—several hundred thousand troops, their families, and numerous large military bases—bound to offend national-istic sensibilities. The combination of this large military presence with the geographical location of the German Federal Republic has made the country especially vulnerable in the event of an armed conflict between NATO and the Warsaw Pact countries. This may also best explain why Germany produced the most active and widely supported peace move-ment in Western Europe and the most intense popular apprehensions not only of nuclear weapons but also nuclear power generation. Nor is it a coincidence that Germany boasts of the largest and best organized polit-ical force in Europe—the Greens—dedicated to unilateral disarmament, neutralism, pacificism, unqualified rejection of nuclear power, an uncom-promising environmentalism, and anti-Americanism [see also Herf in Laqueur and Hunter 1985:366–69].

As in the case of the Campaign for Nuclear Disarmament in England noted earlier, the antinuclear concerns of the Greens are only a part of a far broader anti-establishmentarian agenda and disposition, of a deep and diffuse aversion to modern industrial society, and particularly its cap-italist version. Over three million voters gave electoral support to the Greens in recent years, two-thirds of them under thirty, and the move-ment, transformed into a party, had considerable impact on West Ger-man politics. "All parties in the Federal Republic have become a little bit Green," according to a German academic [Bering-Jensen 1988:34, 35]. The spread of these attitudes was illustrated by a protest demonstration against then Secretary of State Haig in Berlin 1983 organized by the Youth Wings of the Social Democratic and Free Democratic parties, fea-turing "A photo montage of the Secretary of State . . . with his hand over his heart, as if taking an oath, while napalm deformed children stood at his side." Contingents of homosexuals, anarchists, and artists were among the active participants in the demonstration. No reference was made to Soviet contributions to the arms race or world problems; "All the guilt was America's" [Vinocur 1981 September]. Identical attitudes were in evidence at a mock trial organized by the Green party in Nurenberg, called a "Tribunal Against First Strike and Mass Destruction Weapons in East and West." Once more hardly any criticism was directed at the Soviet Union. Symbolizing the affinity between the American and foreign critics of the United States was the presence of Daniel Ellsberg and Philip

Agee at this "tribunal," not surprisingly they accused the United States and its allies of preparing genocide against humanity [Markham 1983].

The influence of the hardcore left in Germany (such as the Greens) has been somewhat similar to the impact of the less organized American protest movements of the 60s which left behind a huge adversarial culture and gave new meanings to concepts such as liberal, conservative, and moderate, although did not give rise to a functioning political party.

In Germany anti-Americanism and critiques of German society have been especially closely integrated in a framework of anti-industrialism, rejection of materialism, affluence, and consumerism, and a generalized questioning of the moral foundation of the Western world. According to a thoughtful German writer,

> . . . a profound change of consciousness . . . took place [in the 60s and 70s] . . . Western industrial society began to question itself . . . The tangible expression of this change was the wave of protest movements that, kindled by a variety of causes, burst upon the political life of many Western countries, the Federal Republic in particular, toward the end of the sixties. . . . It was not until the rapid emergence of the ecological movement in the seventies that industrial society's protest against itself found an authentic form. A new existential sense arose . . . of living in the shadow of impending catastrophe . . . a fear of the self-destructive power of a civilization created by human beings but no longer controlled by them; a . . . feeling that . . . the established order and existing institutions had nothing more to offer . . .
> . . . a disposition to protest, to reject, to say no to a world to which one no longer feels one belongs . . . [emerged].
> [The rapid rise of the ecological and peace movement reflected] the self-doubt, the self-disgust by which Western industrial society has been gripped for a decade and a half. As far as the Federal Republic is concerned, the peace movement could never have become what it has if from the late sixties a politically active subculture of protest had not developed that was receptive to any cause able to spark resistance against existing reality. [Kielmansegg in Laqueur and Hunter 1985:321, 322, 323]

Thus the peace movement in West Germany drew its strength from three groups, each of which had its own motives for aversion to the United States and what it stood for: the environmentalists, the nuclear pacifists, and the traditional left.

In Germany too American cultural influences broadly defined were among the factors provoking anti-American sentiments. In many ways West Germany has been the most Americanized of all European countries and its national identity most threatened by the multiplicity of

American influences (and the widespread receptivity toward them), hence there has been an especially virulent reaction against these processes. As John Vinocur, for many years a *New York Times* correspondent in Germany and France, put it, ". . . in West Germany . . . the idea that the United States is in the way of the country's finding a truer, purer identity now has . . . institutionalized roots" [Vinocur 1984:62].

At last there is the factor of the memories of Nazism and the unease among the younger generations over its widespread past acceptance by the German people. Attitudes of guilt, shame, and anger over such a past indirectly contribute to a vocal anti-Americanism once the United States is identified as a source and symbol of political evil in our times. Guilt over such a past deepens outrage over perceived political injustice in the present and lends a compensatory intensity and moral fervor to public protest and social criticism. Besides the intellectuals the other group particularly susceptible to these attitudes has been the clergy: "Haunted by its failure to resist Nazism, wounded by its lost resonance in national life, the clergy has sought, perhaps unconsciously, to run ahead of all the 'progressive' trends in West Germany over recent years" [Vinocur 1981 November:122]. If so their social and political activism resemble those of the mainline churches in the United States, although they did not have to atone for Nazism.

Guilt over the past is also likely to play a part in embracing the current symbols of victimization: the Third World in general, Marxist guerillas in Latin America, Palestinian Arabs, and for some even members of the violent terrorist groups which were more active in the 1960s and 70s, such as the Bader-Meinhof gang.

But there is yet another possible connection between certain apsects of Nazism and anti-Americanism: both represent in some measure protests against modernity and a nostalgia for a more authentic and fulfilling past. If for the Nazis the Jews were the most visible and reprehensible agents of modernity (and capitalism), for the recent generation of left-wing social crtitics it is the United States, which represents corresponding unwelcome social forces.

West German detractors of the United States excelled in the moral equation of the Superpowers—an equation that in their case too tilted toward the Soviet Union ostensibly because of a belief that the United States has become a more dangerous, aggressive, irresponsible, and erratic country, even one with "the most perfect police apparatus in history, probably more perfect than the Russians'," according to the playwright Rolf Hochhuth [Hochhuth 1970:26]. Whereas the Soviet Union is more stable, peace-loving, and predictable. As Vinocur wrote, ". . . a picture has been created of the Russians as difficult but basically reasonable, while the Americans have been seen as living with the injustice, decomposition and confusion of Vietnam, Watergate and the Carter Presidency" [Vinocur 1981 July and November].

Another interpretation of this attitude is fear: the Soviet Union is more feared and therefore to be propitiated whereas the United States can be attacked and vilified without adverse effects. More than that, the United States is more responsive to protest and pressure than is the Soviet Union. (As a Dutch journalist put it: "If people shout at the United States, it is because only the United States might listen " [Caarten 1981].)

It is especially in its incarnation as trigger-happy warmonger that the United States has been most frequently attacked in West Germany (as in much of Western Europe). A cover page of *Stern*, "the country's largest general interest magazine, showed an American nuclear missile piercing the heart of a dove of peace" [Vinocur 1981 July]. Earlier *Stern* has written about the American sense of mission "degenerat[ing] into naked imperialism" [Liedtke 1976:32]. Prominent West German politicians also freely expressed such attitudes. Oskar Lafontaine, deputy co-chairman of the SPD (Social Democratic party), called the U.S. "an aggressor nation." Rudolf Hartnung, chairman of the youth organization of the SPD, accused the United States of "ideologically inspired genocide" in Central America, among other places. Another SPD politician, state legislator Jurgen Busack, had this to say: "The war-mongers and international arsonists do not govern in the Kremlin. They govern in Washington. The USA must lie, cheat and deceive in an effort to thwart resistance to its insane foreign policy adventures. The USA is headed for war" [Keithly 1990:68–69].

Thus among the vanguard of the West German detractors of the United States even the pretense of moral equivalence has been abandoned. At the time of the Soviet invasion of Afghanistan Gunter Grass, perhaps the most vocal among the well-known German critics of the United States, insisted that "the United States was disqualified from making moral judgements about anything" [Vinocur 1984:73]. He also drew a parallel between resistance to the deployment of American medium-range missiles (in 1983) and resistance to the rise of Nazi power [Markham 1985]. For Grass, as for many other critics, the rejection of the United States and rejection of his own society became intertwined; he detested West German society primarily because it was becoming Americanized, that is, materialistic, greedy, and polluted physically as well as spiritually. Grass also typified the Western intellectual fiercely critical of and cynical toward his own society but remarkably credulous of the claims of political systems he regards as victims of the West. This was well illustrated in his reactions to the tour of a model prison in Nicaragua (chaperoned by police minister Tomas Borge) quoted earlier when he rhapsodized about the influence of Christ on the policies of the Marxist-Leninist authorities [Grass in Diskin ed. 1983:246–47].

Grass was by no means unique in holding the United States responsible for the danger of nuclear war and more generally the ills of the world. "A petition called the Krefeld Appeal, sponsored by left-wing organizations, including the Communist Party, judges the United States to be the sole cause of global insecurity . . . It has been signed by 1.5 million people." Those who signed included other prominent intellectuals such as Noble Prize-winning writer Heinrich Boll, as well as popular entertainers [Vinocur 1981 November:116].

German aversion toward the United States had less political expressions as well. "A full-page advertisement in a West German national magazine . . . said, right in the first paragraph, that 'almost nothing that is sold or used in our restaurants comes from America.' Their enterprise was German, the advertisers insisted, with German interests, German management, German workers and German suppliers" [Vinocur 1981 July]. Ironically the advertisement was placed by McDonald's, which had been attacked in the official newspaper of the Social Democratic Party for its "primitive American nourishment," for "recreating USA hegemony," and for "gastronomic conservativism" [Ibid.]. A soft-drink manufacturer, Afri Cola, likewise sought to increase sales by advertising its non-American origin [Vinocur 1984:60].

For many Italians too McDonald's became a symbol of American cultural penetration, and the opening of one of its restaurants in Rome in 1986 was greeted with widespread protest:

> several thousand people rallied in the picturesque piazza. . . . The gathering organized by the "Save Rome" committee featured Italian singers, actors and politicians speaking out against the coming of the all-beef hamburger. . . . They proclaimed the "degradation of Rome" and the "Americanization" of Italian culture if McDonald's was allowed to continue doing business here . . . a local politician called McDonald's "the principal cause of degradation of the ancient Roman streets" . . . [Suro 1986]

The German rejection of and mistrust toward the United States (and the associated neutralism and pacifism) have been especially pronounced among the younger generation. Surveys show that the younger the people the less they support NATO. Moreover, "The image of the United States beset by economic decline, limited social opportunities, excessive materialism and given to interventionism . . . has increased rapidly in recent years especially among young adults." Some 38% of the postwar generation regards these domestic problems as serious enough to disqualify the United States from a leading role in world affairs [Kramer and Yago 1982].

West German anti-Americanism—and its counterparts in the rest of Western Europe—have been closely associated with the political movements and beliefs of the 1960s, although, as noted earlier, it had more distant roots as well. According to a German commentator the direct stimulants of German (and West European) anti-Americanism included the civil-rights conflict in the United States, Vietnam, and Watergate. At the same time "to many Germans all three events had a very special meaning, for they seemed to vindicate those who liked to whitewash their national honor by pointing at the shortcomings of others" [Siemon-Netto 1981:47]. The German sociologist Erwin Scheuch made the same point a decade earlier [Scheuch 1970:19]. If so the burden of the past helps us to understand the particular relish with which some Germans dwell on the flaws of the United States.

As in most other countries, in West Germany too the well-defined and clearly articulated anti-Americanism, as distinct from ambivalence, has been more characteristic of intellectuals than the general public. This should be no cause for surprise given the general propensity of Western intellectuals to be in some degree estranged from their societies and suspicious of capitalism and of the United States, regarded as the mainstay of the global status quo. As was pointed out earlier these general predispositions have been strengthened in Germany by the problems of the past, an exposed geographic-military position, and a tradition of romantic antimodernism. The outpouring of warmth toward Gorbachev on his visit to West Germany in 1989 and survey results showing that he was far more favorably regarded than President Reagan are further indications of anti-American sentiment.

Anti-Americanism occasionally also provided the psychological basis of more specific and damaging actions against the United States and the Western alliance as in the case of Arne Treholt, the Norwegian spy for the Soviet Union. He was described as a member of the student generation that "grew up on anti-Americanism because of the Vietnam War" and it was also observed that "his strongest ideology was anti-Americanism." Like many foes of the United States he too succumbed to rationalizing Soviet misconduct, "saying that Moscow was forced to protect its borders because of constant threats from the West" [Nordheimer 1984]. In turn a group of Western European peace activists touring the United States insisted that the whole "idea of an enemy must be removed. . . . The world must be built on human trust." This suggestion apparently did not apply to the U.S. as one member of the same delegation voiced dark suspicions of the United States, claiming that the missiles the United States was going to install in Western Europe "would be aimed at the Middle East to 'defend the petrol routes' for American business" [Hartman 1984].

IV

French anti-Americanism, greatly diminished in the 1980s, used to be intense throughout the entire post-World War II period and especially during the 1960s and 70s. It was closely associated with the influence of the French Communist party, sympathy toward the Soviet Union, and the attitudes and beliefs of a largely monolithic stratum of leftist intellectuals. Its most prominent feature was a disdain for American culture. It is this cultural anti-Americanism that has remained the most pronounced among the manifestations of French anti-Americanism, persisting even at a time when its political roots atrophied.

The decline of French anti-Americanism that combined both nationalistic and Old Leftist elements may be traced to two factors. The first was de Gaulle's assertion of French political independence culminating in France leaving NATO [see also Gnesotto in Laqueur and Hunter 1985:246–47]. The second was the upsurge of anti-Soviet feeling resulting apparently from the publication of the works of Solzhenitsyn and the Soviet intervention in Afghanistan. The progressive discreditation of the Soviet Union among French intellectuals and public opinion went hand in hand with the dwindling influence and popularity of the French Communist party.

There have been no American troops or military bases in France since 1967 and no American or NATO nuclear weapons. (Nor has there been public opposition to the creation of a French nuclear force.) The departure of American troops removed a major insult to national dignity that could nourish anti-Americanism. But the departure of American troops was welcome on other grounds as well, reflecting once more the cultural roots of these sentiments. Chronicling the closure of the largest American base in France, an Italian newspaper wrote:

> . . . what will Americans leave behind after fifteen years of residence? . . . Inside the battlements, the American way of life; outside the mysterious, mythic, disturbing entity which is France, where they speak a language so incomprehensible it isn't even worthwhile trying to learn it. "They don't want to learn anything at all, not how to drink wine, not even to eat as we do," says one French lady. . . . "And then some of them complain that in fifteen years not one person in Chateauroux has invited them to dinner. How can we ask them to dinner? They have never had onion soup, steak à la madeira; and if at the end of the dinner, you offer cognac they ask for soda pop!" . . .
>
> Only the electricity and sewers [on the base] are French . . .
>
> All the rest—conditioned, frozen, cellophaned and boxed—comes from the States. Even the bread . . .

The truth is, the Chateaurousians do not like the Americans. They nourish the primordial feelings of the cultivated poor confronted by the rich barbarian. [Monicelli 1966:34, 35, 36]

A French journalist summed it up: "The idea that American values are taking over . . . is, rightly, unbearable to the French" [Suffert 1967:19].

Aversion to American cultural influences has survived from the 1960s and in the 1980s became a particular concern of France's Minister of Culture Jack Lang. At a UNESCO conference in Mexico in 1982 he took a leading role in attacking American cultural imperialism:

The dominance of American pop songs, movie and TV serials, he said, was due to "an immense empire of profit." He called for "real cultural resistance, a real crusade against—let's call things by their name—this financial and intellectual imperialism which no longer grabs territory, or rarely, but grabs consciousness, ways of thinking, ways of living . . . We must act if tomorrow we don't want to be nothing but the sandwich board of the multinationals." [Lewis 1982]

A reporter noted that these remarks were made a week after Lang had a cordial visit with Castro in Cuba [Vinocur 1983].

Similar critiques of American culture were also a major topic at an international conference in Paris organized by the French government in 1983 which sought "to explore the role of culture in resolving the world's economic crisis." Besides the theme of cultural imperialism (there was particular consternation about the popularity of the televsion serial *Dallas*) the United States was criticized for the lack of federal support for the arts. Susan Sontag said, "In our country we don't have a Minister of Culture, and if we did, we wouldn't have someone like Jack Lang. We'd have Clint Eastwood"—a remark which once more illustrates the confluence of the foreign stereotypes of the United States with the criticism of its native intellectuals [Dionne 1983]. In turn "Lang declared war on 'the invasion of fabricated images, prefabricated music, and standardized productions which are destroying national cultures." Even an Israeli participant complained about American cultural domination of Israel [Echikson 1983].

In a letter to the *New York Times* several American participants defended the Paris conference against what they regarded as unfair criticism and pointed out that if *Dallas* was a preoccupation at the conference it was because it "became a symbol of the sort of cultural levelling that leads to the overwhelming of local cultures by worldwide film and television distribution networks" [Bishop, Mailer, Sontag, and Styron 1983]. The aforementioned were impressed by the fact that Mitterand, "an intellectual himself," addressed them, and contrasted wistfully the munificence of the French government in matters cultural to their own—a longstanding grievance of estranged intellectuals in the United States.

The penetration of American cultural products is also troublesome for the conservative voices in France. The conservative magazine *Le Point* asked: "Is European culture in danger, and is American culture supplanting it?" The paper also expressed concern over the impact of American satellite transmissions, the dominant position of two American news agencies, the Associated Press and United Press International, and the prevalence of American television programs among those imported from abroad [Billard 1985:34]. In 1989 France led the campaign (headed by Minister Jack Lang) to impose quotas on the number of American television programs shown in Western Europe "to stop the advance of . . . American cultural imperialism and to preserve European values" [Greenhouse 1989]. In late 1990 ". . . 11 socialist deputies attributed France's troubles to its 'progressive Americanization,' which they described as growing individualism, the impoverishment of the state, the omnipotence of television, untempered consumer spending and the emerging power of lobbies" [Riding 1990].

Western European concern with the effects of the American media and television in particular was not limited to France. Small countries such as Iceland were also apprehensive at least from the early 60s. According to a Danish newspaper,

> In the past two and a half years American TV has become an increasingly serious problem. There are no native TV stations . . . The American TV station . . . threatens not only the movie houses in Iceland but even more important, the Symphony Orchestra, the National Theatre and the local legitimate theatres . . . In March 1964 sixty intellectuals and professors, all pro-NATO, sent an appeal . . . urging that the station's broadcasting be limited to the base itself. [Magnusson 1965:308]

One year later an Icelandic newspaper wrote: "The most troublesome issue today in Icelandic cultural life is bound up with the fact that a great foreign power has pushed its way into Icelandic society with the help of the most powerful propaganda instrument ever invented. I refer to the American television station which has brought a more mischievous influence into our national life than we have ever experienced before"[Lindal 1966:241–42].

Despite the concern with American cultural penetration, anti-Americanism in France is at a far lower level than in Germany, Britain, the

Netherlands, and some of the Nordic countries. Moreover in France "the most *pro-American* group consisted of those between the ages of 15 and 25." In another poll of French students 56% thought that European values were superior to Soviet values but only 26% believed that they were superior to American ones; 44% thought they were equal to American, and close to a quarter regarded American values to be superior [Dionne 1984].

Variations in Western European anti-Americanism can be traced to either the anti-Americanism of the Old Left (linked usually to established communist parties) or to the generation of the 1960s that used to be known as the New Left. The anti-Americanism of the former was a direct outgrowth of its support for the Soviet Union and Soviet policies. A former Jesuit, Francisco Garcia Salve, and organizer of a pro-Soviet communist party in Spain, conceded that ". . . the Soviet Union is capable of making mistakes but . . . American imperialism is far worse than all of the Soviet Union's mistakes" [Markham 1982]. Mikis Theodorakis, the popular Greek composer and longtime supporter of the Soviet Union (and the pro-Soviet Greek communist party), explained his pro-Soviet attitudes by the quaint argument that "The Western worker strives hard and eventually gets the so-called modern comforts. But he is never free of anguish, unlike the Eastern European worker who has all the basic needs in life secured for him by the state" [Anastasi 1979].

While supporters of the New Left also disdained "the so-called modern comforts" which the deluded masses of the West strove for, such attitudes did not rest on pro-Soviet beliefs. The New Left was attracted to the postulate of moral equivalence between the Superpowers and inclined to a benefit-of-doubt approach toward the Soviet Union, perceived as the weaker and more peace-loving of the two and consequently the lesser evil. It was the more advanced technology and the capitalist, consumer economy of the United States that alienated the New Left and allowed it to be marginally more sympathetic toward the Soviet Union (even before Gorbachev).

It is among the puzzling aspects of anti-Americanism in Western Europe that France and Italy, two Catholic countries, apparently display the least, whereas all the Protestant nations seem to have higher levels of it in conjunction with far more popular and active peace movements and other adversarial groups. Perhaps these attitudes are interrelated; in the Protestant countries of Western Europe there may in general be higher expectations regarding public rectitude, the body politic, and the attainability of lofty moral principles. The frustration of such aspirations may in turn contribute to higher levels of moral indignation and criticism directed in equal measure at domestic institutions, the evils of capitalism, and the United States.

The cultural anti-Americanism of Western Europe, stimulated by the public receptivity toward American mass culture, has its counterparts around the globe. A Jamaican cultural adviser to the government complained, not without reason, about American "cultural penetration" of the entire Caribbean region in which the media played an "ominous" part, enhanced of late by cable television and satellite dishes. Such developments in his view posed "the threat of conscious conditioning of important segments of the population away from a Caribbean sensibility" [Singh 1986]. More recently an Australian author noted that Australian television features more than 60 American programs a week, that "Australia has by far the highest number of McDonald's restaurants per capita outside North America," and, more generally speaking, "Australia has thus become an advanced laboratory of the accelerating global homogenization . . . The U.S. has come to hold . . . an insidiously elevated place in the Australian consciousness" [Sheehan 1990].

If this is the case we must further inquire into the sources of receptivity toward things American which are apparently as deep as the animosity and ambivalence the same receptivity and its visible results provoke.

V

The preceding limited regional overview of anti-Americanism focused mainly on the symptoms and more accessible explanations of the phenomenon. Less was said about the deeper sources of each particular variety although it was clear enough that anti-Americanism has regional patterns and causes. The Third World variety is different from what we find in Western Europe and further distinctions can be made within both Western Europe and the Third World. Arab anti-Americanism is nurtured for the most part by different motives and grievances than Latin American. Even within the Arab world different variables sustain the same phenomenon: American support of Israel is one thing, the modernizing influences emanating from the United States another. The latter alarm and antagonize all those who seek to protect the Islamic heritage, far removed from the immediacy of the Arab-Israeli conflict. Anti-American and anti-Israeli sentiment do of course converge since both countries are justifiably seen as agents of modernization and Westernization.

Western Europeans are less concerned with the American subversion of their traditional religious beliefs but are far more apprehensive of their countries becoming potential nuclear battlefields due to American military strategy, while the Arabs are not preoccupied with the threat of nuclear annihilation or blame the United States for it. Nor is it easy to detect either in Arab countries or in much of Latin America the kind of romantic anti-industrialism which gives rise to a militant environmentalism that flourishes in Western Europe and is rich in anti-American themes and implications.

Since anti-Americanism has many forms and originates in many disparate conditions and parts of the world it would be unrealistic to attempt to propose a single theory or explanation. What holds its varieties together is that it is a response to some kind of collective or group frustration or grievance which finds relief in holding the United States (or a particular aspect of it) responsible for the grievances in question.

We may get closer to the core of animosity the United States arouses by examining a few characteristic personal statements of prominent critics which amplify and highlight the essential attributes of the anti-American mindset and impulse.

Jan Morris, the British author, wrote:

> Something snapped in me, and I faced up to a conviction I had been trying to stifle for years: the reluctant and terrible conviction that the greatest threat to the peace of humanity is the United States . . .
>
> . . . I can no longer stomach America's insidious meddlings across the face of the world . . . wherever I go I find myself more and more repelled by the apparently insatiable American urge to interfere in other people's business . . .
>
> . . . nowadays I hardly believe a word official America says. I didn't believe your spokesmen about the Korean airliner . . . about Grenada and certainly do not believe them about Soviet intentions . . . the Soviets are less likely to trigger a World War III than you are yourselves.
>
> Of course you are both paranoiac—two ideologically stunted giants . . . whose preposterous dinosauran posturings menace the survival of everyone. But the Russians have cause to be paranoiac! . . . they are a grand and tragic nation . . .
>
> But you! The most powerful, the most enviable, the richest, the most fortunate nation of the world. You have no excuse for paranoia . . . [Morris 1983]

Morris provides an impressive summary of the major grievances against the United States shared by many intellectuals around the globe. As other impassioned critics she evidently harbored excessively high expectations of the United States which no country can live up to. Disclaiming anti-Americanism bolsters the credibility of the critic: since anti-Americanism implies a prejudiced state of mind, the critic hastens to make clear that he is free of it. The critic may even confess—as in this case—that she brings herself with great reluctance and pain to criticize this great country.

Morris is enraged because she reached the conclusion that the United States is led by dangerous maniacs motivated by a wholly irrational fear and loathing of the Soviet Union and communism, ready to destroy the planet she lives on. She is also disturbed by what she sees as the omnipresence of the United States. She cannot resist two venerable stereotypes of all things American: "vulgar and naïve." Equally revealing and stereotyped is her metaphor of the dinosaur: a huge, awesomely powerful creature guided by a pea-brain, just as the frightening American military and technological colossus is inadequately controlled and guided by a suitable intellect and values. (This imagery has been popular with other critics of the United States as well; another English author called American society "one of the least reflective on earth," adding that "many foreigners . . . behold the U.S. in the image of some great college football player—a vast and imposing mountain of muscle and power from the neck down, surmounted by a head that would never have got on the team if academic prowess came into the selection" [Hastings 1986:37].)

Morris makes explicit what underlies much of the hostility toward the United States but is rarely acknowledged: that it is a rich, unscathed, fortunate, and enviable country. Morris (like other critics) holds it against the United States that it has not suffered enough, that lacking such experience has impoverished its people and culture [see also Fairlie 1975:36].

Her version of moral equivalence, as is often the case, shades into a charitable view of the Soviet Union and a bitterly critical one of the United States. The Russians are a tragic nation, they earned their right to paranoia and sympathy; the Americans are lucky, bloated philistines undeserving of compassion. She has not been the only critic of the United States, American culture and character irritated and antagonized by the alleged naïveté and shallowness of Americans that assume especially frightening proportions when associated with the custody of nuclear weapons. (Graham Greene's portrait of the "Quiet American" has been a major contribution to the archetype, or myth of the naïve but exceedingly dangerous American.) Underneath these stereotypes lurks a social determinism familiar from other contexts of social criticism: the forces of evil (the rich, the capitalists, the West, or the United States) are in full control of their destiny; they don't deserve sympathy. On the other hand the underdogs, the true victims (the poor, the minorities, the Third World, the Russians, and so on) merit compassion; they are buffeted by the winds of history, helplessly tossed about by social forces; they may err but cannot help it. Through the prisms of such a selective social-cultural determinism compassion and contempt are allocated in a highly selective and idiosyncratic way.

Morris like most other critics of American society believes that the profit motive and the corruptions the love of money bring are uniquely American deformities; she also expects Americans to live up to their principles:

> . . . if in theory the American nation is devout, in practice there can hardly be a society more riddled with insincerity and opportunism . . . Watergate was not a phenomenon, only an example. Every day in America, every city, every ward, knows its own corruption. The bribe, the bug, the lie, the evasion, the doubletalk are strands of the American texture, part of life, part of the system.

For good measure Morris adds, "I write only out of love" [Morris 1975:32, 33]. If so her remarks illustrate the displeasure and bitterness of the disappointed lover whose object of ardor did not (and could not) measure up to her expectations. Similarly unrealistic expectations (or double standards) may account for the sentiments of another English writer who reported on "the essential pointlessness and dreary similarity of many American lives"—attributions which invite the question, Compared with what? With the essential meaningfulness and variety of the lives of English factory workers? Indian peasants? French shopkeepers? [Winchester 1981:45].

If American corruption, hypocrisy, dreariness inspire such loathing it is because the indignant critic had believed that this was or was going to be a superior society without the flaws of others known in history. Apparently American culture has succeeded in inculcating such destructively high expectations in not only its own members but also in its critics abroad.

Anti-Americanism is the most seamless and coherent when the withering critiques of institutional arrangements and policies are joined to a correspondingly negative and scornful view of American culture and even individual Americans, perceived as hopelessly deformed by their system, by the culture. For example, Nehru of India observed in 1953: "As far as I can see . . . there is neither breadth nor depth about the average American . . . The United States is hardly the place where one would go at present in search of the higher culture" [Hutchins 1990–1991:96]. This has been a type of criticism that often predates the more recent animosity stimulated by the global influence and power of the United States.

America as uncivilized, lacking in culture, and obsessed with things material and economic are longstanding critiques. Knut Hamsun, the Norwegian writer, was struck (in the second half of the 19th century) by the United States as a country "where everything is so torn up and inharmonious." He also observed:

> . . . America is a very backward country culturally. . . .
> A way of life has evolved in America that turns exclusively upon making a living, acquiring material goods, a fortune. Americans are so absorbed in the scramble for profit that all their faculties are devoted to it; all their interests revolve around it. Their brains are trained exclusively to grapple with monetary values and columns of figures . . .
> . . . a commercial nation devoted to buying and selling, not an artistic or art-loving nation.
> . . . a country in which art means dining-room decorations. [Hamsun 1969:15, 19, 78, 88]

Hamsun also found Americans invincibly and smugly ignorant of "foreign peoples and foreign achievements," "a nation so taken with itself [that it] knows curiously little about others," where "a justifiable national pride [is transformed] into an unjustifiable arrogance . . ." [Ibid.:8, 9, 20]. While the specifics of these century-old critiques are dated, their spirit survives in the image of the basically unsophisticated, immature, naïve, and insensitive nation. "The garish vulgarity" of American civilization in particular has remained a favorite commentary among foreigners, especially from Western Europe [see for example Clement 1976:36].

Maxim Gorky, the Russian writer, visiting the United States in the early 20th century, a few decades after Hamsun, came away with similar but still darker images and impressions:

> . . . the passionate idealism of the young democracy had . . . become covered with rust, like the bronze statue, eating away the soul with the corrosive of commercialism. The senseless craving for money . . . is a disease from which people suffer everywhere. But I did not realize that this dread disease had assumed such proportions in America.
> . . . It is the first time that I have seen such a huge city monster; nowhere have the people appeared to me so unfortunate, so thoroughly enslaved to life, as in New York . . . nowhere have I seen them so tragicomically self-satisfied . . .
> . . . It seems to me that what is superlatively lacking to America is a desire for beauty, a thirst for those pleasures which it alone can give to the mind and to the heart. [Stearn ed. 1975:174, 176, 178]

The contrast between material wealth and spiritual poverty is another venerable theme in the critiques of the American way of life. Bertrand Russell observed half a century after Gorky: "When I look at the faces

of people in opulent cars . . . I don't see that look of radiant happiness
. . . In nine cases out of ten, I see instead a look of boredom and discontent and an almost frantic longing for something that might tickle the
jaded palate" [Feinberg and Kasrils eds. 1983:335]. Such "cheerless luxury" has been an attribute of the American way of life many visitors have
detected [see for example Sullerot 1967:47].

If the presumed cultural superiority of the European critics is a major
source of the kind of reproaches quoted above, in more recent times it
has been the impoverished condition of countries in the Third World
which has stimulated similar condemnation. It may come naturally to
those who find few sources of pride in the material accomplishments of
their society to emphasize its more intangible spiritual assets and benefits.
This leads to a "stress on feeling, soul and depth vis-à-vis the cold rationality of an imperialist civilization," also seen as "the perennial response
to the experience of inferiority and backwardness of one society towards
more powerful rivals" [Kroes 1984:4, 3].

It is safe to say that anti-Americanism is almost invariably more
intense when it originates in traditional or partly traditional societies, or
modernizing societies anxious to preserve some of their traditional attributes. A visitor to the United States from communist China spoke for
many Third World critics displeased with the American way of life that
challenges and violates traditional ways and values:

> So you have your car and your house and your position . . . but what is it
> all for? Spiritually, you are quite poor. You don't have a sense of belief . . .
> It seems young people are mainly concerned with sex, and the society lacks
> beautiful and noble love between men and women.
> . . . Your young people learn quickly, but they learn selfish goals. In China,
> young people put their country first . . . the younger generation should give
> their hearts to better their country—and it is the responsibility of the older
> generation to give their children such a sense of purpose. ["China's Epic
> Novelist Looks at the U.S. . . . ." 1982:75]

Thus the familiar critique of individualism—and that of modernity
which is inseparable from individualism—merges with the critique of
American society and culture.

It takes little effort to discover that a large portion of all critiques of
the United States and American society are as much critiques of modernity as they are of American foreign policy or economic rapaciousness.
And there is a convergence in these matters too, between the voices of
the domestic and foreign critics.

George F. Kennan, better known as an architect and subsequent critic
of American foreign policy after World War II, personifies the type of

domestic social-cultural criticism that is also widespread abroad among those who are offended by American culture and threatened by the onslaught of modernity:

> What was in England an evil of the upper classes seemed to have become the vice of the entire populace [in the Untied States]. It was a sad climax of individualism, the blind-alley of a generation which has forgotten how to think or live collectively . . . I could not help but feel that one ought to welcome almost any social cataclysm . . . that would . . . force human beings to seek their happiness and their salvation in their relationship to society as a whole rather than in the interests of themselves . . . [Kennan 1989:43]

Kennan also shared with foreign critics the concern over the human consequences of American affluence, opportunities, and permissiveness:

> Here it is easy to see that when man is given . . . freedom from both political restraint and want, the effect is to render him childlike . . . fun-loving, quick to laughter and enthusiasm, unanalytical, unintellectual . . . given to seizures of aggressiveness, driven constantly to protect his status . . . by an eager conformism . . . Southern California together with all that tendency of American life which it typifies, is childhood without the promise of maturity. [Ibid.:149–50]

Kennan describes the American character as "one-dimensional" (as had Herbert Marcuse), unreflective, lacking in the capacity for anguish, casually cheerful, immersed in the present [Ibid.: 169–70]. Aesthetic, environmentalist concerns add to a far-reaching indictment of American culture and life (as is often the case in the writings of many visitors from abroad). Thus from his comments on the "'asphalted desolation" unfolding outside the windows of his motel Kennan is led to observe that in this "lonely, air-conditioned world" there is

> Not a touch of community; not a touch of sociability. Only the endless whirring . . . of the air conditioners, the wild wasting of energy, the ubiquitous television set, the massive bundle of advertising pulp that masquerades under the name of a Sunday newspaper. All unnatural; all experience vicarious, all activity passive and uncreative. And this wasteland extending, like a desert, miles and miles in every direction. [Ibid.:289]

That Kennan sounds like a sensitive European touring the United States probably has to do with his being something of a stranger in his own country, having spent the best years, decades, of his life in Europe as a diplomat—a career choice in itself reflecting some discomfort with the home setting, one may conjecture.

Another American critic of American culture and character whose outlook resembles that of both Kennan and the critics abroad (Western Europeans in particular) is Dwight Macdonald. Returning to New York in 1957, he wrote,

> after a year in London and two months in Tuscany, I felt I had crossed a boundary wider than the Atlantic. We are an unhappy people (I felt), a people without style, without a sense of what is humanly satisfying. Our values are not anchored securely, not in the past (tradition) and not in the present (community). There is a terrible *shapelessness* about American life. These prosperous Americans look more tense and joyless than the people in the poorer quarters of Florence. Even the English seem to have more *joie de vivre.*
>
> . . . *There:* a community, each person differentiated by status and function but each a part of an orderly social structure. *Here:* everybody "equal" in the sense that nobody respects anybody else . . . *There:* continuity with the past. . . . *Here:* no bottom, no continuity, no level: a jungle in which anything can happen without anybody's thinking it out of the ordinary. Each individual makes his own culture, his own morality . . .
>
> . . . Americans appear to other nations to be at once gross and sentimental, immature and tough, uncultivated and hypocritical, shrewd about small things and stupid about big things. [Macdonald 1974:44, 47–48, 49]

There is a certain logic to connecting the critiques of political and economic institutions to those of culture and national character. Yet many of the less consistent critics of America insist on liking individual Americans and contrasting them favorably with the corrupt institutions of their society, the influence of which they mysteriously escaped.

Inauthenticity is another theme in the critiques of American society endlessly dwelt upon by its native critics which has found ready acceptance abroad. It is the divergence between word and deed, theory and practice, of which Americans were found uniquely guilty. Freud upon his visit in 1909 lamented the "prudery, the hypocrisy, the national lack of independence! There is no independent thinking in America, is there?" He also advised his interlocutor, Max Eastman, that he "write a book about the monstrous thing that America turned out to be. . . . The word is 'miscarriage.' *The Miscarriage of American Civilization*—that shall be the title of your book . . . find out the causes and tell the truth about the whole awful catastrophe" [Stearn ed. 1975:222].

The theme of the gap between aspiration and achievement also looms large in a historical summary of the critiques of America,

... as a land of contradication and hypocrisy, where whites enslaved blacks under a supposedly democratic constitution; where violence and instability reigned in place of kings; where feudal degradation gave way to capitalist oppression; where corruption became synonymous with universal (white) male suffrage; where feminine idiosyncrasies counterpointed male vulgarity; where culture was frail and mediocrity dominant. [Stearn 1975:xii]

Stanley Hoffman of Harvard University (himself a longtime critic of American foreign policy) claims that "Much of the ambivalence toward the U.S. stems from the contradiction between official U.S. ideology—the Declaration of Independence and the Bill of Rights—and American actions at home and around the world. Many see what the U.S. is doing and conclude it does not practice what it preaches" [Powell 1985:27]. While it is not easy to separate what Hoffman thinks of such matters from what he attributes to other critics (abroad), his remark highlights, once again, the high expectations which underlie much of the criticism of the United States.

One may wonder why people abroad have accepted at face value the promise of America and come to judge the United States by higher standards (based on its ideals) than most other countries. The Soviet Union too generated vast amounts of impressive rhetoric about the ideals and promises of its social system yet it has not become a country of which huge numbers of people around the world expected a great deal, not even in its revolutionary heyday. (Only relatively small numbers of Western and Third World intellectuals harbored high expectations of the Soviet system, and, as a rule, not for long.) Nor did high expectations toward the Soviet system ever find expression in vast numbers of people seeking to live in that country, as has been the case with the United States.

High expectations of America certainly have endured for a long time and with them a tendency to ambivalence (when tested against reality). Ambivalence in turn has often been transformed into fierce rejection. A study of British writers' views of this country captures the contradictory nature of these expectations. Peter Conrad writes:

Geographically America was imagined in advance of its discovery as an arboreal paradise, Europe's dream of verdurous luxury ... the political founders of the United States ... constituted America as a promised land, a conjuration of the liberal hopes or aristocratic fears of Europe. They saw the new kind of state ... not a natural growth of history but the actualization of an idea.

... To the European, the enchantment of America is the variegation of its reality ... America is centerless, not a claustrophobic, centripetal society like those in Europe ... but a chaos of disparate realities ... In England these writers would have had to share the same congested, incest-ridden space. America disperses them, relegating each to a location aptest to his imagination.

The reality for America is selective, optional, fantastic: there is an America for each of us. [Conrad 1980:3, 4]

These reflections help to grasp the depth of feeling and ambivalence America inspires especially in artists and intellectuals, in people of high expecations in search of self-realization and nonmaterial fulfillment. America, as Peter Conrad put it, has for them become a state of mind rather than a country or society. In a similar spirit William Pfaff, an American writer who lives in France, has written that "What these successive visions of America have had in common is the conviction that America is a place where constraining reality—indeed history itself—is defied and the limits of Europe do not prevail . . ." [Pfaff 1989:181]. If so, it is easier to understand why at least a certain type of anti-Americanism is a response to disappointment bred by high expectations.

But if the promise of America has been taken so seriously this suggests that the American experiment has not been a total failure or fraud, that it has not been written off, that there remains something that continues to attract and intrigue, a promise partially fulfilled that continues to fuel ambivalence.

In more recent times it has been the political failures (real or alleged) of the United States and especially those of its foreign policy which aroused the most critical attention and have been found to provide the favored explanation of hostility abroad. Stanley Hoffman has not been the only American commentator focusing on the sins of the United States in seeking to account for such negativity. The editor of a collection examining the putative estrangment of the United States from the rest of the world posed these questions:

How much of our dilemma is our unconscious ethnocentrism, grating on the nerves of those whom we are presumed to lead and instruct?

How much is traceable to our economic and social failure at home measured against our frequently self-righteous stance abroad?

. . . How much of our estrangement proceeded from America's military misadventures and defeats of recent years?

How much of it reflects our reemerging know-nothingism, the atavistic stirrings on our political-cultural scene?

How much derives from our styles of presidential leadership and the confusions these create abroad? [Ungar ed. 1985:xi]

The burden of these rhetorical questions—and of the answers they elicited—was that the United States is ultimately responsible for its unpopularity in the world.

A somewhat similar line of argument is pursued by William Pfaff. He suggests that an excessive interventionism, prompted by missionary zeal and an all-too-serene belief in the superiority and exportability of American values—the United States "as model for mankind, source of idealism, seat of justice"—are responsible for American unpopularity abroad. He is properly critical of "the breathtaking conviction [of Americans] that people everywhere shared the fundamental ambitions and values of Americans" [Pfaff 1989:10, 13].

A more specific form of such reproaches is the claim, embraced with particular relish by both domestic and foreign critics, that the United States and American policy-makers are "insensitive" to foreign nations and especially those in the Third World. Ali Mazrui, a professor both at the University of Nigeria and the University of Michigan (mentioned earlier in Chapter 3 as a star academic chased by many institutions), wrote:

> . . . because Americans are bad listeners, they have resisted being humanized, in the sense of learning to respond to the needs and desires of the rest of the world.
> . . . the Reagan administration has not listened to the groans of the world's poor . . . Using its power to reduce [the World Bank] International Development Association's effectiveness is an instance of singular American insensitivity. Similarly the United States withdrew from UNESCO, having decided that it does not want to listen to some of the messages emanting from UNESCO. . . .
> . . . The messages from abroad that the United States has been least prepared to listen to during the postwar era are those of Marxism and Islam. [Ungar ed. 1985:181, 182, 189]

Similar indictments of the alleged American "faiure to understand the political, cultural and socioeconomic realities of other societies" [e.g., Hamid in Rubinstein and Smith 1985:108] have often been put forward both abroad and in the United States by those predisposed to the criticism of American policies on other grounds as well. Implicit in this line of argument is the premise that the United States unlike most other nations is under a special moral obligation to various countries and especially those regularly berating it and make various demands on it. In this therapeutic model of international relations, countries (or some of them) are presumed to listen carefully to one another, anxious to understand the other's point of view and respond positively. It is a belief most assiduously cultivated in the United Nations, where it is promoted, indeed institutionalized, by the Third World majority. A somewhat similar position used to be taken among American policy-makers and specialists in years past toward the Soviet Union—a point of view which stressed the need to listen, understand and avoid being "judgmental." This author called it the "therapeutic approach" to American-Soviet relations [Hollander 1988:59–62].

The charge of American insensitivity toward foreign nations ranges all the way from scholarly critiques through the standardized denunciations in the U.N. (discussed earlier); it also found literary expression in the once famous novel, *The Ugly American* (number 6 on the bestseller list in 1959), a thinly fictionalized chronicle of American insensitivity, ineptness, and bungling in Southeast Asia. It was the highly popular message of the book that Americans abroad, and officials in particular, were both totally ignorant of local customs, social norms, and culture and cheerfully insensitive to the feelings and beliefs of the peoples they were seeking to patronize and defend from the communist threat. "The Ugly American" became a stereotype of the American abroad universally disliked. It was a novel that did much to popularize and illustrate the notion of ethnocentricity that has since become enshrined in popular sociology and psychology courses. (Ethnocentric Americans judged other cultures in terms of their own and preferred their own to others; this too was presented as a singularly American failing.) The novel also conveyed that the few Americans who were knowledgeable of and interested in foreign countries are systematically weeded out from foreign service. The novel's Ambassador Sears thinks of the natives as "little monkeys" and had no idea where the country was located in which he was given the job as a political reward. He was among the American officials described by one of the articulate natives as people who cannot grasp the power of ideas (unlike the communists) and who were sent over to "try to buy us like cattle." Another American official "drives a big red convertible which he slews around corners and over sidewalks. And he's got exactly the kind of loud silly laugh that every Asian is embarrassed to hear."

Americans are recruited to these posts abroad by the prospect of an easy life, surrounded by servants and perks of many kinds. In the words of another native critic, "A mysterious change seems to come over Americans when they go to a foreign land. They isolate themselves socially. They live pretentiously. They are loud and ostentatious" [Lederer and Burdick 1958:12, 24, 69, 145]. It is the message of the book (supported by "a factual epilogue") that the failures of American foreign policy are rooted in the ignorance, incompetence, insensitivity, and arrogance of Americans who represent this country abroad as well as of those making policy at home.

In *The Quiet American,* Graham Greene develops the same theme in a more serious manner and on a higher literary plane. This time the American abroad is a far more appealing character full of good intentions (determined to "improve the whole universe") which unfortunately have deadly consequences. He is above all innocent and naïve, totally lacking in intellectual sophistication but overflowing with an insipid earnestness. Once more this American innocent meddles destructively in the affairs of the natives (the Indochinese) whom he is incapable of understanding; he is equally "incapable of conceiving the pain he might cause others." He and his people "are trying to make a war with the help of people who just aren't interested." He is "impregnably armoured by his good intentions and ignorance" and makes "the mistake of putting his ideas into practice." In doing so he personifies the hopeless ineptitude of the United States in world affairs [Greene 1955:10, 63, 99, 183, 186]. Greene's barely concealed contempt and condescension are especially aroused by what he takes to be the puritanical core of the American character.

It is noteworthy that the charge of "insensitivity" has also become extremely popular at home, one of the major critiques of domestic policies and institutional arrangements, especially in the context of the alleged mistreatment of minorities. "Insensitivity" has virtually displaced "oppression" or "exploitation" as the major trait of the social order and its rulers. Presumably this development has something to do with the easier applicability of the concept to a wider range of more intangible grievances which surfaced in the 1980s and replaced more observable and clear-cut forms of mistreatment or deprivation.

The gist of present-day anti-Americanism is captured in the observations of a Dutch author who locates it in the discontents of contemporary life, an attitude that has some elements in common with the vehement anti-modernizing hostility the United States ("the Great Satan") arouses in Islamic societies.

Rob Kroes argued that "'America' [is] a construct of the mind, a composite image based on the perception of dismal trends which are then linked to America as the country and culture characteristically but not uniquely displaying them" and that "the 'America' which one now rejects is really a code word—a symbol—for a much wider rejection of contemporary society and culture" [Kroes 1984:1, 12]. At the same time Kroes also sees anti-Americanism as a "highly defensive" response to threats to national and national cultural identity in Western Europe [Ibid.:3]. It was the European reactions to the Vietnam war followed by the fears of nuclear conflagration on European soil that gave a clearer focus to all such diffuse sentiments and crystallized disaffection from the United States.

Another Dutch author, Jan Van Houten, characterized Western European anti-Americanism as in large measure a response to the anti-Americanism of Americans, and intellectuals in particular. He also suggested that anti-Americanism, although stimulated by Vietnam and the deployment of intermediate missiles in Western Europe, has been on the rise ever since the death of President Kennedy, and that

> The fiercest denunciations of America have been home-grown. In the past 20 years, the U.S. exported anti-Americanism just as it did Coca-Cola, . . . hamburgers and "Peyton Place" . . . only a small number are infected with the anti-American virus . . . The problem is that the minority consists of the people in the consciousness industry—the churches, the schools, the universities and the mass media.

Van Houten also sees anti-Americanism less a response to specific American policies and actions (which nonetheless can increase it) than a symptom of "the disease of intellectuals" which is the rejection of Western society: "As the leader and symbol of the West, the U.S. is naturally their No. 1 enemy . . . The root of the matter is the alienation of the intellectuals from the institutions and values of their own society" [Van Houten 1983].

It should be emphasized that this argument is quite different from that which explains anti-Americanism as a defensive response to some type of American enchroachment—economic, political, or cultural. The intellectuals in question have little interest in protecting the values and institutions of their own society which they *also* reject as part of the complex of Western values and institutions. Rather than separating the values of their own society from those of an encroaching United States, they see continuity between the despised values of their own social system (e.g., "consumerism") and those of the United States, which represents the furthest development of the trends they abhor. These homegrown attitudes are in turn enriched and certified by similar sentiments and critiques radiating from American social critics equally unhappy with their own social institutions and values.

In a single article a British writer reporting from the United States benefitted from the vision and opinion of several American social critics such as Congressman Ronald V. Dellums, arguably the most radical elected official in office; E. L. Doctorow, the writer; John Kenneth Galbraith, the economist (and sometime admirer of Mao's China [see Hollander 1981:306–7, 320]); and Grace Paley, another left-of-center author identified in the article as "a veteran of good American causes" [Webb 1983:26]. J. B. Priestley, the well-known English writer, disclosed that "We also dislike the society they ['disillusioned young Americans'] dislike." He thought that "Americans weren't better than most people; they were mostly much worse; they were in no position to teach other people anything except advanced and dangerously suspect technology. It is now time the U.S. started all over again and did much better" [Priestley 1980:18].

Kenneth Minogue, one of the handful of authors who explicitly addressed the phenomenon of anti-Americanism, has made a similar point:

> . . . a great deal of anti-Americanism in Britain is picked up from Americans themselves, for whom the sentiment is the local modification of a long-standing Western tendency towards civilizational guilt and self-dislike . . . Indeed the point of departure for anyone who wants to understand anti-Americanism is that it is most intense . . . in America itself. What foreigner could match, for sheer intensity of hatred, the response of many left-wing Americans to the Vietnam war? It is Americans themselves who supply most of the materials of anti-Americanism. [Minogue 1986:44, 47]

Minogue suggests that (as is also the belief of this author) "the most familiar and recognizable anti-Americanism [is] that of the left." Its hallmarks are the proposition that the United States is a "profit-crazed country blinded by hatred of progressive or left-wing governments"; it is "dangerously unpredictable" (an especially powerful argument when the Untied States has so many fingers on the nuclear trigger); and always "on the wrong side of any liberation struggle"; the U.S. is, furthermore, obsessed with technology while incapable of solving human problems at home or abroad [Ibid.:47].

Such sentiments on the part of left-wing intellectuals are an integral part of the type of estrangement alluded to by the Dutch authors cited; its American forms were discussed at some length in the first part of this book. Left-wing anti-Americanism is permeated by anticapitalism since the intellectuals in question regard capitalism as the most repugnant social-economic system (holding it responsible for the corruption of human nature and character), and they correctly identify capitalism with the United States. Left-wing anti-Americanism is also more conspicuous and consequential because it is widely disseminated in the mass media which in Western Europe as in the United States is very accessible to these intellectuals and their followers.

Arthur F. Burns, U.S. ambassador to West Germany in the early 1980s, also reached the conclusion that ". . . America—with its untiring propensity for self-criticism—exported to Europe its own version of anti-Americanism." He noted that the American mass media and television in particular provide much of the raw material for the critiques of the United States by concentrating on "violence, exploitation and bigotry." He too found the root of the phenomenon in the broader anti-Western disposition of "Europe's educated classes." In their eyes "America is seen correctly as the bulwark of everything they despise—parliamentary democracy, dynamic capitalism, modern technology and robust anti-Communism" [Burns 1983].

Not only does anti-American sentiment abroad derive sustenance from similar critiques at home, the United States also suffers from an inability to project a more attractive image even on the part of those who are not its habitual detractors. George Urban, an English writer, made this point forcefully:

> It is a political curiosity of our time that the nation that invented Madison Avenue should be so poor conveying the truth . . . about the real nature of American society, the values Americans cherish . . .
>
> Sitting among delegates at the United Nations or listening to the Dutch or Mexicans talking among themselves, one is struck by a puzzling phenomenon: the totalitarian world has succeeded in . . . defining the terms in which American society is described and often describes itself.
>
> America, in this light, is rapacious, exploitative, imperialistic, vacuous and lacking compassion. [Urban 1984]

Urban believes that this situation arose in part because American political culture is basically democratic and defensive and Americans are inexperienced in articulating American values and the positive features of American society; they are also handicapped by "a lack of self confidence in dealing with foreigners." Moreover, American elite groups lost confidence in American society and institutions. If so the estranged critical sensibility at home and hostility abroad reinforce one another. A social system continuously engaged in self-denigration (or apparent self-denigration) inspires little trust and confidence abroad. Anti-Americanism not only feeds on the lurid television programs and trashy movies produced in the United States, it also derives support and justification from the rejection of American institutions produced by the flourishing industry of more scholarly social criticism (sampled in Chapter 1).

The late Henry Fairlie, an English author transplanted to this country, was among the few who paid attention to the phenomenon here discussed. He wrote:

> I am not speaking of the steady criticism that any nation—and particularly its intellectuals—ought to maintain of its own society, but of a virulence of tone . . . which seems to spring from self-doubt into self-hate.
>
> . . . during the late 1960s and to some extent since then, whatever the provocations, the repulsion of many Americans from their own country . . . has not been merely virulent, not only monotonous, but itself a kind of sickness, which in turn needs diagnosis.

... the higher up one goes the more searching becomes the self-criticism ... [Fairlie 1975:29]

Fairlie identifies among the features of this self-critical disposition the readiness of individual Americans to feel personal guilt for the historical past:

> No American alive today enslaved the Negroes ... just as no Englishman alive today carried on the slave trade ... Yet whereas no Englishman today feels any guilt or other responsibility for the deeds of his ancestors, the American is apparently expected to go on—and on—crying *mea culpa* for every misdeed that has been committed in his land since Christopher Newport turned his three ships into James River almost four hundred years ago. [Ibid.:30]

Such feelings of guilt seem to increase with education, and the elite institutions appear to be the most committed to inculcate and nurture them.

While anti-Americanism abroad is nourished by the self-laceration of American social critics it is also a response to other processes set into motion by the United States. The latter has been successfully, if unintentionally, exporting to many parts of the world—along with television programs, fast food, and blue jeans—byproducts of modernization which are far more disturbing. Fairlie is right in suggesting that it is "the impact of Americanization that is at the core of anti-Americanism" [Ibid.:48–49]. But what is at the core of Americanization?

Most obviously Americanization amounts to the export of American cultural products, consumer goods, and recreational activities; it does indeed entail a degree of cultural homogenization (as the critics say) and threat to traditional values and social distinctions. But as one digs deeper Americanization and modernization begin to shade into one another. Unhappily modernization means more than the introduction of machines, mass production, and new ways of communication; it also produces social and geographic mobility, the growth of individualism, social isolation, problems of identity, the decline of community, secularization, and the unthinking acceptance of change.

In the late 1970s I wrote [Hollander 1983:308–10] that what many foreigners despise and dislike most about American society and regard among its most threatening or distasteful aspects (as the case may be) is the confused groping for values and standards, at once admirable and pathetic. The American spectacle of a moral, ethical, aesthetic free-for-all (the most recent expression of which is a somewhat mindless veneration of "diversity" in higher education [see also Shanker 1991]), the rapid changes in moral fashions; the determined and self-conscious quest for self-expression, self-realization, as well as popularity—these are among the more intangible aspects, the fruits of America and Americanization which are often met with dismay, unease, bewilderment, or at least ambivalence abroad. The unqualified "openness to change" in particular—regarded as a self-evident virtue in American culture—inspires incomprehension or apprehension and is frequently associated with suggestibility, instability, inability to discriminate, and moral confusion—all of which are abundant in American society. Hence Americanization of other countries and cultures also means the export of confusion, high expecations (easily frustrated), ethical relativism, insecurities which have no discernible material origin, and a shapeless spiritual malaise.

These objections too have deeper roots and were aptly voiced by a fictional representative of French aristocracy in an Edith Wharton novel published in 1913:

> . . . you lay hands on things sacred to us . . . And you're all alike . . . every one of you . . . You come among us from a country we don't know . . . a country you care for so little that before you have been a day in ours you've forgotten the very house you were born in—if it wasn't torn down before you knew it! . . . you come from hotels as big as towns, and from towns as flimsy as paper, where the streets haven't had time to be named, and the buildings are demolished before they're dry, and the people are so proud of changing as we are of holding to what we have—we're fools enough to imagine that . . . you understand anything about the things that make life decent and honourable for us! [Wharton 1987:485]

My own impressions of and objections to some of these more intangible aspects of American life and culture are relevant here. In my first years in this country over thirty years ago (during 1959–60) I certainly qualified as a hostile critic of American society and what I took to be the quality of personal and social relations and the values guiding the lives of people. In a plaintive article written for the student magazine of the London School of Economics (my alma mater) I thus complained:

> What bothered me more [than my encounters with academic bureaucracy at the University of Illinois in Champaign-Urbana] was the much talked about blend of superficiality, conformity, lack of spontaneity and the "other-directedness" which characterises a good deal of . . . relationships in this country . . .
> . . . There is no question about the proverbial American friendliness and hospitality. It does exist but it strikes me as having one regrettable flaw: it is wholly casual and *impersonal* . . . Americans have hundreds of "friends" . . . Knowing somebody for one week or one year does not seem to alter the quality of these relationships . . .

I do not want to be on "friendly" terms with the whole world because I consider this impossible and meaningless. Americans do not . . .

. . . I am yet to understand why of all nations the USA is the most haunted by . . . insecurity, why, for example should going to college in this country be a "traumatic" experience for many students . . .

. . . what I least like in this country and on the campus . . . is what strikes me as the total lack of spontaneity in human relations, in social activities, in the attitudes towards learning [or] leisure . . .

[Then] There is of course conformity, in some ways more deadly than that which is enforced by the security police in totalitarian states, because to all intents and purposes it seems to be spontaneous and consequently more efficient and penetrating. Its root lies in the fact that people . . . feel more at ease if . . . if they resemble each other in attitudes, ways of dressing, hair style, interests and conversational techniques.

Having rediscovered (and exaggerated) Tocqueville before I read him I proceeded to confess to these rather dated expecations:

. . . I not only expect the USA to have better . . . missiles than the USSR . . . but I also expect her to have a society and culture morally . . . superior in every respect to that of a police state . . . [Hollander 1960:44, 45, 46]

Even if one makes allowances for factors which colored these youthful critiques (the social isolation felt in the new American setting and the rather dramatic contrasts between life in London and Champaign-Urbana), a core of criticism remains that has been the familiar staple of the reproaches directed at American life and values. This is not political criticism, but social and cultural. What precisely did I (and others) mean about the lack of spontaneity and other problems of personal relations? I think I had in mind certain pragmatic-practical aspects of the ways in which Americans relate to one another; for example the "mixing of business with pleasure," the deliberate policy not to antagonize others by expressing opinions which deviate from those prevailing in a given subculture or setting, the *policy* of doing small favors to others in the expectation that they will reciprocate (Tom Wolfe called this "the favor bank" [Wolfe 1987]), and other ways of trying to be well liked by all. At the time I wrote about these matters I did not realize that these forms of behavior and manners are promoted by the relentless geographic and social mobility that prevails, that they are forms of adaptation to these processes. (But thirteen years later I recognized more fully the forces shaping and misshaping friendship patterns in this society [Hollander 1973:282–88].)

I had of course vastly exaggerated in that early article both the quantity and quality of conformity and was largely unaware at the time that

American society and culture encompassed a wide range of variation in people's beliefs and values, even if in particular subcultures—be they of teenagers or college professors—there is indeed conformity.

The longstanding critiques of American society and culture gather a special force as the critics recognize that their own society is not immune to the influences of Americanization, that the trends conspicuous in the Untied States are inexorably spreading. Arthur Koestler wrote:

> I loathe processed bread in cellophane, processed towns of cement and glass, and the Bible processed as a comic strip; I loathe crooners and swooners, quizzes and fizzes, neon and subtopia, the Organization Man and the *Reader's Digest*. But who coerced us into buying all this? The United States do not rule Europe as the British ruled India; they waged no Opium War against us to force their revolting "coke" down our throats. Europe bought the whole package because it wanted it. The Americans did not Americanize us—they were merely one step ahead . . . [Koestler 1961:277]

A French writer asked, "Could this America, this *other* world looming on the horizon, be our own future? . . . The taste for imitation is so strong today in Europe that . . . we may also inherit Americanism and all its sorry products . . . the United States projects on the screen of our future a universe of appalling ugliness" [Royer 1965:306, 307]. More matter of factly, an English commentator noted, "The great interest for a foreign visitor to America today is that he is able to peer forward through a priceless telescope at the economic forces that are most likely to influence all other countries' futures" [Macrae 1969:20]. Italian analysts of American culture reached similar conclusions: "The fact that the United States is the most technologically advanced country, and thus in some ways prophesies our future, tends to increase Europeans' aversion. Modern life at times seems to profane what we were yesterday . . . America's degenerate aspects . . . are created by something much more vast: modern industrial civilization" [Fornari and Luraghi 1968:50, 51]. Herbert Soderstrom, a prominent Swedish journalist, wrote: "America is a country where we can find most of our problems blown up and exaggerated . . . It is a country that is somewhat ahead of us in testing and marketing both problems and solutions." He also concluded that "I have tried to find some critiques of the United States that is uniquely Swedish, but I have not found a single opinion, a single nuance that has not already been expressed by American critics . . ." [Soderstrom 1974:36, 35].

It may now be possible to summarize the most likely explanations of anti-Americanism abroad without rank-ordering them.

Clearly a precondition for the development of these attitudes is a certain amount of information about the Untied States which can become the raw material out of which hostile critiques can be constructed. By any comparative historical standard more people know more about the United States than has ever been known of any country by people not living in it; that much of this information is shallow, stereotyped, or distorted does of course help to account for the phenomena here examined.

Such a widespread awareness, if not genuine familiarity with the United States or things American, has its roots in the pervasive global presence of the United States that combines economic, political, military, and cultural forms. The cultural presence in particular, conveyed by the mass media, is most apt to provoke criticism at any rate among elite groups of the countries affected. ("'America' stands for a threat to the autonomy of traditional elites. To be anti-American is to defend one's right against the presumptiveness of the marketplace psychology . . ." [Scheuch 1970:20].) Resentment over such cultural penetration can rest on various political values. Most commonly, as was shown earlier, it reflects nationalistic concerns over the undermining of what is felt to be the uniqueness of a national culture, its "levelling" or "homogenization." Such concerns may be intensified by both a leftist hostility to the products and tentacles of American capitalism and the distaste of traditional elite groups for the new competitor in the marketplace of ideas, art forms, and values.

One aspect of the United States that is the most readily grasped abroad is its wealth. In combination with other attributes of American society—especially its social problems, aesthetic and educational deficiencies—affluence becomes a potent source of envy and derogation. It is among the major unacknowledged sources of anti-Americanism. As Erwin Scheuch, the German sociologist, pointed out, ". . . the most powerful industrial nation in the world (and the richest society the world has ever known) naturally attracts the resentments of the less successful countries . . . Sociological research . . . shows that anti-Americanism becomes shriller in a country when its own conditions become more insecure . . ." [Scheuch 1970:19].

That the United States is also subject to a steady barrage of *domestic criticism* is another powerful factor in the growth and persistence of anti-Americanism abroad. To emphasize this factor is not to suggest that anti-American critiques abroad are no more than echoes or imitations of the domestic ones or that without the themes and information provided by the domestic critiques the foreign ones would not emerge or would wilt. At the same time there is little doubt that the domestic critiques deepen the confidence of the foreign critics (in their own judgment) and help to authenticate their aversion. ("The self-hate of many Americans is giving

West Europe's cultural intelligentsia grounds for new arrogance" [Scheuch 1970:21].) But even when Americans are not bitterly critical of the failings (real or imagined) of their culture and institutions, they are still susceptible to criticism from abroad. It is a susceptibility that can coexist, peculiarly enough, with the belief in the goodness of American ideals. Not only is there an acute awareness of the difference between ideal and reality at the bottom of this self-critical propensity, there is also "a sense of national incompleteness as we constantly change our lives . . . [a] lack of inner security when our optimism begins to seem unfounded or betrayed. Our optimism is perhaps a necessary compensation for a pervasive insecurity, which derives from the physical and economic origins of American society . . ." [Pfaff 1989:51].

There is at last a further stimulant of anti-Americanism, namely that the United States can be abused and vilified without adverse effects—a condition that stimulates and benefits both native and foreign critics. This state of affairs has the most tangible connection with the post-Vietnam image of the United States, a "paper tiger" image of a powerful country with a weakened will to use its power and a long list of failed foreign policy objectives. In this perspective the United States is a nation which suffered a string of national humiliations ranging from a major one, such as the defeat in Vietnam, to the recurrent manifestations of impotence in the face of hostage takings and other forms of terrorism. The military power of the Untied States has failed to translate into political power during the past quarter-century. As a British journalist put it, "Militarily the U.S. is a musclebound giant. You deploy nineteen warships off the coast of Lebanon and a couple of aircraft carriers—but you cannot use that force . . . The U.S. is unwilling to take casualities, so you have soldiers all over the place but won't use them for fear one may get shot" [Dale 1984:23]. Since these observations were made, the level of military assertiveness of the United States has risen considerably, as reflected in the dispatch of troops to Grenada, Panama, and the Persian Gulf.

A final reminder of how high expecations, disappointment, and ambivalence blend in attitudes toward the United States was recently expressed by Martin Amis, the popular English writer:

Countries go insane like people go insane . . . America had her neuroses before, like when she tried giving up drink, like when started finding enemies within, like when she thought she could rule the world; but she had always gotten better again. But now she was going insane . . .

In a way she was never like anything else . . . America had to mean something . . . hence her vulnerability—to make-believe, to false memory, false destiny. [Amis 1989:366]

Anti-Americanism encompasses a great variety of attitudes, beliefs, and circumstances. It may arise out of nationalism, anti-Western sentiment, anticapitalism, the rejection of science, technology, and urban life, fear of nuclear war, general disgust with modernity, the defense of traditional ways of life, and the cultural condescension of established elites. Whatever its origins it tends to acquire an irrational dynamic of its own that springs form the need of human beings to explain and reduce responsibility for the misfortunes in their lives.

9

Mexican and Canadian Intellectuals

In the mid-1980s I attempted to learn more about the foreign critiques of the United States among intellectuals and to probe attitudes which are not necessarily addressed in secondary sources. I decided to study these attitudes among Mexican and Canadian academic intellectuals. In both the United States and abroad academic intellectuals in the humanities and social sciences tend to be the harshest critics of the United States. Moreover to the best of my knowledge a comparison of the attitudes of Mexican and Canadian intellectuals toward the United States has never been undertaken. I assumed that anti-Americanism in both settings would be quite abundant, suggesting that it may exist in countries quite similar to the United States (such as Canada) *and* totally dissimilar to it (such as Mexico).

Since these two countries border on the United States it seemed of particular interest to examine closely whatever anti-American sentiments can be found among their intellectuals. It is a widely held optimistic liberal belief that various kinds of prejudice, especially ethnic or racial, diminish as people of different groups get to know one another, that proximity, information, and personal contact help to overcome bias and stereotypes.

For example, an English writer reported that he arrived in the United States full of negative preconceptions which up to a point he succeeded in confirming by his experiences. However, after a year these prejudices crumbled under the impact of closer knowledge of American life. He concluded that "Anti-American prejudice ... tends to vary in inverse proportion to the extent to which the individual knows America" [Magee 1990:4]. One may ask, however, Which America? Surely the visitor, even if long-term, who settles in one of the enclaves of the adversary culture will have all his negative preconceptions confirmed and greatly enriched. Former prime minister of Greece Andreas Papandreou, as noted earlier, spent many years in the United States in academic settings and he returned to Greece a confirmed and hostile critic of the United States. Many students from Third World countries with a leftist disposition gravitate to Americans of similar inclination and will also succeed in solidifying their beliefs and critiques of the United States. Not only do visitors have different experiences and personal contacts in the United States, they also are different people and even the same experience may produce different results.

It was of further interest to learn about the differences and similarities between attitudes toward the United States in these two countries given the enormous differences between them. About the only thing Canada and Mexico have in common are the long borders with the United States and a substantial American cultural and economic presence in both. While they are profoundly different from one another they both regard the United States as the dominant partner in their respective relationships and as a result they share many grievances.

Canada is of course a wealthy country and a stable political democracy populated primarily by European immigrants of either British or French origin. It has a population about one-third of that of Mexico (about 25 million versus some 85 million) and a huge land area several times that of Mexico. It has had reasonably friendly relations with the United States since achieving statehood in the last hundred and twenty years. Canada has never been invaded by American troops (at any rate not since the War of 1812, which predated statehood) and its foreign policy has generally followed that of the United States in this century. Unlike Mexicans, Canadians enter the United States only as tourists and not as illegal immigrants; nor are Canadians seeking to enter legally in significant numbers. Also unlike Mexico, Canada is neither producer nor shipper of drugs to the United States; nor is it known for its political corruption. In Lipset's words, Americans and Canadians "are probably as alike as any other two peoples on earth" [Lipset 1989:2]. But it has also been pointed out that ". . . only Canada owes its very existence to a conscious rejection of the American Dream—without the United States to rebel against there would be no Canada" [Axworthy 1982:x].

Canada also differs from Mexico by being among the handful of countries of the world which have both well-established democratic political institutions and a high standard of living. In its social structure and major institutions Canada is often regarded as quite similar to the United States (more so by Americans than Canadians), sharing the dominant English language, a federal government, high levels of urbanization and industrialization, and similar patterns of social stratification. Like the United States, Canada has also been addressing the problems of its minorities— Native Americans in particular—through a wide array of compensatory programs. On the other hand, unlike the United States, Canada has little ethnic conflict (except for Quebec) and little crime.

Various authors have called into question the distinctiveness of the Canadian nation, suggesting for example that Canada "is not a nation" but "essentially [a] part of a greater English-speaking North American nation" (with the exception of Quebec, of course) [Peter Brimelow quoted in Lipset 1989:6]. Not that this is the view of most Canadians or Canadian intellectuals. As Lipset sees it, "Many English-speaking Canadians argue the existence of a distinct national value system which is less materialistic and culturally superior to that of the United States." He also believes that "Canada has been a more class aware, elitist, law-abiding, statist, collectivity-oriented and particularistic (group-oriented) society than the United States" [Lipset 1989:6–7, 8]. A Canadian academic noted among the distinctive characteristics of Canada:

> more deference for authority, a tendency to prefer order over liberty . . . a communitarian and somewhat paternalistic impulse to provide social security for individuals. This combination . . . makes Canada at once more conservative in its political structures, more interventionist in its economic policies, and more progressive in its social services than the United States. [Coe 1988:853]

Several among the respondents in the survey of Canadian attitudes toward the U.S. discussed below also conveyed their belief in the distinctiveness of Canadian cultural values. In response to a question about the sources of tension between the two countries one of them pointed to "The inability of Canadians to accept lower *material* standard of living in exchange for higher *quality* of life . . . [and] the tendency for Americans to assume that everyone wants the same things they want [No. 82].

Given the historical and social conditions in Canada and in the light of the sources of anti-Americanism sketched earlier, one would expect fewer reasons for intense or bitter anti-American sentiment to exist in Canada. If indeed anti-Americanism abroad is a form of nationalistic scapegoating that often combines with a generalized protest against aspects of the modernization process, or modernity itself, Canadians have fewer serious collective grievances which should call forth this scapegoating reflex. On the other hand nationalism can flourish even in a wealthy and stable country which has a small population and is situated next to a very big and powerful state. As two American authors put it: "Knowledgeable Americans soon learn that their greatest sin as a nation, from the Canadian perspective, is their geographic location next door to Canada . . . [and] that they cast a political and economic shadow that is ten times as long as Canada's" [Doran and Sewell in Thornton ed. 1988:109].

Thus it is the powerful American economic and cultural influences (domination, according to many) which are at the root of the animosity toward the United States in Canada, exactly as is the case in Mexico. The threat of cultural domination in particular—associated with matters of national identity—becomes a source of friction and suspicion. As a student of Canadian-American relations put it:

> There is also the imperialism of trend setting, by which what happens in America today is fearfully thought to happen in Canada tomorrow. If there is murder on the streets of New York today there will be murder on the streets of Toronto tomorrow. One imagines a creeping virus labelled Americanism making its slimy way across the border . . .
> There is also the imperialism of popular culture. Here is a favorite Canadian charge against Americans: they are a Republic of Junk. [Winks 1979:72]

Lipset also observed: "What they [Canadian intellectuals] fear is that their country will be flooded with American cultural products, and that the distinct character of its intellectual output will be lost . . ." [Lipset 1989:5]. Such observations are echoed in an article in the *National Geographic* magazine:

> So Canada frets and braces itself against the weight of the United States, with its seductive popular culture and sense of righteousness. As former Prime Minister Pierre Trudeau told the U.S. Congress: "Living next to you is in some ways like sleeping with an elephant: No matter how friendly and even-tempered the beast, one is affected by every twitch and grunt." [Vesilind 1990:97]

Such "gross disparity in power" has always been "an overriding reality," as a Canadian author put it, in the relationship of the two countries, similarities notwithstanding [Nelles 1982:29]. The American tendency to overlook the distinctiveness of Canadian culture and society further contributes to the urge for cultural and political assertiveness. This imbalance in the relationship of the two countries has also been captured by Margaret Atwood, the Canadian writer, who suggested that

> the cliché about the world's longest undefended border should be replaced by a more accurate metaphor—the world's longest one-way mirror. Canadians continually press their noses to the glass, looking with equal parts amazement, admiration and outrage at the antics of the great republic,

while Americans remain serenely oblivious to everyone but themselves. [Axworthy 1987:xi]

To be sure the fears of cultural takeover are the preoccupation of the intellectual elite rather than the mass public [Doran and Sewell in Thornton ed. 1988:110]. But it is not only the cultural takeover and American economic preponderance that worries some Canadians, even more tangible and symbolic is the growth of American ownership of Canadian land [see for example Marshall in Innis 1972].

A Canadian observer distinguished between two kinds of anti-Americanism. The older grew out of an identification with British traditions and cultural values and was in fact a form of cultural superiority. From the late 1960s it has been replaced by a new anti-Americanism that "begins with the proposition that the United States is a colossal empire and a corrupt one, and that its imperial designs are forcing its corrupt nature on us, crushing the Canadian Spirit" [Fulford in Innis 1972:91]. This distinction (between the old and new anti-Americanism) corresponds to the anti–Americanism of the right (conservative in its inspiration) and to that of the left, the more recent variant that stresses the combined menace of a political and economic imperialism, in addition to cultural concerns. As one observer put it, ". . . 'Canadian nationalism,' . . . is basically a local variant of international Left-wing and anti-American attitudes" [Brimelow 1990:19].

In Canada as in Mexico, hostility to the United States or American culture appears most pronounced among intellectuals. As Canadian author Mildred A. Schwartz put it, "The locus of anti-Americanism is primarily in the intellectual community—in universities, in publishing houses, and among those concerned with the dissemination of ideas and popular culture" [Quoted in Lipset 1989:230]. By contrast a Canadian author suggested that regular "Canadians have just as much difficulty believing that the pervasive American presence in their lives is a threat to their cultural survival . . . as they do apprehending U.S. protectionism as a threat to their economic survival" [Clarkson 1982:221].

Why intellectuals in both of these and many other countries are the most antagonistic toward the United States has already been alluded to. Insofar as they are of leftist persuasion they object to the exploitativeness they associate with the most powerful representative of capitalism and the commercialization of cultural values; if they are conservative, they see themselves as custodians of national culture and identity and are most sensitive to threats to these values.

In Third World countries such as Mexico, nationalism is an essential part of the (ambivalent) protest against Westernization or some aspects of it. On the other hand intellectuals are not especially nationalistic in most Western countries, hence their nationalism in a country like Canada requires special explanation.

As already noted much of Canadian anti-Americanism reflects an apprehensive concern with a somewhat fragile national identity. This anti-Americanism has been justifiably characterized as "low-grade" rather than intense and broadly based, taking, as a rule, the form of "complaints about neglect or insensitivity" [Doran and Sewell in Thornton ed. 1988:107].

Canadian anti-Americanism, as was said earlier of anti-Americanism in general, resembles and reflects the domestic critiques of the United States and its policies abroad:

> ... half truths about or hostile caricatures of U.S. government policy held by Canadians are almost always likewise held by some sector of U.S. opinion. Can Americans themselves be anti-American? ... Americans can sometimes be lamentably misinformed about themselves to the point of hostile caricature and ... Canadians should not entirely be blamed if some of this misinformation rubs off on them.... Many of the roots of the newer anti-Americanism are indigenous to North America. [Ibid.:108, 116]

The same conclusion was reached by a reviewer of a book written by a prominent Canadian critic of the United States: "No significant criticism of American culture [Robin] Mathews can make has not been made— and is not being made—by Americans" [Raible 1989].

A specific factor in the newer anti-Americanism has been the arrival of Vietnam-era draft-evaders, many of them former students, who became part of the Canadian academic-intellectual community, confirming and possibly deepening its apprehensions about the United States and infusing it with especially vehement critical sentiments toward American society.

Whatever the nature of the Canadian grievances toward the United States, and more will be said about them below, they are dwarfed by those of Mexico.

Mexico is a country that has not only been defeated and humiliated by the United States (and lost half of its land to it) but is riddled with vast problems of its own. It is overpopulated in relation to its resources, employment opportunities, and infrastructure; its political system is reputed to be fairly corrupt and mildly authoritarian; its poverty difficult to reduce let alone erase; and much of its population is poorly educated. It faces vast economic problems. Unlike Canada it differs from the United States in every major respect: language, history, cultural tradition, system of government, ethnic composition, demographic patterns. Mexican nationalism has been nurtured by the characteristic combination of weakness, past humiliation, and lingering resentment.

In Mexico too the torchbearers of anti-Americanism are the intellectuals and aspiring intellectuals, that is, students. These attitudes are neither new nor limited to Mexico but have been present in other Latin American countries as well, and apparently develop or intensify during attendance at a university. In a study of six Latin American countries in 1971 (Argentina, Brazil, Colombia, Ecuador, Mexico, and Venezuela) it was found that anti-American attitudes increase with education and that university students, more often than any other population group, named the United States "as a country least liked" ["Image of the U.S." 1972:17].

The anti-Americanism among Latin American intellectuals arises in part, as elsewhere, from the association between the critiques of the United States and domestic social criticism. Intellectuals specialize in giving expression to collective grievances, or what they presume to be such grievances. Anti-Americanism often goes hand in hand with a negative view of indigenous social institutions. The social criticism of these intellectuals is also often stimulated by the results and byproducts of modernization; with good reason the United States is universally seen as a most powerful agent and symbol of modernization.

On the other hand, intellectuals under certain historical conditions can also be in the forefront of articulating nationalistic feelings and collective grievances which are *unrelated* to the critique of domestic institutions. A sense of victimization is always a part of nationalistic feelings. When this is the case, domestic problems and shortcomings are blamed on outside forces, and the impulse to domestic social criticism is diminished. At the same time the nationalism of Mexican intellectuals is probably also strengthened by their occupational association with the state. As an American student of contemporary Mexican politics observed, "the Mexican Revolution provided numerous opportunities for Mexicans with every conceivable skill to enter public service and occupy leadership roles . . . Many young intellectuals answered the call . . ." On the other hand in more recent times some Mexican intellectuals have also developed doubts about the desirability of holding public office [Camp 1981 "Intellectuals—Agents of Change":311].

Although less pronounced than in Mexico, the association of Canadian intellectuals with the state may also be a factor in their political attitude formation. According to Peter Brimelow, Canadian social-political conditions and divisions "have facilitated the growth of an unusually powerful public class . . . and unusually healthy specimen of what Irving Kristol called 'the New Class' . . ." [Brimelow 1990:22]. A Canadian sociologist observed that ". . . Anglo-Canadian intellectuals had become the handmaidens of the state bureaucracy rather than its rivals." Such association, as in Mexico, might stimulate anticapitalist or anti-private-sector sentiments. At the same time the same author also portrays a part of this intelligentsia, the Anglo-Canadian social scientists, as inhabiting a "comparatively politically neutralized and socially isolated academic world." Perhaps the paradox is resolved by his belief that the intellectuals associated with the state bureaucracy shed many of their intellectual attributes, and while "the Canadian political system . . . favors the production of publicly-employed intellectuals . . . [their] open advocacy of partisan policy options is severely constrained by the norms of government bureaucracy" [Brym and Myles 1989:443, 446, 447–48].

Either or both the social critical and nationalistic sentiments of intellectuals may rest on grievances peculiar to their own position and interests. In less developed countries, such as Mexico, economic opportunities for intellectuals are generally more limited and their standard of living relatively low, resulting in a sense of marginality (no longer experienced by intellectuals in more prosperous Western societies, Canada of course included). Such conditions are likely to contribute to the scapegoating impulse, the urge to find an emotionally satisfying explanation of limited opportunities, misfortune, or relative deprivation. The latter comes especially readily to intellectuals who are at home in the world of ideas and hence are more capable and tempted to compare their actual condition with those which exist elsewhere or in their imagination.

The greater dependence of Mexican intellectuals on the state for employment may also contribute to their nationalistic attitudes. Being a highly centralized and bureaucratized state, Mexico provides many (but not necessarily well-paid) jobs for intellectuals in its multitude of government agencies and government-controlled institutions of higher education. An American specialist on Mexican intellectuals wrote: "The most distinctive characteristic of the Mexican intellectual's relationship to the state is the simple fact that the majority of the leading intellectuals since 1920 have served the government, or followed government careers." Among the various historical and economic reasons for this has been that "Proportionately fewer intellectuals in Mexico today, as compared to the United States, can make a living solely from their intellectual pursuits. The demand for written work, art, music and other products is . . . limited." Likewise intellectuals have rarely worked in the private sector and especially in business [Camp 1981 "Intellectuals and the State":2, 6]. On the other hand, as in other countries including much of Latin America where sharp inequalities in educational attainments prevail, the prestige of intellectuals in Mexico is nonetheless high [Camp 1981 August:301]. These circumstances combine to impart a fluctuating and ambivalent self-conception to Mexican intellectuals and lead to disagreements as to what role they should play in public life [Camp 1981 August:303].

The Mexican Intellectuals
In the light of the considerations noted above Mexican intellectuals were expected to display the most intense, indeed ideal-typical anti-American-ism. I decided to test this all-too-plausible hypothesis on a small group of Mexican academic intellectuals since general attitude surveys do not sin-gle out intellectuals as a distinct category. My resources did not permit the selection of a full-scale, representative sample. However, on the prin-ciple that something is better than nothing, a survey of small groups of academic intellectuals (in the social sciences and humanities teaching in Mexico City) was undertaken. The respondents were from (a) the facul-ties of political and social sciences or their respective research institutes of the UNAM (National Autonomous University of Mexico) and (b) the division of social sciences and humanities of the Ixtalapa campus of UAM (Metropolitan Autonomous University). This was not a mail survey but one carried out with the assistance of interviewers who approached fac-ulty members with the questionnaire and wrote down the answers. It was conducted in Spanish and subsequently translated into English. I was advised against a mail survey on the assumption that few questionnaires would be returned even if stamped, self-addressed envelopes were pro-vided. Of some 150 individuals approached, 104 responses were received. Those refusing to be interviewed often alluded to their concern with pos-sible CIA funding of the project. (This was pure fantasy since nothing whatsoever associated with this project suggested such connections.)

It has to be made clear that this might have been a highly unrepre-sentative group given its small size and concentration in one city, Mexico City, and the particular institutions chosen. (A Mexican academic friend subsequently pointed out that at universities such as ITAM, Iberoameri-cana, and Tecnológico de Monterrey, responses would have been far more pro-American.) On the other hand the opinions expressed followed closely many characteristics of the left-wing intellectual climate of opin-ion which prevailed in the early and mid-1980s among academics when the study was undertaken. It should also be pointed out that in several instances the overwhelming consensus on certain issues suggests the gen-erality of attitudes going beyond the group selected.

Many of the questions used were identical with or similar to those used in the survey of Canadian academic intellectuals that followed.

The questionnaire began with a series of statements (not all will be summarized below) about various American institutions and values and characteristics of American society.

The first statement proposed that "American society, more than most others, has failed to live up to its own ideals." The reader may be surprised that only 35.5% agreed (to what appears to be an indictment of American society); 14% were not sure, and 51% disagreed. In evaluating the meaning of the responses we should keep in mind that, unlike most Americans, the Mexicans did not necessarily regard these ideals as self-evidently praiseworthy hence living up to them is not necessarily a good thing. Quite possibly many among them felt that American society does live up to its ideals but if the ideals themselves are flawed this did not make it a good society. By contrast for Americans and especially the social critics it is axiomatic that the gap between ideals and their realization is a most serious indictment of the social system since the desirability of these ideals is taken for granted.

The second statement proposed that "There is more freedom of expression in the U.S. than in any other country past or present." Some 34% agreed; 10% were unsure; and more predictably 57% were not willing to grant that this was the case.

A related proposition brought forth more widespread critical sentiments: "The American mass media is a servant of the status quo as it seeks to divert attention from pressing social-political problems." A total of 80% agreed; 8% were not sure; and 12% dissented from what apparently is the conventional wisdom in such matters. Possibly the high level of agreement also reflected a generally negative attitude toward the American media among intellectuals.

The statement "Big corporations, especially the multinationals, are today the prime enemies of freedom and social justice around the world" elicited, not surprisingly, a high degree of assent: 75% (of which 40% agreed very strongly); 8% were not sure; and 17% disagreed (only 3% strongly). Such anticapitalist sentiments, as other sources besides these findings also indicate, are widespread among the Mexican intelligentisia and are intertwined with anti-Americanism for reasons discussed before.

The most negative views of the United States emerged in its relations to the Third World (of which Mexico is a part). This was made clear by responses to the statement "The U.S. bears responsibility for much of the suffering and deprivation rampant in the Third World": 87% agreed (48% very strongly); 4% were not sure; and 10% disagreed. The only other question with a comparable, indeed higher rate of agreement regarding some negative aspect of the United States was directed at its militarism (see below). Evidently the group of intellectuals surveyed responded most strongly to the image of the United States as a victimizing force.

Not surprisingly 94% of the respondents answered affirmatively the question "Do you think the U.S. is responsible for any/many of the world's problems?"; 6% disagreed. When asked which problems those who agreed had in mind, the answers could be grouped as follows: economic problems 48%, political problems 12%, cultural problems 12%, war, repression 19%, other 9%.

Intense aversion to American military power is likely to explain the nearly unanimous belief of the respondents that "Current expenditures on the military in the U.S. are excessive." A total of 94% agreed (71% very strongly); 2% were not sure; and 4% thought otherwise. No other question elicited such a level of agreement, which suggests a persisting apprehension of American military power (rooted in Mexican history) even though its contemporary use in Mexico is barely conceivable. Aversion to American intervention anywhere in the region also explains the huge majority which regarded U.S. invasion of Grenada as unjustified: 92% versus 4% who thought it was justified; 4% were not sure.

Apprehensions about American intervention were not limited to the region. When respondents were presented with the statement "The U.S. should provide military assistance (weapons, supplies) to the anti-government guerillas in Afghanistan," only 13% agreed; 10% were not sure; and 78% disagreed.

The same statement was offered in regard to similar assistance "to the anti-Marxist, anti-Cuban guerillas in Angola." It elicited similar responses: 11% were in favor of such assistance; 9% were not sure; and 81% were opposed.

Responses to a statement that questioned a major criticism of American society, namely that "The persistence of racism and sexism in the U.S. has been greatly exaggerated," were thought-provoking. It was presumed that those critical of the U.S. would regard racism and sexism as major, persisting flaws of American society and would not find their persistence exaggerated, perceiving them as widespread and deeply rooted in American culture, as do many professional social critics in the United States. Perhaps it was a mistake to join these two attributes (sexism and racism) in the same question since it is possible that Mexicans in general (and not only males) have different attitudes toward each: they may not regard sexism as a major evil. If so they would be less sensitive to its presence in general and in the United States in particular and would be more likely to find its persistence exaggerated. Some 54% believed that these attributions were exaggerated (thereby diminishing the importance of the phenomenon); 20% were not sure; and only 26% disagreed, that is, found allegations of the persistence of racism and sexism correct. It should also be noted that these attitudes are not central to social criticism in Mexico.

On the other hand Mexican intellectuals resonate strongly to the critique of American cultural values. It was proposed that "American culture and society, dedicated to competitiveness and material gain, nurture indifference to one's fellow human beings." Some 79% agreed; 3% were not sure; and 17% disagreed.

When the respondents were given a list of attributes which would "best describe American society" and asked to pick four of a list of 15, the following were selected by the percentages indicated: imperialist 20.5%, racist 14%, exploitative 12%, cold, impersonal 11%, unjust and oppressive 9%, warps individual growth 8%. Among the negative attributes only 2% chose "sexist," supporting the earlier interpretation.

Among the positive responses 7% chose "no worse than most other societies," and 6% "provides both free expression and decent standards of living"; 4% chose "democratic", and 3% "allows much personal freedom." Altogether 78% chose negative attributes and 22% favorable ones.

The respondents were also asked to rate their own disposition toward the United States in the question "Do you consider yourself very critical/critical/neutral/friendly/very friendly toward . . .": 19% rated themselves very critical, 60% critical, 14% neutral, 6% friendly, and 1% very friendly. These ratings fully support the more specific attitudes elicited by the various other statements and questions.

To explore further these attitudes respondents were also asked, "How do you think the U.S. is regarded today by most people in the world?" Of 10 attributes provided they were asked to choose three. In order of magnitude they were: (with) criticism 29%, hatred 17.5%, ambivalence 12%, admiration 12%, envy 9%, perplexity 5%, curiosity 3.5%, sympathy 2.8%, and pity 2.8%. Nobody chose "affection." Negative attributes totaled 49.5%, positive 15%, neutral (curiosity, perplexity) 8.5%; ambivalence 12%.

Further light was shed on the political attitudes of the respondents in connection with a series of statements suggesting that "Western reports of repression in the Soviet Union/China/Cuba are greatly exaggerated." It was assumed that those sympathetic to these systems do not regard them as repressive and would be inclined to dismiss Western reports of repression as unreliable and exaggerated. It should also be pointed out that these questions were asked in 1984, well before the decline of repression associated with Gorbachev.

Some 72% agreed that Soviet repression was greatly exaggerated in the West (that is to say, at a time when it was not); 17.5% were not sure; and only 11% disagreed. It may be safe to infer that it was the same percentage, 11%, who would regard Soviet society repressive. I found these responses and their pro-Soviet implications surprising given the disillusionment with the Soviet Union that has prevailed for decades even among leftists in the West. Perhaps one must remember that the Soviet Union had something of a special relationship with Mexico going back to the revolutionary beginnings of both systems which coincided chronologically. In regard to repression in China, 66% did not find its Western depiction credible; 24% were not sure; and only 10% did not find these reports exaggerated.

Not unexpectedly Cuba was seen most favorably in such matters, with 77% *not* finding Western reports of its repressive policies credible; 10% were not sure; and 13% found them credible. In other words over three-quarters of the respondents were reluctant—to say the least—to regard Cuba as repressive; close to three-quarters had the same attitude in regard to the Soviet Union and two-thirds about China.

Generally positive attitudes toward these systems were also brought forth by the response to the statement "Whatever the shortcomings of the Soviet/Chinese/Cuban political system, at least one knows that its leaders are committed to abolishing material inequalities and to improving the life of their people." Roughly the same percentages who did not find them repressive were also prepared to attribute these commendable motives to their leaders. As far as the Soviet Union was concerned: 66% agreed; 10% were not sure; and 13% disagreed. The positive view of Chinese leaders was shared by 68%; 16% were not sure; and 18.5% disagreed. Once more Castro's Cuba got the best ratings, with 81% holding the benign view, 7% expressing uncertainty, and 13% disagreeing.

Despite a generally positive view of these putatively socialist countries the overall moral superiority of such systems (over the capitalist countries and the United States) was not overwhelmingly endorsed. This came to light in response to the question which proposed that "Although many socialist countries are poor, they are morally superior to the capitalist ones, including the U.S." Only 49% agreed, for reasons difficult to explain given the much higher percentages of those expressing hostility toward capitalism and the U.S. in other contexts; 17% were not sure; and 33% disagreed. It should also be pointed out that this study was carried out in 1984 well before the self-critical revelations associated with Gorbachev erupted and made the moral superiority of socialist systems more questionable than ever before. Possibly the questioning of such superiority might be associated with the greater cynicism of Mexican intellectuals, greater than that of correspondingly alienated American intellectuals who might be more tempted to endorse poor but seemingly virtuous systems which call themselves socialist.

Such cynicism may also explain the otherwise puzzling response to the statement "Nicaragua has emerged as the most authentic socialist regime in the world today." Given the depth of hostility toward the United States and especially its interventions in Central America and the close support given by Castro to Nicaragua, it was expected that most respondents would have a more favorable attitude toward Nicaragua, perceived as a prime victim of current American foreign policy. But even if these beliefs were present they did not translate into strong support for the statement perhaps because of the high standards incorporated in it ("most authentic . . . in the world today"). Only 19% agreed; 34% were not sure; and 47% disagreed. To be sure neither the disagreement nor the doubts can be faulted. Nicaragua was indeed a long way from being an authentic socialist system but so were the other countries claiming socialist credentials. Nicaragua at least, more than others, had seemingly better excuses for not becoming more truly socialist.

Further light was shed on these matters when the group of Mexican intellectuals were asked, "In your opinion which countries in the world come closest to living up to the ideals of socialism?" Again Cuba got the most favorable ratings: 23.5%, next came China with 10%, followed by the Soviet Union with 9.5%, Yugoslavia with 5.5%, Sweden with 4.5%, and Nicaragua with only 4%. But significantly 31.5% thought that "none" of the countries in the world today came close to living up to socialist ideals.

Generally speaking the ideals of socialism appeared more attractive than its existing embodiments. It was proposed that "The ideals of socialism offer the best hope for peace and social justice in the world": 68% agreed; 14% were not sure; and 16.5% disagreed.

The dissociation of theory from practice was also brought home by the response to the question: "Do you think that the ideas of Marxism-Leninism are helpful for understanding and solving the problems of Mexico? Some 68% believed they were and 32% did not (there was no "not sure" option in this case).

The political sympathies of the group were further probed in the question "Which country (countries) and political systems in the world today do you admire most?" Cuba was at the top, being mentioned by 20.5%, followed by France 12%, Sweden 7%, Nicaragua 5%, and many others not achieving significant representation (55% chose other countries each by less than 5%). The relative popularity of France under Mitterrand's socialist government and of Sweden may be ascribed to the sympathy, among these respondents, toward a democratic as opposed to a state socialist system.

Respondents were also asked, "Which countries and political systems in the world today do you find most unappealing?" The U.S. topped the list with 17%; followed by Chile with 14%; "Dictatorships" 10%; the Soviet Union 10%; "socialist systems" 8%; Uruguay 7%; "capitalist systems" 6%. A total of 27% mentioned others but these responses were too fragmented to be worth reporting.

The respondents were also asked to list five "political leaders in the world today (or in recent history) you admire most and least." These were the results for the most admired: Castro 13%, Allende 7%, Gandhi 7%, Gonzales (prime minister of Spain) 5%, Mao 5%, Lazaro Cardenas (of Mexico) 3.5%. The least admired were Reagan 16.5%, Pinochet 13.5%, Thatcher 7%, Hitler 5%, Lopez Portillo (of Mexico) 4%, Somoza 4%.

When provided with the opportunity to identify their own political attitudes by using designations provided in the questionnaire, 21% choose leftist, 38% moderate leftist, 35% centrist-neutral, 3% moderate right-wing, and 4% right-wing. These forms of self-identification were commensurate with most of the other responses reported above and also made plausible by the reported familiarity with the ideas of Marxism: 89% had such familiarity, 11% did not (the degree of familiarity was not questioned; it was merely asked if they read anything by "Marx, Engels, Lenin and their followers).

When asked about exposure to "the ideas of Marxism as part of a course," 83% reported that these ideas were indeed "presented" by their teachers in high school or college; 14% did not have this experience; and 3% were not sure.

In seeking to explain the attitudes and beliefs this survey brought to light (or confirmed), the simplest "variable" to fall back on is the long prevailing tradition of suspicion of and resentment toward the United States among the Mexican intelligentsia and their instinctive sympathy toward political systems (such as communist Cuba and the Soviet Union) which have challenged American power. Not unlike the climate of opinion on many college campuses in the United States, a highly critical disposition toward American society and foreign policy is part of the climate of opinion, of the conventional wisdom among many Mexican academic intellectuals. The continued influence and prestige of Marxism can also be explained along these lines: as anti-Americanism and anticapitalism merge, Marxism becomes (or remains) attractive because it helps to sharpen and make more coherent these sentiments.

Although the type of anti-Americanism encountered in these attitudes amounts to a reflexive disposition, indeed a form of bias, it does not rest—as is often assumed of other kinds of biases—on ignorance, unfamiliarity, distance, or lack of communication and contact with Americans and the United States. When asked, "Do you personally know Americans?" only 10% did not; 48% knew Americans "superficially," and 42% "closely." To be sure we do not know about the nature of the "close" relationships and about the type of American who befriended the respondents. It is quite possible that many Americans the Mexicans knew were themselves critics of the United States, especially likely if they were attending college in Mexico and/or preparing for a career in Latin American studies—a field that seems to attract those with well-developed critical sensibilities toward the United States. On the other hand if the Mexicans got to know Americans in the course of their studies in the United States similar processes might also have been at work as the more estranged Americans would sympathetically gravitate toward the Mexican students, perceived as belonging to a major Third World country victimized by the United States.

As far as their overall familiarity with the United States is concerned, 79% had visited the country, but no questions were asked about the duration and purpose of the visit.

Despite the many critiques directed at the United States 40% of the sample would consider living there and 60% said they would not. This makes an interesting contrast to a clear majority of those surveyed who entertained highly critical or unfavorable attitudes toward the United States. (Those displaying favorable attitudes toward the U.S. rarely exceeded 10 to 15% but apparently three times their number would consider living in the much criticized country.)

Some 60% of the respondents regularly watched television programs originating in the United States or dealing with it, thus getting exposure to a rich if dubious source of information about American culture. Rather than a beneficial tool of learning and understanding such exposure could actually have contributed to negative sentiments toward American society or confirmed critical dispositions and stereotypes. (In personal conversations several Mexican intellectuals expressed contempt for American television programs while also admitting that they watched them—an attitude similar to that of many native critics of American society.)

It may be concluded that ignorance or lack of contact per se were *not* major determinants of attitudes and biases toward the United States or American society. On the other hand selective exposure and skewed information may well have confirmed critical predispositions deeply rooted in Mexican political culture and history.

The Canadian Intellectuals
The attempt to learn about the comparable attitudes of Canadian intellectuals was made several years after the Mexican survey (in the spring of 1989), which called for certain modifications in some questions. A mail questionnaire was used, but the same qualifications which applied to the Mexican survey also apply in this instance. Again, this was not a representative sample of Canadian intellectuals or academic intellectuals but a small group drawn from leading Canadian universities.

I selected with the advice of some Canadian academics six major Canadian universities: the universities of Alberta (Edmonton), Simon Fraser (Barnaby, B.C.), Carleton (Ottawa), McGill (Montreal), Quebec (Montreal), and the University of Toronto. These choices offered some regional diversity as they included institutions both from the two most populous provinces (Ontario and Quebec) and two Western provinces (Alberta and British Columbia) and one institution (Carleton) from the capital of the federation (Ottawa).

Given my interest in academic intellectuals more typically found in departments of humanities and social sciences (rather than in the sciences and engineering or business schools), the questionnaires were sent to members (all, half, or one-third, depending on size) of departments of English, history, anthropology, psychology, and sociology. Respondents were randomly selected from the catalogues of the universities listing faculties by name and departmental affiliation. A total of 360 were chosen from a pool of a total of 914 listed in all these departments. 135 questionnaires were returned completed, a response rate of 38%. There is little reason to believe that those not responding were more favorably disposed toward the United States since some of those returning the questionnaire uncompleted enclosed notes expressing their aversion toward any such research project originating in the United States.

A number of respondents volunteered negative comments about the whole enterprise either in enclosed notes or on the questionnaire itself. (There were a handful of positive ones too.) For example: "In answer to your circular . . . I must point out to you that I do not assist U.S. scholars in work concerning Canada." Another academic wrote: "Anything so badly written—really illiterate—scarcely inspires confidence or deserves an answer." Another respondent in a long letter wrote: "Do you know how mistrusting Canadians are of such inquiries? Memories of CIA projects continue here . . . That is why I did not answer fully the biographical questions" (nor did many others). Needless to say the questionnaire was anonymous.

Even among those who completed the questionnaire many could not resist a few negative or hostile comments and expressions of suspicion about the enterprise. For example: "This is a flawed questionnaire . . . it is not the *people* of the USA that are responsible for 3rd world suffering but its capitalist class . . . and its govt. controlled by that class" [No. 127]. Another comment: "This is not a very good questionnaire . . . it has no place for the U.S. as a militarist society or Americans as gun worshippers" [No. 118]. I was also reproached for using terminology (in the structured questions) which was allegedly "consumer-oriented, superficial, chauvinistic, narcissistic and ethnocentric" [No. 113].

Several respondents complained about the questions concerning colleges attended, departmental affiliation, parents' occupation, ethnicity, and religiosity on the ground that such information could be used to identify the respondents. Some of these reactions were very similar to those reported from Mexico at the time when the project was under way; rumor had it that the CIA sponsored the whole project. Such were my initial intimations of the similarities between certain attitudes toward the United States in these two very different countries. (It is likely that some of the highly suspicious attitudes were displayed by those of American origin who settled in Canada during the Vietnam war to avoid the draft and regarded themselves as fugitives and potential victims of CIA intrigues.)

Several Canadian respondents commented negatively on the project on methodological rather than ideological grounds, pointing out that a questionnaire with many precoded, or structured, answers cannot capture the complexity of sentiments and attitudes of the respondents. Presumably many of these comments came from those in the humanities.

One major difference between the two groups of respondents (those in Canada and Mexico) and a probable determinant of some of their attitudes is that a high proportion of the Canadians in the group, 31%, were born in the United States. It is likely that many of them belong to the Vietnam era generation of draft-resisters and critics of the United States who moved to Canada in the 60s and early 70s. This would also help us to better understand the highly critical attitudes toward the United States the survey found. The plausibility of this supposition is indirectly supported by a report which found that, already in 1968, 25% of the Canadian faculties were foreign-born and the trend was up [Winks 1979:71]. Another high proportion, 15%, were born in England and they too are likely to have left (unless taken as children by their parents) because of dissatisfaction with some aspects of life in Britain. If so almost half of the sample might have consisted of individuals estranged in some respect from their homeland and especially the policies and political trends personified by Reagan and Thatcher. (Extremely hostile attitudes toward these two leaders, shown below, confirm this supposition.)

Not surprisingly, critical attitudes toward the United States dominated the responses and were expressed most forcefully by ratios of one-half to two-thirds of the respondents. This roughly corresponds to and reflects political self-identification: 28% choose to describe themselves as "radical" and "radical-liberal," and 36% as "liberal-moderate." This adds up to a total of 64% who may thus be labeled as left-of-center.

Respondents were presented a list of statements for the most part identical with those used in the Mexican project, but fewer in number. "American society, more than most others, has failed to live up to its own ideals" was the first of such propositions designed to tap the mainspring of the social-critical sentiment which often focuses on the gap between lofty ideals and sordid realities, or on the hypocrisy of social systems which promise a great deal but deliver little. A total of 52% agreed; 16% were not sure; and 33% disagreed. As was suggested in the Mexican case it is also possible that some of the respondents do not think highly of the ideals themselves; hence their disagreement—which amounts to belief in a *congruence* between ideal and reality—is not necessarily an endorsement of the American social system.

Over half, 52%, agreed that "big corporations and especially multinationals are today the prime enemies of freedom and social justice around the world"—a belief which is a cornerstone of the left-of-center outlook associated with the prevailing, updated versions of anticapitalism. Some 16.5% were not sure and 31% disagreed. (A full three-quarters of the Mexican group agreed to this proposition.)

Given the view taken of multinationals (and presumably of various Western countries) it was not surprising that most respondents would not assign responsiblity for the problems of the Third World to its own elites. The statement proposed that "The economic problems of the Third World countries are largely due to the corruption and incompetence of their leaders and elites." Only 23% agreed; 21% were unsure; and 56% disagreed. Interestingly enough 67% of the Mexicans agreed with the same statement, thus taking a far less charitable view of their elites than did their Canadian counterparts—an attitude that is likely to be rooted in the Mexicans' own experiences and a less romantic view of Third World realities.

The military expenditures of the United States were found to be "excessive" by an overwhelming 90% of the respondents; 7.5% were not sure; and only 2% disagreed (none of them strongly)—a response very similar to those of the Mexican respondents, 94% of whom took this position. In both cases the responses reflect strong apprehension about the abuse or misuse of American power. It should not come as a surprise that a similarly large proportion, 85%, found the U.S. invasion of Grenada unjustified, and 13% justified (92% of the Mexicans found it unjustified).

Since racism and sexism are among the major critiques of American culture and society, agreement with the suggestion that their persistence has been exaggerated would point to a greater acceptance of these evils. In fact only 14% agreed that such exaggeration has taken place (as opposed to 54% of the Mexicans); 19% were unsure; and an overwhelming 67% disagreed, presumably believing that racism and sexism persist unchecked—a major difference between Canadian and Mexican groups probably due to different responses to these attitudes, especially sexism.

It has been another article of faith of the critics of the United States that "American culture and society, dedicated to competitiveness and material gain, nurtures indifference to one's fellow human beings": 61% agreed (79% of the Mexicans did); 14% were uncertain; and 23.5% disagreed.

As in the Mexican case it was a matter of interest to learn what, if any, connection there was between critical attitudes toward the United States and toward other countries that used to be its rivals or adversaries. It was thus put to the respondents that "Despite changes under Gorbachev the Soviet Union remains a repressive society": 66% agreed, 19% were not sure; and 15% disagreed. These attitudes were quite different from those of the Mexicans; as may be recalled 67% of them found Western reports of repression in the USSR exaggerated, and this was *before* the Gorbachev reforms when political repression was largely unchecked. The Canadian attitudes toward Cuba were more favorable than toward the Soviet Union and less clearly defined, as suggested by the responses to the proposition "Western reports of political repression in Cuba are greatly exaggerated": 24% agreed; 42% were not sure; and 34% disagreed. (Not surprisingly the Mexicans were far more pro-Cuban, as 77% of them did not find Western reports of Cuban political repression credible.)

A somewhat more favorable view (compared with views regarding its repressiveness) of the Soviet system emerged from the reactions to the statement suggesting that ". . . its leaders are committed to abolishing material inequalities and to improving the life of their people": 33% agreed; 25% were unsure; and 42% disagreed.

The same proposition applied to the Cuban leader's egalitarian policies yielded an agreement of 51%; 28% were unsure; and only 20% disputed the existence of these benevolent policies, making clear that many Canadian leftists—as those in the United States and Western Europe— continue to entertain far more favorable views of Cuba than of the Soviet Union. This is all the more remarkable since Cuba's economy is as mismanaged and inefficient as any in the "Socialist Commonwealth," its shortages glaring, the repression undiminished, and critical intellectuals especially harshly dealt with. To be sure all these flaws might in theory be compatible with policies designed to "abolish material inequalities and improve the life of its people," but there has been little evidence of this happening. Presumably the Canadian sympathies toward Cuba (as those of the Mexicans) feed, in some measure, on the hostility toward the United States and on the persisting revolutionary mystique of Cuba associated with the durability of Castro and his charisma—at least as seen by sympathetic foreigners. Several of these responses, including those which follow, suggest that in the case of these academics—unlike those in Mexico sampled earlier—strong critical sentiments toward the United States do not reflexively translate into widespread support or sympathy for the Soviet Union or other state socialist systems, except perhaps Cuba. This was also demonstrated by the responses to the suggestion that "Although many socialist countries are poor, they are morally superior to the capitalist ones, including the U.S." Only 11% agreed; 24% were unsure; and 62% disagreed—another finding this author would not have anticipated.

Critical attitudes toward the United States were especially strong when it was perceived as victimizer of poor countries. It was proposed that the United States was responsible "for much of the suffering and deprivation rampant in the Third World": 51% agreed (87% of the Mexicans did); 15% were undecided; and 34% disagreed.

Interestingly enough while only 11% found existing socialist countries morally superior to capitalist ones (as noted above), attitudes were quite different when it came to socialist ideals. It was proposed that "The ideals of socialism offer the best hope for peace and social justice in the world": 40% agreed; 25% were not sure; and 37% disagreed (68% of the Mexicans agreed). Those affirming these ideals presumably did not wonder why existing socialist systems have not been able to put these ideals to such laudable uses, and if they were incapable, why this did not reflect in some manner on the ideals themselves.

I was also interested to learn about the respondents' view of these ideals. They were asked: "In your opinion what are [three] essential ideals or characteristics of a socialist political or economic system?" The first response was as follows:

Material equality: 33%, equal opportunity 7%, equal access to health 6.5%, Participatory democracy 6.5%; redistribution of property 4%. When all responses (first, second, third) were combined the results were: Material equality 20%, humane values/social justice 10%, central planning 8%, participatory democracy 8%, equal access to health 7%, equal opportunity: 6%.

As these responses indicate, for approximately two-thirds of these intellectuals, equality and the various pathways to it remain the key attraction of socialism. Central planning too is likely to be seen as instrumental for equality and social justice, as is "participatory democracy" for power sharing.

Did familiarity with and interest in the theories of Marxism play a part in the presence of these attitudes? One question addressed this issue: "Is Marxism a major/moderate/minor influence in your research or teaching?" As far as research was concerned the responses were: minor influence 44%, moderate 17.5%, major 9.5%; in regard to teaching the influence of Marxism was: minor 45%, moderate 19%, major 9%.

There are different ways to interpret these findings. It may be argued that generally speaking these academics had little use for Marxism since for barely 10% was Marxism a "major" influence either in research or teaching. On the other hand it could also be argued that for approximately two-thirds it plays a moderate or major role in their work and thinking. At last it is also possible that Canadian academic intellectuals, as their American counterparts, have since the 1960s absorbed certain basic ideas of Marxism to a degree that they can treat them as self-evident truths (e.g., the evils of capitalism and the inequalities it perpetuates) rather than specific propositions of Marxism. If so they need not think of themselves as "Marxist"—in the sense of wielding a specific and elaborate conceptual apparatus—while sharing some of its basic premises. Thus Marxism, or some aspects of it, may have become conventional wisdom rather than a distinct theoretical orientation.

The realism of the respondents in judging existing socialist systems was further shown in their response to the proposition that "Nicaragua has emerged as the most promising socialist system in the world today." (The question was put to them before the electoral victory of the opposition in February 1990.) A mere 7.5% agreed; 31% were not sure, and 60% rejected the idea (19% of the Mexicans rated it as "the most authentic socialist system in the world today"). The very small proportion of those entertaining such beliefs about Nicaragua may also be explained in connection with the phenomenon of reaction formation. Unlike in the United States in Canada the government has been relatively friendly toward Nicaragua, thus it did not create the victim-victimizer relationship that elicited much of the sympathy in the United States toward a country under attack by the Reagan administration. The "my enemy's enemy is my friend" syndrome did not apply in Canada partly because of lesser hostility toward the federal government on the part of these intellectuals and partly because these authorities themselves did not conduct policies hostile toward Nicaragua. The open-ended question "Which countries in the world come closest to living up to the ideals of socialism?" confirmed that most of these respondents were not enamored with the existing state socialist systems of the Marxist-Leninist one-party variety. Some 50% mentioned Sweden first; 8% "Scandinavian countries"; and 4% Cuba. (Among the Mexicans Cuba led by 23.5%, followed by China with 10%, and the USSR with 9.5%; Sweden was nominated by a mere 4.5%.) For 15% no country came close to these ideals (31.5% of the Mexicans took the same position, once more suggesting a greater realism or cynicism among the Mexican respondents).

These preferences were confirmed by the replies to the question "Which country (countries) and political systems in the world do you admire most?" Again, among those first mentioned (three responses were requested), Sweden led with 28%, Canada 23%, the United States 10%, Switzerland 6%, Britain 4%, New Zealand 4%. To obtain a better idea of the strength of the attraction to such countries, the question was added: "Under what conditions would you consider living there?" A total of 60% mentioned various conditions. For 34.5% secure employment was such a condition; 13% answered, in various ways, that they already lived in the country they admired most, that is, Canada; for 8% mastery of the language would be the precondition of moving there; 6% were not going to contemplate such a move under any conditions; and 5.5% would contemplate such a move under some form of pressure.

If indeed a third of the respondents would have considered moving to another country (most likely Scandinavian) if they had a comparably satisfying job, it might be taken as an indication of what Karl Mannheim called the "free floating" character of intellectuals not strongly attached to place or country and possibly an indication of a degree of estrangement from the social setting inhabited.

To round out the political universe of our academics they were also asked, "Which countries or political systems in the world do you find most unappealing?" They were again asked to mention three. Among those *first mentioned* the percentages were as follows: South Africa 14%, Israel and United States tied with 12%, Chile 9%, Cuba 5%, Romania 4%, Haiti 3%. Here of course the striking fact is the unpopularity of the United States and Israel; hostility toward Israel presumably being a reflection of a broader "Third Worldism" rather than of latent antisemitism. In this perspective Israel might be seen as a premier Western-style victimizing country oppressing Arabs in the occupied territories. (In the Mexicans' ranking the United States led the list of the most unappealing with 17%, followed by Chile 14%, Soviet Union 10%, "dictatorships" 10%, "capitalist systems" 6%.)

The relatively high degree of aversion shown toward Israel by the Canadian academics sampled and its apparent irrelevance to the Mexicans as a symbol of injustice is noteworthy. The hostility toward Israel suggests a complementary sympathy toward Arab countries and populations. One may wonder why Canadian intellectuals are more pro-Arab then the Mexicans. It is possible that these attitudes are concentrated among the American contingent of the Canadian sample, more generally critical of U.S. foreign policy and more keenly aware of U.S. support for Israel; another possibility is that there was a high proportion of Jews among the American-born Canadians who are considerably left of center and therefore also hostile to Israel and pro-Third world.

To shed further light on the political attitude of the respondents they were also asked to "list a few [5] political leaders in the world today—or in recent history—[they] admire most and least." First listed among those most admired was Pierre Trudeau with 19% followed by Gorbachev with 15.5%, Gandhi 6%, John Diefenbaker 4%, and Daniel Ortega, Churchill, and Olav Palme tied with 3%, (The Mexican list had Castro at the top with 13%, Allende 7%, Gandhi 7%, Gonzalez (of Spain) and Mao each with 5%. It should be recalled that the Mexican survey was administered before Gorbachev's rise to power.)

The cumulative results of all references to appealing leaders was as follows: Gorbachev 13%, Trudeau 10%, F.D. Roosevelt, J.F. Kennedy, and Martin Luther King, Jr., 3.5%. These choices lend further credence to the characterization of the majority of those in the Canadian sample as "liberal" (in the more recent sense of the word) or left-of-center.

The same orientation was still more remarkably revealed in the selection of the least admired political leaders. According to the choices made by these Canadian intellectuals Reagan was far more reprehensible than Hitler, Stalin, Idi Amin, Pol Pot, or the Ayatollah Khomeni, and so were Nixon and Thatcher. Thus Reagan was nominated by 29%, followed by Hitler as distant second with 10%, Stalin 8.5%, Nixon and Thatcher were tied with 6%, Pinochet of Chile 5%. Still further down only 4% nominated the Ayatollah Khomeni, 2% Pol Pot, 3% Idi Amin. Yitzhak Shamir of Israel was thought to be more reprehensible than Idi Amin or Pol Pot (3.4% vs. 2.6% and 1.7% respectively). That the most outstanding mass murderers of our times, Stalin and Pol Pot, were given such low ratings remains among the mysteries of political attitude formation.

Another way to look at these tabulations is that approximately half of the unappealing leaders nominated were Western, fewer than 10% associated with communist systems, and an even lower percentage with Third World countries.

The cumulative references (all five listings combined) yield the following: Reagan 15%, Thatcher 19%, Stalin 8%, Khomeni 7%, Nixon 6%, Amin 4%, Shamir 3%, Pol Pot 1.5%. (The Mexicans too placed Reagan at the top with 16.5%, followed by Pinochet 13.5%, Thatcher 7%, and Hitler 5%. Others were mentioned by still smaller proportions, including Stalin and Pol Pot.)

At last the political-moral dimensions of the worldview of the respondents was probed by asking them the open-ended question, which were "the most shocking historical-political events in this century?"

It was my belief that outrages chosen would reflect more on the political-ideological values held by the respondents than the quantitative dimensions of the outrages involved. (The same of course also applied to the most disliked political leaders: why would the names of Reagan and Thatcher come more readily to mind than those of Stalin or Pol Pot? Certainly not because the Canadian academics were unfamiliar with the historical roles and misdeeds of the latter.) In other words moral outrages (and politicians associated with them) are apparently rated or ranked on the basis of how they fit into the general universe of moral judgments and concerns of an individual. People exhibit different degrees of sensitivity toward moral outrages depending on their relationship to their own moral values. Thus, for example, religious persecution will bother less those who do not find religion an important or desirable social institution; those who find racism a major evil will display greater indignation toward its manifestations than those who rank it lower among existing evils; those hostile to capitalism and the United States will reflexively reach for the names of Reagan and Thatcher when asked to name the least admirable politician of their times rather than attempt some more or less objective ranking of political outrages and leaders associated with them.

Not surprisingly (because it is the best documented and most widely publicized among the shocking recent historical events of this century) the Holocaust rated the highest with 52% mentioning it in the first place. The other choices were more unexpected: World War I chosen by 15%, (perhaps those of English background?), the bombing of Hiroshima and Nagasaki by 10%, World War II by 6%. Nobody mentioned (at least in statistically significant numbers) outrages associated with the Soviet system: Soviet concentration camps, the purges, show trials, the "terror famine," collectivization of agriculture, relocation of ethnic groups, the crushing of popular uprising in Eastern Europe and Afghanistan, and so on. Nor were similar outrages associated with communist China mentioned, including the so-called Cultural Revolution.

The second ranking outrage was selected by these percentages: World War II 18%, Stalinist purges 15%, Hiroshima-Nagasaki 11%, Holocaust 11%, Vietnam 9%. Other percentages were all under 3%. When all three responses were combined the results were as follows: Holocaust 24%, World War II 11%, Hiroshima 9%, World War I 8.5%, Vietnam 7%, repression in Cambodia 4%.

Aversion toward the United States—well established by now—nonetheless did not predispose these Canadians to blame the United States for *all* major contemporary disasters and outrages, such as the boat people. It was proposed that "It is the political system prevailing in Indochina since the end of the war that is responsible for the outpouring of the boat people"—a statement that many American social critics would find unacceptable persuaded as they are that such responsibility lies wholly with the U.S. They reach this conclusion by blaming the outpouring of the people on the war and its after-effects, including the sorry state of the Vietnamese economy—and in turn by blaming both the war and the state of the economy on the U.S.

Contrary to such inclinations 41% of the respondents here surveyed found the communist authorities responsible; 36% were undecided; and 21% disagreed to such an attribution of responsibility.

At the same time, responding to another open-ended question, 91% found the U.S. "responsible for many world problems." Asked to specify the problems, among those first mentioned 24% chose environmental deterioration; 23% poverty and exploitation in the Third World; 21% arms trade and race; 10% promoting instability in Central America;

6% support for regional military conflicts; 6% international debt crisis; 5% waste of resources. Again an image of American aggressiveness emerges from approximately one-third of the answers. Concern with American irresponsibility and wastefulness is reflected in holding the U.S. responsible for environmental problems and Third World poverty. It may be noted here that the very tangible and widely publicized contribution the U.S. makes to Canadian air and water pollution by acid rain has undoubtedly sensitized Canadians to such activities in general.

Attitudes toward the United States were further probed in questions which consisted of lists of attributes, three of which the respondents were asked to circle (not rank ordered). They were asked first, "How do you think the U.S. is regarded by most Canadians?" "ambivalence" was marked by 85%, "criticism" 55%, "envy" 24%, "admiration" 22%, "perplexity" 21%, "affection" 15%, "sympathy" 13%, "curiosity" 10%, "pity" 7%, and "hatred" 4%. To what extent these attributions were projections of the feelings of the respondents is not easy to tell; given the elitist self-conception of many intellectuals it is possible that they would sharply differentiate their own attitudes and values from those of average or ordinary people, "most Canadians" in this case.

The next question did not ask for attributions but proposed that "American society may be described as . . ."; once more respondents were asked to mark (four) of the most appropriate of a list of 13. The results were as follows: "Imperialist" was chosen by 56%, "exploitative" 51%, "racist" 47%, "allows much personal freedom" 41.5%, "one of the handful of free and materially prosperous countries in the world" 40%, "provides free expression and decent standards of living" 33%, "no worse than most other societies" 31%, "basically flawed" 19%, "unjust and oppressive" 16%, "sexist" 14%, "allows too much personal freedom" 12%, "cold, impersonal, bureaucratized" 8%, "warps personal growth" 3%.

While a total of one-third to 40% chose positive attributes, the single highest attribution was a negative one, imperialist (56%), as was the second most popular choice, exploitative (51%), and the third, racist (47%).

As already noted, despite such generally unfavorable attitudes toward the United States 76% of the respondents had contemplated living there under various conditions, which included: good job or research opportunities 45%, study 2%, and retirement 4%. (Only 40% of the Mexicans had considered living in the United States, which is not surprising given the language difference.)

One-quarter of the respondents noted that they had previously lived in the United States and 10% actually were U.S. citizens. Only 1% said that they would under no conditions live in this country. Thus we have indications of a generally positive or positive-utilitarian attitude toward the United States as far as the possibility of residence is concerned. The United States may be viewed with distaste or strong criticism but this does not deter over half the respondents from entertaining the prospect of living there if career opportunities were promising. Possibly such attitudes are more pronounced among those of American origin in the sample. It would not be surprising if there was some ambivalence among Canadian academics about the large number of their American colleagues who found employment at Canadian universities and have thus intensified competition for scarce jobs. If so, academics of American background would have additional reasons to consider relocating in their native country under appropriate conditions.

Since it is often assumed that lack of personal contact and communication is the principal source of negative stereotypes—at any rate this is a prevalent view among students of racial and ethnic relations and prejudice—respondents were also asked (as in the Mexican cases) about their experience of the United States and contacts with Americans. For 29%, such contacts (and U.S. residence) were due to a period of study; 26% regular visits or vacations; 17% short visits; and 6% visiting appointments. From such figures one may conclude that some two-thirds of them had quite thorough exposure to American society and culture. Another 22% reported other contacts, most of which involved having been born there.

Not surprisingly 94% in the sample reported knowing Americans closely—further indication that lack of contact was not a factor in the development of their attitudes toward the United States. Again, as in the case of Mexican academics, it is likely that many such contacts were made with American academics in similar fields (humanities and social sciences), themselves critically disposed toward American society and foreign policy.

I was also interested in learning something, within the obvious limits of a brief questionnaire, about attitudes toward Canadian society. One reason was to find out whether in the respondent's view the United States was implicated in any of the flaws and problems of Canada; the second was to see if there were any similarities between critiques of Canadian and American society. It was also of interest to learn whether or not criticism of the United States was part of a generally social-critical disposition or rather a reflection of nationalistic concerns and grievances.

In the first of these open-ended questions it was asked, "What do you regard as the most serious problems of Canada?" The first mentioned were as follows: economic or political domination by the United States 18%, rift between Quebec and rest of Canada 9%, acid rain/environmental problems 8%, increasing national debt 8%, regionalism 5.5%, language 5%.

In the cumulative tabulation of all answers, economic and political domination by the U.S. led with 13%, followed by Quebec 12%, acid rain 7%, national debt 6%, free trade 5%.

In another open-ended question it was asked, "What do you regard as the major defects of Canadian society?" Interestingly enough, "prejudice and racism" topped the list among the defects first mentioned with 12%; it was followed by "economic and political domination by the U.S." 7%, tied both with the Quebec problems and "regionalism," which for some meant domination of regions by central provinces. Canadian "insularity" and poverty was mentioned by 5%.

The cumulative tabulation of all defects mentioned produced the following results: prejudice and racism 11%, regionalism 6%, smugness and complacency 6%, U.S. domination 5%, Quebec problems 5%, native rights and land claims (meaning their denials) 5%. Defects mentioned by proportions under 5% included lack of strong central government, Canadian inferiority, insularity, weak national identity, extreme multiculture, intolerance toward immigrants, conservative political ideas, and homelessness.

It may be concluded that except for the attribution of prejudice and racism (presumably directed at native populations and new immigrants of color) most of the defects mentioned had more to do with the Canadian political than social structure and with problems of Canadian national identity. Thus one respondent wrote in response to this question (regarding major defects): "There is a Canadian joke: we could have had American business, French culture and British politics. Instead, we have American culture, British business and French politics" [No. 73]. The United States was implicated in several of the perceived defects of Canadian society, for example, environmental and trade problems and various ways of dominating Canada.

At last it was asked what the respondents regarded as the major sources of the tensions in Canadian-American relations. The responses brought to surface a wide range of grievances and made clear that the overwhelming majority held the United States responsible for these tensions. Thus first mentioned among the sources of tensions: pressure for economic integration 16%, environmental issues 13.5%, disproportionate power 12%, ignorance of Canada 12%, American threats to social programs and culture 7%, U.S. arrogance 6%, U.S. control of energy and water 4%.

Those selecting other sources of tension (in smaller percentages) followed the same trend: American responsibility dominated these suggestions as well.

As is often the case, some of the actual comments (subsequently compressed into the coding categories) conveyed attitudes with far greater richness than summary coding categories would allow. For example, one respondent [No. 106] had this to say about the sources of tension between the two countries: "Americans don't like the idea that there are foreigners with ideas of their own. Canadians don't like the knowledge that in any dispute with the U.S.A., they have no power or leverage worth mentioning."

The terminology used in the replies to this question was also revealing. Canada was frequently characterized as actually or potentially "swamped," "swallowed," "dominated," and in fear of becoming the 51st state; "subordinated" to the U.S. and its economic, cultural, or political interests. Frequent references were also made to U.S. "hegemony," "economic aggression," "imperialism," and "cultural imperialism." The two countries were sometimes described as "the mouse next to the elephant." On the other hand one respondent made this unusual comment concerning the sources of tension: "Acid rain is about the only one I can think of; the rhetoric concerning the fear of American take-over in economic matters is largely fake, in my opinion" [No. 110].

The Canadian intellectuals here surveyed were for the most part united in regarding American policies and influences harmful to Canadian national and economic interest and culture. If there was any recognition of the Canadian contribution to what these respondents saw as a troubled relationship, it did not emerge from the responses. It is plausible enough to come to the conclusion that the many negative conceptions, indeed stereotypes, of the United States encountered are linked to the perceptions of its specific policies and influences as harming Canada. On the other hand it is also possible that perceptions of the threats and harmful influences and policies derive at least in part from negative preconceptions and predispositions which color the assessment of specific policies. It is especially difficult for those with a negative predisposition to entertain the possiblity that there may be areas of common interest between the two countries and that not every policy proposed or pursued by the United States is automatically and self-evidently self-serving.

In their suspiciousness and apprehensiveness toward the United States Canadian respondents resemble their Mexican colleagues to a far greater extent than this author had anticipated.

It remains to comment further on the characteristics and representativeness of the sample. While it may be said that the six universities selected cannot be considered representative of Canadian higher education *as a whole* they arguably are representative of the major and most respected among these institutions. If so, this was something of an elite sample, but then throughout this study no secret has been made of my interest in the attitude of elite groups.

Among the characteristics of the sample the reader may wish to know the gender distribution. It consisted of 75% males and 17% females; the missing 8% failed to provide this information. They described their ethnic background as: Anglo-Saxon 45.5%, French Canadian 9%, Jewish 7%, Canadian 6.5%, Scottish 6.5%, German 6%. Some 60% of the respondents did not consider themselves religious and 17% did, while 23% opted for "somewhat religious"; 26% declared the parents' religious affiliation as Catholic, 22% Anglican, 10% Protestant, 10% Jewish, 6.5% Presbyterian, 4% United Church.

Some 35% of the respondents attended American colleges (again, a figure roughly corresponding to the reported place of birth, confirming the supposition that those born in the United States emigrated to Canada as adults or young adults). As to graduate school, 50% in the sample attended American graduate schools; 23% declined to respond to this question.

Regarding departmental affiliation, 24% were in history, 21% in sociology, 20% in English or literary studies, 19% in psychology, and 12.5% in anthropology.

At last some final speculations may be in order concerning those who did not respond. It is unlikely that many among the nonrespondents entertained more positive attitudes toward the United States than those who chose to respond; indeed nonresponse may be another form of protest, an expression of negative sentiments toward a research project originating in the United States and seeking to gather information about Canadian attitudes toward the United States; such refusal to cooperate is far more likely to be associated with generally negative attitudes toward the United States than with favorable ones.

Although the two samples were in some ways asymmetrical (the Canadian was larger and the respondents were drawn from predominantly elite institutions from different parts of the country whereas the Mexican sample was smaller and limited to Mexico City and included one institution of more modest reputation, the Metropolitan Autonomous University) a few generalizations may be attempted.

It is obvious that in both groups the level of critical sentiment toward the United States was high. American foreign policy, culture, and the association of the United States with capitalism and its role in the alleged exploitation of the Third World were central to the critiques in both instances. Most respondents from both countries were fully persuaded that the United States threatens these countries in various ways, especially economic and cultural, that it is ignorant of and insensitive toward them and misuses its overwhelming power in relating to them.

The unexpected finding for this author was the similarity of the type and degree of criticism directed at the United States by both groups, as I expected the Canadians to be a good deal less critical than the Mexicans and suffering fewer resentments and nationalistic grievances. This clearly was not the case. It may in part be explained by the fact that, unlike in the Mexican sample, hostility toward the United States among the Canadians was intensified by the presence, among those sampled, of a large contingent of American emigrants, many of whom may have regarded themselves as political refugees of sorts. The timing of the questionnaire might have contributed to such negative attitudes on the part of the Canadians: they were sent out in the spring of 1989 at a time when the impending free trade agreement with the United States was publicly debated and stirring up nationalistic concerns. Conceivably, at more tranquil times less apprehension and aversion toward the United States might have been found. (But economic friction has been growing in recent decades and intensified during the Reagan presidency, as was shown in a study commissioned by the Canadian Institute for Economic Policy [see Clarkson 1982].)

It would also be difficult to overestimate continued Canadian concern with Americanization, defined as "the transfer of American cultural and economic values abroad" [Ibid.:221], and the grave apprehensions of the impact of American media, television in particular, on Canadian cultural-national identity. ("The consumption of television is the dominant cultural activity of Canadians ... But the national identity and culture Canadians learn about in front of their TV screens is of foreign origin ... overwhelmingly American" [Ibid.:224].) So strong are the concerns about national identity that according to the current prime minister, Brian Mulroney, without bilingualism (that is, Quebec) Canada would be no more than an adjunct to the United States ["Canada's Independent Streak" 1990].

What is also worthy of note is that quite different cultural and historical circumstances can lead to similar attitudes. Thus if in the Canadian case a problematic or weak national identity was among the factors leading to a beleaguered, apprehensive, and finally hostile disposition toward the United States, it would be hard to argue that Mexican national identity and culture are similarly indistinct and could easily be confused with the North American. Likewise if difficult economic conditions—including mass poverty, illiteracy, and unemployment—were a factor in generating resentment toward a wealthy neighbor, such conditions clearly cannot be found north of the border.

In both sets of responses it was possible to discern, besides aversion, something slightly more positive: ambivalence. The large numbers of both Canadians and Mexicans who visited this country, who studied in it, and would be willing to live here is among the indications that feelings toward the United States do not reduce to mere hostility. Somewhat

unexpectedly the observations of a Canadian author might apply, with
some obvious modifications to Mexico as well:

> Ever since 1775, when the Americans broke away from Britain . . . we have
> had a love-hate relationship with the United States . . . We are both
> delighted and appalled by the United States, often simultaneously. So con-
> scious are we of the presence and power of our big neighbor that the
> nationalism of Canadian people often seems anti-American rather than
> pro-Canadian. [Innis 1972:1]

10

Conclusions: Anti-Americanism, Decadence, and the Collapse of Communism

> ... at the very moment in history when the East is looking toward the West and its civilization as a model, or as a promise, or as a vital alternative, we find in the West a situation that may be described simply as decadence and intellectual civil war.
>
> *Hilton Kramer*

> Like communism, capitalism is a materialist and utopian faith; also like communism, it has shown itself empty of a moral imperative or spiritual meaning. To the questions likely to be asked by the next century, the sayings of Malcolm Forbes will seem as useless as the maxims of Lenin.
>
> *Lewis H. Lapham, 1990*

> It matters that there are influential, highly educated Americans who think that the United States is a cold, careless society in debt and decline.
>
> *Jeane Kirkpatrick, 1990*

It has been shown in this study that the domestic and foreign critiques of the United States and American society are quite similar in their substance, although arising out of dissimilar circumstances and geographic locations. It is also clear that both within the United States and abroad intellectuals are the most committed and passionate critics of American society and not merely because they are the best equipped to formulate such critiques but also because they believe in them most wholeheartedly. More unexpectedly on further reflection it appears that not merely the themes but the deeper sources and motives behind these critiques are also similar.

As may be recalled, anti-Americanism abroad has three major types or subspecies: there is anti-Americanism as nationalism, as anticapitalism, and as protest against modernity. These three forms may appear jointly or, less often, singly. One need not be a disciple of Marx to recognize that capitalism is a modernizing force, hence linking the protest against capitalism and modernity has an indisputable logic; in turn the problems created by modernization add to the store of nationalistic grievances.

The domestic critiques, as was made clear, also incorporate an abundance of anticapitalist themes. On the other hand, being citizens of the United States, domestic critics cannot by definition be motivated by nationalistic grievances of their own (as the term is generally understood) but they can sympathize with nationalist critiques abroad which label the United States imperialist and a menace to the independence and integrity of smaller and weaker nations. As far as the protest against modernity is concerned, the domestic and foreign versions also converge although there are differences as to what aspects of modernity provoke hostility within and outside the United States and what remedies are being sought and proferred against this process.

Americanization—that is, the spread of American values and ways of life threatening traditional values and ways of life—stimulates a defensive anti-Americanism around the world; it often evokes what Peter Berger called counter-modernizing impulses, most clearly exemplified by the Islamic religious revival in Iran and Arab countries.

The aversion to modernity discernible in the domestic critiques of the United States is less a protest against the decline of traditional values than an expression of anguish or anger directed at the decline of sustaining bonds of community and at life in a materially rich, secular, and individualistic society which offers little help in finding and grasping the ends of existence. This may be called *anti-Americanism as a crisis of meaning.* Unlike, for example, anti-Americanism in Arab countries, this type of protest against modernity does not propose and postulate a return to well-defined traditional values and ways of life, it only conveys distress over existing social arrangements, over life as it is.

In the spring of 1990 when this is being written it may appear that the global conditions breeding anti-Americanism have significantly changed. It is tempting to think that the decline of communist systems during the late 1980s will have, or already had, an impact on anti-Americanism. These changes may be interpreted not merely as repudiation of political-economic systems antithetical to those of the United States (and other Western countries) but also as amounting to an implicit endorsement of the political practices, social values, and cultural beliefs of the West, and pre-eminently the United States. Not only had most of the communist or post-communist states—with some notable exceptions—ceased or significantly reduced the production and distribution of anti-

American propaganda; what is more important, they demonstrated that the major putative alternative to the political pluralism of the West offers little. More than that, the people living in the formerly or by now partially communist systems have displayed a great yearning for everything American (and Western), from clothing to music, from free enterprise to American-style checks and balances, and ideals of a civil society. Would not these developments deal a blow to anti-Americanism both in the United States and around the world?

Unfortunately this need not be the case. Anti-Americanism has never been primarily a product of Soviet or communist propaganda although the latter helped to nurture it. Much of the hostility toward the United States abroad had indigenous sources which the Soviet Union (and other communist powers) tried to stimulate and exploit, but did not create. Nationalism in particular remains a potent force through much of the Third World, and the decline of Soviet power and the attractions of Soviet communism will do little to reduce it. Likewise the decline of Soviet-type systems has little relevance to the persistence of poverty in much of the Third World, although this decline may indirectly contribute to adopting new policies aimed at the reduction of this poverty. On the other hand these developments may put a damper on anticapitalist sentiment often associated with anti-Americanism among Third World elites (as in the West). If the Soviet socialist or state socialist model holds fewer attractions, anticapitalism and anti-Americanism may lose some of their intensity.

Even more important is the question of what conclusions Third World intellectuals will draw from these developments as to the validity and promise of Marxism as a charismatic ideology. There was, well before the recent developments in the Soviet bloc, a wealth of information to discredit self-styled Marxist-Leninist systems and to inspire reflection about the flaws of a theory that has so stubbornly resisted application or became so readily distorted in the process. Yet, as a Mexican intellectual observed a few years ago, ". . . for the university lecturer in Mexico and Peru, as in other Third World countries, Marxism, with its many variants, still holds its old Messianic prestige" [Krauze 1986:141]. To what degree will these intellectuals attempt and succeed in separating the now publicly acknowledged failures of state socialist systems and their rapid decline from the flaws of the beliefs which inspired and allegedly guided them? The reaction of American social critics discussed below (more readily accessible at this point in time) is not encouraging; already arduous efforts are under way to distance the theory from the practices it was used to legitimate and to salvage faith.

The disruptions caused by modernization will certainly not abate and neither will the associated mood of anti-Americanism. Moreover these days a country need not be greatly modernized for anti-modernizing impulses to be set into motion; a major form of modernity, easily acquired and most relevant for subverting values and traditions, the mass media of communications, readily penetrates even otherwise backward societies, raising expectations and mobilizing the concerns of the guardians of traditional cultural values.

Nationalistic grievances are not likely to decline either, as specific interests of the United States and those of various countries will continue to collide, for instance in matters of trade or with regard to the presence of American military installations and troops on foreign soil, always a powerful incentive for nationalistic indignation and protest. At the present time this is well illustrated by events in the Philippines and South Korea, two countries where public anti-Americanism is prominent and linked to the presence of American troops and bases. In South Korea in particular an observer called "the ferocity of anti-Americanism . . . striking" and its growth spectacular during the 1980s [Kristof 1987] while the country was successfully modernizing and democratizing, processes fueling both the nationalistic and antimodernizing grievances. Young intellectuals and students in particular relished a fervent hostility toward the United States colored by a left-wing radicalism.

Insofar as the contrast between the wealth of the United States and the poverty of many countries around the world is also going to persist, it will predictably replenish hostilities and the scapegoating impulse. Americans travelling abroad will continue to personify these contrasts, although no more so than similarly well-heeled tourists from Western Europe or Japan.

Another stimulant of anti-Americanism abroad dwelt on earlier, the aversion of American social critics to their own society (and its communication to many corners of the world), will probably also persist and continue to provide models and raw materials for fashioning the foreign critiques. Why these domestic critiques and the underlying sentiments are likely to persist at a time when communist systems are in profound disarray is a more thought-provoking phenomenon than the corrresponding anti-Americanism in underdeveloepd countries. Indeed, as noted in the beginning, domestic anti-Americanism is an altogether more puzzling, and possibly more consequential phenomenon than its counterparts abroad. In concluding this study there is reason to ask what connections there may be between these critiques and the phenomenon of decadence or decline—an issue that has not been addressed earlier in this book.

Decadence itself may be the target of the social critics; their main objection to the society they live in may rest on the charge that it is decadent (rather than unjust or exploitative, though of course all such critiques may be combined). But the social critics may also look hopefully

upon decadence as vindication of their critiques or as the process herald-
ing the collaspe of the inhumane and corrupt system they opposed all
along. Attributions of decadence on the part of the critics may also have
a more specific and not so hidden agenda; they may be used to support,
on prudential grounds, an isolationist posture in foreign policy. It has
thus been argued during the 1980s with growing frequency and conviction that a society in decline cannot afford to overextend itself in foreign
ventures; the recent school of decline vigorously supports American
retreat from global affairs on such grounds. In all probability such isolationism also rests on a distaste for what the critics see as excessive and
unwholesome American influence or "hegemony" abroad. Not surprisingly some of the decline theorists are also critics of the Reagan era and
its policies:

> Kennedy's "Rise and Fall" and Mead's "Moral Splendor" are particularly
> bare-knuckled in their condemnation of American politics in the 1980s.
> Kennedy devotes much of his . . . eighth chapter to a grim accounting of
> the long-term strategic costs of budget and trade deficits, trillion-dollar
> defense budgets and dwindling rates of private investment. [Schmeisser
> 1988:67]

The immense media attention lavished on Kennedy's book in particular suggests that the decline thesis found favor both among those critical
of what they see as American imperialism and those who wishfully contemplate the demise of a social order they so heartily dislike. On the other
hand it has also been said of these writings that they "shake all of us from
complacency" [Ibid.]—a peculiar claim in a culture that during the past
quarter-century has been immersed in waves of self-critical scrutiny and
collective breast beatings over its unresolved social and economic problems and wrongheaded foreign policies.

There are additional grounds for skepticism about some highly publicized attributions of decline, as such claims in the recent past often had
other, ulterior motives. Readers will not find it difficult to recall several
elections in which rival contenders pointed to symptoms of decline (falling behind the Soviet Union militarily, behind Japan economically, being
destroyed by domestic social problems, and so on) only to brandish their
own remedies. Attributions of decline have provided excellent points of
departure for both ambitious politicians and disaffected intellectuals for
promoting and justifying their own policies and promises.

There are also those who openly welcome a diminished status of the
United States in global affairs. A *New Yorker* editorial spoke for many:

> now we need a president who can calm a national appetite for global swag-
> gering and develop a national willingness to look at who we are, with our

> homeless, our poor schools, our struggling industries . . . there is actually
> something appealing . . . in the prospect of a more modest United States
> . . . burdened by neither the corruptions of militarism nor those of self-
> righteousness . . . ["Notes and Comment" 1990:34]

Decadence and social criticism may be linked in other ways too: certain kinds of social criticism may by themselves be regarded as symptoms of decadence as the endless elaboration of collective guilt and national failures which such critiques entail might contribute to less tangible forms of social-cultural decline by eroding the self-confidence of both the elites and the rest of the nation.

Discussions of decadence and decline have not been confined to the United States but often address the broader process of the alleged decline of the West—a form of inquiry that has been with us in a self-conscious form at least since the late 19th century. A French student of America believed that "The general impression and confusion that seems so depressing in America today is . . . felt all over the West," but he had "No doubt there is a crisis in America today" and that "The whole country seemed to have lost its bearings" [Crozier 1984:142, 139, xviii]. For Octavio Paz, the Mexican writer and philosopher, the traits of such decline include "an emptiness of faith, a superficial nihilism, renunciation, resignation, a lowering of vital tension, greed, abandonment, moral surrender, vulgarity . . . rebirth of superstitions. 'We now live longer' writes Paz, 'but they are hollow and empty years'" [Krauze 1986:142]. For Robert Nisbet, the process began in 1914 with World War I and led to the isolation of the individual and all the pathologies associated with it:

> During the 70 years since the war, Americans have seen a constantly
> increasing emphasis placed upon the individual as separated from the
> social order, as in revolt against the ties of family, church, and in due time
> university, the living tradition of classics, even objective reality itself. [Nis-
> bet 1988:17]

What Nisbet here explains is not so much decadence (though he probably would agree that the processes he described culminate in it) but rather the alienation or estrangement of the individual ("this self-obsessed being") that underlies much social criticism and the convergence of personal unhappiness with the rejection of the social world.

Aaron Wildavsky, seeking to explain "anomalies in the American welfare state," finds the key factor in

> The disintegration of institutions . . . accompanied on the personal level
> by diminuition of distinctions that once separated moral from immoral

behavior, authority from disorder. Even a short list of eroded distinctions is impressive: those between male and female fashions; young and old; various types of sexual orientation and experience; the roles of parents and children, teachers and students. [Wildavsky 1982:46]

Many analyses of the difficulties of contemporary American society— relevant to the matter of decadence—take a similar position by focusing on the growth of ethical, moral, and aesthetic relativism and its obvious result: the reluctance to differentiate, to make vital, value-based distinctions. Leszek Kolakowski wrote:

> We have gotten used to shrugging off many horrors of our world by talking about cultural difference. "We have our values, they have theirs" is a saying we frequently hear when dealing with the atrocities of totalitarianism, or of other forms of despotism . . . When we extend our generous acceptance of cultural diversity to include all the rules of good and evil, when we aver, for example, that the human rights idea is a European concept, unfit for and ungraspable in societies that share other traditions, do we mean that Americans rather dislike being tortured and packed into concentration camps but Vietnamese, Iranians and Albanians do not mind . . . ? And if so, what is wrong with the racial laws of South Africa . . . ? [Kolakowski 1986:31]

Such relativism, and the social-cultural determinism that underlies it, is not consistently applied but more characteristically when it is aimed at discrediting Western values. As such, the attitude here considered is similar to the moral equivalence approach that used to link the United States and the Soviet Union, and which, on closer inspection, turned out to be less than "equivalent" and far more critical of the United States. Schools of cultural-political relativism and diversity on closer inspection also reveal a far greater tolerance and sympathy for non-Western or anti-Western values and ways of life than for those of the Western tradition. This author had commented in another work on the corresponding (politically motivated) alternation between moral relativism and moral absolutism so characteristic of our times [Hollander 1981:424–28]. More recently Kolakowski had this to say on the matter:

> More often than not we are simply inconsistent, less for cognitive than for political reasons: we like to profess our relativistic complacency in cases that we prefer . . . and to reserve our moral intransigence and "absolute values" for other cases. Thus it can be congenial to be moralists about South Africa but realpolitikers and courteous relativists about communist systems, or vice versa. [Kolakowski 1986:31]

The embrace of such relativism has numerous expressions and applications in American domestic matters. While on the one hand this outlook cautions about being "judgmental" about ethnic minorities, non-Western cultures, or "alternative" sexual preferences, it celebrates "diversity" without providing clear criteria as to what among the vast diversity of human values, ways of life, and cultural products is deserving of such celebration.

"Diversity" in matters cultural and educational has become something of a code word, as moral equivalence used to be; the much recommended supsension of standards of judgment is partial, and behind the apparent refusal to make distinctions and to discriminate, political preferences are not hard to find. It turns out that it is perfectly acceptable (in academic life) to freely express vigorous aversion toward things Western, American, "Eurocentric," or associated with the intellectual efforts of "dead white males." As Peter Shaw observed, "When it comes to [Western] civilization . . . the eye that looks benignly on the disposition of the mentally ill in Nigeria—turns suddenly censorious and judgemental" [Shaw 1989 *The War Against Intellect*:152–53]. The selective embrace of "diversity" or "multiculturalism" has also been energetically pursued by major foundations increasingly championing non-Western, non-European art [Lipman 1990].

The selective relativism here discussed also has significant moral ramifications in current discussions of crime and criminals. Here again the hidden dimensions of this partial or incomplete relativism (and its affinity with social criticism) can be detected; not only is the burden of responsibility lifted from criminals (or certain types of criminals) but it is shifted to other actors and entities. As George Will put it, "We have here another triumph of the social science of victimology. Its specialty is the universalization of victimhood, the dispersal of responsibility into a fog of 'socio-economic factors' . . . The ambition of the modern mind is to spare itself a chilling sight, that of the cold blank stare of personal evil" [Will 1989 May 1]. Crime so relativized allows for a far more satisfactory and moralistic indictment of the social system as a whole and sometimes of particular individuals as well, representing the evil system. By contrast it is difficult to recall critical assessments of the performance or attributes of, say, Ronald Reagan as President that stressed the degree to which he was a product of his environment and therefore had little choice but press ahead with his unfortunate policies which, however deplorable they might have been, could be understood with reference to a wide range of social factors and circumstances which shaped them.

The issue of personal responsibility becomes central in any discussion of decadence because of its linkage to morality and its presumed role in human affairs. A culture that diminishes or dismisses the part played by personal responsibility (informed by moral standards) in social affairs may indeed be in decline. Examples of such dismissal of personal responsibility assault us daily from every direction. Consider the psychologist interviewed on the CBS evening news (on April 24, 1990) about the phenomenon of black teenagers killing one another for the possession of fashionable jackets and sneakers. It was the view of this expert that these articles of clothing should not have been advertised, because through such advertising the temptation to acquire them becomes irresistible, presumably creating an uncontrollable urge to murder those unwilling to part with them. The expert also pointed out that if similar atrocities had taken place in a white middle-class neighborhood (instead of black ghettos) the offending commercials would have been stopped immediately. It was clearly his message that individuals, or culturally and economically disadvantaged individuals (black teenagers in big cities), are helpless victims of the media; their behavior could be improved and their murderousness curtailed if they were not to tempted by commercials extolling articles of clothing. The matter of the moral values and impulse control was not raised, nor the possibility that the offenders had a measure of control over, and hence responsibility for, their actions.

The findings of a report that "New York City schools spent more than $120 million in the last four years to prevent students from dropping out, but most of the participants did not improve their attendance or academic work" also led to conclusions which excluded any notion of the responsibility of the students for their performance. The board of education officials believed that "the findings pointed to a need to make instruction more appealing to students" rather than to the possibility that the motivation, discipline, and values of the students had some bearing on their levels of academic performance [Berger 1990:B1].

Time and again when minorities had performed poorly on various tests it was automatically concluded that the tests were biased (rather than those taking them unprepared) even after they had been revised to remove alleged "cultural bias." Hence renewed calls for changing the tests or restructuring the environment. Thus, for example,

> Despite the involvement of minority officers in helping prepare a new promotion examination for the New York City Police Department virtually all of the latest group of officers promoted to sergeant are white . . . Now the Police Department is bracing for a possible new round of lawsuits, this time over the 1988 sergeants' test . . . [As to the idea that the low test scores had anything to do with educational deficiencies] . . . many Hispanic people and blacks reject this explanation as racist, arguing instead that low scores may reflect a hidden agenda by bureaucrats . . . to keep minority advancement . . . to a minimum. [Pitt 1988:B1, 6]

In another case, test results were challenged because they had a "disparate impact" on minorities, that is, a high proportion of them failed.

According to a Justice Department official the tests were discriminatory because they included "questions that had no bearing on police work and dealt generally with an applicant's cognitive ability. Scores on these non-job-related questions reflected an 'adverse impact on blacks and Hispanics,' he said" [Hanley 1988:27]. Declaring cognitive ability irrelevant (or non-job-related) to police work may be viewed as part of a broader trend to revise standards downward discernible in many areas of life and connected with the erosion of support for personal responsibility.

The question of how far the principle of social determinism should extend has great significance. More often than not the refusal to make important distinctions—moral or intellectual—and social determinism are linked. As Kolakowski observed,

> The belief that human beings are entirely society-made has a number of alarming consequences . . . if I am totally definable in the "objective" terms of social relationships then indeed there is no reason why "I," rather than the abstraction "society," should be responsible for anything. [Kolakowski 1986:32]

George Will characterized as "Unlimited tolerance in the form of indiscriminate compassion" Cardinal O'Connor's decision to visit both the victim and alleged perpetrator of the notorious rape in Central Park. He added: "It is an age of egalitarian distribution of esteem as well as compassion. In such an age indiscriminateness is a moral imperative. In such an age, there will be clerics, who, as a sign of tender sensibility, will not 'single out' the brutalized from the brutes" [Will 1989 May 15].

The rapid expansion of diseases included in the *Diagnostic and Statistical Manual* of the American Psychiatric Association is an example of both the effectiveness of the lobbying by various interest groups and the successful drive to further narrow personal accountability for criminal behavior. "Post-traumatic stress disorder" spawned the battered woman syndrome, rape trauma syndrome, and child abuse syndrome, each widely used in courts to limit responsibility. Newly proposed diseases that would further reduce criminal responsibility of selected groups

> include "Post-Abortion Syndrome," "Oppression Artifact Syndrome" (said to afflict blacks, gays, lesbians and other oppressed groups) and "Victimization Disorder."
>
> These aspiring disorders can be expected to receive powerful lobbying support. Together, the mental health professionals who define new diseases and the lawyers who labor to broaden their definitions form an emerging industry that recasts people's unfortunate life histories as the root causes of ailments, which can then win insurance compensation or

civil awards for the victims, or insulate them from criminal responsibility. [Saletan and Watzman 1989:91]

Again, as these designations suggest, the drive to diminish personal and magnify social responsibility is not universal. While these efforts utilize the general cultural trend toward relativization and the new affinity toward social and situational determinism, the trend does not seek to reduce individual responsibility on sociological grounds across the board. This was pointed out already in 1971 when Michael Lerner wrote:

> The violence of the ghetto is patronized as it is "understood" and forgiven; the violence of a Cicero racist convinced that Martin Luther King threatens his lawn and house and powerboat is detested without being understood. [Likewise] . . . elite intellectuals . . . show immediate "understanding" for the ghetto black's hatred of the policeman yet find police violence directed at a partially upper class demonstration a sure sign of incipient fascism. [Lerner 1971:146, 155]

The admiration of violent criminals on the part of distinguished intellectuals and social critics further suggests that moral relativism by itself is not the sole explanation of the phenomena here examined. On the contrary sympathy toward these criminals amounts to an assertion of a particular set of values: their crime is misidentified as social protest and its perpetrator as authentic social critic. Thus Norman Mailer, the main champion of Jack Henry Abbott, a violent criminal, wrote in the introduction to Abbott's book: ". . . not only the worst are sent to prison, but the best—that is, the proudest, the bravest, the most daring, the most enterprising, and the most undefeated of the poor" [Munson 1981:22].

The two most notable illustrations (in recent times) of the confluence of social criticism with sympathy toward violent criminals were those of George Jackson, the black convict in California (killed in the course of an attempted violent prison break) and that of Jack Henry Abbott, Mailer's protégé. Both were transformed by their supporters into virtuous victims and credited with literary talent. *Soledad Brother: The Prison Letters of George Jackson* (1970) (with an introduction by Jean Genet) received rave reviews, as had the selection of prison letters of Abbott entitled *In the Belly of the Beast* (1981). Jackson's innocence was treated as axiomatic and he was perceived and celebrated as a fighter for racial justice and profound self-taught thinker, though originally he was imprisoned for crimes that had little to do with matters political. While Jackson was black and Abbott white, their political philosophies and personalities appeared similar. What was said of Abbott may apply to Jackson, as well as to lesser figures regarded with similar sympathy in the adversary culture:

... Abbott's grisly depiction of prison life was treated as gospel truth, his grandiose and paranoid self-portrait accepted as evidence of a noble soul, and his expressions of violent impulses interpreted as "rage" against society.

Indeed that rage was undoubtedly the secret of Abbott's success. For his insistence that he bears no responsibility for his actions, that he is no more than a creature of "the state," and that freedom, equality and justice in America are mere shams might be said to express perfectly . . . the ideology dear to the hearts of New York's fashionable intelligentsia . . . Abbott's admirers accepted without question the underlying political message that capitalist America is a sick and evil society. [Munson 1981:20]

The rights of prisoners was yet another issue that shed light on the transformation of American society between the 1960s and the 1980s. It was part of the "rights revolution" that begin with civil rights and continued with women's rights, those of homosexuals, AIDS victims, and the disabled, and included—at the other end of the political spectrum—the rights of the unborn, potential victims of abortion [for a book-length critique of the "rights industry" see Morgan 1984]. While these developments can be applauded, their excesses shed light on the collapse of common sense and the growing difficulty that came to attend to the exercise of authority at almost every level. The legal profession often spearheaded these initiatives, sometimes propelled by the profit motive, other times by an adversarial idealism. It thus became possible for convicted prisoners to file lawsuits (funded by the taxpayer) for almost any reason, no matter how frivolous or trivial. In Massachusetts "Inmates have sued because scrambled eggs were too hard, fruit was overripe and lightbulbs dim . . . Approximately 2000 suits by inmates are pending. The Correction Department has hired more than 20 lawyers since the early 1970s to deal with the increased number of suits . . ." ["State Countersues Jailhouse Lawyers" 1990]. The trends were the same across the nation.

What Michel Crozier called "the delirium of due process" or the "fanatical commitment to the formalism of due process" [Crozier 1984:98, 118] may also be added to the symptoms of decadence as these tendencies increasingly interfere with rational decision-making and societal efficiency.

Race relations are another area where the initial determination to discard irrational and unjust discrimination led to a suspension of standards of judgment—as in the case of black criminals perceived as innocent victims of social forces and even more so in the gradual transformation of nondiscrimination into reverse discrimination, discussed earlier. Here the issue is not merely one of justice (toward those who suffer the results of reverse discrimination) but also the maintenance of standards and quality.

It is indicative of the climate of opinion in such matters that Jesse Jackson felt entitled to weigh in in the Harvard Law School dispute (centered on demands to hire without delay a black woman faculty member as a role model) and dismiss Harvard's attempts to maintain academic standards as "'cultural anemia.'" "'We cannot just define who is qualified in the most narrow, vertical academic terms,' he said. 'Most people in the world are yellow, brown, black, poor, non-Christian and don't speak English, and they can't wait for some white males with archaic rules to appraise them'" [Butterfield 1990].

It has also been a legacy of the 1960s that egalitarian beliefs increasingly interfere with the cultivation of excellence and talent at every level of education and in the world of the arts as well. Even the word "quality" has come to be viewed with deep suspicion by many artists and critics who associate it with elitism and the underrepresentation of minorities [Brenson 1990]. When concern for the lagging academic performance of minorities combines with the fears of elitism—as is the case in many school systems across the country which have abandoned ability grouping (or "tracking")—it is "hard times for educating the highly gifted child," as a recent article pointed out. "The issue of elitism . . . haunts the field of gifted education . . ." [Wernick 1990]. Such a refusal to recognize and cultivate exceptional talent for fear of offending or undermining the self-esteem of the less talented—a major argument in favor of removing ability grouping—may also be added to the signs of decline.

The trend toward reverse discrimination over the past quarter-century that persisted through different presidencies is also relevant to an understanding of the morale of American elite groups. It is these elite groups which have been promoting or acquiescing in reverse discrimination (and the lowering of standards entailed), retreating step by step in face of recurring demands for more of the same. The mentality of these elite groups—politicians, educators, churchmen, civil servants, miscellaneous intellectuals—helps to explain the entrenchment of policies predicated on a selective social determinism and refusal to make often vital distinctions. It is likely that—besides the commendable impulse to make amends for the injustices of the past—a deep uncertainty about the social order and its basic values is one of the factors that predispose these elites to acquiesce to the demands of formerly victimized groups.

It should also be noted here that no issue in American society in recent times has generated more pious rhetoric, unctuousness, and sheer hypocrisy than race relations and racial problems. It is indeed the case, as Martin Peretz remarked, that in the United States today "we can no longer truthfully talk about race" [Peretz 1990:42]. A society that cannot truthfully confront one of its most critical problems cannot entertain realistic hopes for solving or reducing it. Nor does such refusal to be truthful reflect favorably on the body politic and the soundness of the prevailing climate of opinion.

As one continues to reflect on the attitudes and outlook of elite groups in relation to the (real or alleged) decline of the United States and the intractability of American social and cultural problems, reference must be made to the issue of authority and the sense of legitimacy underlying it. Ever since the late 1960s there has been a smouldering crisis of legitimacy as far as these elites are concerned as indicated more by their own actions (and inactions) than by vigorous public delegitimation, although public mistrust of elite groups has also increased. This phenomenon has more typically been referred to as a crisis of leadership than of legitimacy but they reinforce one another. Its most obvious expression is a government by public opinion poll and the related aversion to doing anything that might irritate or displease any vocal constituency, or the public in general. One author called the phenomenon a "flight from power"—a flight linked to uncertainty as to the grounds upon which power can be exercised. The decline of authority has extended across the entire spectrum of society, from the president to politicians, teachers, policemen, prison guards, academic deans, physicians, parents, and all other conventional authority figures. The process has not been without consequences as far as the governability of the nation is concerned. In the words of one observer, "We have gradually transformed our system of government into a town meeting of 250 million people, in which everyone has an equal right to *prevent* things from being done . . ." [Korda 1982:9; see also Burnham 1978 and Hacker 1971].

A foreign observer writing in the Swiss *Neue Zuricher Zeitung* linked these trends to Vietnam and especially Watergate: "The outcome of the Watergate affair did more than merely expose and radically eliminate excesses in the Executive's use of power. It also cast general suspicion on the act of governing per se . . ." [Luchsinger 1975:30].

Another area of American life that may plausibly be linked to decadence is that of risk-taking and, again, the associated progressive limitation of personal responsibility for the many misfortunes and accidents which may befall the individual. Although the legal profession has been in the vanguard of these developments, its endeavors could not have been so successful without the support and encouragement of the broader social-cultural environment. Henry Fairlie was among those addressing this problem:

> . . . the desire for a risk-free society is one of the most debilitating influences in America today, progressively enfeebling the economy with a mass of safety regulations and a widespread fear of liability rulings . . .

The origins of the widespread refusal to accept a sometimes high level of risk as a normal and necessary hazard of life lie in the early 1970s. As America lost heart in the prosecution of war in Vietnam, the energy of the dissenters . . . turned to the lavish care for the environment . . . and their own exquisite . . . physical and emotional well-being. The simultaneous loss of faith in American technology was part of the same phenomenon . . .

. . . one pernicious moral effect of America's growing fear of risk: a commensurate diminuition of the notion of individual responsbility for one's action . . .

. . . It is reasonable . . . to assume a link between the attitudes that have led to the slowing of such new and promising industries as space technology and nuclear power, the gross development of liability law and litigation, the concern about environmental pollution, and the finicky attention to one's bodily health, comfort, and even purity.

. . . The risk-averse groups are drawn from a privileged class . . .

. . . these groups could not have been so destructively successful if Americans had not already suffered a loss of faith in their nation . . . the Vietnam War Memorial . . . is a monument to a loss of life that is seen as wasteful and dishonorable. The feelings it excites reflect a nation that is coming to believe that even wars should be fought without risk . . . [Fairlie 1989: 14, 16, 17, 19; for a book-length treatment of these issues see also Douglas and Wildavsky 1982].

It is not without significance that the renewed fears of various catastrophes—environmental, nuclear, weather-related, and so on—followed the manifest decline of the radical political movements which originated in the 1960s. It was almost as if the decline of domestic social-political turbulence prompted the former activists to find substitute issues and problems, some more realistic than others. Sometimes it appeared that American society became one of those ". . . that have been distracted from the actual dangers they faced by the allure of disasters wholly imaginary" [Shaw *Commentary* 1989:52]. A *New York Times* columnist, commenting on outbreaks of panic over alleged contamination of apples and grapes, speculated on possible public reaction to nuclear blackmail by terrorists or some deranged but well-armed dictator:

What would be our reaction? A public that overnight will stop eating apples on the remote chance that 4% of them contain what might possibly be a carcinogen, and will cut off a billion dollars of fruit imports on suspicious evidence in two grapes, is not a public that will back its Government in resisting nuclear blackmail. [Safire 1989]

Ronald Steel, the historian, was also moved to reflect, in the aftermath of the grape scare, on the broader meaning of such events:

Though we still honor the image of the brave frontiersman who rode off into the wilderness to confront danger, we do so in front of the TV, behind the security of double-locked doors and barred windows. We down our bran in hopes of eternal life and remove books from our shelves because some religious fanatic in the Middle East has decided he doesn't like the author. [Steel 1989]

The last point is a reminder of another important dimension of decadence: the problematic relationship of our elites to what used to be deeply held cultural values. The robust affirmation of such values has been replaced by a dubious "open-mindedness," ethical relativism, and a tolerance more clearly rooted in the inability to make moral, ethical, or intellectual choices and distinctions than in the rejection of fanaticism. Former President Carter's pleading for a sympathetic understanding of those who clamored for the head of the writer Salman Rushdie was a telling expression of this attitude. Carter cautioned that "we should be sensitive to the concern and anger that prevails even among the more moderate Moslems." He was apparently led to this position in part because "their seemingly radical statements and actions are obviously sincere" [Carter 1989].

It should be asked why the sincerity of the bloodthirsty fanatics should make much difference. It is worth dwelling on this point as it has also been among the legacies of the 1960s that whatever attitudes and emotions are sincere and strongly felt deserve respectful hearing—although "sincerity" by itself tells us nothing about the validity, quality, or ethical substance of the feelings and attitudes involved. Presumably "sincerity" came to be perceived and appreciated as an antidote to the impersonality and inauthenticity of modern society the social critics habitually attacked.

As the views examined suggest, decadence and decline have many meanings and aspects, both domestic and international. A declining country would certainly cease to be a major power, let alone superpower. The prospects of this type of decline in the foreseeable future are slim given the far more obvious and accelerated decline and disintegration of the Soviet Union and its empire. But even if the United States could maintain its relative military strength with the proposed cutbacks, its loss of economic power may still undermine its position as a preeminent power. In particular the growing trade and budget deficit, the imbalance between consumption, saving, and production, reduced competitiveness on international markets, inadequate research and development, shortage of scientists and engineers (and the decline in the number of Americans studying the sciences [see De Palma 1990])—all these are cited when the decline of the United States is publicly discussed.

There are other symptoms of decadence, a concept which, more than that of decline, has deeper cultural or value implications. A decadent society (late Rome, 20th-century Weimar) has no faith in itself and its future and is recognizable by the spread of hedonism and the wide variety of escapism, the refusal to defer gratification, the *carpe diem* mentality. The spread of antisocial behavior, especially criminal violence and mental illness, is also among the familiar indicators of decay. Both escapism and antisocial behavior are connected with family instability and disintegration and the decline of value-based communities. There is an abundance of all these in American society although it is hard to specify how much these types of behavior may be compatible with a stable and healthy society.

Underlying several of the ills noted above is the more elusive and immeasurable process of the intensifying individualism that contributes both to the "ungovernability" of society and its larger units and to the erosion of marriages and families. Individualism itself is, for the most part, a product of the even more pervasive and momentous development not limited to the United States: the continued process of secularization that undercuts traditional bonds between groups and individuals and deprives people of accessible sources of meaning in life. (It should be noted here that some empirical investigations led to the questioning of the advance of secularization, more narrowly interpreted as decline of professed religious belief and participation; see Greeley 1989.)

The growth of individualism may then be added to these intangible processes which include the decay of sustaining values, loss of national purpose, decline of collective self-esteem, loss of will and nerve of important elites, and the related weakening of authority in the political as well as cultural-educational sphere.

Although the domestic critiques of the American social system have sturdy indigenous roots (as was shown in much of this book), it is appropriate to ask at the end of the 1980s what if any impact developments in formerly communist countries had on the adversary culture and the community of social critics.

To be sure there is no necessary connection between the decline and evils of communism and the evils of capitalism. There is no reason to expect that as the defects of communist systems are further revealed, and these systems are being swept away on tides of massive popular disaffection, critics of the United States should revise their estimates of American society.

On the other hand it is beyond dispute that a seemingly essential counterpart of anti-American, anti-Western social criticism has always been some measure of sympathy for, or outright admiration of, political systems which claimed socialist credentials and were certainly anticapitalist. Over time such enthusiasms declined but were never totally abandoned; the lingering, smoldering hope and expectation that a new anticapitalist, authentic socialist system will somewhere arise has been a temptation to which the Western left never ceased to be totally immune. Before Nicaragua came along, "Cuba seemed like a much needed breath of fresh air . . . [and] revived the exhausted utopias of the Old World . . . the socialist abstraction had to be defended at all costs and its horrors in the Soviet Union written off to the barbarous customs of Russia, to its isolation, even to its weather" [Cruz 1990:40]. Likewise the belief that Marxism remains somehow intact, relevant, and applicable to the understanding of the social world and the humane reconstruction of modern societies has also survived and quite vigorously—an attitude foreshadowed by that of the late Raymond Williams, the famous English Marxist scholar. It was said of him that "He knew the chief historical predictions of Marxism had been falsified by events, and clung all the harder, for that reason, to its conceptual framework" [Watson 1990:54].

In the light of these observations it need not be a cause for great surprise that the collapse or substantial transformation of East European (and other) communist systems failed to deal a fatal blow to those who harbored illusions about existing socialist systems and to their belief in the applicability of Marxism to contemporary social reconstruction or to more humane and efficient methods of modernization. The failure of these alternatives to their own much despised social system did not deprive the social critics of their fund of grievances and sources of resentment. As Irving Kristol among others pointed out,

> . . . the sources that feed such rebellions [against the West—P.H.] remain. Which is to say that our American democracy, though seemingly triumphant, is at risk, and it is at risk precisely because it is the kind of democracy it is, with all the problematics . . . that fester within such a democracy. Among such problems is the longing for community, for spirituality, a growing distrust of technology, the confusion of liberty with license and many others . . . [Kristol 1989:28]

Perhaps most remarkable about the adversarial responses to the events in Eastern Europe was the freely expressed alarm that the demise of communist systems might be used to legitimate capitalism, or American society, and the corresponding insistence that the discreditation of communism had no relevance whatsoever to the sins of capitalism. Thus

Paul Sweezy proclaimed hopefully in *The Nation:* "As far as global cap-italism is concerned, its internal contradictions will hardly be effected one way or another . . . these contradictions, as in the past, continue to multiply and intensify, with all indications pointing to the maturing of one or more serious crises in the not-so-distant future" [Sweezy 1990:278]. A similarly aged but less well-known old-leftist in a California retirement home for former left-wing political activists (commenting on changes in Eastern Europe) averred that "'Organized capitalism is an evil thing in itself . . . It's profits versus people'"; he was convinced that "his hero, Lenin, would have approved" of the changes ["Political Idealists" 1990:B10]. A professor of sociology from Illinois expressed irritation with "all the self-righteous, sanctimonious celebration of the 'victory' of cap-italism over Communism precipitated by the upheavals in Eastern Europe." She was not content to remind the readers of the evils of cap-italism but also extolled the accomplishment of these East European sys-tems: "These governments . . . constructed massive social service delivery systems that eliminated illiteracy, petty street crime, prostitution and a myriad of other social cancers . . . Though disadvantaged in consumer gadgetry, their populations are well educated and healthy" [Gross 1990] —claims which would have greatly surprised residents of these countries. Richard Falk (encountered earlier) was among those for whom the trans-formations in the Soviet Union provided new opportunity to highlight the shortcomings of the United States as compared with the emerging virtues of the Soviet Union: "It is Moscow, not Washington, that is providing the peoples of the world with some basis to hope for the avoidance of warfare and nuclear destruction, for a safer and more equitable world . . ." [Raskin and Hartman eds. 1988:317–18].

Typically, many such musings—aimed at putting the events in East-ern Europe into the proper perspective—would begin with the destruc-tion of the Berlin Wall and then move rapidly to the innumerable evils of American society, as exemplified by a *New York Times* op-ed piece by the comedian Jackie Mason. The tour of inequities included McCarthy-ism, the denial of rights to women, the problems of homosexuals, the uselessness of free expression "if we can't leave the house to buy a news-paper," the burdens of leading "an unpopular life style," and of course "poverty, inequality and discrimination," among other things. He con-cluded:

> . . . perhaps Mikhail Gorbachev could do for us what he did for East Ger-many. Maybe he could make us aware of the fact that we too could unbur-den ourselves from our own forms of oppression. He might remind us that we could be a free country once again. [Mason 1990]

For another writer the joys of the demolition of the Berlin Wall inspired reflections about the sorrows of "more subtle, elusive walls" including "the wall of doubt that takes over from within," which interfere with self-realization in America. The author (who had earned a graduate degree and worked for a large New York law firm) had many complaints, as for instance an insufficient salary level, limited career choices, worries of divorce in case she gets married, concerns about child care in case she had children, indignation over her lack of funds to buy a house in her hometown in California [Rector 1989]. While such writings may be dismissed as the idiosyncratic complaints of a spoiled New Yorker, the *New York Times* deemed it worthy of publication and some editor must have thought that the article captured some deeper and more substantial discontent of our times, which it may well have. By contrast the president of NBC was saddened over the current failure of American youth to complain and protest—compared with those in Eastern Europe—and he was concerned that they may turn out to be as apathetic as the generation of the 1950s [Will 1989 December].

Tom Wicker began an article by quoting a Czech celebrating the newly won freedom in Prague and immediately moved on to a listing of violent crimes, accidents, "traffic incidents . . . , drunkenness, drug abuse, vandalism and other human vagaries" which occurred on New Year's Eve in New York and the United States while the Czechs were celebrating their freedom. He concluded: "Freedom is . . . not a panacea; and that Communism failed does not make the Western alternative perfect, or even satisfying for millions of those who live under it" [Wicker 1990 January 5]. In another piece he applied the same perspective to foreign affairs: "Why not draw the lesson of Eastern Europe . . . and leave the Sandinistas to the Nicaraguan people? Or would that be too 'new' a world for a U.S. still bent, as in Panama, and as always, on dominating its so-called 'backyard'?" [Wicker 1990 January 2]. In the same spirit a *New Yorker* editorial advised that given the decline of the Cold War the United States might as well let events take their course in El Salvador ["Notes and Comment" 1989:44], a course that would greatly increase the chances of the communist victory—anachronistic as it would be at a time when communist regimes elsewhere crumble.

Anthony Lewis suggested that while the whole world from Eastern Europe to South Africa is embarked on beneficial change, "one great country is not confronting its problems . . . That country is the United States." He too then proceeded to the usual litany of the ills of America [Lewis 1990].

Yet another editorial writer in the *New York Times* used the East European re-examination of the past political crimes as a point of departure to introduce the suggestion that the "Cold War's [American] victims deserve a memorial" and that "America shields its secret government" and refuses to reveal all the innocent victims of nuclear tests and other environmental atrocities. He concluded by quoting Vaclav Havel, suggesting that his remarks about the communist system apply to the United States. Havel's quote went as follows: "The previous regime, armed with a proud and intolerant ideology, reduced people into means of production . . . Out of talented and responsible people . . . it made cogs of some great, monstrous, thudding, smelly machine . . ." [Rochberg-Halton 1990].

It was in the same spirit that an article in *The Nation* which began with a discussion of the changing political map in Europe concluded that

> . . . the Western left should get on with its job. It must attack the very foundation of our own system . . . its incapacity to conceive of growth for any purpose other than profit, with the attendant environmental destruction; its commercialization of art, culture and even human relationships; its exploitation of the Third World; and its perpetuation of social, sexual and racial inequities.

The author also suggested that the people of Eastern Europe, presently beguiled by capitalism, needed a bit of consciousness-level-raising [Singer 1989 December:720]. Elsewhere Mr. Singer was led from his survey of developments in Eastern Europe to the conclusion that ". . . our task is to spread the conviction that a radical change of society in all its aspects is on our own historical agenda. In the long run, the collapse of the Stalinist model should help us in this search for a socialist alternative" [Singer 1989 November:600].

Sheldon Wolin in an article also pondering the political changes in Eastern Europe found occasion to note that "In the past decade the perception and sensibilities of many Americans have been Reaganized, shaped by counterrevolutionary concerns regarding welfare, race relations, health care, ecology, government regulation of business . . . the rights of minorities and women . . ." By contrast, "Even acknowledging gross distortions, Communist regimes have been the only ones that professed, and to some degree achieved, a commitment to equality" [Wolin 1990:373].

Other social critics took a more sanguine view of the situation, concluding in effect that the people of Eastern Europe have been closet Marxists or socialists all along. One unmistakable piece of evidence was that

> The exodus of . . . East Germans . . . cannot be interpreted, as some Western commentators would have it, as an abandonment of the teachings of Karl Marx . . . the country to which they are traveling . . . is not Thatcher's Britain or *après*-Reagan America.

... the new emigrants have chosen capitalism with a human face [i.e., West Germany] ... And so the newcomers have gone from Stalin back to Marx. ["Borderline Marxists" 1989:1]

The latter was precisely the conclusion Paul Robeson, Jr., reached: "This is the death of Stalinism and the birth of Marxism" [Baer 1990:27].

The Nation's interpretation of these migrations deserves to be enshrined in some yet-to-be-written encyclopedia of political absurdities. Apparently it did not occur to the editorial writer that the East Germans had little choice but to go to West Germany, which also happened to be the most convenient and sensible thing to do; they were not invited to Thatcher's England or the the United States; their choice of West Germany might also have been influenced by matters such as the language, automatic citizenship, and proximity!

Some academic Marxists—such as Sam Bowles, a professor of economics at the University of Massachusetts at Amherst, and Philip Green, professor of government at Smith College in Northampton, Massachusetts—chose to express relief at the events in Eastern Europe, insisting rather unconvincingly, that "For the first time in history there is a chance of a true socialist and democratic state, one based on the writings of Karl Marx ..." They further averred that "'Eastern Europe now will lead the way to creating the first truly socialist nations ... The soil in Eastern Europe is prime for true socialism to take root'" [Grabar 1989:11].

If we recall that many intellectuals used to be capable of believing that the Soviet Union under Stalin or China under Mao were the purest embodiments of everything Marx had wished for, then perhaps the belief that East Europeans long for socialism and Marxism will not be so astonishing. (It may be noted here that East Germans wasted little time changing the name of Karl Marx City back to its original, Chemnitz; that Czech students called their new freedom from studying the classics of Marxism "a ... dream come true ... For the first time we are not learning nonsense ..." [Fowler 1990; see also Kamm 1989]. In both Hungary and East Germany, in their first free elections, even the very mildly leftist social-democrats were badly beaten and right-of-center parties voted in. These are a few examples illuminating the attitudes of East Europeans in these matters.

Thus several highly patterned responses to the collapse of communism have emerged among the critics of American society. The first has been an affirmation of their unrelenting hostility toward capitalism and the American social order; it is indeed possible that such hostility increased rather than diminished notwithstanding the absence of plausible and available alternatives to the abhorred system. Kenneth Minogue, the English political scientist, observed that "... it has been one of the

curiosities of the last two decades that as radicals have lost plausible utopias of one kind or another—from the Soviet Union to Cuba—they have
become more ferociously intolerant of the society in which they actually
live" [Minogue 1990:4]. Short of such an increase of hostility, developments in Eastern Europe were used to affirm the moral equivalence theory, even on the part of more moderate critics of the United States. Thus
Todd Gitlin wrote that

> East-West confrontation apparently reduced all choices to one either/or
> choice: Light versus Dark, Freedom versus Slavery, Godliness versus Athe-
> ism, Capitalism versus Socialism, Democracy versus Dictatorship . . . Vir-
> tue and paranoia fused to make us the Good Guys. Our cars, kitchens,
> families, schools, synagogues and churches were all defended in the name
> of our goodness . . . For more than forty years . . . it was virtually impos-
> sible to talk about America without talking about its Enemy . . . [Gitlin
> 1990:28]

Gitlin also appears to convey that the presence of such an enemy interfered with or unduly restrained the critiques of American society, again
a peculiar proposition given the vast amount of criticism that had been
aimed at American institutions and their defects over the past quarter-
century.

Second, there is the insistence that the collapse of existing socialist
systems had nothing whatsoever to do with the theory which inspired,
legitimated, and allegedly guided these failed experiments. Eugene Genovese pointed out, "To this day it has not occurred to radical leftists and
Left-liberals that the central contradiction in the socialist countries has
been the vain attempt to combine an unrealizable goal of personal liberation with a form of social organization that, above all, requires maximum
social discipline" [Genovese 1990:49]. Some suggested that "The theory
would have worked if only the comrades who put it into action hadn't
fallen prey to the temptations of corruption" [Baer 1990:27]. Such durable affection for the theory is also illustrated by the report that "tourists
and pilgrims of the left are flocking in greater numbers to the Marx grave-
site in Highgate Cemetery . . ." One among them observed: "'We come
here for hope . . . We come here for inspiration'" [Kuntz 1990]—sentiments which lend further support (if more is needed) to the conclusions
of thinkers such as Raymond Aron and Leszek Kolakowski, who had
noted some time ago the pre-eminently religious functions Marxism had
performed for Western intellectuals.

Third, and still more daring, some insist that in some peculiar way
events in Eastern Europe actually vindicated Marxism or cleared the way
to its successful implementation. Hence the continued insistence that

"socialism . . . is far from dead" while allowing for the need to "recast socialism in a contemporary idiom" [Birnbaum 1989:150, 152]. Increasingly this recasting enterprise proceeds by holding up the most generalized and watered-down conception of Marxism which affirms every conceivable human right and value and opposes every widely abhorred political or economic practice or personality trait (e.g., greed, avarice, selfishness, dishonesty).

There was also concern among some Western intellectuals, such as Gunter Grass, "about the survival of the socialist economic system and way of life in the GDR [East Germany] . . . Peter von Oertzen . . . a member of the SPD [Social Democratic Party of West Germany] warns the Soviet Union not to give in to capitalism" [Hacker 1989:3].

All these reactions to the events in Eastern Europe—and the immense resistance to admitting their true significance—appear to be rooted in the adherence to some vague but morally bracing version of socialism which continues to play an important part in the sense of identity and righteousness of the critics of American (and Western) society. Again, as Minogue pointed out,

> To be a socialist in this ideological sense is not to be a person holding opinions which might be rationally modified . . . It is to affirm a self-identity as a particular kind of moral *thing* . . . Socialists . . . are basically committed not to any positive improvement in the human condition, but to the pleasure of struggle against the world in which they live . . . Western socialists never for a moment contemplated fleeing to the socialism, which in principle they so admired. Nothing stopped them from setting up socialist commmunes within capitalist societies, but few did so . . . A socialist life was widely recognised by many socialists . . . as not really suitable for themselves. Hence the inescapable revelation from Eastern Europe that living under socialism is profoundly boring and impoverished is hardly likely to affect Western socialists. . . . the less plausible any ideological reconstruction of society comes to be seen, the more enthusiastically will ideologists rush for the higher ground. They will identify themselves with Peace, Nature, Rights, Compassion etc.—and take up an enthusiastically negative posture towards the established society in which they live . . . [Minogue 1990:3, 12]

Another reaction to the events in the Soviet bloc—not incompatible with those noted above—has been to ignore them altogether and to burrow deeper into academic Marxism, concentrate on the more esoteric critiques of American society and capitalism, and chart new approaches toward their delegitimation. At a conference on matters literary at the University of Utah in 1990, topics included "the erotic politics of the female body," "postmodern terrorism," "post-colonial body politics," and "postmodern feminism and Madonna." Those who "once occupied buildings and marched on Washington . . . these days are more apt to use the arcane and specialized language of literary criticism to expose what many see as the evils of 'late' . . . capitalism." At the same conference in a rare reference to Eastern Europe a speaker warned that it "must fend off the capitalist threat" [Bernstein 1990 April].

A famous academic literary critic, Frederic Jameson, continues to repeat what a reviewer called the "thuggish pieties of the Marxist left," holding forth about "'counterinsurgency warfare and neocolonialism . . . as deeper and more ominous necessities of the American system . . ." while cherishing and defending memories of the Chinese Cultural Revolution! [Bromwich 1990:35]. A group of younger historians who came of age in the 60s is rewriting the history of the American West to reveal that it was "distorted, misleading, exclusive, chauvinistic . . . racist and sexist . . . [and to show that] There was suffering and oppression . . ." Their work "stresses the darker themes." An account of their activities and attitudes pointed out, putting it rather mildly, that they are willing ". . . to find the invisible worm eating away at the once blushing rose of the American self-image" [Bernstein 1990 March:34, 59].

At last among the more bizarre responses to the collapse of communist systems the fantasies of revolutionary change in the United States must also be included. The *Village Voice* began a section entitled "Perestroika, USA—Can It Happen Here?" with the following pipe-dream:

> Summer 1993. America is in the 25th month of the . . . Great Depression II. George Bush . . . was carried off by a heart attack . . . the Federal Deposit Insurance corporation declared bankruptcy just days into his second term . . . President . . . Quayle . . . has his hands full. In the second year of a massive drought induced by the greenhouse effect, America has become a food importer . . . prices are skyrocketing. Gasoline rationing has immobilized the American workforce . . . highways are littered with abandoned cars. Armies of the unemployed . . . trudge the polluted streets in search of nonexistent jobs. President Quayle . . . ordered federal troops to fire on food rioters at Christmas . . .
> . . . The Close the Pentagon Movement . . . has gripped the imagination of the country. . . . general strikes have immobilized cities from coast to coast . . . America is in the streets. [Ireland 1990:22]

The author called it "an optimistic fantasy." He explained: "With whole peoples on the march these days from the Danube to the Don, America's relative passivity and quiescence make a stark and disillusioning contrast" [Ibid.]. His unstated premise, needless to say, was that the American people had just as good, if not better, reasons to march and protest as the East Europeans.

Another contributor suggested still more wishfully that the East European revolutions struck fear into "our own bureaucrats . . . Revolution is contagious" [Willis 1990:32]. Other contributors to the special section were led from reflecting on the decline of communism in Eastern Europe to voice their demand for abolishing "immediately" all state sodomy laws, and to "begin the process of striking homophobia and heterosexual bias from our education systems" [Weinstein 1990:31]. Barbara Ehrenreich found an "obvious connection" between "the prodemocracy demonstrations" in East Germany and demonstrations in the United States for reproductive rights, which also represent, in her view, "a vast and angry prodemocracy movement" [Ehrenreich 1990 December:28]. The same author was among those who regarded the 1980s as "the worst years of our lives" and a "decade of greed" [Ehrenreich 1990].

We must take leave of the seemingly endless eruptions and wishful fantasies of the social critics for whom everything ends and begins with the unsurpassed corruptions of America.

In the end one is compelled to return to the idea proposed earlier, that the restlessness of estranged intellectuals and the hostility of the adversary culture are in all probability generalized responses to the discontents of life in a thoroughly modernized, wealthy, secular, and individualistic society where making life meaningful requires great ongoing effort and remains a nagging problem—at any rate for those whose attention does not have to be riveted on the necessities of survival. These conditions have been aggravated by the expectations which American culture has always bred and which were commented upon earlier. As Michel Crozier put it: "Might not the trouble with America, in the final analysis, come right out of the American dream?" [Crozier 1984:xx]. In such a society there is also a great temptation and pressure to link personal unhappiness to the failings of social institutions.

The more one learns about the varied discontents sampled in this study and of the readiness to lapse into moral indignation (an attitude most characteristic of the adversary culture) the harder it becomes to escape the conclusion that these impulses point to something both more general and deep-seated than dissatisfaction with the deficiencies of American institutions and ways of life in the second part of the twentieth century. The distress and indignation of the critics of America—at home more than abroad—remain nurtured by the continued frustration of their determined efforts to find meaning in life.

Thus anti-Americanism as a crisis of meaning is unlikely to disappear even if domestic social reform and attacks on social injustice become more determined and successful; and even if the significance of the failure of communist systems would be confronted by the critics of America.

References

Chapter 1. Persistence of Radical Critiques

Abbey, Edward (1971), *Desert Solitaire,* New York: Ballantine.

Alpert, Jane (1981), *Growing Up Underground,* New York: Morrow.

Applebome, Peter (1990), "Hoax Suspected Over Allegation of Racial Crime," *New York Times* (NYT below), June 1.

Ayvazian, Andrea (1986), "A Profile of Tireless Frances Crowe," *Daily Hampshire Gazette* (Northampton, Mass.) (DHG below), July 12.

Babize, Mollie (1978), "Bucking the System—Or, How I'm Learning to Live with Money," *Valley Advocate* (Northampton, Mass.), Dec. 6.

Baker, Russell (1990), "Don't Mention It," NYT, May 30.

Baritz, Loren (1988), *The Good Life: The Meaning of Success for the American Middle Class,* New York: Knopf.

Barnard, Ellsworth (1984), Letter, DHG, Nov. 12.

Barnet, Richard J. (1975), "Not Just Your Corner Drug Store" (op-ed), NYT, June 19.

Barrett, Steven P. (1983), Letter, DHG, May 14.

Barron, James (1984), "Feminist Seeks Presidency for Citizens Party," NYT, Aug. 12.

Barth, John (1987), *The Tidewater Tales,* New York: Putnam.

Bell, Daniel (1976), *The Cultural Contradictions of Capitalism,* New York: Basic.

Bellah, Robert, et al. (1985), *Habits of the Heart: Individualism and Commitment in American Life,* Berkeley: Univ. of California Press.

Berman, Paul (1988), "Neocon Frenzy!," *Village Voice,* Dec. 6.

Bernstein, Richard (1982), "Nuclear Foes Ponder Fate of the Earth," NYT, Oct. 22.

——— (1987), "Critic of Academe Fears Catch-22 on His Success," NYT, Dec. 28.

Berrigan, Daniel (1969), *Night Flight to Hanoi,* New York: Macmillan.

Birnbaum, Norman (1958), "America, a Partial View," *Commentary,* July.

——— (1988), *The Radical Renewal: The Politics of Ideas in Modern America,* New York: Pantheon.

——— (1989), "Hope's End or Hope's Beginning? 1968—And After," *Salmagundi,* No. 82, Winter.

Bishop, Katherine (1990), "Finding the Right Dog for a Left-Leaning City," NYT, May 2.

Boorstin, Daniel (1961), *The Image,* New York: Harper Colophon.

Brint, Steven (1984), "'New Class' and Cumulative Trend Explanations of the Liberal Political Attitudes of Professionals," *American Journal of Sociology,* July.

Britton, Ann (1986), "Ex-congresswoman Calls for Activism," *Massachusetts Daily Collegian* (Amherst), Dec. 3.

Broder, David (1978), "Children of the 60s Grow Up on Proposition 13," *Washington Post,* July 17.

Brown, Greg (1985), "Student Strikes to Shun Militarism," *Mass. Daily Collegian,* April 26.

Brown, Judson (1988), "Rosenbergs Still a Source of Pain," DHG, Nov. 8.

———— (1989), "'Outsider' Activist Heading for New Life," DHG, March 16.

Buchanan, Todd (1982), Letter, DHG, Nov. 30.

Bunzel, John (1983), *New Force on the Left—Tom Hayden and the Campaign Against Corporate America*, Stanford: Hoover Press.

Caldeira, Mark (1984), "A Brainwashed Democracy," *Mass. Daily Collegian*, Dec. 13.

Camus, Albert (1974), *Resistance, Rebellion and Death*, New York: Vintage.

Canby, Vincent (1990), "After 20 Years What Has Changed at Kent State?," NYT, May 17.

Carnoy, Martin, and Henry M. Levin, "A Strategy for Education," in Marcus G. Raskin, ed. (1978), *The Federal Budget and Social Reconstruction*, Washington, D.C.: Institute for Policy Studies.

Carrol, Charles Francis (1988), "Anticommunism and the Rosenbergs: A Lesson from the Past?," *Valley Advocate* (Northampton, Mass.), Nov. 7.

Chomsky, Noam, and Edward S. Herman (1977), "Distortions at Fourth Hand," *Nation*, June 25.

———— (1988), *Managua Lectures*, Boston: South End Press.

Clecak, Peter (1983), *America's Quest for the Ideal Self*, New York: Oxford Univ. Press.

Cockburn, Alexander (1985), "Excusing U.S. Capitalism by Denying Its Presence," *Wall Street Journal*, Dec. 12.

Collier, Peter, and David Horowitz (1985), "Goodbye to All That," *Contentions*, May.

———— (1989), *Destructive Generation: Second Thoughts About the '60s*, New York: Summit.

Corry, John (1985), "Writers, Politics and Reality," NYT, Jan. 12.

Cousins, Norman (1987), "Saga of SDI Suggests Ike Was Right," DHG, Feb. 20.

Cowan, Paul (1970), *The Making of an Un-American*, New York: Viking.

Cronkite, Walter (1983), "Orwell's '1984' Nearing?" (op-ed), NYT, June 5.

Crozier-Hogle, Lois (1986), "An Open Letter on Values: Where Have We Gone Wrong?," *Palo Alto Weekly*, July 2.

Curtis, Charlotte (1986), "The Nation at 120," NYT, April 29.

Daly, Mary (1978), *Gyn/Ecology: The Metaethics of Radical Feminism*, Boston: Beacon.

Davis, Angela (1974), *An Autobiography*, New York: Random House.

Dempsey, Jennifer (1987), "Chomsky Discusses World Terrorism," *Mass. Daily Collegian*, Feb. 26.

Dhillon, Harmeet K. (1988), "Letter from the Editor," *Dartmouth Review*, Oct. 28.

Diamond, Stanley (1988), "Reversing Brawley," *Nation*, Oct. 31.

Dickstein, Morris (1988), "Columbia Recovered," NYT *Magazine*, May 15.

Dionne, E. J., Jr. (1989), "Poll Finds Public Favors Sharp Cut in Arms Funds," NYT, March 12.

Dipalazzo, John (1985), "Chaplain for A-bomb Crews Is Now Convert to Peace," DHG, Oct. 5.

Dixler, Elsa (1986), "Back to the 1960s," *Nation*, April 26.

Doctorow, E. L. (1983), "It's a Cold War Out There, Class of '83," *Nation*, July 2.

———— (1989), "'Gangsterdom of the Spirit,'" *Nation*, Oct. 2.

Doran, Charles F., and James Patrick Sewell, "Anti-Americanism in Canada?," in Thomas Perry Thornton, ed. (1988), *Anti-Americanism: Origin and Context*, Annals of the Academy of Political & Social Studies, May.

Draper, Theodore (1987), "The Myth of the Communist Professors," *New Republic*, Jan. 26.

Dworkin, Andrea (1974), *Woman Hating*, New York: Dutton.

Ehrenreich, Barbara (1986), "Is the Middle Class Doomed?," NYT *Magazine,* Sept. 7.

Eisenstein, Zillah R., ed. (1979), *Capitalist Patriarchy and the Case for Socialist Feminism,* New York: Monthly Review Press.

Elfin, Mel (1988), "The Haves, the Have-Nots and the Have-Somewhats," NYT *Book Review,* Oct. 8.

Elliott, Brendan (1987), "Marines Retreat—But They Will Return," DHG, March 3.

Engel, Jacqueline H. (1989), Letter, DHG, April 28.

Engel, Michael (1986), Letter, DHG, Jan. 8.

Epstein, Joseph (1989), "The Joys of Victimhood," NYT *Magazine,* July 2.

Etzioni, Amitai (1977), "The Neoconservatives," *Partisan Review,* No. 3.

Euben, Peter J. (1989), "Fanfare for the Common Complaints," NYT *Book Review,* Jan. 8.

Evanier, David, and Harvey Klehr (1989), "Anticommunism and Mental Health," *American Spectator,* February.

Falk, Richard (1983), Interview in *Prospect* (Princeton, N.J.), November.

Farber, Leslie H., Robert Jay Lifton, and others (1972), "Questions of Guilt," *Partisan Review,* Fall.

Farber, M. A. (1982), "Behind the Brink's Case: Return of the Radical Left," NYT, Feb. 16.

Feron, James (1989), "400 Honor Seegers' Folk Protest," NYT, March 19.

Fields, Suzanne (1988), "Dr. Spock Can't Separate Pediatrics from Politics," *Washington Times,* Aug. 15.

Flacks, Richard (1988), *Making History,* New York: Columbia Univ. Press.

Frankfort, Ellen (1983), *Kathy Boudin and the Dance of Death,* New York: Stein and Day.

Franks, Lucinda (1981), "The Seeds of Terror," NYT *Magazine,* Nov. 22.

French, Howard W. (1988), "Job for Radical Reflects Role of Brooklyn Group," NYT, Jan. 10.

French-Lankarge, Vicki (1985), "Carlo Valone—Fighting the Good Fight," *Hampshire Life,* March 15.

Friedman, John S., ed. (1983), *The First Harvest—The Institute for Policy Studies 1963–1983,* New York: Grove Press.

Fromm, Erich (1955), *The Sane Society,* New York: Rinehart.

Galitsky, Josh (1989), "In Our Society . . . Enough Is Enough," *Mass. Daily Collegian,* Nov. 9.

Gamarekian, Barbara (1983), "20 Years of Decidedly Liberal Views," NYT, April 22.

Gaylin, Willard (1986), "Accountability for Sale, Cheap" (op-ed), NYT, Nov. 16.

Gibson, Elise (1990), "Food as a Substitute for Thought," DHG, Feb. 28.

Gitlin, Todd (1981), "White Heat Underground," *Nation,* Dec. 19.

——— (1987), *The Sixties: Years of Hope, Days of Rage,* New York: Bantam.

Glanzer, Katie (1983), "Marge Piercy Speaks of History's Oppression," DHG, March 3.

Goldstein, Robert J. (1978), *Repression in Modern America: From 1870 to the Present,* Cambridge: Schenkman.

Goode, Stephen (1986), "Pro Bono: To Whose Good?," *Insight,* Feb. 10.

Goodman, Walter (1983), "For a Spirited Audience at Town Hall, 'The Rosenberg File' Remains Open," NYT, Oct. 22.

Gross, Bertram (1980), *Friendly Fascism: The New Face of Power in America,* New York: Evans.

Haddad, Anne (1990), "High School Keeps SI [*Sports Illustrated*] Swimsuit Issue in Library," DHG, Feb. 14.

Hankiss, Elemer (1988), Letter to author, Jan. 9.

Hanley, Robert (1990), "Black Poet Says Faculty 'Nazis' Blocked Tenure," NYT, March 15.

Hartley, Anthony (1989), "Saving Mr. Rushdie?," *Encounter*, June.

Hartman, Chester, ed. (1983), *America's Housing Crisis*, Boston: Routledge.

Harwood, Richard (1990), "Dealing With the Perception of 'Isms,'" DHG, Feb. 14.

Hayden, Tom (1980), *The American Future: Visions Beyond Old Frontiers*, Boston: South End Press.

———— (1988), *Reunion: A Memoir*, New York: Random House.

Hechinger, Fred M. (1986), "Alarm Over Alienation of the Young," NYT, March 25.

Heilbronner, Robert (1985), *The Nature and Logic of Capitalism*, New York: Norton.

Helms, J. Lynn (1984), Letter, NYT, Nov. 24.

Hitchens, Christopher (1983), "American Notes," *Times Literary Supplement*, Sept. 23.

Hochschild, Arlie Russell (1983), *The Managed Heart: Commercialization of Human Feeling*, Berkeley: Univ. Press of California.

Hollander, Paul (1983), *The Many Faces of Socialism*, New Brunswick: Transaction.

———— (1986), "The Survival of the Adversary Culture," *Partisan Review*, No. 3.

———— (1988), *The Survival of the Adversary Culture*, New Brunswick: Transaction.

Holt, Margaret G. (1988), Letter, DHG, Feb. 3.

Hook, Sidney (1987), "Communists, McCarthy and American Universities," *Minerva*, Autumn.

Horn, Joseph (1990), "Robbed by a Young Black . . ." (op-ed), NYT, May 15.

Horowitz, David (1988), *The Fate of the Jews and the Radical Left* (address at the Pacific Jewish Center), Nov. 5.

Howe, Irving (1978), "Some Romance!," *NY Review of Books*, April 6.

———— (1989), "An American Tragedy," *Dissent*, Fall.

Hundley, Kris (1987), "Behind the Revolutionaries," *Valley Advocate*, Aug. 24.

Institute for Policy Studies Annual Report (1983), Washington, D.C.

Jacobs, Harold (1989), "Tom Hayden: The Waning of the Political Vision," *Tikkun*, Vol. 4, No. 3.

Jacoby, Russell (1987), *The Last Intellectuals: American Culture in the Age of Academe*, New York: Basic.

Johnson, Dirk (1989), "City Embraces Symbol of Its More Radical Past," NYT, April 18.

———— (1990), "Challenge at Home for Adept Player of Racial Politics," NYT, March 11.

Johnson, Paul (1988), "Spreading the Western Disease," NYT *Book Review*, Jan. 24.

———— (1988), *Intellectuals*, New York: Harper and Row.

Kaplan, Craig, and Ellen Schrecker, eds. (1983), *Regulating the Intellectuals: Perspectives on Academic Freedom in the 80s*, New York: Praeger.

Katz, Jack (1989), *Seductions of Crime*, New York: Basic.

Kazin, Alfred (1989), "God's Own Little Squirt," NYT *Book Review*, March 12.

Kelliher, Judith (1989), "Amherst's GWEN [Ground Wave Emergency Network] Group Goes on the Road," DHG, Jan. 14.

Kennan, George F. (1988), "The Buried Past," *NY Review of Books*, Oct. 27.

Kilson, Martin (1990), "Realism About the Black Experience," *Dissent*, Fall.

King, Wayne (1989), "Abbie Hoffman Committed Suicide," NYT, April 19.

Kinsley, Michael (1985), "Conservatives Meet to Dine on Red Herrings," *Wall Street Journal*, May 9.

Klare, Michael (1972), *War Without End: American Planning for the Next Vietnams*, New York: Knopf.

———— (1989), Letter, NYT *Magazine*, Aug. 13.

Klehr, Harvey (1988), *Far Left of Center: The American Radical Left Today*, New Brunswick: Transaction.

Kolakowski, Leszek (1977), "Marxism, A Summing Up," *Survey*, Summer.

Kozol, Jonathan (1975), *The Night Is Dark and I Am Far from Home*, Boston: Houghton.

—— (1988), *Rachel and Her Children*, New York: Crown.

Kramer, Larry (1989), *Reports from the Holocaust: The Making of an AIDS Activist*, New York: St. Martin's.

Krassner, Paul (1989), "Abbie," *Nation*, May 8.

Kreilkamp, Thomas (1976), *The Corrosion of the Self*, New York: New York Univ. Press.

Kristol, Irving (1983), *Reflections of a Neoconservative*, New York: Basic.

Lander, Louise, "National Health Insurance," in Marcus G. Raskin, ed. (1978), *cited*.

Lasch, Christopher (1978), *The Culture of Narcissism*, New York: Norton.

—— (1984), *The Minimal Self*, New York: Norton.

—— (1989), "The I's Have It for Another Decade" (op-ed), NYT, Dec. 27.

Leavitt, David (1989), "The Way I Live Now," NYT *Magazine*, July 9.

Leonard, John (1982), Review of Joel Kovel, *The Age of Desire*, NYT, Jan. 14.

Lester, Julius (1989), "Banalities from the Far Left," *WashingtonTimes*, March 20.

Lewin, Tamar (1988), "Judge Refuses to List AIDS as a Sexual Disease," NYT, Nov. 16.

Loisel, Laurie (1985), "Boycotting Thanksgiving," DHG, Nov. 26.

Loury, Glenn C. (1989), Letter, *New Republic*, Sept. 4.

Lukas, Anthony J. (1989), "In Chicago a Holy War Over the Flag" (op-ed), NYT, March 16.

Lewis, Anthony (1985), "The Sore Winners" (op-ed), NYT, Dec. 16.

Lipset, S. M., and William Schneider (1983), *The Confidence Gap: Business, Labor and Government in the Public Mind*, New York: Free Press.

—— (1985), "The Elections, the Economy and Public Opinion: 1984," *PS*, Winter.

Lynd, Staughton, and Gar Alperowitz (1973), *Strategy and Program: Two Essays Toward a New American Socialism*, Boston: Beacon.

Mager, Andy (1985), "I Won't Register for the Draft" (op-ed), NYT, Jan. 15.

Margolick, David (1987), "Up from McCarthyism: At 50 the Left-Wing National Lawyers Guild Is Bigger Than Ever," NYT, Dec. 11.

Marwell, Gerald, Michael T. Aiken, and N. J. Demerath III (1987), "The Persistence of Political Attitudes Among 1960s Civil Rights Activists," *Public Opinion Quarterly*, Vol. 51.

Marx, Gary T. (1986), "The Iron Fist and the Velvet Glove: Totalitarian Potentials Within Democratic Structures," in James F. Short, ed., *The Social Fabric*, Beverly Hills: Sage.

Matteson, John H. (1981), Letter, DHG, Feb. 14.

McCann, Michael W. (1986), *Taking Reform Seriously: Perspectives on Public Interest Liberalism*, Ithaca: Cornell Univ. Press.

McCarthy, Colman (1987), "From Yale to Jail," *Washington Post*, Feb. 21.

McConnell, Scott (1987), "Resurrecting the New Left," *Commentary*, October.

McDermott, Deborah (1987), "The CIA Trial Verdict," DHG, April 16.

—— (1987), "Trial, Verdict Send a Message," DHG, April 16.

McFadden, Robert D., et al (1990), *Outrage: The Story Behind the Tawana Brawley Hoax*, New York: Bantam.

Mckay, Betsy (1982), "Faculty Protest Recruiting by CIA," DHG, Nov. 2.

—— (1982), "Radical Black Leader Criticizes Capitalist Economic System," DHG, April 6.

Melville, Samuel (1972), *Letters from Attica*, New York: Morrow.

Menashe, Louise, and Ronald Radosh, eds. (1967), *Teach-Ins: USA,* New York: Praeger.

Miller, Jim (1987), "Tears and Riots, Love and Regrets," NYT *Book Review,* Nov. 8.

Mitgang, Herbert (1990), "Decade of Changing American Values," NYT, May 16.

Mohr, Charles (1981), "Disclosing Intelligence Agents' Names," NYT, Feb. 6.

Moyers, Bill (1989), *A World of Ideas,* New York: Doubleday.

Moynihan, Daniel Patrick (1978), "The American Political Elite," *Washington Review,* January.

Myers, Robert M. (1985), Letter, DHG, July 9.

Neuhaus, Richard John (1987), "Prophets With Tenure," *Commentary,* July.

Nisbet, Robert (1982), "No End to the Process of Creating Victims" (op-ed), NYT, Aug. 15.

Parenti, Michael (1978), *Power and the Powerless,* New York: St. Martin's.

—— (1986), *Inventing Reality,* New York: St. Martin's.

Parkin, Frank (1968), *Middle Class Radicalism: The Social Bases of the British Campaign for Nuclear Disarmament,* Manchester: Manchester Univ. Press.

Pear, Robert (1981), "War on Poverty Is Difficult to Call Off," NYT, Nov. 29.

Pemberton, Richard, Jr. (1986), Letter, NYT *Book Review,* March 9.

Peretz, Martin (1986) "Cambridge Digest" *New Republic,* April 7.

Piercy, Marge (1979), *Vida,* New York: Summit.

Piven, Frances Fox, and Richard A. Cloward (1982), *The New Class War,* New York: Pantheon.

Pollard, Peter (1987), "From Observer to Vocal Activity," DHG, Jan. 10.

Pollitt, Katha (1986), "Hers," NYT, Jan. 23.

Potter, David M. (1973), *History and American Society,* New York: Oxford Univ. Press.

Powell, S. Steven (1988), *Covert Cadre: Inside the Institute for Policy Studies,* Ottawa, Ill.: Green Hill.

Puddington, Arch (1987), "Gorbachev's Russia," *The Social Democrat,* June.

Purdum, Todd S. (1986), "Police Trap Major Graffiti Suspect," NYT, Aug. 21.

Radosh, Ronald, ed. (1976), *The New Cuba,* New York: Morrow.

Raskin, Marcus G. (1969), "National Security State," *Progressive,* June.

—— (1974), *Notes on the Old System,* New York: McKay.

—— , ed. (1978), *The Federal Budget and Social Reconstruction,* Washington, D.C.: Institute for Policy Studies.

Reed, Roy (1983), "Dr. Spock, at 80, Still Giving Advice," NYT, May 2.

Rich, Adrienne (1979), *On Lies, Secrets and Silence,* New York: Norton.

Rimer, Sara (1988), "Columbia's Ex-Radicals Retake It for a 20th Reunion," NYT, April 25.

Rockman, Jane, ed. (1979), *Peace in Search of Makers,* Valley Forge: Judson.

Rosenthal, Andrew (1987), "'60s Protesters Hold Bittersweet Reunion in Park," NYT, May 18.

Rossi, Peter (1987), "No Good Applied Social Research Goes Unpunished," *Society,* November–December.

Rothfeld, Charles (1990), "Minority Critic Stirs Debate in Minority Writing," NYT, Jan. 5.

Rothstein, Edward (1989), "Broken Vessel," *New Republic,* March 6.

Russell, Diana E. H. (1975), *The Politics of Rape,* New York: Stein & Day.

—— (1984), *Sexual Exploitation: Rape, Child Sexual Abuse and Workplace Harassment,* Beverly Hills: Sage.

Sanger, David E. (1985), "Curb on Campus Computers: Pentagon vs. Academia," NYT, Aug. 17.

Schlesinger, James (1980), "American Power and the Survival of the West," *Parameters,* June.

Schulz, Bud and Ruth (1989), *It Did Happen Here—Recollections of Political Repression in America*, Berkeley: Univ. of California Press.

Schumpeter, Joseph (1950), *Democracy, Capitalism and Socialism*, New York: Harper & Row.

Shabecoff, Philip (1987), "Political Activists Weigh U.S. 'Green' Movement,'" NYT, July 6.

Simon, John (1989), *The Sheep from the Goats: Selected Literary Essays*, New York: Weidenfeld and Nicolson.

Singer, Amy (1982), "Spray Paint Rage," *Valley Advocate*, Aug. 4.

Sobran, Joseph (1983), "A Pervasive Philosophy," DHG, Jan. 24.

Sontag, Susan (1968), *Trip to Hanoi*, New York: Farrar, Straus & Giroux.

——— (1982), "Communism and the Left," *Nation*, Feb. 27.

Sowell, Thomas (1985), *Marxism: Philosophy and Economics*, New York: Morrow.

——— (1990), *Preferential Policies: An International Perspective*, New York: Morrow.

Speier, Hans (1952), "Risk, Security and Hero Worship," in *Social Order and Risk of War*, New York: Stewart.

Stark, Steven (1984), "The Harvard Strike," *Boston Magazine*, March.

Strozier, Matthew (1988), "How Gentrification Broke My Nose" (op-ed), NYT, Dec. 3.

Taubman, Philip (1980), "Gadfly Stings CIA by 'Naming Names' of Its Agents," NYT, July 19.

Teltsch, Kathleen (1990), "Founded by Idealists, Group Thrives on Need," NYT, Jan. 30.

Thomas, Jo (1980), "Jamaicans Weathering Economic and Social Storm," NYT, July 6.

Ticker, William (1990), Letter, NYT, Nov. 22.

Tipton, Steven M. (1982), *Getting Saved from the Sixties*, Berkeley: Univ. of California Press.

Tolchin, Martin (1983), "For Blacks, Racism and Progress Mix," NYT, March 11.

Tonelson, Alan (1986), "Institutional Structure Blues," NYT *Book Review*, May 11.

Tucker, Robert W. (1971), *The Radical Left and American Foreign Policy*, Baltimore: Johns Hopkins Univ. Press.

Updike, John (1989) "On Not Being a Dove," *Commentary*, March.

Vidal, Gore (1982), *The Second American Revolution*, New York: Random House.

Vonnegut, Kurt (1986), Letter, NYT, May 18.

Wachtel, Paul L. (1983), *The Poverty of Affluence: A Psychological Portrait of the American Way of Life*, New York: Free Press.

Walzer, Michael (1988), *The Company of Critics*, New York: Basic.

Wattenberg, Ben (1985), "Exaggeration Won't End Illiteracy," NYT, Sept. 1.

Watts, Lisa (1985), "The Legacy of the New Left," *Northeastern University Alumni Magazine*, May–June.

Weaber, Gerald C., Jr. (1985), Letter, NYT, July 24.

Weinraub, Bernard (1983), "Titan of the Senate Still Gives Counsel," NYT, Oct. 11.

Weiss, Philip (1988), "The Education of Chancellor Green," NYT *Magazine*, Dec. 4.

Whalen, Jack, and Richard Flacks (1989), *Beyond the Barricades: The Sixties Generation Grows Up*, Philadelphia: Temple Univ. Press.

Whitman, David (1988), "Who's Who Among the Homeless," *New Republic*, June 6.

Wicker, Tom (1984), "A Damning Silence," NYT, Sept. 7.

Wildavsky, Aaron (1982), "The Three Cultures: Explaining Anomalies in the American Welfare State," *Public Interest*, Fall.

Will, George (1987), "Homelessness and the Community," DHG, Nov. 18.

Wilson, Suzanne (1984), "Williamsburg Anti-nuclear Protester May Be Sentenced on Her Birthday," DHG, Feb. 8.

Wise, Helen (1984), "Ex-militant Now Persuades by Words and Film," *The Alumnus* (Univ. of Massachusetts), June–July.

———— (1985), "Our Way of War, Our Way of Life: Facing the Issue," *The Alumnus,* April–May.

Wolfe, Alan (1978), *The Seamy Side of Democracy: Repression in America,* New York: Longman.

Wolfe, Tom (1977), *Mauve Gloves & Madmen, Clutter & Vine,* New York: Bantam.

Wrong, Dennis (1989), "The Passing of 60s Radicalism," *Contemporary Sociology,* September.

Other Sources

"Anticommunism and the U.S.—History and Consequences" (1988), *Conference Program,* Cambridge, Mass.

"Benefit for Indian Activist Draws Support" (1987), Associated Press (AP below), DHG, Oct. 28.

"Berkeley in Sanctuary Move" (1985), NYT, Feb. 21.

"CIA Calls Off Visit to Columbia" (1983), NYT, April 12.

Colloquium on "Prospects for Peace and War" (1982), Washington D.C.: IPS/TNI.

"Come Home, Anti-Communism" (1989), *Contentions,* January.

"Evidence Points to Deceit by Brawley" (1988), NYT, Sept. 27.

"Faculty Opposes Army's Study Center at CalTech" (1984) (AP), NYT, Feb. 1.

"'Free Speech Orator' Savio Gives Call to Action" (1984) (AP), DHG, Oct. 3.

"Gallup Finds Support for Military Cutbacks" (1985), NYT, March 9.

"Grenada Debate" (1984), DHG, Oct. 26.

"Guilty or Innocent? Rosenberg Debate Becomes Heated" (1983) (AP), DHG, Oct. 21.

"House in '88 Rated Most Liberal in 40 Years" (1989) (AP), NYT, Jan. 25.

"Local Action/National Strength" (1987), *Conference Program* for 18th National Conference on Women and Law, March.

"Miss America: 'Society Has Lost Its Bearings'" (1988) (AP), DHG, Nov. 29.

"Necessity Defense" (1984) (AP), DHG, Nov. 29.

"No Business as Usual April 29" (1985), *Leaflet,* Univ. of Massachusetts at Amherst.

"Notes on People" (1981), NYT, Dec. 15.

"Our Anti-Government Government Radio" (1982), *AIM Report,* April-II.

"Police Don't Applaud William Kunstler" (1984), DHG, March 15.

"Protesters' Unusual Defense Ends in Controversial Victory" (1984) (AP), NYT, Dec. 4.

"The Responsibility of Intellectuals—A Discussion" (1986), *Salmagundi,* Spring/Summer.

"Student Movement of '64 Remembered at Berkeley" (1984), NYT, Oct. 7.

TRB (1985) "Dohrn Again," *New Republic,* Oct. 14.

"2500 Rally at UN to Oppose Invasion" (1983) (AP), NYT, Oct. 27.

Chapter 2. The Churches

Armstrong, James, and Russell Dilley (1977), "A Report from Cuba," rpt. in *Time for Candor: Mainline Churches and Radical Social Witness,* Washington, D.C.: Institute for Religion and Democracy.

Austin, Charles (1982), "Ministers Seeking to Revitalize Preaching," NYT, Oct. 24.

———— (1982), "300 Church Leaders Protest U.S. Policies in Central America," NYT, Nov. 28.

Baldizon, Alvaro Jose (1985), "Nicaragua's State Security: Behind the Propaganda Mask" (Briefing Paper), Washington, D.C.: Institute for Religion and Democracy.

Berger, Peter L. (1983), "The Third World as a Religious Idea," *Partisan Review,* No. 2.
—— (1985), "Can the Bishops Help the Poor?," *Commentary,* February.
Berrigan, Daniel (1987), *To Dwell in Peace: An Autobiography,* San Francisco: Harper & Row.
——, and Robert Coles (1972), *The Geography of Faith—Conversations between Daniel Berrigan and Robert Coles,* New York: Bantam.
Berryman, Philip (1984), *The Religious Roots of Rebellion,* Maryknoll: Orbis.
—— (1987), *Liberation Theology,* New York: Pantheon.
Billingsley, K.L. (1990), *From Mainline to Sidelines: The Social Witness of the National Council of Churches,* Washington, D.C.: Ethics and Public Policy Center.
Bloom, Alan (1987), *The Closing of the American Mind,* New York: Simon & Schuster.
Branigin, William (1986), "Philippine Rebels Targeting Right Groups," *Washington Post,* Oct. 18.
Briggs, Kenneth A. (1981), "Catholic Bishops Criticize Aid to El Salvador," NYT, Nov. 20.
—— (1982), "U.S. Catholic Bishops Opposing Administration's Salvador Policy," NYT, Feb. 21.
—— (1982), "Billy Graham, Back Home, Defends Remarks," NYT, May 20.
—— (1983), "World Churches Back U.N. Afghanistan Plan," NYT, Aug. 11.
—— (1984), "Political Activism Reflects Churches' Search for a Role in a Secular Society," NYT, Sept. 9.
—— (1984), "Activism Affirmed by Catholic Order," NYT, Dec. 10.
Brock, David (1986), "Movement Seeks Sanctuary for Itself as Well as Aliens," *Insight,* Aug. 11.
Buxton, D. F. (1928), *The Challenge of Bolshevism: A New Social Ideal,* London: Allen and Unwin.
Casey, William Van Etten, and Philip Nobile, eds. (1971), *The Berrigans,* New York: Avon.
Chira, Susan (1983), "Catholic Church Consciousness-Raising About Nuclear Arms," NYT, Dec. 16.
Chomsky, Noam, and Edward S. Herman (1977), "Distortions at Fourth Hand," *Nation,* June 25.
Coffin, William Sloane, Jr. (1983), "Nicaragua Is Not an Enemy" (op-ed), NYT, July 31.
—— (1985), *Living the Truth in a World of Illusions,* San Francisco: Harper & Row.
Crowe, Francis (1974), Letter, *Peacework,* No. 24, Oct.
—— (1986), Letter, DHG, July 23.
—— (1988), Letter, DHG, Oct. 7.
Davenport, Rusty (1981), "Cuba: A Land of Contrast," quoted in *A Time for Candor: Mainline Churches and Radical Social Witness,* Washington, D.C.: Institute for Religion and Democracy.
Demerath, Jay (1990), Letter to author.
Duggan, Ervin S. (1986), "A Church in the Political Thicket," *Public Opinion,* Summer.
Ehrenreich, Barbara (1986), "Is the Middle Class Doomed?," NYT *Magazine,* Sept. 7.
Ferber, Michael (1985), "Religious Revival on the Left," *Nation,* July 6/13.
Frawley, Joan (1983), "Religious Activists Tour Nicaragua," *National Catholic Register,* July 24.
—— (1983), "Revolutionists Win Converts Among Catholic Missionaries," *Wall Street Journal,* Oct. 7.
Georgiana, Sharon (1988), "Human Rights Violations in Cuba," *Religion and Democracy,* July.
Glynn, Patrick (1983), "Pulpit Politics," *New Republic,* March 14.

Golden, Renny, and Michael McConnell (1986), *Sanctuary: The New Underground Railroad*, Maryknoll: Orbis Books.

Goldman, Ari L. (1985), "Clerics Offering Support on AIDS—Christian and Jewish Leaders Join to Urge Compassion for Victims of Disease," NYT, Feb. 24.

—— (1988), "Church Council, Losing Appeal, Adopts Changes," NYT, Nov. 4.

Gray, Francine du Plessix (1970), "Acts of Witness," *The New Yorker*, March 14.

Griffith, Carol Friedley, ed. (1981), *Christianity and Politics*, Washington, D.C.: Ethics and Public Policy Center.

Hadden, Jeffrey (1969), *The Gathering Storm in the Churches*, Garden City: Doubleday.

Hart, Benjamin (1984), "George Washington Ortega?" (Letter), *Policy Review*, Summer.

Hedges, Christopher (1990), "For Mainline Protestantism, the Inner City Grows Remote," NYT, May 31.

Herbut, Paula (1983), "75 Leaders Lobby on Hill for End to Military Aid for Central America," *Washington Post*, May 24.

Hershey, Robert D. (1982), "Military Men Say Congress Cuts Too Close to Bone," NYT, Feb. 21.

Himmelfarb, Gertrude (1971), "The Intellectual in Politics: The Case of the Webbs," *Journal of Contemporary History*, No. 3.

Hitchcock, James (1983), "Through Soviet Glasses," *National Catholic Register*, April 27.

Hollander, Paul (1981), *Political Pilgrims*, New York: Oxford Univ. Press.

—— (1983), *The Many Faces of Socialism*, New Brunswick: Transaction.

—— (1983), "Sojourners in Nicaragua: A Political Pilgrimage," *National Catholic Register*, May 29.

—— (1988), "Socialist Prisons and Imprisoned Minds," *National Interest*, Winter.

Hunsinger, George (1985), "Barth, Barmen and the Confessing Church Today," *Katallagate*, Summer.

Ingwerson, Marshall (1984), "From Actors to Advocates, Americans Are Flocking to Nicaragua," *Christian Science Monitor*, Nov. 23.

Isaac, Rael Jean and Erich (1981), "Sanctifying Revolution: Protestantism's New Social Gospel," *American Spectator*, May.

Johnson, Hewlett (1940), *The Soviet Power*, New York: International Publishers.

Jones, Gary (1988), "Hundreds Convene for Peace," DHG, Oct. 3.

Kennedy, Moorehead (1986), quoted in the review of his *The Ayatollah in the Cathedral*, NYT *Book Review*, Aug. 6.

King, Florence (1990), "George Will Collection," *Washington Times*, Nov. 5.

Kinsler, Ross F. (1986), "Observing Nicaragua Through Different Lenses," *Monday Morning* (a magazine for Presbyterian ministers), March 10.

Lefever, Ernest W. (1979), *Amsterdam to Nairobi—The World Council of Churches and the Third World*, Washington, D.C.: Ethics and Public Policy Center.

—— (1987), *Nairobi to Vancouver: The World Council of the Churches and the World, 1975–87*, Washington, D.C.: Ethics and Public Policy Center.

Lerner, Robert, and Stanley Rothman (1988), *Political and Theological Views of Religious Elites* (manuscript).

Lewy, Guenter (1988), *Peace and Revolution—The Moral Crisis of American Pacifism*, Grand Rapids: Eerdmans.

Lindsey, Robert (1984), "Bishops Protest Train Carrying Atom Weapons," NYT, Feb. 24.

Martin, David (1983), "The Clergy, Secularization and Politics," *This World*, Fall.

Marzani, Carl (1982), "The Vatican as a Left Ally?," *Monthly Review*, July–August.

Maurer, Marvin (1977), "Quakers in Politics: Israel, PLO and Social Revolution," *Midstream*, November.

—— (1979), "Quakers and Communists—Vietnam and Israel," *Midstream*, November.

Michaelsen, Robert S., and Wade Clark Roof, eds. (1986), *Liberal Protestantism*, New York: Pilgrim Press. .

Meconis, Charles A. (1979), *With Clumsy Grace: The American Catholic Left, 1961–1975*, New York: Seabury Press.

Minogue, Kenneth (1990), "Societies Collapse, Faiths Linger On," *Encounter*, March.

Monroe, Ann (1985), "Devout Dissidents," *Wall Street Journal*, May 24.

Motavalli, Jim (1985), "Ortega Takes Manhattan," *Valley Advocate*, Nov. 6.

Munoz, Natalia (1988), "Coffin Speaks on Disarmament," DHG, Oct. 10.

Muravchik, Joshua (1983), "Pliant Protestants," *New Republic*, June 13.

Myers, Kenneth A., ed. (1988), *Aspiring to Freedom—Commentaries on John Paul II's Encyclical "The Social Concerns of the Church" With the Complete Text of the Encyclical*, Grand Rapids: Eerdmans.

Nickel, Herman (1980), "Crusade Against the Corporation—Church Militants on the March," *Fortune*, June 16.

Novak, Michael (1982), "Arms and the Church," *Commentary*, March.

—— (1982), "A Stunning Survey: Notes and Comments," *This World*, Summer.

—— (1984), "The Case Against Liberation Theology," NYT *Magazine*, Oct. 21.

Oliva, Milagros (1983), "En Cuba no hemos visto ningun signo de violacion de los derechos humanos" (In Cuba we have seen no sign of human rights violations), *Granma Weekly Review*, May.

Pogson, Jane M. B. (1986), Letter, NYT, Aug. 3.

Powell, Loey (1988), "My Visit with Cuban Women," *Common Lot*, New York: United Church of Christ Coordinating Center for Women in Church and Society, Winter.

Preston, Richard (1983), "The Reign of God Has Arrived in Nicaragua," *Catholic Weekly*, March 25.

Quass, Susan (1985), Letter, NYT, Jan. 7.

Radosh, Ronald, ed. (1976), *The New Cuba: Paradoxes and Potentials*, New York: Morrow.

Ramming, Todd (1985), "Arrested Protester Reflects on Civil Disobedience," *Campus Report* (Stanford), June 5.

Raskin, Marcus G. (1983), "War, Peace and the Bishops," *Nation*, April 19.

Robb, Ed and Julia (1986), *Betrayal of the Church*, Westchester, Ill.: Crossway Books.

Robbins, William (1981), "Judge Bars 4 Defense Witnesses in Berrigans' Trial," NYT, March 5.

Roelofsma, Derk Kinnane (1986), "Missionaries with a Leftist Mission," *Insight*, May 19.

Roof, Wade Clark (1982), "America's Voluntary Establishment: Mainline Religion in Transition," *Daedalus*, Winter.

—— (1988), "Campaign '88's Silent Majority" (op-ed), *Wall Street Journal*, Feb. 24.

—— , and William McKinney (1987), *American Mainline Religion*, New Brunswick: Rutgers Univ. Press.

Russell, Bertrand (1950), *Unpopular Essays*, London: Allen & Unwin.

Ryan, William (1971), *Blaming the Victim*, New York: Pantheon.

Schall, James V. (1981), "The Changing Catholic Scene," in Carol F. Griffith, ed., *Christianity and Politics—Catholic and Protestant Perspectives*, Washington, D.C.: Ethics and Public Policy Center.

Scherer, Peggy (1984), "Journey to Central America," *Catholic Worker*, January–February.

Schmemann, Serge (1982), "Graham Preaches at Church in Moscow," NYT, May 10.

Schultz, Kathleen (1984), "An Analysis of Christian Left in the United States," *Monthly Review,* July–August.

Seabury, Paul (1978), "Trendier Than Thou—the Episcopal Church and the Secular World," Washington, D.C.: Ethics and Public Policy Center Reprint Series, No. 14.

Shapiro, Margaret (1985), "The Roots of O'Neill's Dissent," *Washington Post,* June 5.

Steinfels, Peter (1988), "U.S. Bishops Oppose Anti-Missile Plan," NYT, April 15.

——— (1989), "AIDS Provokes Theological Second Thoughts," NYT, Nov. 19.

Sysyn, Frank E. (1985), "Clergy and Commissars," *New Republic,* June 10.

Tamayo, Juan (1983), "Sandinistas Aim Soft Sell at Activists," *Miami Herald,* Dec. 14.

Tanham, George K. (1988), "Subverting the South Pacific," *National Interest,* Spring.

Teltsch, Kathleen (1985), "Activist Trend Found in Religious Charities," NYT, Jan. 26.

Turner, Wallace (1982), "Tax Refusal Completes Prelate's Moral Journey," NYT, April 19.

Valladares, Armando (1983), "For the Record," *Washington Post,* July 17.

Vecsey, George (1978), "Riverside Church Conference Seeks Arms Cutback," NYT, Dec. 10.

Vree, Dale (1975), "'Stripped Clean': The Berrigans and the Politics of Guilt and Martyrdom," *Ethics,* July.

Wallis, Jim, ed. (1987), *The Rise of Christian Conscience,* San Fransciso: Harper & Row.

Wieseltier, Leon (1982), "Passionate Compassion," *New Republic,* June 16.

Wolfe, Tom (1977), *Mauve Gloves & Madmen, Clutter & Vine,* New York: Bantam.

Other Sources

"AIDS Quilt to Visit Amherst, Umass" (Briefs) (1990), DHG, March 26.

"American Bishops Visiting Nicaragua" (1985) (AP), DHG, Feb. 25.

"Chronicle" (1990), NYT, March 24.

"Church Coalition Assails Utility Ads Favoring Nuclear Power" (1984) (UPI), NYT, Jan. 5.

Church Support for Pro-Sandinista Network (1984) (pamphlet), Washington, D.C.: Institute for Religion and Democracy.

"The Churches and the Cold War" (1990) (editorial), *First Things,* April.

"Excerpts from Draft of Bishops' Letter on the U.S. Economy" (1984), NYT, Nov. 12.

"Excerpts from Final Draft of Bishops' Letter on the Economy" (1986), NYT, Nov. 14.

"An Interview with Clark Pinnock" (1985), *Religion and Democracy,* January.

"Letter from Corinto" (1984), *Nicaraguan Journal* (pamphlet), published by AFSC, St. Louis area, December.

"NCC Policy Statement on Peace and the Reunification of Korea," quoted in *Religion and Democracy* (1988), September–October.

"NCC Shaken by Crisis" (1989), *Religion and Democracy,* January.

"The NCC on South Africa" (1986), *Religion and Society Report,* December.

"Nicaragua: A Fragile Future" (1983), *Sojourners,* March.

"Nicaragua Visited" (1984), *The Churchman,* April–May.

Nuclear Weapons and Intervention in Central America and the Caribbean (pamphlet), n.d., AFSC, Northampton, Mass.

"Quaker College in Indiana Aiding Draft Resisters" (1982) (AP), NYT, Oct. 10.

"Quaker Group Reports Rights Curbs in Grenada" (1984), NYT, Jan. 10.

"Quakers Leading Tax Protest Against Support for Military" (1983) (AP), NYT, April 17.

Pledge of Resistance (n.d.).

"Religious Figures Protest Contra Aid" (1986) (AP), NYT, March 5.

"Religious Freedom and the WCC" (1983), *Religion and Democracy,* June–July.

"The Sanctuary Movement: A Time for Reappraisal" (1985), *Religion and Democracy,* March.

"Sandinista Makes His Case on a Brooklyn Church Visit" (1985), NYT, July 28.

"Secretary of Navy Critical of Some Disarmament Views" (1982) (AP), NYT, March 9.

Statistical Abstract of the United States (1988), Washington, D.C.: Government Printing Office.

Theology Faculty Survey (1982), *This World,* Summer.

"36 Religious Leaders Urge Fight on Poverty" (1985) (UPI), NYT, Feb. 17.

"Truth in Book Advertising" (1987), *Religion and Society Report,* December.

"World Church Assembly Proves Bias" (1983), *Religion and Democracy* (August–September), Washington, D.C.: Institute for Religion and Democracy.

World Peacemakers, "Our Call and Program" (n.d.), Pamphlet listing publications and activities.

Chapter 3. Higher Education

Adelson, Joseph, and Chester E. Finn, Jr. (1983), "Terrorizing Children," *Commentary,* April.

Anyon, Jean (1979), "Ideology and United States History Textbooks," *Harvard Educational Review,* August.

Atlas, James (1987), "MIA at the MLA," *New Republic,* Jan. 26.

——— (1988), "Battle of the Books," NYT *Magazine,* June 5.

Balch, Stephen H., and Herbert I. London (1986), "The Tenured Left," *Commentary,* October.

Barringer, Felicity (1989), "The Mainstreaming of Marxism in U.S. Colleges," NYT, Oct. 25.

Beer, William R. (1987), "Resolute Ignorance: Social Science and Affirmative Action," *Society,* May–June.

——— (1988), "Sociology and the Effects of Affirmative Action: A Case of Neglect," *American Sociologist,* Fall.

Begley, Adam (1990), "Black Studies' New Star," NYT *Magazine,* April 1.

Berger, Brigitte (1988), "Academic Feminism and the 'Left,'" *Academic Questions,* Spring.

Berger, Joseph (1990), "Now the Regents Must Decide If History Will Be Recast," NYT, Feb. 11.

——— (1990), "Pessimism Lurks as Schools Try Affirmative Action," NYT, Feb. 27.

Berlin, Isaiah (1986), *Four Essays on Liberty,* New York: Oxford Univ. Press.

Bernstein, Richard (1990), "Literary Critics Find Politics Everywhere," NYT, Jan. 1.

Blanton, James (1989), "Limits to Affirmative Action?," *Commentary,* June.

Bloom, Alan (1987), *The Closing of the American Mind,* New York: Simon and Schuster.

Bowers, C. A. (1977), "Emergent Ideological Characteristics of Educational Policy," *Teachers College Record,* September.

Bowles, Samuel, and Herbert Gintis (1976), *Schooling in Capitalist America,* New York: Basic.

Brock, David (1985), "The Big Chill: A Report Card on Campus Censorship," *Policy Review,* Spring.

——— (1985), "Combating Those Campus Marxists," *Wall Street Journal,* Dec. 12.

Bunzel, John H. (1983), "Campus 'Free Speech'" (op-ed), NYT, March 13.

——— (1990), "Minority Faculty Hiring," *American Scholar,* Winter.

Burawoy, Michael, and Theda Skockpol (1982), "The Resurgence of Marxism in American Sociology," *American Journal of Sociology,* Supplement.

Burns, Michael (1986), "How Should History Be Taught" (op-ed), NYT, Nov. 22.

Cantor, Norman F. (1988), "The Reagan Right: No Bark, No Bite" (op-ed), NYT, Aug. 22.

Carlson, Valerie (1986), "Mount Holyoke Stages 'Teach-in,'" DHG, April 24.

Cheney, Lynne V. (1988), *American Memory: A Report on the Humanities in the Nation's Public Schools,* Washington, D.C.: National Endowment for the Humanities.

Chomsky, Noam (1966), "Some Thoughts on Intellectuals and the Schools," *Harvard Educational Review,* Fall, No. 4.

Cole, John W., and Gerald F. Reid (1986), "The New Vulnerability of Higher Education," *NEA Higher Education Journal,* Winter.

Coleman, James S. (1989), "Response to the Sociology of Education Award," *Academic Questions,* Summer.

Collins, Glen (1987), "Spelman College's First 'Sister President,'" NYT, July 20.

Csorba, Les, III (n.d.), *Appeasing the Censors—A Special Report on Campus Free Speech Abuses,* Washington, D.C.: Accuracy in Academia.

Custred, Glynn (1990), "Onward to Adequacy," *Academic Questions,* Summer.

Cuzan, Alfred G. (1985), "LASA Spreads Disinformation on Nicaragua," *Times of the Americas,* Jan. 30.

Daley, Suzanne (1990), "Inspirational Black History Draws Academic Fire," NYT, Oct. 10.

Dastidar, Pratip (1990), "Patterns of History Reflected in Leader's Life," *Mass. Daily Collegian,* Nov. 27.

Dershowitz, Alan (1989), "Campus Speech Control," *Boston Herald,* May 2.

Detlefsen, Robert R. (1989), "White Like Me," *New Republic,* April 10.

Draper, Theodore (1987), "The Class Struggle," *New Republic,* Jan. 26.

Egan, Timothy (1988), "Challenge in Women's Course Roils Washington U. Campus," NYT, April 6.

Eitzen, Stanley D. (1983), *Social Problems,* Needham: Allyn and Bacon.

Ellington, Athleen (1986), "Smith Siege Ended," DHG, March 3.

Elliot, Brenda (1987), "Smith Survey Finds Elitism," DHG, Nov. 6.

Epstein, Joseph (1986), "A Case of Academic Freedom," *Commentary,* September.

Feron, James (1989), "College Agrees to Demands of Protesters," NYT, March 18.

Finn, Chester E., Jr. (1989), "The Campus: 'An Island of Repression in a Sea of Freedom,'" *Commentary,* September.

———, and Joseph Adelson, (1985), "Terrorizing Children," *Commentary,* April.

Fiske, Edward B. (1985), "3 Year Survey Finds College Curriculum in U.S. in 'Disarray,'" NYT, Feb. 11.

Fitzgerald, Frances (1979), *America Revised,* Boston: Little, Brown.

Giroux, Henry A. (1980), "Teacher Education and the Ideology of Social Control," *Boston University Journal of Education,* Winter.

Glazer, Nathan, and Reed Ueda (1983), *Ethnic Groups in History Textbooks,* Washington, D.C.: Ethics and Public Policy Center.

Gonzales, Daniel (1988), "Controversial Textbook Draws National Attention," DHG, July 13.

Goode, Stephen (1988), "Studied Furor in Required Reading," *Insight,* March 7.

——— (1988), "The Rights Response to Radicalism," *Insight,* Dec. 12.

Gordon, Robert A. (1988), "Thunder from the Left" (review of *Storm Over Biology: Essays on Science, Sentiment and Public Policy* by Bernard D. Davis), *Academic Questions,* Summer.

Grabar, Robert (1990), "Dishing Out the A's," DHG, April 14.

—— (1990), "College Troubled by Racist Act," DHG, Dec. 26.

Greene, Elizabeth (1985), "Students Ponder Life Without a Future as Courses on Peace and War Proliferate," Chronicle of Higher Education, Nov. 6.

—— (1986), "Distruptive Tactics of Spartacus League Annoy and Frustrate Other Student Leftists," Chronicle of Higher Education, Feb. 12.

Gutman, Amy (1988), "Principals, Principles," New Republic, Dec. 12.

Hacker, Andrew (1989), "Affirmative Action: The New Look," NY Review of Books, Oct. 12.

—— (1990), "Trans-National America," NY Review of Books, Nov. 22.

Hechinger, Fred M. (1984), "Censorship Rises in Nation's Public Schools," NYT, Jan. 3.

Hentoff, Nat (1989), "Free Speech on Campus," Progressive, May.

Herz, Martin F. (1978), How the Cold War Is Taught, Washington, D.C.: Ethics and Public Policy Center.

Hewitt, Hugh (1982), Letter, Commentary, November.

Hill, Laura (1987), "Peace Activist Leads Effort to Remove Textbook," DHG, Oct. 17.

Himmelfarb, Gertrude (1988), "Stanford and Duke Undercut Classical Values" (op-ed), NYT, May 5.

Hollander, Paul (1988), "Introduction: The Puzzle of Alienation," The Survival of the Adversary Culture, New Brunswick: Transaction.

Hook, Sidney (1988), "The Attack on Western Civilization: An Interim Report," Measure, February.

Horowitz, Irving Louis (1987), "Disenthralling Sociology," Society, January–February.

Howe, Irving (1988), "What Should We Be Teaching," Dissent, Fall.

Hurn, Christoper J. (1985), The Limits and Possibilities of Schooling, Boston: Allyn and Bacon.

Kampf, Louis (1969), "Notes Toward a Radical Culture," in Priscilla Long, ed., The New Left, Boston: Porter Sargent.

Kaplan, Craig, and Ellen Schrecker, eds. (1983), Regulating the Intellectuals: Perspectives on Academic Freedom in the 80s, New York: Praeger.

Kimball, Roger (1986), "Debating the Humanities at Yale," New Criterion, June.

—— (1990), Tenured Radicals, New York: Harper & Row.

Klehr, Harvey (1988), Far Left of Center: The American Radical Left Today, New Brunswick: Transaction.

Koppett, Leonard (1987), "At Princeton, They Call It an Education" (op-ed), NYT, Aug. 15.

Kors, Alan C. (1988), "Thought Reform and Education: A View from the University of Pennsylvania," Academic Questions, Fall.

Kozol, Jonathan (1976), "The Search for an Adjective That Will Kill Discrimination" (op-ed), NYT, Feb. 2.

Kristol, Irving (1986), "American Universities in Exile," Wall Street Journal, June 17.

Kuklick, Bruce (1980), "The People? Yes," Nation, May 24.

Langfur, Hal (1984), "Colleges Launch Peace Studies Program," DHG, Nov. 1.

Langiulli, Nino (1989–90), "Sifting the Rubble at Yale," Academic Questions, Winter.

Leacock, Eleanor (1982), "Marxism and Anthropology," in B. Ollman and E. Vernoff, eds., The Left Academy: Marxist Scholarship on American Campuses, New York: McGraw-Hill.

Lefever, Ernest W., ed. (1978), Values in an American Government Textbook, Washington, D.C.: Ethics and Public Policy Center.

Levin, Margarita (1988), "Caring New World: Feminism and Science," *American Scholar,* Winter.

Levin, Michael (1985), Women Studies, Ersatz Scholarship," *Coalition Newsletter,* October.

Lewy, Guenter (1982), "Academic Ethics and the Radical Left," *Policy Review,* Winter.

——— (1983), *False Consciousness,* New Brunswick: Transaction.

Lilla, Elizabeth (1986), "Who Is Afraid of Women's Studies?," *Commentary,* February.

Lindsey, Robert (1987), "1960's Activists Jailed in New Causes," NYT, May 18.

Lipset, Seymour Martin (1982), "The Academic Mind at the Top: The Political Behavior and Values of Faculty Elites," *Public Opinion Quarterly,* Vol. 46.

———, and Everett Carll Ladd, Jr. (1972), "The Politics of American Sociologists," *American Journal of Sociology,* July.

——— (1986), Letter, *Campus Report,* July.

London, Herbert I. (1987), *Armageddon in the Classroom: An Examination of Nuclear Education,* Lanham: Univ. Press of America.

Long, Priscilla, ed. (1989), *The New Left,* Boston: Porter Sargent.

Lyall, Sarah (1988), "Pressed on Animal Rights, Researcher Gives Up Grant," NYT, Nov. 22.

Maeroff, Gene I. (1981), "Highly Qualified City U. Teachers Now Used for Remedial Studies," NYT, March 16.

——— (1981), "Klan's Critics Split on Educational Response," NYT, Oct. 25.

Main, Robert S. (1978), "The Treatment of Economic Issues in High School Government, Sociology, U.S. History and World History Texts," *Journal of Economic Education,* Spring.

Mannheim, Karl (1936), *Ideology and Utopia,* New York: Harvest.

McFadden, Robert D. (1987), "3d Manual Says Whites Are Racists," NYT, May 16.

McKay, Betsy (1982), "Hampshire College President Says Schools Have Role in Social Change," DHG, Oct. 22.

McKinley, James C., Jr. (1989), "Minority Students Walk Out Over a Teacher's Remark," NYT, Oct. 4.

Monteverde, Elliot (1990), "My Letter to Che" and "Cuba, the Media and the Fallacy of the New World Order," *Mass. Daily Collegian,* Oct. 9.

Navarro, Mireya (1989), "Racial Tensions in New York Blamed for Disruption," NYT, Oct. 5.

Neth, Michael J. (1987), Letter, *Commentary,* April.

Nettler, Gwynn (1973), "Wanting and Knowing," *American Behavioral Scientist,* September–October.

Nix, Crystal (1987), "Contra Leader's Harvard Appearance Disrupted," NYT, Oct. 4.

Novak, Michael, Jeane Kirkpatrick, and Ann Crutcher (1978), *Values in American Government Textbooks,* Washington, D.C.: Ethics and Public Policy Center.

Oppenheimer, Martin (1988), Letter, NYT, Nov. 30.

Ollman, Bertell, and Edward Vernoff, eds. (1982), *The Left Academy: Marxist Scholarship on American Campuses,* New York: McGraw-Hill.

Podhoretz, Norman (1986), "Academic Tyranny in the Ivy League," *NY Post,* April 5.

——— (1988), "Fundamentalism at Harvard," *NY Post,* Oct. 25.

Powers, Stephen P., David J. Rothman, and Stanley Rothman (1990), "The Myth of Low Black Self-Esteem," *World and I,* March.

Proefriedt, William (1980), "Socialist Criticisms of Education in the United States: Problems and Possibilities," *Harvard Educational Review,* November.

Raskin, Marcus G. (1971), *Being and Doing,* New York: Random House.

Ravitch, Diane (1990), "Multiculturalism," *American Scholar,* Summer.

Ravo, Nick (1988), "Yale Move to Make Cum Laude Mean More," NYT, May 22.

Richardson, David B. (1982), "Marxism in U.S. Classrooms," *U.S. News and World Report,* Jan. 25.

Ricketts, Glenn M. (1990), "Multiculturalism Mobilizes," *Academic Questions,* Summer.

Rosdil, Donald L. (1988), "Altruism and Social Determinism: The Paradox of Recent Social Movements," Paper Presented at Midwestern Political Science Association Meeting, Chicago, April.

Rosenberg, B., and E. Goldstein, eds. (1982), *Creators and Disturbers,* New York: Columbia Univ. Press.

Rossie, David (1989), "SUNY Bids $500,000 for One Prof," *Press & Sun Bulletin,* May 28.

Rothman, Stanley (1986), "Academics on the Left," *Society,* March/April.

Ryerson, Andre (1988), "How Eight Colleges Teach American Foreign Policy," *Academic Questions,* Fall.

Sanoff, Alvin P. (1989), "60s Protestors, 80s Professors," *U.S. News and World Report,* Jan. 16.

Schlesinger, Arthur, Jr. (1990), "When Ethnic Studies Are Un-American," *Social Studies Review,* No. 5, Summer.

Schmidt, William E. (1990), "Art and Ire Mix Again, This Time Over Race," NYT, April 20.

Searle, John (1990), "The Storm Over the University," *New York Review of Books,* Dec. 6.

Shaw, Peter (1989), *The War Against the Intellect,* Iowa City: Univ. of Iowa Press.

Shils, Edward (1969), "Plenitude and Scarcity," *Encounter,* May.

Short, Thomas (1988), "'Diversity' and 'Breaking of Disciplines': Two New Assaults on the Curriculum," *Academic Questions,* Summer.

———— (1988), "A 'New Racism' on Campus?," *Commentary,* August.

Simon, William E. (1988), "To Reopen the American Mind," *Wall Street Journal,* July 8.

Skerry, Peter (1981), "Race Relations at Harvard," *Commentary,* January.

Smith, Thomas B. (1985), *Education for Disaster: The Nuclear Spectre in American Classrooms,* Evanston: Mark Books.

Snyderman, Mark, and Stanley Rothman (1988), *The IQ Controversy, the Media and Public Policy,* New Brunswick: Transaction.

Sowell, Thomas (1989), "Campuses Grant Free Speech Only to Ideologically Correct," *San Jose Mercury News,* July 24.

Steele, Shelby (1990), "A Negative Vote on Affirmative Action," NYT *Magazine,* May 13.

Stewart, Charles (1986), Letter, NYT, May 28.

Sullivan, Andrew (1990), "Racism 101," *New Republic,* Nov. 26.

Terry, Don (1990), "John Jay Grants Students Amnesty," NYT, June 3.

Thernstrom, Abigail (1989), "Permafirm Action," *New Republic,* July 31.

Thomas, Daniel C. (1987), *Guide to Careers & Graduate Education in Peace Studies,* Amherst: Five College Program in Peace and Security Studies, Hampshire College.

Tucker, William (1988), Letter, NYT, May 21.

Vitz, Paul C. (1986), *Censorship: Evidence of Bias in Our Children's Textbooks,* Ann Arbor: Servant Books.

Washburn, Wilcomb (1982), "Leftist Academics and Ethnic Minorities," *Washington Times,* Dec. 30.

———— (1984), Letter, *Anthropology Newsletter,* January.

———— (1985), Letter, *Anthropology Newsletter,* January.

———— (1988), "The Academic Profession and Contemporary Politics," *Minerva,* Fall.

Weiss, Samuel (1990), "John Jay's Head to Accede to Some Student Demands," NYT, May 16.

Weissberg, Robert (1989), "Political Censorship: A Different View," *Academic Questions,* Fall.

—— (1989–90), "Safe-Bashing," *Academic Questions,* Winter.

Whitmoyer, Walter C. (1988), "More on the Social Honor Code," *Princeton Alumni Weekly,* Jan. 13.

Wilkerson, Isabel (1989), "Discordant Notes in Detroit: Music and Affirmative Action," NYT, March 5.

Wills, Garry (1989), "In Praise of Censure," *Time,* July 31.

Winkler, Karen J. (1985), "Scholars Ask Boycott of Pentagon Plans for Research on Third World Nations," *Chronicle of Higher Education,* May 8.

—— (1988), "Sociologists Accused of Forsaking Problems of Society, Abandoning 'Critical Bite,'" *Chronicle of Higher Education,* Sept. 7.

Other Sources

"Boston Schools Called Insensitive" (1988) (AP), DHG, Nov. 21.

"Communist Heads UMass Student Body" (1988), DHG, March 30.

The Condition of the Professoriate, Attitudes and Trends 1989, Princeton: Carnegie Foundation for the Advancement of Teaching.

"Cultural Revolutions" (1987), *Chronicles of Culture,* July.

The Curriculum of Inclusion (1989), Report of the Task Force on Minorities, Albany, N.Y.: State Education Dept.

Equity Institute Report (1987), reproduced by Smith College, Northampton, Mass.

"Facing the Challenge of Cultural Diversity" (1990), *Higher Education Advocate* (newsletter), April 19.

"InCAR—A Reincarnation of SDS?" (1987), *Measure,* June.

Institute of Latin American Studies, University of Texas at Austin (brochure), 1986–87.

"Maine Faculty Votes CIA Ban" (1987), NYT, Nov. 15.

"Minority Hiring by Yale Is Criticized in Study" (1989), NYT, Oct. 4.

"Mount Holyoke: Students Rally to Overcome Discrimination" (1990), NYT, Nov. 11.

"New Brand of Campus Activism Is Emerging" (1983) (AP), NYT, Nov. 28.

"New Courses to Focus on Cultural Diversity" (1990), NYT, Dec. 9.

"Penn State Will Drop Charges Against 89 Students" (1988) (AP), NYT, April 19.

Policy on Discrimination and Discriminatory Harassment (Memorandum) (1989), Univ. of Michigan.

"Politically Correct" (1990) (editorial), *Wall Street Journal,* Nov. 24.

"Radical Changes in Schools Sought" (1990) (AP), DHG, Nov. 13.

Report of the Latin American Studies Association Delegation to Observe the Nicaraguan General Election of November 4, 1984, LASA Secretariat, Univ. of Texas, Austin.

"Righting the Leftist Tilt at U. of Colorado" (1986), *Campus Report,* August.

"Smith College Croquet Court Elitist?" (1988) (AP), DHG, April 7.

"Talk of the Campus" (1985), *In Other Words,* Feb. 8.

What Students Should Know About Discrimination and Discriminatory Harassment (n.d.) (Booklet), Affirmative Action Office of the President, Univ. of Michigan.

Women's Studies Course Offerings Fall 1987, University of Masschusetts at Amherst.

Advertisements for Textbooks

Curran, Daniel J., and Claire M. Renzetti (1987), *Social Problems: Society in Crisis,* Boston: Allyn and Bacon.

Eitzen, Stanley D. (n.d.), *Social Problems,* 4th ed., Boston: Allyn and Bacon.

Lauer, Robert H. (n.d.), *Social Problems and the Quality of Life,* 3rd ed., Dubuque: Brown.

Liazos, Alexander (n.d.), *Sociology: A Liberating Perspective,* Boston: Allyn.

Neubeck, Kenneth J. (1986), *Social Problems: A Critical Approach,* New York: Random House.

Pavalko, Ronald M. (n.d.), *Social Problems,* Ithaca: Peacock.

Skolnick, Jerome H., and Elliott Currie (n.d.), *Crisis in American Institutions,* 6th ed., Boston: Little, Brown.

Zastrow, Charles (n.d.), *Social Problems: Issues and Solutions,* Chicago: Nelson-Hall.

Chapter 4. Mass Media

Barnes, Fred (1989), "Flics Mix in Politics," *New Republic,* Oct. 30.

Basler, Barbara (1987), "'Bad Guys' Wear Pin Stripes," NYT, Jan. 29.

Bellah, Robert, et al. (1985), *Habits of the Heart,* Berkeley: Univ. of California Press.

Bernstein, Carl (1989), *Loyalties,* New York: Simon & Schuster.

Bernstein, Richard (1990), "The Arts Catch Up With a Society in Disarray," NYT, Sept. 2.

Bishop, Katherine (1990), "Berkeley in the 60's Brings Back the Future," NYT, Sept. 23.

Blau, Eleanor (1984), "The Ethnic Authenticity of 'Moscow,'" NYT, May 22.

Blonsky, Marshall (1988), "Ted Koppel's Edge," NYT *Magazine,* Aug. 14.

Boorstin, Daniel J. (1961), *The Image: A Guide to Pseudo-events in America,* New York: Harper & Row.

Boyer, Peter J. (1986), "ABC Delays 'Amerika,' Discloses Soviet Warning," NYT, Jan. 9.

Chanoff, David (1985), "Biased Series on Vietnam," *Boston Globe,* June 25.

Christian, Shirley (1982), "Covering the Sandinistas—The Foregone Conclusions of the Fourth Estate," *Washington Journalism Review,* March.

Collier, Peter (n.d.), "The Left in America After Reagan," *Policy Forum,* Washington, D.C.: National Forum Foundation.

Corry, John (1983), "TV: Documentary Film Examines Amiri Baraka," NYT, June 28.

——— (1983), "'The Day After': TV as Rallying Force," NYT, Nov. 20.

——— (1985), "Sorting Out Coverage of Hanoi's Celebration," NYT, May 2.

——— (1985), "Cuba's Revolution at 25," NYT, July 25.

——— (1985), "'Human Rights' on PBS, British Documentary," NYT, Oct. 29.

——— (1986), *TV News and the Dominant Culture,* Washington, D.C.: Media Institute.

——— (1986), "A PBS Documentary on Guatemala," NYT, Jan. 13.

——— (1986), "'Frontline' Examines Nicaragua's Contras," NYT, March 18.

——— (1986), "A Documentary Series, 'Hammer and Cross,'" NYT, Aug. 7.

——— (1986), "'The Hammer and the Cross': A Series of Distortions," NYT, Aug. 17.

——— (1986), "'The Africans': An Attack on Western Values," NYT, Oct. 26.

——— (1986), "The Uses of Television and the Pitfalls of Politics," NYT, Dec. 7.

——— (1987), "Jumping the Gun on 'Amerika,'" NYT, Jan. 25.

——— (1988), "Russia Through Rose-Colored Lenses," NYT, March 20.

Coser, Lewis, Charles Kadushin, and Walter W. Powell (1982), *Books: The Culture and Commerce of Commercial Publishing,* New York: Basic.

D'Souza, Dinesh (1984), "Retreat from Radicalism," *Policy Review,* Fall.

Ehrenreich, Barbara (1990), "The Wretched of the Hearth," *New Republic,* April 2.

Epstein, Edward Jay (1973), *News from Nowhere,* New York: Vintage.

Farber, Stephen (1984), "Docudrama Aims to Reopen a Case," NYT, Sept. 2.

——— (1988), "AIDS Groups Protest Series Episode," NYT, Dec. 8.

Friendly, Jonathan (1984), "Transition in 'Alternative' Press Focus of Meeting," NYT, June 17.

Gans, Herbert J. (1980), *Deciding What's News: A Study of CBS Evening News, NBC Nightly News, Newsweek and Time,* New York: Vintage.

——— (1985), "Are U.S. Journalists Dangerously Liberal?," *Journalism Review,* December.

Gerard, Jeremy (1989), "Walter Cronkite: Speaking His Mind Instead of Just News," NYT, Jan. 8.

Gergen, David R. (1984), "The Message to the Media," *Public Opinion,* April/May.

Gitlin, Todd (1980), *The Whole World Is Watching: The Mass Media in the Making and Unmaking of the New Left,* Berkeley: Univ. of California Press.

——— (1987), *The Sixties—Years of Hope, Days of Rage,* New York: Bantam.

Goldberg, Bernard (1989), "TV Insults Men Too" (op-ed), NYT, March 14.

Goode, Stephen (1988), "Long-lived, the Revolutionary Press," *Insight,* Oct. 17.

Goodman, Walter (1986), "Screen: 'Salvador' by Stone," NYT, March 5.

——— (1990), "3 Women in High-Security Prison," NYT, June 25.

Greenfield, Meg (1985), "Why We Are Still Muckraking," *Washington Post,* March 20.

Grenier, Richard (1991), *Capturing the Culture: Film, Art and Politics,* Washington, D.C.: Ethics and Public Policy Center.

Harmetz, Aljean (1983), "5 Films with Political Statements Due in Fall," NYT, Sept. 10.

Harrington, Mona (1989), "'Working Girl' in Reagan Country" (op-ed), NYT, Jan. 15.

Herman, Edward S., and Noam Chomsky (1988), *Manufacturing Consent: The Political Economy of the Mass Media,* New York: Pantheon.

Holden, Stephen (1990), "AIDS Dominates Nonfiction Series of Film and Video," NYT, April 6.

Hollander, Paul (1981), *Political Pilgrims,* New York: Oxford Univ. Press.

——— (1983), *The Many Faces of Socialism,* New Brunswick: Transaction.

——— (1988), *The Survival of the Adversary Culture,* New Brunswick: Transaction.

Hughes, John (1985), "How Vietnam Manipulated TV," DHG, May 16.

Jones, Alex S. (1990), "An Editorial Stirs Newsroom Feud," NYT, Dec. 21.

Katz, Susan (1987), "Unwelcome Chronicle of a Prison in Hanoi," *Insight,* June 8.

Kennan, George, and His Critics (1978), *Decline of the West?,* Washington, D.C.: Ethics and Public Policy Center.

Kerr, Peter (1988), "Campus Radicals Count the Cost of Commitment," NYT, Sept. 4.

Koppel, Ted (1986), "Koppel Warns Against False Values Celebrated by the Media," *Campus Report* (Stanford Univ.), June 18.

Kowet, Don (1985), "Journalists See Red at 'Pink' Label," *Insight,* Dec. 9.

Kristol, Irving (1978), "The New Demagogic Journalism," in *The Press and American Politics,* Washington, D.C.: Ethics and Public Policy Center Reprint No. 15.

Lacayo, Richard (1983), "Who Breaks the Law on TV?," NYT, March 6.

Lasky, Melvin J. (1985), "Toward a Theory of Journalistic Malpractice," *Encounter,* November.

Legault, Suzanne Ramey (1989), Letter, NYT, Feb. 3.

Lerner, Robert, and Stanley Rothman (1989), "The Media, the Polity and Public Opinion," in Samuel Long, ed., *Political Behavior Annual,* Vol. 2, Boulder: Westview.

Lichter, Robert S., Stanley Rothman, and Linda S. Lichter (1986), *The Media Elite,* Bethesda: Adler & Adler.

MacDougall, A. Kent (1989), "Memoirs of a Radical in the Mainstream Press," *Columbia Journalism Review,* March/April.

Maslin, Janet (1988), "Sentimentalizing 60's Radicalism," NYT, Sept. 18.

Michaels, Albert (1986), "The Media as an Adversary Culture," *World Media Report*, Vol. 1, No. 1.

Milgram, Stanley (1977), "Reflections on News," *Antioch Review*, Spring–Summer.

Miller, Arthur H., Edie N. Goldenberg, and Lutz Erbring (1979), "Type-Set Politics: Impact of Newspapers on Public Confidence," *American Political Science Review*, March.

Montaner, Carlos Alberto (1991), "Rhetoric Obscures Cause of Puerto Rican Plight," *Wall Street Journal*, Jan. 4.

Muravchik, Joshua (1988), *News Coverage of the Sandinista Revolution*, Washington: American Enterprise Institute.

Navarro, Mireya (1990), "Comments on Puerto Ricans Provoke Boycott of Network," NYT, Dec. 31.

Noelle-Neumann, Elisabeth (1984), *The Spiral of Silence: Public Opinion—Our Social Skin*, Chicago: Univ. of Chicago Press.

O'Connor, John J. (1978), "Two Views of Vietnam Today," NYT, April 30.

―――― (1986), "Real World Impinges on 'Miami Vice,'" NYT, Oct. 19.

―――― (1987), "CBC Presents 'My Dissident Mom,'" NYT, Jan. 14.

―――― (1988), "Debated Episode on AIDS," NYT, Dec. 13.

Parenti, Michael (1986), *Inventing Reality: The Politics of the Mass Media*, New York: St. Martin's.

Robinson, Michael J. (1976), "Public Affairs Television and the Growth of the Political Malaise: The Case of 'The Selling of the Pentagon,'" *American Political Science Review*, June.

Rosenberg, Bernard, and David Manning White, eds. (1957), *Mass Culture: Popular Arts in America*, Glencoe: Free Press.

Rosenthal, A. M. (1987), "New Villains at the Movies" (op-ed), NYT, March 26.

Rothman, Stanley (1979), "The Mass Media in Post-Industrial Society," in S. M. Lipset, ed., *The Third Century: America as a Post-Industrial Society*, Stanford: Hoover Press.

―――― (1987), "Hollywood's America: How Motion Pictures Portray American Institutions" (Research Proposal).

Schudson, Michael (1978), *Discovering the News: A Social History of American Newspapers*, New York: Basic.

Shils, Edward (1974, first pub. 1956), *Torment of Secrecy*, Carbondale: Southern Illinois Univ. Press.

Shore, Elliot, Patricia J. Case, and Laura Daly, eds. (1982), *Alternative Papers—Selections from the Alternative Press, 1979–1980*, Philadelphia: Temple Univ. Press.

Smith, Ted J., III (1988), *Moscow Meets Main Street—Changing Journalistic Values and the Growing Soviet Presence on American Television*, Washington, D.C.: Media Institute.

Snyderman, Mark, and Stanley Rothman (1988), *The IQ Controversy—The Media and the Public*, New Brunswick: Transaction.

Stein, Ben (1979), *The View from Sunset Boulevard*, New York: Basic.

Stoler, Peter (1986), *Against the Press: Politics, Pressure and Intimidation in the 80s*, New York: Dodd, Mead.

Szamuely, George (1988), "'1969' Reverses Generation Role," *Insight*, Dec. 5.

―――― (1989), "'Believer' Can't Make Up Its Mind," *Insight*, March 6.

Taitz, Sonia (1989), "'True Believer' Makes a Case for Idealism," NYT, Feb. 12.

Theberge, Leonard J., ed. (1981), *Crooks, Conmen and Clowns: Businessmen in TV Entertainment*, Washington, D.C.: Media Institute.

Tyrmand, Leopold (1975–76), "The Media Shangri-La," *American Scholar*, Winter.

Updike, John (1989), "On Not Being a Dove," *Commentary*, March.

Watson, Francis M., Jr. (1979), *The Alternative Media*, Rockford: Rockford College Institute.

Wattenberg, Ben J. (1984), *The Good News Is the Bad News Is Wrong*, New York: Simon and Schuster.

Weintaub, Bernard (1986), "ABC Admits an Error in Airing Russians' Views," NYT, Feb. 28.

Weissberg, Jacob (1990), "Public Television's Cuba Problem," *New Republic*, Aug. 13.

White, Theodore H. (1969–70), "America's Two Cultures," *Columbia Journalism Review*, Winter.

Whiteside, Thomas (1975), "How ABC Buttered Up the Russians—And, Maybe, Why," NYT, Nov. 23.

Wolin, Merle Linda (1990), "Hollywood Goes Havana," *New Republic*, April 16.

Other Sources

"Documentary Discusses Social Change" (1985), DHG, Jan. 17.

"First-Strike Chic" (1985) (editorial), *Wall Street Journal*, Jan. 30.

"Group Criticizes Violence in 'Red Dawn' Saying It Teaches 'Barbaric Ethic of Hate'" (1984) (AP), DHG, Sept. 6.

Video Home Entertainment Guide (1986), Syosset: National Video Clearinghouse.

Undated Mail Advertisements of Documentary Films

Catticus Corporation, Berkeley, Calif.

Cine Research Associates, Boston, Mass.

Community Media Productions, Dayton, Ohio

Downtown Community Television Center, New York, N.Y.

Films for Humanities and Sciences, Princeton, N.J.

First Run Features, New York, N.Y.

New Day Films, Wayne, N.J.

New Day Films (offering Richter Productions), New York, N.Y.

Utne Reader, Marion, Ohio (periodical)

Chapter 5. The Pilgrimage to Nicaragua

Arce, Bayardo (1985), *Secret Speech before the Nicaraguan Socialist Party (PSN)*, trans. from *La Vanguardia* (Barcelona), Washington, D.C.: Dept. of State.

Baldizon, Alvaro Jose (1985), "Nicaragua's State Security: Behind the Propaganda Mask," Briefing Paper, Washington, D.C.: Institute on Religion and Democracy, September.

———— (1986), *Inside the Sandinista Regime: A Special Investigator's Perspective*, Washington, D.C.: Dept. of State.

Barnes, Fred (1986), "The Sandinista Lobby," *New Republic*, Jan. 20.

Barnet, Richard (1985), "The U.S. Left and Nicaragua," *Nation*, April 20.

Belli, Humberto (1982), "The Sandinista Regime Today," *Freedom at Issue*, November–December.

———— (1985), *Breaking Faith—The Sandinista Revolution and Its Impact on Freedom and Christian Faith in Nicaragua*, Westchester, Ill.: Crossway.

Bensky, Larry (1990), "Campaigning with the Sandinistas," *Nation*, March 5.

Benson, Harry (1986), "Rosario's Revolution," *Vanity Fair*, July.

Berman, Paul (1986), "Nicaragua 1986—Notes on the Sandinista Revolution," *Mother Jones*, Dec. 20.

———— (1989), "Double Reality—People's Revolution vs. Sandinista Revolution," *Village Voice*, Dec. 5.

Bonpane, Blase (1988), Letter, NYT, Oct. 5.

Brentlinger, John (1985), "Needed: A Clear Impression," *Massachusetts Daily Collegian*, Nov. 7.

Burbach, Roger (1980), "Nicaragua: The Course of the Revolution," *Monthly Review*, February.

Burns, Bradford E. (1983), "Progress Too, in Nicaragua," *In These Times*, June 14.

Carson, Tom (1987), "The Long Way Back," *Village Voice*, May 12.

Chamorro, Jaime Cardenal (1988), *La Prensa—The Republic of Paper*, New York: Freedom House.

Chamorro, Violeta (1989), "Keep Watch on Our Elections," *Washington Post*, Nov. 8.

Chavez, Linda (1987), "Nicaragua Is Aided by Sister City Projects," NYT, *News of the Week*, Feb. 1.

Chomsky, Noam (1985), *Turning the Tide—U.S. Intervention in Central America and the Struggle for Peace*, Boston: South End Press.

———— (1987), *On Power and Ideology: The Managua Lectures*, Boston: South End Press.

Christian, Shirley (1985), "Nicaragua Police Criticized on Rights," NYT, April 5.

———— (1986), *Nicaragua—Revolution in the Family*, New York: Vintage.

————, (1987), "Covering the Sandinistas," *Washington Journalism Review*, March.

Cockburn, Alexander (1985), "Why We're Getting Psyched Up for War," *Wall Street Journal*, Jan. 31.

Cody, Edward (1985), "Americans Pay Homage to a Revolution," *Washington Post*, July 23.

Coffin, William Sloane, Jr. (1983), "Nicaragua Is Not the Enemy" (op-ed), NYT, July 31.

Collier, Peter, and David Horowitz, eds. (1989), *Second Thoughts—Former Radicals Look Back at the Sixties*, Lanham, Md.: Madison.

———— (1989), *Destructive Generation: Second Thoughts About the 60s*, New York: Summit.

Copeland, Jerry (1990), Letter, *New Republic*, March 26.

Decker, Christine C. (1987), "Women Head for Nicaragua," DHG, March 31.

Denton, Jim (1985), "A Lobbying Drive Began in Managua," *Wall Street Journal*, April 23.

Diskin, Martin, ed. (1983), *Trouble in Our Backyard*, New York: Pantheon.

Donziger, Steven (1988), "The Nicaragua Connection," *Atlanta*, February.

Dowd, Maureen (1985), "Reporter's Notebook: Ortega Chic," NYT, Oct. 25.

Dreifus, Claudia (1983), "Playboy Interview: The Sandinistas," *Playboy Magazine*, September.

Driscoll, Frances (1983), "Poet Adrienne Rich Mixes Poetry, Politics in Talk at UMass," DHG, Sept. 29.

Falcoff, Mark (1986), "Revolutionary Tourism," *Public Opinion*, Summer.

Falk, Richard (1979), "Trusting Khomeni" (op-ed), NYT, Feb. 16.

———— (1983), Interview, *Prospect* (Princeton, N.J.), November.

———— (1985), "The U.S. Left and Nicaragua," *Nation*, April 20.

Fehrenbach, Jean (1984), "Nicaraguan People 'Tremendous,'" *Green Bay Catholic Compass*, July 21.

Foley, Jack (1984), "Nicaragua Is Invaded by American Visitors," *San Jose Mercury News*, Oct. 7.

Frawley, Joan (1985), "Pilgrims from the Heartland," *American Spectator*, August.

Garvin, Glen (1986), "U.S. Citizens Work for Sandinistas," *Insight,* Dec. 8.

Goldman, Francisco (1987), "Poetry and Power in Nicaragua," NYT *Magazine,* March 29.

Goodman, Walter (1986), "At PEN a Feeling of Community," NYT, Jan. 20.

Grove, Lloyd (1986), "Rosario's Revolution," *Vanity Fair,* July.

Harrington, James C. (1984), "Picando los ojos in Honduras," *Texas Observer,* Sept. 28.

Harrington, Michael (1981), "Economic Troubles Besetting Nicaragua" (op-ed), NYT, July 16.

Harris, Art (1984), "Nora Astorga's Revolutionary Journey," *Washington Post,* Oct. 4.

Heard, Alex (1989), "Inaugural Anthropology," *New Republic,* Feb. 13.

Hollander, Paul (1981), *Political Pilgrims,* New York: Oxford Univ. Press.

———— (1983), "Sojourners in Nicaragua: A Political Pilgrimage," *National Catholic Register,* May 29.

———— (1985), "The Newest Political Pilgrims," *Commentary,* August.

———— (1986), "Political Tourism in Cuba and Nicaragua," *Society,* May–June.

———— (1987), "Socialist Prisons and Imprisoned Minds," *National Interest,* Winter.

Hollyday, Joyce, and Jim Wallis (1983), "A Fragile Experiment," *Sojourner,* March.

Hoover, Larry (1986), "Attorney Visits Nicaragua—II," *Daily News Record* (Harrisonburg, Va), Jan. 4.

Ingwerson, Marshall (1984), "From Actors to Advocates, Americans Are Flocking to Nicaragua," *Christian Science Monitor,* Nov. 23.

Jenkins, Tony (1990), "The Unmaking of Dona Violeta," *Nation,* Feb. 26.

Johns, Michael (1987), "Department of Disinformation—Tribute to Totalitarianism," *Policy Review,* Winter.

Kennedy, Edward M. (1984), "Support the Peace Effort of Nicaragua's Indians" (op-ed), NYT, Nov. 27.

Kinzer, Stephen (1985), "Sandinistas' Visitors: Motives Touch Off Dispute," NYT, July 4.

———— (1985), "Sandinista Portrait: Poet, Militant, Bible Devotee," Sept. 3.

———— (1987), "Managua Cracks Down on Group That Presses for Prisoners' Rights," NYT, April 5.

———— (1987), "2 U.S. Senators Tour Nicaraguan Security Jail," NYT, Dec. 8.

———— (1988), "For Sandinista, a Strong Literary Escort," NYT, Jan. 16.

———— (1988), "Managua Jails 2 Economists, Stirring Fears," NYT, Oct. 2.

Kramer, Steven Philip (1987), "Coming to Terms with Nicaragua" (op-ed), NYT, March 6.

Kriele, Martin (1985), *Nicaragua—America's Bleeding Heart,* Mainz, Germany: Hase & Koehler.

Lanier, Alfredo S. (1984), "Pilgrims for Peace," *Chicago,* October.

Leiken, Robert S. (1984), "Nicaragua's Untold Stories," *New Republic,* Oct. 8.

———— (1985), "The Nicaraguan Tangle," *NY Review of Books,* Dec. 5.

————, and Barry Rubin, eds. (1987), *The Central American Crisis Reader,* New York: Summit Books.

Lewis, Anthony (1986), "By Hate Possessed" (op-ed), NYT, March 24.

———— (1989), "Would We Suffer in Silence?" (op-ed), NYT, Nov. 5.

Lindauer, Susan (1984), "Public Attitudes Shape U.S. Policy," DHG, Oct. 22.

Livingston, Joan (1987), "Worthington Man Visits Nicaragua," DHG, Aug. 14.

Llosa, Mario Vargas (1985), "In Nicaragua," NYT *Magazine,* April 28.

Lobenstein, Margaret (1987), "Brigada Companeras Builds Hope," *Valley Women's Voice* (Amherst, Mass.), February.

Luxenburg, Norman (1984), Letter, NYT, Feb. 20.

Lynd, Staughton (1985), Letter, NYT, Nov. 3.

Lyons, Stephen (1983), "Two City Women Back Home," DHG, Nov. 26.

Markham, George F. (1987), Letter, DHG, April 23.

Massing, Michael (1985), "Hard Questions on Nicaragua," *Nation,* April 6.

——— (1988), "Who Are the Sandinistas?" *NY Review of Books,* May 12.

McDowell, Edwin (1986), "PEN Congress to Open Without Soviet Writers," NYT, Jan. 11.

Miller, Marc S. (1987), "View of the Contra-Sandinista War from Tiny Wiwili," *Christian Science Monitor,* June 3.

Miller, Marjorie (1986), "Nicaragua's Tourism Up Despite War," *Los Angeles Times,* March 12.

Moore, John (1986), "Reporting Nicaragua," *National Interest,* Summer.

Morrison, James (1986), "Managua," *Washington Times,* March 20.

Muravchik, Joshua (1988), *News Coverage of the Sandinista Revolution,* Washington, D.C.: American Enterprise Institute.

Neier, Aryeh (1986), "Alleged Conspiracies in the 50s and Now" (op-ed), NYT, March 15.

Nielson, Gary (1985), "Rock 'n' Roll Rebels," *Valley Advocate,* Jan. 23.

O'Brien, Conor Cruise (1986), "God and Man in Nicaragua," *Atlantic Monthly,* August.

Oney, Steve (1984), "Stars Over Central America: How the Sandinistas Sought the Hearts and Minds of Susan Anspach and Daryl Hannah," *California Magazine,* July.

O'Rourke, P. J. (1987), "Sightseeing in Sandinistaland," *Rolling Stone,* Dec. 3.

Ozer, Stuart (1986), "Back from the Future: Notes on the Central America Movement," *Socialist Review,* March–April.

Ozick, Cynthia (1986), "Literature Lost" (op-ed), NYT, Jan. 22.

Payne, Douglas W. (1985), "The 'Mantos' of Sandinista Deception," *Occasional Bulletins,* Puebla Institute, July.

Peretz, Martin (1986), "Cambridge Diarist—Out of Line," *New Republic,* April 7.

Powell, S. Steven (1987), *Covert Cadre: Inside the Institute for Policy Studies,* Ottawa, Ill.: Green Hill.

Preston, Julia (1990), "The Defeat of the Sandinistas," *NY Review of Books,* April 12.

Purcell, Susan Kaufman (1985), "Behind a Revolution," NYT, July 20.

Radosh, Ronald (1986), "Nicaraguan Myths," *Partisan Review,* No. 1.

Radu, Michael, ed. (1988), *Violence and the Latin American Revolutionaries,* New Brunswick: Transaction.

Ray, Ellen, William Schaap, and Louis Wolf (1985), Letter, *Nation,* April 27.

Riderour, Ron (1986), *Yankee Sandinistas: Interviews with North Americans Living and Working in the New Nicaragua,* Willimantic, Ct.: Curbstone Press.

Rodriguez, Linda (1984), Letter, *The American Statesman* (Austin, Texas), June 13.

Rohmer, Harriet (1987), "Managua's First Book Fair," *Publisher's Weekly,* Sept. 4.

Rohter, Larry (1985), "Outlook Grim for Squatters in Nicaragua," NYT, Feb. 18.

——— (1985), "Managua Rule Seen as Leftist Hybrid," NYT, March 3.

——— (1985), "Ortega Faces the People But Most Are Friends," NYT, Oct. 26.

——— (1990), "Stunned Sandinistas Seek to Define Their New Role," NYT, March 1.

——— (1990), "Ortega Spurned in an Old Stronghold," NYT, March 5.

——— (1990), "Sandinistas' Foreign Legion is Faithful in Defeat," NYT, March 13.

Sanders, Dylan (1990), "Observers Begrudgingly Endorse Sanctity of Vote," DHG, March 6.

Shapiro, Margaret (1985), "The Roots of O'Neill's Dissent," *Washington Post,* June 5.

Shea, Nina (1986), "'Justice' in Nicaragua" (op-ed), NYT, Oct. 31.

Shepherd, Fred and Geoffrey (1984), "On the Ground in Nicaragua," *Amherst,* Winter.

Singer, Michael (1980), "Nicaragua: Public Dreams," *Village Voice,* July 30–Aug. 5.

Smith, Lois M. (1987), "New Film Documents Citizens' Quest for Truth," *Times of the Americas,* Feb. 25.

Smolowe, Jill (1986), "Conversion of a Timely Kind," *Time,* April 21.

Stone, Keith (1987), "In Nicaragua: Professor Returns from Tour of Prisons, Talks to Inmates," DHG, April 1.

Stone, Norman (1990), "Anti-Americanism Is at the Root of Support for the Defeated Sandinistas," *Sunday Times* (London), March 4.

Sullivan, Cheryl (1987), "U.S. Volunteers Head for Nicaragua," *Christian Science Monitor,* June 2.

Swaim, Loring (1985), "Betrayal for Those Who Seek Freedom," DHG, April 29.

Tamayo, Juan (1983), "Sandinistas Aim Soft Sell at Activists," *Miami Herald,* Dec. 14.

Thatcher, Rebecca (1984), "UMass Graduate Discusses Nicaraguan Struggle," *Massachusetts Daily Collegian,* Nov. 26.

Uncapher, Jo (1987), *Nica Journal: Five Weeks in Esteli,* mimeograph.

Vinocur, John (1984), "Herzog Introduces a Political Issue at Cannes," NYT, May 15.

Volsky, George (1988), "A Freed Contra Leader Tells of 4 Years in Sandinista Jails," NYT, April 14.

West, Diana (1986), "About Face on the Sandinistas," *Insight,* July 21.

Williams, Dan (1984), "U.S. Citizens Help Build Revolution in Nicaragua, Protest Reagan Policy," *NY Herald Tribune,* Aug. 28.

Woodhull, Albert S. (1988), Letter, DHG, July 27.

Other Sources

Ambulances for Nicaragua (mail solicitation), Los Angeles, n.d.

"Americans Work for Free in Nicaraguan Fields" (1985) (AP), DHG, Jan. 24.

"Ben Linder" (1987) (obituary), *Village Voice,* May 12.

"Letter from Nicaragua" (1984), *New America,* June–July.

Marazul Tours Cover Letter and Tour Descriptions (1983), September.

"The Meaning and Destiny of the Sandinista Revolution" (1987), *Policy Forum,* Washington, D.C.: National Forum Foundation, August.

"The Myths of Revolution" (1985) (editorial), *New Republic,* April 29.

Nicaragua in Focus (1987), Washington, D.C.: Puebla Institute, July–August.

"Nicaraguan Defector Details Sandinista Repression" (1985) (Newsletter), Washington, D.C.: Council for Democracy in the Americas, December.

"Nicaraguans Want Property Back" (1990), DHG, April 10.

"On Traveling to Nicaragua" (1986), NYT, July 12.

"The 'Other Side' of the Sharpening Confrontations" (1983) (AP), DHG, Sept. 30.

"Perspectives" (1987), *Nicaragua in Focus,* Puebla Institute, July–August.

Report on Human Rights Defenders in Nicaragua (1986), New York: International League for Human Rights.

Report on Travel Seminar Conducted by Center for Global Service & Education, Augsburg College, Minneapolis, Minn. (1985), *Congressional Record,* April 16.

"Sandinista Holiday" (1988), *New Republic,* Nov. 21.

"Spoils of War" (1990) (editorial), *Nation,* March 19.

Statement Regarding the Prison Situation (1986), Nicaraguan Permanent Commission on Human Rights, September.

"Two Return from Trips to Nicaragua" (1984–85), *The Alumnus* (Univ. of Massachusetts at Amherst), December–January.

"Washington Talk: Briefing—Trying to Avert a 'Vietnam'" (1984), NYT, Dec. 17.

Chapter 6. College Students

Barrow, Clayton, and Julie A. Lam (1988), *The Entering Class at U.Mass, Fall 1988*, Amherst: Student Affairs Research and Evaluation Office, Univ. of Massachusetts.

Boyer, Ernest L. (1987), *College: The Undergraduate Experience in America*, New York: Harper & Row.

Johnson, Haynes (1990), "The Sad, Tragic Legacy of Kent State" (Times-Post News Service), DHG, May 9.

Karlen, Neal, et al. (1985), "The Conservative Student," *Newsweek on Campus*, March.

Landers, Robert K. (1986), "No Sharp Turn Right by Today's Students" (Editorial Research Reports, Washington), DHG, Sept. 3.

MacDougall, Kent A. (1989), "Memoirs of a Radical in the Mainstream Press," *Columbia Journalism Review*, March/April.

Meyer, Thomas J. (1985), "Freshmen Are Materialistic but Not Conservative," *Chronicle of Higher Education*, Jan. 16.

Moynihan, Daniel Patrick (1975), *A Dangerous Place*, Boston: Little, Brown.

Shils, Edward (1974, first pub. 1956), *The Torment of Secrecy*, Carbondale: Southern Illinois Univ. Press.

———— (1989), "Liberalism: Collectivist and Conservative," *Chronicles*, July.

Shribman, David (1983), "Polls Show Support for Presence of U.S. Troops in Lebanon and Grenada," NYT, Oct. 29.

Other Sources

"Political Attitude Survey" (1986), Project Pulse, Amherst: Student Affairs Research and Evaluation Office, Univ. of Massachusetts, May.

"Students Views on Social and Educational Issues" (1986), *Chronicle of Higher Education*, Feb. 5.

"Survey Finds No Big College Swing to Right" (1986), NYT, Oct. 31.

Chapter 7. The Third World

Aksyonov, Vassily (1985), *In Search of Melancholy Baby*, New York: Random House.

Barzun, Jacques (1965), "The Man in the American Mask," *Foreign Affairs*, April.

Bauer, P. T. (1976), "Western Guilt and Third World Poverty," *Commentary*, January.

Berger, Peter (1976), *Pyramids of Sacrifice*, Garden City: Doubleday.

Berlin, Isaiah (1972), "The Bent Twig: A Note on Nationalism," *Foreign Affairs*, No. 51.

———— (1979), "Nationalism: Past Neglect and Present Power," *Partisan Review*, Vol. 46, No. 3.

Berlow, Alan (1990), "The Filipinos' American Fixation—Way Off Base," *New Republic*, Dec. 31.

Bernstein, Richard (1983), "Behind U.N. Vote: How Much Anti-Americanism?," NYT, Nov. 4.

———— (1984), "The U.N. versus the U.S.," NYT *Magazine*, Jan. 22.

———— (1984), "Report Says U.S. Is Often in U.N.'s Minority," NYT, March 14.

Bittman, Ladislav (1972), *The Deception Game*, Syracuse: Syracuse Univ. Research Corporation.

Bruckner, Pascal (1986), *The Tears of the White Man: Compassion as Contempt*, New York: Free Press.

Buckley, William F. (1989), *On the Firing Line: The Public Life of Public Figures*, New York: Doubleday.

Collier, Peter, and David Horowitz, eds. (1989), *Second Thoughts: Former Radicals Look Back at the Sixties,* Lanham, Md.: Madison.

Conrad, Peter (1980), *Imagining America,* New York: Oxford Univ. Press.

Crespi, Leo P. (1979), "The Extent of Anti-Americanism Abroad," *Foreign Opinion Note,* Washington, D.C.: U.S. Information Agency, Dec. 3.

——— (1981), "The Extent of Anti-Americanism Abroad in the Perspective of Past Agency Surveys" (Mimeographed Report), USIA, Washington, D.C., Sept. 18.

Cuzan, Alfred G. (1985), "LASA Spreads Disinformation on Nicaragua," *Times of the Americas,* Jan. 30.

Dionne, E. J., Jr. (1983), "In Paris, Celebrities Talk of Arts and the Economy," NYT, Feb. 14.

Fairbanks, Charles, Jr. (1990), "Gorbachev's Global Doughnut," *National Interest,* Spring.

Fairlie, Henry (1975), "Anti-Americanism at Home and Abroad," *Commentary,* December.

Falcoff, Mark (1989), "Semper Fidel," *New Republic,* July 3.

Feher, Ferenc, Agnes Heller, and Gyorgy Markus (1983), *Dictatorship Over Needs,* New York: St. Martin's Press.

Freedman, Samuel G. (1986), "The Writer as an Exile: A Voice Far from Home," NYT, Jan. 18.

Godson, Joseph (1986), "Anti-Americanism Grows New Roots" (op-ed), NYT, June 11.

Goldin, Harrison J. (1990), "Hussein's Support: Deeper Than We Think?" (op-ed), NYT, Aug. 28.

Grass, Gunter (1989), *Show Your Tongue,* New York: Harcourt, Brace.

Greene, Graham (1984), *Getting to Know the General: The Story of an Involvement,* New York: Simon and Schuster.

Hameed, Mazher (1984), "Arab Anger at U.S." (op-ed), NYT, Feb. 20.

Handlin, Oscar (1981), *The Distortion of America,* Boston: Little, Brown.

Harries, Owen (1983), "U.S. Quit UNESCO" (op-ed), NYT, Dec. 21.

Hartley, Anthony (1989), "Saving Mr. Rushdie?," *Encounter,* June.

Haseler, Stephen (1985), *The Varieties of Anti-Americanism,* Washington, D.C.: Ethics and Public Policy Center.

Hollander, Paul (1984), Interviews in Mexico City, February.

Horowitz, Irving Louis (1985), "Latin America, Anti-Americanism and Intellectual Hubris," in Rubinstein and Smith, *cited.*

Howard, Michael (1985), "The Bewildered American Raj," *Harper's,* March.

Humbert, Maximo (1970), "ABC-TV Has Just Bought Latin America" (*Analisis,* Santiago, Chile), trans. *Atlas,* January.

Kamm, Henry (1985), "Papandreou: The Politics of Anti-Americanism," NYT *Magazine,* April 7.

Kristof, Nicholas D. (1990), "Painting America: The Unbeautiful and Damned," NYT, April 12.

Laqueur, Walter (1980), *The Political Psychology of Appeasement,* New Brunswick: Transaction.

———, and Robert Hunter, eds. (1985), *European Peace Movements and the Future of the Western Alliance,* New Brunswick: Transaction.

Lefever, Ernest W. (1987), *From Nairobi to Vancouver: The World Council of Churches and the World,* 1975–1987, Washington, D.C.: Ethics and Public Policy Center.

Lewis, Paul (1989), "U.N. Support for U.S. Hits New Low," NYT, May 16.

——— (1990), "U.S. Gaining Ground at U.N., State Department Study Says," NYT, April 3.

Luck, Edward, and Peter Fromuth, "Anti-Americanism at the United Nations: Perception or Reality?," in Rubinstein and Smith (1985), cited.

Mead, Robert G., Jr. (1974), "Images North and South of the Border: The United States and Latin America Today and Tomorrow," Hispania, May.

Minogue, Kenneth (1986), "Anti-Americanism: A View from London," National Interest, Spring.

Montaner, Carlos Alberto (1976), "The Americanization of the Planet" (El Nacional, Caracas, Venezuela), trans. Atlas, November.

Morgan, Thomas B. (1967), The Anti-Americans, London: Michael Joseph.

Moynihan, Daniel P. (1975), "The U.S. in Opposition," Commentary, March.

––––––– (1978), A Dangerous Place, Boston: Little, Brown.

Nossiter, Bernard D. (1981), "U.S. as Whipping Boy," NYT, Oct. 5.

Parenti, Michael (1969), The Anti-Communist Impulse, New York: Random House.

Pastor, Robert A., and Jorge G. Castaneda (1988), Limits to Friendship: The United States and Mexico, New York: Knopf.

Payne, Douglas W. (1988), "North American Scholars Seen as Misrepresenting the Sandinistas," Nicaragua in Focus, April.

Paz, Octavio (1972), "Eroticism and Gastrosophy," Daedalus, Fall.

Pilon, Juliana Geran (1982), "Through the Looking Glass: The Political Culture of the U.N.," Backgrounder, Washington, D.C.: Heritage Foundation.

Powell, Stewart (1985), "How the World Views America," U.S. News & World Report, July 15.

Rangel, Carlos (1977), The Latin-Americans: Their Love-Hate Relationship with the United States, New York: Harcourt, Brace.

––––––– (1986), Third World Ideology and Western Reality: Manufacturing Political Myth, New Brunswick: Transaction.

Reid, John (1989), "Peru Sojourn 'Revitalizes' Teachers," DHG, Aug. 29.

Riding, Alan (1982), "Mexico's Middle Class Turns to Disco and Burgers," NYT, Jan. 13.

––––––– (1985), Distant Neighbors: A Portrait of Mexicans, New York: Knopf.

Rohter, Larry (1989), "Uproar Over Envoy Strains Ties with Mexico," NYT, Feb. 14.

Rubinstein, Alvin Z., and Donald E. Smith, eds. (1985), Anti-Americanism in the Third World: Implications for U.S. Foreign Policy, New York: Praeger.

Russell, Bertrand (1967), War Crimes in Vietnam, London: Allen and Unwin.

Schrieberg, David (1990), "Dead Babies," New Republic, Dec. 24.

Stockton, William (1986), "Mexicans in Poll View U.S. as Friend," NYT, Nov. 17.

Thompson, E. P., and Dan Smith (1981), Protest and Survive, New York: Monthly Review Press.

Thornton, Thomas Perry, ed. (1988), Anti-Americanism: Origins and Context, The Annals, May 1988.

Vermaat, Emerson, J. A. (1989), The World Council of Churches and Politics 1975–1986, New York: Freedom House.

Van Houten, Jan (1983), "Why Intellectuals Abroad Love to Hate America," Wall Street Journal, Aug. 3.

Vinocur, John (1984), "Europe's Intellectuals and American Punks," NYT Magazine, April 29.

West, Richard (1967), The Gringo in Latin America, London: Cape.

Other Sources

"Anti-Communism and the U.S.—History and Consequences," Conference Program, Cambridge, 1988.

"CIA Chief's Phrases Turned to Intervention" (1989) (El Dial), trans. Insight, March 27.

"The Climate of Opinion in Mexico City in Mid-1983" (1983) (Research Report), USIA, Washington, D.C.

"Image of the U.S. in Six Latin American Countries" (1972), U.S. Information Agency, Office of Research, Washington, D.C.

"Korean Students Attack U.S. Site—Firebombs Are Thrown After Cultural Center Reopens" (1990), NYT, June 13.

Chapter 8. Western Europe

Amis, Martin (1989), *London Fields,* London: Jonathan Cape.

Anastasi, Paul (1979), "Greek Conducts Music—and Leftist Drive," NYT, Nov. 25.

Bering-Jensen, Henrick (1988), "Struggle for the Soul of the Greens," *Insight,* Jan. 11.

Bethel, Tom (1983), "The Lovelies of Greenham Common," *American Spectator,* April.

Billard, Pierre (1985), "Europe Fights 'Americanization'" (Le Point, Paris), trans. *World Press Review,* October.

Bishop, Tom, Norman Mailer, Susan Sontag, and William Styron (1983), Letter, NYT, Feb. 27.

Burns, Arthur F. (1983), "Looking into Anti-Americanism" (op-ed), NYT, Dec. 27.

Caarten, Michiel Bicker (1981), "The European Protests" (op-ed), NYT, Nov. 25.

Campbell, Duncan (1984), "U.S. Bases in Britain," *Sanity* (London), May.

Clement, Alain (1976), "An Uneasy Calm" (*Le Monde,* Paris), trans. *Atlas,* July.

Conrad, Peter (1980), *Imagining America,* New York: Oxford Univ. Press.

Crespi, Leo P. (1983), *Long Term Trends in Some General Orientation Toward the U.S. and U.S.S.R in West European Public Opinion* (Report), Washington, D.C.: USIA, July.

Dale, Reginald (1984), "America Adrift in the World" (Financial Times, London), rpt. in *World Press Review,* May.

Dionne, E. J., Jr. (1983), "American in Paris Who's Disenchanted by UNESCO," NYT, April 21.

——— (1984), "What D-Day Means for Today's Youth in Europe: The Moods Are Many," NYT, June 8.

Echikson, William (1983), "Intelligentsia in Paris Ponder 'Dallas'" (Christian Science Monitor News Service) DHG, February 22

Esslin, Martin (1990), "Between Propaganda & Reality: Views on George Urban's 'Paradox,'" *Encounter,* April.

Fairlie, Henry (1975), "Anti-Americanism at Home and Abroad," *Commentary,* December.

Feinberg, Barry, and Ronald Kasrils, eds. (1983), *Bertrand Russell's America: A Documented Account* (vol. 2), Boston: South End Press.

Finn, James (1990), "Graham Greene as Moralist," *First Things,* May.

Fornari, Franco, and Raimondo Luraghi (1968), "Why Don't They Like Us—A Dissection" (*La Fiera Letteraria,* Milan), trans. *Atlas,* February.

Gelb, Norman (1981), "Europe's New Anti-Americanism," *New Leader,* Nov. 16.

Godson, Joseph (1986), "Anti-Americanism Grows New Roots" (op-ed), NYT, June 11.

Goodman, Walter (1988), "Politics of the Philosopher," NYT, Dec. 29.

Grass, Gunter (1983), "Epilogue: America's Backyard," in Martin Diskin, ed., *Our Backyard,* New York: Pantheon.

Greene, Graham (1955), *The Quiet American,* New York: Viking.

——— (1967), "The Writers Engage in Battle" (Letter), *Times* (London), Sept. 4.

——— (1984), *Getting to Know the General: The Story of an Involvement,* New York: Simon and Schuster.

Greenhouse, Steven (1989), "The Television Europeans Love, and Love to Hate," NYT, *News of the Week*, Aug. 13.

Hamsun, Knut (1969, first pub. in 1889), *The Cultural Life of Modern America*, Cambridge: Harvard Univ. Press.

Hartman, Holly (1984), "Loyalty to Peace Urged," DHG, Feb. 4.

Hastings, Max (1986), "Feeling Self-Satisfied" (*Sunday Times*, London), rpt. *Atlas*, February.

Havel, Vaclav (1987), "Search for the Human Dimension" (*New Socialist*, London), rpt. *World Press Review*, May.

Hochhuth, Rolf (1970), "A German Playwright Depicts a Coup d'Etat in the U.S." (*Die Weltwoche*, Zurich), trans. *Atlas*, June.

Hollander, Paul (1960), "Letter from America," *Clare Market Review* (London), Spring.

——— (1973), *Soviet and American Society: A Comparison*, New York: Oxford Univ. Press.

——— (1983), "Reflections on Anti-Americanism in Our Times," in *The Many Faces of Socialism*, New Brunswick: Transaction.

——— (1988), *The Survival of the Adversary Culture*, New Brunswick: Transaction.

Hook, Sidney (1987), *Out of Step*, New York: Harper & Row.

Humbert, Maximo (1970), "ABC-TV Has Just Bought Latin America" (*Analisis*, Santiago, Chile), trans. *Atlas*, January.

Hutchins, Francis G. (1990–1991), "The Odd Couple," *National Interest*, Winter.

Ionescu, Eugene (1985), "Truth Dwells in the Imaginary," *Chronicle of Culture*, January.

Johnson, Paul (1988), *The Intellectuals*, New York: Harper & Row.

Johnson, R. W. (1984), "KAL 007: Unanswered Questions" (*Guardian*, London), rpt. *World Press Review*, March.

Keithly, David M. (1990), "The German Fatherland—Of the Left," *Orbis*, Winter.

Kennan, George F. (1989), *Sketches from a Life*, New York: Pantheon.

Koestler, Arthur (1961), *The Lotus and the Robot*, New York: Macmillan.

Konrad, George (1984), *Antipolitics, an Essay*, New York: Harcourt, Brace.

Kramer, David, and Glenn Yago (1982), "Germans' Hostility to the U.S." (op-ed), NYT, June 7.

Kroes, Rob (1984), "The Great Satan Versus the Evil Empire: Anti-Americanism in the Netherlands" (Manuscript).

Laqueur, Walter, and Robert Hunter, eds. (1985), *The European Peace Movement and the Future of the Western Alliance*, New Brunswick: Transaction.

Lederer, William J., and Eugene Burdick (1958), *The Ugly American*, New York: Norton.

Lefever, Ernest W. (1987), *Nairobi to Vancouver: The World Council of Churches and the World, 1975–87*, Washington, D.C.: Ethics and Public Policy Center.

Lelyveld, Joseph (1986), "In Britain, Anti-Americanism Rises After Strikes on Libya," NYT, April 26.

Lewis, Flora (1982), "Motes in Both Eyes" (op-ed), NYT, Sept. 17.

Liedtke, Klaus (1976), "The U.S. Licks Its Wounds" (*Stern*, Hamburg), trans. *Atlas*, July.

Lindal, Sigurd (1966), "Wasteland in Iceland" (*Morgunbladid*, Reykjavik), trans. *Atlas*, April.

Macdonald, Dwight (1974), *Discriminations*, New York: Grossman.

Macrae, Norman (1969), "The Neurotic Trillionaire" (*Economist*, London), rpt. *Atlas*, July.

Magnusson, Sigudur A. (1965), (untitled excerpt from *Perspektiv*, Copenhagen), trans. *Atlas*, May.

Markham, James M. (1982), "Communist Rivals in Spain Plan New Parties," NYT, Feb. 7.

——— (1983), "The A-Bomb Is 'Convicted' in Nuremberg," NYT, Feb. 23.

Minogue, Kenneth (1986), "Anti-Americanism: A View from London," *National Interest*, Spring.

Monicelli, Mino (1966), "Au Revoir with a Shrug" (*L'Europeo*, Milan), trans. *Atlas*, September.

Morris, Jan (1975), "Land of Paradoxes," *Encounter*, rpt. *Atlas*, July.

———— (1983), "Down, Down on America" (op-ed), NYT, Nov. 13.

Nordheimer, Jon (1984), "Portrait of Spy as Golden Young Man," NYT, Jan. 29.

Papandreou, Andreas (1987), "If Capitalism Can't, Can Socialism?," *New Perspectives Quarterly*, Fall.

Parkin, Frank (1968), *Middle Class Radicalism: The Social Basis of the British Campaign for Nuclear Disarmament*, Manchester: Univ. of Manchester Press.

Pfaff, William (1989), *Barbarian Sentiments: How the American Century Ends*, New York: Hill and Wang.

Powell, Stewart (1985), "How the World Views America," *U.S. News & World Report*, July 15.

Priestley, J. B. (1980), "I Feel Sorry for America" (*New Statesman*, London), rpt. *Atlas*, March.

Pryce-Jones, David (1989), "Graham Cracker," *New Republic*, Jan. 23.

Riding, Alan (1990), "France Questions Its Identity as It Sinks into 'Le Malaise,'" NYT, Dec. 23.

Royer, J. (1965), "Ugliness—Made in U.S.A." (*Nouvelle Frontière*), rpt. *Atlas*, May.

Rubinstein, Alvin Z., and Donald E. Smith, eds. (1985), "Anti-Americanism: Anatomy of a Phenomenon," in Rubinstein and Smith, eds., *Anti-Americanism in the Third World: Implications for U.S. Foreign Policy*, New York: Praeger.

Russell, Bertrand (1951), "Democracy and the Teachers," *Manchester Guardian*, Oct. 30.

———— (1967), *War Crimes in Vietnam*, London: Allen & Unwin.

———— (1968), *Autobiography*, Vol. II, London: Allen & Unwin.

Ryan, Alan (1988), *Bertrand Russell: A Political Life*, New York: Hill & Wang.

Scheuch, Erwin K. (1970), "Hating America—The World's Favorite Pastime" (*Die Welt*, Hamburg), trans. *Atlas*, September.

Shanker, Albert (1991), "Multicultural and Global Education: Value Free?," NYT, *News of the Week*, Jan. 6.

Sheehan, Paul (1990), "The Americanization of Australia" (op-ed), NYT, May 5.

Siemon-Netto, Uwe (1981), "On the Brink: The Myth of German Anti-Americanism," *Yale Literary Magazine*, No. 3.

Singh, Rickey (1986), "Media Seen Aiding U.S. Cultural Penetration in Region," *Daily Gleaner* (Kingston, Jamaica), April 22.

Soderstrom, Herbert (1974), "Through a Swedish Mirror" (*Svenska Dagbladet*, Stockholm), trans. *Atlas*, October.

Stearn, Gerald Emanuel, ed. (1975), *Broken Image: Foreign Critiques of America*, London: Allen & Unwin.

Suffert, Georges (1967), "Are We Becoming Americans?" (*L'Express*, Paris), trans. *Atlas*, November.

Sullerot, Evelyen (1967), "'Oppression'—A French Report" (*Reforme*, Paris), trans. *Atlas*, April.

Suro, Mary Davis (1986), "Romans Protest McDonald's" (op-ed), NYT, May 5.

Thompson, E. P. (1978), *The Poverty of Theory and Other Essays*, New York: Monthly Review Press.

———— , and Dan Smith (1981), *Protest and Survive*, New York: Monthly Review Press.

Ungar, Sanford J., ed. (1985), *Estrangement: America and the World*, New York: Oxford Univ. Press.

Urban, George (1984), "Where America Fears to Tread" (op-ed), NYT, Nov. 18.
––––– (1989), "The Paradox of Truth Telling," *Encounter,* November.
Van Houten, Jan (1983), "Why Intellectuals Abroad Love to Hate America," *Wall Street Journal,* Aug. 3.
Vermaat, J. A. Emerson (1989), *The World Council of Churches and Politics 1975–1986,* New York: Freedom House.
Vinocur, John (1981), "Anti-Americanism in West Germany Appears in Many Guises," NYT, July 5.
––––– (1981), "Violence in Berlin Marks Haig's Visit," NYT, Sept. 14.
––––– (1981), "The German Malaise," NYT *Magazine,* Nov. 15.
––––– (1983), "Will French Culture Be More French?," NYT, *Arts & Leisure,* Jan. 9.
––––– (1984), "Europe's Intellectuals and American Power," NYT *Magazine,* April 29.
Walden, Brian (1989), "Why America Is Always Wrong in Clouded Eyes?," *Sunday Times* (London), Jan. 1.
Webb, W. L. (1983), "In Search of American Optimism" (*Guardian,* London), rpt. *World Press Review,* June.
Welles, Edward O. (1986), "A Conversation with Paul Theroux," *Boston Globe,* Nov. 9.
Wharton, Edith (1987, first pub. 1913), *The Custom of the Country,* New York: Macmillan.
Winchester, Simon (1981), "The Road from Pleasantville" (*Sunday Times,* London), rpt. *World Press Review,* May.
Wolfe, Tom (1987), *Bonfire of the Vanities,* New York: Farrar, Straus, Giroux.

Other Sources
"British Anti-Americanism" (1986) *(Sunday Times),* Insight, March 10.
"China's Epic Novelist Looks at the U.S.—and the Report Card Is Mixed" (1982), *People,* March 22.
"CIA Chief's Phrases Turned to Intervention" (1989) *(El Dia),* Insight, March 27.
"Greenham Women Against Cruise Missiles" (pamphlet), n.d., New York: Center for Constitutional Rights.
"We Love You, We Love You Not: Gosh, Isn't Life Confusing" (1986), *Economist,* April 26.

Chapter 9. Mexican and Canadian Intellectuals

Axworthy, Thomas S., ed. (1987), *Our American Cousins,* Toronto: Lorimer.
Brimelow, Peter (1990), "The Maple Leaf Forever?," *Encounter,* April.
Brym, Robert J., and John Myles (1989), "Social Science Intellectuals and Public Issues in English Canada," *University of Toronto Quarterly,* Summer.
Camp, Roderic A. (1981), "Intellectuals—Agents of Change in Mexico?," *Journal of Interamerican Studies and World Affairs,* August.
––––– (1981), "Intellectuals and the State in Mexico, 1920–1980, the Influence of Family and Education," VI Conference of Mexican and United States Historians, Chicago.
"Canada's Independent Streak" (1990) (editorial), *Globe and Mail,* March 15.
Clarkson, Stephen (1982), *Canada and the Reagan Challenge—Crisis in the Canadian-American Relationship,* Toronto: Lorimer.
Coe, Richard M. (1988), "Anglo-Canadian Rhetoric and Identity: A Preface," *College English,* December.
Doran, Charles F., and James Patrick Sewell (1988), "Anti-Americanism in Canada?," in

Thomas Perry Thornton, ed., *Anti-Americanism: Origin and Context, The Annals,* May.

Fulford, Robert, "The New Anti-Americanism," in Hugh Innis, ed., *Americanization* (1972), Toronto: McGraw-Hill & Ryerson.

"Image of the United States in Six Latin American Countries" (1972), U.S. Information Agency, Office of Research, Washington, D.C.

Innis, Hugh, ed. (1972), *Americanization,* Toronto: McGraw-Hill & Ryerson.

Lipset, Seymour Martin (1989), *Continental Divide—The Values and Institutions of the United States and Canada,* New York: Routledge.

Magee, Brian (1990), "New World Symphony," *Weekend Guardian* (London), Sept. 22–23.

Marshall, Douglas, "Where Has All Our Best Land Gone? Guess," in Innis (1972), *cited.*

Nelles, Viv (1982), "The U.S. and Canada: A Gathering Storm," *Saturday Night* (Toronto), rpt. *World Press Review,* April.

Raible, Chris (1989), "Our Elusive Identity Remains Elusive" (review of R. Mathews, *Canadian Identity*), *Saturday Magazine,* Feb. 25.

Rubinstein, Alvin Z., and Donald E. Smith, eds. (1985), *Anti-Americanism in the Third World,* New York: Praeger.

Vesilind, Priit, J. (1990), "Common Ground, Different Dreams," *National Geographic Magazine,* February.

Winks, Robin W. (1979), *The Relevance of Canadian History: U.S. and Imperial Perspective,* Toronto: Macmillan of Canada.

Chapter 10. Anti-Americanism, Decadence, and Communism's Collapse

Baer, Donald (1990), "Leftists in the Wilderness," *U.S. News and World Report,* March 19.

Berger, Joseph (1990), "Dropout Plans Not Working, Study Finds," NYT, May 16.

Bernstein, Richard (1990), "Unsettling the Old West," NYT *Magazine,* March 18.

———— (1990), "Academic Left Finds the Far Reaches of Postmodernism," NYT, *News of the Week,* April 8.

Birnbaum, Norman (1989), "Hope's End or Hope's Beginning? 1968—And After," *Salmagundi,* No. 82, Winter.

Brenson, Michael (1990), "Is Quality an Idea Whose Time Has Gone?," NYT, *Art & Leisure Section,* July 22.

Bromwich, David (1990), "The Professor of Necessity" (review of F. Jameson, *The Ideologies of Theory*), *New Republic,* Feb. 19.

Burnham, Walter Dean (1978), "Thoughts on the 'Governability Crisis' in the West," *Washington Review,* July.

Butterfield, Fox (1990), "At Rally, Jackson Assails Harvard Law School," NYT, May 10.

Carter, Jimmy (1989), "Rushdie's Book Is an Insult" (op-ed), NYT, March 5.

Crozier, Michel (1984), *The Trouble with America,* Berkeley: Univ. of California Press.

Cruz, Arturo, Jr. (1990), "Low Fidelity" (review of H. Padilla, *Self Portrait of the Other*), *New Republic,* March 26.

DePalma, Anthony (1990), "Foreigners Flood U.S. Graduate Schools," NYT, Nov. 29.

Douglas, Mary, and Aaron Wildavsky (1982), *Risk and Culture: An Essay on the Selection of Technological and Environmental Dangers,* Berkeley: Univ. of California Press.

Ehrenreich, Barbara (1990), "Democracy 101, Fighting for the Right to Choose," *Village Voice,* Dec. 19.

———— (1990), *The Worst Years of Our Lives: Irreverent Notes from a Decade of Greed,* New York: Pantheon.

Fairlie, Henry (1989), "Fear of Living," *New Republic*, Jan. 23.

Fowler, Brenda (1990), "New Courses and Even Votes at Czechoslovak Universities," NYT, March 31.

Genovese, Eugene D. (1990), "The American 80's: Disaster or Triumph?," *Commentary*, September.

Gitlin, Todd (1990), "After the European Revolutions: A Jump Start to History?," *Tikkun*, March–April.

Grabar, Robert (1989), "Marxists in Area Predict Better Time for Socialism," DHG, Feb. 8.

Greeley, Andrew M. (1989), *Religious Change in America*, Cambridge: Harvard Univ. Press.

Gross, Harriet E. (1990), Letter, NYT, Jan. 7.

Hacker, Andrew (1971), *The End of the American Era*, New York: Atheneum.

Hacker, Reinhart (1989), "British Media Have Mixed Feelings as East German Refugees Vote with Their Feet," *German Tribune*, October.

Hanley, Robert (1988), "Justice Dept. Accuses Jersey of Bias in Police Hiring Test," NYT, Nov. 26.

Ireland, Douglas (1990), "Perestroika, USA," *Village Voice*, Dec. 19.

Kamm, Henry (1989), "For Prague's Institutes It's Goodbye to Marxism," NYT, Dec. 14.

Kirkpatrick, Jeane J. (1990), "The American 80's: Disaster or Triumph?," *Commentary*, September.

Kolakowski, Leszek (1986), "The Idolatry of Politics," *New Republic*, June 16.

Korda, Michael (1982), "The Gradual Decline and Total Collapse of Nearly Everyone," *Family Weekly, Burlington Free Press*, Aug. 29.

Kramer, Hilton (n.d.), *Does the West Still Exist?*, New York: Orwell Press.

Krauze, Enrique (1986), "The Past Explained," *Salmagundi*, Summer.

Kristof, Nicholas D. (1987), "Anti-Americanism Grows in South Korea," NYT, July 12.

Kristol, Irving (1989), "Response to Fukuyama," *National Interest*, Summer.

Kuntz, Tom (1990), "In Highgate Cemetery, Marx Is Safe on a Pedestal," NYT, March 14.

Lapham, Lewis H. (1990), "Notebook," *Harper's*, October.

Lerner, Michael (1971), "Respectable Bigotry," in Murray Friedman, ed., *Overcoming Middle Class Rage*, Philadelphia: Westminster.

Lewis, Anthony (1990), "But We Close Our Eyes" (op-ed), NYT, Feb. 20.

Lipman, Samuel (1990), "Backward and Downward with the Arts," *Commentary*, May.

Luchsinger, Fred (1975), "The Reluctant Superpower" *(Neue Zuricher Zeitung)*, trans. *Atlas*, July.

Mason, Jackie (1990), "America, Land of the Unfree" (op-ed), NYT, March 23.

Minogue, Kenneth (1990), "Societies Collapse, Faiths Linger On," *Encounter*, March.

Morgan, Richard E. (1984), *Disabling America: The "Rights Industry" in Our Time*, New York: Basic.

Munson, Naomi (1981), "The Literary Life of Crime," *New Republic*, Sept. 9.

Nisbet, Robert (1988), "Reversing the Decline," *Crisis*, November.

Peretz, Martin (1990), "Washington Diarist," *New Republic*, May 28.

Pitt, David E. (1988), "After New York Test, Most New Sergeants in Police Are White," NYT, Jan. 13.

Raskin, Marcus, and Chester Hartman, eds. (1988), *Winning America: Ideas and Leadership for the 1990s*, South End Press (Boston) and the Institute for Policy Studies (Washington, D.C.).

Rector, Lucinda (1989), "Some Walls, Like Mine, Don't Fall" (op-ed), NYT, Dec. 1.

Rochbergh-Halton, Eugene (1990), "Cold War's Victims Deserve a Memorial" (op-ed), NYT, March 10.

Safire, William (1989), "Madness of Crowds" (op-ed), NYT, March 23.

Saletan, William, and Nancy Watzman (1989), "Marcus Welby, J.D.," *New Republic*, April 17.

Schmeisser, Peter (1988), "Is America in Decline?," NYT *Magazine*, April 17.

Shaw, Peter (1989), "Apocalypse Again," *Commentary*, April.

——— (1989), *The War Against Intellect*, Iowa City: Univ. of Iowa Press.

Singer, Daniel (1989), "Revolutionary Nostalgia," *Nation*, Nov. 20.

——— (1989), "Europe in the Post-Yalta Era," *Nation*, Dec. 11.

Steel, Ronald (1989), "Peel Me a Poison Grape" (op-ed), NYT, March 21.

Sweezy, Paul M. (1990), "Is This Then the End of Socialism?," *Nation*, Feb. 26.

Watson, George (1990), "Memoir—The Return of the Sage," *Encounter*, January–February.

Weinstein, Jeff (1990), "Duking It Out, a Gay and Lesbian Mandate," *Village Voice*, Dec. 19.

Wernick, Sarah (1990), "Hard Times for Educating the Highly Gifted Child," NYT, May 30.

Wicker, Tom (1990), "The New 'Sooners'" (op-ed), NYT, Jan. 2.

——— (1990), "Freedom for What?" (op-ed), NYT, Jan. 5.

Wildavsky, Aaron (1982), "The Three Cultures: Explaining Anomalies in the American Welfare State," *Public Interest*, Fall.

Will, George (1989), "Behind Social Science of Victimology," DHG, May 1.

——— (1989), "A Tragedy of Perfunctory Compassion," DHG, May 15.

——— (1989), "Liberals Can't Deal with New East Bloc," DHG, Dec. 11.

Willis, Ellen (1990), "Radical Change's Pleasure Principle," *Village Voice*, Dec. 19.

Wolin, Sheldon (1990), "Beyond Marxism and Monetarism," *Nation*, March 19.

Other Sources

"Borderline Marxists" (1989) (Editorial), *Nation*, Oct. 2.

"Notes and Comment" (1989), *New Yorker*, Dec. 11.

"Notes and Comment" (1990), *New Yorker*, Feb. 5.

"Political Idealists Trying to Hold Back the Night" (1990), NYT, April 12.

"State Countersues Jailhouse Lawyers" (1990) (AP), DHG, May 23.

Index